THE
OTHER
CITY
CARLO
SCARPA
DIE
ANDERE
STADT

THE OTHER CITY

CARLO SCARPA

DIE ANDERE STADT

THE ARCHITECT'S WORKING METHOD
AS SHOWN BY THE BRION CEMETERY
IN SAN VITO D'ALTIVOLE

DIE ARBEITSWEISE DES ARCHITEKTEN
AM BEISPIEL DER GRABANLAGE BRION
IN SAN VITO D'ALTIVOLE

ERNST & SOHN

Conception/Konzeption
Philippe Duboy, Peter Noever

Editorial work/Redaktion
Johannes Wieninger, Regina Haslinger

Design/Gestaltung
Dorner & Monti

© 1989

Wilhelm Ernst & Sohn, Verlag für Architektur und technische Wissenschaften, Berlin
Gesellschaft für österreichische Kunst, Wien

ISBN 3-433-02097-3

All rights reserved, especially those of translation into other languages
Alle Rechte vorbehalten, besonders die der Übersetzung in andere Sprachen

Overall production/Gesamtherstellung:
Ueberreuter Buchproduktion, Korneuburg

Editor/Herausgeber
Peter Noever
Österreichisches Museum für angewandte Kunst, Wien

Project committee/Projektkomitee
Manlio Brusatin, Philippe Duboy, Peter Noever,
Nini Scarpa, Tobia Scarpa,
Hiroyuki Toyoda, Johannes Wieninger

Carlo Scarpa during his lecture in Vienna in 1976/Carlo Scarpa während seiner Vorlesung 1976 in Wien

REMINISCENCES

One of my first encounters with Carlo Scarpa was in the "American Bar" in Vienna by Adolf Loos. We had hardly entered when he began to express his passionate admiration for what he saw. Gradually his eyes wandered from the ceiling—which had caught his attention first—into the room itself. He noticed the women who were sitting at the bar, approached them, and bowed with a smile. At once he found himself the center of a group of people who quite obviously were interested in everything but architecture. Scarpa ordered champagne for them and a measuring tape for himself. He was fascinated by Adolf Loos and his architecture. He joked with the guests as he surveyed every detail of the room with his eyes and hands. He assumed unexpected positions, and eventually started—with the aid of the ladies—to take exact measurements of the "Loos" bar. He was inspired by the proportions and details and wanted to know the diameter of the bar rail down to the last millimeter. He finally proclaimed the room a place of "singular spiritual and emotional quality."

He had quickly summed up the perfection of the room—the underlying intellectual idea as well as its material manifestation—without feeling any reserve in expressing his honest admiration and great enthusiasm. Scarpa, an individual among architects, also sought perfection in his own work—from the overall construction of a building to the design and precise completion of all pertaining details.

All his life he defended the utopian visions of his architecture against "the real world" and the powers that be. He never went near politicians, never allied himself with any of them. He saw life itself as a kind of art form. If, for example, he thought the Venetian culture of cooking and eating somehow in danger, it might happen that he would burst into the kitchen of a restaurant to demonstrate to the astonished chef as well as to the guests how to prepare a "real" pasta. Even to this sort of activity he dedicated his utmost concentration. He was convinced that everything had to be done at just the right moment, every motion had to be right. Scarpa knew how to enjoy himself like few others. He took pleasure in everyday things just as much as in the arts. He could unexpectedly and surprisingly produce a situation in which the simple encounter would turn into a celebration, an unforgettable experience.

Back then in the "Loos" bar, more than fifteen years ago, we also spoke about the possibility of organizing the first comprehensive Carlo Scarpa show in Vienna. Scarpa was immediately enthused by this idea. Despite the fact that he was in Vienna for the first time, he had always had a special relationship to this city. Joseph Marie Olbrich and Josef Hoffmann, he maintained, had served as his childhood models.

The exhibit never came off. Instead Scarpa gave an impressive talk under the title "Can Architecture be Poetry?" at the Academy of Fine Arts. In high spirits, with his own characteristic body language, always a bit ironic and lighthearted, completely undidactic and yet profound and captivating, he presented himself as the "Professore" from Venice. He meant to give a summary of his œuvre and ended up with an *ex tempore* development of his theory, method, and attitude toward architecture. This despite the fact that he had always avoided formulating such theories.

The very complex and ingenious work of Scarpa uses a highly formal language characterized by its feel for details and an absolute mastery of the materials at hand. Scarpa understood architecture to be poetry; poetry that was fully realized when the form reached the maximum of its expression. Still, he disliked terms such as "poetic architecture" or "environmental planning" or "urban studies", rejecting them because he felt their meaninglessness led to a sort of sterility. Scarpa, who never stopped learning himself, was perhaps not well enough known as a great teacher. His charisma and generosity were not limited to the academic world, in fact, the thought of symposia, architectural conferences and debates almost made him panic. He had no interest in taking part in what he called the "battlefield of arguments."

Undoubtedly, the Brion tomb at San Vito d'Altivole is the architect's masterpiece, and at the same time it also became his own monument. The first mass for the dead to be held at the chapel was—in a twist of fate, like his own deadly fall over the stairs in Sendai, Japan—his own. He had already selected his own tomb during his lifetime. At San Vito, in a secluded and barely accessible place, a sort of "no man's land" between the graveyard he had built for the family Brion and the old village cemetery lies the grave of the "maestro"—as he was known in that region. Scarpa had determined all the details pertaining to his grave—by means of a tube embedded in the earth he meant to assure ongoing contact with the living after death.

What Carlo Scarpa created in San Vito, a fertile plain situated in front of the small elevated town of Asolo with its jagged range of hills, is not so much a mausoleum as a sacred district. He was mainly concerned that this place remind one not only of the transitoriness of mortality, but rather testify to life after death. He even once suggested jokingly that one might just as well lie on the lawn of the cemetery with a good glass of wine and from there enjoy the view over the fertile landscape and the village of San Vito.

The appearance of this graveyard with all its surprising details and implied references to mythology, poetry, and symbolism is primarily characterized by the dimensional formation of its main body; i.e. through the recurrent yet often varied stair—motif so characteristic for Scarpa. In the staccato arrangement of the steps, in the labyrinth of passages and carefully considered gate constructions, in the lively water and vegetation which seem to burst through the concrete—in short, everywhere one looks one feels the signature of the poet and symbolist Carlo Scarpa. Every change in light and season gives the Brion cemetery a new look. The Austrian writer Alfred Kolleritsch writes in his latest novel "Allemann":

"The green lawn, the sparse plants, and this mixed gray of black and white concrete structures together built an isolated area. Its framework was like a conversation with Death where no God is present. The stairs that determined the organization of the buildings and details were the most powerful trademarks of Scarpa's formal language—and they happened to be stairs to death. Moss nestled in some of them, here and there they were ravaged by fissures. They prevented the making of excuses, machinations against understanding. The life that had disappeared had determined this layout; at its frontier memory and future met. It was the moment when truth ended." (our translation)

Just as poetry is no architectural discipline—although architecture may well develop a poetic form—this exhibition arranged together with Tobia Scarpa and the other members of the exhibition committee is not the usual monumental show to be expected of such a famous architect. Instead this exhibition attempts to bring back the memory of Scarpa's sensual and spiritual world through concentration on one amply illustrated subject.

Peter Noever

VENEZIA–WIEN

This is the second important exhibition of my father's works to be held to date: the first was in Venice, and now this one in Vienna.

During the last century, Venice was united with Vienna, and not only in the political sense. Thus this could be, or seems to be, a continuation of the history of the subtle and pervasive adventure of Venice's interaction with Central Europe. This interaction was not allowed to continue; it did, however, leave traces with which my father grew up. I therefore find this exhibition in the Austrian Museum of Applied Arts highly significant; this topic was very dear to him.

Curator of this exhibition was Philippe Duboy, a perceptive Frenchman who loves my father's work so much that he has assumed the responsibility for this task. Of the number of original drawings I have preserved, 600 have been selected from a single work in order to permit a scrutiny less superficial than the usual present-day interpretation of a topic as complex as architecture. I am in complete agreement with this choice, and therefore wish this initiative the greatest possible success.

I wish to thank all those who have been so enthusiastic in contributing their efforts, with special thank-yous to Manlio Brusatin, Peter Noever, Hiroyuki Toyoda and Johannes Wieninger.

Tobia Scarpa

POINTS OF REFERENCE

I first met Carlo Scarpa in 1962. I was a good friend of his son Tobia at the time: both of us were vitally interested in the cultural and moral upheaval of those years.

For me, young and full of enthusiasm for the adventure I had plunged into, this meeting was like entering a new and fascinating universe. Carlo Scarpa, on the other hand, was on the threshold of mastery in his field, in a career which had matured step by step, far from ephemeral glitter: an international point of reference.

I have always held fast to Carlo Scarpa's conception of architecture, one which I also recognize in Tobia. And it was the latter, together with his wife Afra, who designed and carried out all the Benetton offices, factories and shops.

This is why my part in bringing about the exhibition at the Austrian Museum für angewandte Kunst means much more to me than paying tribute to one of the greatest architects of our century: it is the most natural thing in the world, like fondly remembering the father of a close friend, or one's teacher.

Luciano Benetton

ERINNERUNGEN

Eine meiner ersten Begegnungen mit Carlo Scarpa hatte ich in der „American Bar" von Adolf Loos in Wien. Kaum eingetreten drückte er temperamentvoll seine Bewunderung aus. Dann wanderte sein Blick allmählich von der Decke – die zuallererst seine Aufmerksamkeit fesselte – in den Raum, er registrierte die an der Bar sitzenden Damen, ging auf sie zu, verneigte sich lächelnd. Sogleich war er Mittelpunkt einer Gesellschaft, die ganz offensichtlich andere Neigungen als die Hingabe zur Architektur verfolgte. Scarpa bestellte Champagner für alle und ein Metermaß für sich. Er war begeistert von Adolf Loos und dessen Architektur, scherzte mit den Gästen, tastete mit Augen und Händen jedes Detail im Raum ab, nahm gänzlich unerwartete Körperpositionen ein, bis er schließlich mit Hilfe der Damen die „Loos Bar" zu vermessen begann. Er war fasziniert von den Proportionen und Details, wollte auf den Millimeter genau den Durchmesser des Barholms wissen und bezeichnete schließlich diesen Ort als „einzigartigen geistig-emotionalen Raum".

So wie er dort augenblicklich die Perfektion des Gedanklichen und Stofflichen aufspürte, keinerlei Scheu zeigte, seiner aufrichtigen Bewunderung und großen Begeisterung Ausdruck zu verleihen, suchte der Einzelgänger unter den Architekten in seiner Arbeit immer wieder die Perfektion – von der Gesamtanlage eines Bauwerkes bis zur Gestaltung und präzisen Vollendung aller Details.

Ein Leben lang verteidigte er seine Architektur, utopische Visionen, gegen die Realität, gegen die Mächtigen. Er suchte nie die Nähe von Politikern, verbündete sich mit keinem von ihnen, verstand vielmehr das Leben selbst als eine Art Kunstform. Selbst wenn er meinte, die venezianische Kultur des Kochens und Essens wäre in Gefahr, konnte es passieren, daß er in die Küche eines Restaurants eindrang und den verblüfften Köchen und Gästen die Zubereitung einer „echten" Pasta demonstrierte. Auch dieser Tätigkeit widmete er sich mit äußerster Konzentration, er war überzeugt, daß alles im richtigen Augenblick passieren, jeder Handgriff perfekt sein mußte. Scarpa konnte wie kaum ein anderer genießen, erfreute sich alltäglicher Dinge genauso wie an Kunstwerken, inszenierte immer wieder unvermutet und überraschend Situationen, die jede Begegnung mit ihm zu einem kleinen Fest, zu einem unvergeßlichen Erlebnis werden ließ.

Damals in der „Loos Bar", vor über fünfzehn Jahren, sprachen wir auch über die Möglichkeit, in Wien eine erste umfassende Carlo-Scarpa-Ausstellung zu veranstalten. Scarpa war sofort begeistert. Er, der zum ersten Mal in Wien war, hatte seit jeher eine besondere Beziehung zu dieser Stadt: Joseph Maria Olbrich und Josef Hoffmann waren für ihn so etwas wie Jugendvorbilder, wie er versicherte.

Die Ausstellung kam nicht zustande, stattdessen hielt Carlo Scarpa an der Akademie der bildenden Künste einen eindrucksvollen Vortrag mit dem Titel „Kann Architektur Poesie sein?". Temperamentvoll, mit der ihm eigenen Körpersprache, immer ein wenig ironisch und zum Scherzen aufgelegt, gänzlich undidaktisch, geistvoll und fesselnd präsentierte er sich ganz als der „professore" aus Venedig, hatte vor, einen Abriß über sein Gesamtwerk zu vermitteln und entwickelte als einer, der keine Theorie besaß – worauf er besonderen Wert legte – bereits in der Einführung seine Theorie, seine Methode und seine Haltung zur Architektur.

Scarpa, dessen Arbeiten von erstaunlicher Komplexität, Ideenreichtum, überraschender Formensprache, dem sicheren Gefühl für Gestaltungsdetails und absoluter Beherrschung der Materialien geprägt sind, begriff die Architektur als Poesie, die dann verwirklicht ist, wenn die Form das Maximum des Ausdruckes erreicht hat. Begriffe hingegen wie „poetische Architektur" oder gar „Umweltplanung" und „Urbanistik" fand er ärgerlich und lehnte sie als unsinnig, weil direkt in die Sterilität führend, ab. Der als großer Lehrer vielleicht zu wenig bekannte Scarpa, der selbst nie aufhören wollte zu lernen, dessen Ausstrahlung und Großmut, zu geben, sich nicht auf akademischen Boden beschränkte, hatte nahezu eine Panik vor Symposien, Architekturkonferenzen und Debatten, wollte sich nicht daran beteiligen, wie ihm auch das „Schlachtfeld der Argumente" zuwider war.

Die Grabanlage Brion in San Vito d'Altivole ist unbestritten das Meisterwerk des venezianischen Architekten und gleichzeitig sein eigenes Denkmal. Die erste Totenfeier, die in der von Carlo Scarpa errichteten Friedhofskapelle stattfinden sollte, war – eine Ironie des Schicksals, wie auch sein tödlicher Sturz über eine Treppe in Sendai, Japan – seine eigene. Bereits zu Lebzeiten suchte er seine Grabstätte aus – in San Vito, in einem abgeschiedenen Winkel, an einer schwer zugänglichen Stelle. In einer Art „Niemandsland" zwischen der von ihm errichteten Grabanlage für die Familie Brion und dem alten Dorffriedhof befindet sich die Grabstätte des „maestro", wie er in der ganzen Region genannt wurde. Die Details seines Grabmals hat er selbst festgelegt: durch ein in die Erde geschlagenes Rohr wollte er auch nach seinem Tod den Kontakt mit den Lebenden nicht missen.

Was Carlo Scarpa in San Vito, einer fruchtbaren Ebene, der hochgebauten kleinen Stadt Asolo mit ihren gezackten Hügelbergen vorgelagert, geschaffen hat, ist weniger ein Mausoleum als ein geweihter Bezirk. Es ging ihm vor allem darum, daß dieser Ort nicht nur an die Vergänglichkeit alles Irdischen mahnt, sondern auch für ein Leben nach dem Tod Zeugnis ablegt. Scarpa meinte auch einmal scherzhaft, auf diesem Friedhof könne man sich genauso gut auf den Grasboden legen, den Blick über die fruchtbare Landschaft und den Ort San Vito schweifen lassen und ein Glas Wein genießen.

Das Erscheinungsbild dieser Grabanlage mit all den überraschenden Details, vermischt mit Mythologie, Poesie und Symbolen ist aber vor allem durch die plastische Durchformung der Baukörper geprägt, etwa durch das in mannigfaltigsten Variationen wiederkehrende, für Carlo Scarpa so charakteristische Treppenmotiv. Im Stakkato der Abtreppungen, im Labyrinth der Durchgänge und wohlüberlegten Torkonstruktionen, im lebendigen Wasser und in der Vegetation, die den Beton zu sprengen scheint – überall spürt man die Hand des Poeten und Symbolisten Carlo Scarpa. Jede Veränderung in Licht und Jahreszeit geben der Grabanlage Brion ein ständig wechselndes Aussehen. Der österreichische Schriftsteller Alfred Kolleritsch schreibt darüber in seinem jüngsten Roman „Allemann":

„Die die Bauten und ihre Details gliedernde Stufen, dem stärksten Zeichen der Formensprache Scarpas, waren Stufen zum Tod. In einigen hatte sich Moos eingenistet, da und dort waren sie von Rissen getrennt. Sie verwehrten jeden Hinweis auf Verzeihung, auf die Umtriebe des Verstehens."

So wie Poesie keine Architekturdisziplin ist, jedoch Architektur zur Poesie werden kann, ist diese nun gemeinsam mit Tobia Scarpa und den Mitgliedern des Ausstellungskomitees realisierte Ausstellung keine, die man sonst von einem so bedeutenden Architekten erwartet: eben eine monumentale Retrospektive; stattdessen zeugt die Schau von dem Bemühen, durch das Konzentrieren auf ein Thema, uns die Sinnen- und Gedankenwelt des Architekten noch einmal in Erinnerung zu rufen.

Peter Noever

VENEZIA–WIEN

Dies ist nunmehr die zweite bedeutende Ausstellung, die über das Schaffen meines Vaters veranstaltet wird. Die erste fand in Venedig statt, diese aber in Wien.

Im vorigen Jahrhundert war Venedig eng mit Wien verbunden, und das nicht nur äußerlich. Im subtilen Spiel der kulturellen Bande Mitteleuropas schien das Abenteuer der Geschichte und des Lebens Venedigs in Wien beinahe seine Fortsetzung zu finden. Dieses Spiel konnte freilich nicht länger währen; es hat aber doch seinen Niederschlag gefunden. In dieser Situation ist mein Vater aufgewachsen, und an der „Moderne" hat er sich versucht, herausgefordert und konfrontiert. Ich halte diese Ausstellung im Museum für Angewandte Kunst – einem Themenbereich, der meinem Vater so wichtig war – für äußerst sinnvoll.

Betreuer der Ausstellung ist Philippe Duboy, ein feinsinniger Franzose, der die Arbeiten meines Vaters so sehr schätzt, daß er die Verantwortung dieses Unternehmens übernommen hat. Aus dem Bestand eigenhändiger Zeichnungen, die sich heute unter meiner Obhut befinden, wurden 600 für ein einziges Werk geschaffene Blätter ausgesucht; dies, um ein weniger überhastetes und somit sinnvolleres Studium der Exponate zu ermöglichen, als dies sonst heute, selbst bei so komplizierten Themen wie der Architektur, üblich ist. Ich kann mich voll hinter die getroffene Auswahl stellen und wünsche dem Unterfangen den größtmöglichen Erfolg.

Ein Dank sei an alle ausgesprochen, die mit großer Hingabe mitgearbeitet haben, insbesondere an Manlio Brusatin, Peter Noever, Hiroyuki Toyoda und Johannes Wieninger.

Tobia Scarpa

BEZUGSPUNKTE

Ich habe Carlo Scarpa im Jahre 1962 kennengelernt. In jener Zeit pflegte ich bereits den Umgang mit seinem Sohn Tobia: Beide waren wir voll des Interesses für die kulturellen und allgemein gesellschaftlichen Regungen jener Jahre.

Für mich, der ich jung war und voller Enthusiasmus für meine damals gerade anlaufenden Unternehmungen, bedeutete das alles das Eintreten in eine neue, faszinierende Welt. Carlo Scarpa hingegen war auf dem Wege zur vollen Reife seines beruflichen Werdeganges, eines Weges, der über sichere Etappen führte, abseits von allen kurzlebigen Sensationen: und gerade deshalb ein Bezugspunkt von internationalem Format.

Ich bin der von Carlo Scarpa vertretenen Architekturauffassung immer treu geblieben, und ich erkenne sie bei Tobia Scarpa wieder. Und er ist es, der es – zusammen mit seiner Frau Afra – übernommen hat, sämtliche Büros, Betriebe und Verkaufslokale der Firma Benetton zu entwerfen und auszuführen.

An der Verwirklichung der Ausstellung im Österreichischen Museum für angewandte Kunst mitzuwirken, ist für mich somit weit mehr, als für die Verbreitung des Werkes eines der größten Architekten unseres Jahrhunderts einen Beitrag zu leisten; es ist geradezu ein Akt der Selbstverständlichkeit: gleichbedeutend mit der herzlichen Erinnerung an den Vater eines Freundes, an den eigenen Lehrmeister.

Luciano Benetton

Carlo Scarpa

CAN ARCHITECTURE BE POETRY?

Revised lecture hold by Carlo Scarpa at the Akademie der bildenden Künste in Vienna, November 16th, 1976

I feel very touched because the geography of my academic background inclined me naturally while being at school to feel closer to the modern trends from Vienna, especially those with the glorious names you all know. Of course, the artist we knew and loved best, one who was able to publish most in German reviews—*Moderne Bauformen, Wasmuth,* etc. come to mind—was: Josef Hoffmann. And Josef Hoffmann had a great sense or feeling for decoration which students were also trained at the academies of Fine Arts (one has to recall, as Ruskin said, that art is decoration). This fact includes a very basic orientation for us both: I am a Byzantine at heart, and in Hoffmann you'll find something of an Oriental too: like a European looking towards the Orient. This may be a difficult way to explain the phenomenon, though those who know this architect's expressive forms will have to agree intuitively with what I say. At this point it doesn't hurt to laugh at these professors who like to flaunt their learning by talking about difficult, obscure or mysteriously arcane matters. And, to tell the truth, I am an heir to the cultural tradition which descends from the Victor Emmanuel II Monument in Rome, because I was the best pupil of my professor who had been the best pupil of his professor who happened to be the architect of this monument. So you are luckier than we were because you have had a homogeneous atmosphere of general, international culture, which is, if I'm not mistaken, called *"International Style."* Unfortunately, during that period Italy suffered from cultural poverty. This was the trouble, let's call it that, because all the figures who taught at schools like this one, académies des beaux arts, belonged to the eclectic taste of the 19th century. So we had a rather hard time getting away from the academic curriculum we had learned, quite apart from the fact that one should always do one's best (even if we had been completely up-to-date in our field) to achieve a certain personal quality, to achieve the sense of moral authority which an individual in the arts has to acquire at a certain point if he wishes to declare himself an artist in that sense. One always has to cut loose from the womb, as it were.

Well then, I had the good fortune to come across a book entitled *Vers une architecture*— everyone knows who the author is—about the time I finished school. This broadened my mind. Infact, this discovery was a genuine instance of what you call *"Sturm und Drang"*—my world view completely changed from that point onwards. So far some periods in the life of someone who does not want to be called a master for it is highly unlikely that we have any masters at present at all: they are all dead. A master is someone who expresses something new and which others listen to and understand if they can. But we, oh, pardon me, I meant to say, I, I do not consider myself a master; our poor heads are full of modern elements of the men I just now claimed—for all of us, sad to say—are all dead. Not one of the great modern architects is still living. The last one, Louis Kahn, passed away rather unpleasantly. And these are grave losses, because, in my opinion, they cannot be replaced.

The question on the small invitation I received was whether architecture could be poetry — I believe this is the correct translation of the German. Yes, of course it can be poetry. Frank Lloyd Wright declared many years ago in a London lecture: "Gentlemen, architecture is poetry." So the answer is yes; architecture is sometimes poetry, therefore poetry is not an everyday thing. It is not enough to say: I will create a poetic work of architecture. Poetry arises from things in themselves if the person who makes it has this nature, or it can derive from various conditions between the goals and the execution of architecture. What I want to say is that sometimes architecture is poetry, it can happen today such as it happened in the old days. I might call the nearby Secession building by Josef Olbrich poetic too, indeed it is full of poetry. Another way of posing the question is to ask: when is an Attic Greek base poetry, and when is another Attic base not poetry? This means that there are huge differences between two of the same object.

You could say that architecture in order to be poetic must have harmony. Harmony is like a face of a beautiful woman in which all the proportions are perfect. One Attic base is poetry, the other not. Architecture is a language very difficult to grasp and to understand. I don't mean you, those of you who are setting out to practice architecture, but in the overall variety of mankind which looks at things painting and sculpture are understood to a large extent, so is perhaps poetry, music very much so, while architecture remains a kind of mysterious language.

It was mentioned before, I think, that I was in Japan. In Japan one can clearly see the difference between those who are Shintoists and those who are Buddhists. Buddhism is a Chinese tendency, that is the influence of China, while Shinto is the genuine, authentic Japan. Our modern taste and our critical categories both favor Shinto, not Buddhism, to such an extent that Chinese architecture, in fact the entirety of this very glorious architecture, is not to our liking. If you look at the books, because it isn't always possible to go to Japan, you will see this difference. Now in my opinion — you can't really say that Shinto is more poetic than Buddhism from an architectural point of view — this is a great reversal of values because the value of a work consists in its greatest expression. When something is expressed very well this value can become very high indeed. But I wouldn't want you to think I've come here to give a sermon. I am a very humble and simple man. I've done work, some work. I am a specialist — I say that with a touch of irony because you should never trust a specialist although the modern world loves specialists — but I have become something of an exhibition designer and an architect of museums. I've done my work, it is not very much, not very important as to dimension. It isn't very grand.

I would like to explain the Tomba Brion because it is a rather recent work. It's very odd, or, perhaps strange and it is not easy to get society to commission this sort of thing: I mean to express oneself freely about highly questionable areas which may exclude modern rational thought, because it could be superfluous to this work.

I consider this work, if you permit me, to be rather good and which will even get better over time. I have tried to put some poetic imagination into it, though not in order to create poetic architecture but to make a certain kind of architecture that could emanate a sense of formal poetry. I mean an expressed form that can become poetry, though, as I said before, you cannot intentionally make poetry. I will attempt to explain this to you through simpler means. A person died in Italy; his family wanted to honor him because he had worked his way up from the lower class through force of will and hard work. So the family wished to honor him with a tomb. The place of the family tomb lay here. The family decided they wanted more space for it. The landowner wanted to sell even more land, not a little. 100 square meters would have been enough for me. And this is 2 200 square meters. So we decided to build shelters for the family-tombs. In short, to protect them from bad wheather. The tomb of the couple Brion is the sunniest place. And it offers the most beautiful view. The deceased had asked to be close to earth since he was born in this village—so I decided to build a small arch, which I will call *arcosolium. (arcosolium* is a Latin term from the time of the early Christians in the catacombs. Important persons or martyrs were buried in them). I used a more costly version. This is what you call arcosolium, it's nothing more than a simple arch from the Catholic tradition. I thought it a good idea for two people who had loved each other to be put in such a way as to be able to greet one another, after death. Soldiers stand erect, movements are human.

The *arcosolium* became an arch, a bridge span, an arch of reinforced concrete and would still have looked like a bridge if I hadn't had it illustrated, I mean decorated. But instead of painting we used mosaics, a Venetian tradition that I interpreted in a different way. This is the path lined with cypresses; small Italian cemeteries have always cypresses. So this path—architects love pathways, there are many, many pathways in Italy—is called *propylaeum*, which means gate, entrance. The first impression you get from the cemeter is by looking through these two "eyes". This piece of land was so large it became a lawn—what we call in French *gazon*—; and to rationalize this expanse of space we thought it useful to add a small temple for funeral services. Still too large. So the wall, I call it sacred ground because you have a beautiful panorama from inside whereas from outside you cannot look inside.

Coming from the village you pass by the funeral chapel. The chapel belongs to the general public. The land is state property, although the family has the only right to use it. Here you have a private atmosphere, a small pavilion in a basin: "Une pavillon pour la méditation." So this sums up what we did. The place for the dead is a garden. After all the 19th century American cemeteries are like the one in Chicago a large park, large parks unlike the typical Napoleonic graveyards (which are awful!). It is a large park where you can drive in with the car; there are wonderful tombs there, some of them by Sullivan. Almost all cemeteries look like boxes, like these shoe-boxes you get at the shoe-maker. There are even cemeteries where the dead are mounted by elevators. Luckily, Veneto is not very densely populated and its people live rather quietly. I wanted to show some ways in which you could approach death in a social and civic way; and further what meaning there was in death, in the ephemerality of life—other than these shoe-boxes. Modern lesiglation should permit to bury men upright and have them wrapped up like in the ancient's day. That's how you could save space—by changing the law. Man should be burried upright, that's all, for we're getting short of space. Instead of ending up with these boxes, they should be used for other things. Virtually everyone in my country, regardless of class, will do anything to have a grave; they are satisfied even with a burial niche called "loculo." This may be a tradition; I think it makes no sense.

Questions

—I was told that Scarpa has taken a place in the cemetery of San Vito. Is that true, and which criteria did you use in choosing it?

—Yes, yes: economic criteria because if you want to be resurrected from beneath the ground modern society wants you to pay. I mean I wanted to save money. No, there's a small spot here, an indentation that goes from here to the old cemetery. So I shall rest here in a no-man's-land, in the municipal copse. No one can deny me this. It's a caprice of mine—will that do for you? Did you read about it in *Architecture d'aujourd'hui*?

—No.

—Then who told you?

—The innkeeper's wife at the village trattoria.

—Oh, so you went there? You know the place? It has become very popular in Veneto: everyone comes to take a look, and it isn't even finished, that's the funny thing. And it still leaks, I guess we could use a good Austrian engineer to show us how to hold back the water. Some of you might think I've sold out to the capitalists. But if you buy a small piece of land in, let's say, Milan or Vienna, or Berlin, or Madrid or Rome in order to build a family tomb, and the regulations say you have to use marble, etc., and if you had the ambition to add a sculpture you would end up spending as much as 150—200 million lire for all this, and even more if you went to a great sculptor: let's say Marino Marini or Manzú or Henry Moore. In that case you'd have to spend more. All of this work costs money: 150 million lire as of now. And they all say I was paid as much as what the costs of the whole work had been. Yet I don't own anything, nor do I want to own something. I am a genuine communist.

—It would interest me to know what you have to say about this kind of burial; I mean if for you and the Italians in general, a certain kind of burial is a guarantee of life after death.

—This is an odd question... no, it's not clear at all. You didn't put it right, what do you mean by "guarantees"? In your opinion, what does "guarantee of death" mean?

—I mean, there are two ways of looking: the importance of a place and, let's say, its mystical sense. Do you believe in it?

—Well, I come from a devout Roman Catholic family. I do not practice, like almost everyone, you see? Many of us forgot the religious instruction we had as children, yet there is still a moral background deeply inside of us which remains. Certain conditions do exist and, let's be clear about this, you're in favor of everyone being cremated? Even the Catholics have begun to permitting it because we have not enough space. We'll have more dead people than living ones, how will it end?

Starting with the French Revolution and the famous Napoleonic laws which allowed, socially speaking, everyone to having a place in the earth—at least for some time, otherwiese this would go on for ever. During the times of the Egyptians, Romans, etc., only the rich and powerful had tombs for themselves. And the poor, what's the expression, la populasse, that is the humble people all over the world, the ones without any power whatsoever, how did they end? In ashes, in dust, in the lost dephts of time. In fact, the Napoleonic laws which could still be called democratic no longer interpret the French Revolution: justly because the French Revolution had proclaimed liberté, egalité, fraternité... that is, we are all equal, we are all brothers, and it turns out—like with communism today—that it isn't true, unfortunately, not a word of it is true. Because the cemeteries interpreted according to the Napoleonic Code meant wall, colonnade and field, campus: hallowed ground *(camposanto)* in the earth, a small token, for the general population. But then local council immediately began with speculations out of practical reasons. They simply sold the space. For one you paid less and for the other more, on the latter you could erect a tomb. So the populasse is here and the well-to-do, that is the new middle class, in there. It all ended up by filling the public space with more and more monumental tombs. This is the tradition as it still exists today...

As I mentioned before it was the family, the wife and daughter, who decided to buy property. Now there are curious circumstances involved. Of course, I could have made a large statue and leave the rest a lawn, but I enjoyed doing things. In fact, I had what I consider a rather socialy-minded idea: a place that belongs to everyone, where children could play for example. I used to go there when I lived in Asolo, which is nearby. It's a place of meditation: peaceful, pagan, if you will, very beautiful. I mean you enjoy being there. That is, it's arranged in such a way that you can visit the dead in a peaceful setting without shoe-boxes, without strong-boxes. I am very upset that Venetian architecture students stole and soiled things and wrote: "Down with the Capitalists" and "Scarpa Mercenary Bastard" on the walls. Well, I never sell myself to anyone: I have never sold myself and will never sell myself, because I have a free spirit; and I can make a coffin, or, if you want me to, a chair for this gentleman. You can make everything. You can design a beautiful tie, or a fountain pen, or a "scarpa" (shoe).—You can design, invent anything—I don't know what "design" means.

—How did the people in the village react to this cemetery?

—Oh, so far the population has, I think, been very happy with it. They go there to look at it, on Sundays. They take walks there, children play, dogs frolic. Here, I must tell you a story. When the priest saw the first model he went like this: "Oh," he said, "all this for only one person!" Then he said: "And what about us poor priests?" I said that I hadn't thought about this problem. I thought that in the country, in Italy, priests were buried inside the church whereas in the cities they have separate sections in the graveyards with nuns on one side, friars on the other. So I divided off a section at this point. I had the ground lowered 10 centimeters and immediately had planted eleven (9,5 meter high) cypresses with water. There is a passage way and a grassy pit where I had seven ribs fractured. Here then we have space for nuns and priests; there will be one, two, three, four, five, six, seven, eight point twenty: that makes 160 yards; plenty space for the priests. That's how we devise the space for the death of the priests. So it's not right to call this a capitalistic centure, quite the contrary. I mean to a certain extent it's like an ancient capital which could afford the luxury of having made beautiful things for the city. It was like that then. Otherwise—from our view-point—we would have to destroy the works of the past since they were made by emperors and kings. And all we do is exclaim "Uh, ah, how wonderful!" out of sheer admiration. The machine has created tremendous problems for the modern social order: everything is mechanized. Despite all the great problems—machines and the like—deriving from our modern social system, that is very mechanical, we should strive to reach the highest ideal, to return to the ancient origins of the Greeks. In this time, the city, *polis,* had believed in the notion of god or state depending on which was esteemed high and holy. For the rest one should try to live as good as one can and to benefit from modern technology. Yet I, being one among the populace, would like to have the wide parks of Versailles for walks, and to have my children and their children to play on. This is the great modern dream, one shared by everyone... and these monuments weren't all that huge after all. And if I may add a personal thought: great works of art are small in size. (This has nothing to do with my cemetery).

—Mrs. Tabarelli once told me that you cook an incredible pasta dish. Is that part of your world view too?

—Me? My wife. Yes, of course, you also have to be a gourmand to be a good architect. I think all the architects like to eat. Now I have to tell you something. When I was thirty or forty I met a number of great architects, truly great architects: Frank Lloyd Wright—no, there I must have been older, I suppose fifty—, and Louis Kahn, Alvar Aalto. Alvar Aalto drank a lot but he didn't eat much, so I supposed a superior mind could not pay much attention to food. When I was your age, as young as you, I weighed 57 kilograms, and now I weigh 90 kilos. I had to tell you this because I thought I would never become a great architect for all the joy I had in good food. I have to add one more thing, a joke by an American playwright, Thorton Wilder: "A glass of wine, sir, to the health of these noble ladies!"

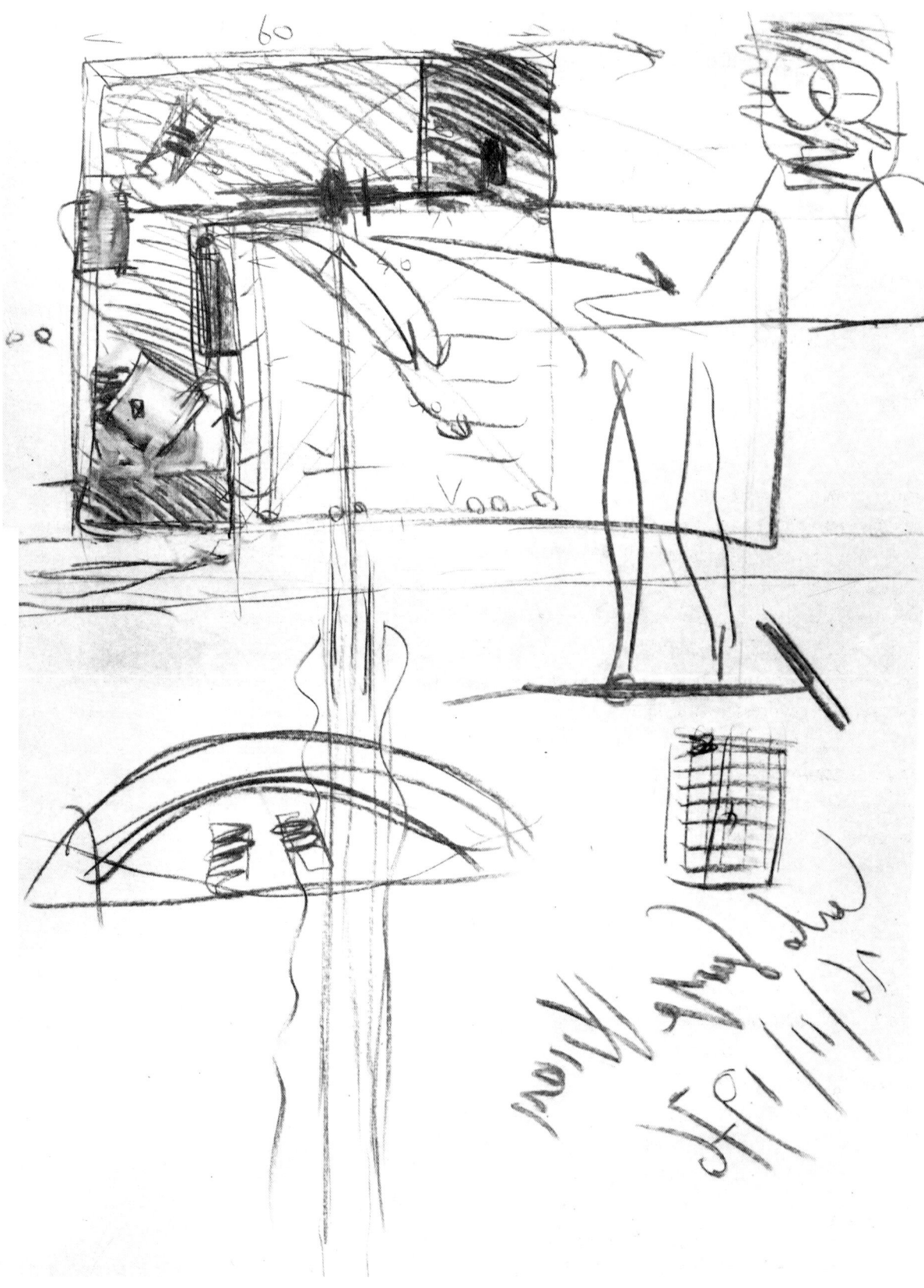

Sketch, made by Carlo Scarpa during his lecture in Vienna
Zeichnung, von Carlo Scarpa während seines Vortrages in Wien angefertigt

Carlo Scarpa

KANN ARCHITEKTUR POESIE SEIN?

Redigierte Fassung eines Vortrags von Carlo Scarpa, gehalten am 16. November 1976 an der Akademie der bildenden Künste in Wien

Ich bin sehr ergriffen, denn die Tradition meiner Studien brachte mich – zuletzt auch durch die geographische Lage – der Wiener Moderne samt ihrer glorreichen Namen, die einem sofort ins Gedächtnis kommen, näher. Selbstverständlich war jener Künstler, den wir am besten kannten und am meisten schätzten, auch der, der am meisten in deutschsprachigen Zeitschriften veröffentlicht wurde, wie z. B. *„Moderne Bauformen"*, *„Wasmuth"* usf., dieser Mann war: Josef Hoffmann. Josef Hoffmann hatte einen ausgeprägten Sinn für das Dekorative, den sich auch die Studenten der bildenden Künste aneigneten (dies erinnert an John Ruskin's These: „Architektur ist Dekoration").

Im Grunde bin ich ein Byzantiner, und im Grunde hat auch Josef Hoffmann etwas von einem orientalischen Charakter, und zwar in dem Sinn, wie ein Europäer sich zum Orientalischen hinwendet. Dies ist vielleicht nicht die richtige Art, ein Phänomen zu erklären; jedoch die, die die expressiven Formen Josef Hoffmanns kennen, werden schon verstehen, was ich meine. Es schadet nicht, hier einmal zu lachen, wenn sich die Professoren so wie Hoffmann immer aufspielen und von ernsten, obskuren und mysteriösen Dingen zu sprechen anfangen. Um die Wahrheit zu sagen, ich bin ein Erbe jener kulturellen Tradition, die zurückgeht auf das Monument des Vittorio Emanuele II in Rom. Ich war nämlich der beste Schüler meines Professors, und dieser wiederum war der beste Schüler seines Professors, der der Erbauer dieses Monuments war. Deshalb seid Ihr glücklicher als wir, denn Ihr hattet den Vorteil eines homogenen Klimas, einer allgemeinen, internationalen Kultur, welche, wenn ich mich nicht irre, *„Internationaler Stil"* genannt wird. Leider war Italien zu dieser Zeit kulturell nicht sehr bedeutend. Ein Grund für die geistige Armut an den italienischen Schulen – an denen für bildende Kunst wie dieser hier – waren die Professoren, die dem eklektischen Geschmack des 19. Jhdts. angehörten. Es fiel uns daher nicht leicht, uns von dem akademischen curriculum wieder zu befreien; abgesehen davon, daß jeder für sich immer das Beste anstreben sollte, auch dann, wenn wir sozusagen ganz up-to-date gewesen wären. Ich glaube nämlich, daß man gar nicht anders kann, als sich vom mütterlichen Schoß zu befreien; irgendwann kommt einmal der Zeitpunkt, wo Fragen der persönlichen Qualität und moralischen Autorität für den Künstler, oder zumindest für den, der es werden will, ganz wichtig werden.

Für mich war es ein großes Glück, daß ich ungefähr zu der Zeit, als ich die Schule abgeschlossen hatte, ein Buch mit dem Titel *„Vers une architecture"* – Sie alle kennen den Autor – fand. Für mich öffnete sich damit ein neuer Horizont. Meine ganze Weltanschauung änderte sich aufgrund dieser Entdeckung, die auch etwas mit einer „Sturm und Drang"-Zeit zu tun hat – so wie Sie das nennen.

Soweit die Etappen eines kleinen Lebens, das eigentlich nicht das Leben eines Meisters sein möchte. Ich glaube vielmehr, daß wir in diesem Moment vielleicht gar keinen Meister mehr haben. Sie sind alle gestorben, sie sind alle tot. Ein Meister ist der, der etwas Neues hervorbringt, und das sich die anderen anhören, oder das sie verstehen, wenn sie können. Aber wir – oh pardon – ich wollte sagen, daß ich mich nicht für einen Meister halte, denn unsere armen Köpfe sind voll von Komponenten der Moderne, von Leuten, von denen ich vorerst behauptete, daß sie leider schon tot seien. Kein einziger großer Architekt der Moderne lebt noch. Als letzter – und auf keine sehr angenehme Weise – ging Louis Kahn von uns; und das sind schwere Verluste, da diese Leute nach meiner Meinung nicht ersetzbar sind.

Die Frage auf meiner Einladung lautet, ob Architektur Poesie sein kann – ja, sie kann ganz sicher Poesie sein. Frank Lloyd Wright sagte auf einer Konferenz in London: „Die Architektur, meine Herren, ist Poesie"! Also, die Antwort ist ja: hie und da ist Architektur Poesie, das heißt nicht immer, weil die Gesellschaft nicht nur nach Poesie verlangt, und deshalb ist Poesie auch nicht etwas für alle Tage.

Es genügt auch nicht zu sagen: „Jetzt mache ich eine poetische Architektur". Die Poesie kommt aus der Sache selbst, wenn der, der sie macht, diese Gabe hat; ansonsten gibt es auch noch bestimmte Bedingungen zwischen der Vorstellung und der Ausführung einer Architektur. In bestimmten Fällen ist Architektur Poesie, so wie in der Antike kann sie es vielleicht auch heute noch sein. Ich sage, poetisch oder voll Poesie ist das Gebäude der Sezession von Olbrich, das sich nur wenige Schritte von der Akademie der bildenden Künste befindet. Die Frage könnte folgendermaßen lauten: „Wann ist eine attische Basis Poesie und wann ist sie es nicht"? Man könnte sagen, daß die Architektur, die wir als poetisch bezeichnen, Harmonie haben sollte; Harmonie ist wie ein wunderschönes Frauengesicht, in dem alle proportionalen Verhältnisse perfekt sind. Die eine attische Basis ist Poesie, die andere ist es nicht. Zwischen zwei gleichen Dingen sind oft immense Unterschiede. Die Architektur ist auch eine Sprache, die nicht leicht zu verstehen ist. Ich meine nicht Euch, die Ihr auf dem Weg seid, Architektur zu machen, aber generell haben die Menschen, wie sie so die Dinge betrachten, die Malerei und die Bildhauerei ganz gut verstanden, vielleicht auch die Dichtkunst, ganz sicherlich aber die Musik – Architektur hingegen ist eine geheimnisvolle Sprache geblieben.

Es wurde erwähnt, daß ich in Japan war. In Japan unterscheidet man zwischen zwei Strömungen: die Shintoisten und die Buddhisten. Der Buddhismus kam als Einfluß von China nach Japan, der Shintoismus dagegen ist authentisch. Unser moderner Geschmack sowie unsere kritische Anschauung bevorzugen den Shintoismus, nicht den Buddhismus. Aus diesem Grunde gefällt uns die chinesische Architektur nicht, auch wenn sie noch so viel geleistet hat. Für den modernen rationellen Verstand mögen diese Probleme vielleicht gar nicht existieren – genauso könnte die Vernunft für den Zweck dieser Arbeit überflüssig sein. Von mir aus gesehen – und von einem architektonischen Standpunkt aus betrachtet kann man ja wirklich nicht sagen, daß der Shintoismus poetischer sei als der Buddhismus – ergibt sich da eine große Wertverschiebung, weil der Wert eines Werkes in dessen Ausdruckskraft besteht. Wenn etwas sehr gut ausgedrückt ist, wird auch der Wert ein sehr großer. Aber natürlich möchte ich nicht den Eindruck bei Ihnen erwecken, ich sei hierher gekommen, um eine Predigt zu halten. Ich bin ein sehr bescheidener und einfacher Mensch. Ich habe gearbeitet, d. h. ich habe ein paar Arbeiten gemacht. Ich bin ein Spezialist – ich sage das nicht ohne einen Anflug von Ironie, denn man muß sich ja vor allen Spezialisten hüten, auch wenn die moderne Welt sie so sehr liebt – für Ausstellungsgestaltung und Museumsbau geworden. Fast wurde ich ein „Museograph". Das was ich gemacht habe, sind kleine Arbeiten, sind keine Monumentalbauten.

Ich würde gerne etwas näher eingehen auf eine meiner Arbeiten, die Tomba Brion; sie ist ziemlich neu und etwas außergewöhnlich. Die heutige Gesellschaft gibt für so etwas, das sich sehr frei über umstrittene Dinge äußert, nicht gerne einen Auftrag. Ich finde diese Arbeit, die ich gemacht habe – wenn Sie erlauben – ganz gut und die, falls sie etwas länger bestehen bleiben wird, auch noch etwas besser werden könnte, und wo ich versuchte, etwas hinzuzufügen – man könnte dies auch poetische Phantasie nennen. Allerdings nicht, um poetische Architektur zu machen, sondern um eine Art Architektur zu machen, von der vielleicht etwas Poesie ausstrahlt. – Und dies geschieht aus formalen Gründen, das heißt, die dargestellte Form kann oder muß sogar Poesie werden. Aber man kann nicht, wie ich schon vorhin sagte, „poetische Architektur" machen wollen.

Ich werde nun versuchen, mit einfachen Strichen am Papier einfache Dinge zu erklären, die jeder versteht. In Italien ist ein Mann gestorbe; seine Familie wollte ihn ehren, weil er Großes geleistet hatte, weil er sich mit eigenem Willen und Können vom Nichts emporgearbeitet hatte. Dies ist der Plan eines kleinen Friedhofs in einem kleinen Dorf in Italien. Die Familie wollte mit einem Grabdenkmal den Mann ehren. Der Ort des Familiengrabes lag hier. Die Familie wollte einen etwas größeren Grund für das Grab des Verstorbenen – mir hätten 100 m² genügt. Der Grundbesitzer aber wollte viel Grund verkaufen: Nun sind es 2200 m². Ich habe dann beschlossen, für die Familiengräber eine große Überdachung zu bauen als Schutz vor dem Wetter.

Das Grabdenkmal des Ehepaares Brion ist der Ort, der der Sonne am meisten ausgesetzt ist – zugleich auch der Punkt mit der besten Aussicht. Der Tote wünschte sich, nahe der Erde zu sein, denn er wurde in diesem Orte geboren. – Und so dachte ich, einen kleinen Bogen zu bauen, den ich „arco solium" nennen möchte. „Arco solium" kommt aus dem Latein, aus der frühchristlichen Zeit der Katakomben. Wichtige Leute oder Märtyrer wurden in einer etwas kostspieligen Weise begraben. Das heißt „arco solium" – und das ist nichts anderes als ein einfacher Bogen. Ich dachte mir, daß sich zwei Personen, die sich zu Lebzeiten liebten, nach dem Tode einander zuneigen sollten, um sich so zu grüßen. Aufrecht stehen die Soldaten; die Bewegung ist menschlicher.

Der „arco solium" wurde zur Brücke; ein kleiner Betonbogen wäre eine Brücke geblieben – und damit es keine Brücke blieb, war es notwendig, diesen Bogen zu ornamentieren. Anstatt einen Maler anzustellen, um das Gewölbe auszumalen, bekleideten wir es mit Mosaik; das ist eine venetianische Tradition. Das Gewölbe wurde also anders, auf meine Art interpretiert. Zum Friedhof führt diese lange Zypressenallee. Es ist eine italienische Tradition, daß kleine Friedhöfe einen „cupressus" haben.

Solche Durchgänge *(percorsi)* wie den vom Gemeindefriedhof lieben die Architekten, aber vielleicht nur in Italien, da ist alles ein „*percorso*". Diesen „*percorso*" bezeichne ich als „*propyleion*", dies ist ein Tor, ein Eingang, ein „*portico*". Den ersten Eindruck vom Friedhof bekommt man, wenn man durch die „zwei Augen" schaut. Die Fläche ist sehr groß und wurde als ein grüne Rasen – „*gazon*" auf Französisch – gestaltet. Um die Dimension des Raumes zu rechtfertigen, dachten wir uns, daß auch ein kleiner Tempel für Totenfeiern notwendig sei. Es war alles immer noch zu groß.

Wir haben das Gelände gehoben, denn von hier aus hat man ein wunderschönes Panorama; von draußen aber sieht man nicht herein.

Vom Dorf kommt man bei der Totenkapelle vorbei auf dieses besondere Grundstück. So kann man den neuen Friedhof betreten. Die Kapelle gehört allen. Der Grund gehört dem Staat. Die Familie hat aber das Recht, hier begraben zu werden. Hier empfindet man eine private Atmosphäre: ein kleiner Pavillon in einem Wasserbecken: „*pavillon pour la meditation*".

Das wäre soweit alles, eine Zusammenfassung von dem, was wir gemacht haben. Dieser Ort für die Toten ist ein Garten. Übrigens sind die großen amerikanischen Friedhöfe aus dem 19. Jahrhundert, wie Chicago zum Beispiel, große Parks; ganz anders als die typischen napoleonischen Friedhöfe, die ganz schrecklich sind. Der Friedhof in Chicago ist ein großer Park, man kann sogar mit dem Auto hineinfahren; es gibt dort wunderbare Grabdenkmäler, einige sind auch von Sullivan entworfen. Im Veneto werden die Toten heute in Schachteln bestattet – Schuhschachteln wie beim Schuster. Es gibt sogar Friedhöfe, wo die Toten mit dem Aufzug verschickt werden. Veneto ist zum Glück dünn besiedelt und die Bevölkerung ist eher ruhig. Ich wollte zeigen, wie man es machen könnte, wie man sich im sozialen und bürgerlichen Sinne dem Tode gegenüber verhalten könnte, was der Sinn des Todes, des Vergänglichen sein könnte – anders als diese Schachtelwirtschaft. Die moderne Gesetzgebung sollte erlauben, daß der Mensch senkrecht begraben werden kann, eingewikkelt wie in der Antike. So könnte man Platz gewinnen, man müßte das Gesetz ändern. Der tote Mensch sollte aufrecht stehen; wir haben keinen Platz mehr. Sonst gibt es halt diese Schächtelchen. Man sollte die Schächtelchen für etwas anderes verwenden. In unserem Land wollen fast alle ein Grab, auch wenn es ganz einfache Leute sind, und deshalb geben sie sich auch mit einem „loculo" zufrieden. Vielleicht ist das eine Tradition... Ich weiß es nicht, ich würde sie schrecklich nennen.

Fragen aus dem Publikum:

– Ich habe gehört, daß sich Scarpa in San Vito auf dem Friedhof einen Platz ausgesucht hat. Stimmt das, und nach welchen Kriterien wurde der Platz ausgesucht?

– Ah ja, ja. Aus ökonomischen Gründen, denn unsere moderne Gesellschaft verlangt auch für das Leben unter der Erde Geld – und da wollte ich sparen. Nein, da gibt es eine kleine Stelle, eine kleine Einbuchtung, die führt zum Ortsfriedhof; und so werde ich hier im Niemandsland schlafen, das heißt weder Brion noch Gemeinde. Und das kann mir von keinem der beiden abgestritten werden. Das ist eine Laune, genügt Ihnen das? Haben Sie das in „l'architecture d'aujourd'hui" gelesen?

– Nein, nein, nein.

– Wer hat es Ihnen dann gesagt?
– Die Wirtin im Gasthaus.
– Ah, Sie kennen sich aus.

Der Friedhof wurde zu einem Anziehungspunkt im Veneto. Alle fahren hin, um sich das anzuschauen, obwohl es noch gar nicht fertig ist. Das ist das Komische daran. Das Wasser rinnt auch noch immer aus, es benötigte vielleicht eines guten österreichischen Technikers, der zeigen könnte, wie man abdichtet. Vielleicht glaubt der eine oder andere, daß ich mich an die Kapitalisten verkauft habe. – Wenn Sie hingegen in Mailand, oder in Wien, oder in Berlin, oder vielleicht in Madrid oder in Rom ein kleines Grundstück kaufen, um ein Familiengrab zu bauen, und die Bauvorschriften sagen, man müsse in Marmor usw. bauen, und wenn Sie dann auch den Ehrgeiz haben, eine Skulptur darauf zu haben – würden auch Sie hundertfünfzig oder zweihundert Millionen Lire ausgeben für diese Sachen. – Vielleicht auch mehr, denn wenn man zu einem berühmten Bildhauer geht, wie zum Beispiel zu Marino Marini oder Manzu oder Henry Moore, muß man noch mehr zahlen – richtig? Diese Arbeit hingegen kostet bis zum heutigen Tag hundertfünfzig Millionen, und alle sage, daß ich dabei soviel verdient habe, wie die ganze Arbeit gekostet hat. Ich aber besitze nichts und will nichts besitzen. – Ich bin ein „authentischer Kommunist".

– Glauben Sie, daß diese Art Leute zu bestatten, das Leben nach dem Tode versichert?

– Das ist eine sehr seltsame Frage, was heißt „versichert", was verstehen Sie unter „versichern"?

– Versichern in zweifacher Hinsicht: erstens in der Bedeutung des Ortes und zweitens in mystischer Hinsicht.

– Glauben Sie daran? Ja, sehen Sie, ich stamme aus einer römisch-apostolisch-katholischen Familie, aber praktiziere nicht, wie fast alle. Viele von uns haben die religiöse Erziehung, die wir in unserer Jugend erhielten, vergessen, verlassen, aber in unserem tiefsten Inneren bleiben bestimmte Wertvorstellungen. – Sie möchten damit sagen, daß wir alle verbrannt werden sollten, die katholische Kirche erlaubt das inzwischen auch, es wird bald keinen Platz mehr geben, es gibt mehr Tote als Lebende, also wie soll das enden? Die Französische Revolution und Napoleon machten, sozial gesehen, großartige Gesetze, die besagten, daß jeder die Möglichkeit haben sollte, einen Platz in der Erde zu haben, zumindest für eine gewisse Zeit, denn sonst würde das ewig weitergehen. – Früher hatten nur die Großen, die Reichen Gräber – bei den Ägyptern, den Römern usw. –, die Armen, „*la populasse*", und das meine ich nicht im schlechten Sinne, das heißt das einfache Volk der ganzen Welt, das überhaupt keine Macht hatte, die sind verschwunden. Sie wurden zu Asche, zu Staub; wie verlorene Zeit weit weg. Die napoleonischen Gesetze sind zwar noch immer demokratische Gesetze, sind aber nicht mehr die richtige Interpretation der Französischen Revolution, denn diese setzte sich für Freiheit, Gleichheit aller ein, das heißt alle sind gleich, alle sind Brüder. Ungefähr wie der Kommunismus heute, und es hat sich gezeigt, daß das nicht wahr ist – leider. Denn die gesetzlichen Bestimmungen für den Friedhof lauteten: Umfassungsmauer, „*porticus*" und Erdenfeld *(Campus, camposanto)*, auf der Erde ein kleines Zeichen für das einfache Volk! Die Behörde aber machte aus praktischen Gründen sofort Spekulationen. Ich sage ja nichts dagegen – sie verkauften die Gräber. Also hier zahlt man weniger und hier zahlt man mehr und dafür kann man ein monumentales Familiengrab errichten. Deswegen ist hier die „*populasse*" und hier sind die Reichen, das heißt, die neue bürgerliche Klasse. Das endet damit, daß auch jenes Feld, das für die normalen Gräber bestimmt war, mit riesigen monumentalen Grabstätten angefüllt wurde. So ist die heutige Tradition.

Weil Giuseppe Brion von diesem Ort stammte, kaufte die Familie, Frau und Tochter, den Grund, wie ich schon vorher erzählte. Da kam es zu diesen kuriosen Umständen. Sicher hätte ich eine große Statue machen und alles ringsherum grün lassen können. Es hat mir Spaß gemacht, diese Dinge zu bauen... Ich möchte sogar sagen, daß ich eine nahezu soziale Idee hatte, nämlich, daß dieser Ort allen gehörte: Die Kinder gehen zum Spielen dorthin. Als ich noch in Asolo wohnte, das nicht weit weg von Altivole liegt, gefiel es mir, hinzugehen. Es wurde ein heiterer Ort der Meditation. Wenn Sie wollen, ist er auch ein bißchen heidnisch und sehr schön. Das heißt, dort fühlt man sich wohl. Das heißt, dieser Ort ist so gestaltet, daß man auch seine Toten mit heiteren Gefühlen grüßen kann – ohne all die Schuhschachteln und die Panzerschränke.

Es hat mich sehr betrübt, daß Architekturstudenten aus Venedig kamen. Sie stahlen, sie beschmutzten und sie schrieben auf die Mauer: „Nieder mit den Kapitalisten – Scarpa Bastard". Ich habe nie etwas verkauft, ich werde nie etwas verkaufen und nie zu kaufen sein, weil mein Geist frei ist. Ich kann sowohl einen Sarg zeichnen oder, wenn Sie wollen, einen Stuhl für diesen Herrn. Nicht wahr, alles kann man machen. Man kann eine schöne Krawatte zeichnen, oder eine Füllfeder, oder eine „scarpa" (Schuh). – Alles kann man zeichnen, erfinden, ich weiß nicht was „design" heißt.

– Wie wurde dieser Friedhof von der Bevölkerung des Ortes aufgenommen?

– Die Bevölkerung ist bis heute – wie mir scheint – sehr zufrieden. Die Leute schauen sich das immer an, sonntags gehen sie dort spazieren; die Kinder spielen; die Hunde laufen überall herum.

Da muß ich Ihnen eine kleine Geschichte erzählen: Als der Pfarrer das erste Modell sah, sagte er: „Uhhh, für eine einzige Person so viele Sachen, und wir armen Geistlichen?" Ich sagte ihm, daß ich wirklich nicht an dieses Problem gedacht hätte. Ich glaubte nämlich, daß in Italien die Geistlichen auf dem Land in der Kirche begraben werden. In den Städten haben die Geistlichen auf der einen Seite des Friedhofs und die Klosterfrauen auf der anderen einen Ort, wo sie begraben werden. Deshalb machte ich diese Abteilung, wo die Erde zehn Zentimeter tiefer ist. Hier pflanzten wir sofort elf Zypressen, die

9,5 Meter hoch sind. Hier ist Wasser. Hier ist ein Übergang und hier ist ein Loch mit Gras, wo ich mir sieben Rippen gebrochen habe. Hier also werden Klosterfrauen und Pfarrer ihren Bereich haben – also: eins, zwei, drei, vier, fünf, sechs, sieben, acht – acht mal zwanzig sind hundertsechzig Jahre. Da haben wir leicht genug für die Pfarrer. Somit haben wir diesen Ort auch für den Tod der Pfarrer bestimmt. Meiner Meinung nach ist es nicht wahr, daß das kapitalistisch ist, es ist nahezu das Gegenteil, so wie sich die Reichen in der Antike den Luxus leisten konnten, schöne Sachen für die Stadt zu bauen. In der Antike machte man das so. Sonst müßte man von unserem Standpunkt aus mit Kanonen alle großen Werke der Vergangenheit zerstören, denn sie wurden von Kaisern und Königen gemacht. Wir sagen jedoch heute: „Uh, wie schön, uh, wie schön!" Nicht wahr? Wir sollten versuchen, trotz der großen Schwierigkeiten von Seiten unserer modernen sozialen Ordnung, wegen der Maschinen und wegen all dem, was sehr mechanisch ist, zum höchsten Ideal, zum antiken Ursprung des Griechentums zurückzukehren, wo man für die Stadt, die „polis", als Ordner ihres Gebietes den Begriff des Gottes oder des Staates, je nachdem, an was man glaubte, für hoch und heilig hielt. Und für den Rest sollte man versuchen, so gut wie möglich zu leben, da es uns die moderne Technologie auch ermöglichen würde. Aber ich, als einer der „populasse", möchte die großen Gärten von Versailles zum Spazierengehen und für meine Kinder und Enkel zum Spielen. Das ist der große Traum, dessen Erfüllung sich alle gewünscht haben. Es waren auch nicht einmal so große Monumente. Und wenn Sie mir erlauben, würde ich Ihnen noch einen kleinen persönlichen Gedanken vorbringen: Ein großes Kunstwerk hat immer kleine Dimensionen. – Das hat nichts mit meinem Friedhof zu tun.

– Frau Tabarelli hat mir einmal gesagt, daß Sie eine unvergleichlich gute „pasta asciutta" kochen können. Gehört das auch zu Ihrem Weltbild?

– Ich? – Meine Frau. – Sicher, man muß auch „gourmet" sein, wenn man ein guter Architekt sein will. Ich weiß nicht, ich glaube alle Architekten essen gerne. Nein, nun muß ich etwas erzählen: Als ich dreißig, vierzig war, habe ich große Architekten kennengelernt, ganz große, wie Frank Lloyd Wright, nein, da war ich älter, fünfzig, auch Luis Kahn, auch Alvan Aalto, aber der „bibebit". Sie alle legten wenig Wert auf das Essen, und so dachte ich mir, daß eine höhere Qualität an Geistigkeit nicht so sehr an die Nahrung gebunden sei. Als ich so jung war wie Sie, wog ich siebenundfünfzig Kilogramm, heute wiege ich neunzig. Und da ich es liebte, gut zu essen, dachte ich: Oh, wie schade, ich werde nie ein guter Architekt werden.

Ich grüße Sie.

Ich muß aber noch etwas sagen, einen Scherz des amerikanischen Dramaturgen Thorton Wilder: „Dem Herrn ein Glas Wein zum Wohle dieser edlen Damen".

Philippe Duboy
THE OTHER CITY

"The following studies are, like others I have previously undertaken, "historical," due to the sphere they deal with and the references they utilize; they are not, however, the work of a "historian." This does not mean that they summarize or synthesize work which may have been done by others; they are—if one wishes to regard them from a "pragmatic" point of view—the record of a long and groping exercise, one which has often had to be revised and begun anew. It was a philosophical exercise; its stakes were to find out the extent to which the effort of thinking about one's own history can liberate the thought of what one thinks in silence, and to allow one to think in a different way."

Michel Foucault, Introduction to *"L'usage des plaisirs,"* Editions Gallimard, 1984, 15.

Locus Solus:

That Thursday in early April, my eminent, learned friend Carlo Scarpa had invited me, together with a few other close friends of his, to visit the vast park which surrounds his beautiful grave in San Vito d'Altivole.

Locus Solus—this is the name of the property—is a calm retreat where Scarpa likes to develop his multifarious, fertile scientific experiences in complete tranquility of mind.

An old, rusty gate opens onto a cypress-lined path leading to a small, square, insignificant and rather gloomy cemetery in San Vito d'Altivole (Treviso Province): a small village in the Veneto plain at the foot of the Asolo hills, containing one of the Brionvega factories (Brinel—architect: Marco Zanuso). This rural cemetery provides the setting for the *mausoleum* which Onorina Brion had built in memory of her husband Giuseppe—Carlo Scarpa makes a point of adding that the deceased was a "cavaliere del lavoro" (an Italian decoration given to important figures in industry)—and his family, thus providing Scarpa with the unique opportunity to plan and build "his most important work" and, at first sight, his most disconcerting.

In all of its banality, the pre-existing cemetery becomes an unforeseen, unexpected, intentionally rectified „*ready-made*": a co-protagonist of Carlo Scarpa's astonishing project, one which underscores how completely it has succeeded.

The only equivalent to this work are the seemingly totally different worlds of Marcel Duchamp and Raymond Roussel. An explicit reference by Aldo Rossi allows us to declare that the best answer to the theoretical problems posed in *architecture of the city* is to be found in Scarpa's works.[1]

Like Roussel's writings or Duchamp's painting, Scarpa's architecture is enigmatic to those who do not wish to understand it; to those who still believe in secret mythologies, however, this architecture requires no critical explanation: it is self-evident. At this point we would like to mention Raymond Roussel's secret wish to become an architect, as evidenced by his realistic *maison roulante,* which puts forward the exact opposite of minimal housing, the same old ideological, revolutionary or opportunistic story of Le Corbusier or the other central avant-garde figures of the Modern Movement. This architecture is an authentic *"maison Voisin,"* a grotesque and ambiguous answer to *"Messieurs les Industriels,"* one enthusiastically received by Il Duce when Roussel presented it to him![2]

"I had the good fortune," Scarpa emphasizes, "of coming across a book entitled *Vers une architecture* right after I had finished school. This dazzling discovery broadened my mind, and my world view completely changed from that point onwards."

But Roussel is not Le Corbusier, nor is Duchamp, who later used Roussel's heavy prose as his main weapon: *"ready-made"*, the subtitle of his insistent, silent architecture. Another Don Quixote is Duchamp who with his skill and architectural draftsman tilts at other verbal windmills, against the *objets à réaction poétique Le Corbusier.* Raymond Roussel and Marcel Duchamp, both marginal figures have come forward and became modern in the last few decades. This is also true of Carlo Scarpa, who doesn't flee his detractors and appears just as he is, undisguised, calm yet disconcerting.

Before he died suddenly at age 72 Scarpa gave a Duchampesque answer to the question of how he felt: "My health isn't bad at all... I am very happy."

The tomb of Giuseppe and Onorina Brion is pure architecture, sublime superfluity. We prefer the sincerity of an architect such as Scarpa who has the courage to work in silent and seemingly anachronistic purity to the mystifications perpetrated through ideological smokescreen. Like Purism, another *cadavre exquis*: "The architect lay behind the desk with his skull smashed in. The light on the overturned desk and the murder weapon (which could have been a valuable piece of evidence, about which, however, the police did not wish to provide details) lay on the ground next to the victim. The latter, it would seem, had been struck from behind facing the library." Let us forget this character in a novel, this architect of whom "half a dozen yellowed projects: a cube towering over a pyramid, a circular temple, a complicated construction with many arches and three domes, a kind of pagoda,"[3] had been lost among the shelves of the archives of the Turin General Cemetery. The initiatory, simple route begins here, in the ugliness of a small provincial cemetery.

The Scarpa drawings presented here are part of his work for San Vito. This was his most prolific period as architect: while working on the cemetery he was also busy with the reconstruction of the Carlo Felice Theatre in Genoa, the building of the head office of the Banca Popolare di Verona, the furnishing of the *villa-palazzetto* in Monselice, the monument commemorating the Fascist massacre in Brescia, the restoration of the great hall of the Faculty of Architecture of the University of Venice, the building of the Borgo Condominium in Vicenza and the Ottolenghi House in Bardolino, he designs various exhibitions: about the painters Giorgio Morandi at the Royal Academy in London and Gino Rossi in Treviso, one-man shows in Vicenza and Paris where he enters the competition for the Picasso Museum, and the "Venice-Byzantium" and the "Giuseppe Samonà" exhibitions in Venice.

At the same time, he is also involved in restoring the San Sebastiano Convent in Venice (office for the Faculty of Literature and Philosophy) in which one of the most important Italian libraries on twentieth-century avantgarde was to be installed—the library of his friend Aldo Camerino.[4] Scarpa was reminded of this friendship by rereading Raymond Roussel's "Locus Solus," which he had first read in the *Pages choisies* (1918) more than 40 years ago during the war while sharing the isolation (517 days) with his close Jewish friend Camerino. Scarpa's library (about 4,000 volumes) not only bears witness to his learning, but is linked to that heroic period as well: the experience of a uniquely modern fantastical nature, as described by Michel Foucault:

"...the nineteenth century discovered an imaginative space whose power the previous age had not suspected in the least. This new place of phantoms is no longer the night, the sleep of reason, the uncertain void which yawns before desire; on the contrary, it is the wakefulness, the unshakeable attention, the zeal of erudition, the attention to what lurks... The imaginary is located between the book and the lamp. It no longer brings the fantastical into the heart, nor is it expected to come from the incongruity of nature, rather it is obtained from the precision of knowledge: its wealth lies waiting in documents. It is not necessary to close one's eyes to dream; all one has to do is read. The true image is knowledge. Words which have already been said, precise reviews, masses of miniscule information, the worst groupings of monuments and reproductions bring the powers of the impossible into such experiences... The imaginary does not arise against the real to negate or make up for it; it extends to the beginnings, from book to book, in the interstice of commonplaces and commentaries; it is born and forms in the cracks between one context and the other. It is a library phenomenon."[5]

"I have read Roussel and I still read him," claims Carlo Scarpa, "I dealt with Duchamp for an exhibition of his works for Gavina during the '60s. That was when I made his acquaintence."

"Dieses ist lange her"

But, given that Marcel Duchamp's most important work, *"Étant donné"*, is hidden in a small room of the Philadelphia Museum of Art, and the San Vito d'Altivole cemetery can also barely be seen despite its location on the plain: two constructs one of which Duchamp's is enigmatic and secret, while the other, Scarpa's is serene and calm. They share a common theme: the gaze; through a small hole of Duchamp's wooden front door is being revealed a brick wall. The entrance to Scarpa's cemetery focuses on an opening-round window "symbol of the union of man and woman; this is the influence of China," Scarpa says. To be exact, it used to be a shop window. Duchamp's hilly American landscape is deliberately Swiss, while Scarpa's is venetian. An aquatic mirror: Scarpa's pool is the opposite of Duchamp's wild one. In Duchamp's work the woman is dead, muffled up and accursed; Scarpa's drawings, on the other hand, teem with the figure of a vital, nude, disturbing muse; away from San Vito, her tomb is empty.

The beginning of Scarpa's path to the Brion Tomb consciously negates the principal function of this garden of death by celebrating the landscape in all its calm beauty: *"Je suis belle, ô mortels! comme une rêve de pierre... je trône dans l'azur comme un sphinx incompris... les poètes, devant mes grandes attitudes, que j'ai l'air d'emprunter aux plus fiers monuments, consumeront leurs jours en d'austères études."* Baudelaire—Carlo Scarpa made a special point of this—was his favorite poet: text as delight, architecture as delight, enjoyment of architecture. *"Qu'est ce que la jouissance? Elle se réduit a n'être qu'une instance négative. La jouissance c'est ce qui ne sert à rien."*[6] But also the enjoyment of woman as shown by all the female figures who crowd Scarpa's drawings.

Roussel, Duchamp, Scarpa: *"Die andere Stadt,"* other ruins, architecture of the city of long long ago: "DIESES IST LANGE HER!"[7]

Scarpa then—after announcing that we already knew all the secrets of his park—continued along the road to the villa, where we all came together soon afterwards at a cheerful banquet. Obtrusive music drowned out his last words:

Tosca (still staring at Scarpia, slowly walks to the table, resolutely sits down across from Scarpia, then asks him with the most profound contempt): How much?!
Scarpia (impassively, filling his glass with wine): How much?
Tosca: The price!
Scarpia: (laughing): Indeed. They call me venal, but I do not sell myself to a fair woman for gold.
Scarpa (shouting): *"Cuisinier on devient, mais rôtisseur on naît"*: an aphorism by Brillat-Savarin as prolegomena to his entire work.

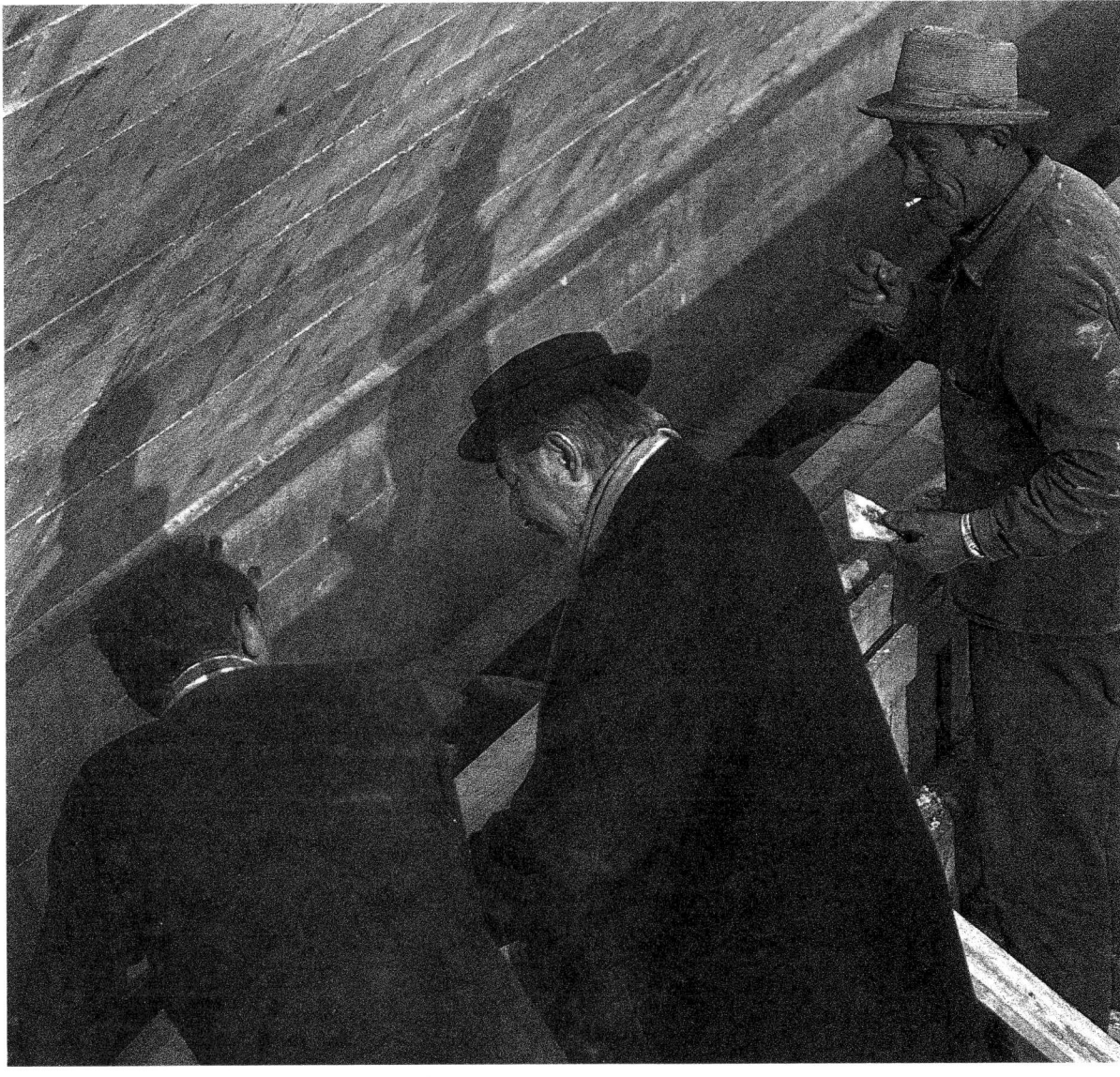

The cemetery Brion under construction / Der Friedhof Brion während des Baus

[1] "We have to begin to talk about our works, about the dream of our experience; of the artists and interpreters of modern culture, the one I think of most often is Raymond Roussel in his book *Comment j'ai écrit certains de mes livres*; this book is fundamental as a theory of composition which desires to master every aspect of artistic creation," Aldo Rossi, *La città come fondamento dello studio dei caratteri degli edicifici (1966) in Scritti scelti sull'architettura e la città 1956—1972*, Milan: Clup, 1975, 325.

[2] Philippe Duboy, *Der Reisende und sein Schatten. Raymond Roussels "Haus auf Rädern"* in *Daidalos*, XXVIII, 1988, 60—64.

[3] Fruttero and Lucentini, *La donna della domenica*, Milan: Mondadori.

[4] Aldo Camerino, *Prosa di Roussel* in *Corriere Padano*, 12 May 1935, French translation in *Les cahiers de la recherche architecturale*, numéro spéciale Carlo Scarpa, XIX, 1986, 114—117.

[5] Michel Foucault, *La bibliotèque fantastique*, introduction to Flaubert, *La tentation de Saint Antoine*, Insel Verlag, 1964.

[6] Jacques Lacan: Le séminaire. Buch II: Encore. Sevil. Paris 1975. 10.

[7] "Dieses ist lange her" is a verse from Georg Trakl's poem "Abendlied", a caption to an AR 75 recording (Aldo Rossi); vid. Ellis Donda, *Rivelazioni su di un luogo analogico* in *Il piccolo Hans*, XXXV, Milan, 1982, 153—184.

Philippe Duboy
DIE ANDERE STADT

„Die folgenden Studien sind, wie andere, die ich früher durchgeführt habe, Studien der ‚Geschichten' zu dem jeweiligen Bereich, mit dem sie sich beschäftigen, und den Bezügen, die sie herstellen; aber sie sind keine ‚historischen' Arbeiten. Das soll nicht heißen, daß sie die Arbeit zusammenfassen, die von anderen gemacht worden wäre; sie sind – wenn man sie unter dem Gesichtspunkt ihrer „Pragmatik" betrachten will – die Aufzeichnung einer langen, tastenden Übung, die sich oft wiederholen und verbessern mußte. Es war eine philosophische Übung; ihr Einsatz war, zu wissen, in welchem Maße die Arbeit, ihre eigene Geschichte zu denken, den Gedanken, an den sie schweigend denkt, freimachen kann und ihm erlauben kann, an anderes zu denken."

Michel Foucault: Einführung zu „L'usage des plaisirs", Editions Gallimard. 1984. S 15

Locus solus:

An einem Donnerstag Anfang April hat mich mein gelehrter Freund, der hervorragende Carlo Scarpa, eingeladen, gemeinsam mit einigen anderen guten Freunden, den riesigen Park zu besichtigen, der sein schönes Grab in San Vito d'Altivole umgibt.

Locus solus – so nennt sich der Besitz – ist ein stiller Ort der Zurückgezogenheit, an dem Scarpa gerne in völliger geistiger Ruhe an seinen vielfältigen und ergiebigen wissenschaftlichen Studien arbeitet.

Auf einem kleinen Landstrich in der Ebene des Veneto, in der Provinz von Treviso, findet man zu Füßen der Berge von Asolo in San Vito d'Altivole eine jener Industrieanlagen von Brionvega, nämlich die „Brinel" des Architekten Marco Zanuso. Ein altes, verrostetes Eisentor öffnet sich auf einen von Zypressen gesäumten Weg hin, der zu einem kleinen, quadratischen Friedhof führt, unbedeutend und mehr noch unheimlich. Er dient dem *Mausoleum* als Rahmen, das Onorina Brion – eine „Heldin der Arbeit", wie Carlo Scarpa sagt – ihrem Mann Giuseppe und ihrer Familie gewidmet hat, und Scarpa den Luxus ermöglichte, „sein wichtigstes Werk" und – auf den ersten Blick – sein verwirrendstes zu planen und zu errichten.

In seiner Banalität wird der Friedhof, ein ganz unvorhergesehenes und unerwartetes *„ready-made"*, willentlich verbessert: Koprotagonist des erstaunlichen Projekts von Carlo Scarpa, der dessen großen Erfolg erst ausmacht.

Wir stellen fest, daß sein Werk nichts Äquivalentes hat – nur in einer scheinbar anderen Welt, jener Marcel Duchamps oder Raymond Roussels. Der ausdrücklich theoretische Hinweis erlaubt uns, zu behaupten, daß die beste Antwort auf die Fragen einer „Architektur der Stadt" das Werk Scarpas selbst ist.[1]

Wie die Schriften Roussels oder die Malerei von Duchamp, so ist die Architektur Scarpas unverständlich für den, der nicht verstehen will; für den aber, der noch an geheime Mythologien glaubt, bedarf es keines kritischen Diskurses, sie ist der Beweis selbst. Hier sei uns erlaubt, auf den geheimen Wunsch Raymond Roussels selbst Architekt zu sein, hinzuweisen, der uns mit seinem realistischen *„maison roulante"* das umgekehrte Bild – die objektive Spiegelung – der kleinsten Wohnung entwarf, die ideologische Wiederholung, revolutionär oder opportunistisch, von Le Corbusier oder anderen avantgardistischen Protagonisten des „Movimento Moderno". Das echte „Maison Voisin", die groteske und zweifelhafte Antwort auf die „Messieurs les Industriels", diese Architektur, die von Roussel selbst vorgeführt wurde, hat beim Duce große Begeisterung erweckt!²

„Also hatte ich großes Glück", betont Scarpa, „als ich – kaum hatte ich mein Studium abgeschlossen – ein Buch mit dem Titel „Vers une architecture" fand, es war eine Eröffnung für die Seele ... diese Entdeckung, Licht, nicht wahr? Von diesem Augenblick an haben sich die geistigen Bedingungen völlig geändert."

Aber Roussel ist nicht Le Corbusier, er ist nicht einmal Duchamp, der die schwerverdauliche Literatur Roussels als wichtigste Waffe benützen wird: „ready-made", Untertitel für seine eindringliche, stille Architektur. Ein anderer Don Quichotte, der mit seinem ganzen Werk von Architekturentwürfen sozusagen gegen andere Windmühlen polemisiert: die „objets à réaction poétique" von Le Corbusier. Daneben fallen Raymond Roussel und Marcel Duchamp auf und wurden erst in diesen letzten Jahrzehnten modern. Das ist auch der Fall bei Carlo Scarpa, der nicht vor seinen Verleumdern flieht, sich ohne Schwindel zeigt, heiter und verwirrend.

Bevor er starb, unerwartet mit 72 Jahren, antwortete er auf die Frage: „Wie geht es Ihnen?" wie Marcel Duchamp: „Es geht mir sehr gut. Mein gesundheitlicher Zustand ist überhaupt nicht schlecht ... ich bin sehr glücklich."

Das Grabmal von Giuseppe und Onorina Brion ist reine Architektur, sublime Zwecklosigkeit. Wir ziehen den mystifizierenden Versuchen, die Arbeit mit einem ideologischen Mantel zu umgeben, die Offenheit eines Architekten wie Scarpa vor, der den Mut hat, mit stiller und scheinbar anachronistischer Reinheit zu arbeiten: nach dem Purismus ein anderer „cadavre exquis": „Der Architekt lag mit eingeschlagenem Schädel hinter seinem Arbeitstisch. Die Lampe auf dem Tisch war umgefallen und die Mordwaffe (ein wichtiges Indiz, über welches aber andererseits die Polizei keine genaueren Angaben machen wollte) lag auf dem Boden, neben dem Opfer. Letzteres, so schien es, ist von hinten erschlagen worden, während es sich gerade der Bibliothek zuwandte." Vergessen wir diese Romanfigur, diesen Architekten mit seinem „halben Dutzend vergilbter Projekte: ein Würfel, der von einer Pyramide überragt wird, ein runder Tempel, eine komplizierte Konstruktion mit vielen Bögen und drei Kuppeln, eine Art Pagode"³, die in den Regalen des Archivs im Turiner Zentralfriedhof verloren gegangen sind. Hier, in der Häßlichkeit des kleinen Provinzfriedhofs, ist die Fortsetzung der Initiation einfach.

Die Zeichnungen Scarpas, die hier gezeigt werden, sind Teil seiner Arbeit für die Realisation von San Vito. Das ist die fruchtbarste Periode seiner Tätigkeit als Architekt: gleichzeitig mit der Planung des Friedhofs beschäftigte er sich mit der Planung der Restaurierung des Teatro Felice in Genua, mit der Planung des Hauptsitzes der Banca Popolare di Verona, mit der Einrichtung der *Villa-palazzetto* in Monselice, mit dem Denkmal für das Faschistenattentat in Brescia, mit der Instandsetzung der Aula des Universitätsinstituts für Architektur in Venedig, mit der Planung des Borgo-Wohnsitzes in Vicenza und mit dem Haus „Ottolenghi" in Bardolino; und er bereitete verschiedene Ausstellungen vor: über die Maler Giorgio Morandi in der Londoner Royal Academy und Gino Rossi in Treviso, Einzelausstellungen in Vicenza und Paris, wo er an einem Wettbewerb für das Picasso-Museum teilnahm, die „Venedig – Byzanz"-Ausstellung und eine über Giuseppe Samona in Venedig.

Zur gleichen Zeit beschäftigte er sich mit der Restaurierung des Klosters San Sebastian in Venedig (dem Sitz der Philosophischen Fakultät), wo er eine der wichtigsten italienischen Bibliotheken über die Avantgarde des 20. Jahrhunderts unterbringen mußte: die seines Freundes Aldo Camerino.⁴ Scarpa erinnerte sich dieser Freundschaft bei der neuerlichen Lektüre des „Locus Solus" von Raymond Roussel, den er schon vor mehr als 40 Jahren während des

Krieges in den *„pages choisies"* (1918), heimlich in 517tägiger Isolation gelesen hatte, die er gemeinsam mit seinem jüdischen Freund Camerino verbrachte. Die Bücher Scarpas (etwa 4000) legen nicht nur Zeugnis über seine Kultur ab, sie haben auch etwas von einem heroischen Moment: die Erfahrung einer außergewöhnlich modernen Phantasie, wie sie Michel Foucault beschreibt:

„... das 19. Jahrhundert hat einen imaginativen Raum entdeckt, dessen ihm innewohnende Kraft das vorherige Zeitalter nicht vermutet hätte. Dieser neue Ort der Geister ist nicht mehr die Nacht, der Schlaf der Vernunft, die unbestimmte, offene Leere vor dem Verlangen: er ist im Gegenteil das Wachsein, die unerschütterliche Aufmerksamkeit, das Bravouröse der Bildung, das Sich-in-acht-nehmen vor Fallen ... Das Imaginäre befindet sich zwischen dem Buch und der Lampe. Es trägt uns nicht das Unwirkliche ins Herz, man erwartet es nicht einmal mehr in der Inkongruenz der Natur, man schöpft es aus der Exaktheit des Wissens: sein Reichtum steckt in der Erwartung des Beweises. Um zu schlafen, muß man nicht mehr die Augen schließen, es genügt, zu lesen. Die wahre Vorstellung ist die Erkenntnis. Bereits gesprochene Worte, präzise Rezensionen, Massen von kleingeschriebenen Informationen, die schlechtesten Teile von Denkmälern und Reproduktionen tragen in einer solchen Erfahrung das Vermögen des Unmöglichen ... Das Imaginäre besteht nicht im Gegensatz zum Realen, um es zu negieren oder zu kompensieren; es erweitert sich in seinen Ursprüngen, von Buch zu Buch, im Zwischenraum von Allgemeinplätzen und Kommentaren; es entsteht und formt sich in der Spalte zwischen einem Kontext und dem anderen. Es ist ein Phänomen der Bibliotheken!"[5]

„Roussel habe ich gelesen, und ich lese ihn wieder", hält Scarpa fest, „mit Duchamp habe ich mich anläßlich einer Ausstellung über ihn bei Gavina in den sechziger Jahren beschäftigt. Und in diesem Moment habe ich ihn verstanden."

„Dieses ist lange her"

Aber, so wie das wichtigste Werk Duchamps, *„Étant donné"*, in einem kleinen Raum des Museums in Philadelphia verborgen ist, so ist auch der Friedhof von San Vito d'Altivole, obwohl in der Ebene gelegen, kaum zu sehen: zwei Konstruktionen, eine rätselhaft und geheimnisvoll – jene von Duchamp –, die andere heiter und still – jene von Scarpa. Das Thema ist das gleiche: der Blick. Durch ein kleines Loch im Holztor von Duchamp wird eine Ziegelmauer sichtbar. Der Eingangsbereich bei Scarpas Friedhof hat in der Mitte einen runden Durchblick, „Symbol für die Vereinigung von Mann und Frau, chinesisch beeinflußt", sagt Scarpa. Den runden Durchblick kennen wir schon von einem Schaufenster. Die Berglandschaft: jene Duchamps in Amerika ist gewollt schweizerisch, jene von Scarpa venezianisch. Der Wasserspiegel: der gebaute Teich Scarpas steht dem wilden von Duchamp gegenüber. Die Frau, vermummt und verdammt, ist im Werk Duchamps tot; lebend und nackt, als beängstigende Muse, besiedelt sie die Entwürfe Scarpas. In San Vito ist sie abwesend, ihr Grab ist leer.

Scarpas Weg der Initiation hebt gewollt die primäre Funktion dieses Gartens des Todes auf, um die Landschaft in ihrer ganzen heiteren Schönheit zu enthüllen: *„Je suis belle, ô mortels! comme un rêve de pierre ... je trône dans l'azur comme un sphinx incompris ... les poètes, devant mes grandes attitudes, que j'ai l'air d'emprunter aux plus fiers monuments, consumeront leurs jours en d'austéres études."* Baudelaire, betont Scarpa, sei sein Lieblingsdichter: Wohlgefallen am Text, Wohlgefallen an der Architektur, Genuß an der Architektur: „Was ist der Genuß? Er leitet sich nicht davon ab, eine negative Instanz zu sein. Der Genuß ist das, was zu nichts dient."[6] Aber auch der Genuß der Frau, wie das alle weiblichen Figuren, die in Scarpas Entwürfen vorkommen, bezeugen.

Roussel, Duchamp, Scarpa: *„Die andere Stadt"*, andere Ruinen, Architektur der Stadt: „DIESES IST LANGE HER"![7]

Dann, nachdem Scarpa verkündet hat, daß wir nun alle Geheimnisse des Parks kennen würden, nahm er wieder die Straße zur Villa, wo wir uns etwas später zu einem fröhlichen Essen einfanden. Eine eindringliche Musik deckte seine letzten Worte zu:

Tosca (Scarpia anstarrend, nähert sich langsam der Tafel, setzt sich entschlossen vor Scarpa hin: dann, mit dem Ausdruck tiefster Verachtung, fragt sie): Wieviel?

Scarpia (gelassen, während er sich zu trinken einschenkt): Wieviel.

Tosca: Der Preis!

Scarpa(lacht): Gewiß, man sagt, ich sei käuflich, aber an eine schöne Frau verkaufe ich mich nicht für schnödes Geld.

Scarpa (schreiend): *„Cuisinier on devient, mais rôtisseur on nait."*

Ein Aphorismus Brillat-Savarins, der seinem ganzen Werk als Prolegomenon dient.

[1] „Es ist notwendig, daß wir über unsere Arbeiten zu sprechen beginnen, über den Traum unserer Erfahrung: ich denke immer unter all den Künstlern und Interpreten der modernen Kultur, die mich beeinflußt haben, an das Buch von Raymond Roussel ‚*Comment j'ai écrit certains des mes livres*'. Dieses Buch ist fundamental in seiner Eigenschaft als Theorie der Komposition, die alle Aspekte der künstlerischen Schöpfung überragen will". Aldo Rossi: *La Città come fondamento dello studio dei caratteri degli edifici. 1966. In: Scritti scelti sull'architettura e la città 1956–1972.* Clup. Mailand 1975. S. 325.

[2] Philippe Duboy: *Der Reisende und sein Schatten. Raymond Roussels „Haus auf Rädern".* In: *Daidalos* Nr. 28. 1988. S. 60–64.

[3] Fruttero/Lucentini: *La donna della domenica.* Mondadori. Mailand.

[4] Aldo Camerino: *Prosa di Roussel.* In: *Corriere Padano.* 12. Mai 1935. Französische Übersetzung in: *Les cahiers de la recherche architecturale.* Sonderheft Carlo Scarpa. Nr. 19. 1986. S. 114–117.

[5] Michel Foucault: *La bibliothèque fantastique.* Einführung zu: Gustave Flaubert: *La tentation de Saint Antoine.* Insel Verlag. 1964.

[6] Jacques Lacan: Le séminaire. Buch II: Encore. Seuil. Paris 1975. S. 10.

[7] „Dieses ist lange her" ist eine Zeile aus dem Gedicht „Abendlied" von Georg Trakl: es steht als Inschrift auf einem Kupferstich AR 75 (Aldo Rossi). Siehe Ellis Donda: *Rivelazioni su di un luogo analogico.* In: *Il piccolo Hans.* Nr. 35. Mailand 1982. S. 153–184.

The cemetery Brion unter construction / Der Friedhof Brion während des Baus

THE OTHER CITY

The cemetery is unquestionably a different place in comparison to usual cultural spaces; nonetheless it is a space linked to the general effect of all the sites of the city or society or village (...)

It was during the age in which civilization became, to put it very roughly, "atheistic" that Western culture ushered in what we call the cult of death (...)

In all events, since the 19th century everyone has had the right to his own little personal decomposition (...)

Cemeteries, then, no longer constitute the sacred and immortal precinct of the town, but rather "the other city". ...

DIE ANDERE STADT

„Der Friedhof ist verglichen mit gewöhnlichen Kulturräumen sicherlich ein anderer Ort; er ist ein Raum, der vor allem in Beziehung zu der Gesamtheit aller Plätze der Stadt, der Gemeinschaft oder des Dorfes steht ...

In der Zeit, in der die Zivilisation, grob gesagt, „atheistisch" wurde, begann die abendländische Kultur gleichzeitig einen bestimmten Todeskult zu feiern ...

Jedenfalls gibt es seit Beginn des 19. Jahrhunderts für jeden das Recht auf seine kleine persönliche Verwesung ...

Die Friedhöfe stellen also nicht mehr den geheiligten und unsterblichen Bezirk der Stadt dar, sondern sind vielmehr „Die andere Stadt" ...

Michel Foucault: Des espaces autres: utopies et hétérotopies. In: L Architettura Nr. 12, April 1968, pag. 822–823

INITIAL PLANS AND FLOOR PLANS

ERSTE ENTWÜRFE UND GRUNDRISSE

1969–1970

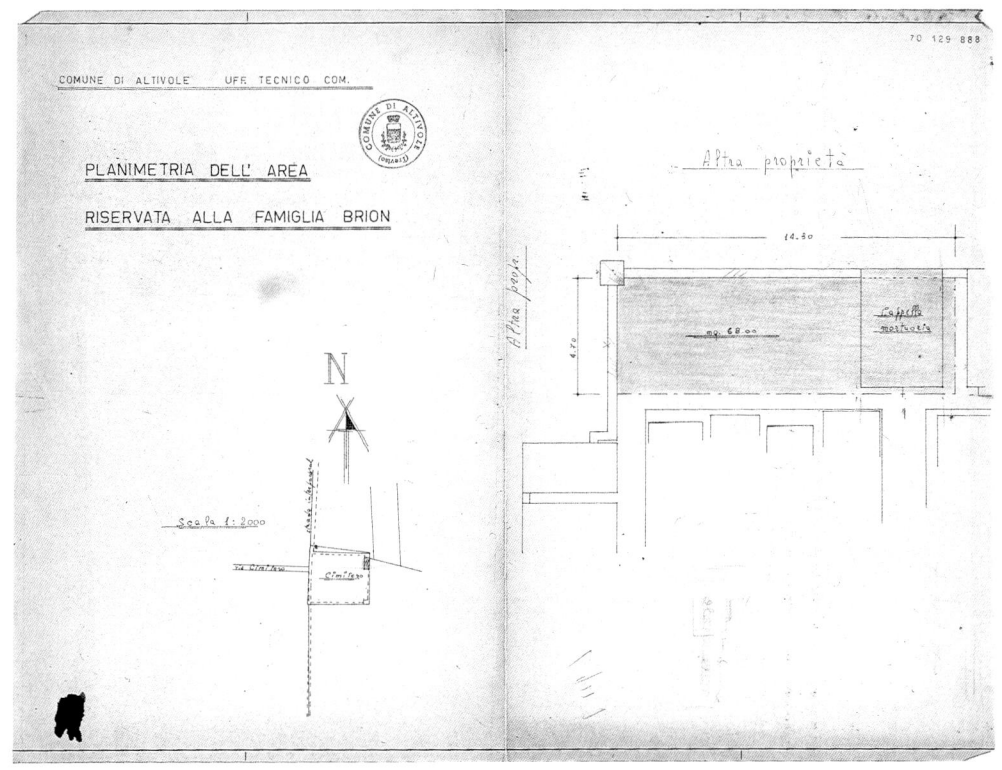

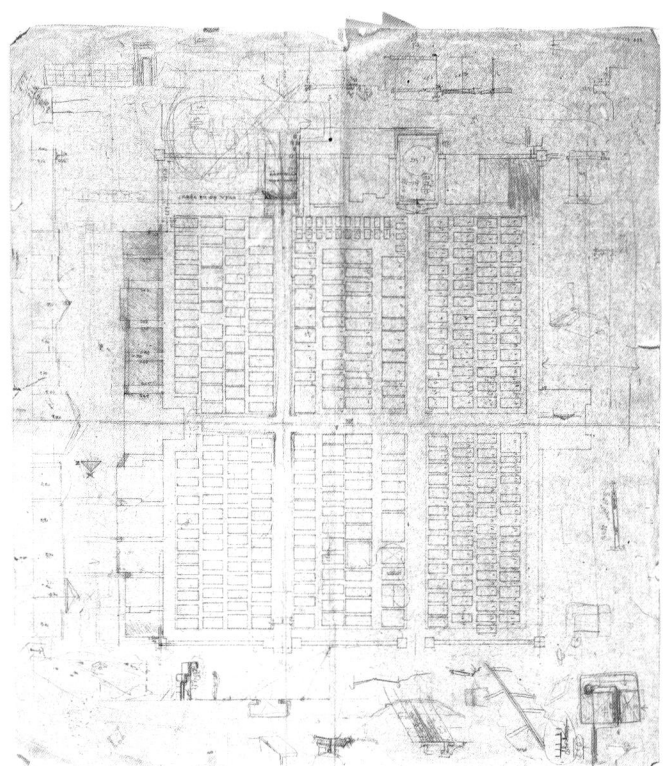

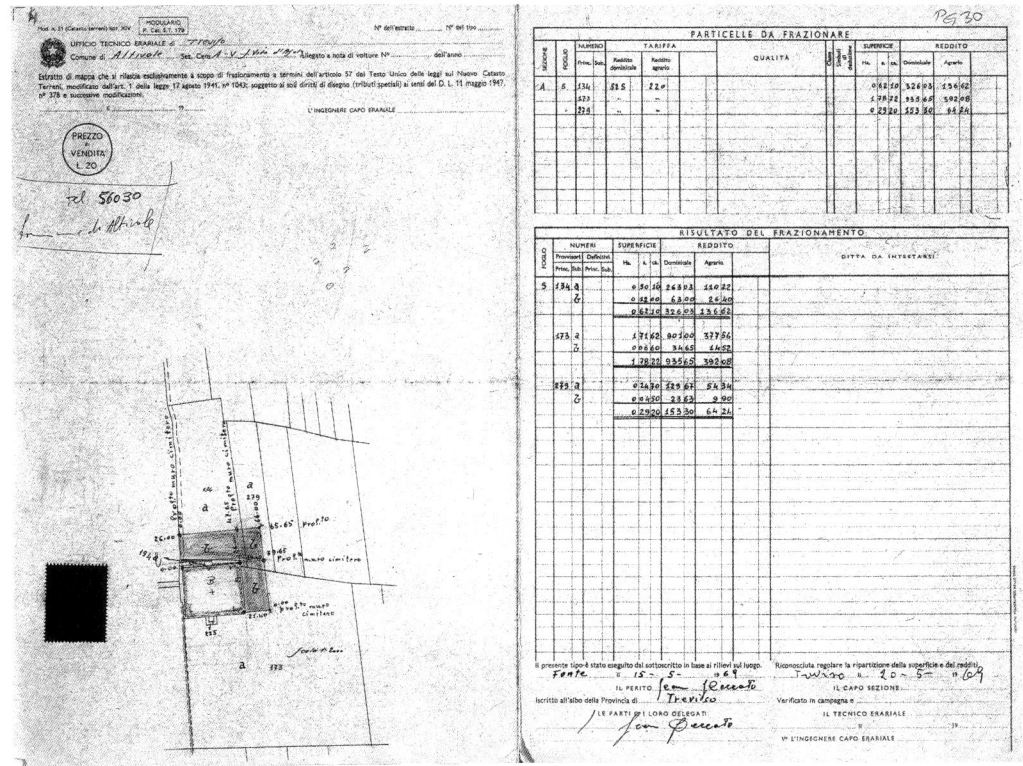

Black notebook/das schwarze Notizbuch

5

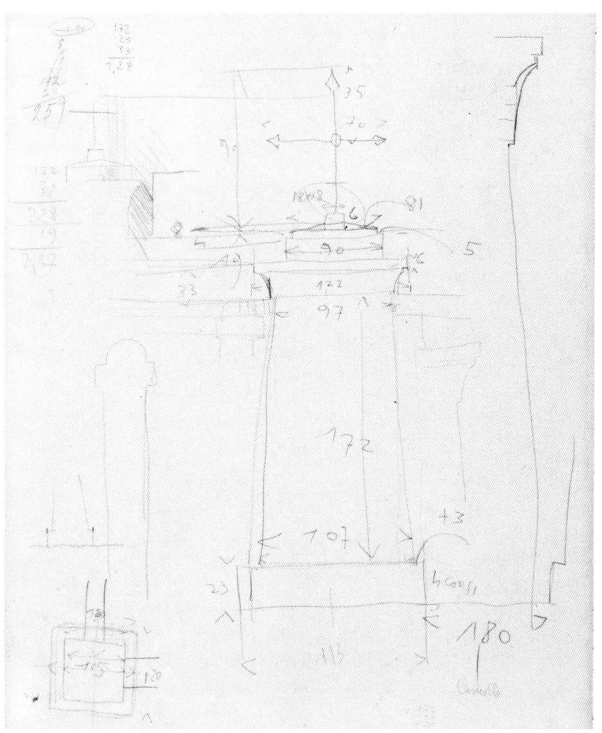

6

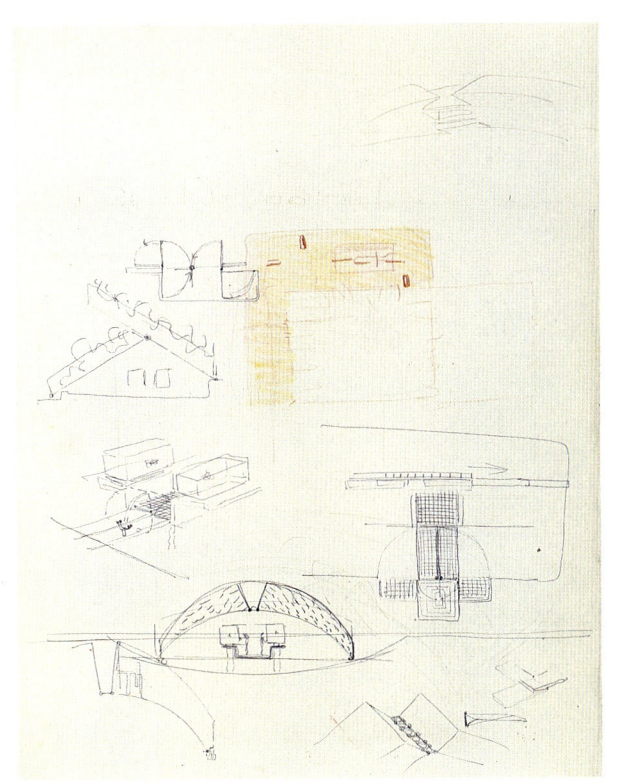

7

8

42

9

10

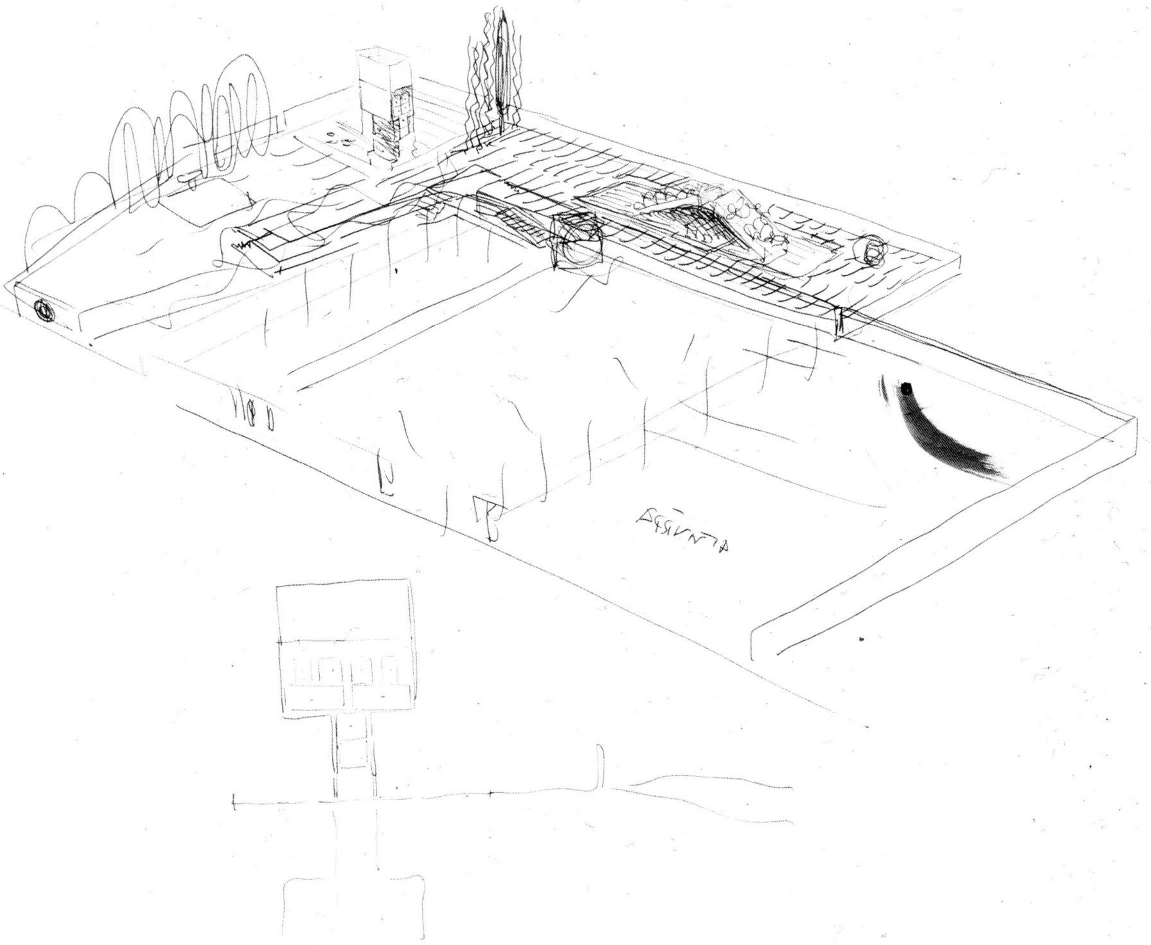

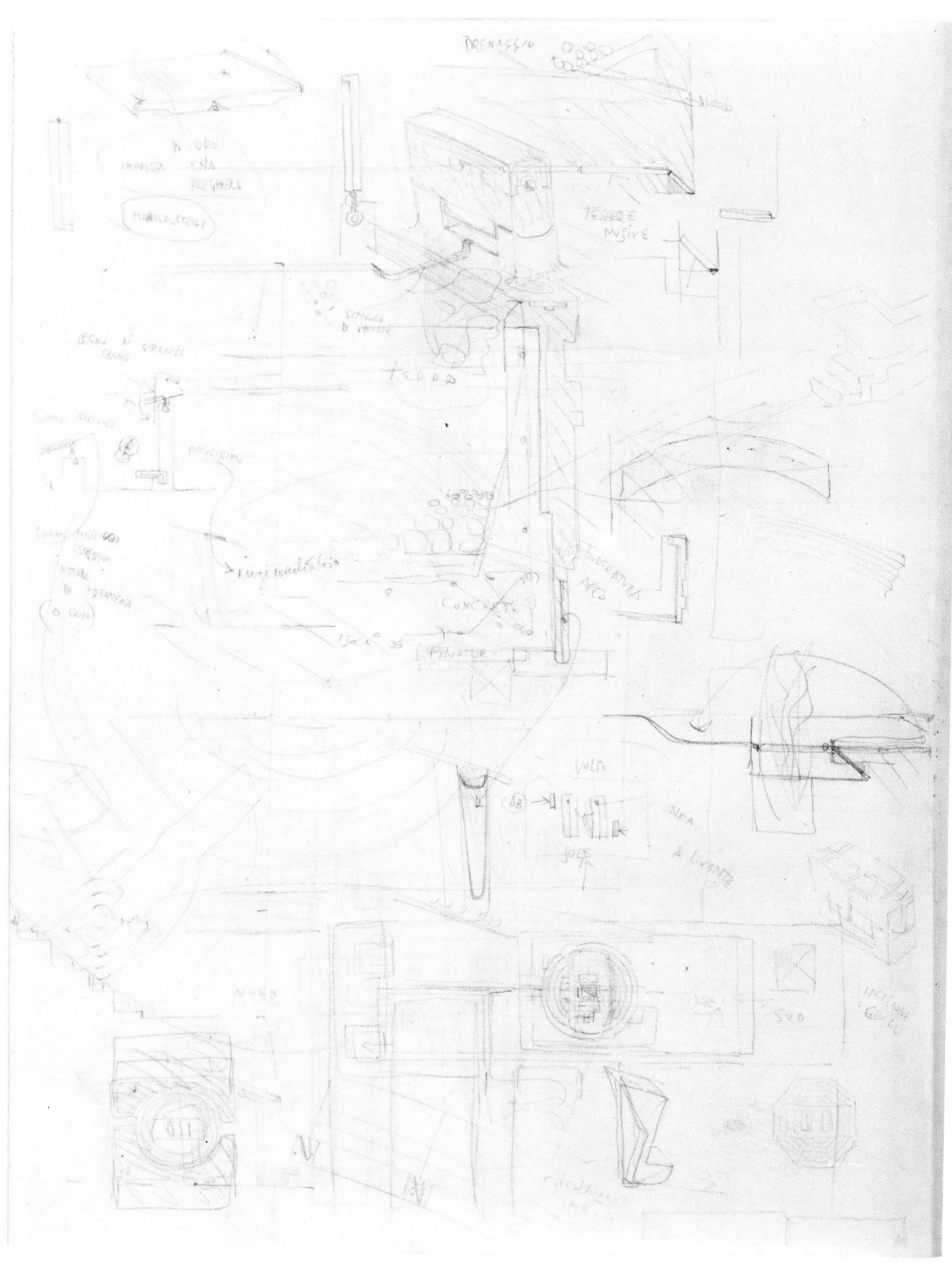

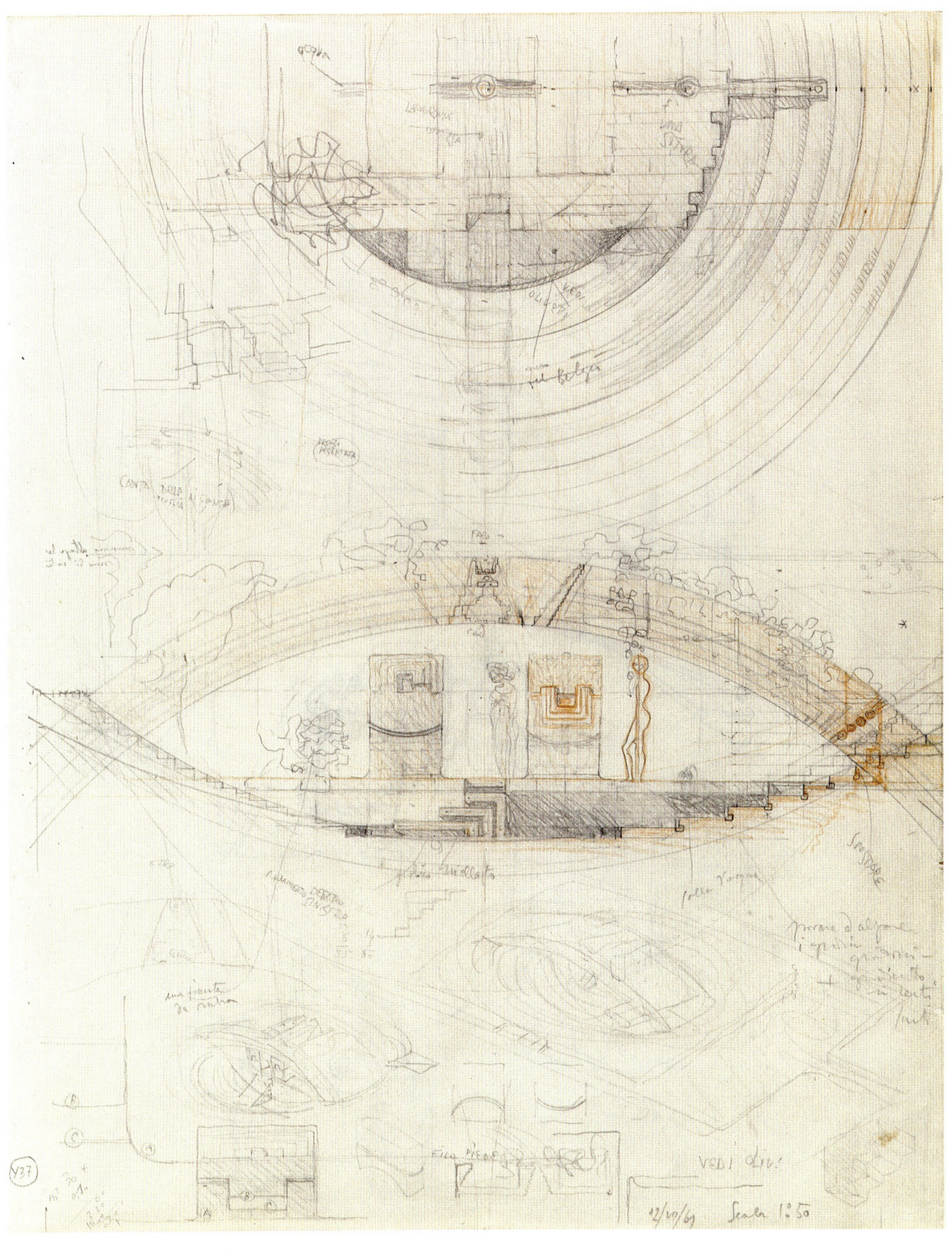

Drawings/Skizzen

46

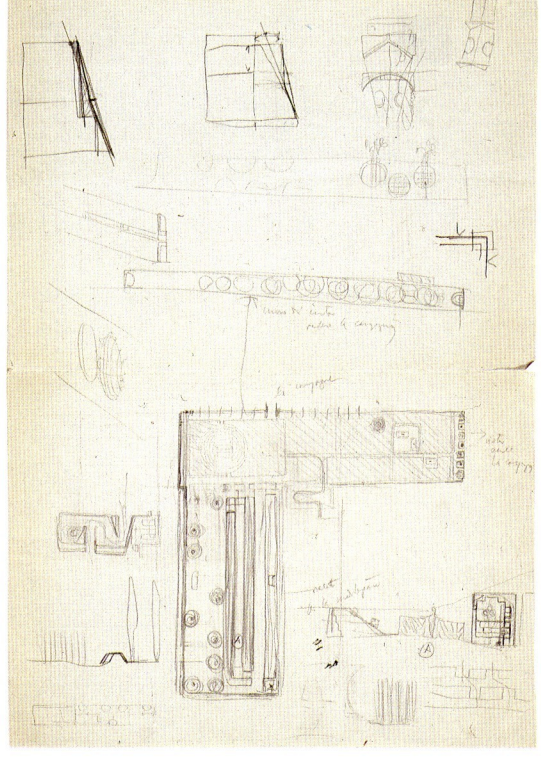

14

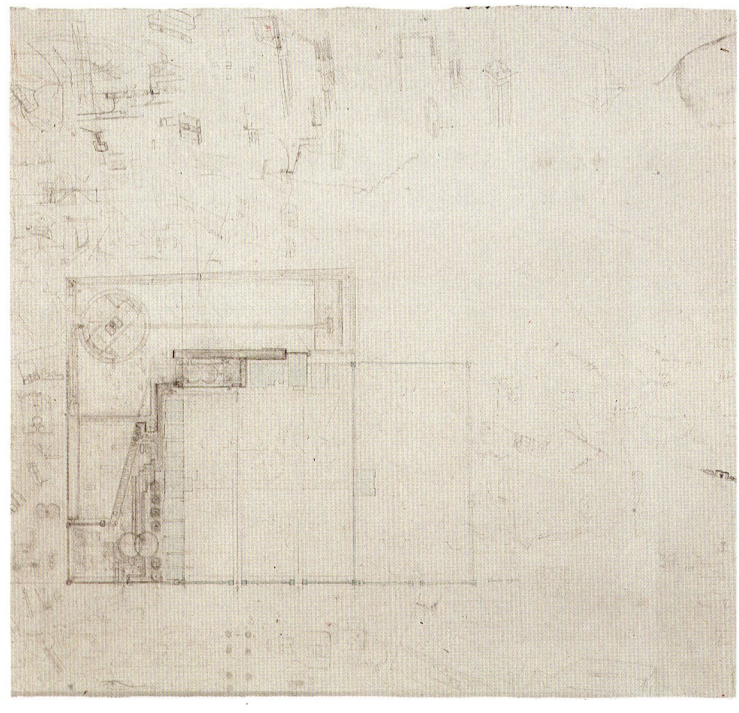

15

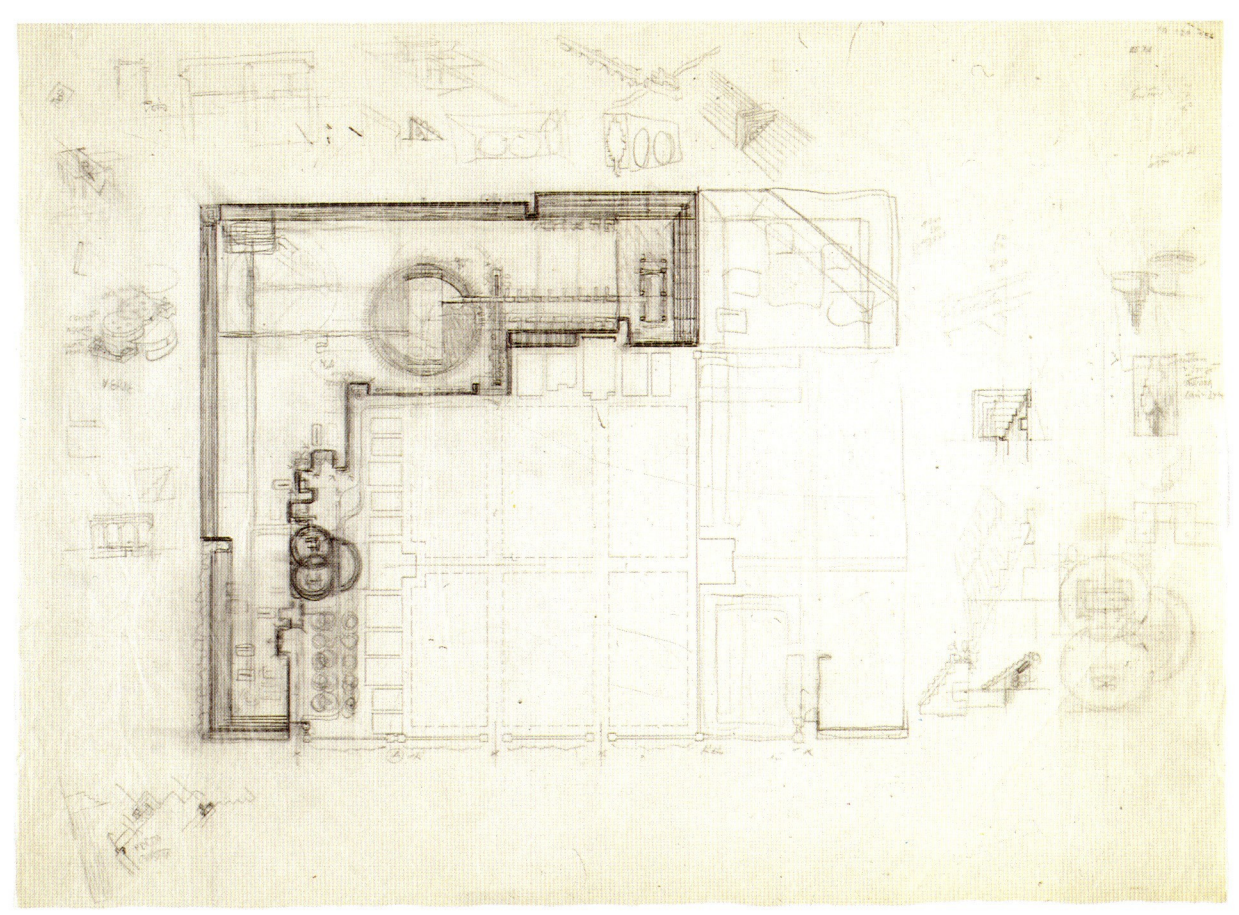

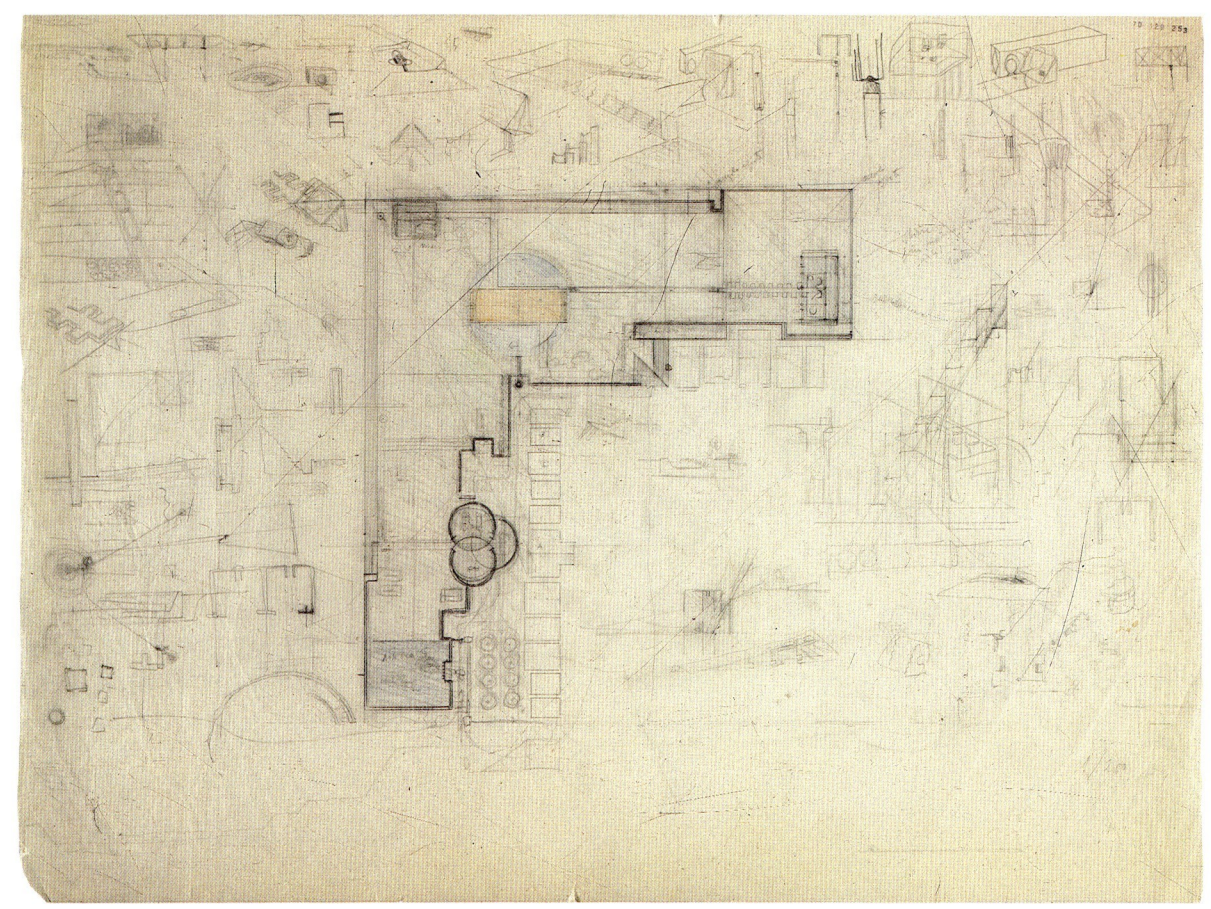

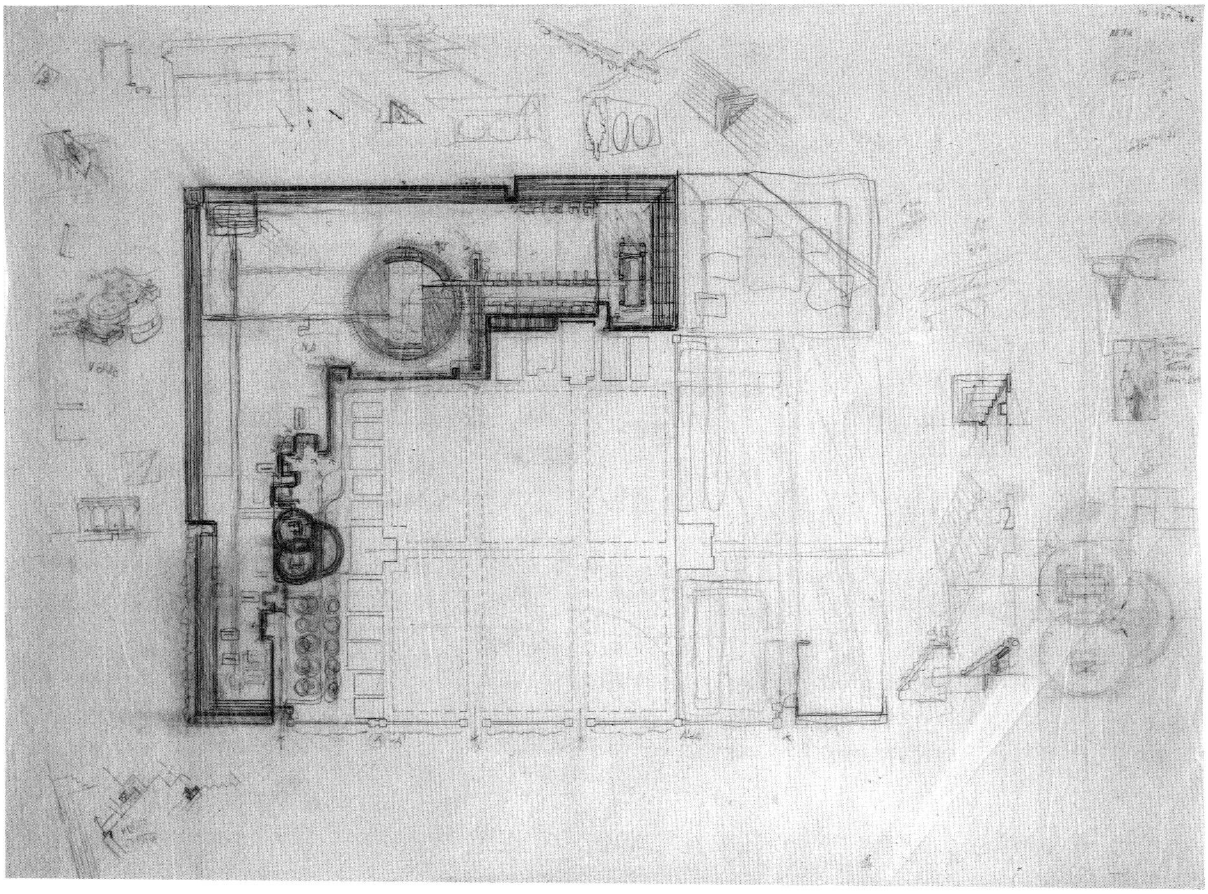

50

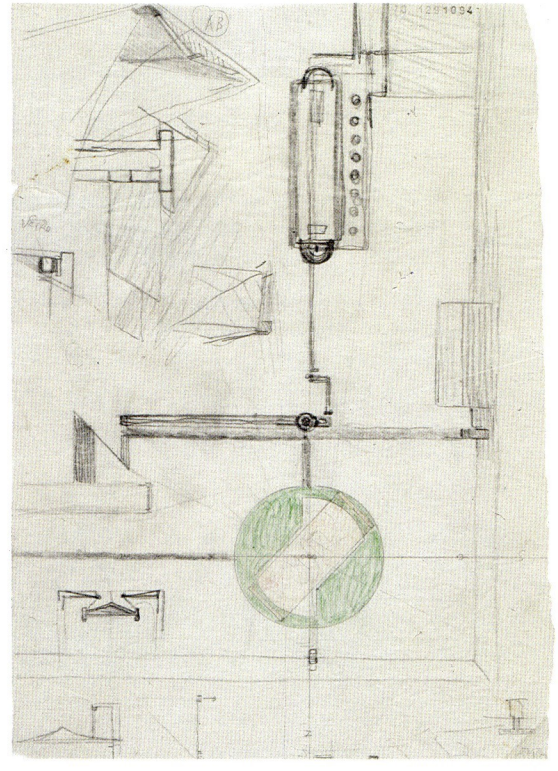

19

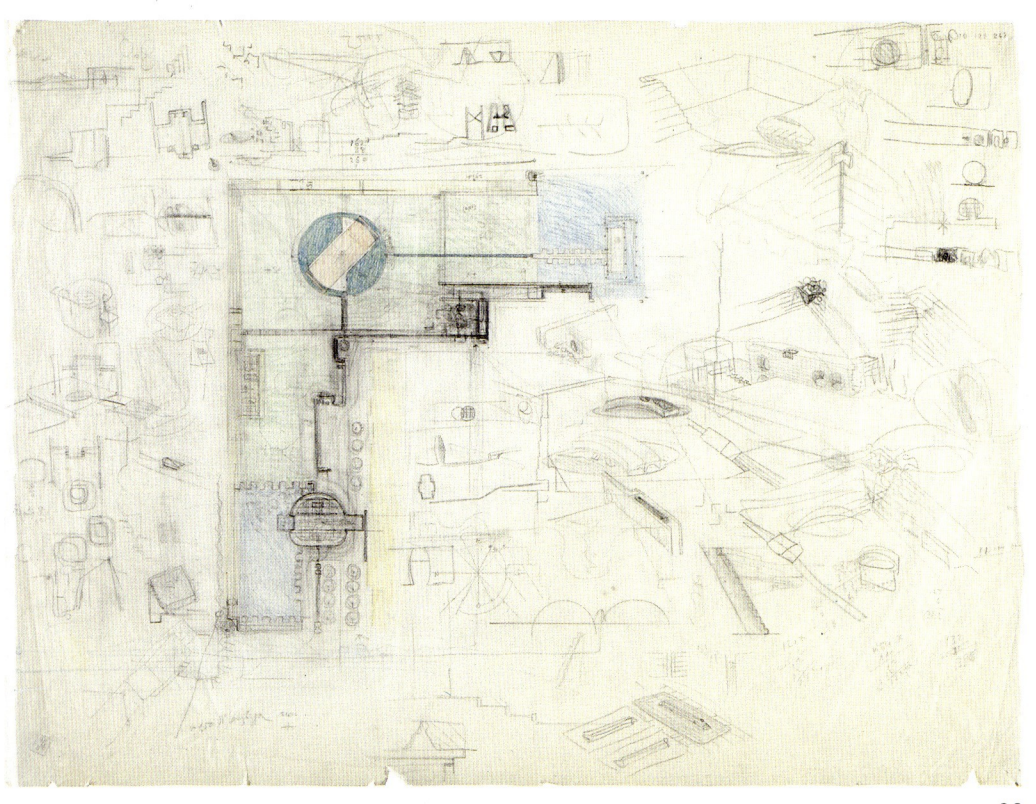

20

6–9 March 1970 project approved by the Altivole town council
6.–9. März 1970 das von der Gemeinde Altivole genehmigte Projekt

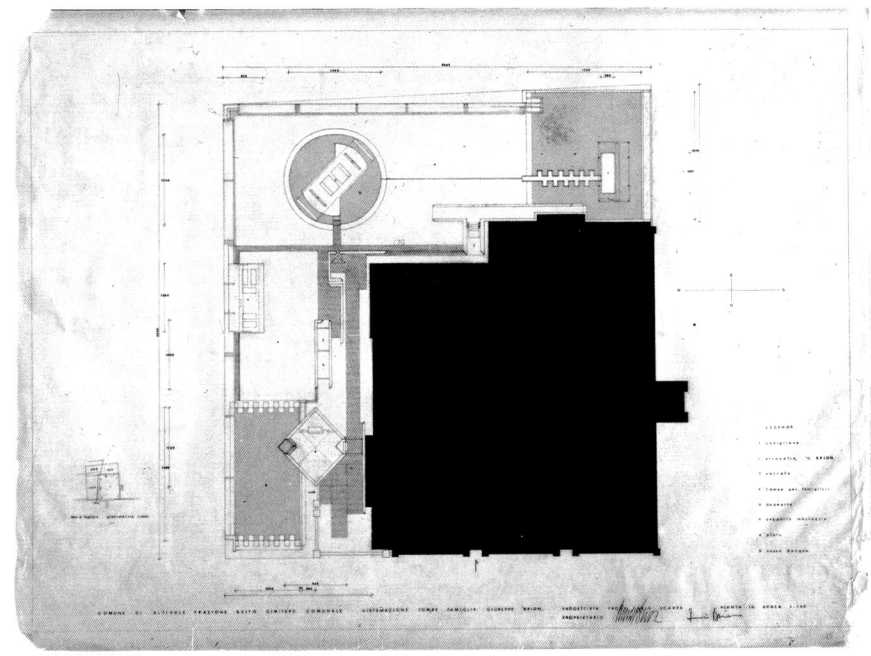

21

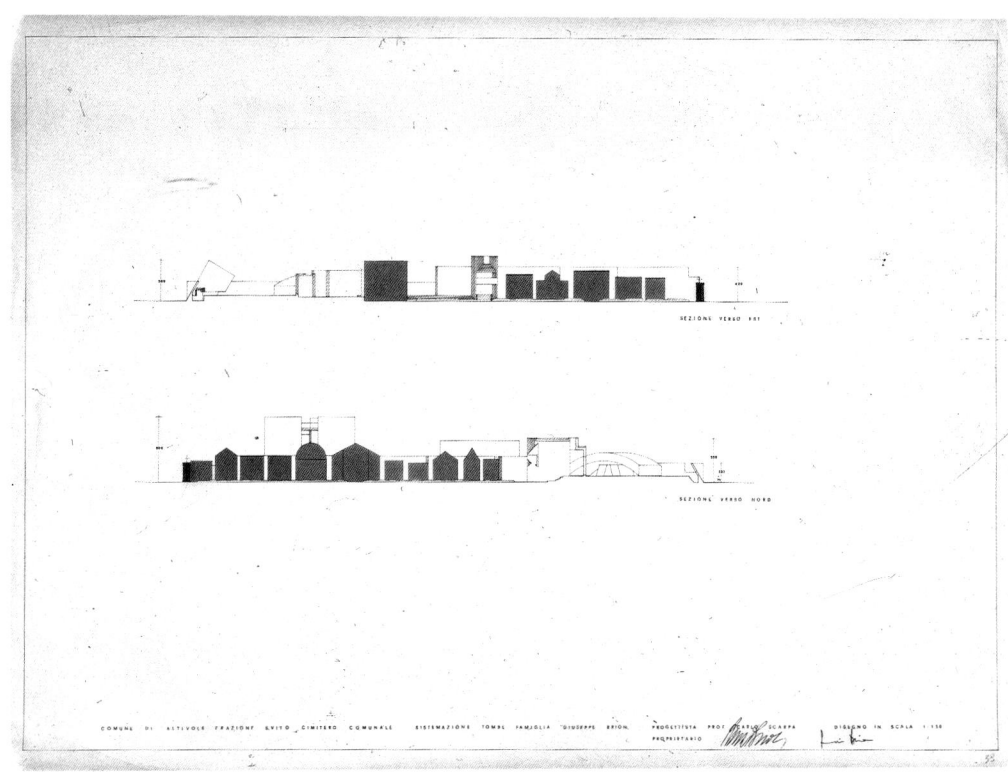

22

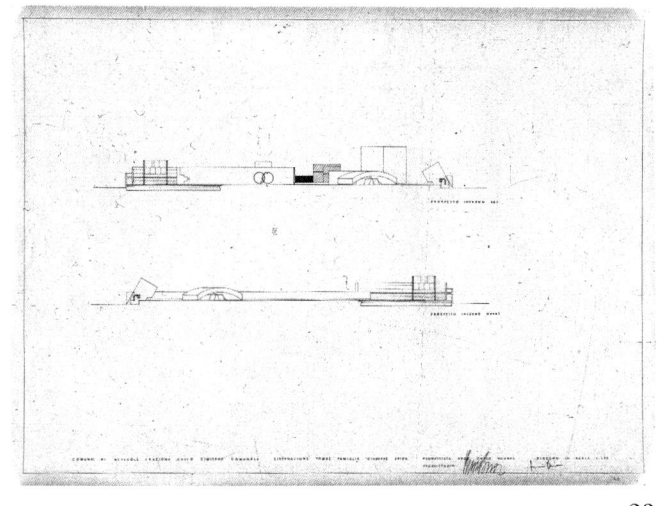

23

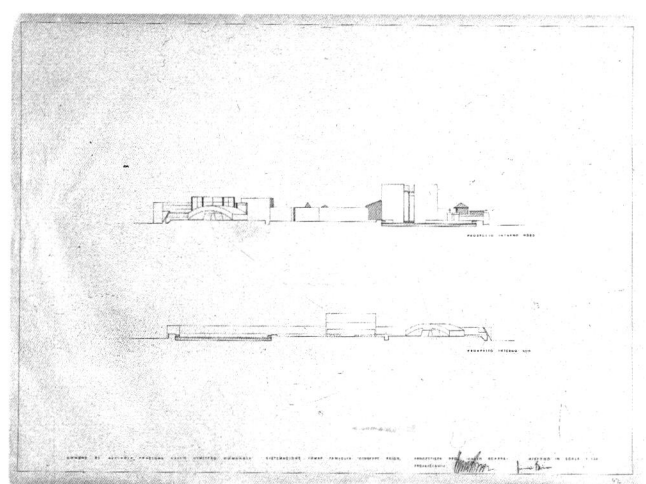

24

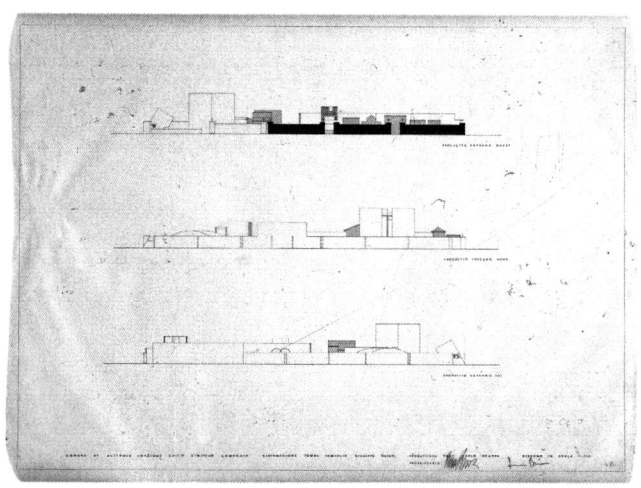

25

ENCLOSING WALL
DIE UMFASSUNGSMAUER

WEST: FACADE ADJACENT TO THE OLD CIMITERY
WESTSEITE: FASSADE GEGEN DEN ORTSFRIEDHOF HIN

Fountain, spring, pool, waterside shed open to the public, northwest corner, Carlo Scarpa's tomb
Brunnen, Quelle, Wasserbecken, allgemein zugängliche Wasserstelle, Nordwestecke,
Grab Carlo Scarpa's

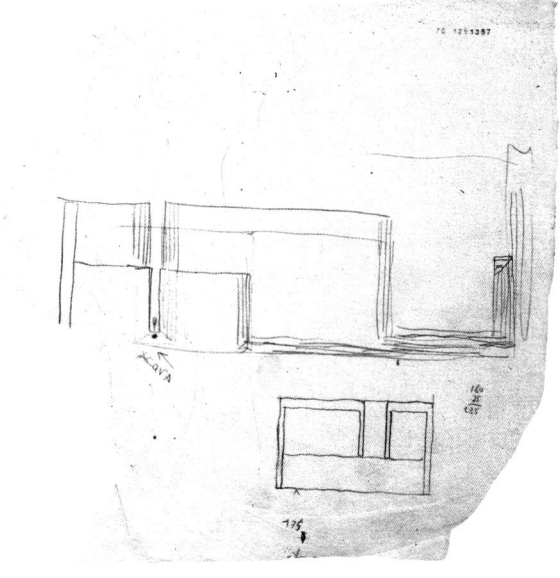

26

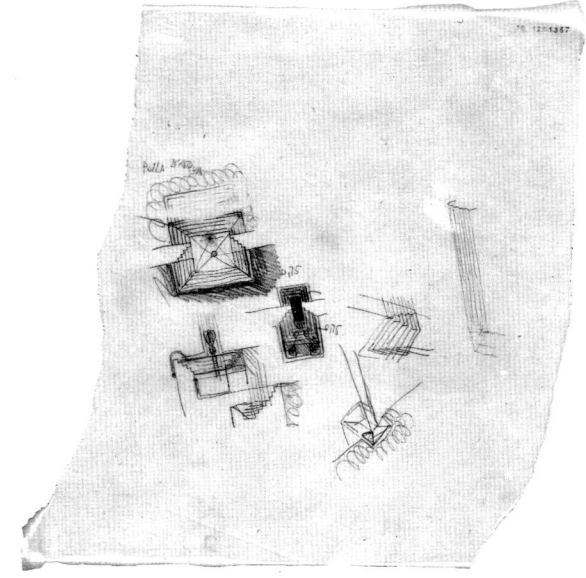

28

27

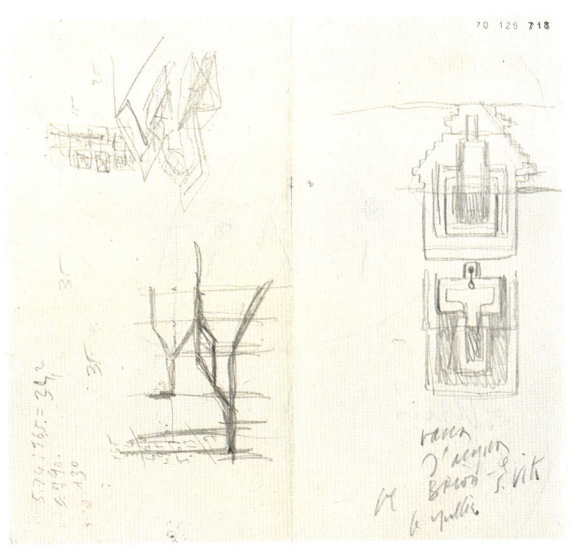

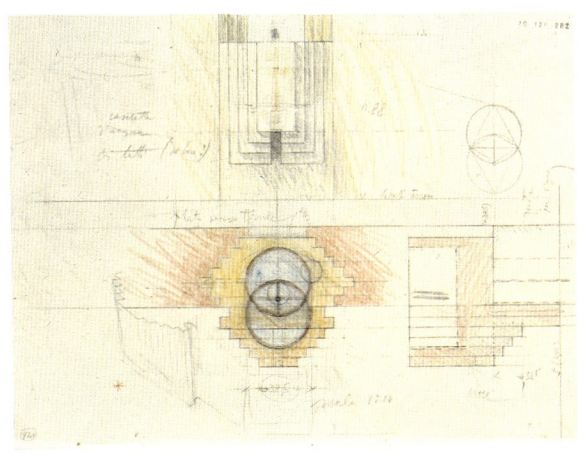

29

30

Propylaeum, entrance, passage, entrance to the chapel (1970–1974)
Propyleion, Eingang, Passage, Zugang zur Kapelle (1970–1974)

Facade facing the old cemetery/Fassade gegen den Ortsfriedhof hin

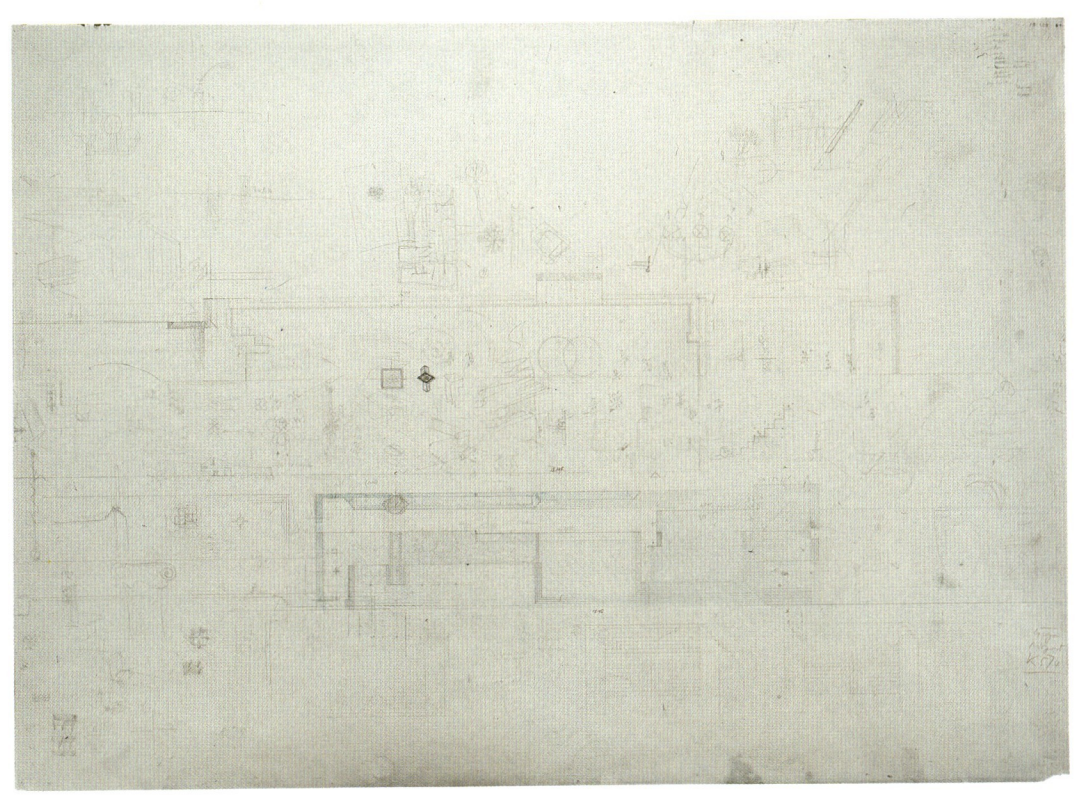

31

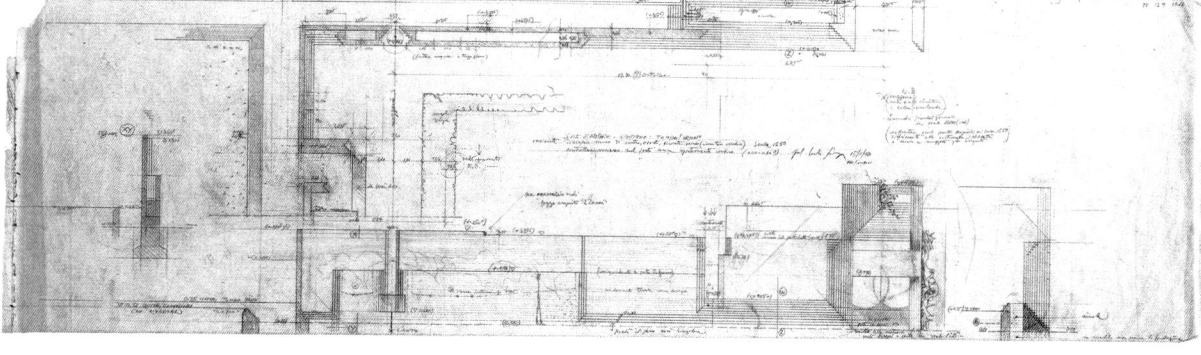

32

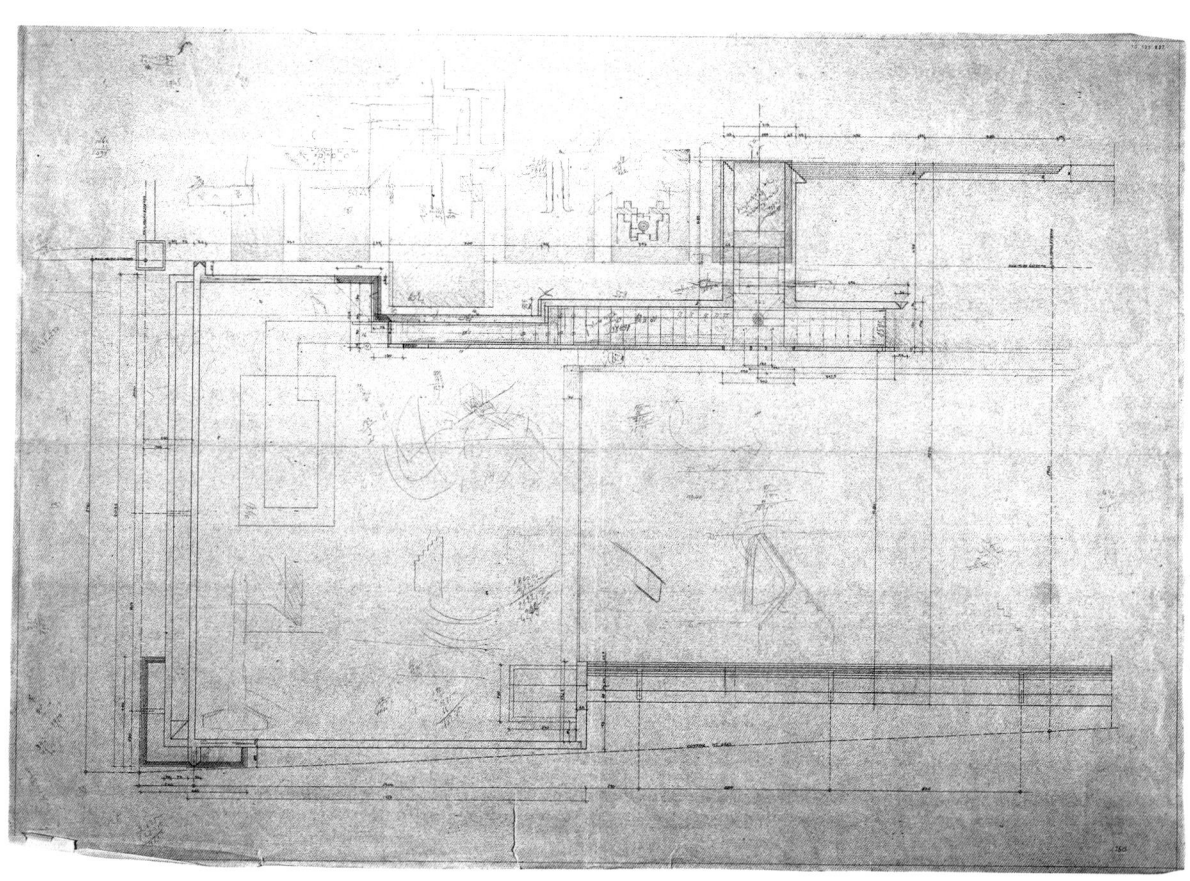

33

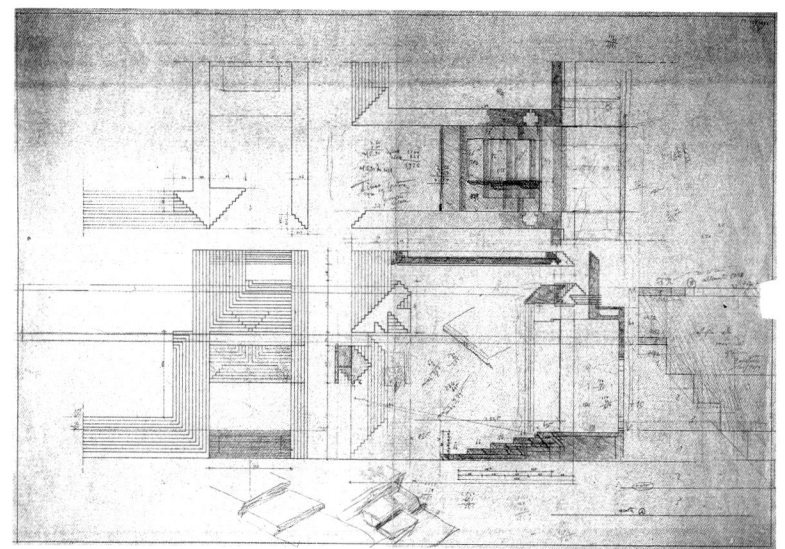

34

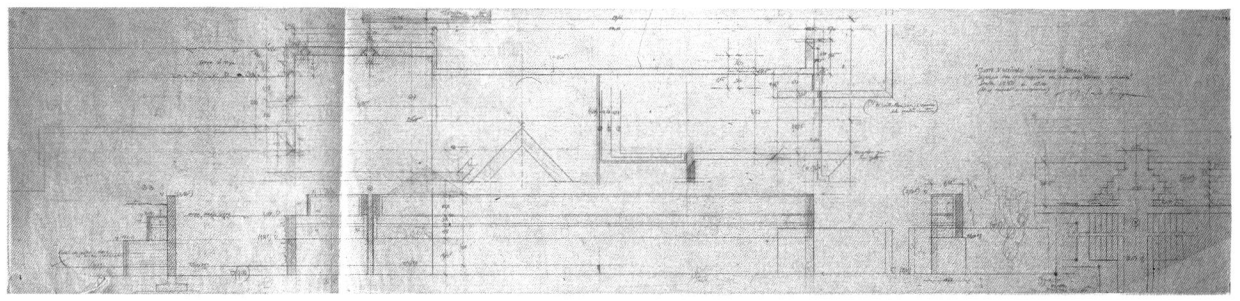

35

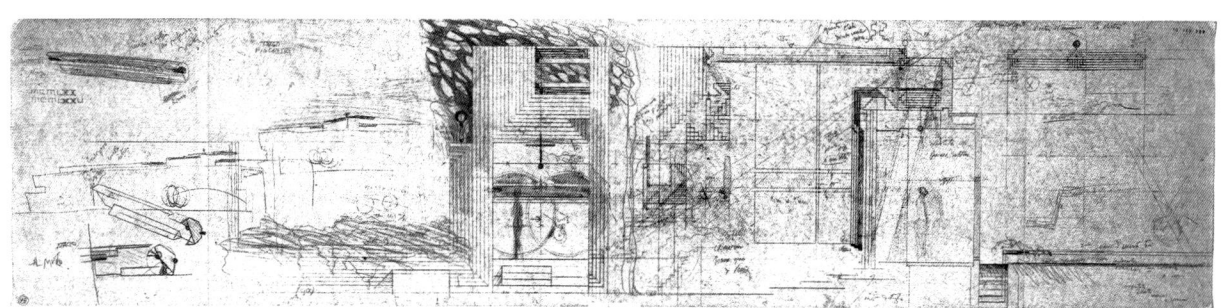

36

58

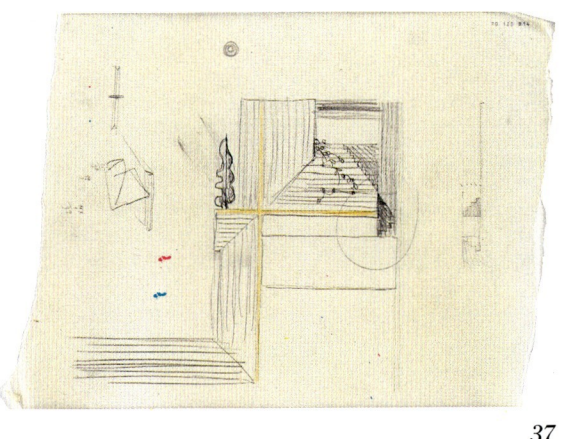

37

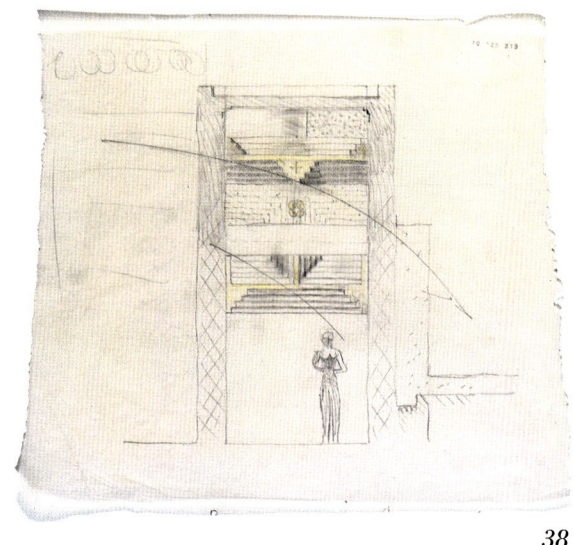

38

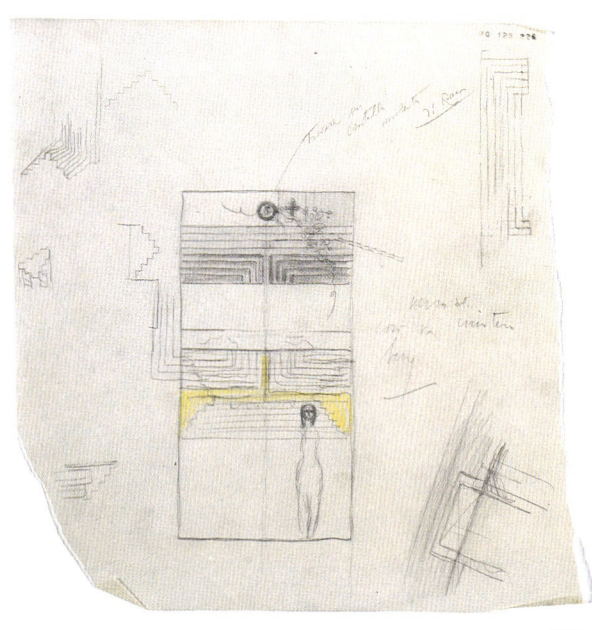

39

40

Steps/Stufen

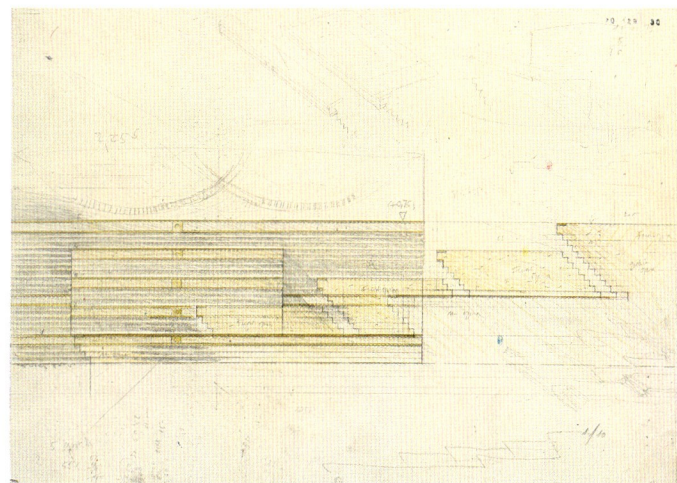

59

41

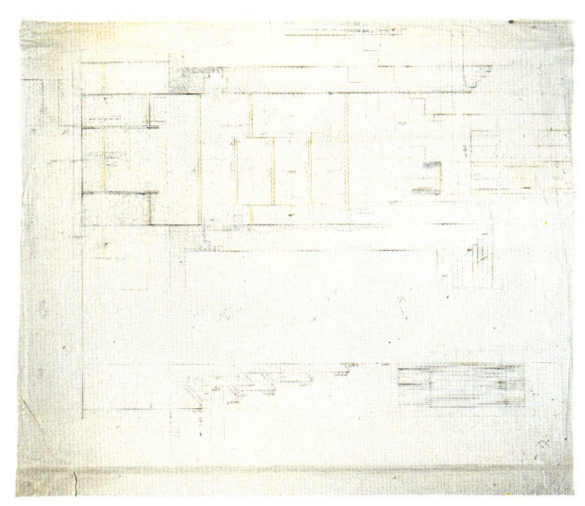

42

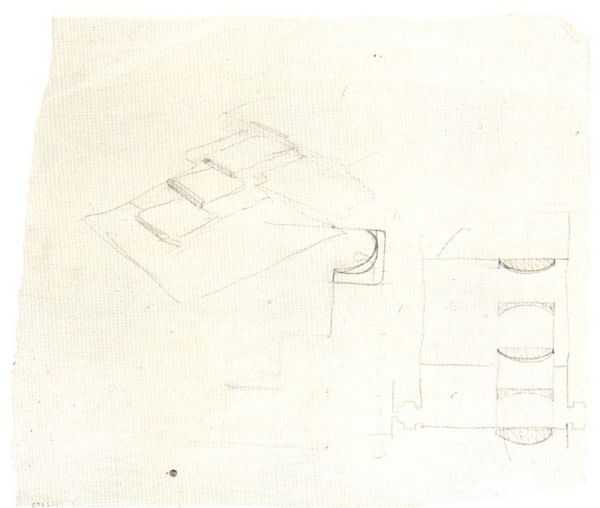

43

East facade/Ostseite

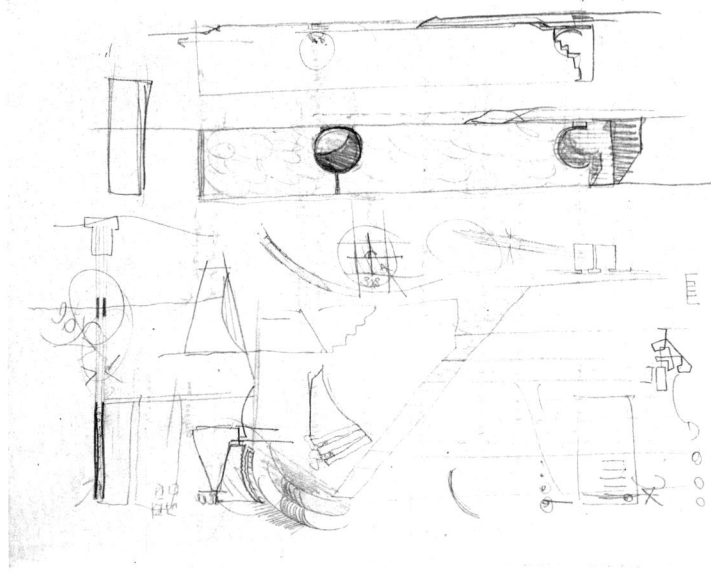

44

45

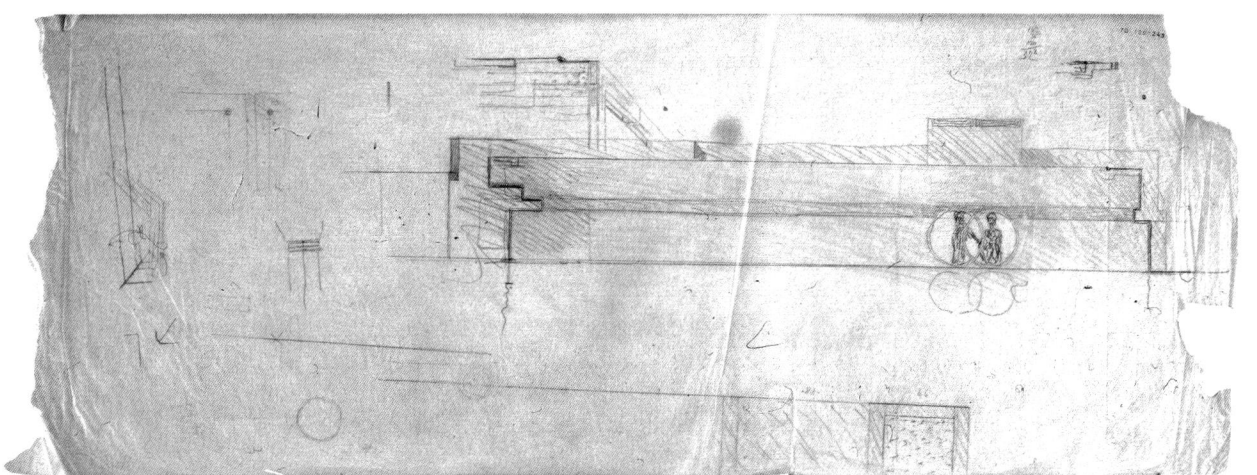

46

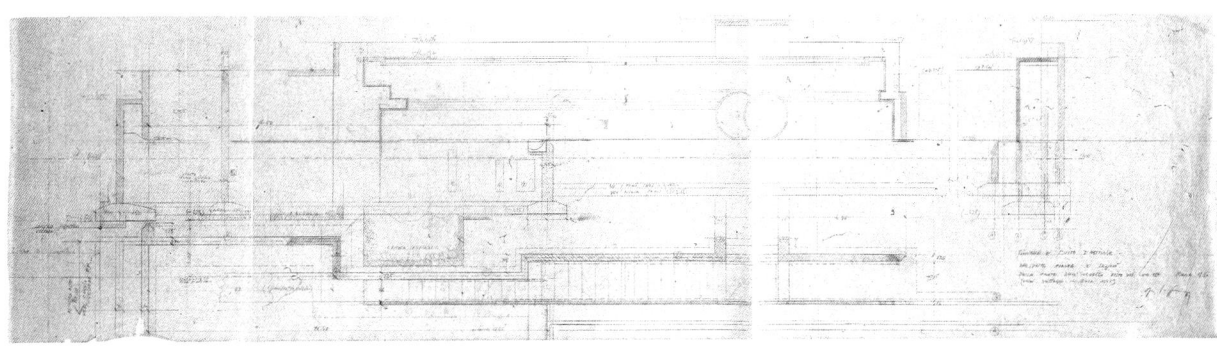

47

Ceiling of the corridor/Decke des Korridors

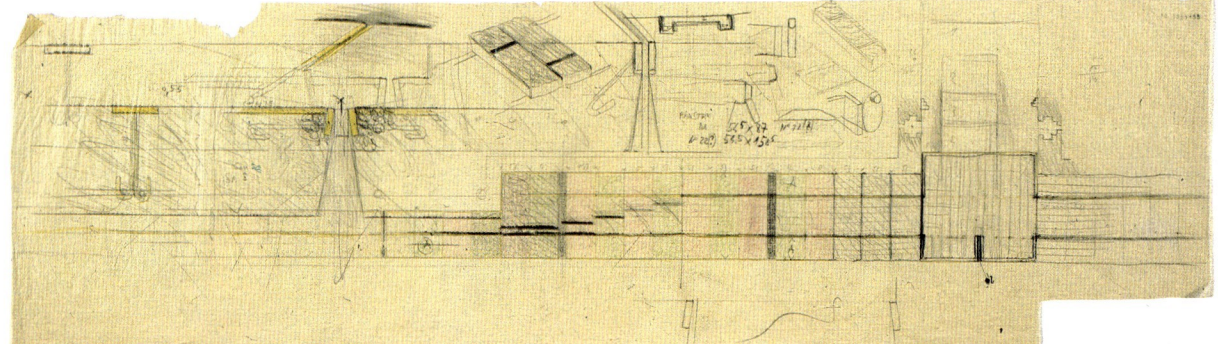

48

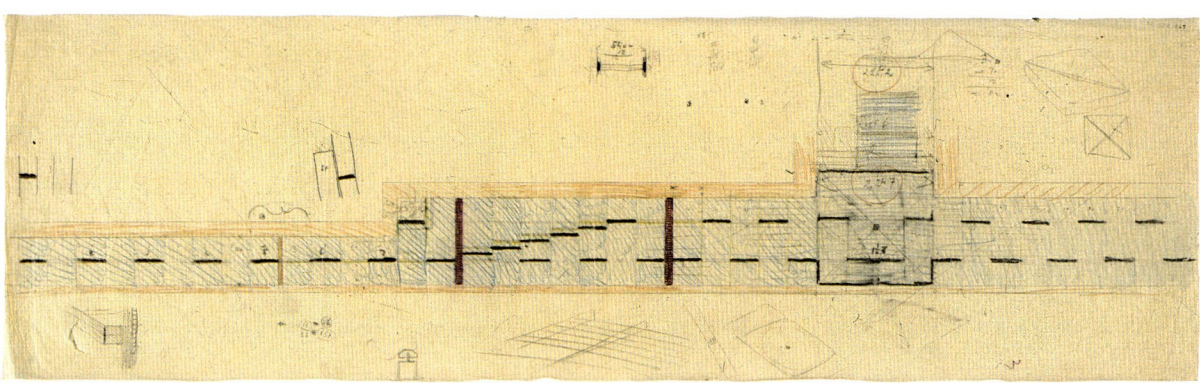

49

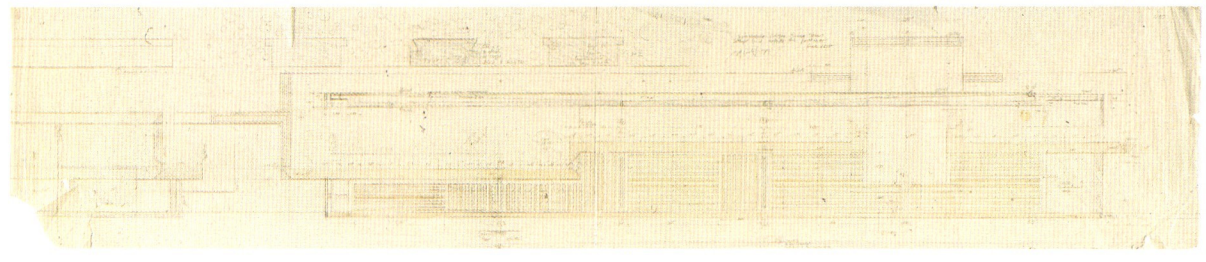

50

Coin-metal moulding at the entrance of the wing and the center of the corridor
Rahmen aus „Muntzmetall" beim Eingang und in der Mitte des Korridors

51

52

64

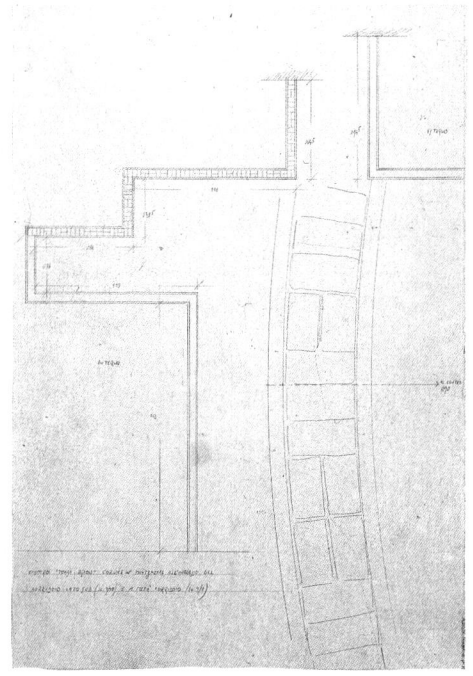

53

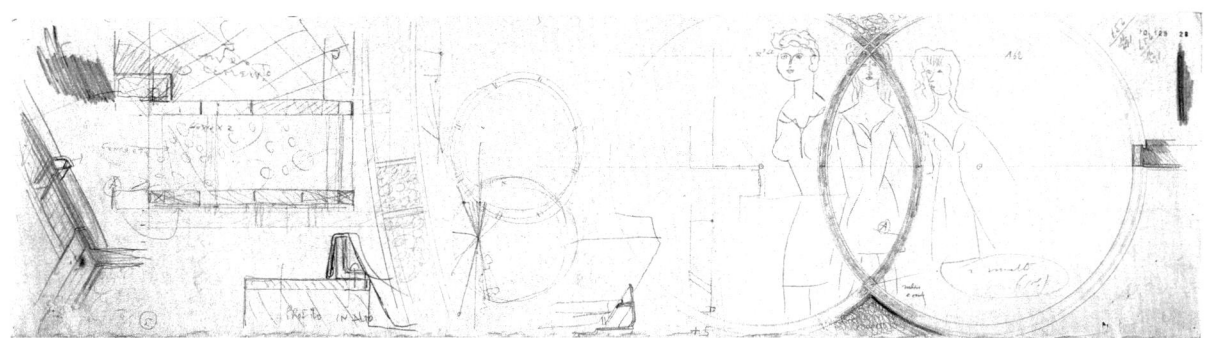

54

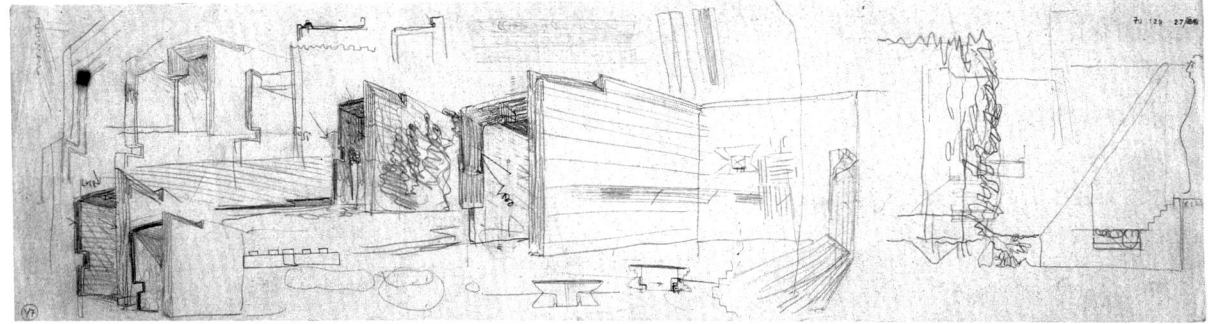

55

Crystal glass and coin-metal doors along the corridor: vertical sliding door to prevent access to the large pool/Türe aus Kristallglas und „Muntzmetall" im Korridor: die vertikale Schiebetür versperrt den Zugang zum großen Wasserbecken

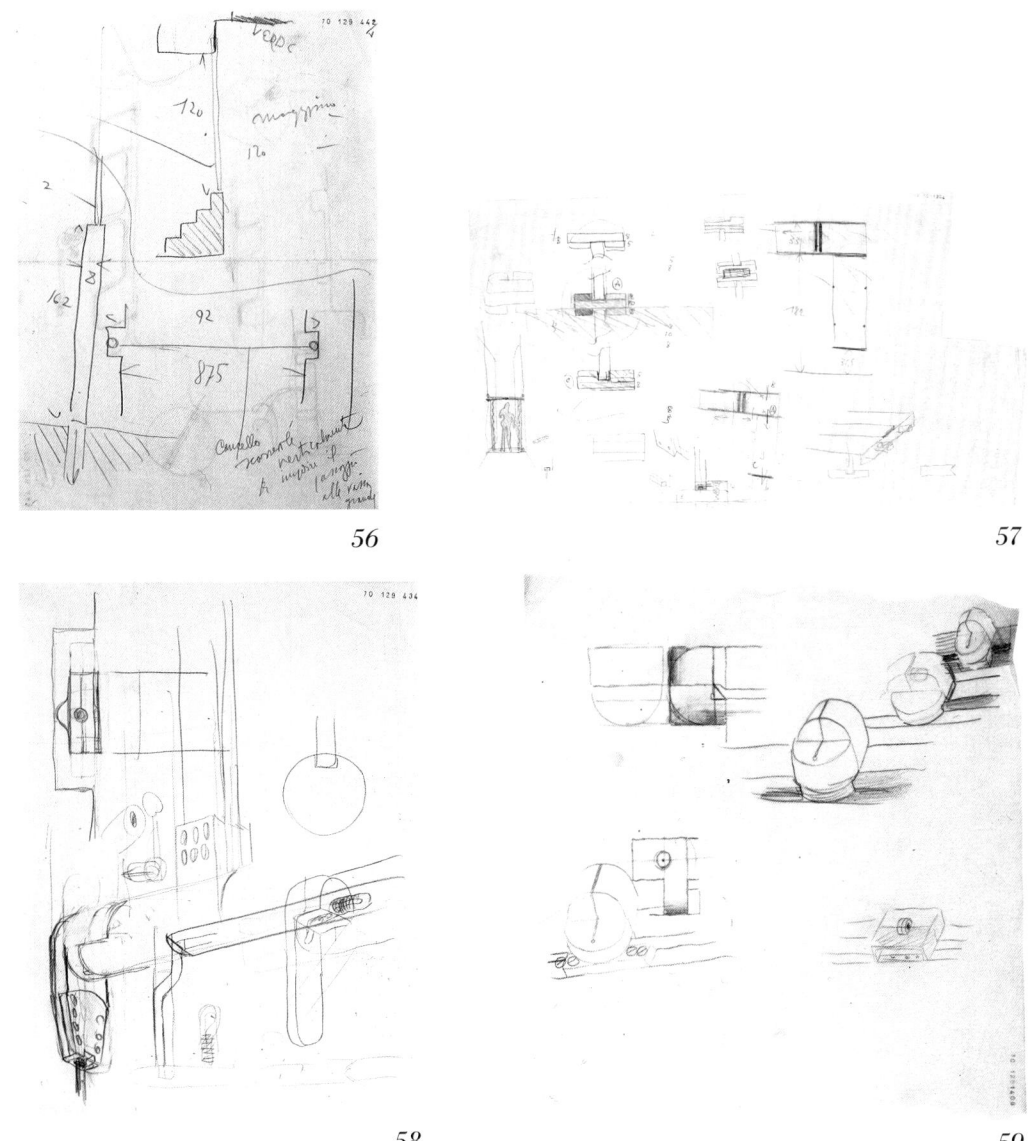

56

57

58

59

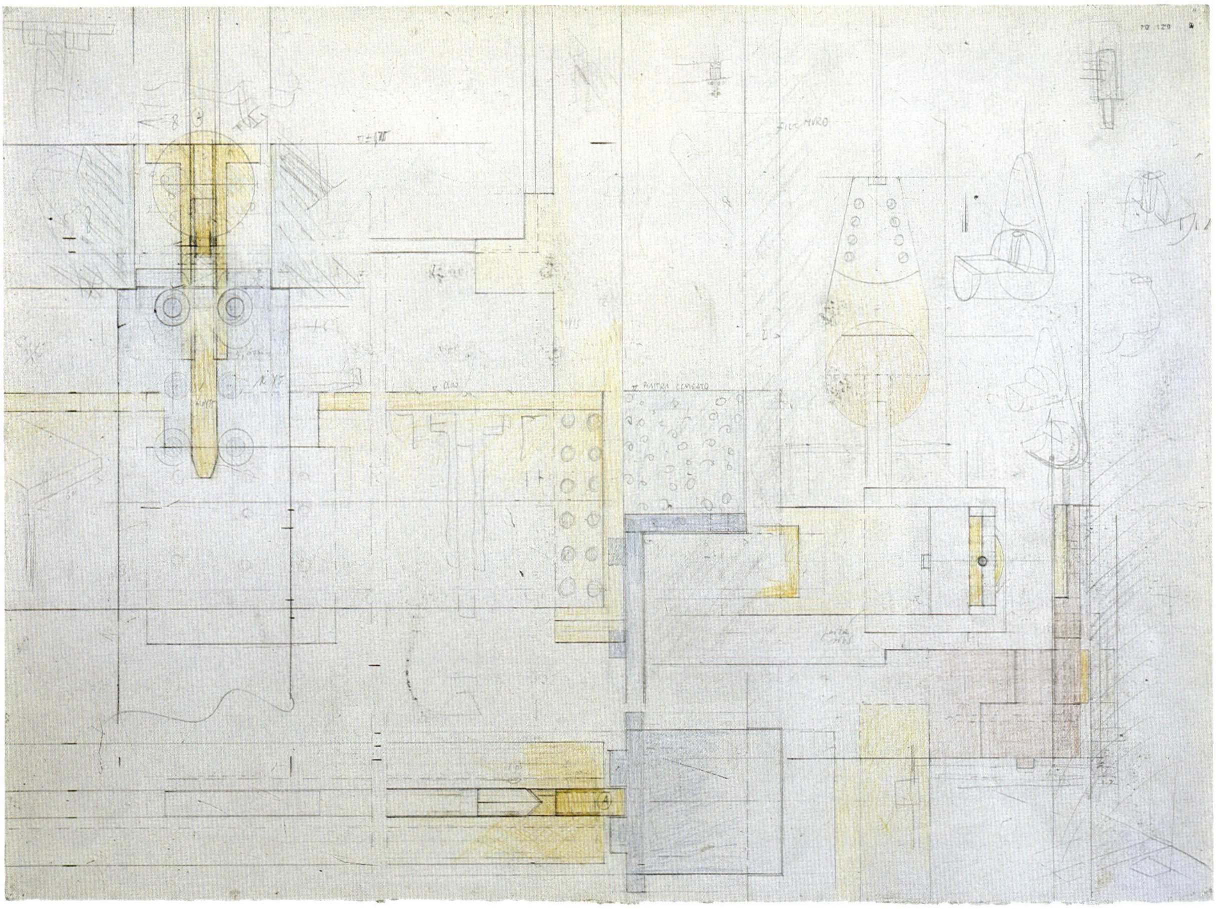

67

61

62

Iron counterweight and bronze and stainless steel sliding door pulley system/Gegengewicht aus Eisen und Rollensystem in Bronze und Inoxstahl für die Schiebetür

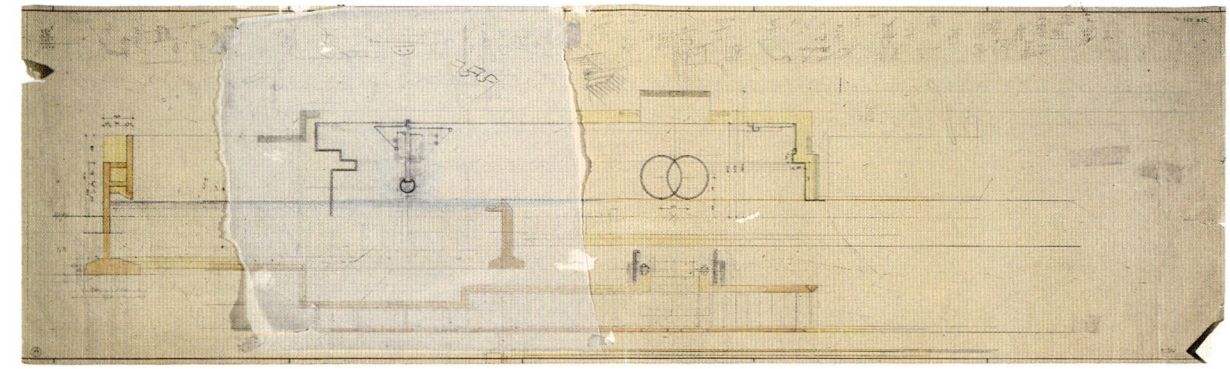

68

63

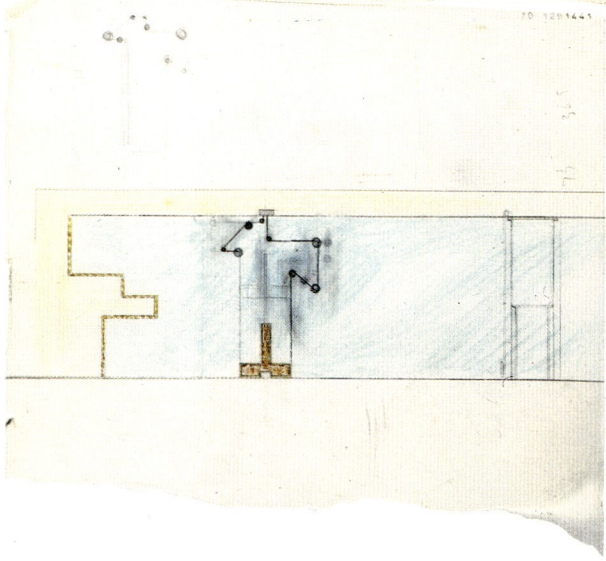

64

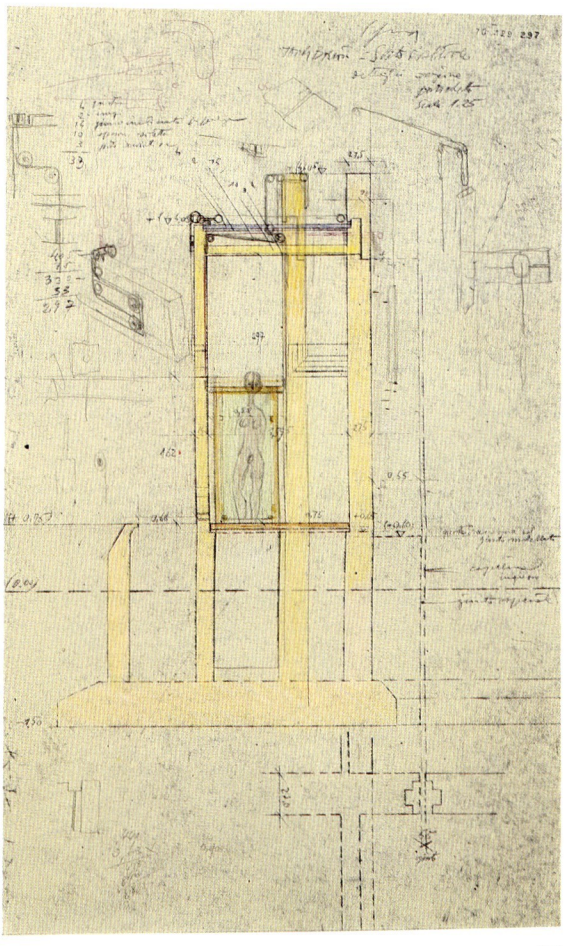

65

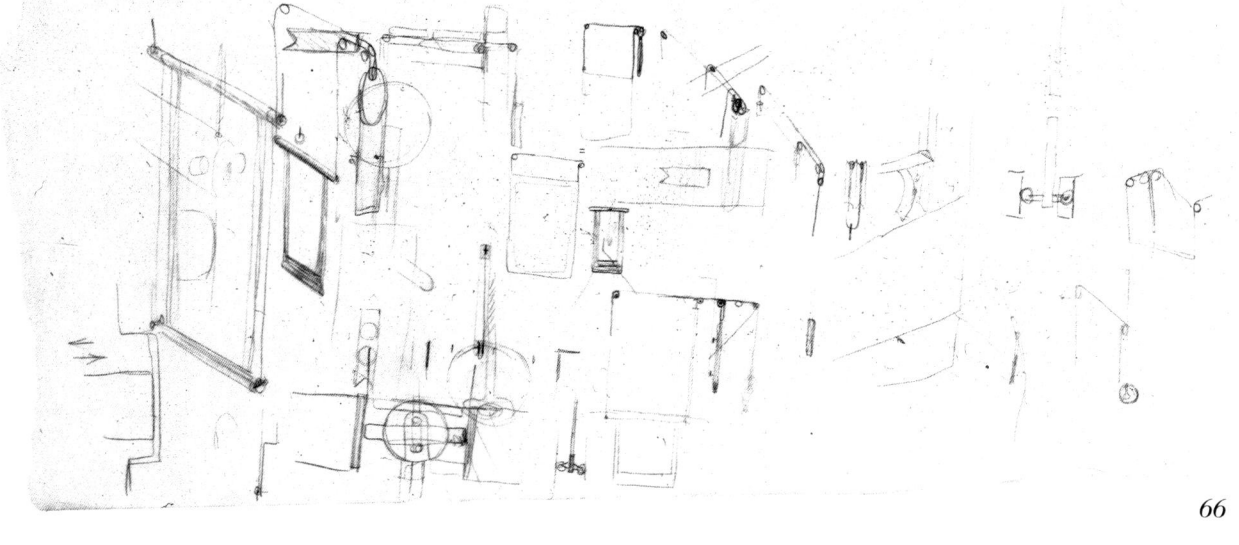

66

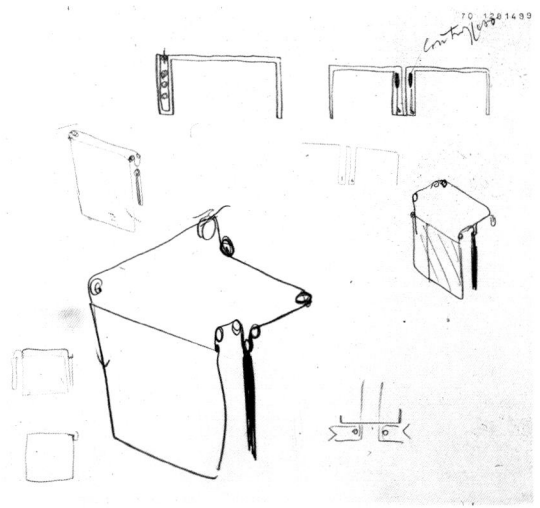

67

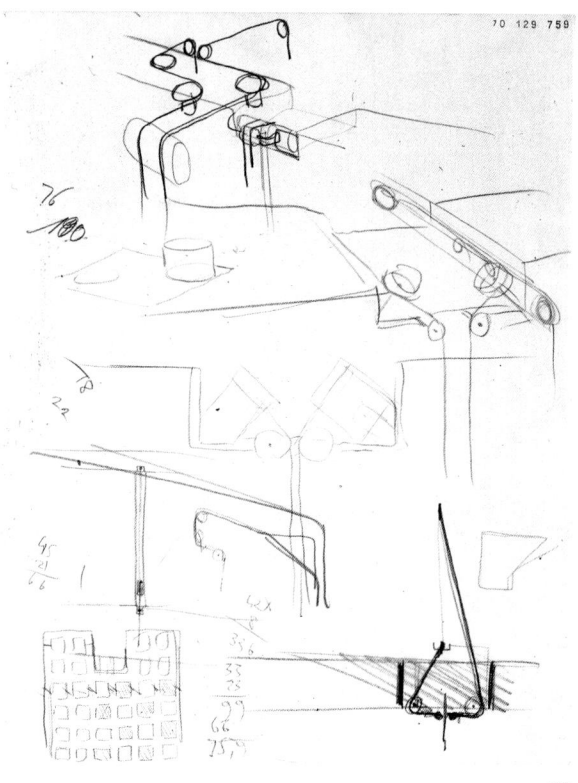

68

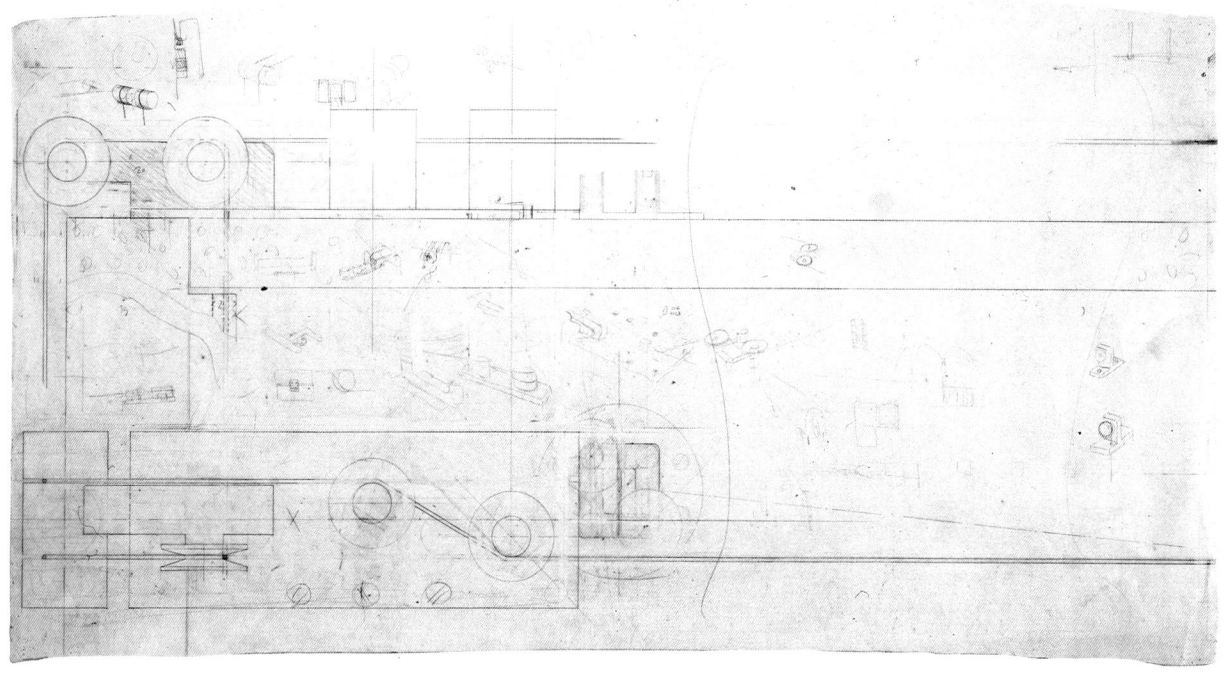

69

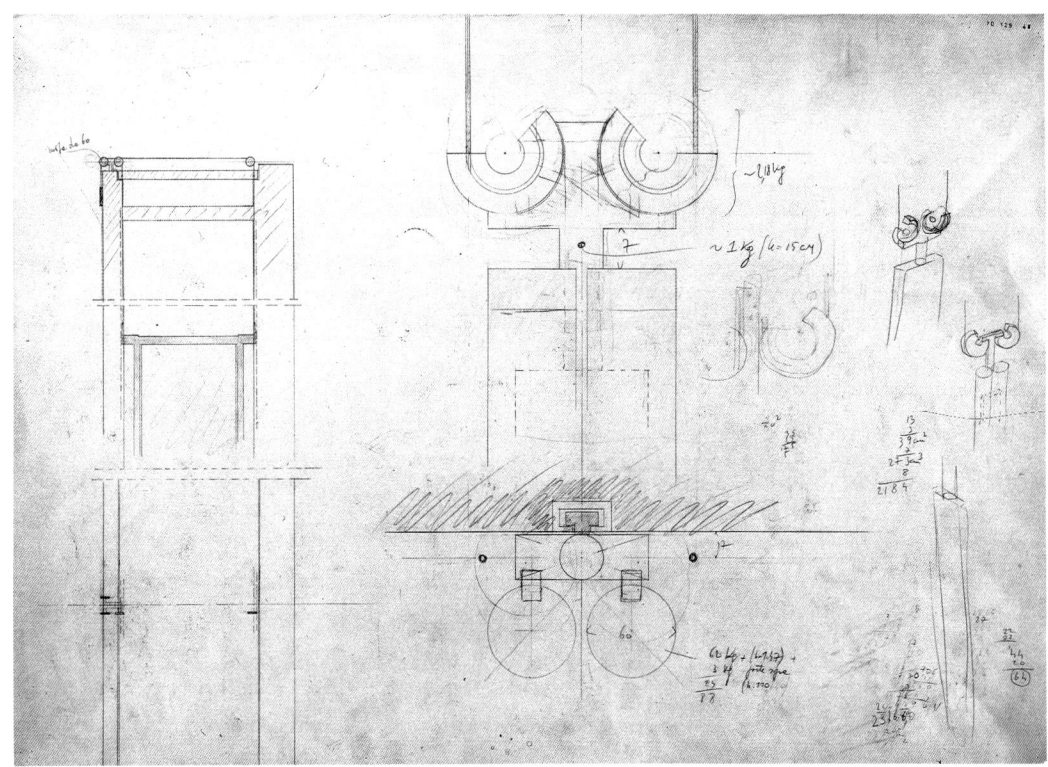

70

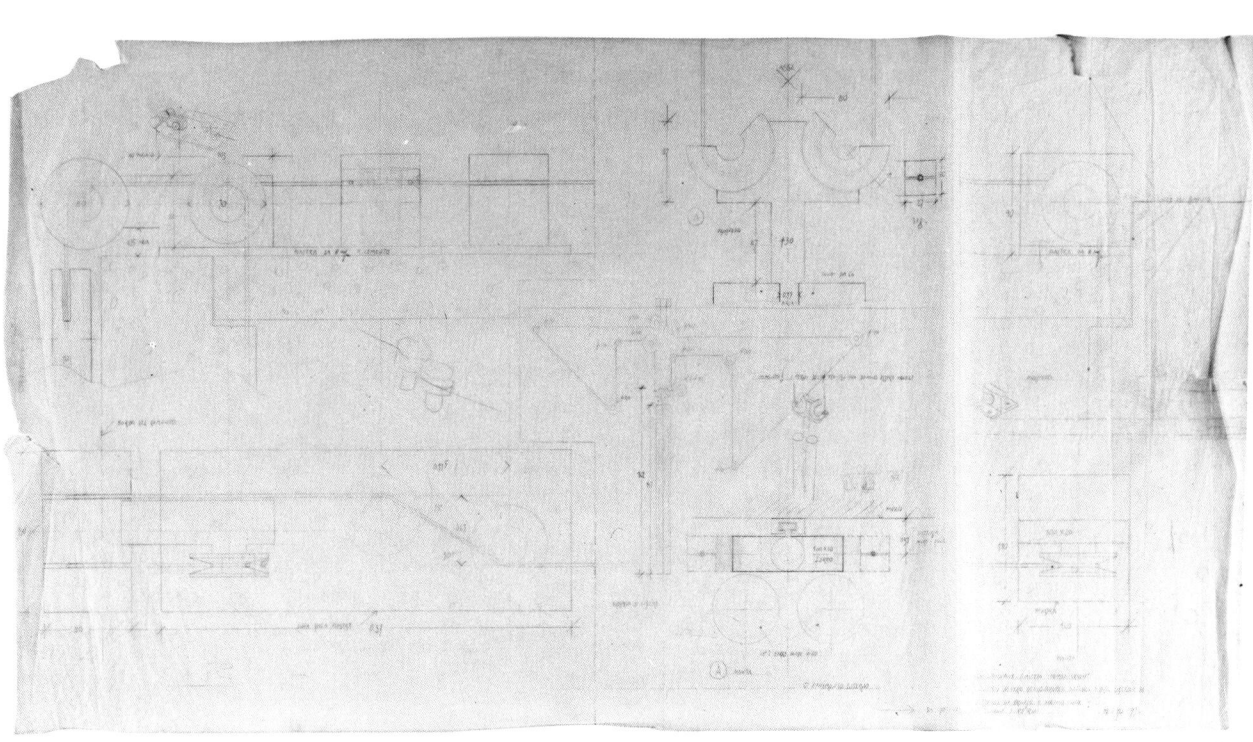

71

Bronze clasp on top of the east facade wall
Bronzeschließe im oberen Teil der ostseitigen Mauer

SOUTH AND EAST/SÜD- UND OSTSEITE
Flower bed/Blumenbeet

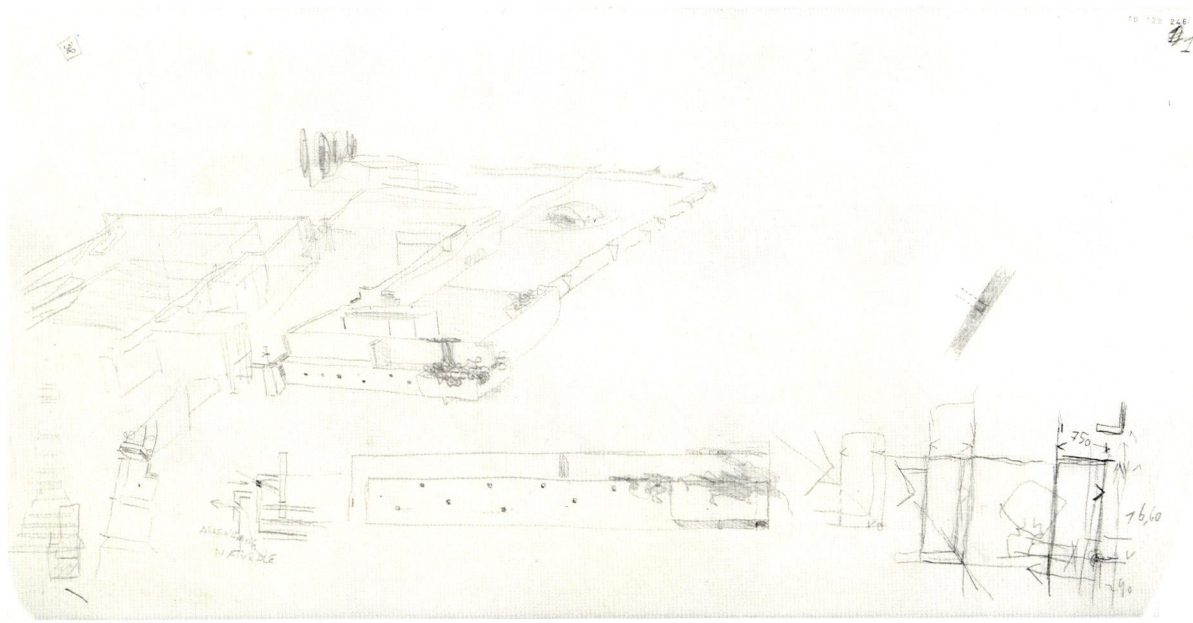

73

73

74

74

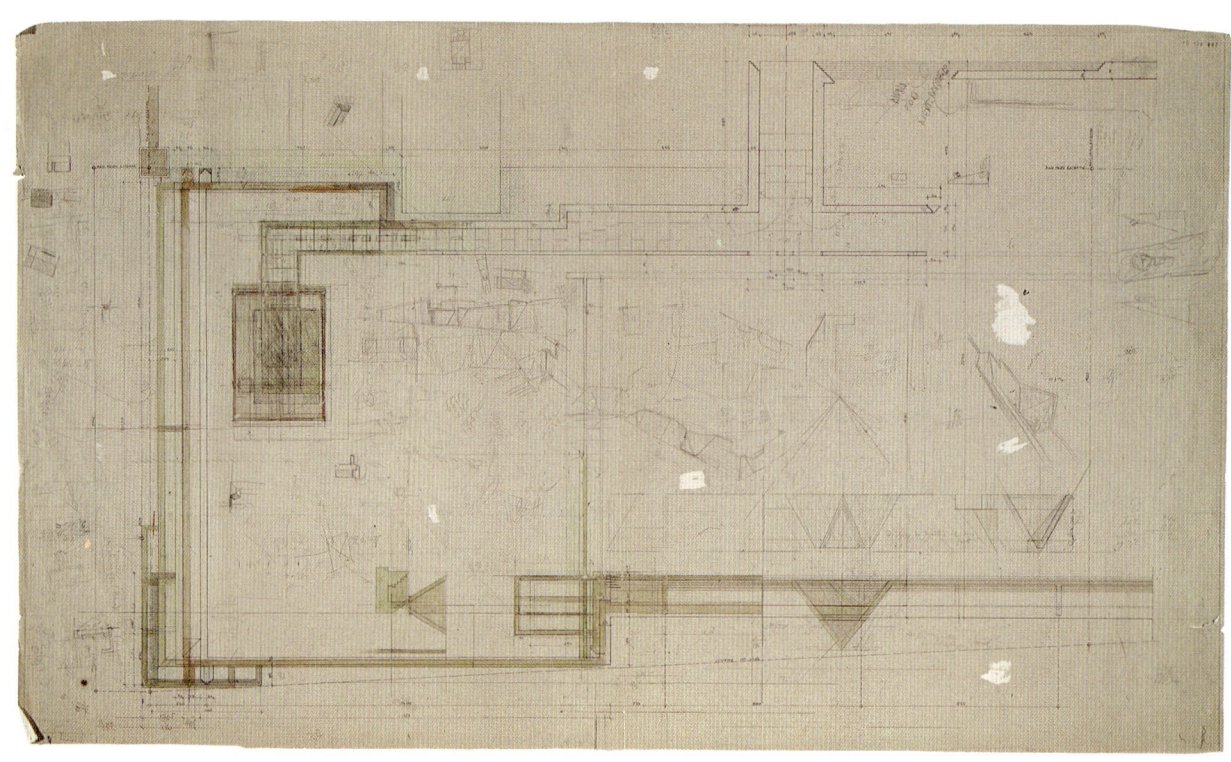

75

Large flower container above the pool/großer Blumenbehälter über dem Wasserbecken

75

76

77

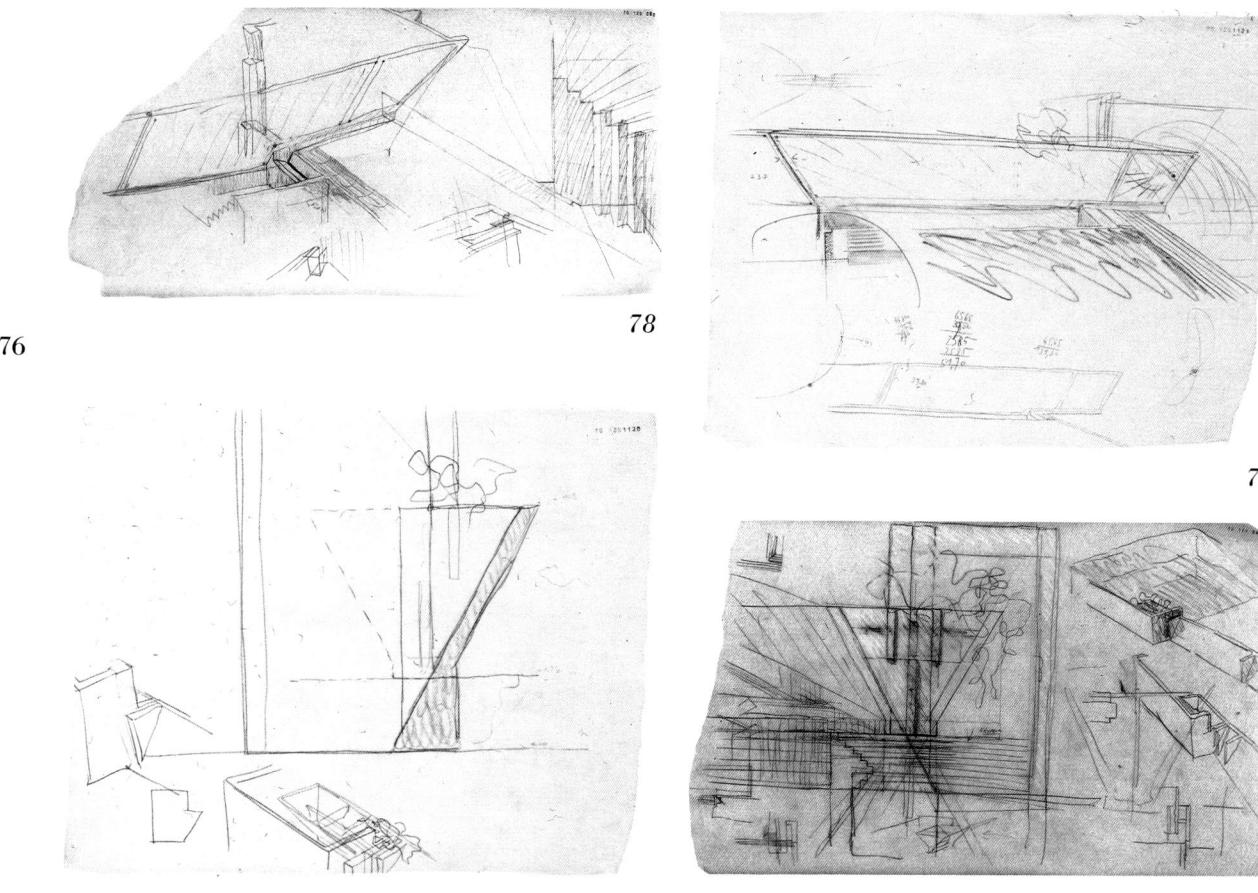

76

78

79

80

81

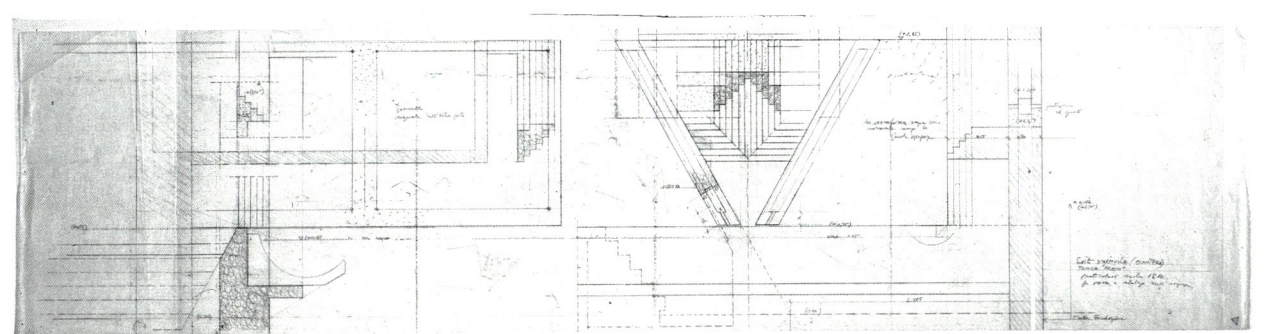

82   77

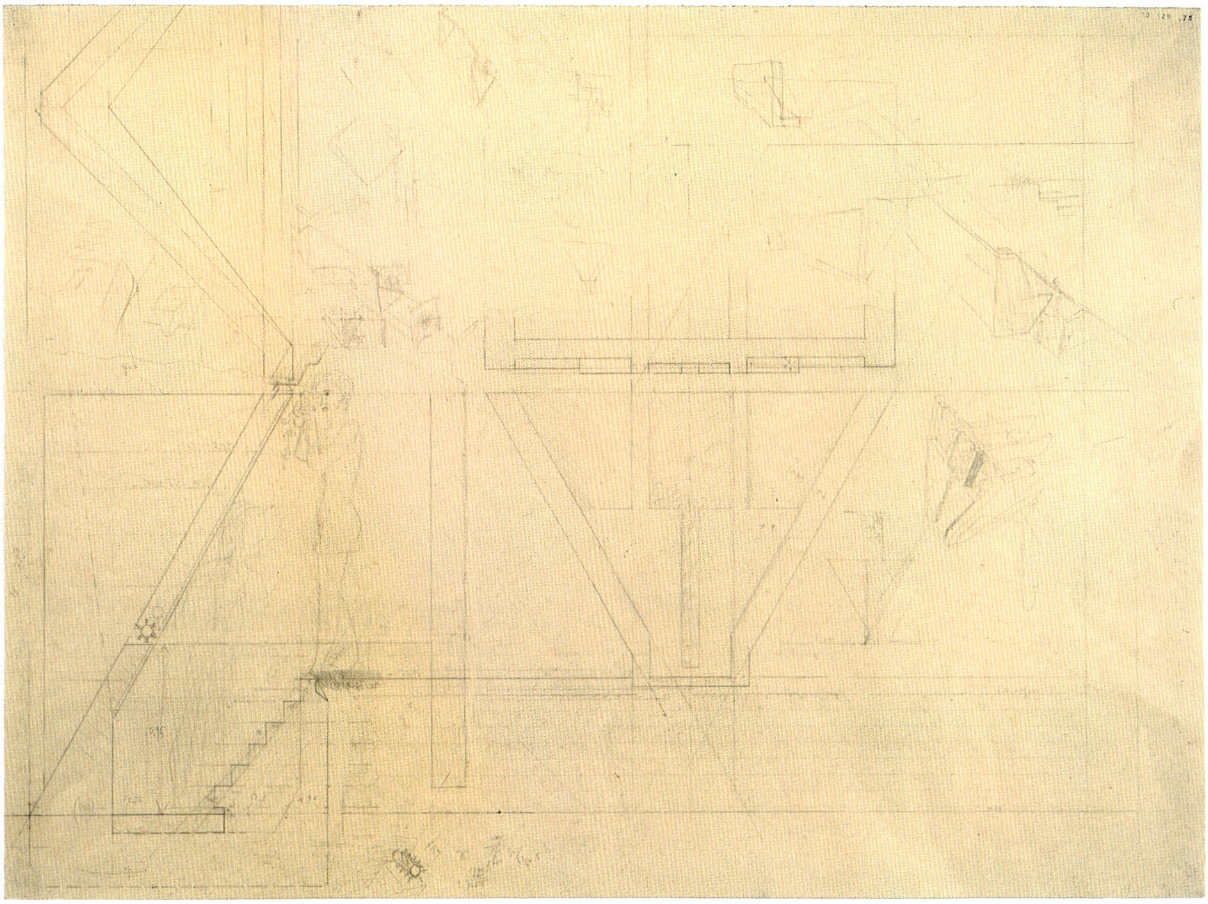

83

Sloping tiered wall/schräge und abgestufte Mauer

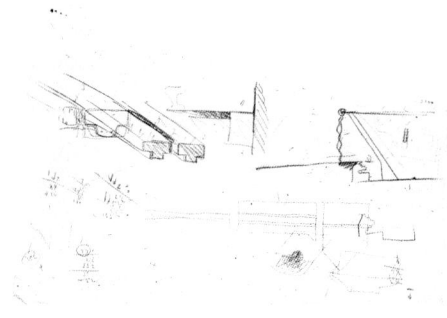

84

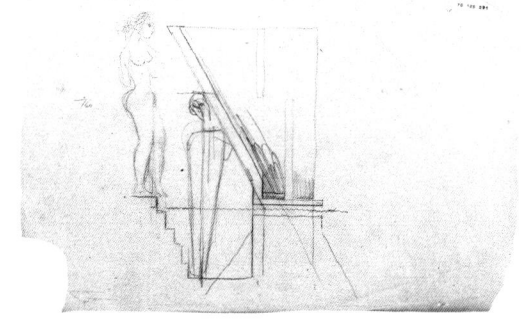

85

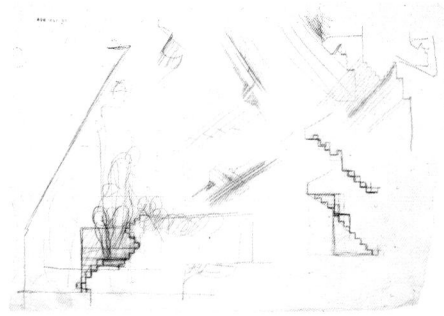

86

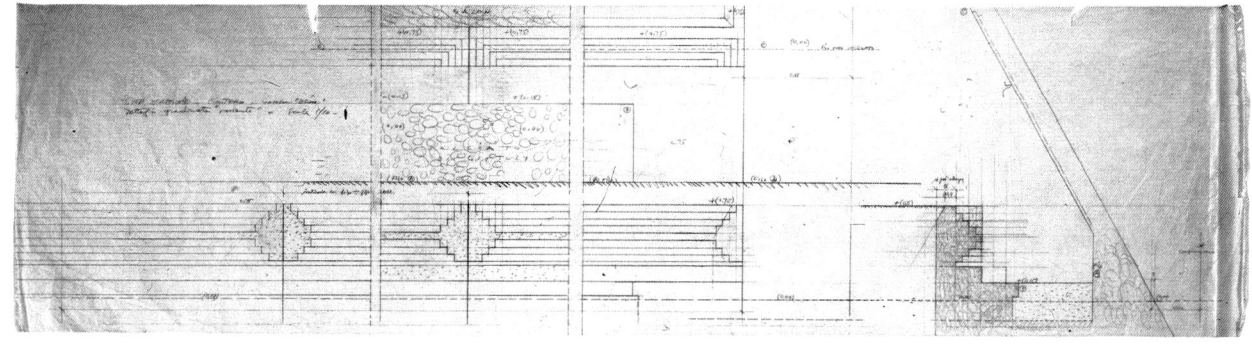

87

NORTH: FAMILY TOMB/NORDSEITE: FAMILIENGRAB

Corner brackets/Ecklösungen

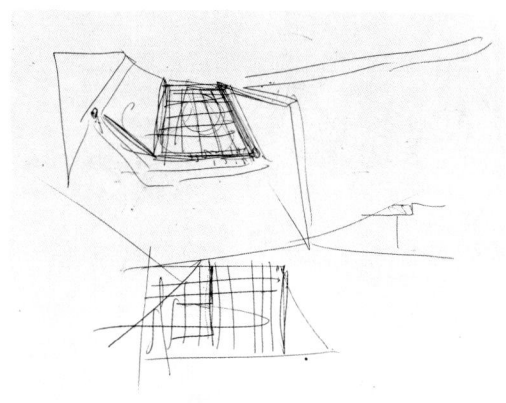

79

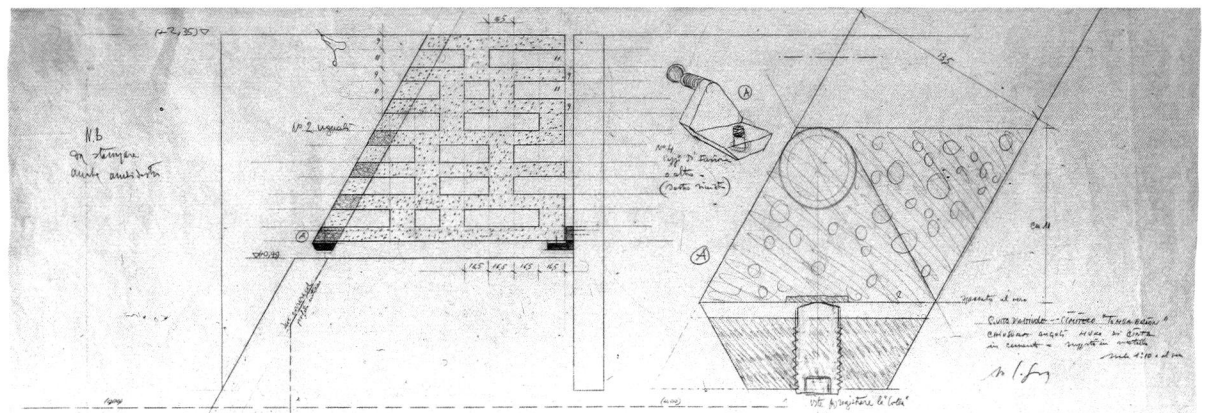

88

89

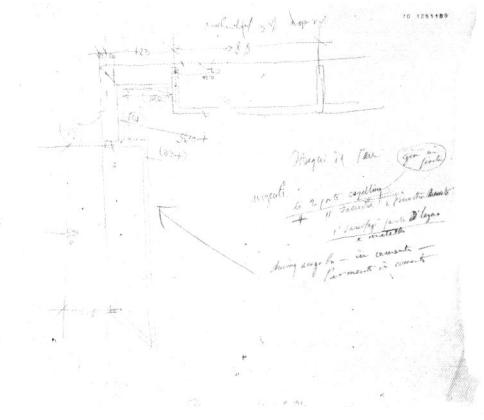

90

80

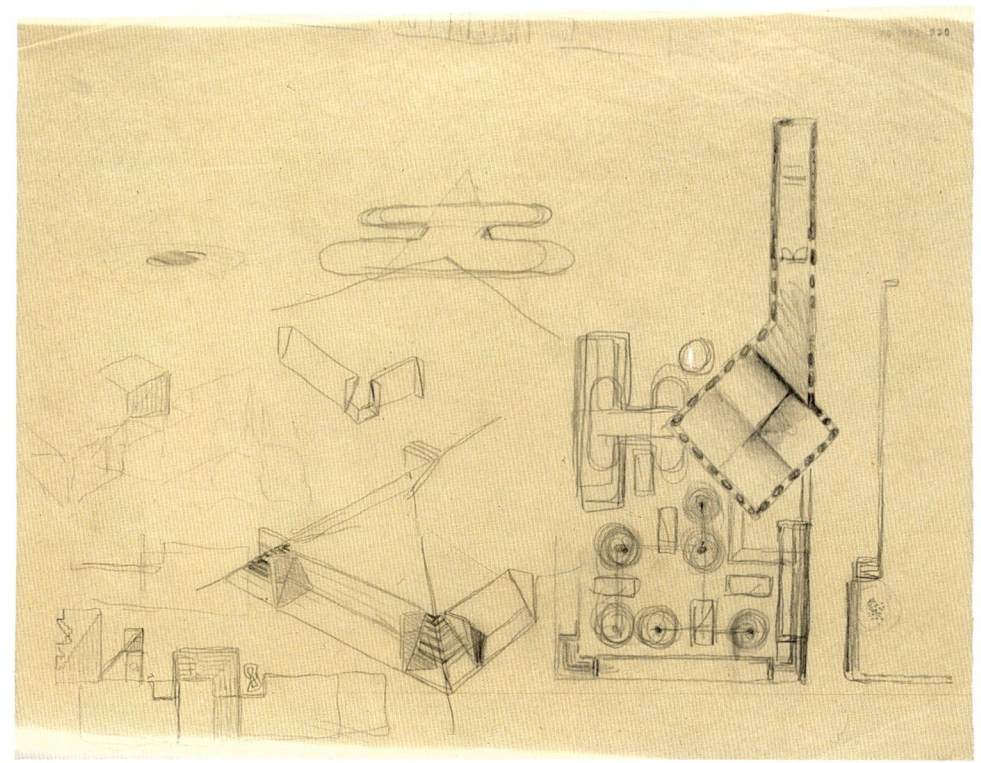

91

92

Family tomb/Familiengrabmal

Exterior view/Außenansicht

93

Sections/Schnitte

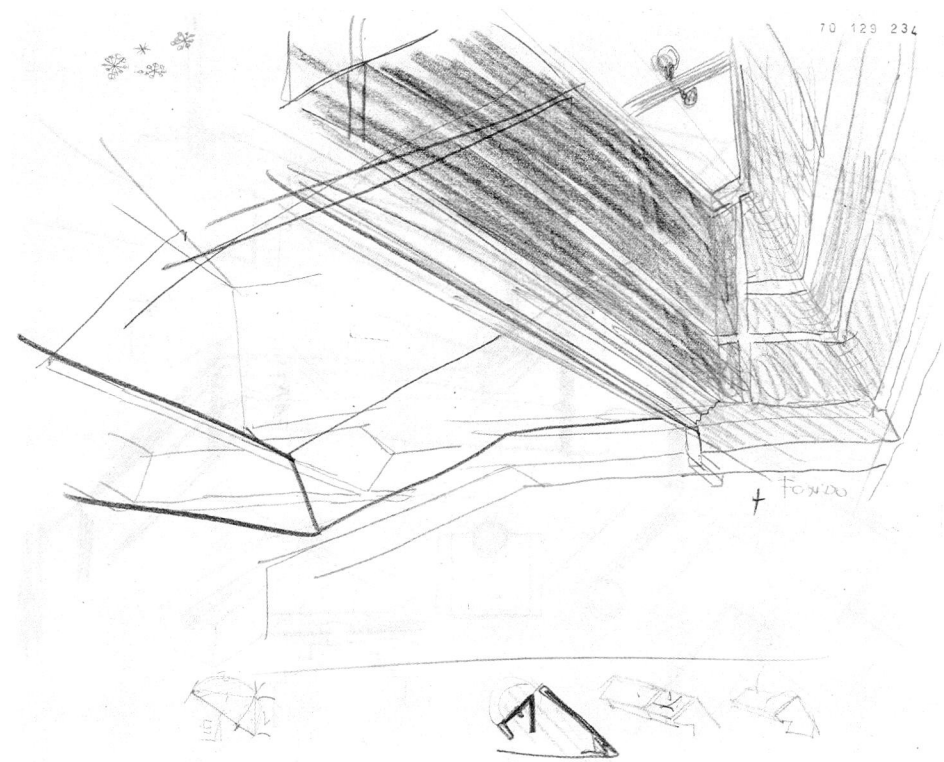

94

82

95

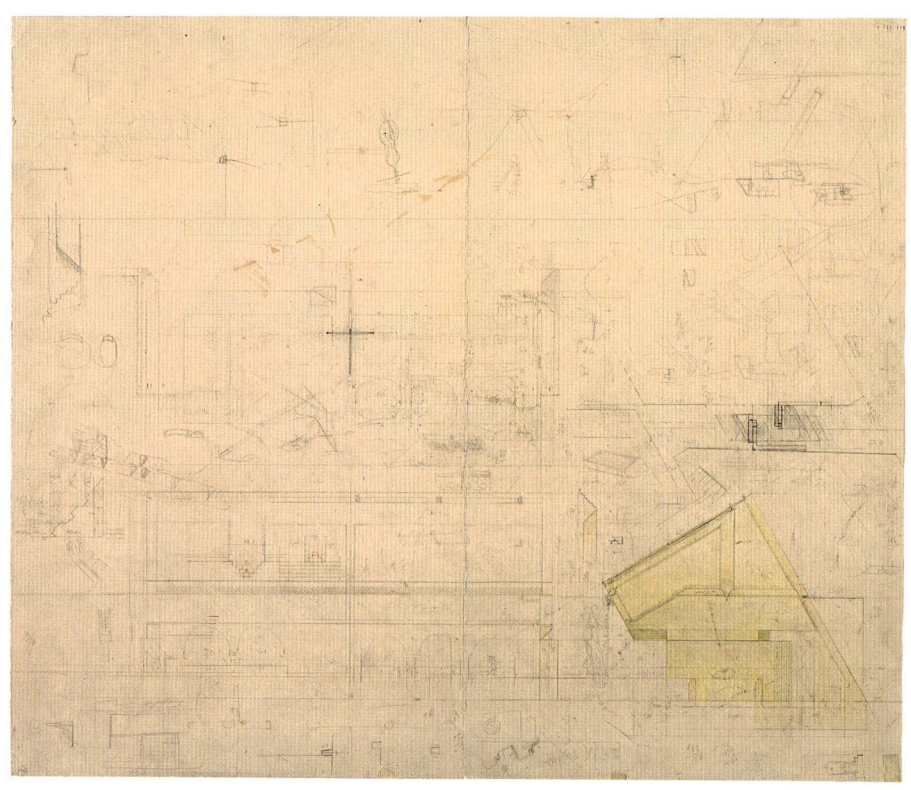

96

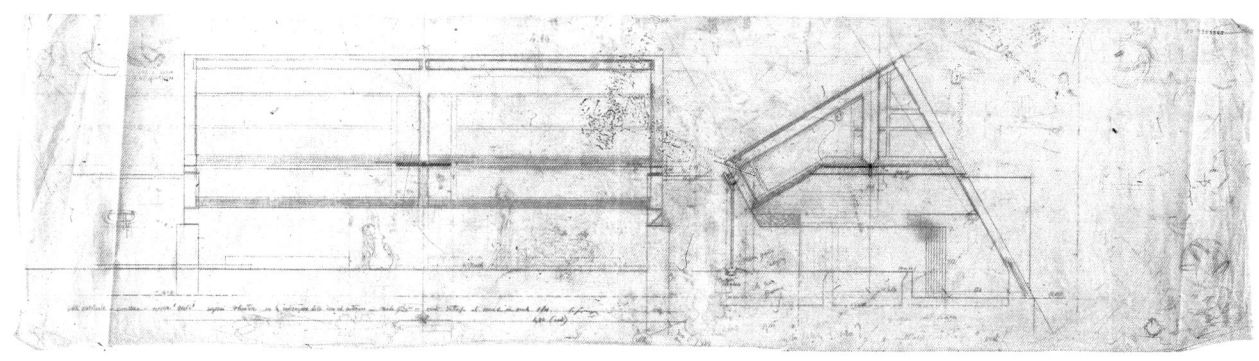

84

98

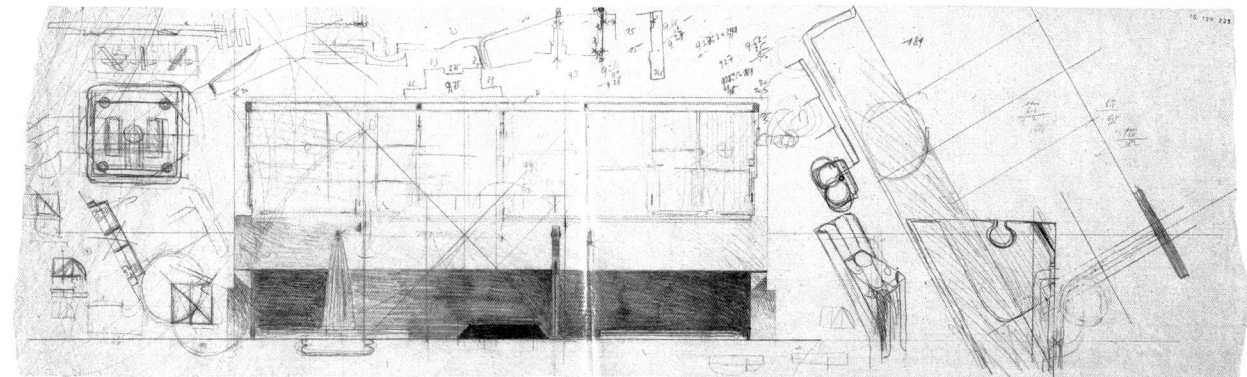

99

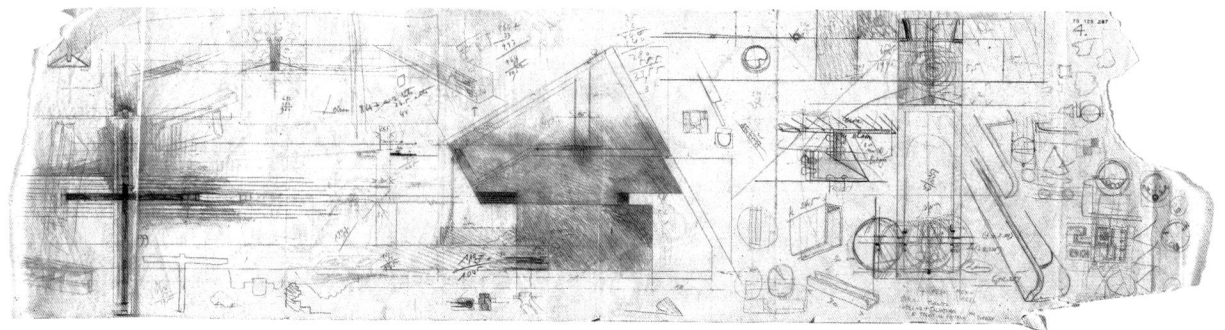

100

Slanted ceilings intrados, covering/Schräge Deckenleibung, Überdachung

101

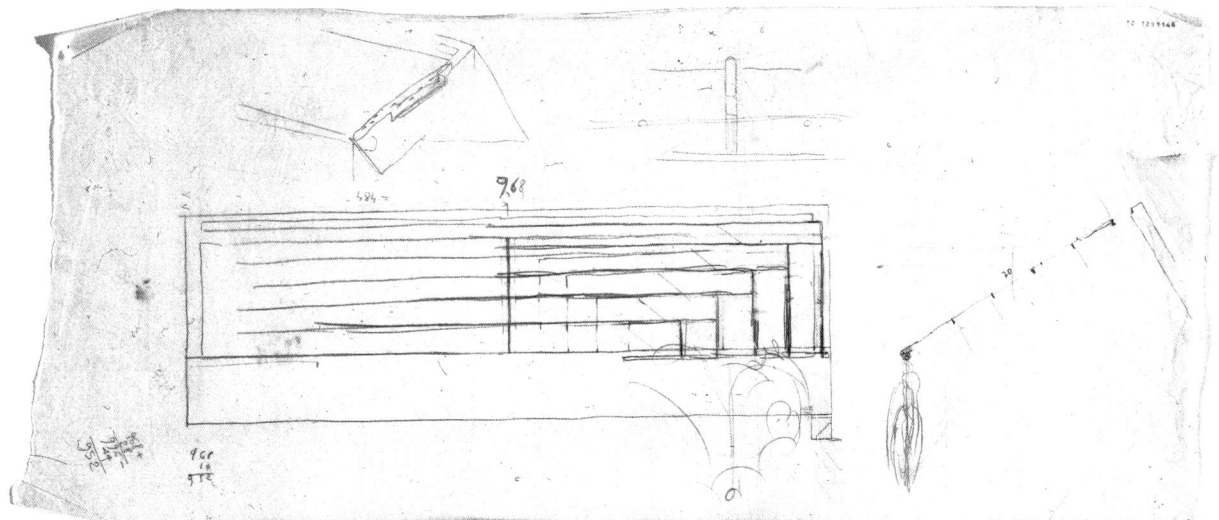

102

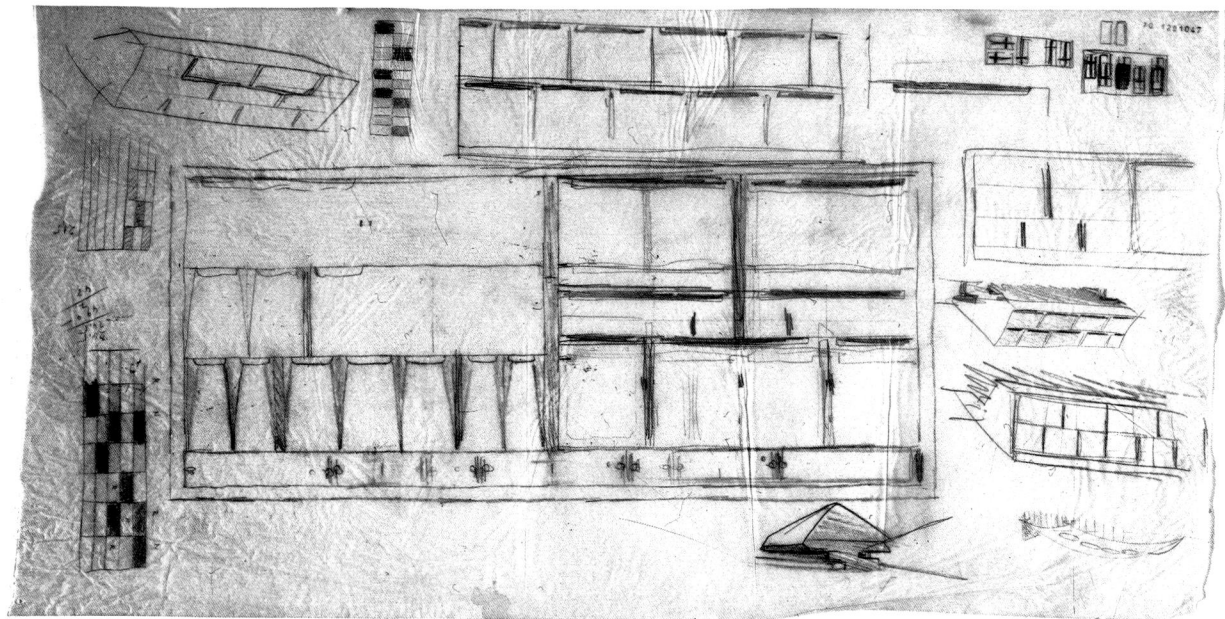

103

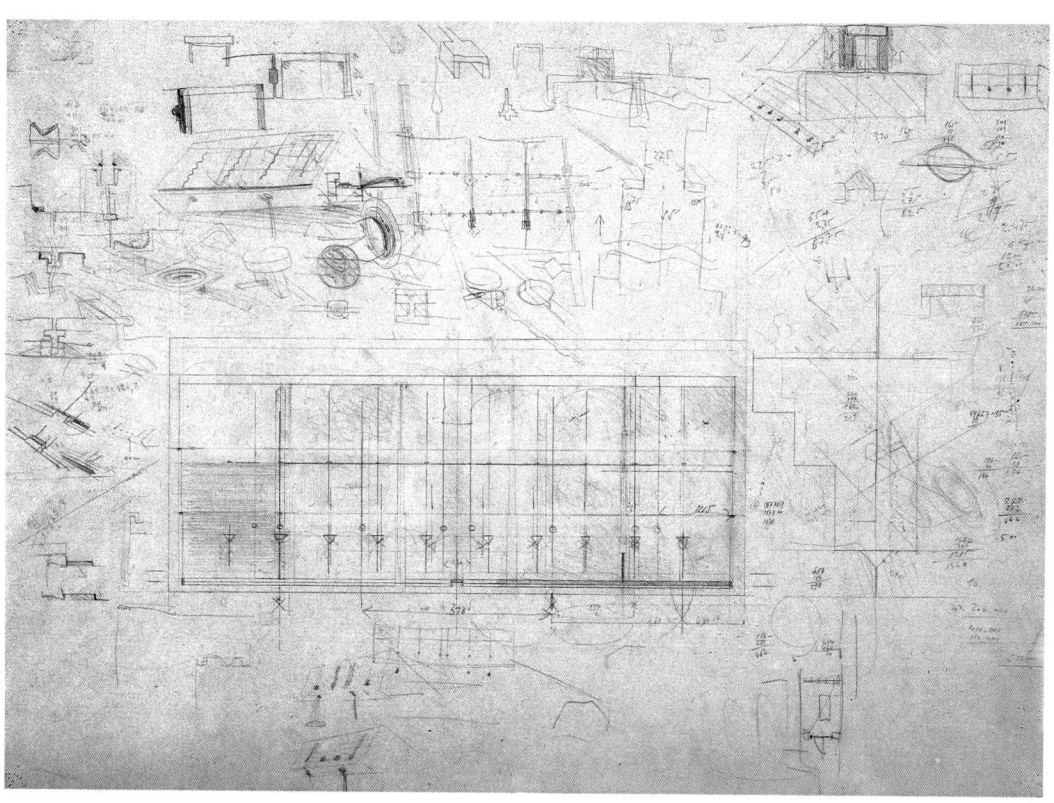

104

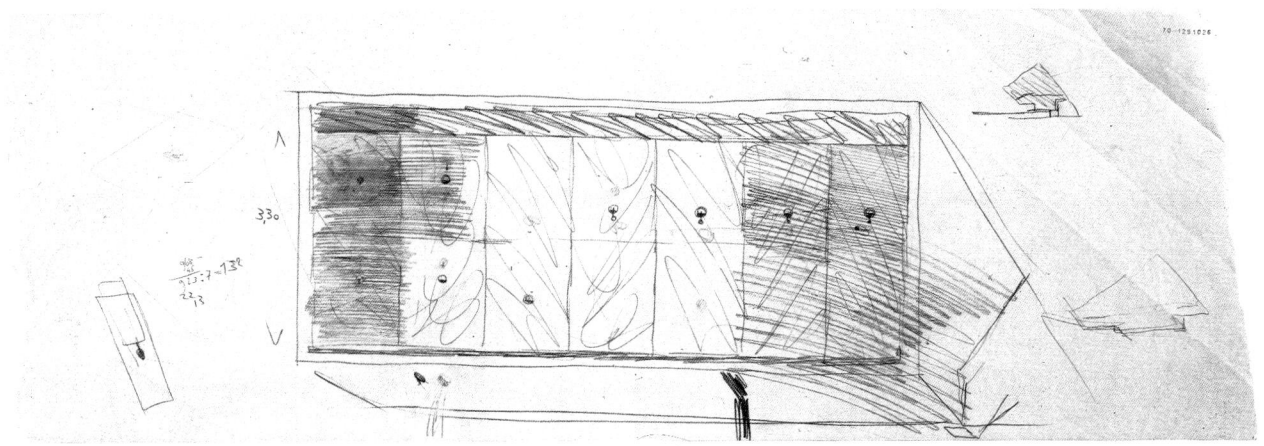

105

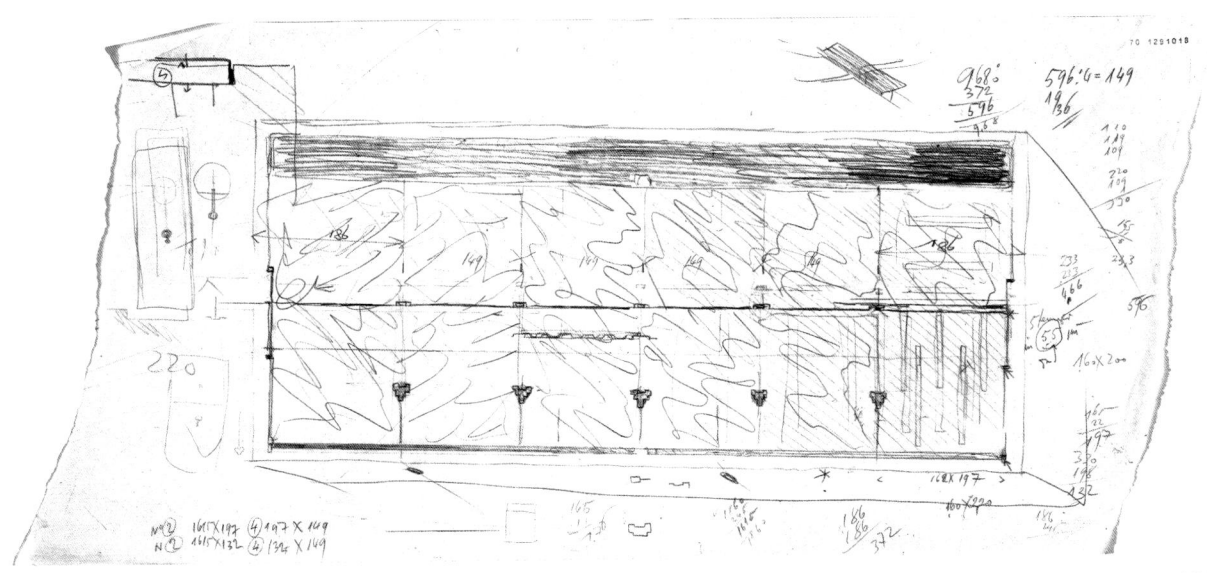

106

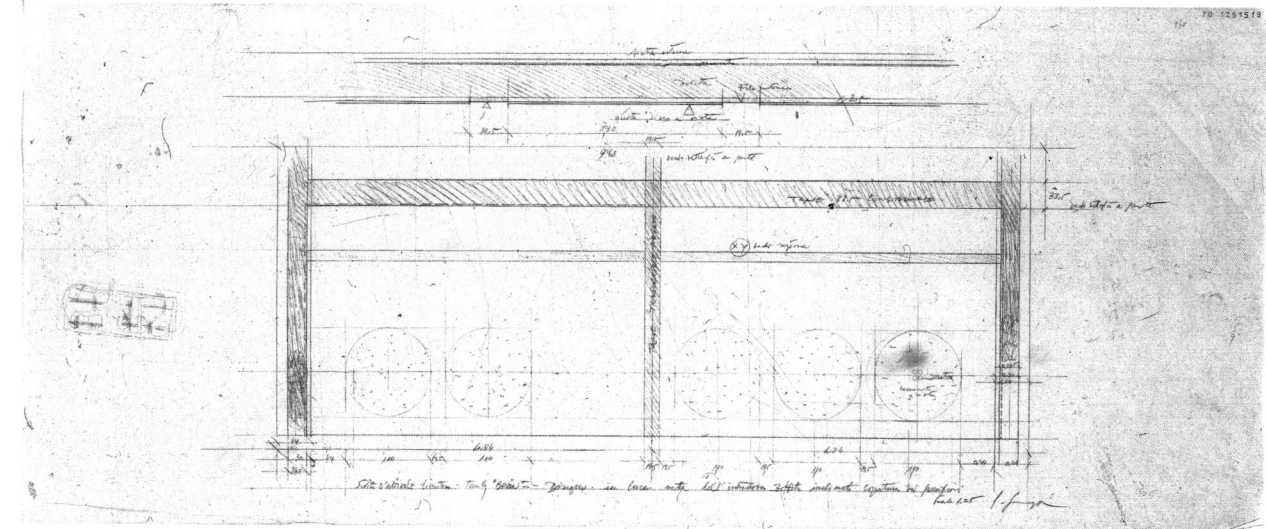

107

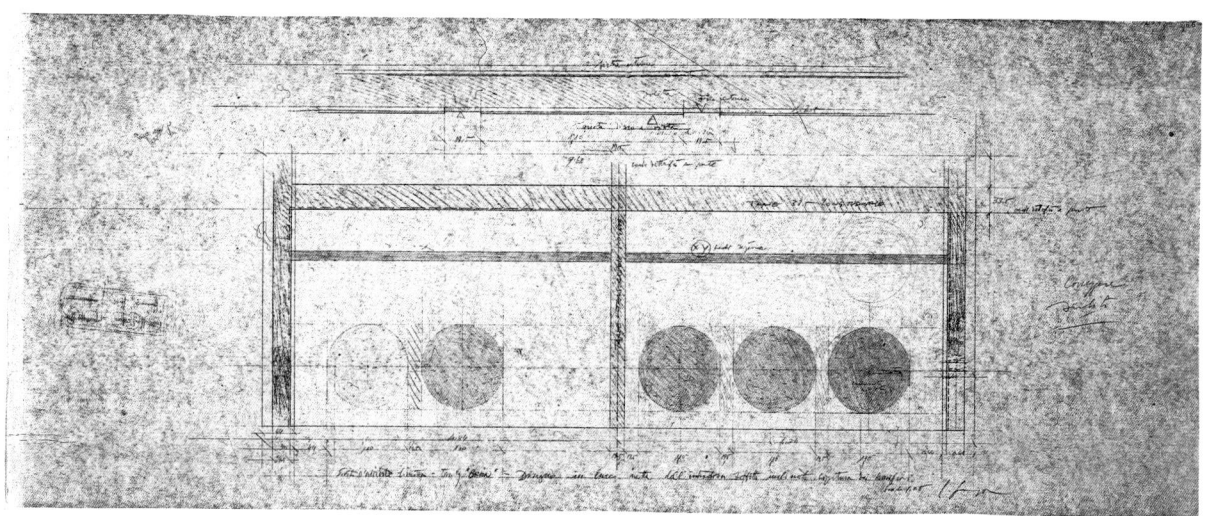

108

Gutter/Dachrinne

89

109

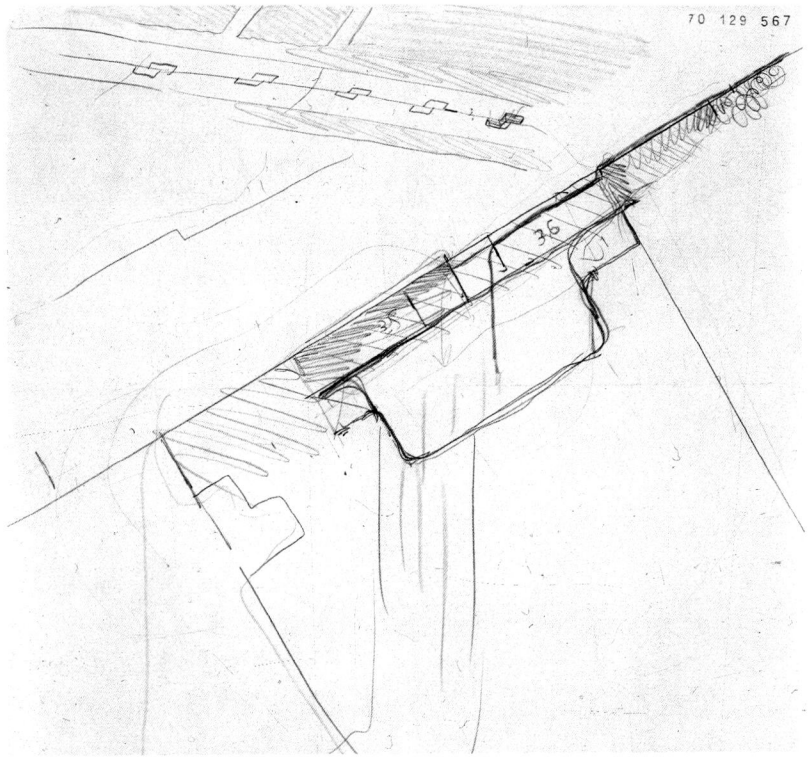

90

110

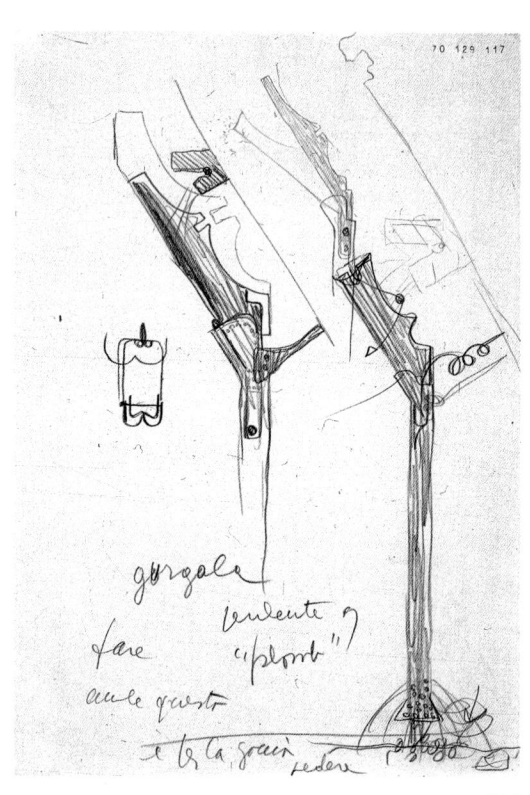

111

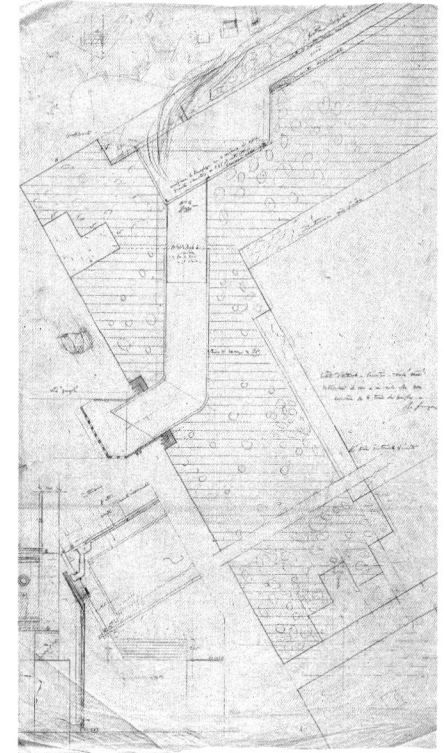

112

Guttae and gold ball/Tropfen und vergoldete Kugel

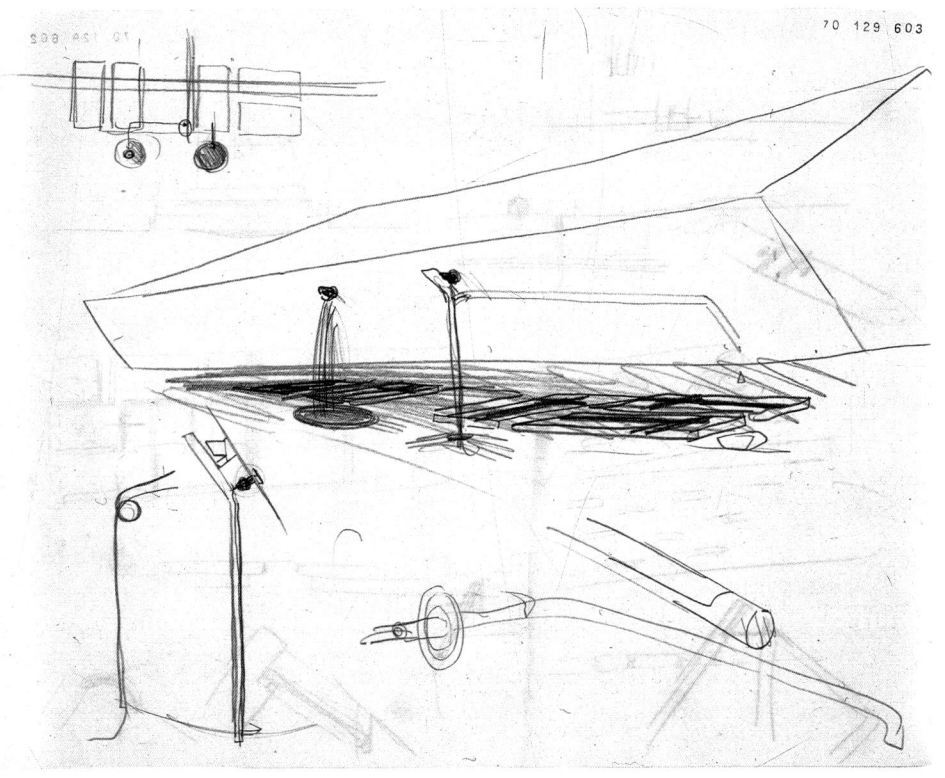

113

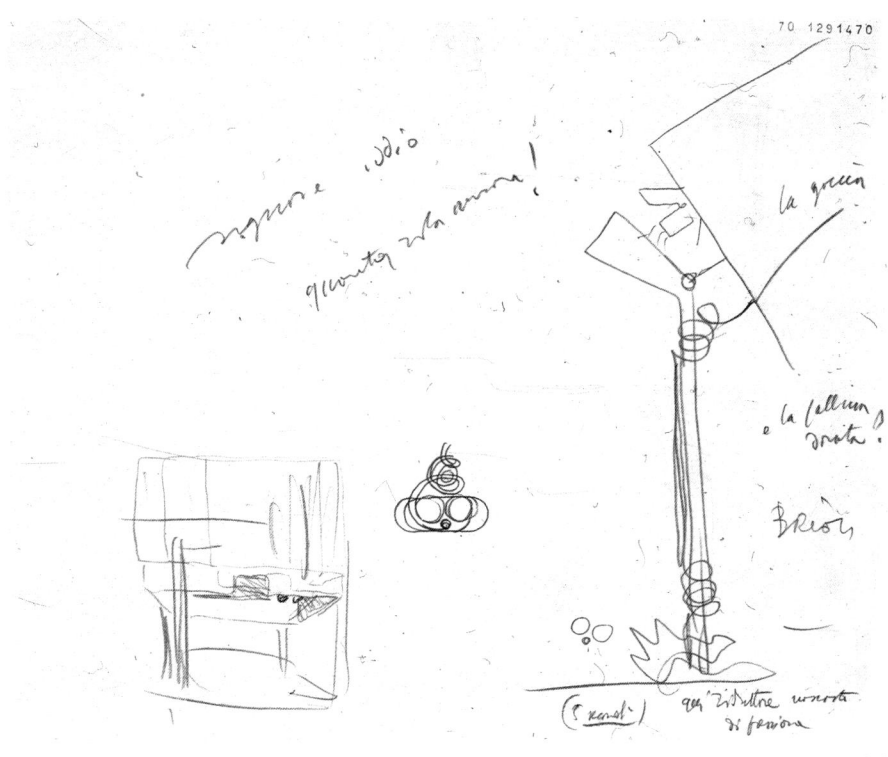

114

92

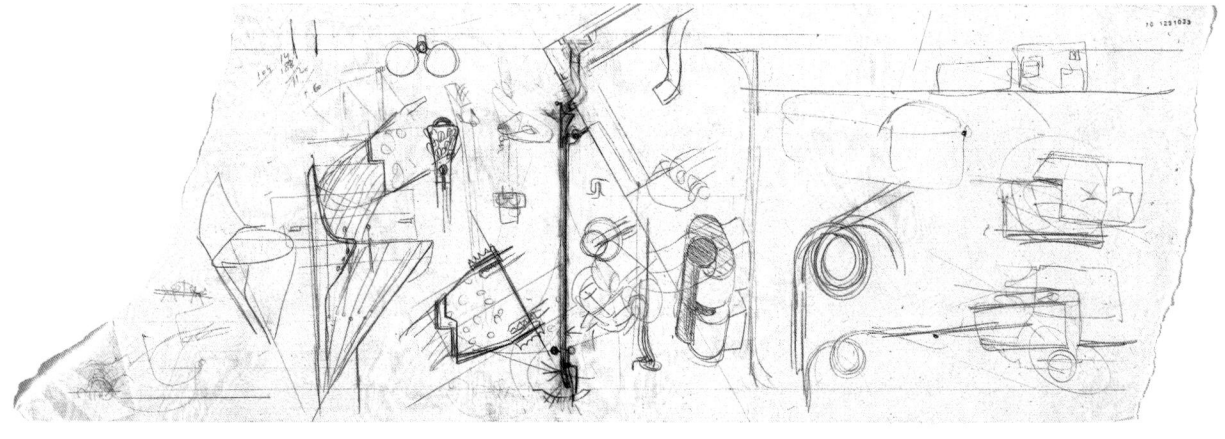

115

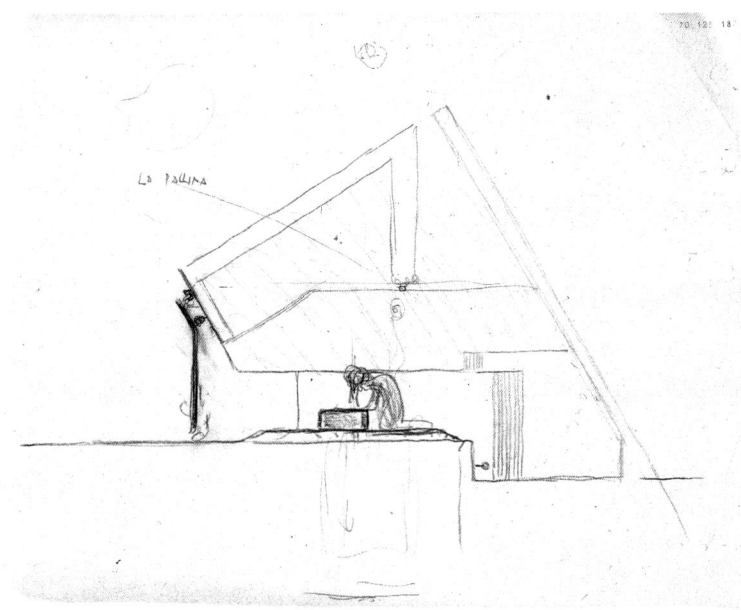

116

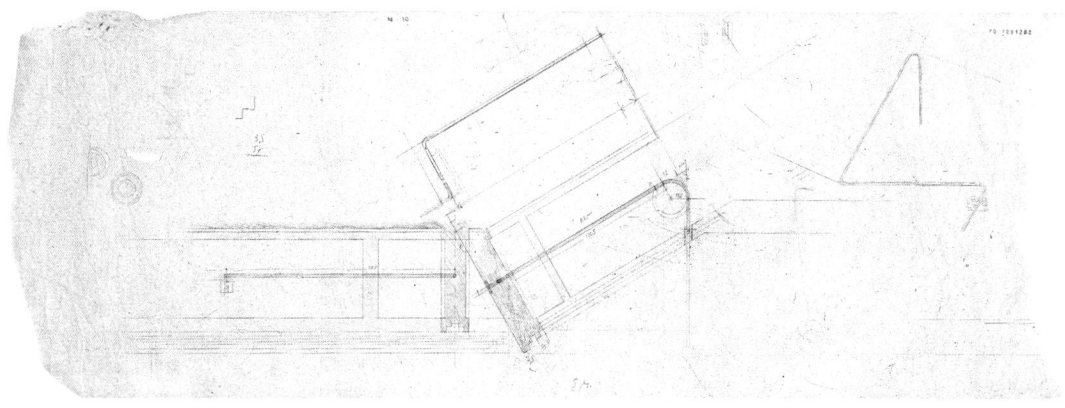

117

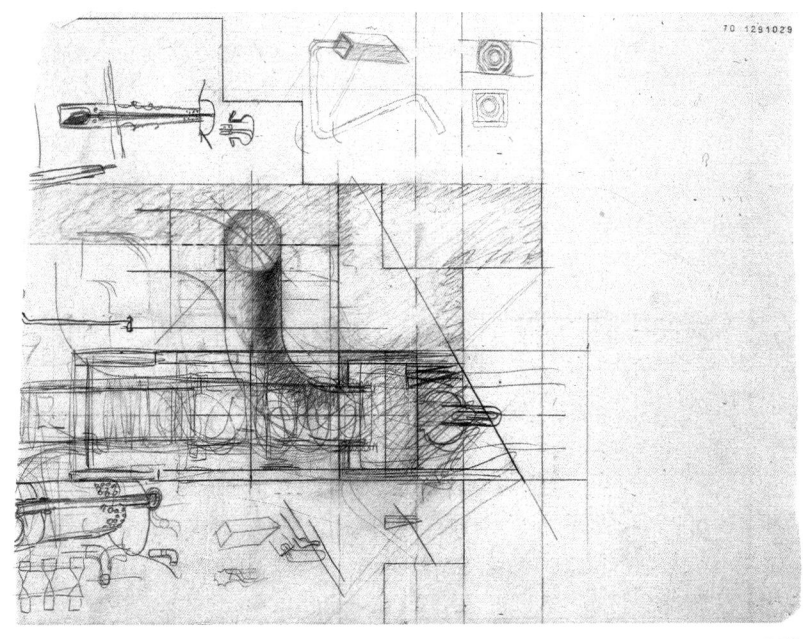

118

Gargoyle/Wasserspeier

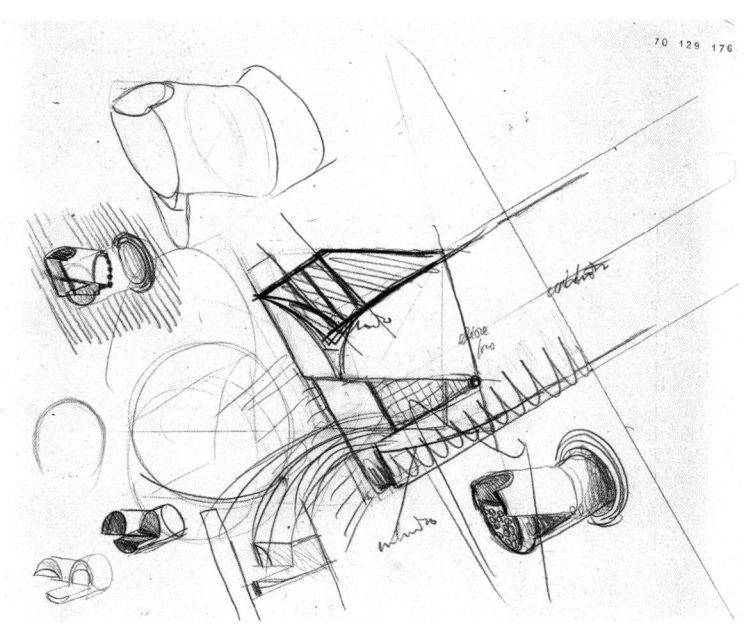

119

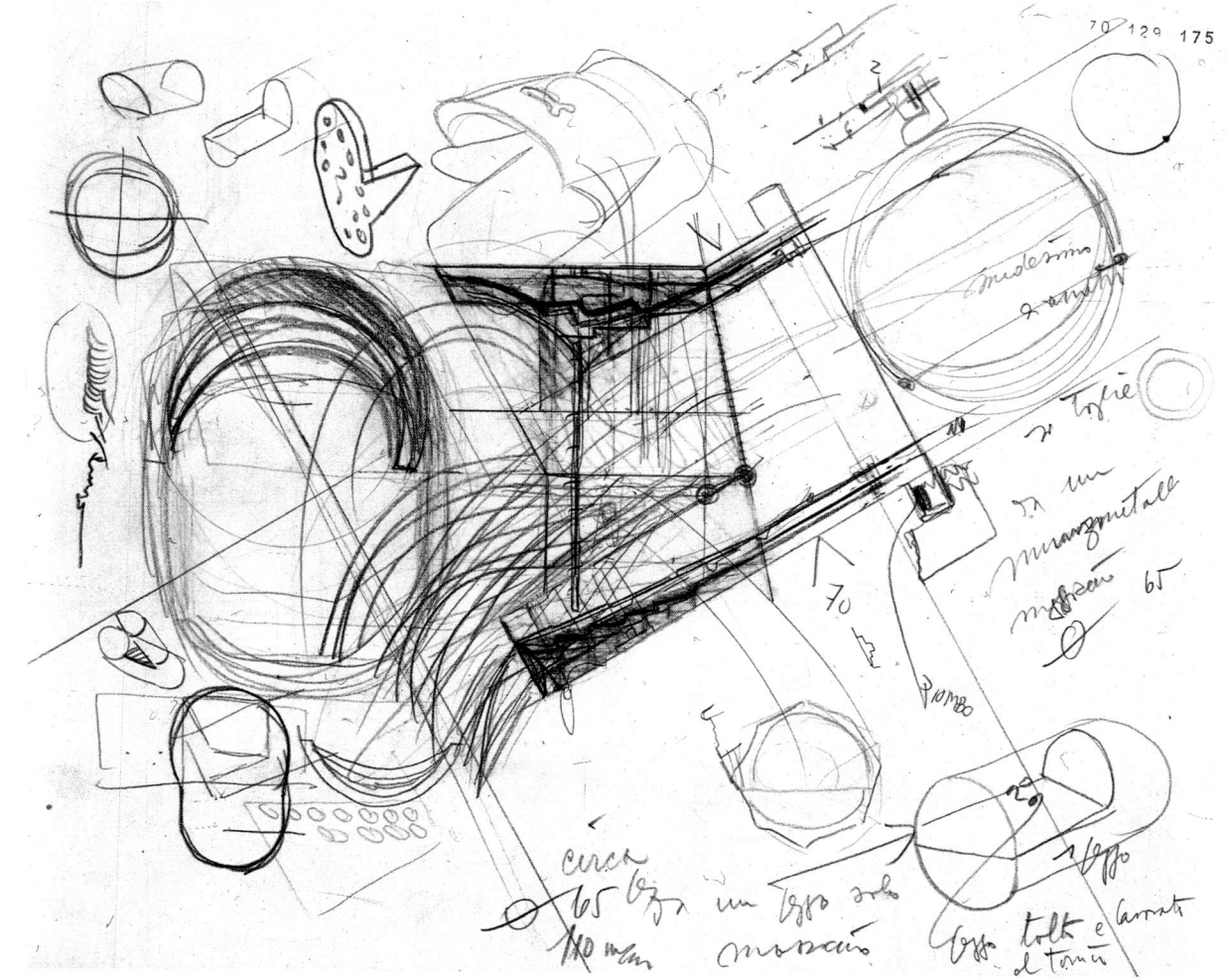

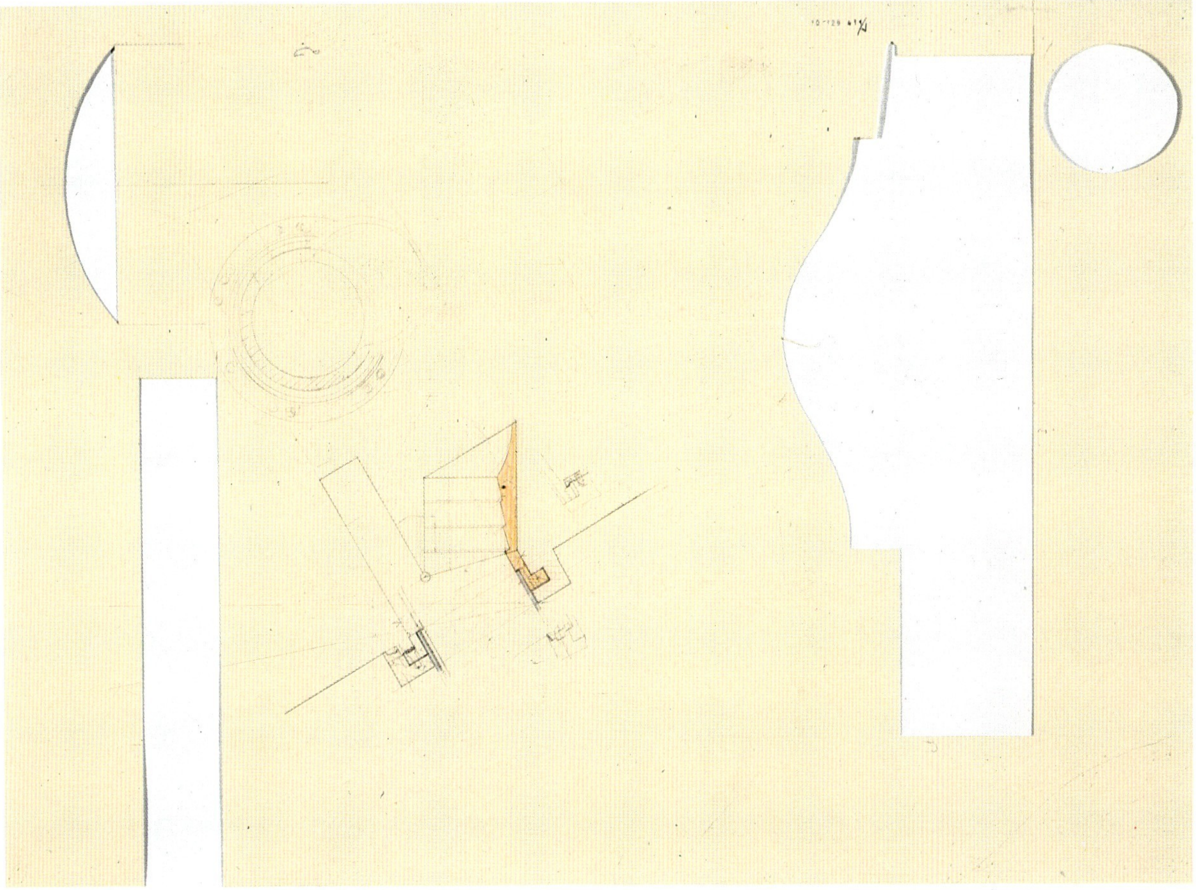

95

121

Plan of the memorial stones/Lageplan der Gedenksteine

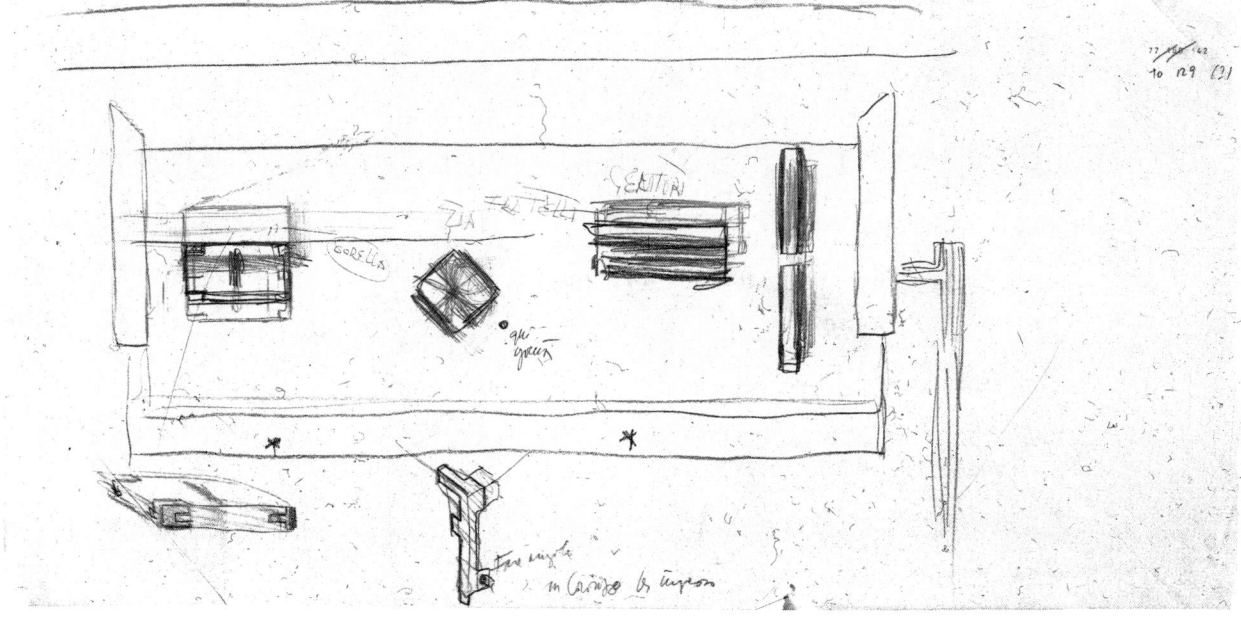

122

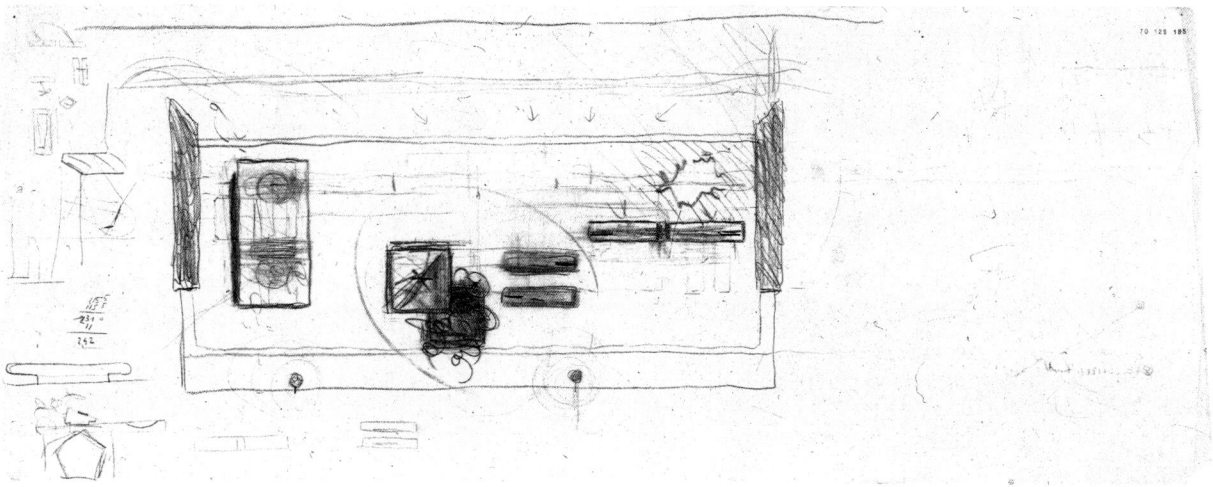

123

Memorial stones/Gedenksteine

97

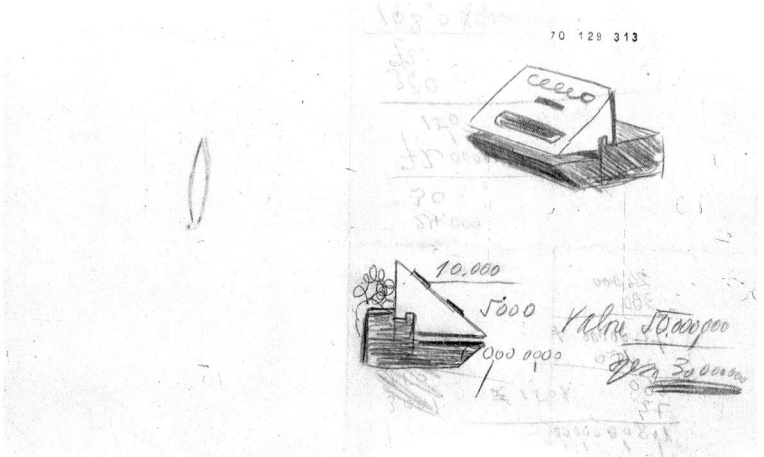

124

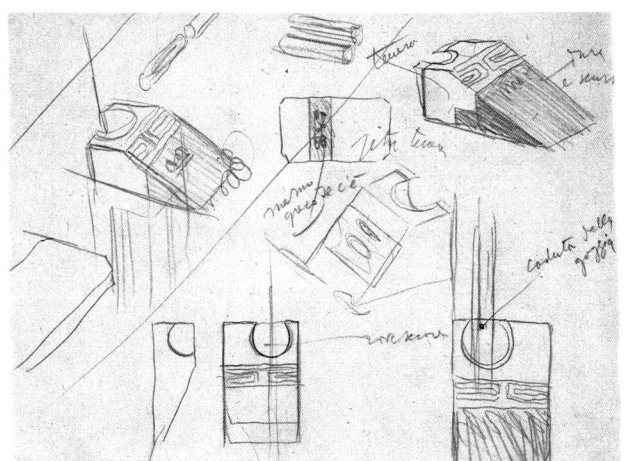

125

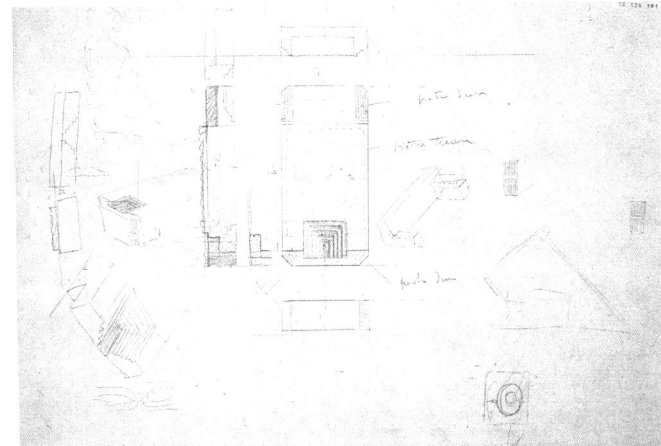

126

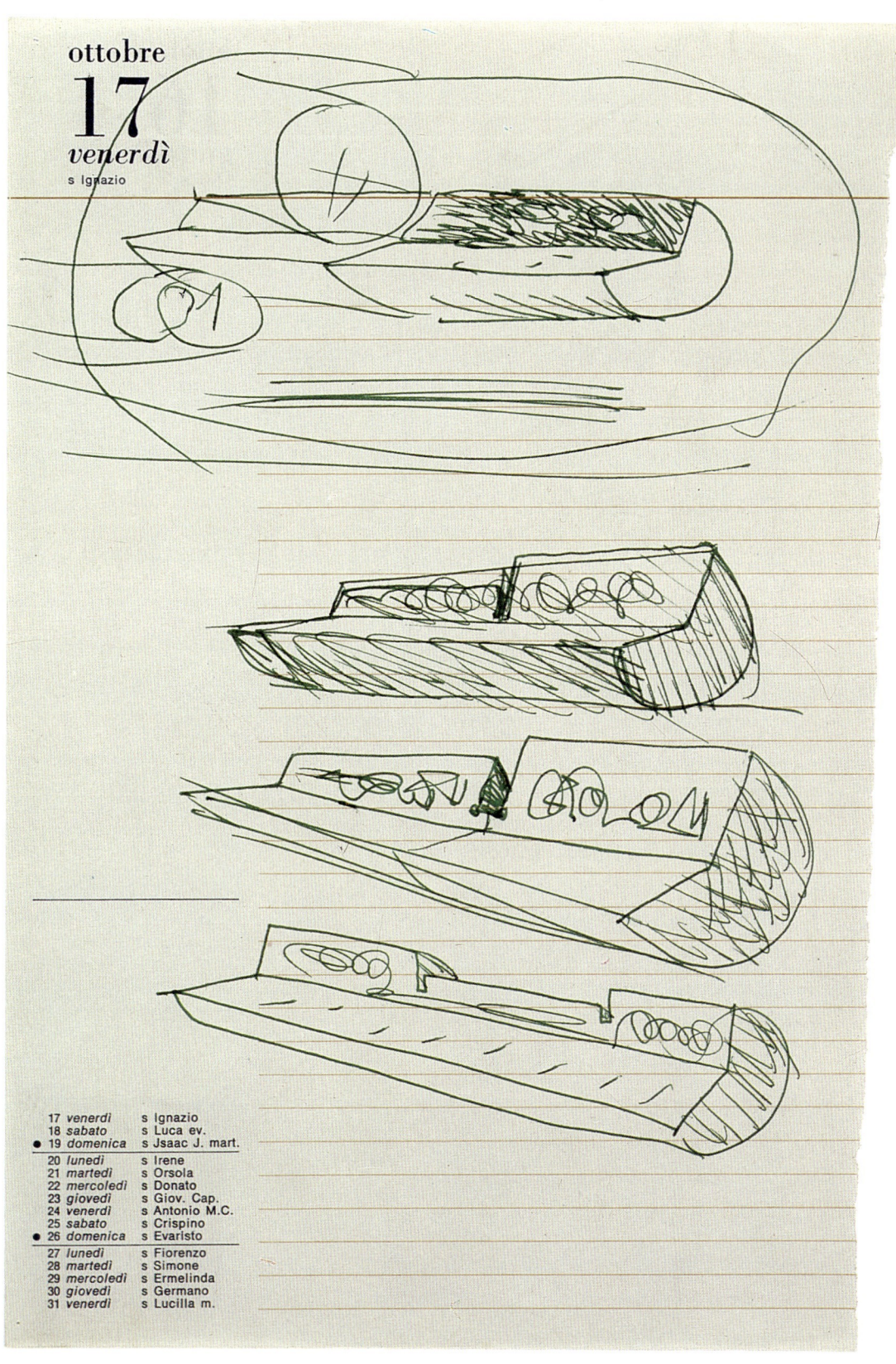

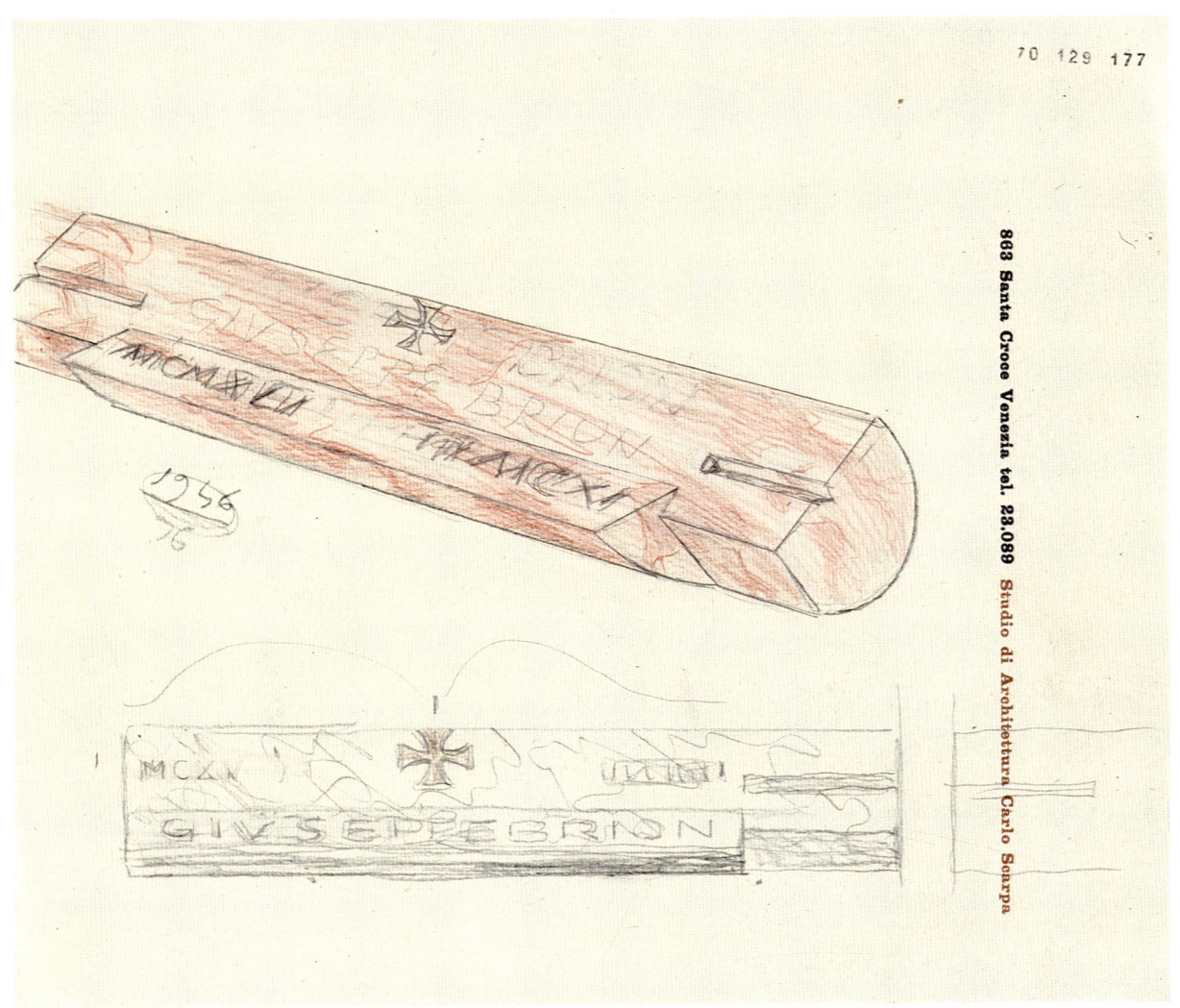

100

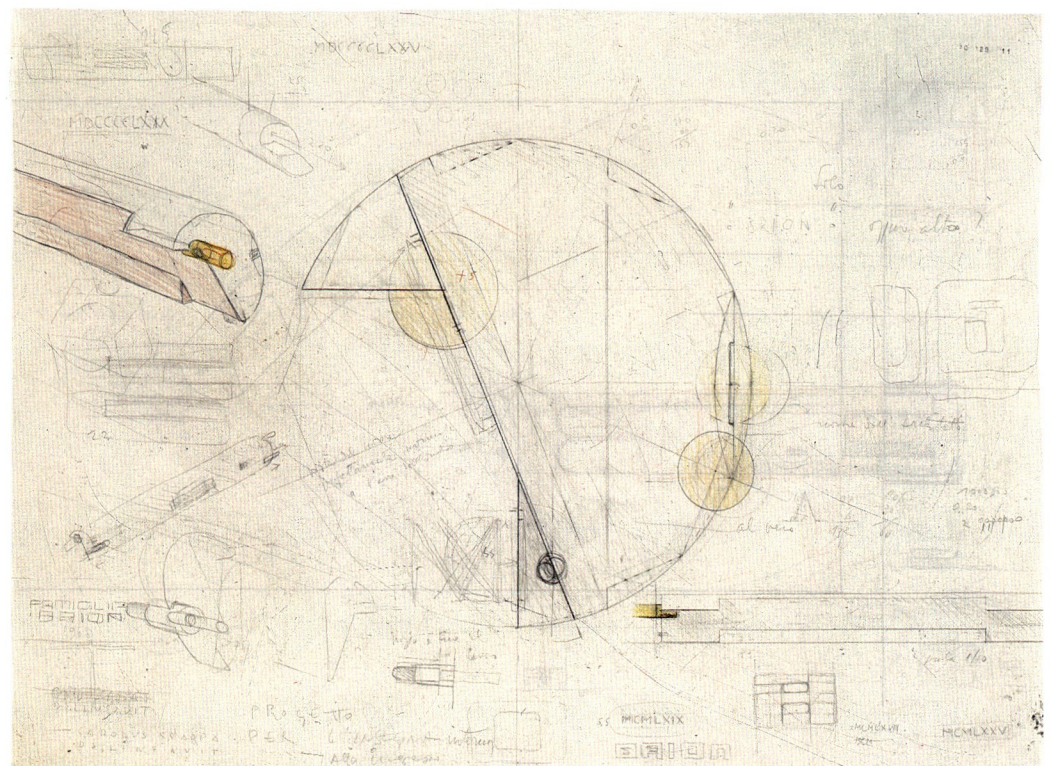

129

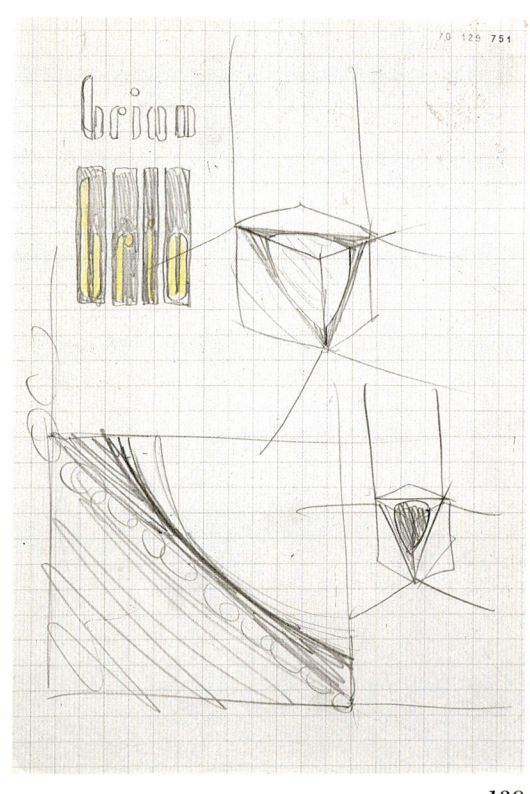

130

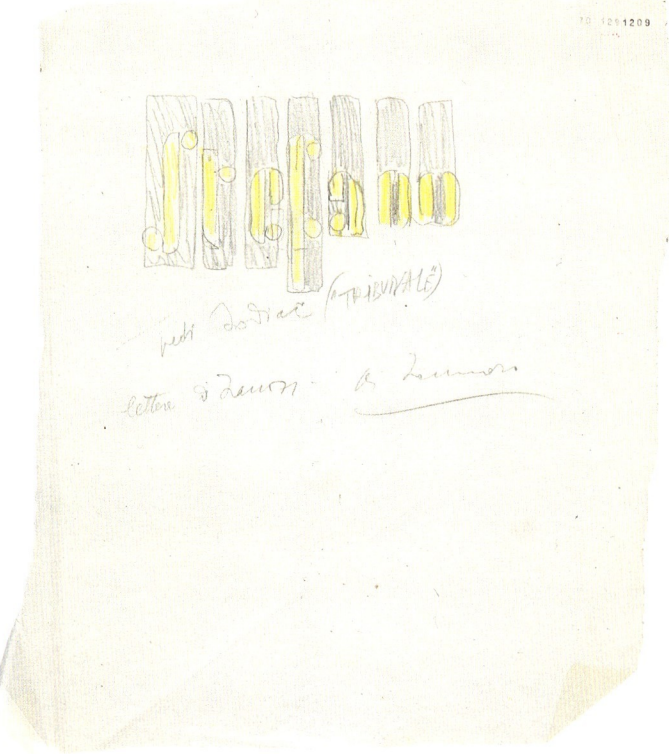

131

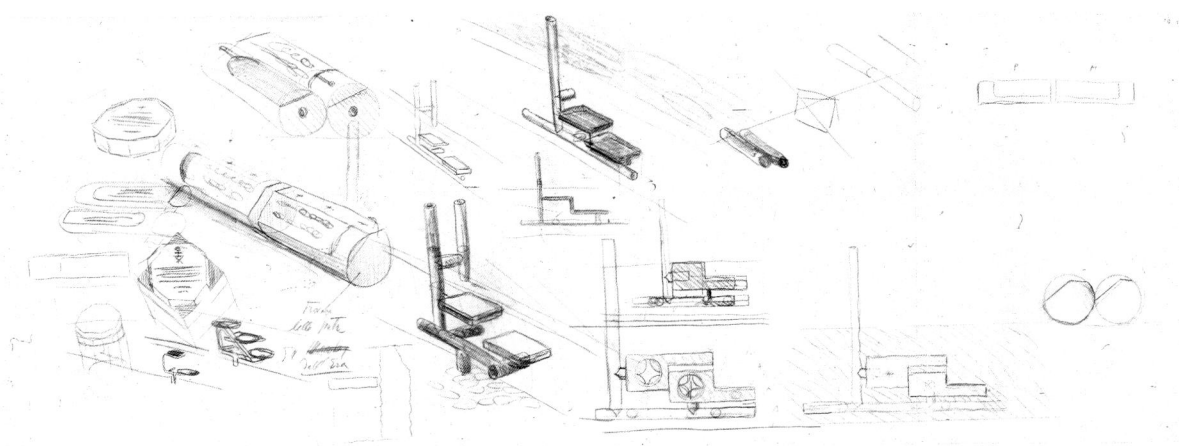

WEST: ENTRANCE OF THE DEAD (CHAPEL AREA)
WESTSEITE: TOR DER TOTEN (BEI DER KAPELLE)

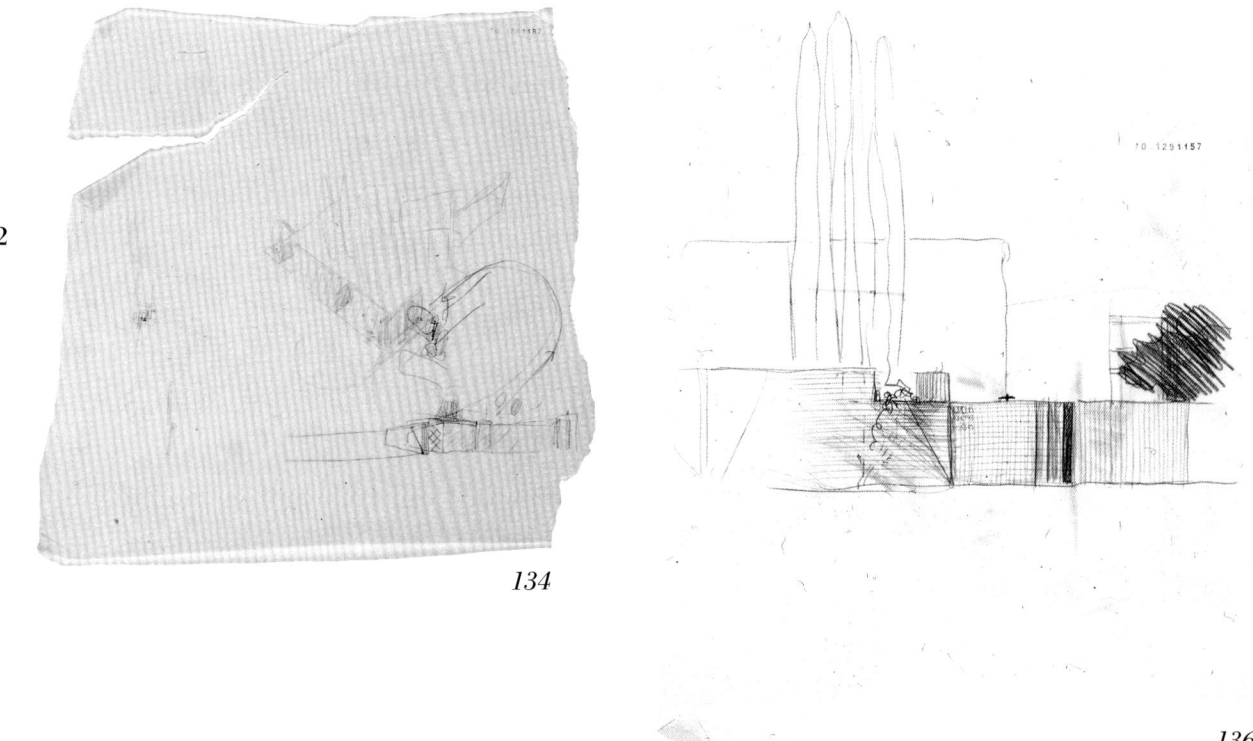

134

136

135

137

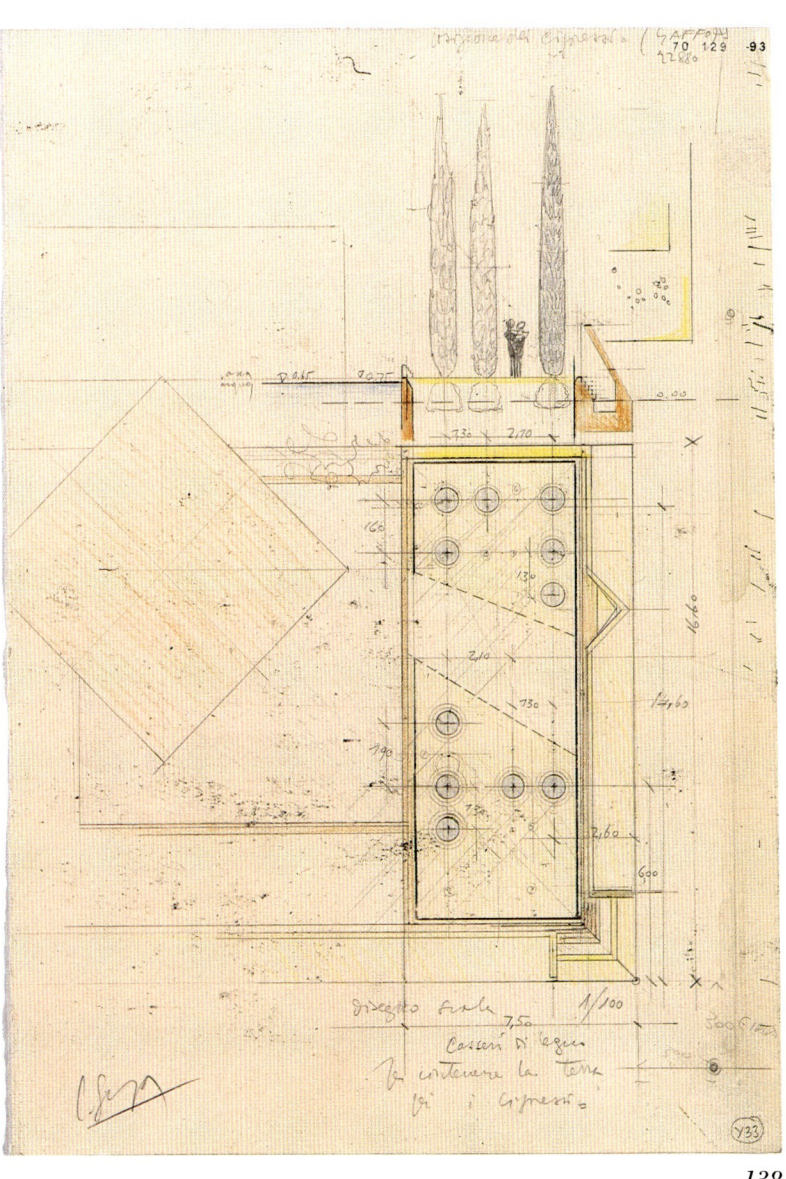

138

104

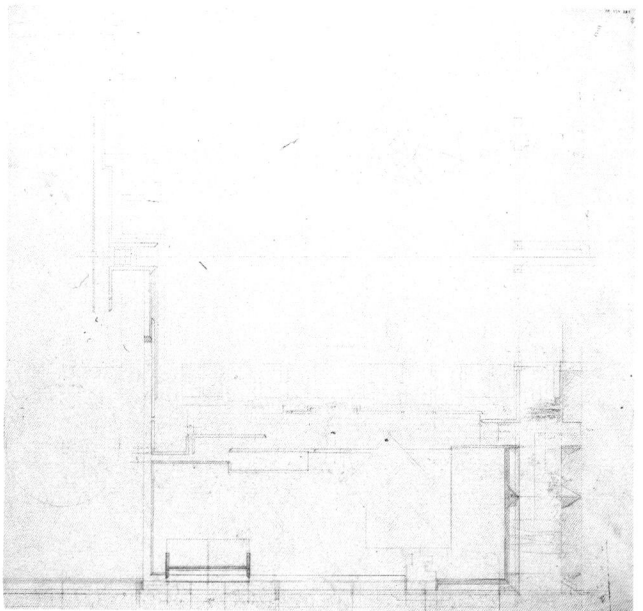

139

Concrete sliding gate/Schiebetüre aus Beton

140

141

142

143

106

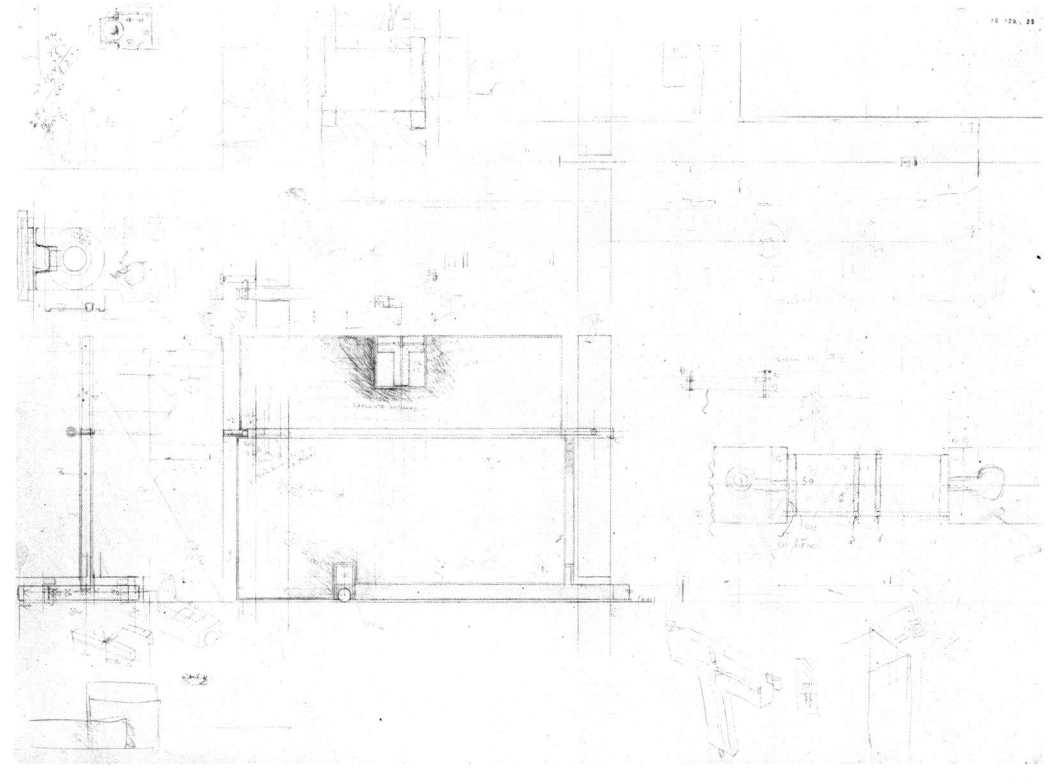

144

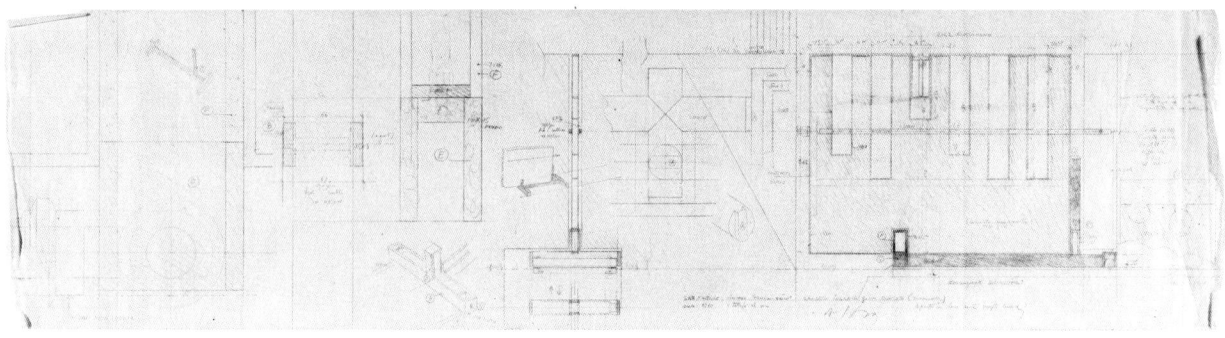

145

NORTH: VIEW TOWARDS THE FUNERAL CHAPELS (OLD CEMETERY)
NORDSEITE: IN RICHTUNG GRABKAPELLEN (ALTER FRIEDHOF)

146

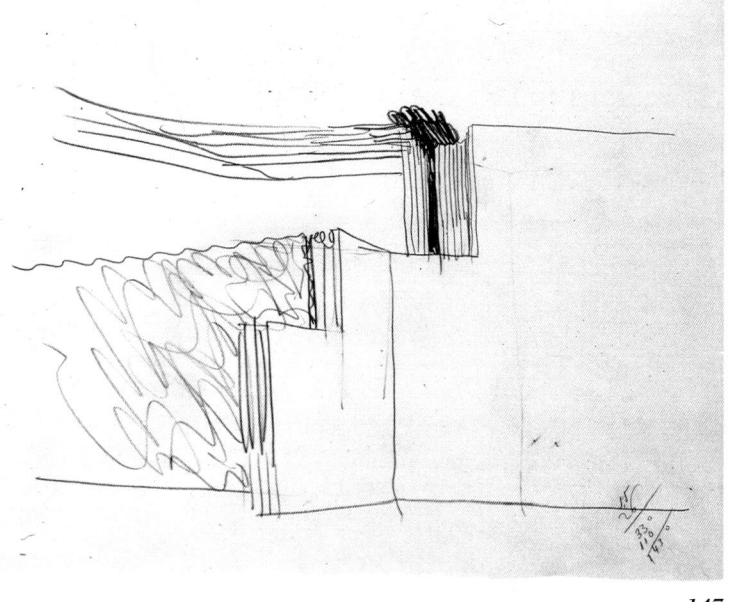

107

147

148

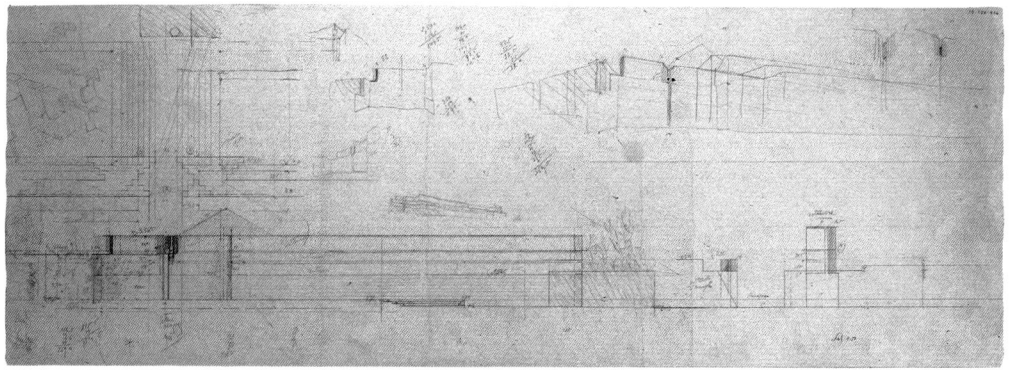

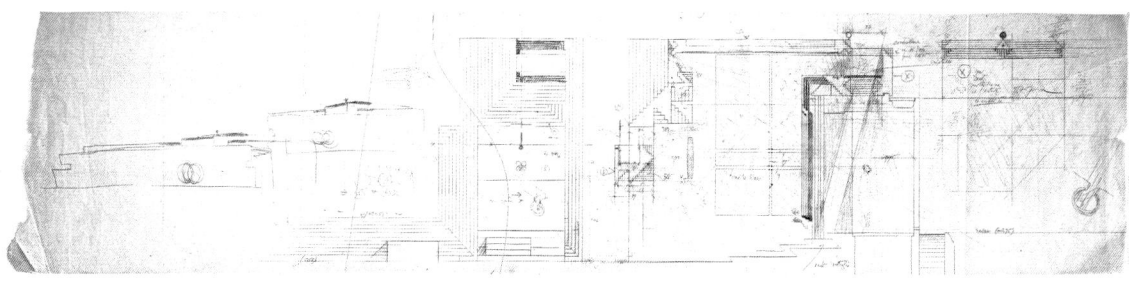

Reinforced concrete "Anta" access to old cemetery (1974)
Eisenbetontür zum Durchgang zum Ortsfriedhof (1974)

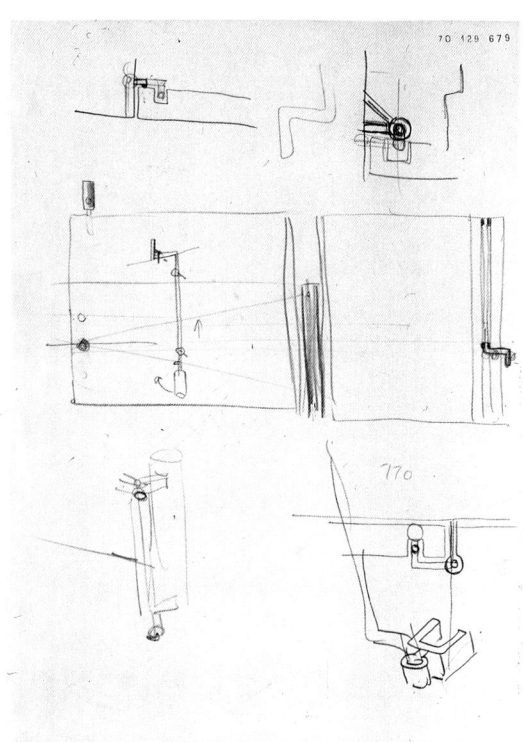

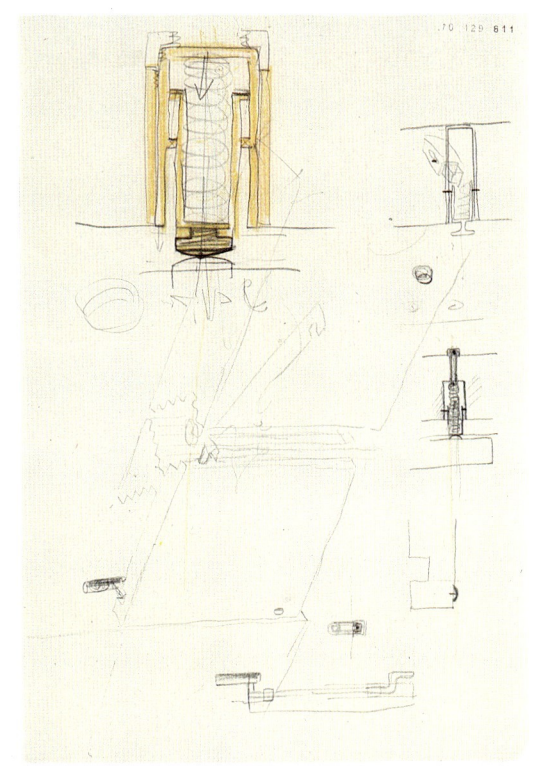

109

153

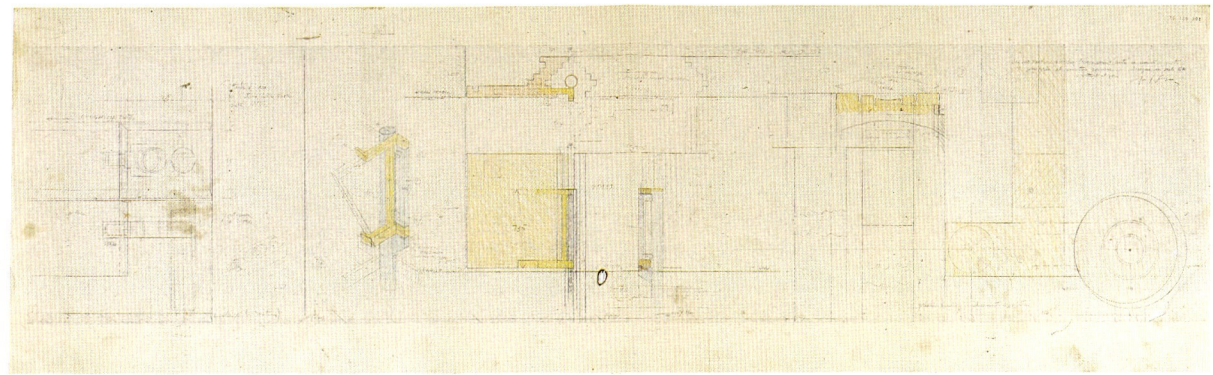

154

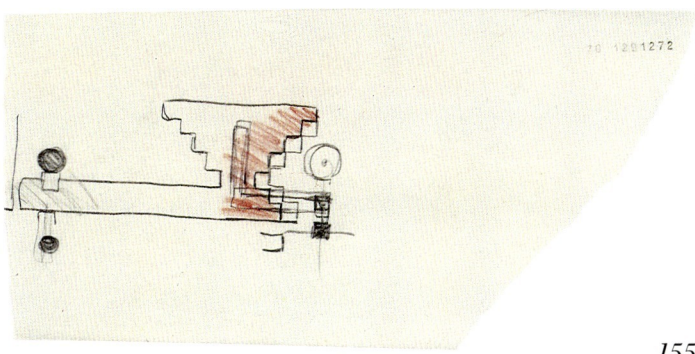

155

Solid brass mounts to hold doors open (1974)
Vorrichtung aus massivem Messing zum Offenhalten der Türe (1974)

156

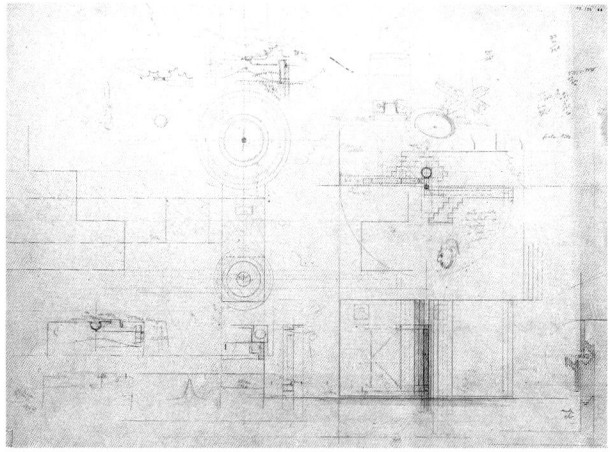

157

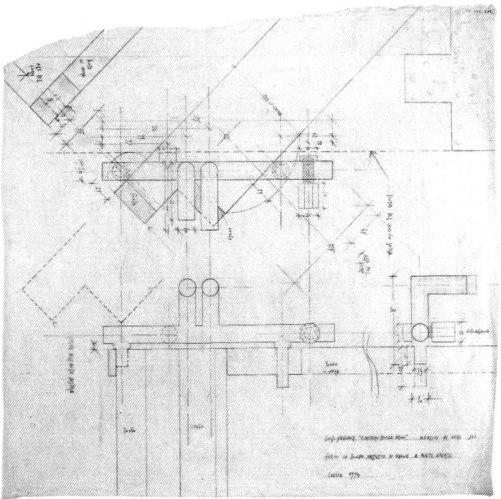

158

ENLARGEMENT OF THE SAN VITO D'ALTIVOLE CEMETERY.
PROPOSAL FOR THE NEW ENCLOSING WALL (1971–1972)

ERWEITERUNG DES ORTSFRIEDHOFES VON S. VITO D'ALTIVOLE.
VORSCHLÄGE FÜR DIE NEUE UMFASSUNGSMAUER (1971–1972)

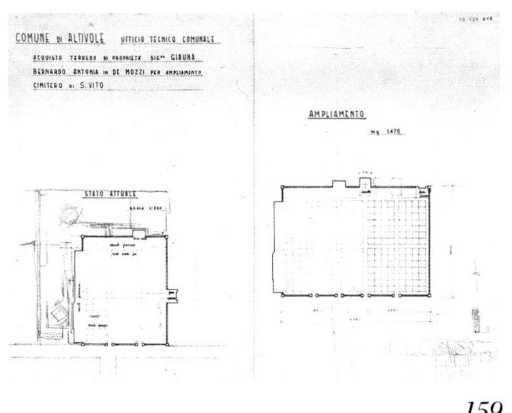

159

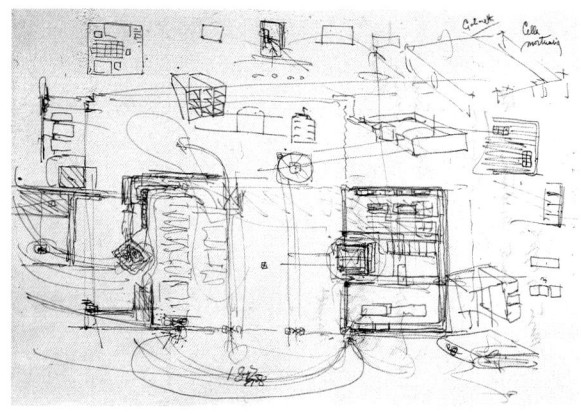

160

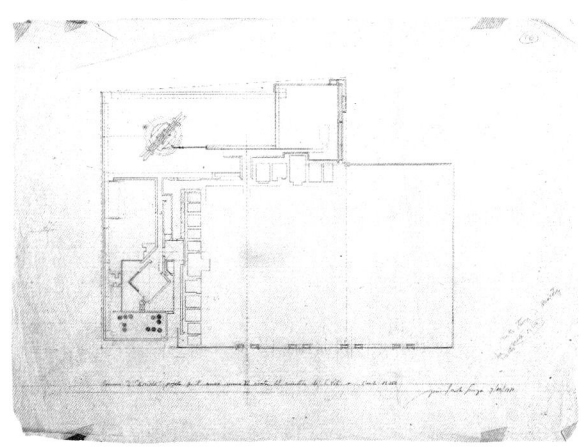

161

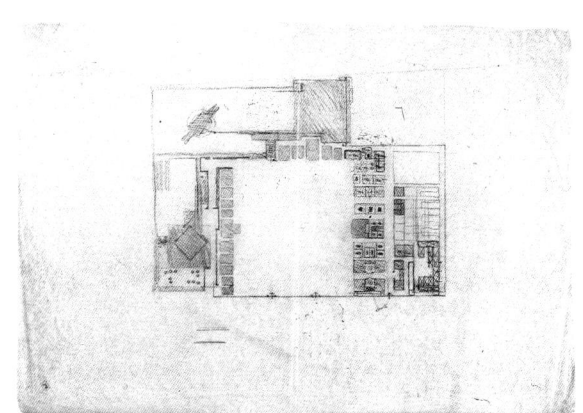

162

West/Westseite

163

164

165

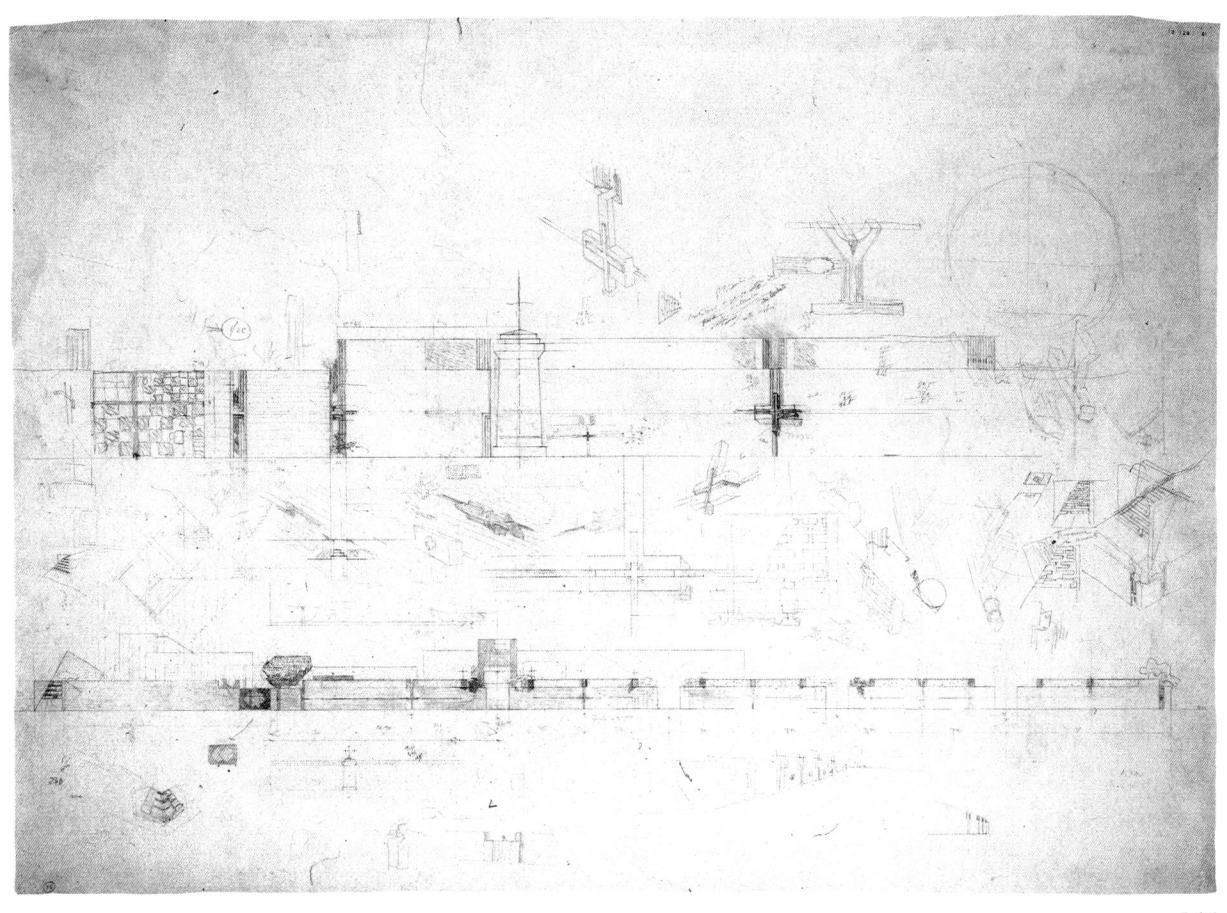

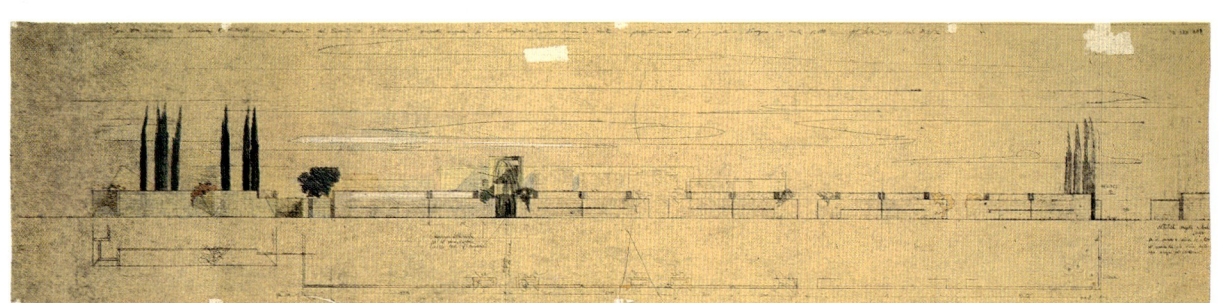

PAVILION

DER PAVILLON

Entrance plate: beam suspended over the large pool
Platte beim Eingang: Balken über dem großen Wasserbecken

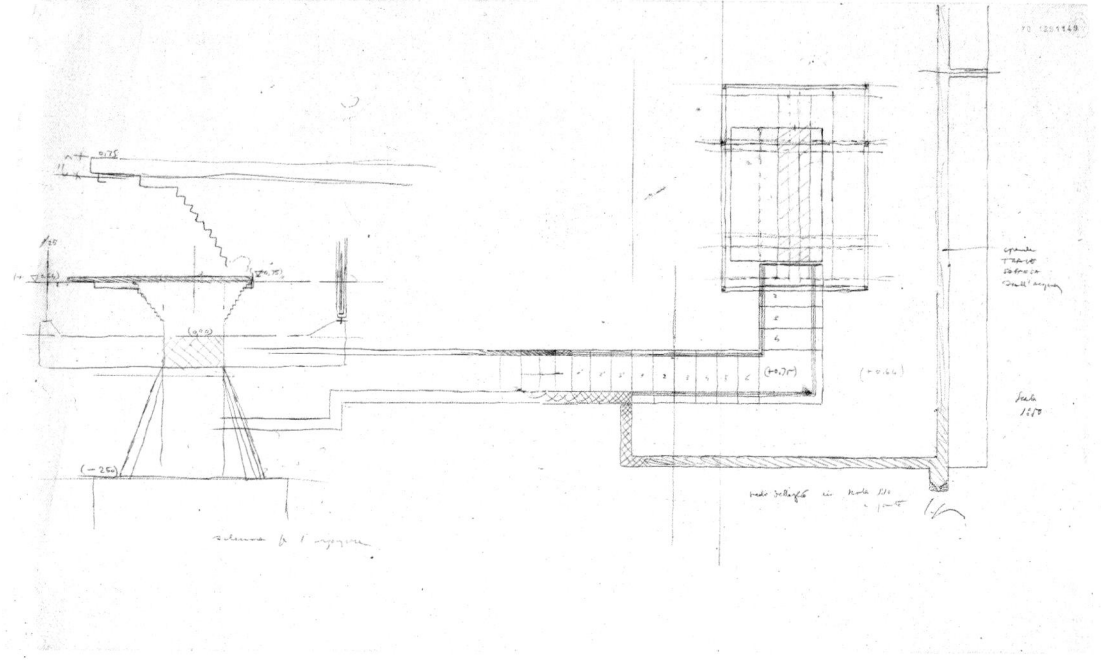

168

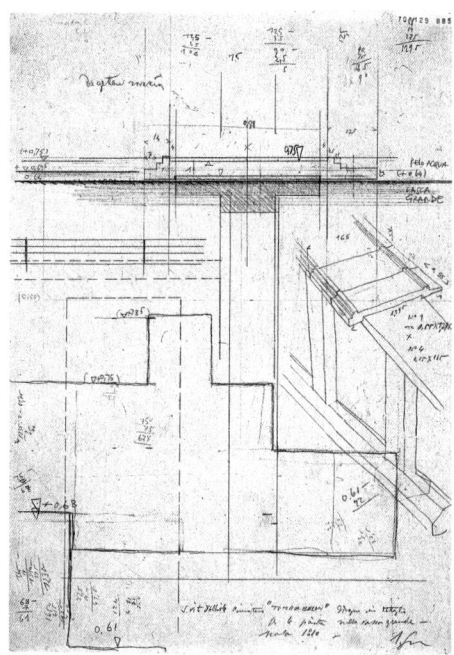

169

Foundation, central plate/Fundament, zentrale Platte

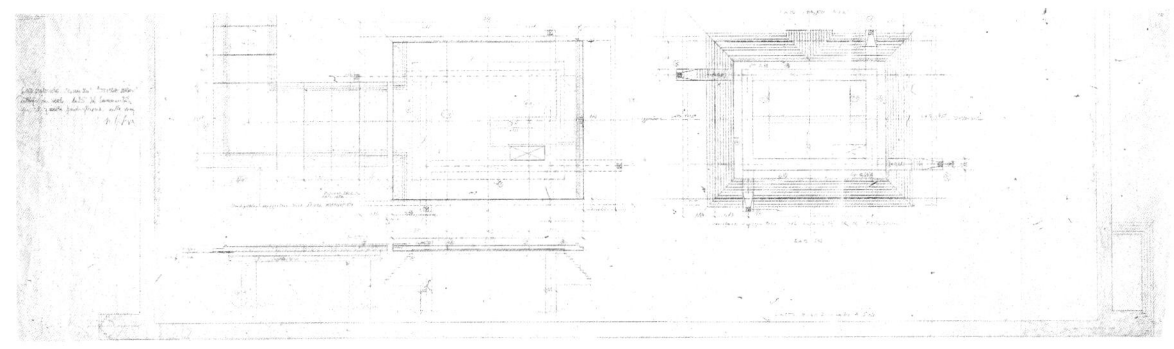

170

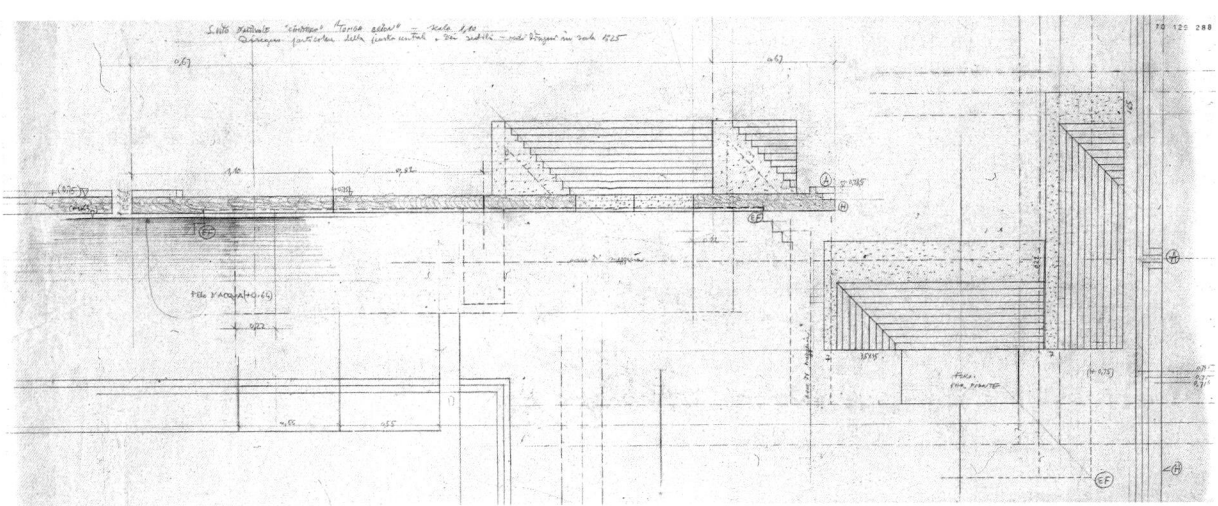

171

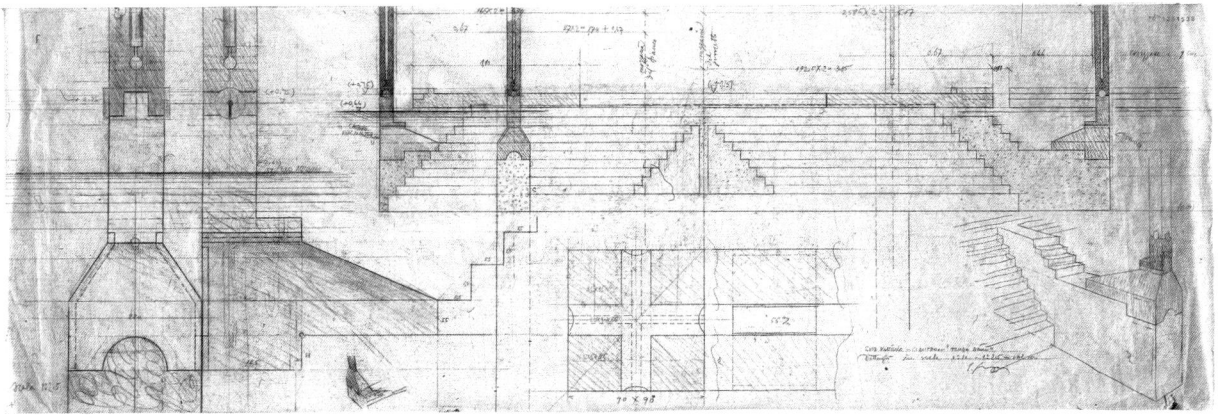

172

Pavilion/Der Pavillon

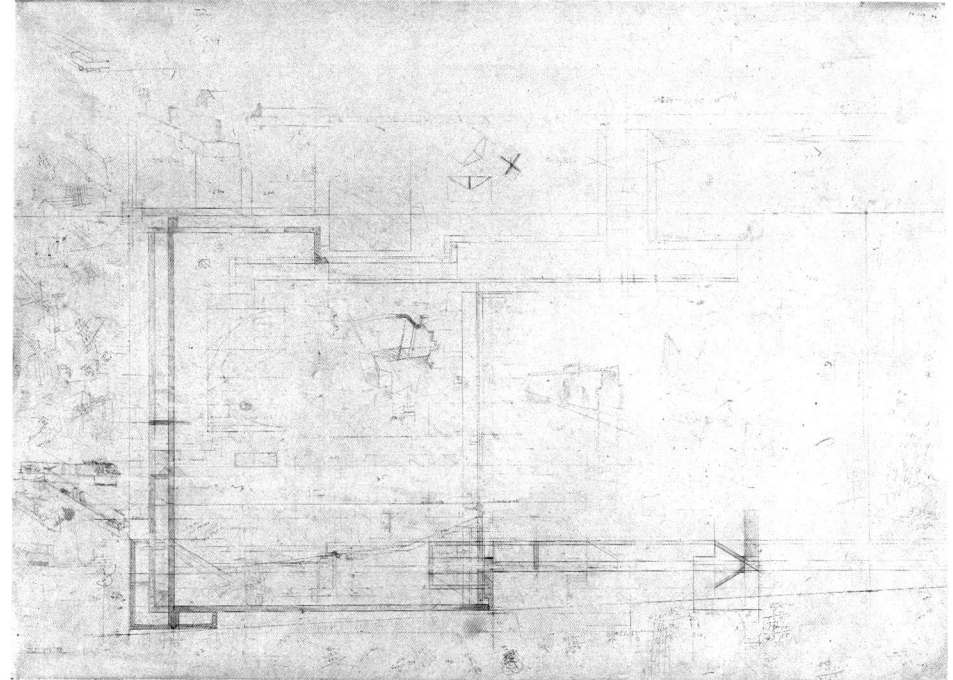

173

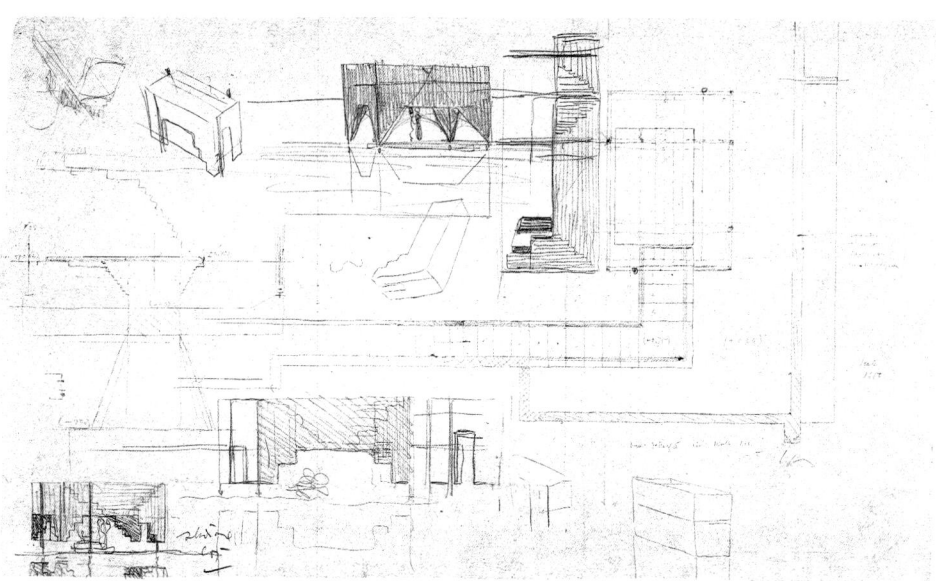

174

175

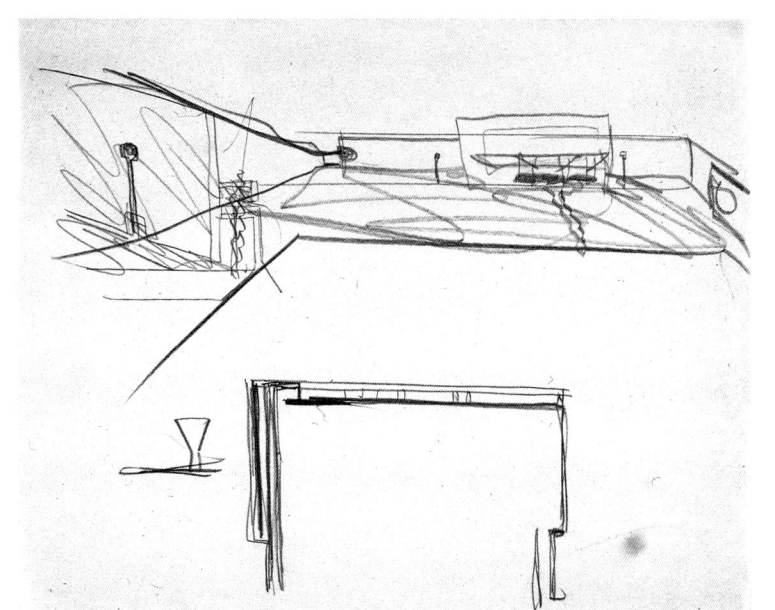

119

176

177

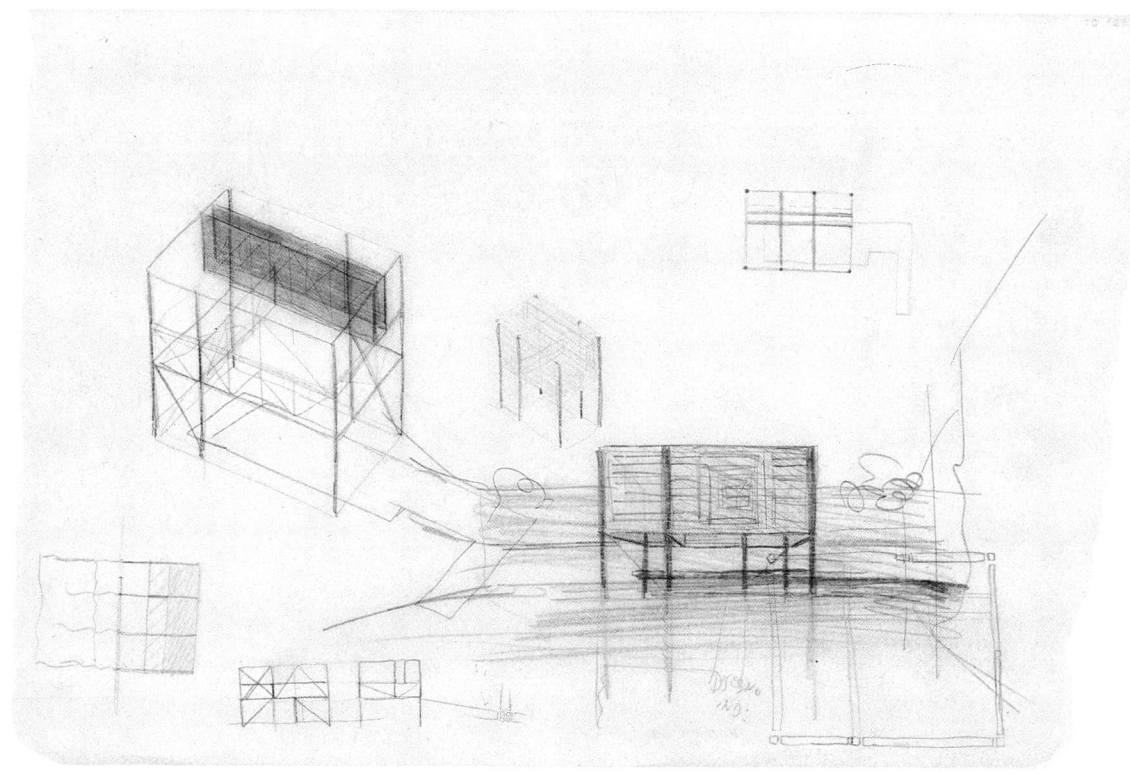

178

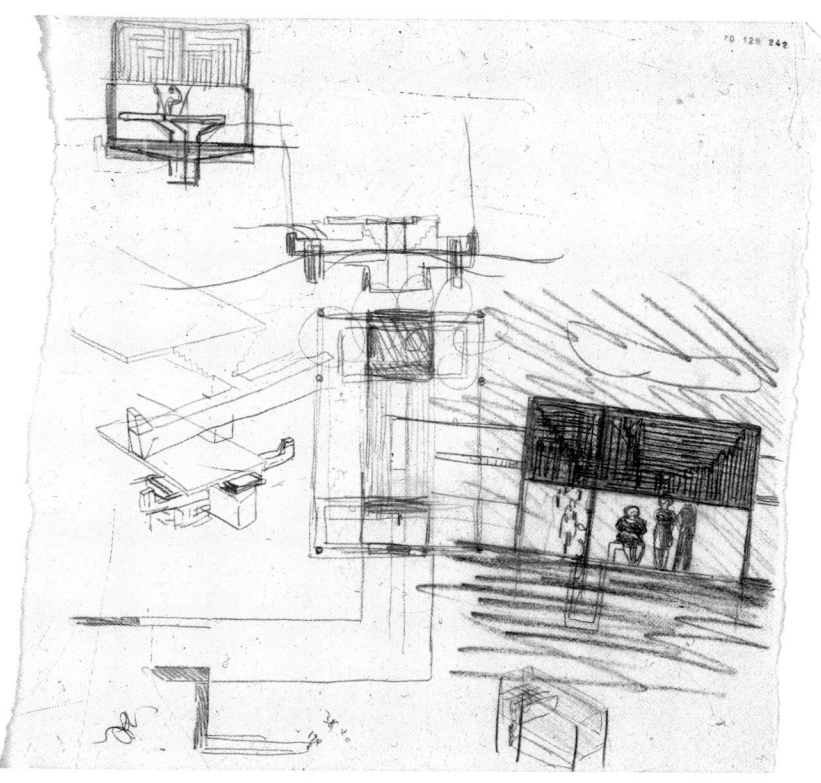

179

180

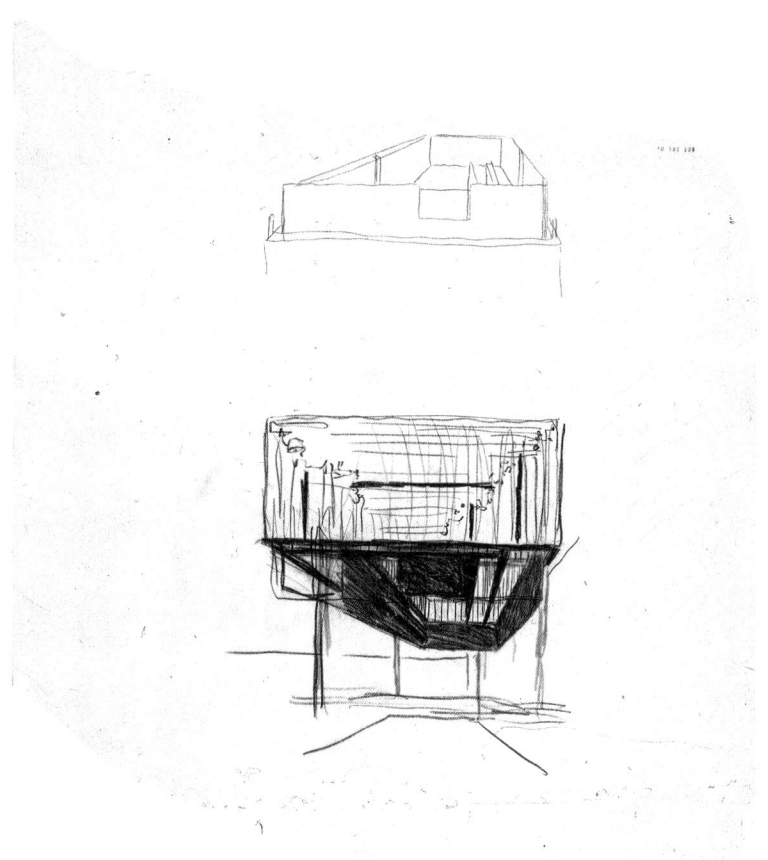

181

182

183

Sections/Schnitte

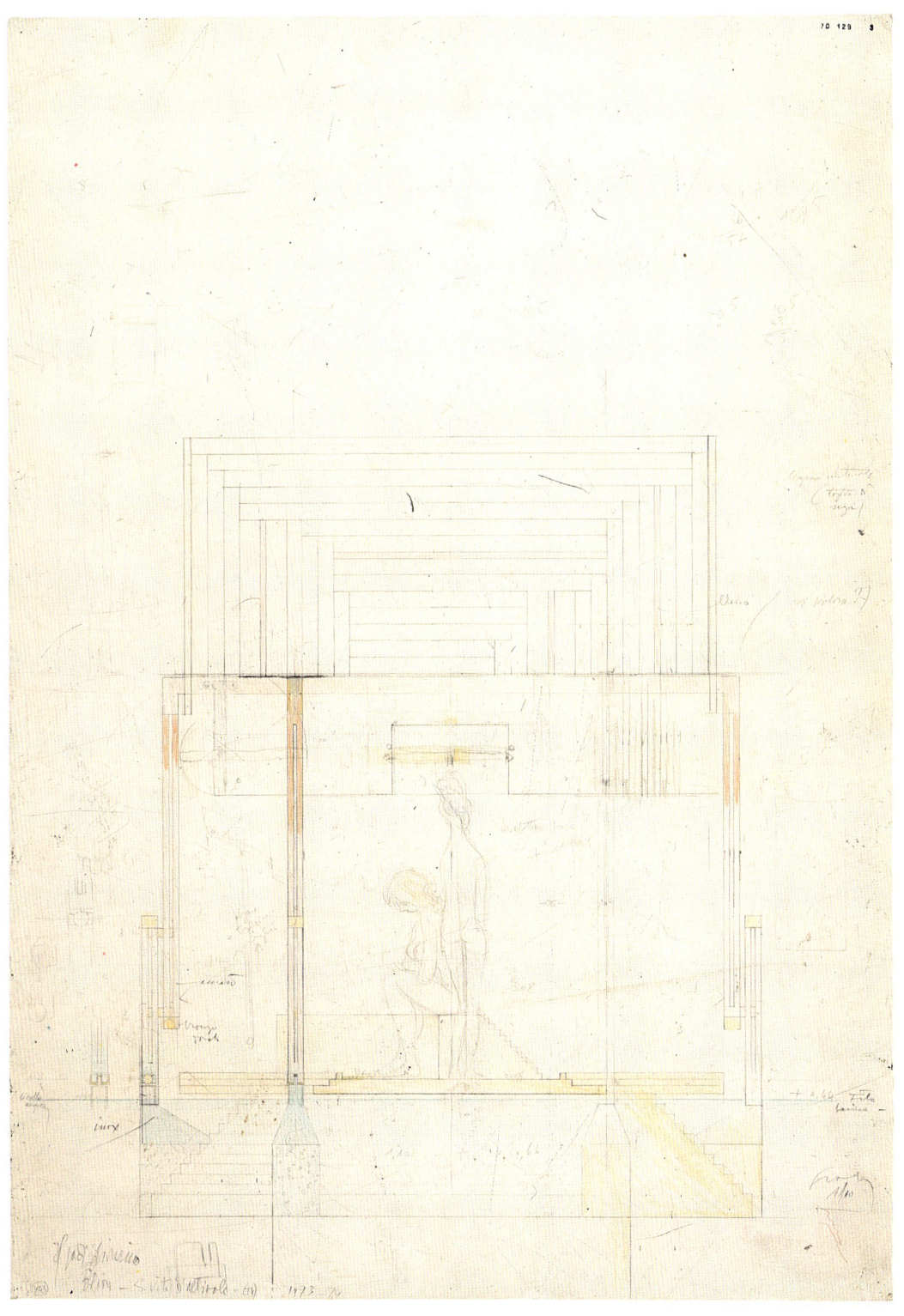

184

124

185

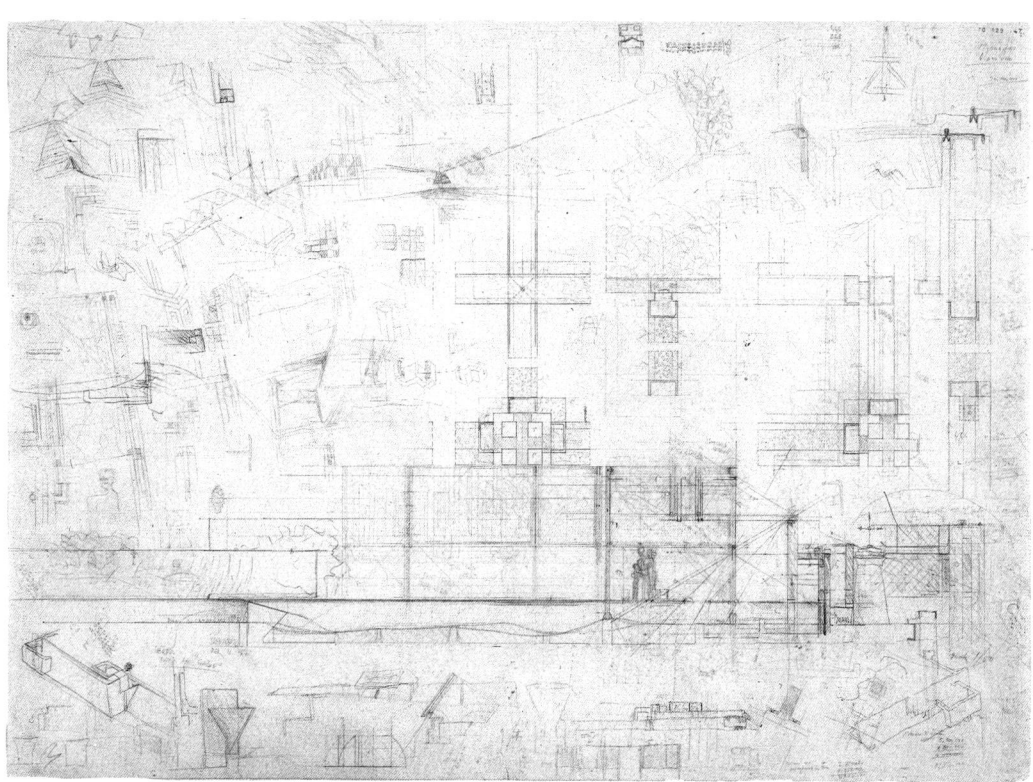

186

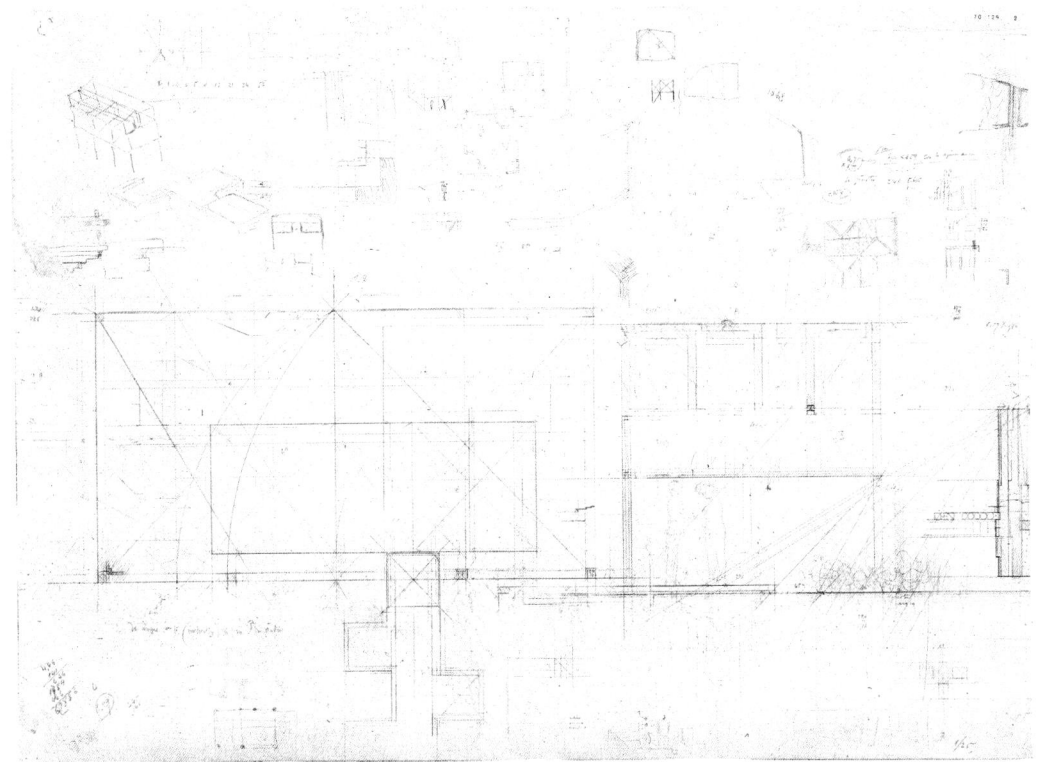

187

188

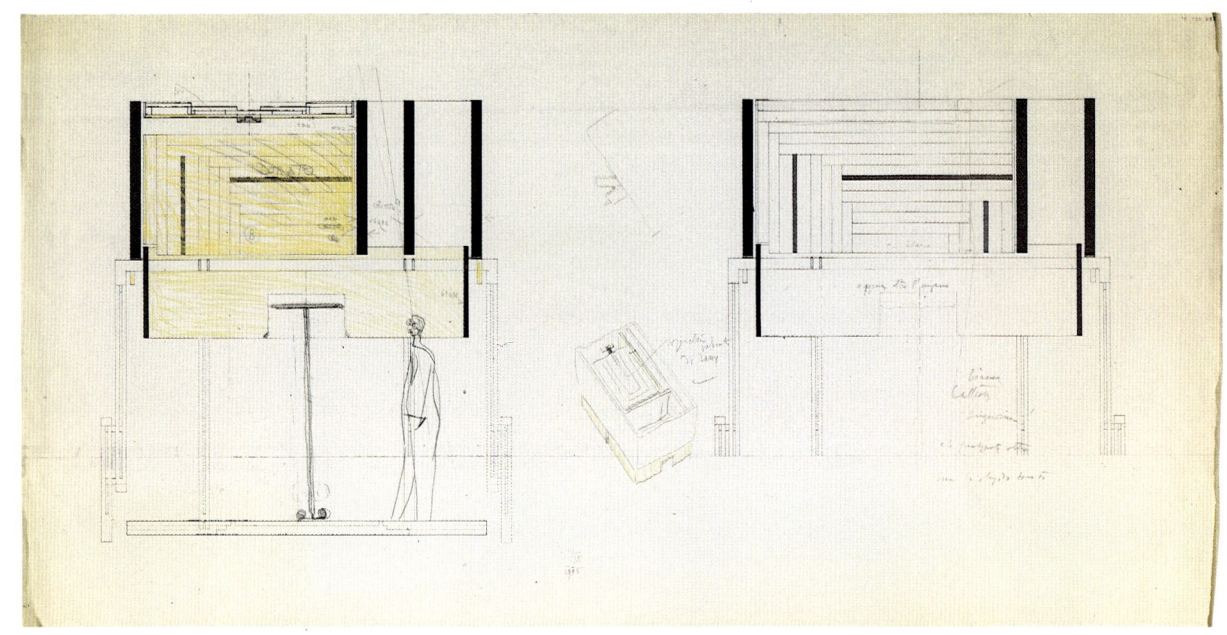

189

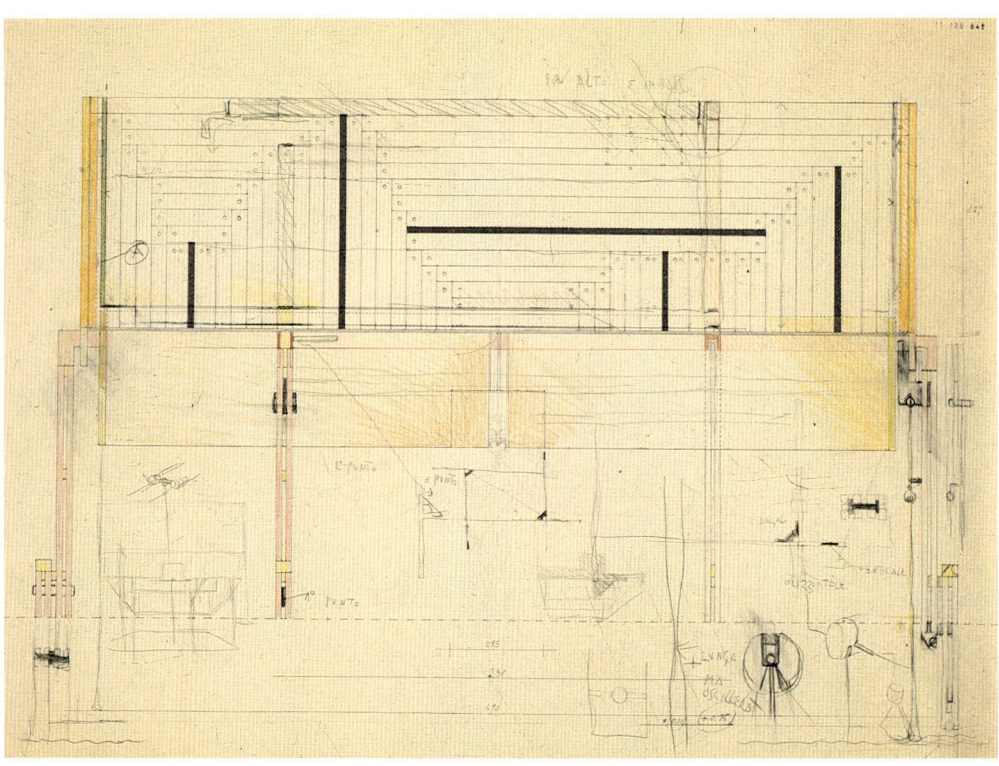

190

Wooden panels: the pavilion "roof"/Holzpanele: „Dach" des Pavillons

Exteriors/Außen

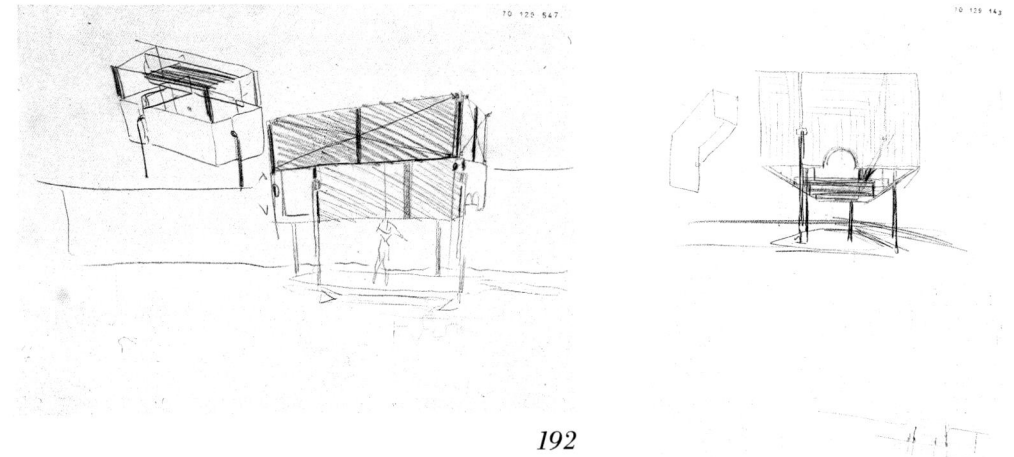

192

191

193

194

195

196

129

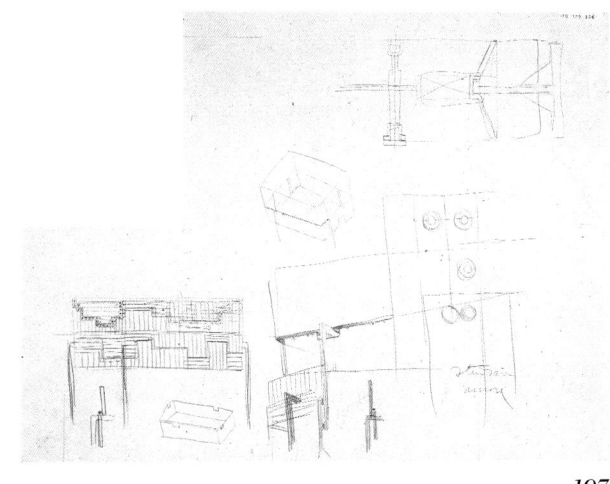

197

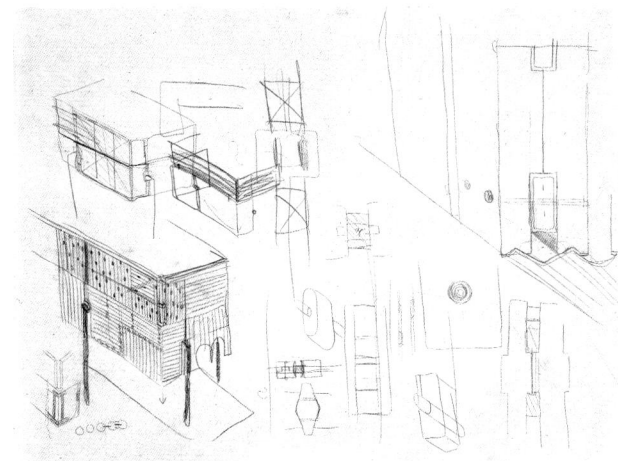

198

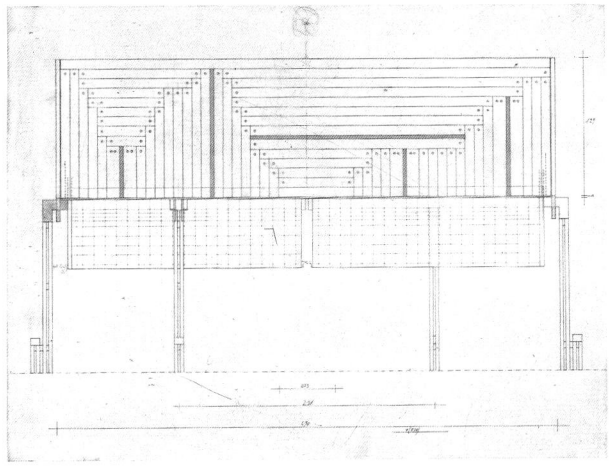

199

Interiors/Innen

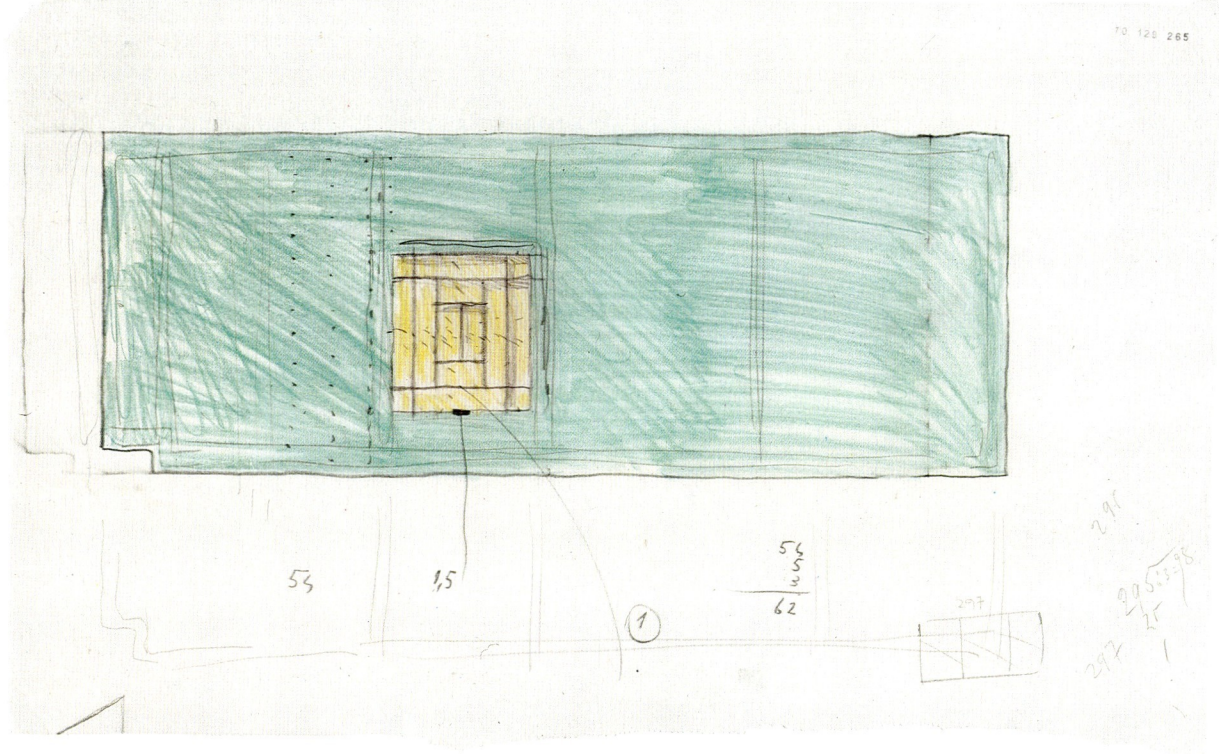

Pilasters/Eckpfeiler

131

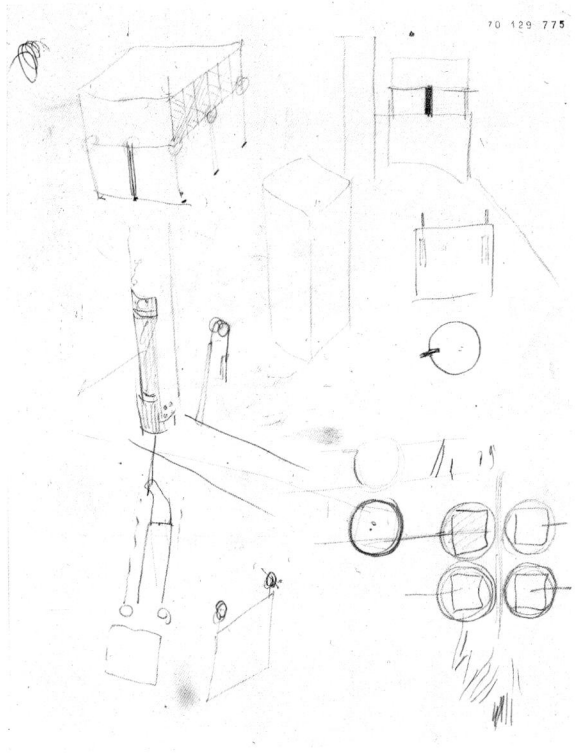

201

202

203

204

205

206

207

208

133

134

209

210

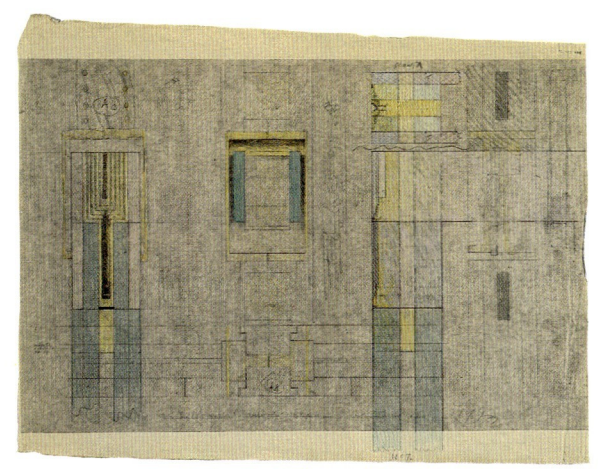

211

Corners/Ecken

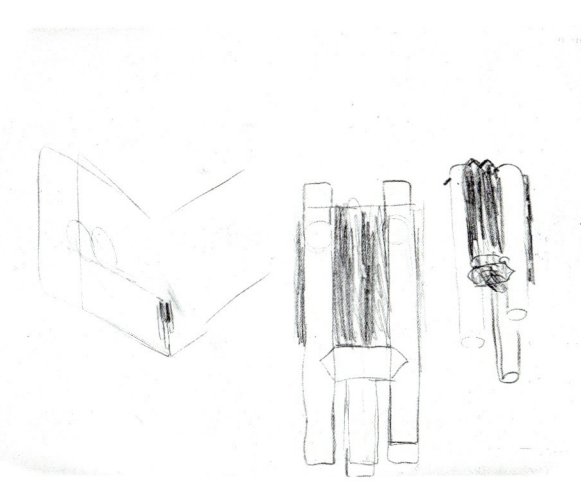

212

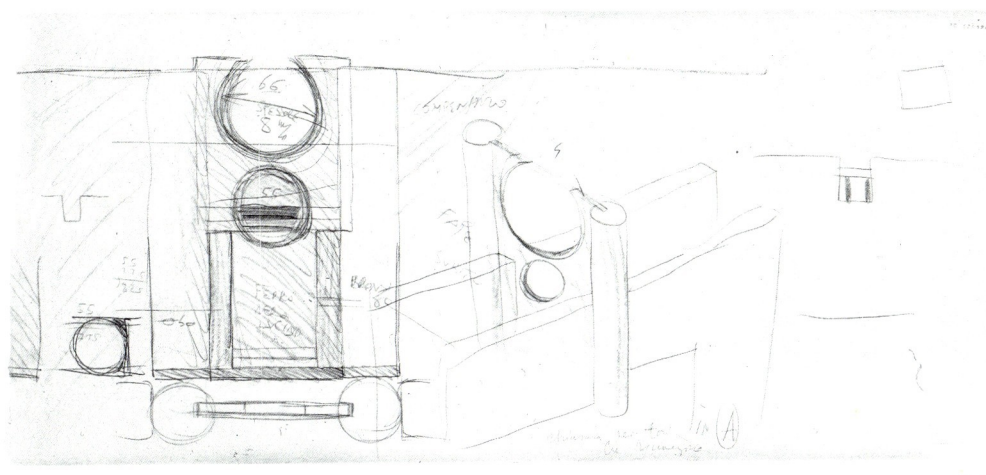

213

136

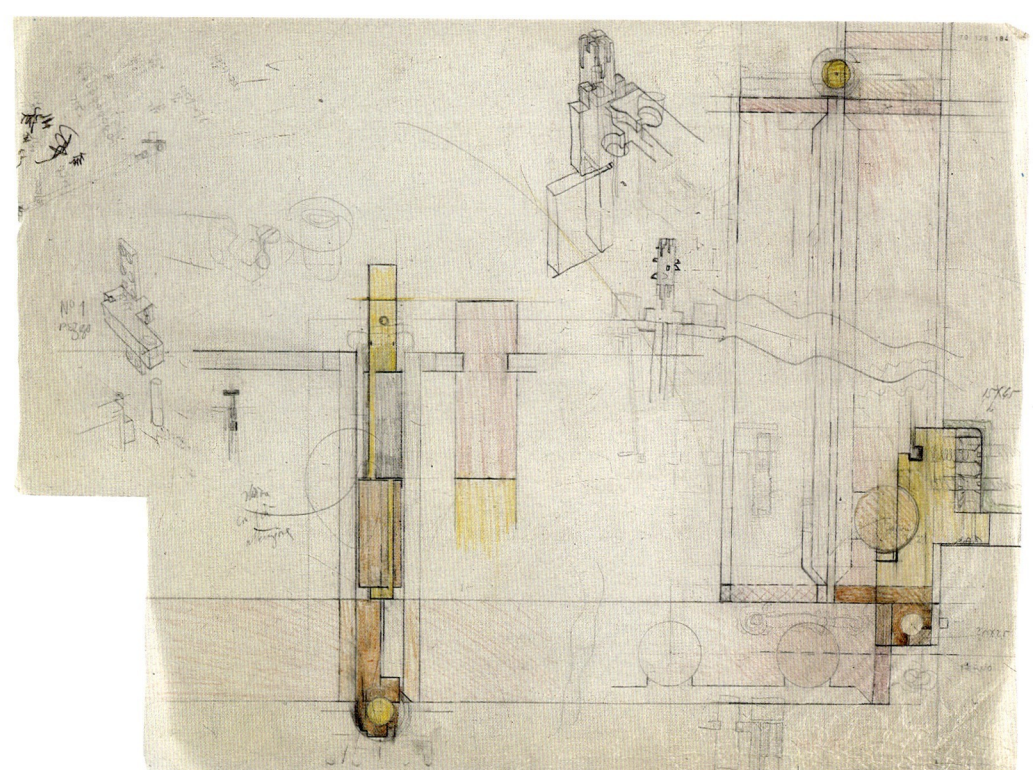

214

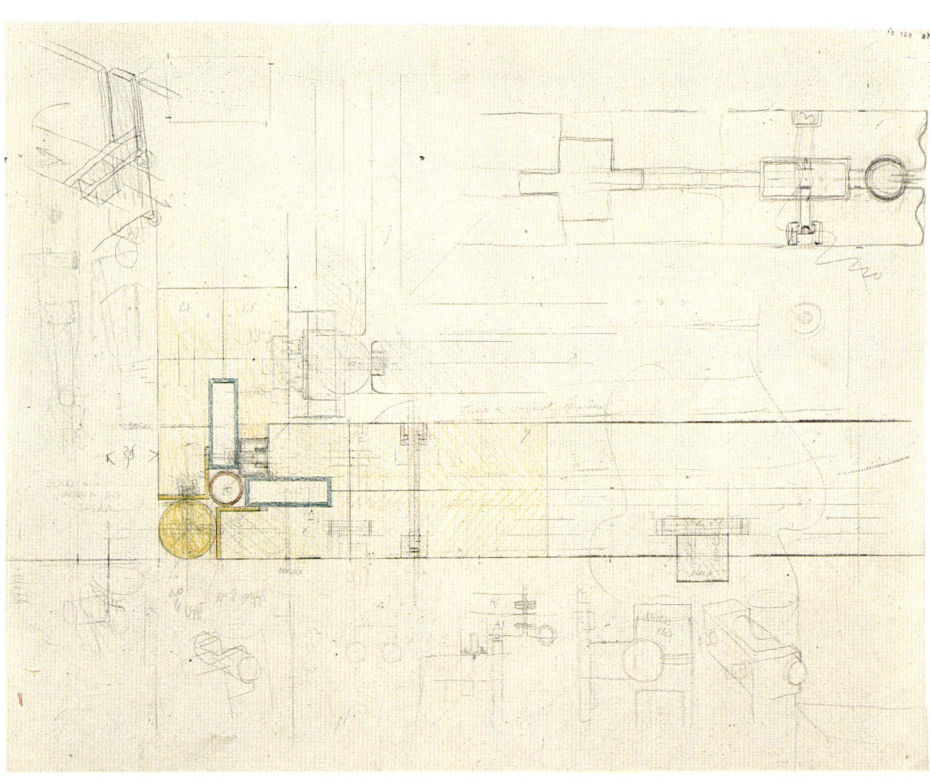

215

Entrance wings opening Durchblick („occhio")

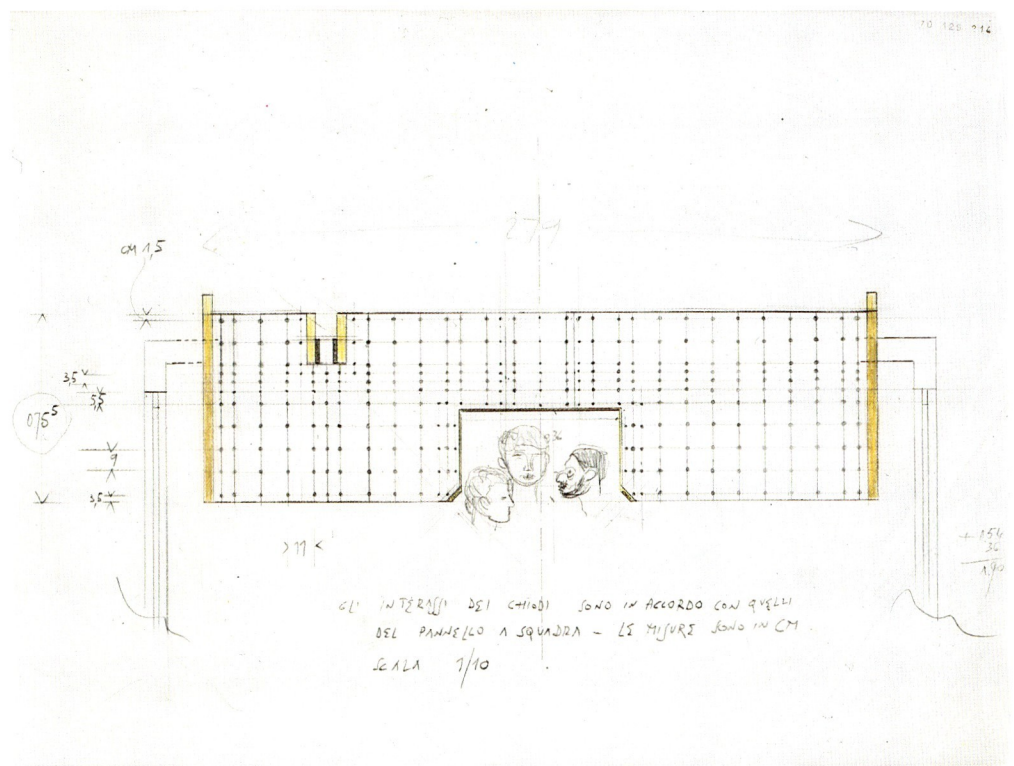

216

217

138

218

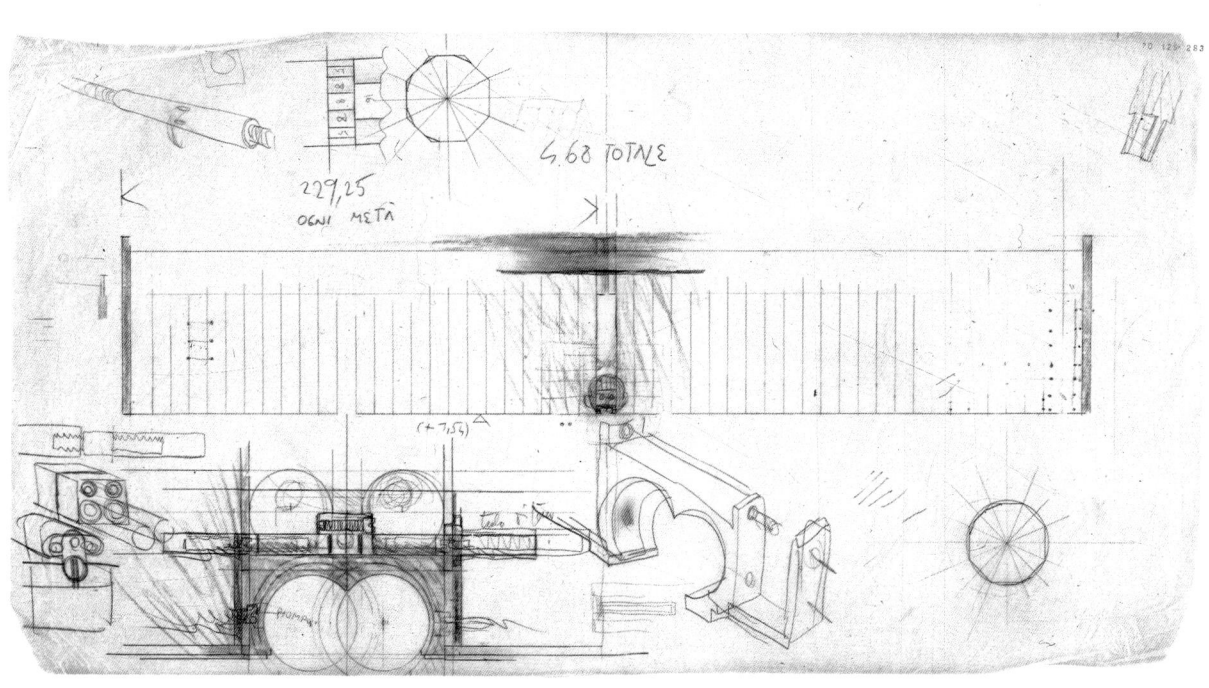

219

Entrance stay bar/Haltestange beim Eingang

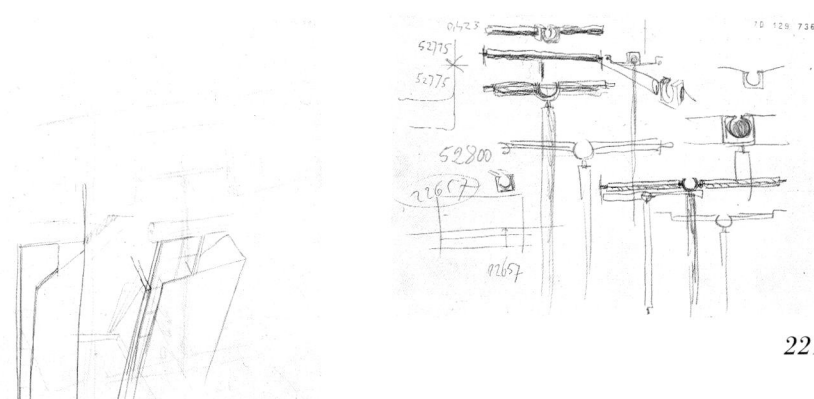

139

221

220

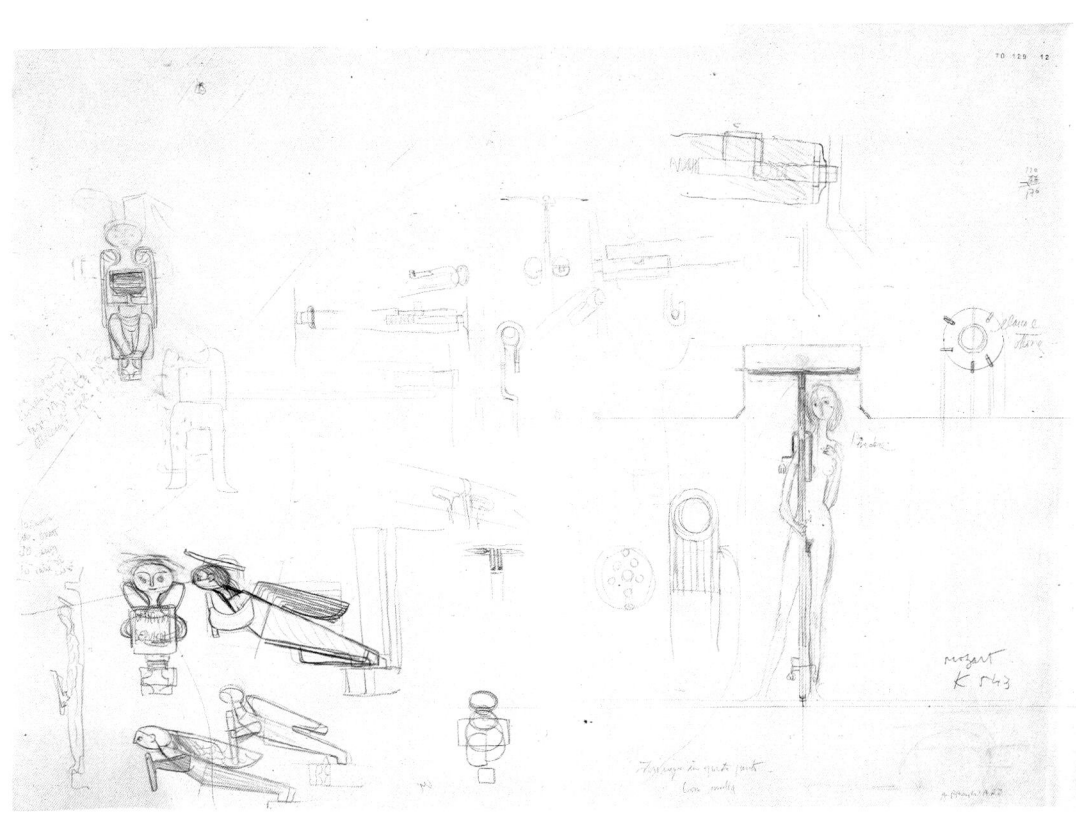

222

140

223

Structure/Struktur

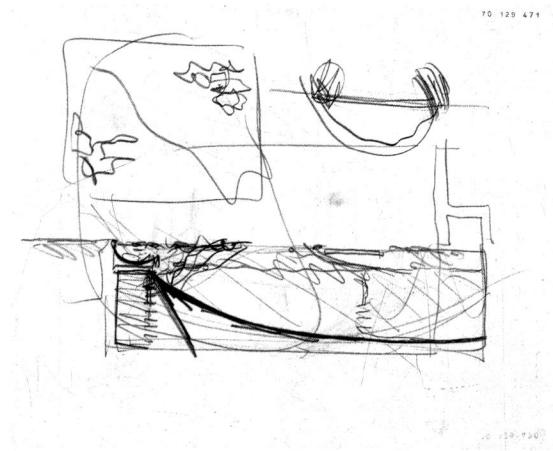

224

141

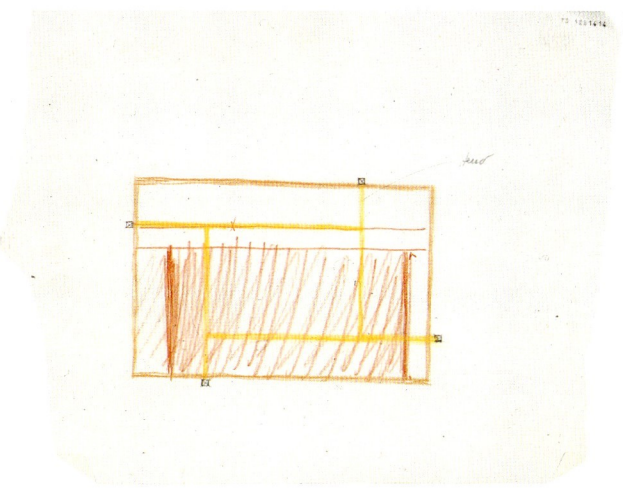

225

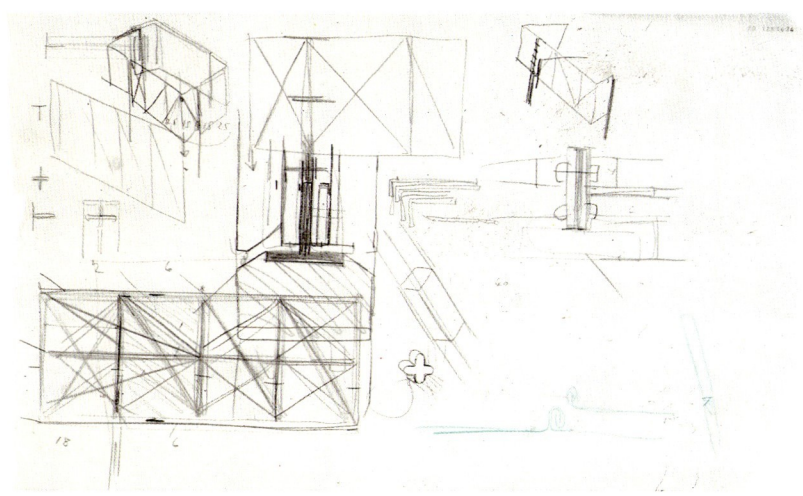

226

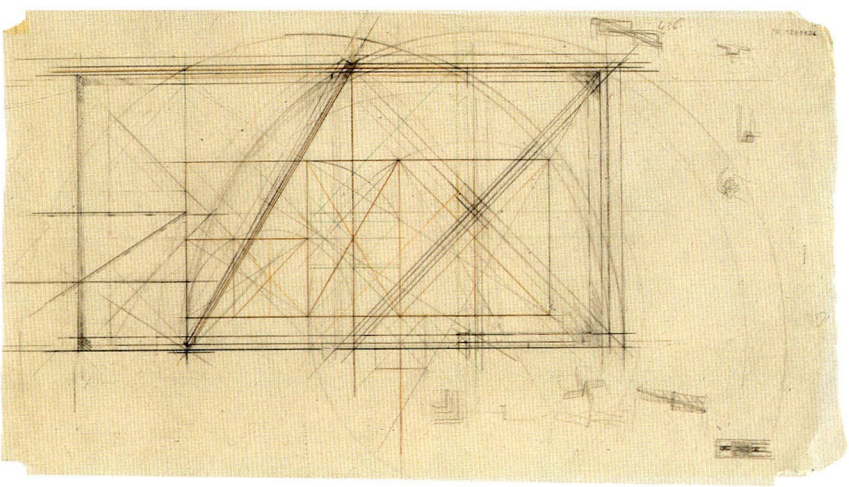

227

142

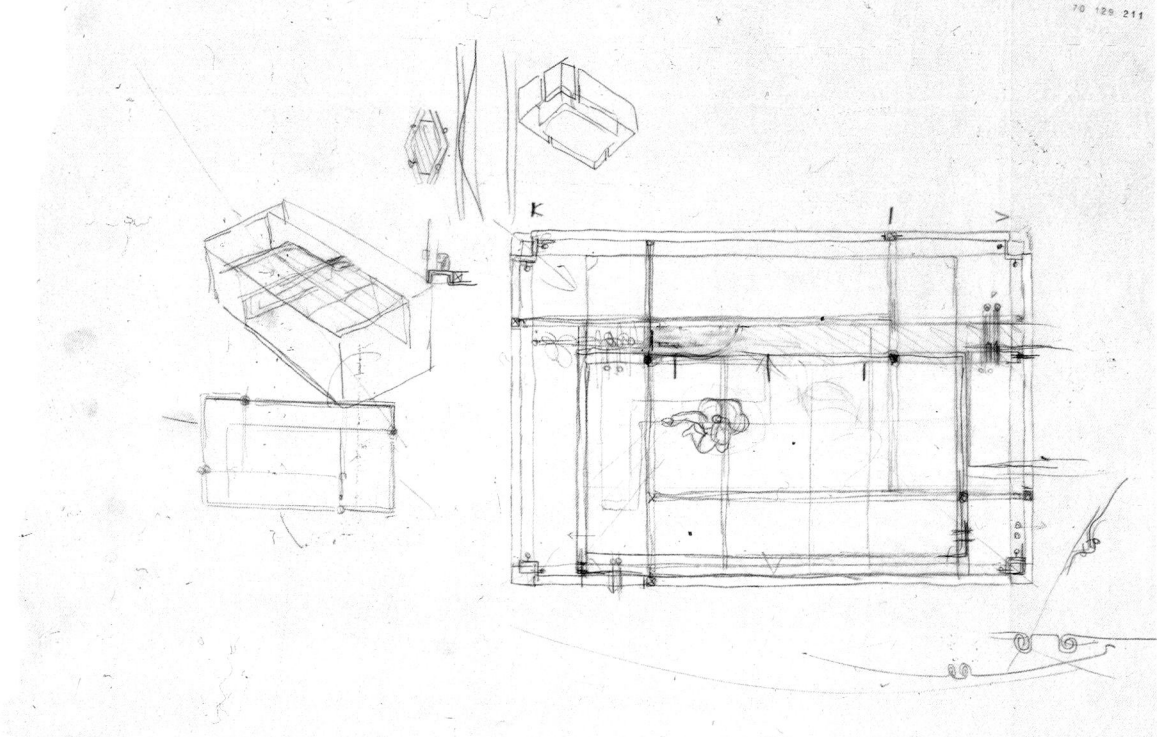

228

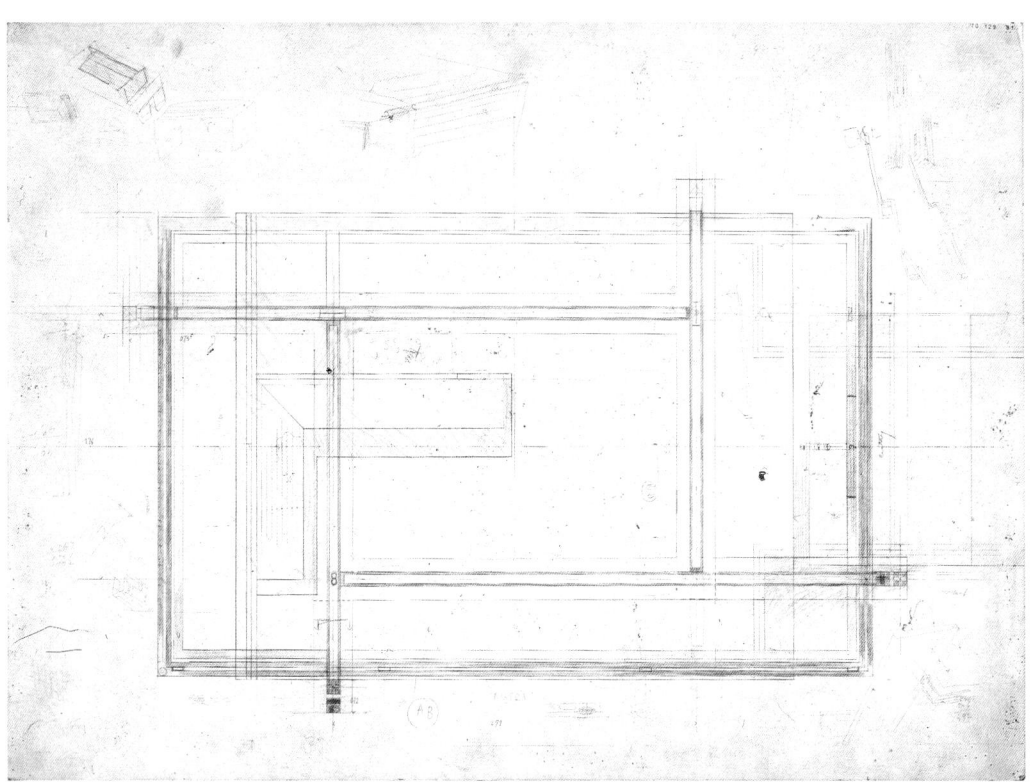

229

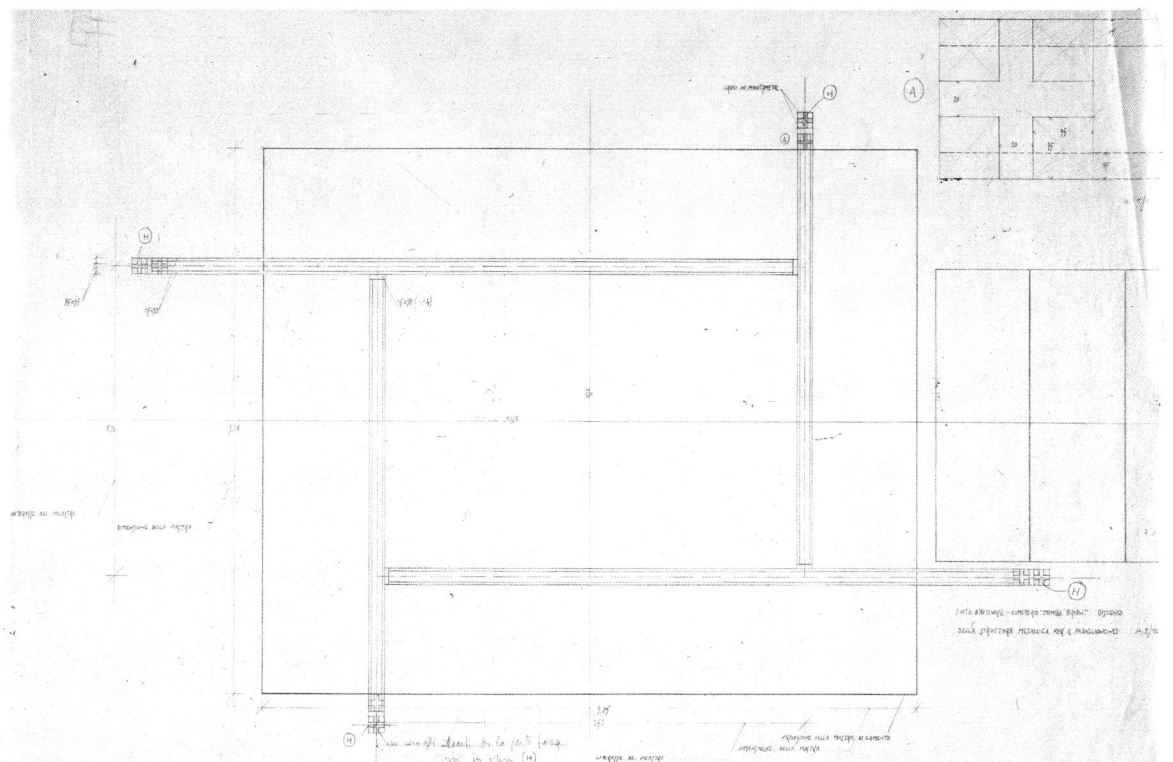

230

231

Lighting/Beleuchtung

144

232

Large pool/großes Wasserbecken

233

234

235

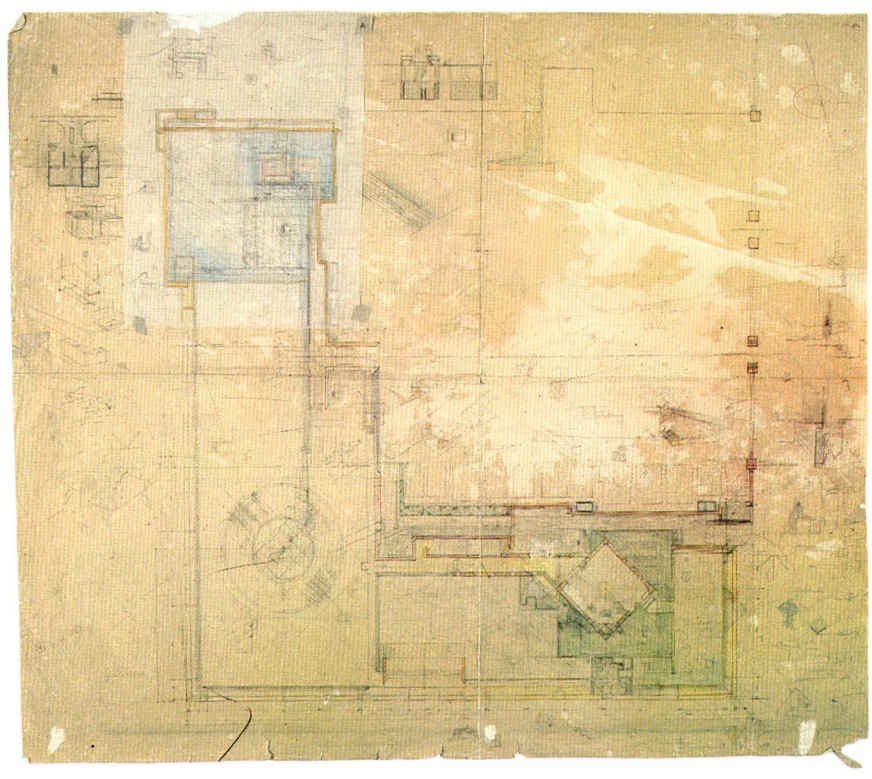

236

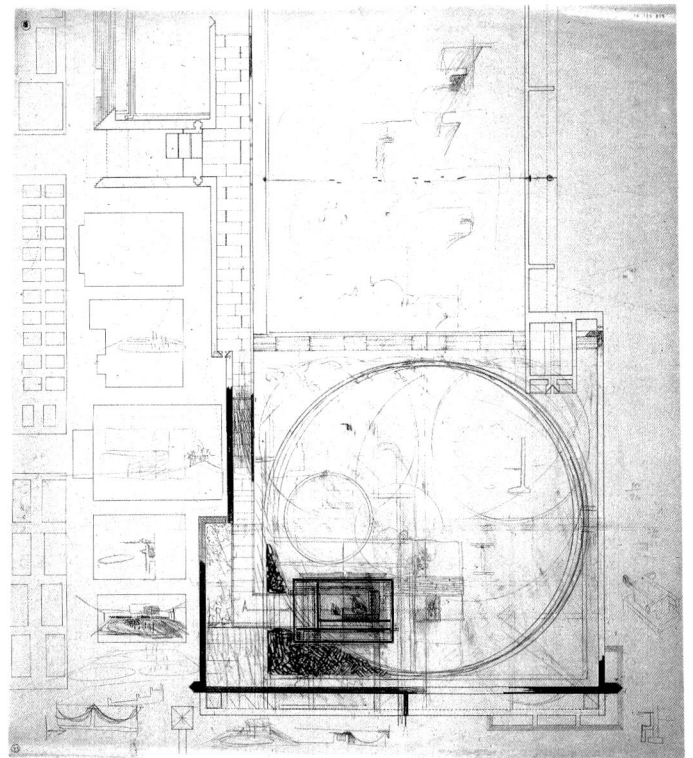

237

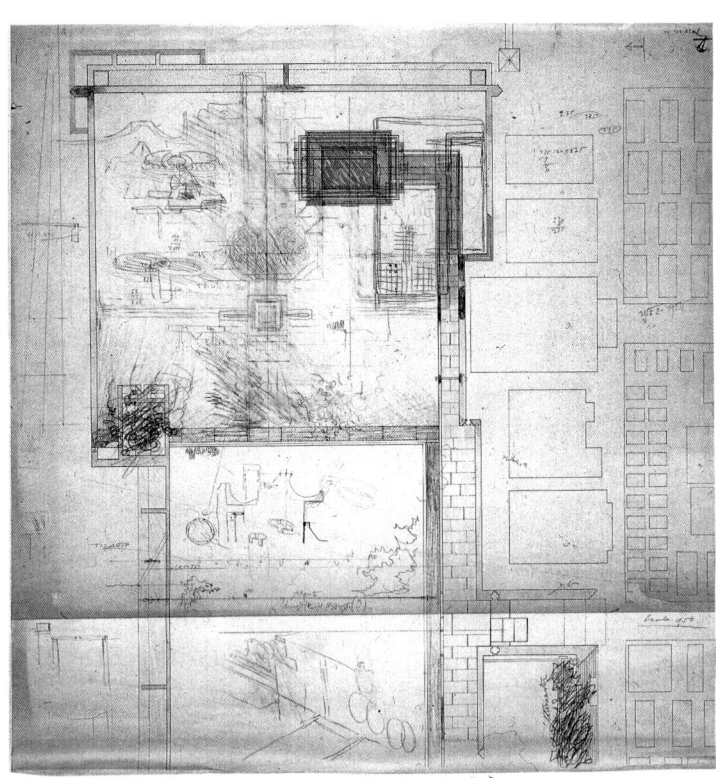

238

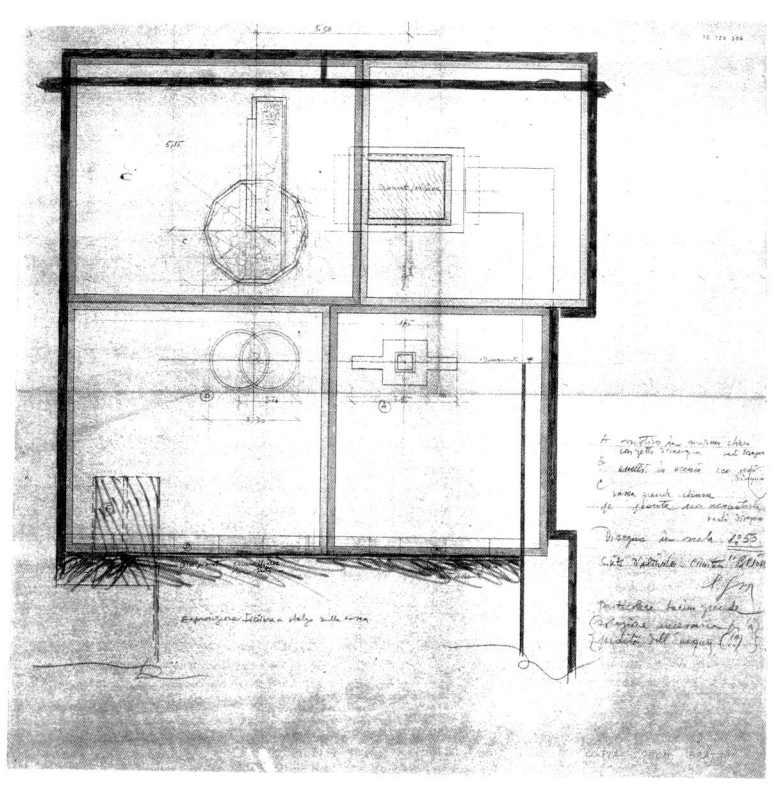

239

Retaining wall near the pool/überhängende Stützmauer

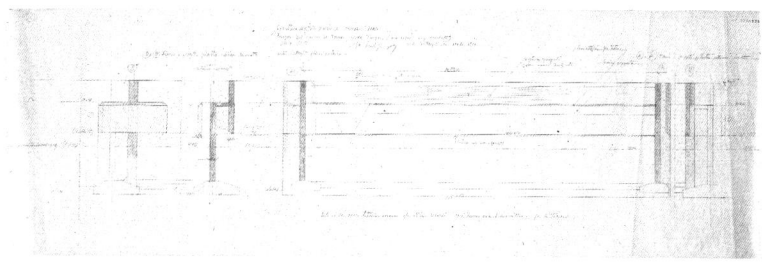

240

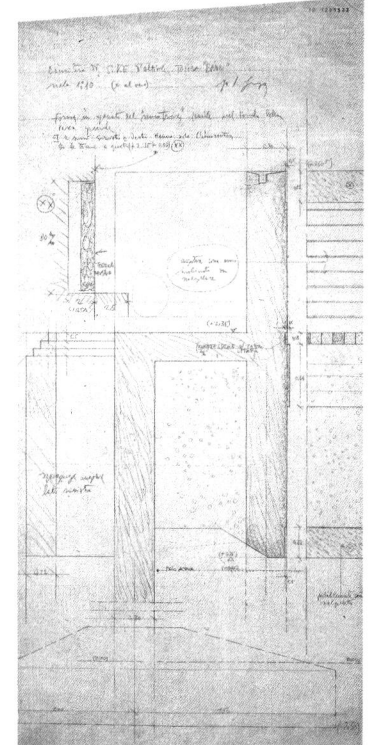

241

Bottom of the pool/Beckenboden

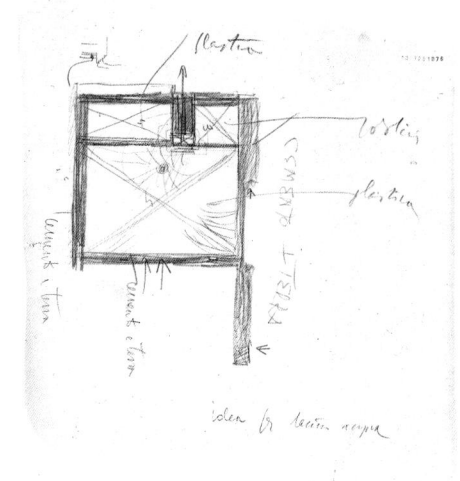

242

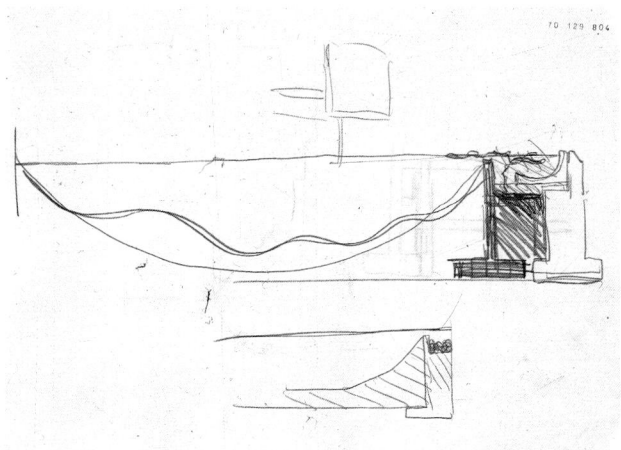

243

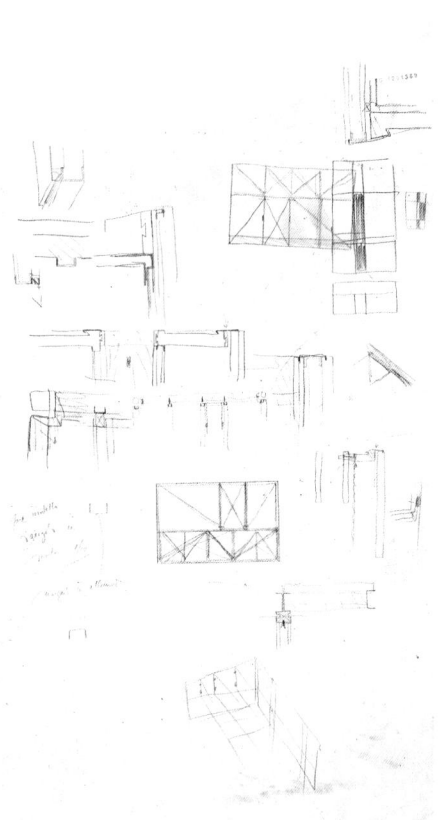

244

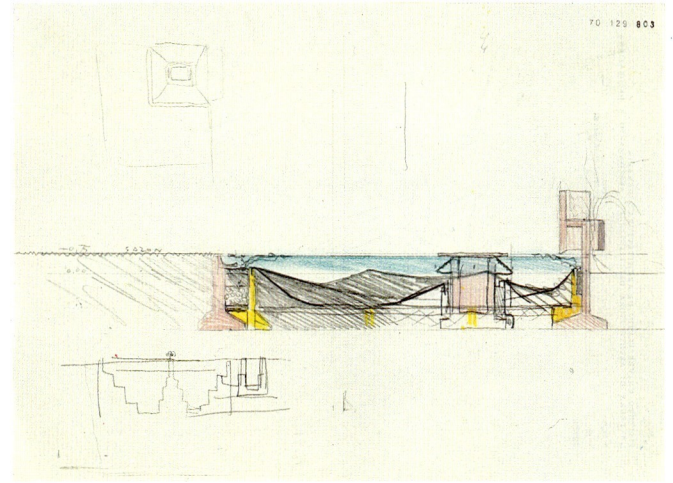

245

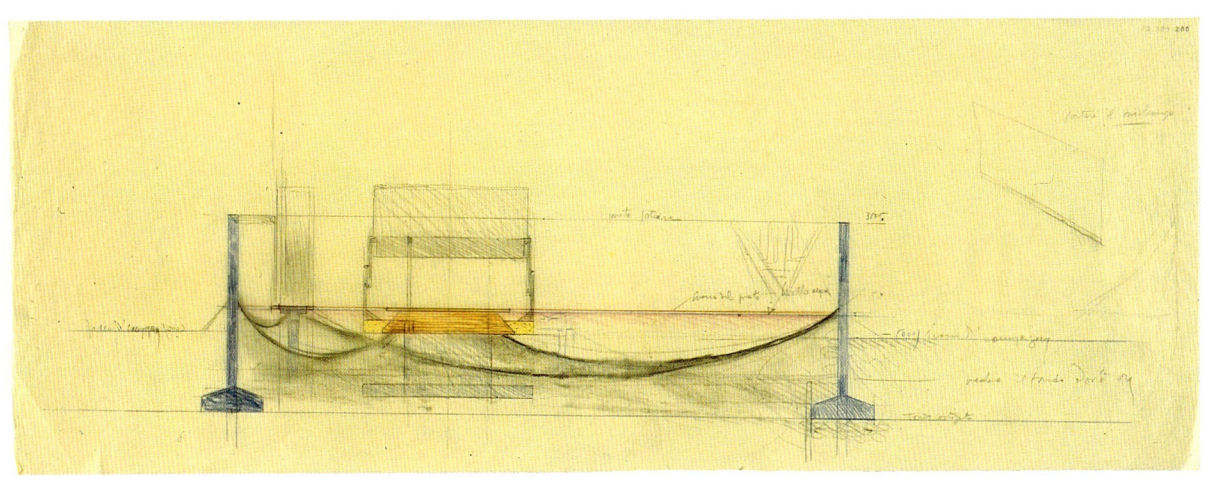

246

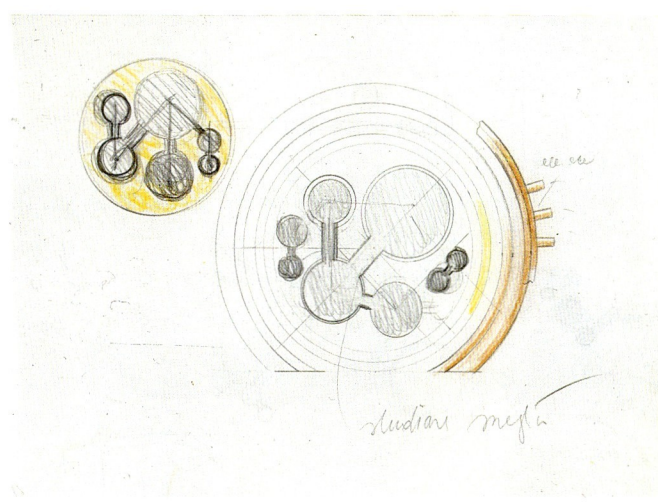

247

Views/Ansichten

248

249

250

Bamboo Island/Bambusinsel

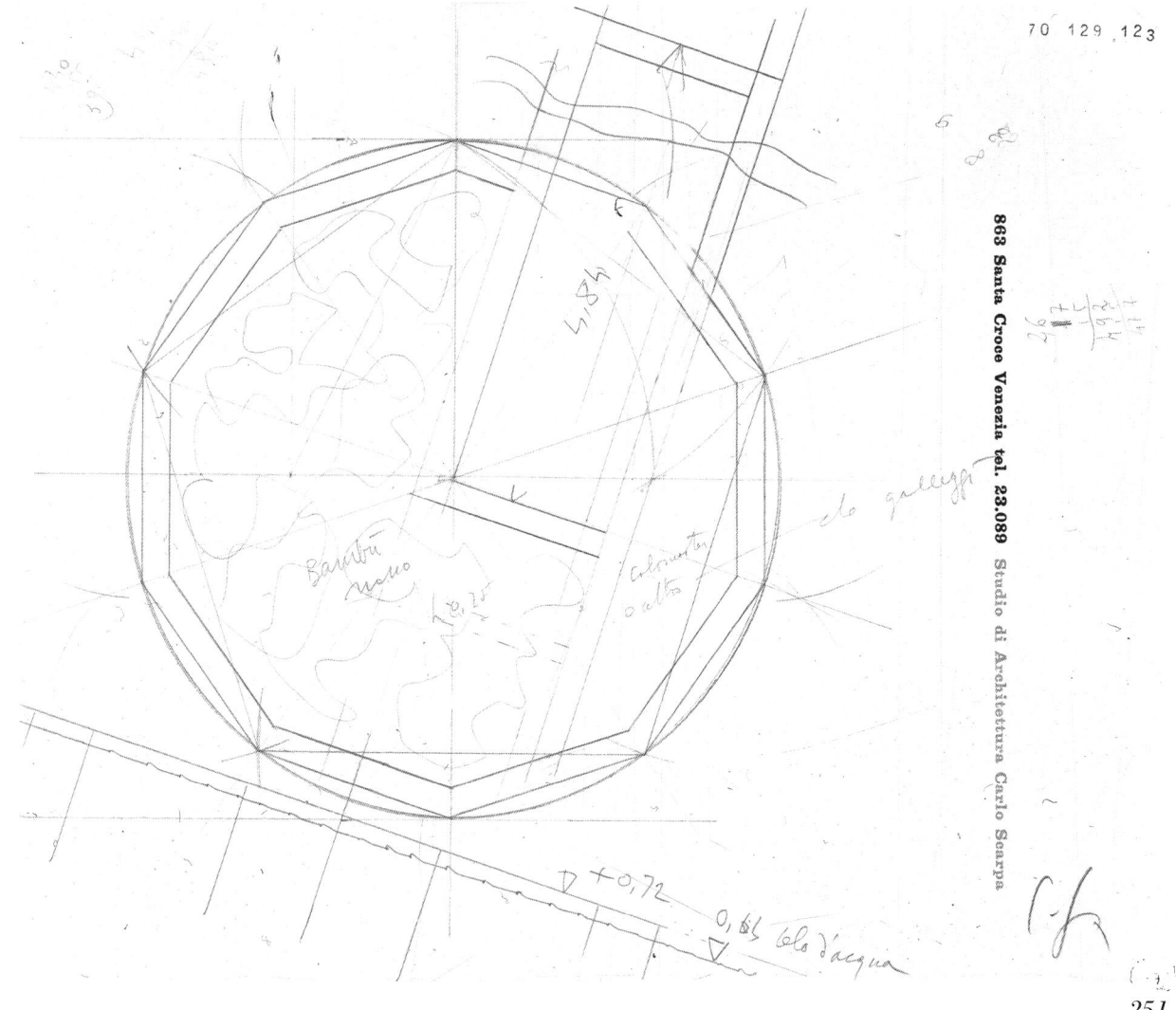

Two rings/Zwei Ringe

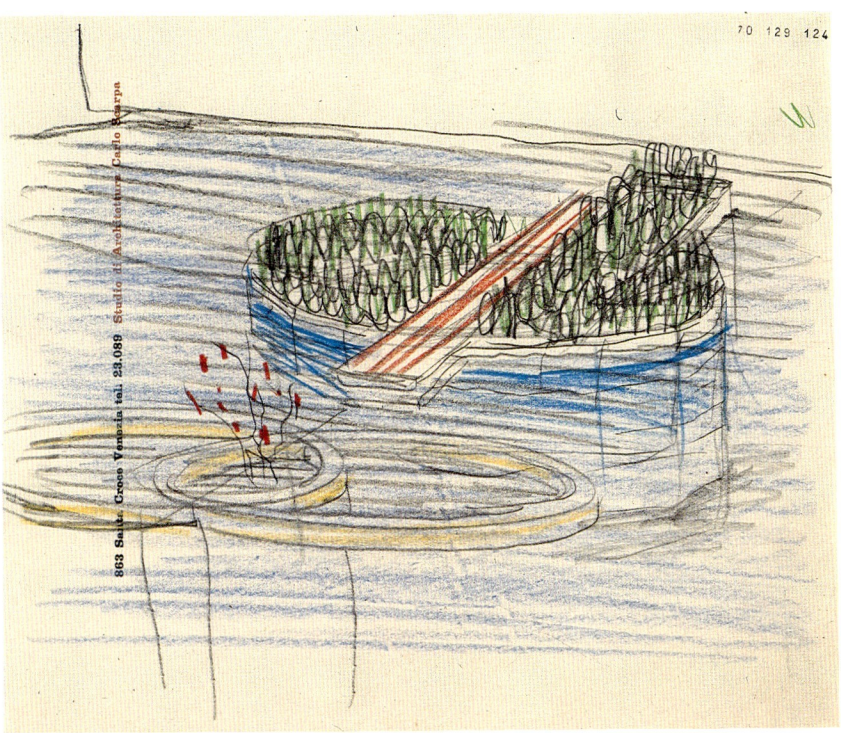

252

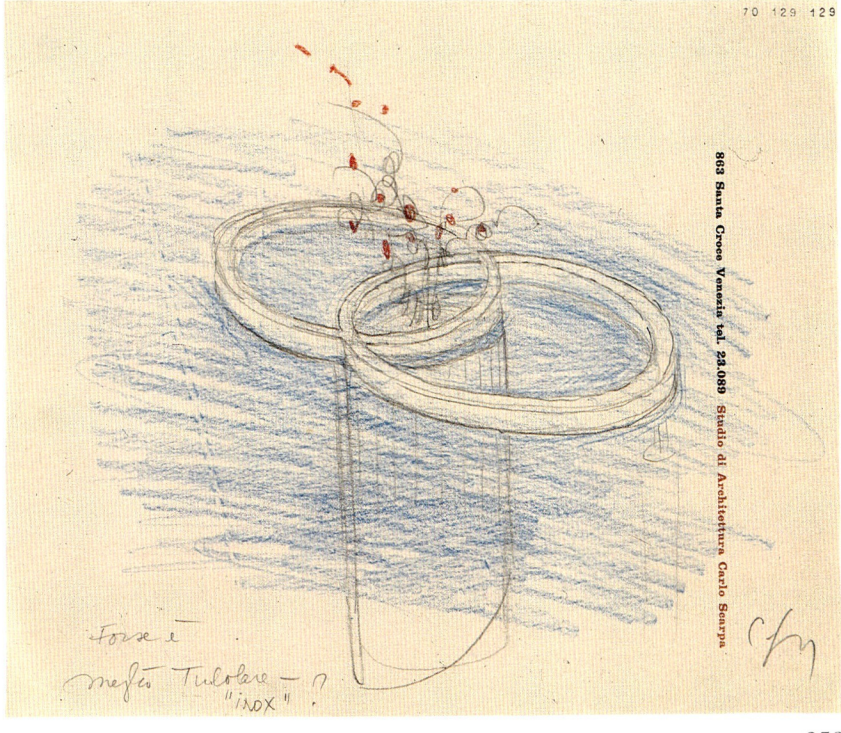

253

154

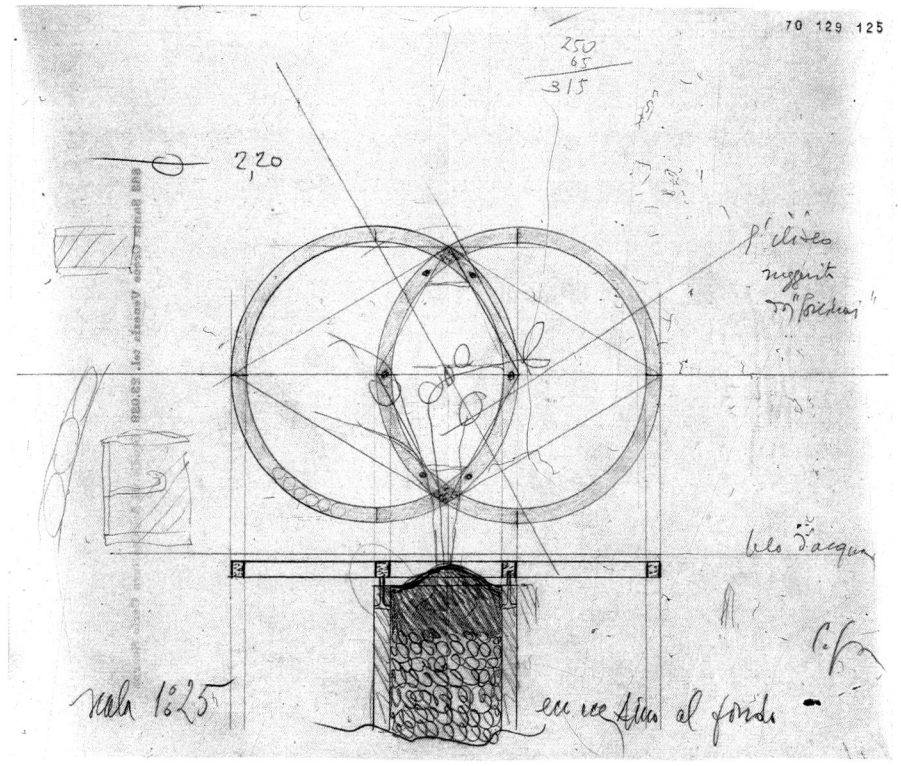

254

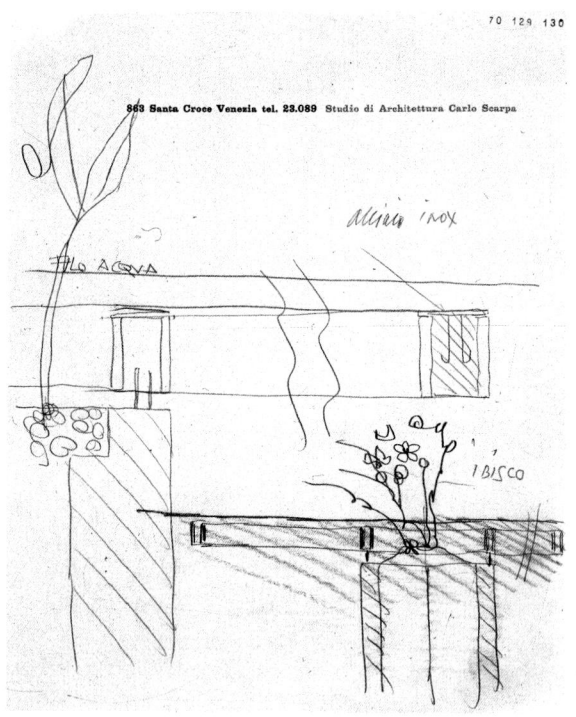

255

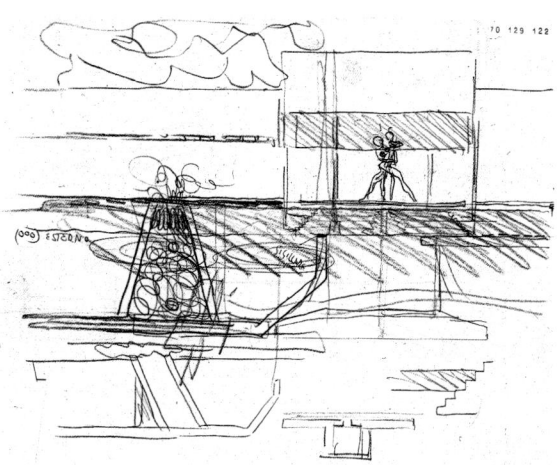

256

Fountain or floating flower box/Springbrunnen oder schwimmende Blumenschale

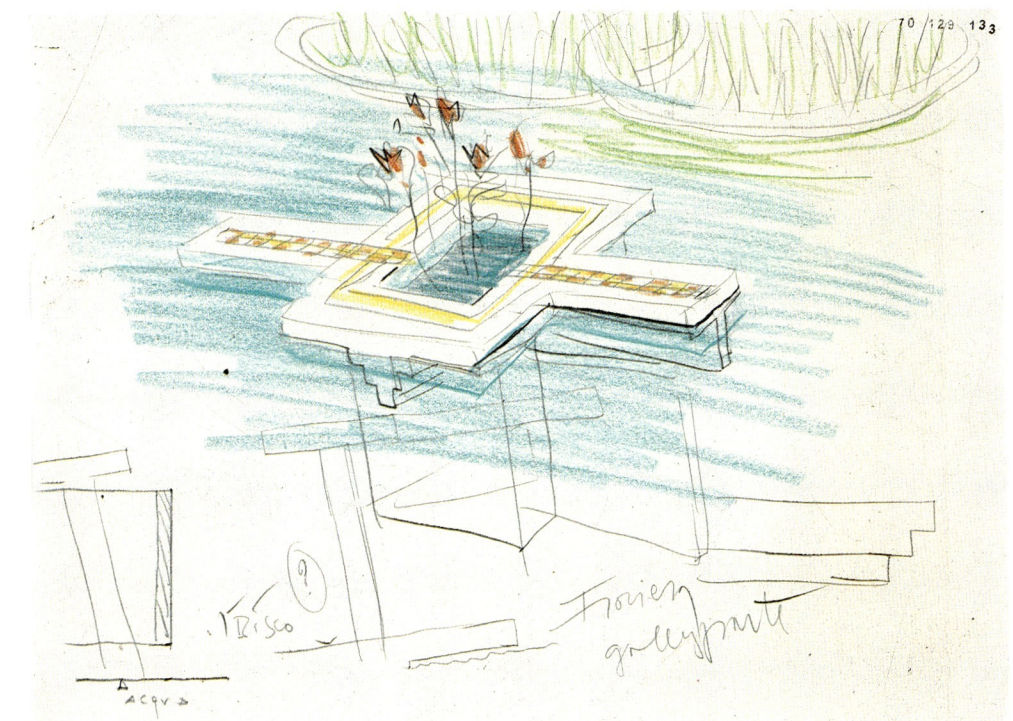

257

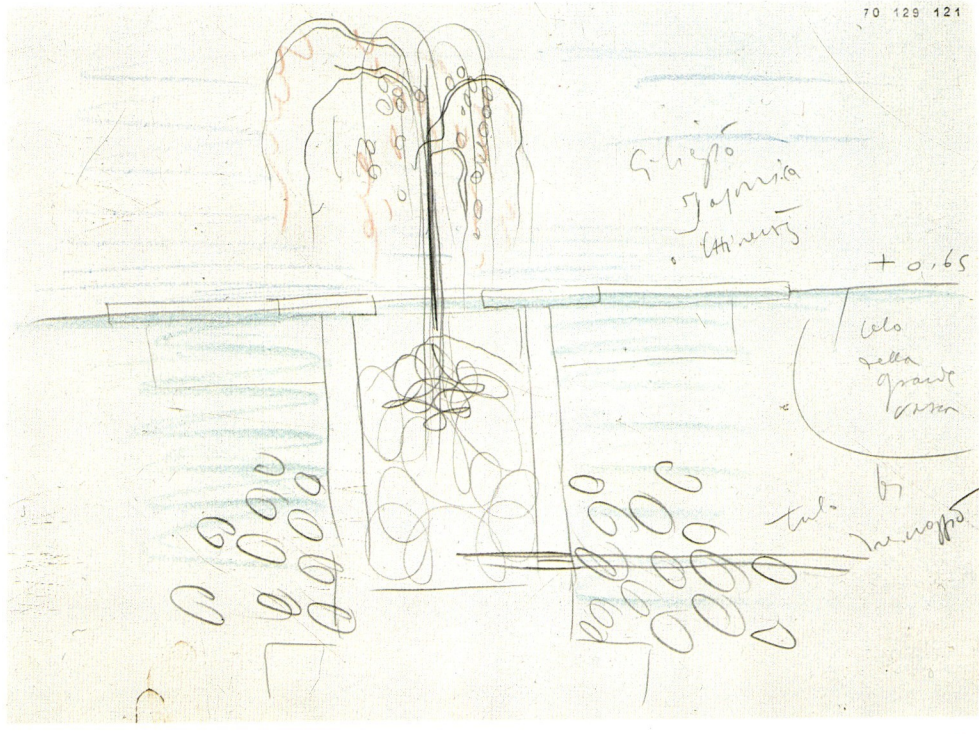

258

156

259

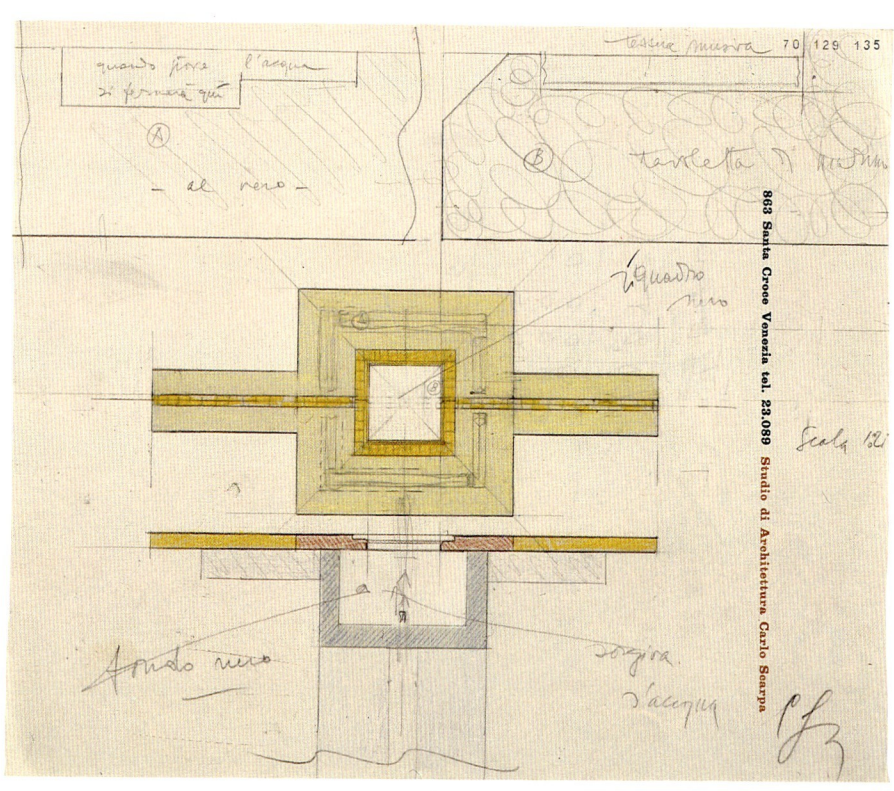

260

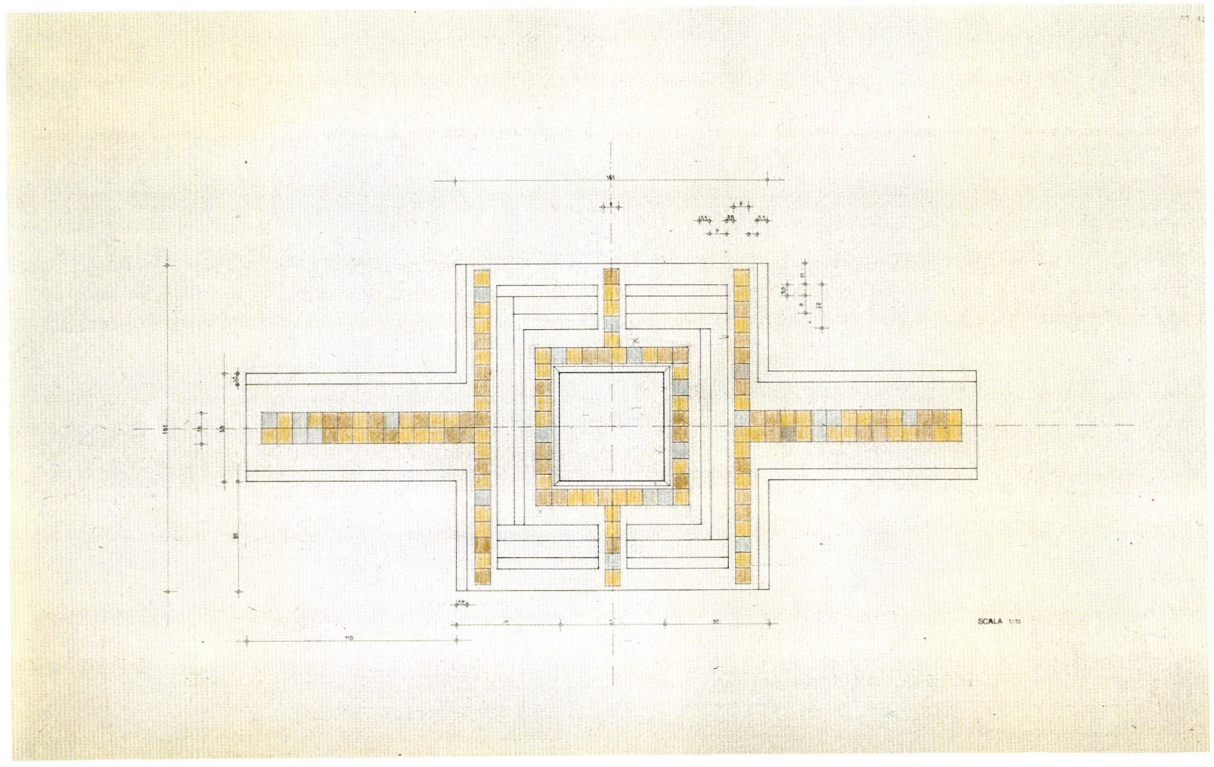

261

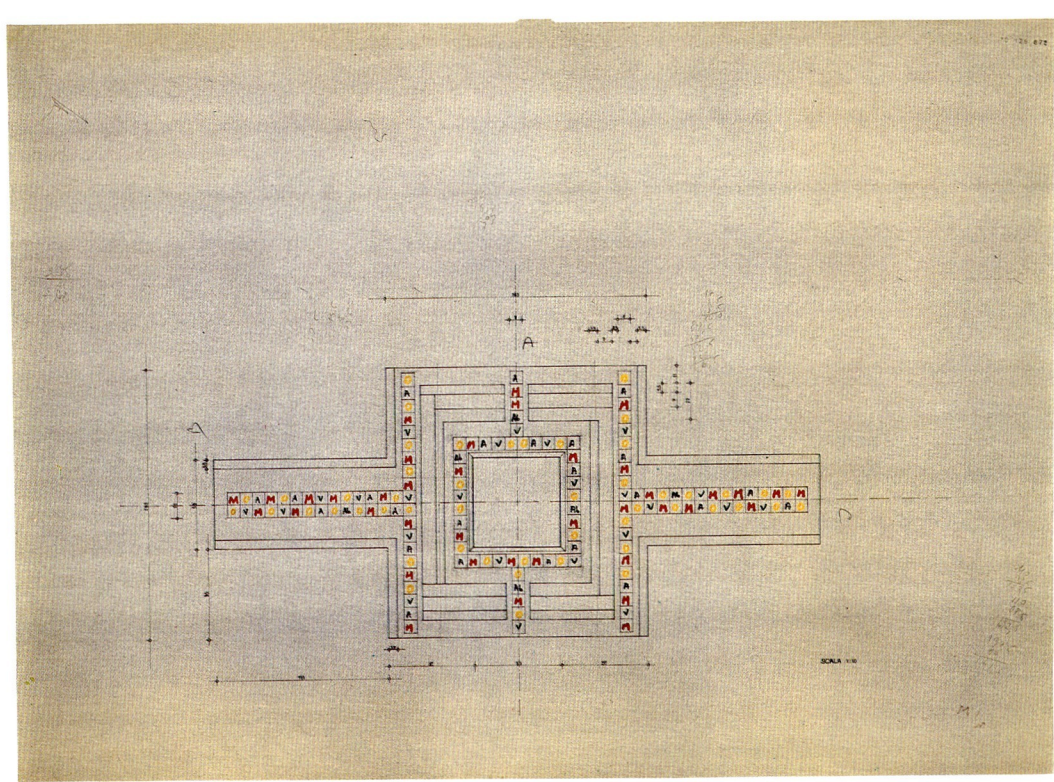

262

158

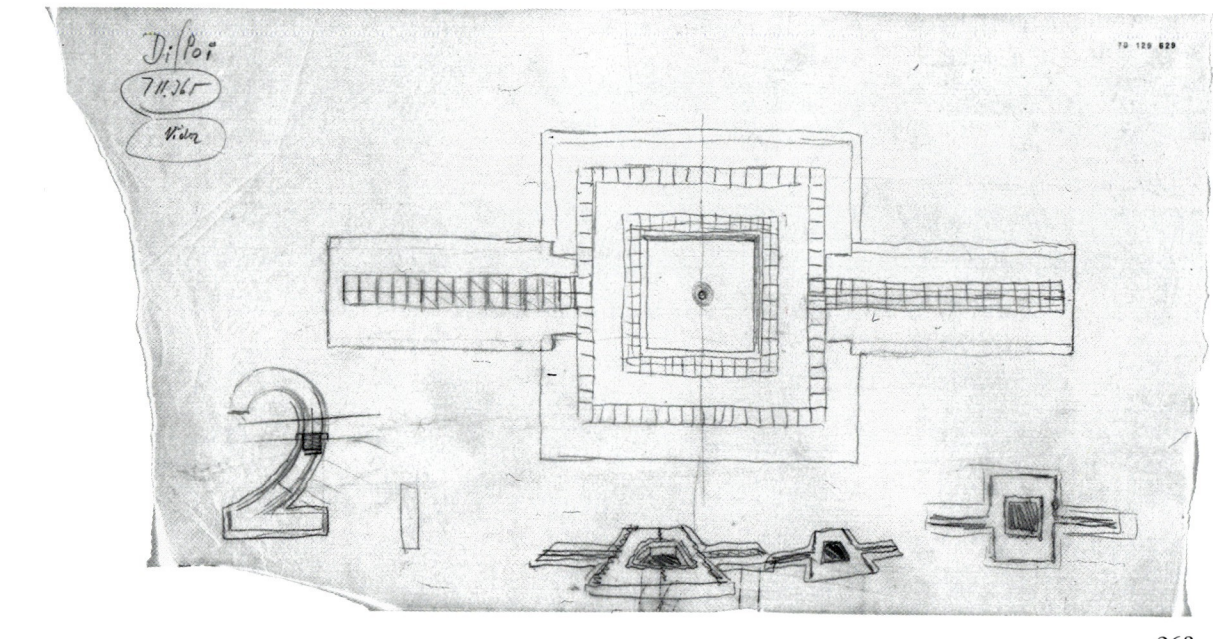

263

Edge of pool/Beckenrand

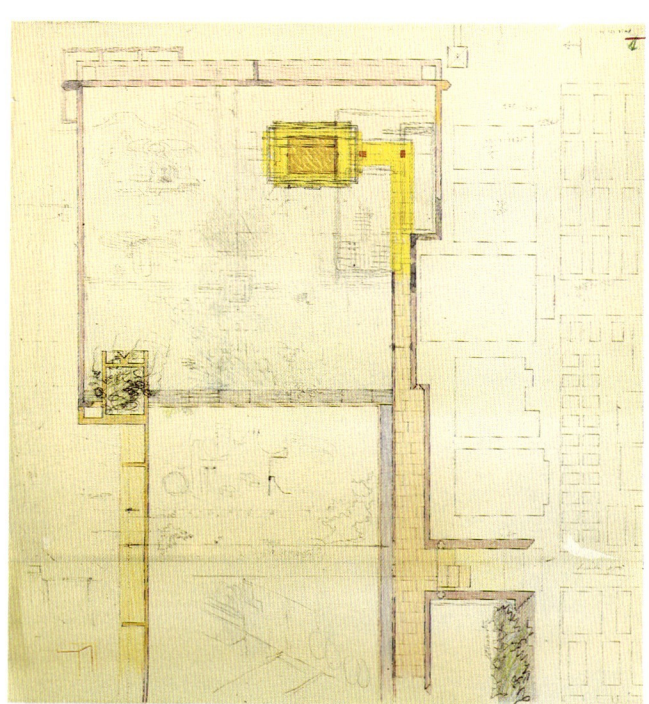

264

Hindrance near the pool: cable barrier across lawn
Absperrung vor dem Wasserbecken: Verspannung über der Wiese

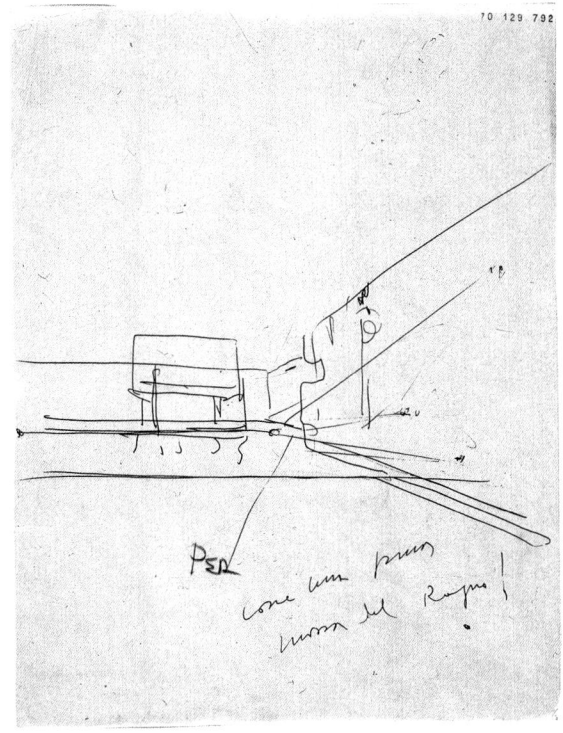

265

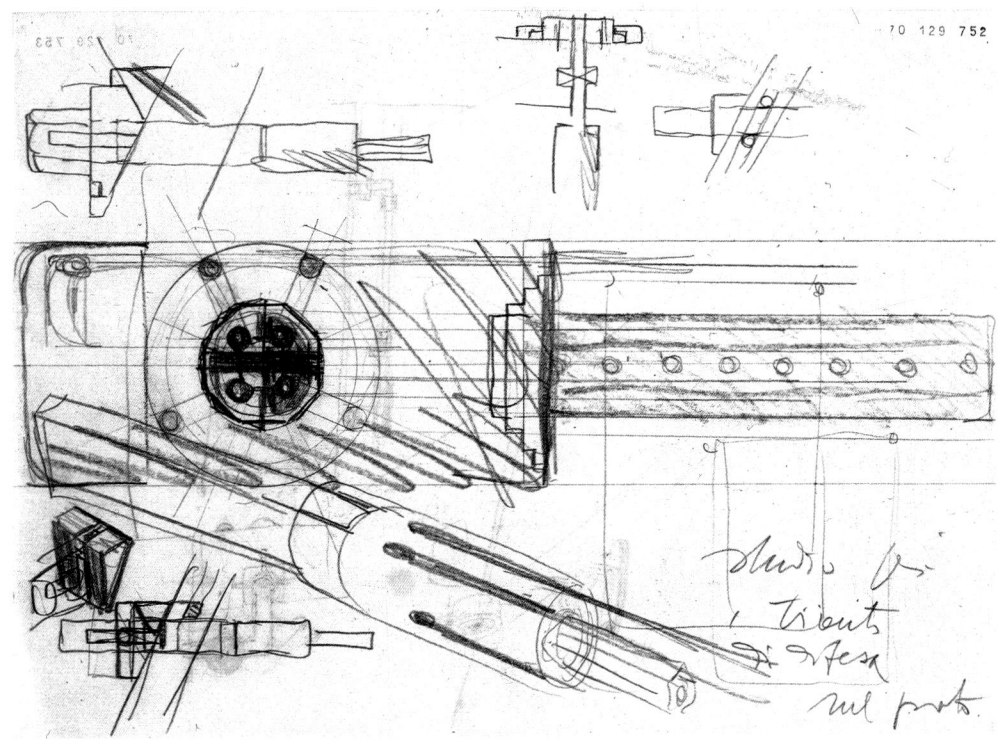

266

160

267

TOMB/DAS GRABMAL

162

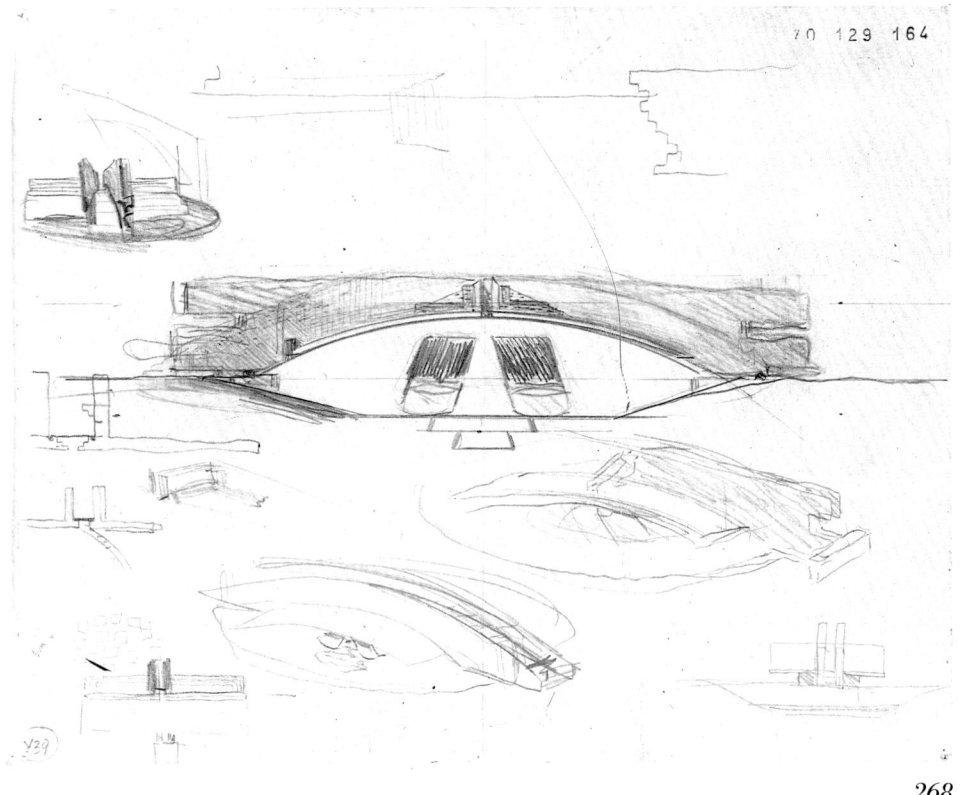

268

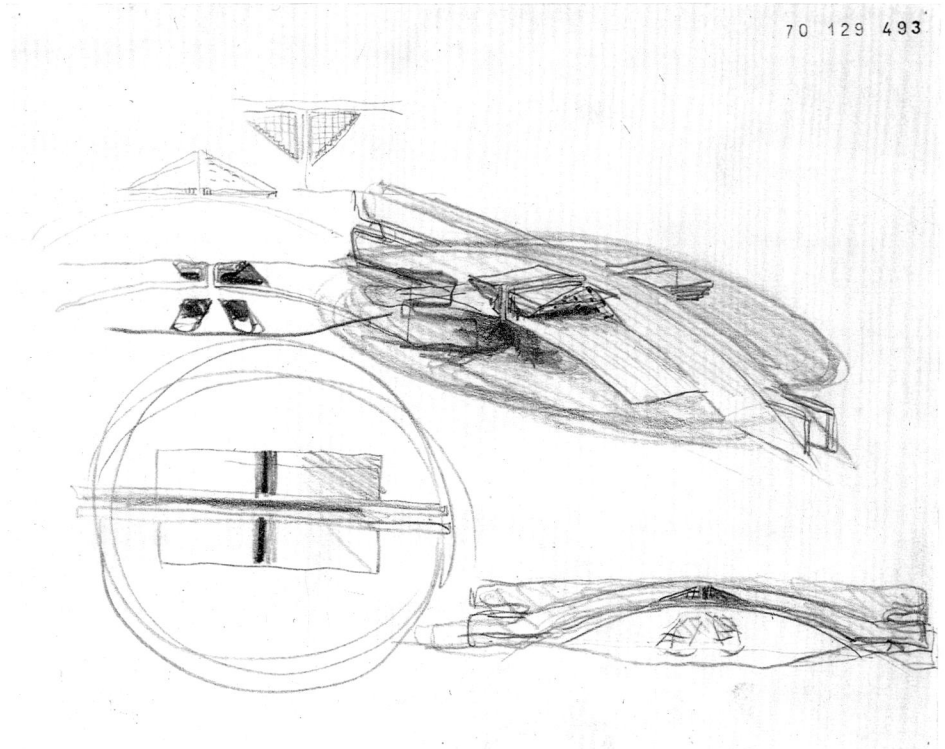

269

6–9 March 1970, project approved by the Altivole town council
6.–9. März 1970, Das von der Gemeinde Altivole genehmigte Projekt

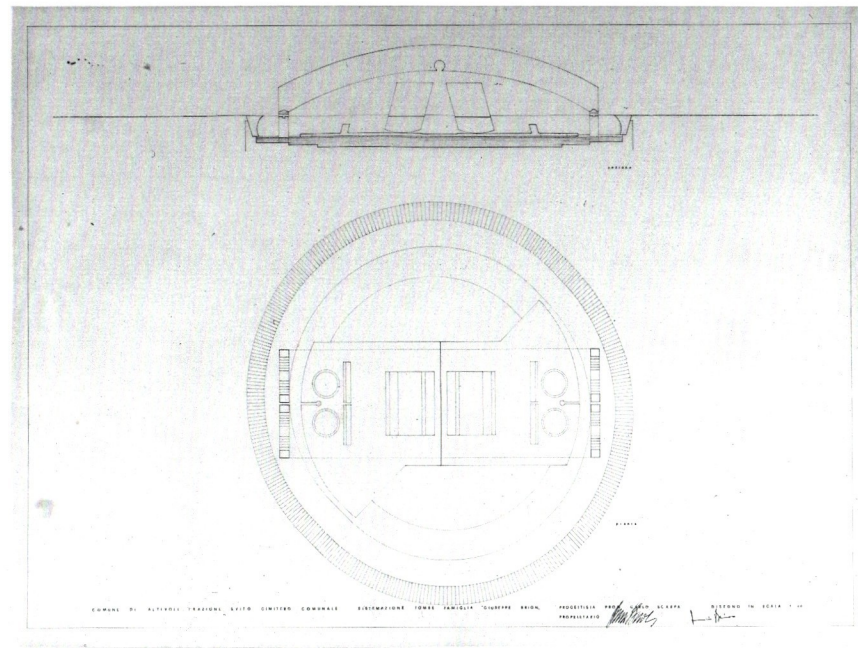

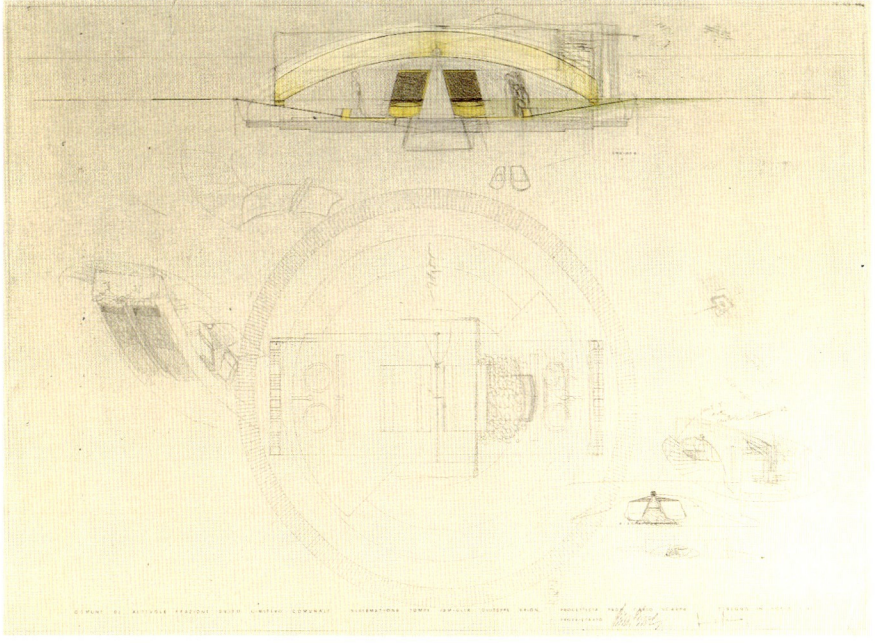

Arch over the sacrophagi: "Arcosolio"/Bogen über den Sarkophagen: „Arcosolio"

Extrados/Bogenrücken

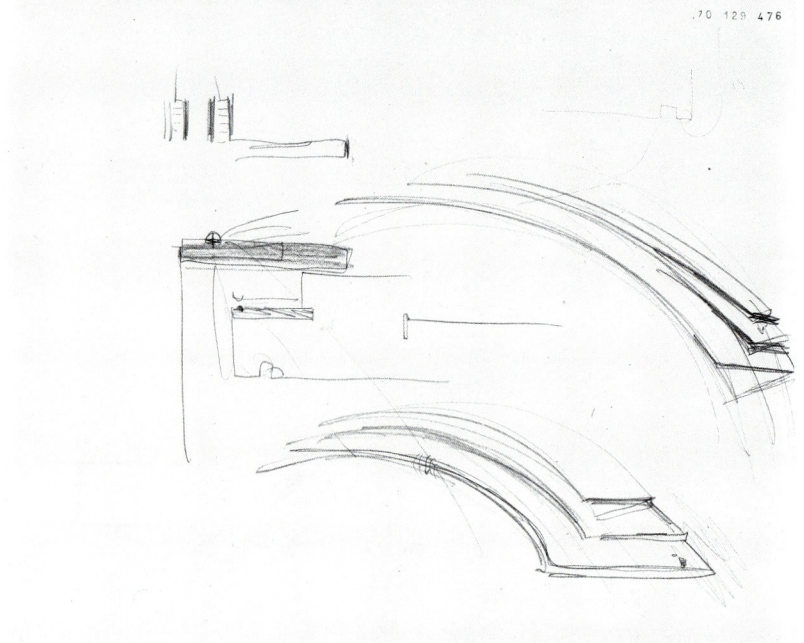

272

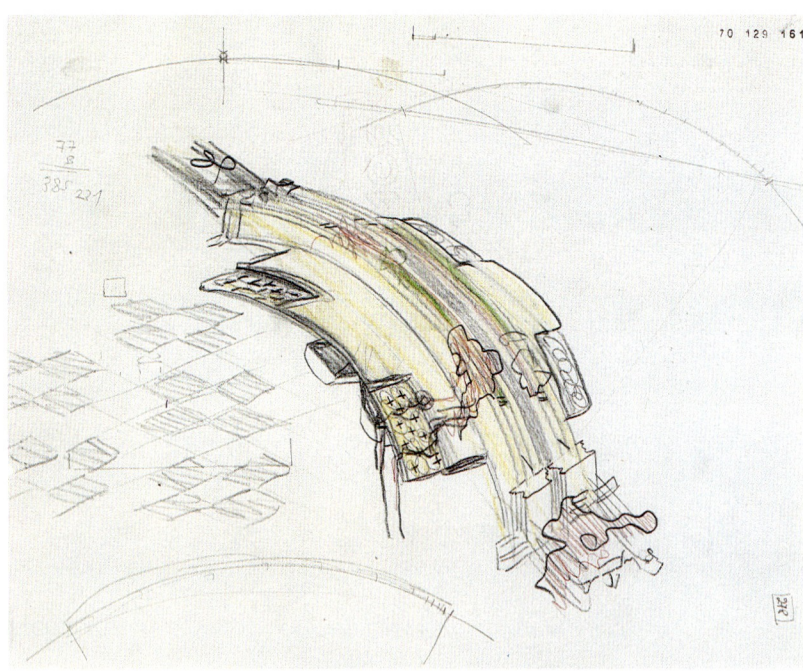

273

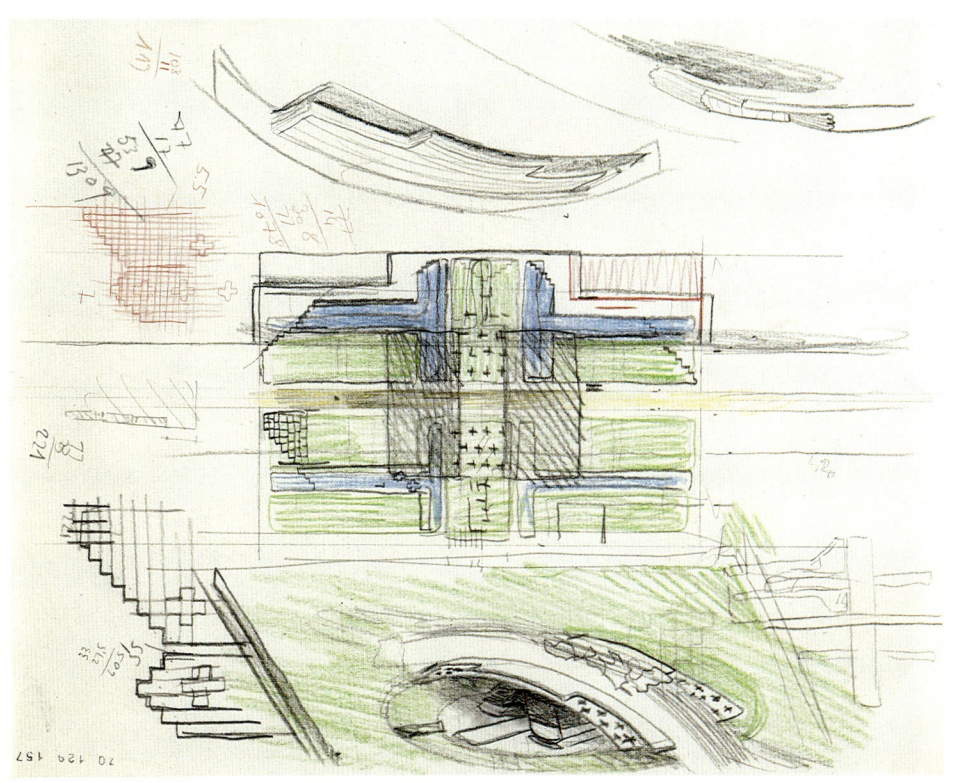

274

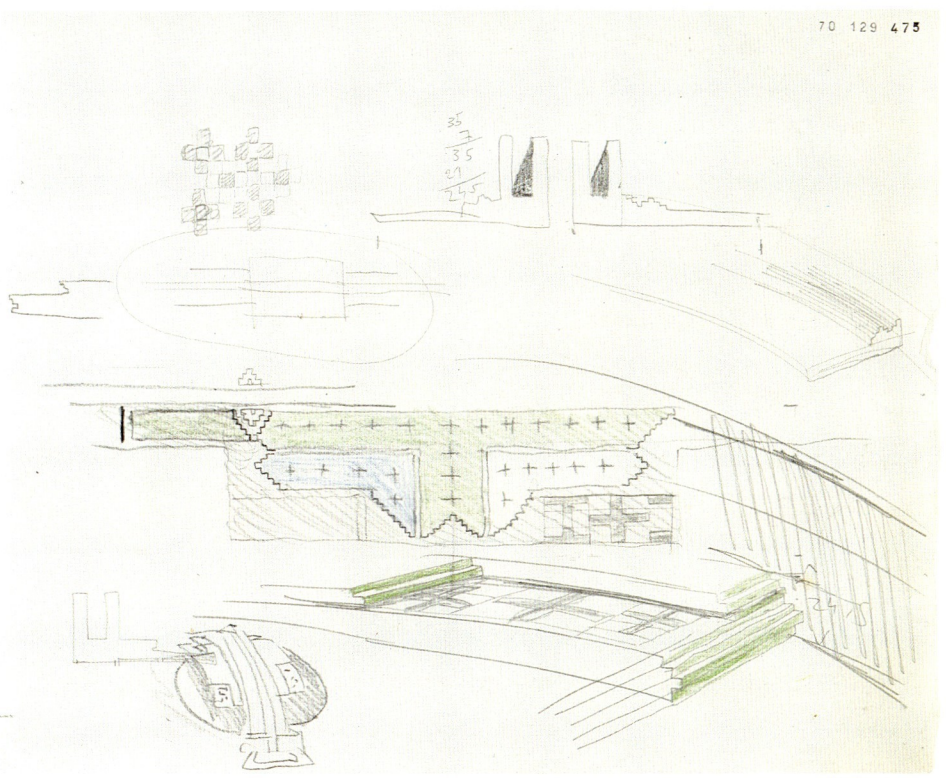

275

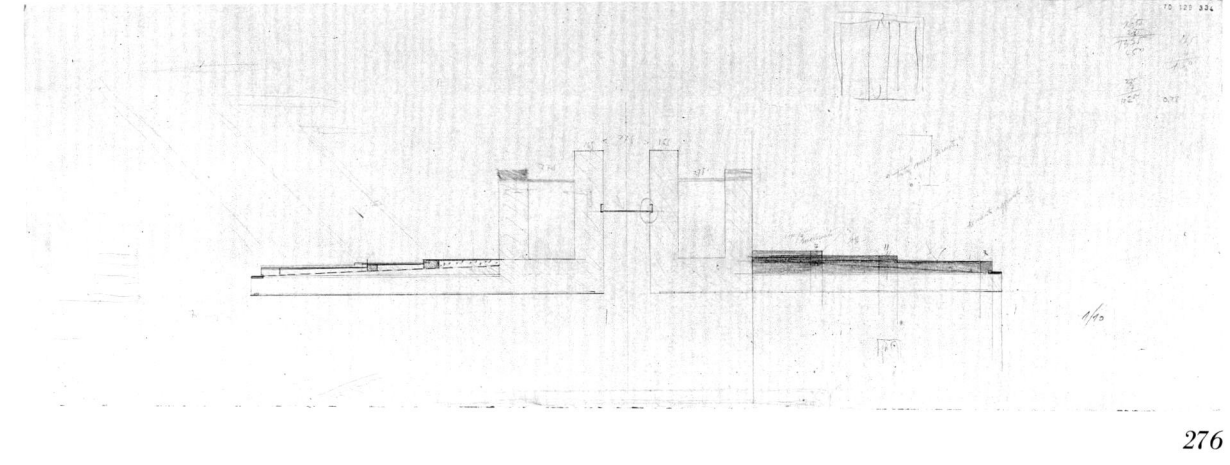

276

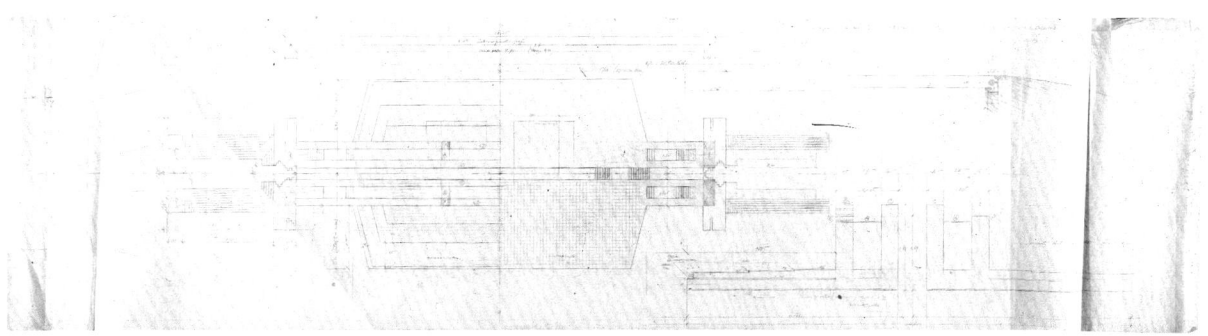

277

Arch brace/Verankerung des Bogens

278

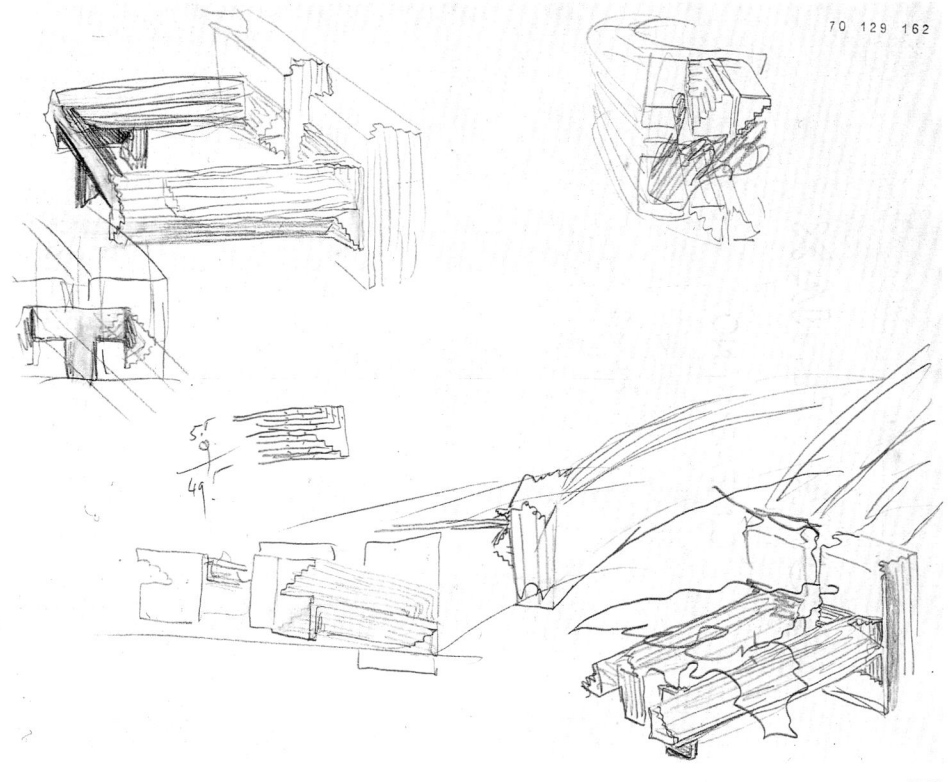

167

279

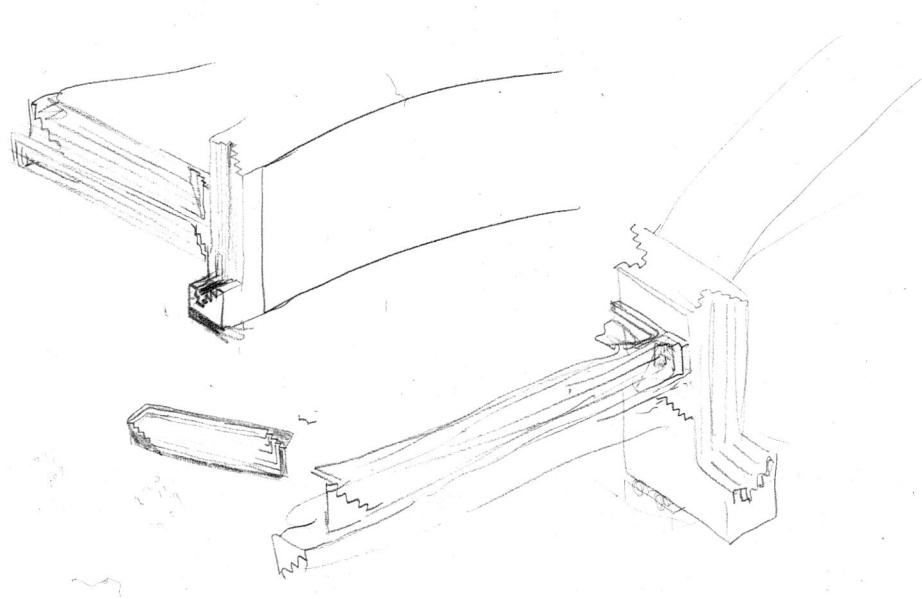

280

168

281

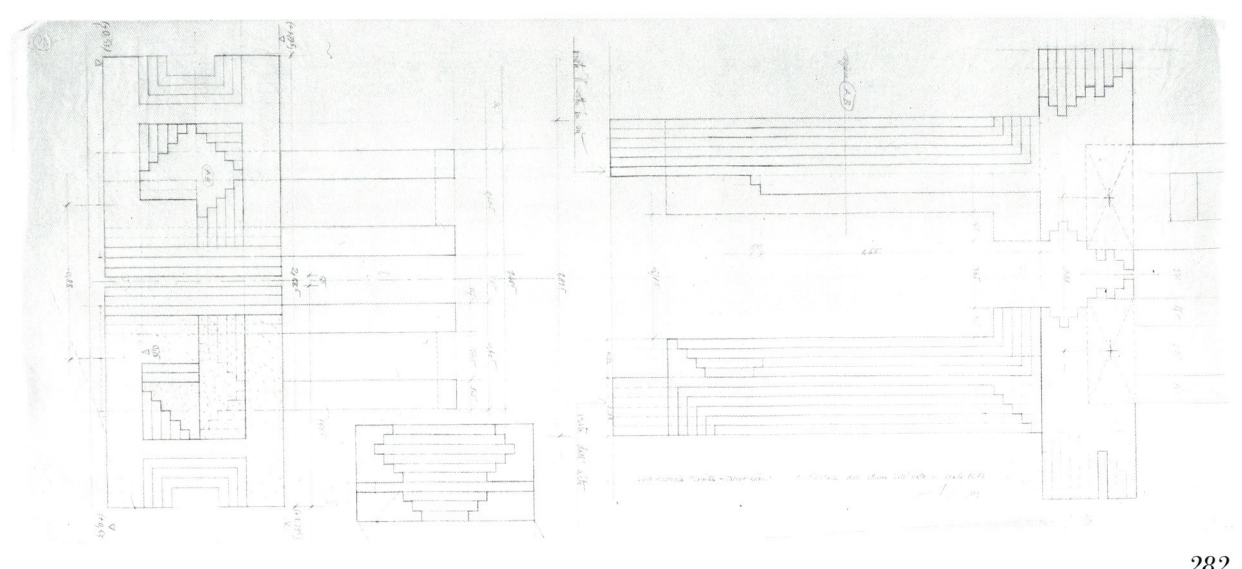

282

Entredos mosaic/Mosaik an der Bogenunterseite

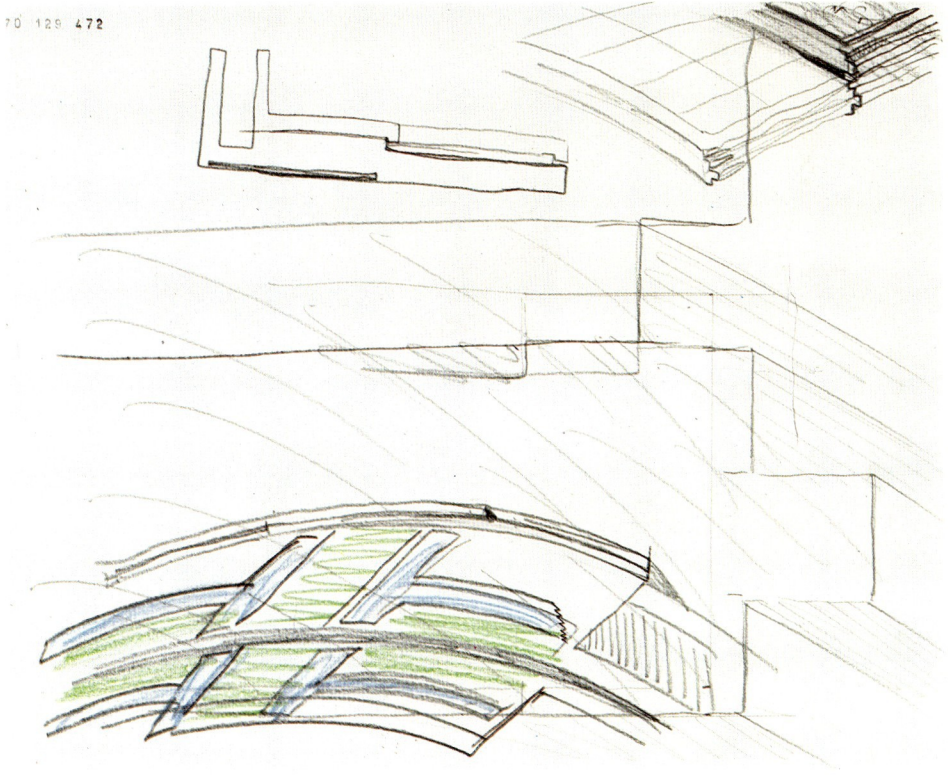

283

170

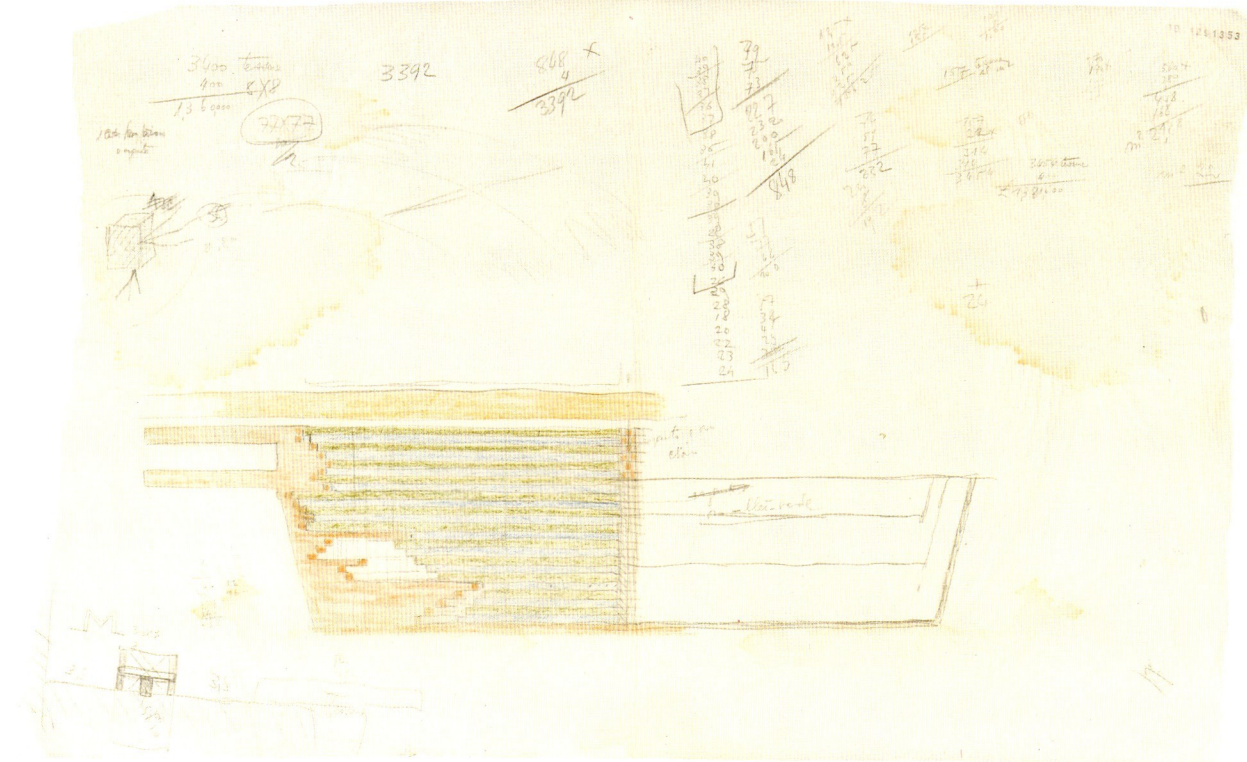

284

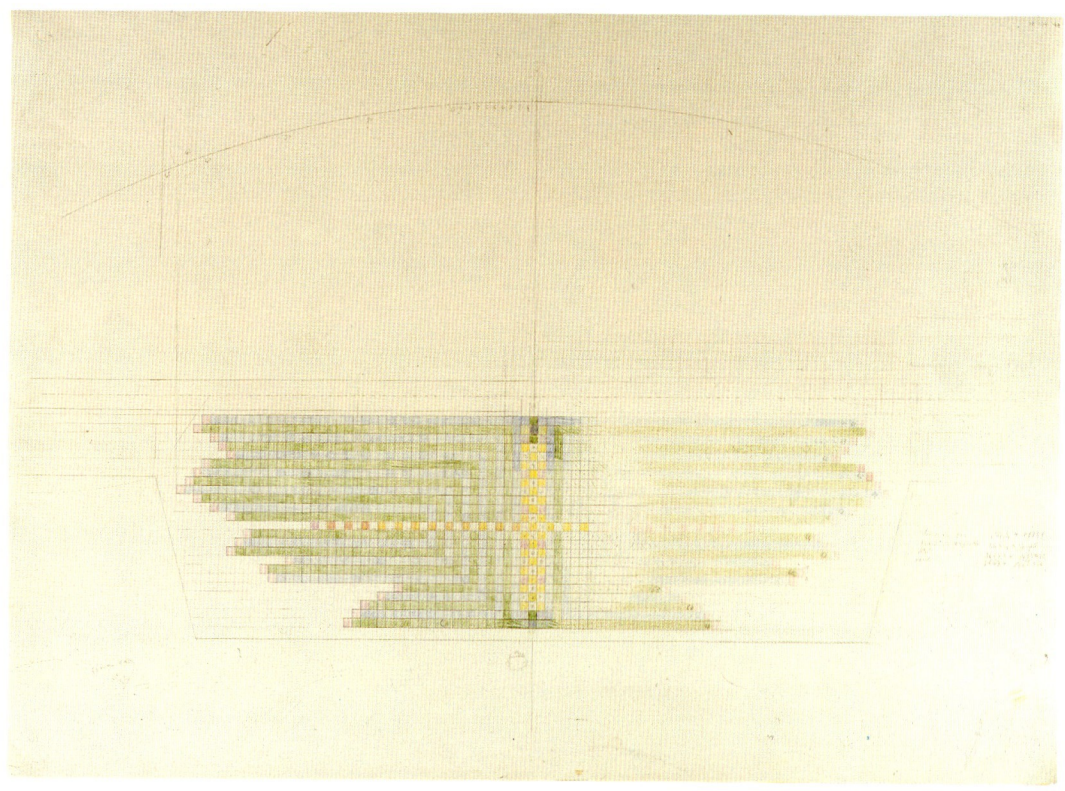

285

Details of the entredos/Details an der Bogenunterseite

286

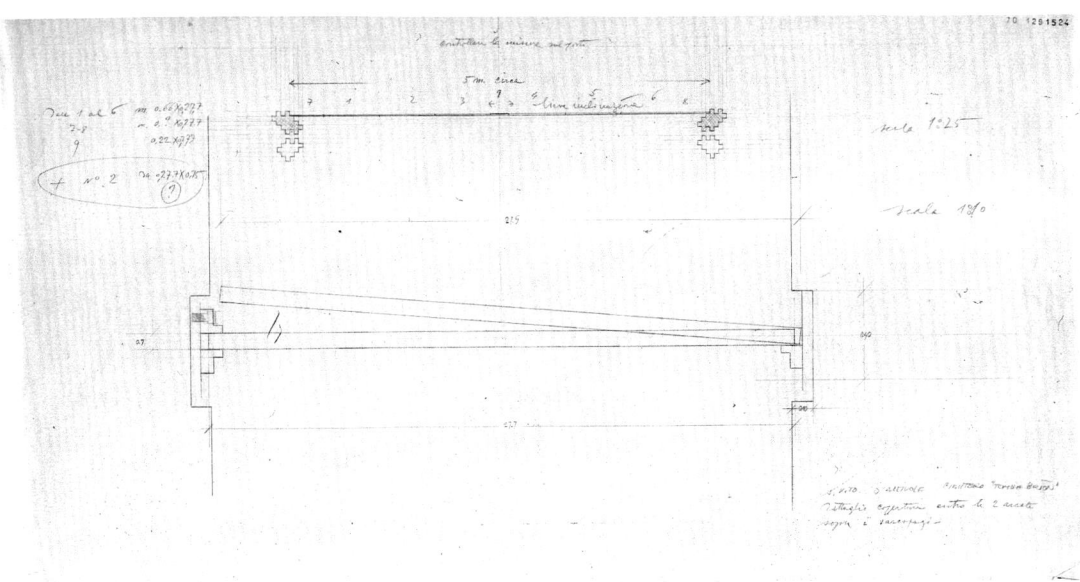

287

Sarcophagi/Sarkophage

172

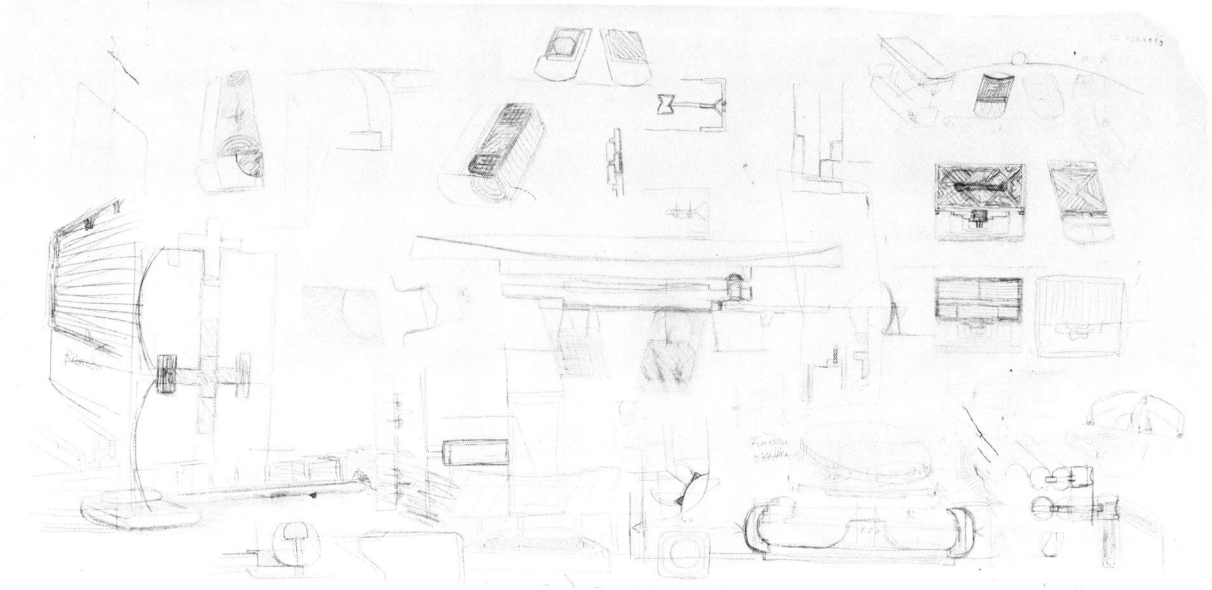

288

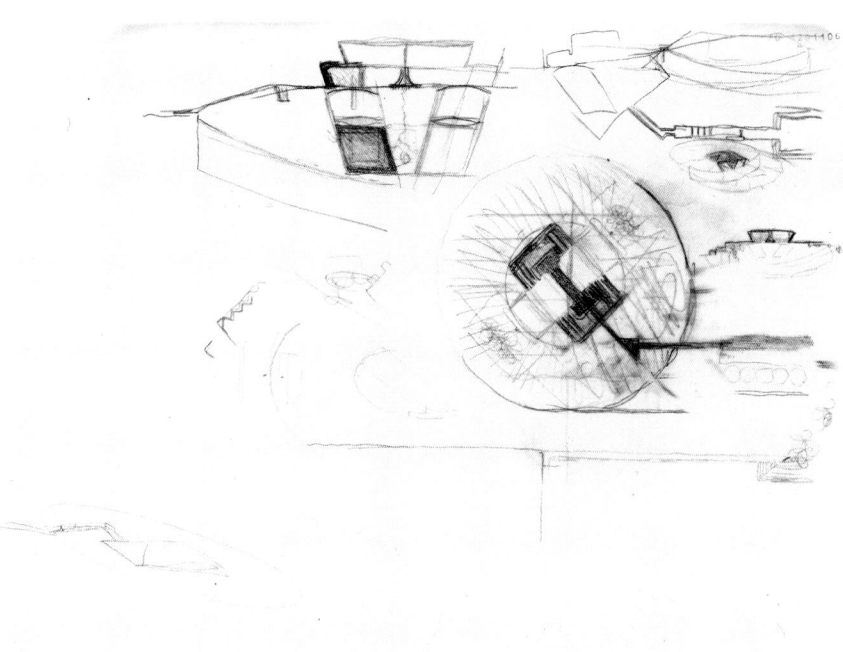

289

174

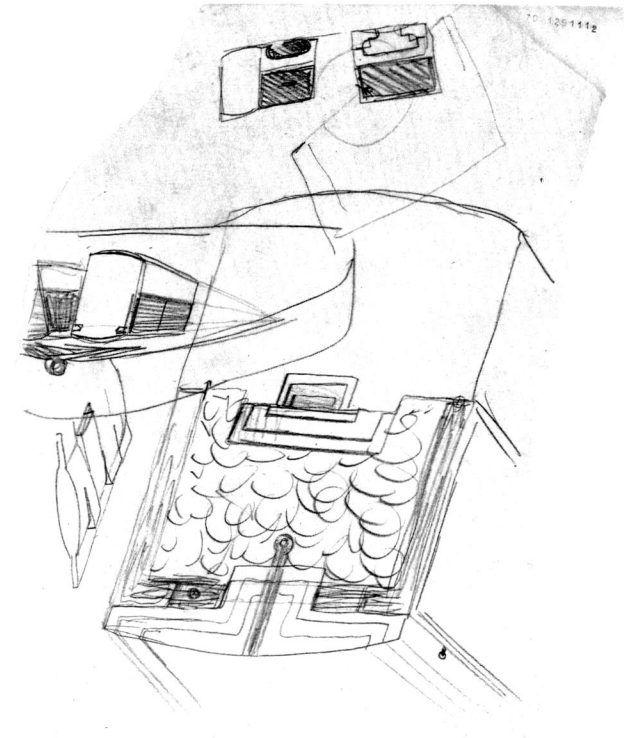

291

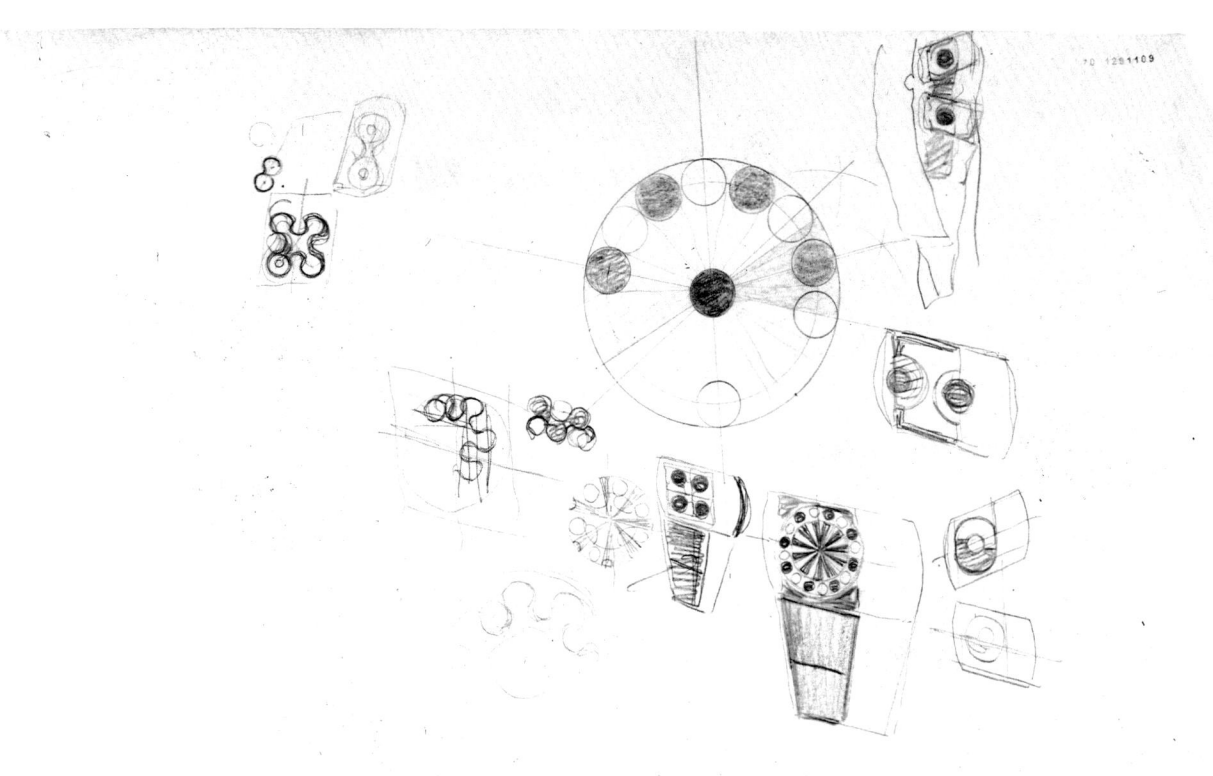

292

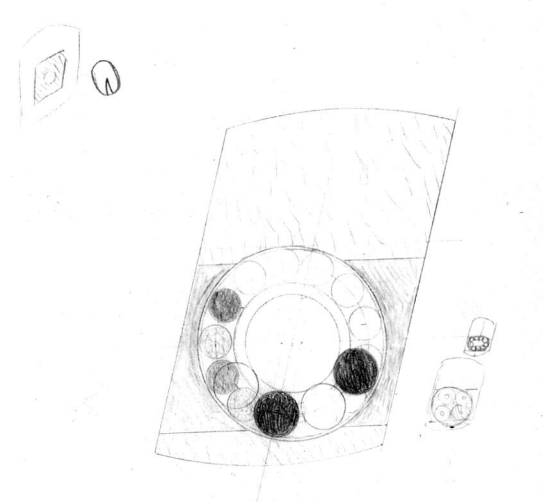

293

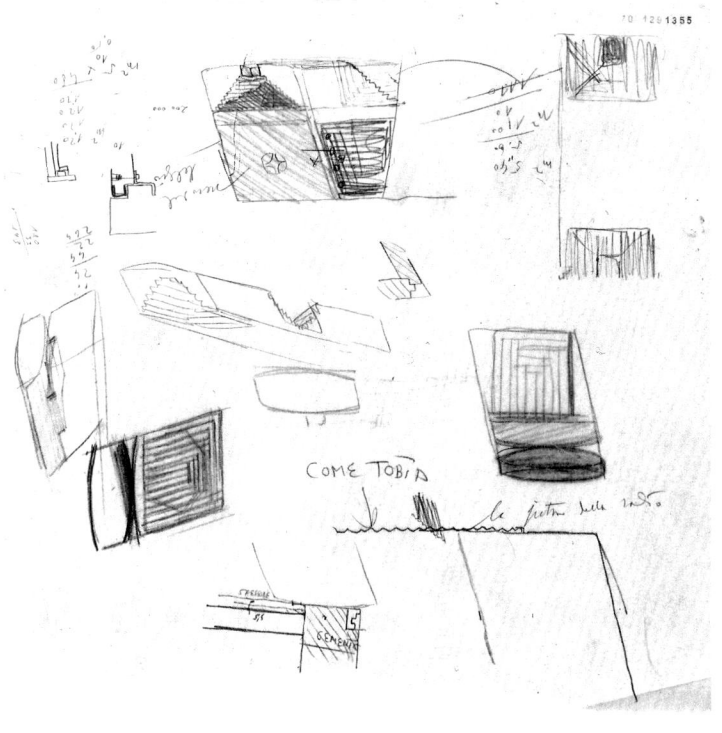

294

295

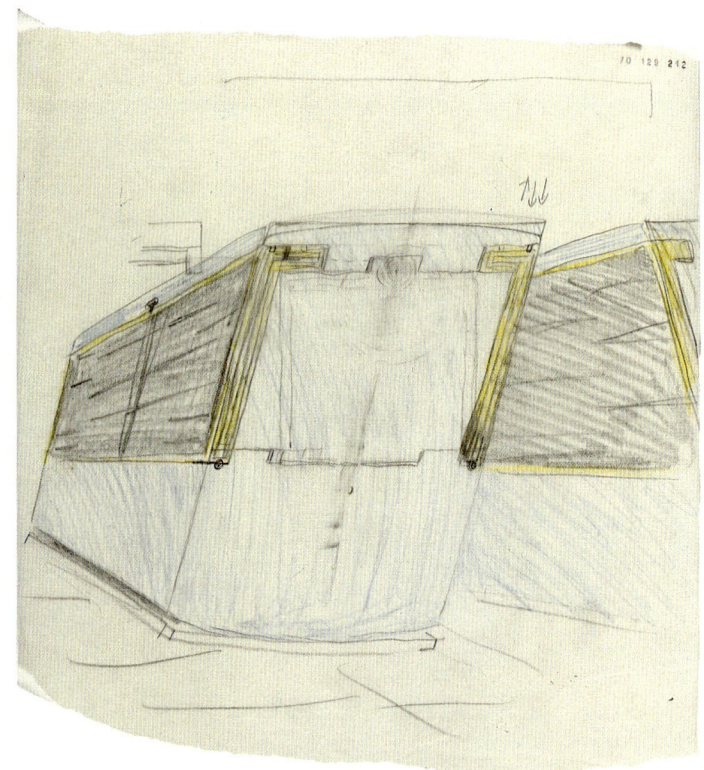

296

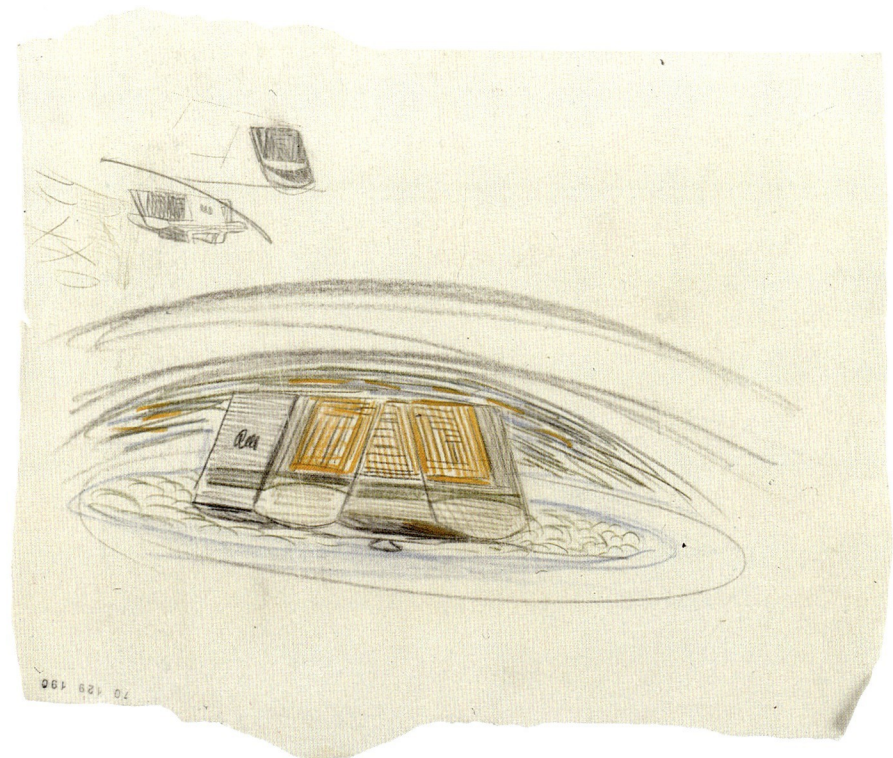

177

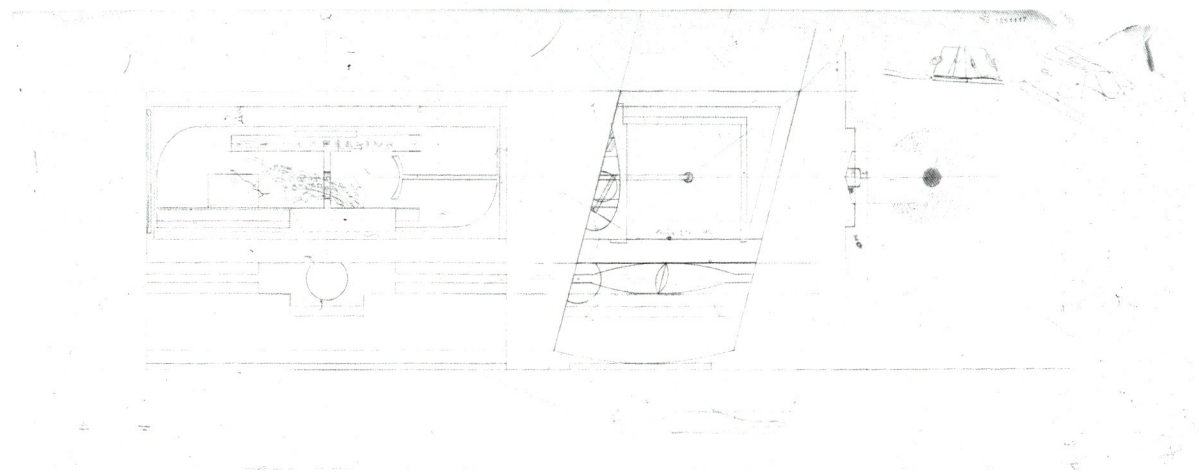

297

298

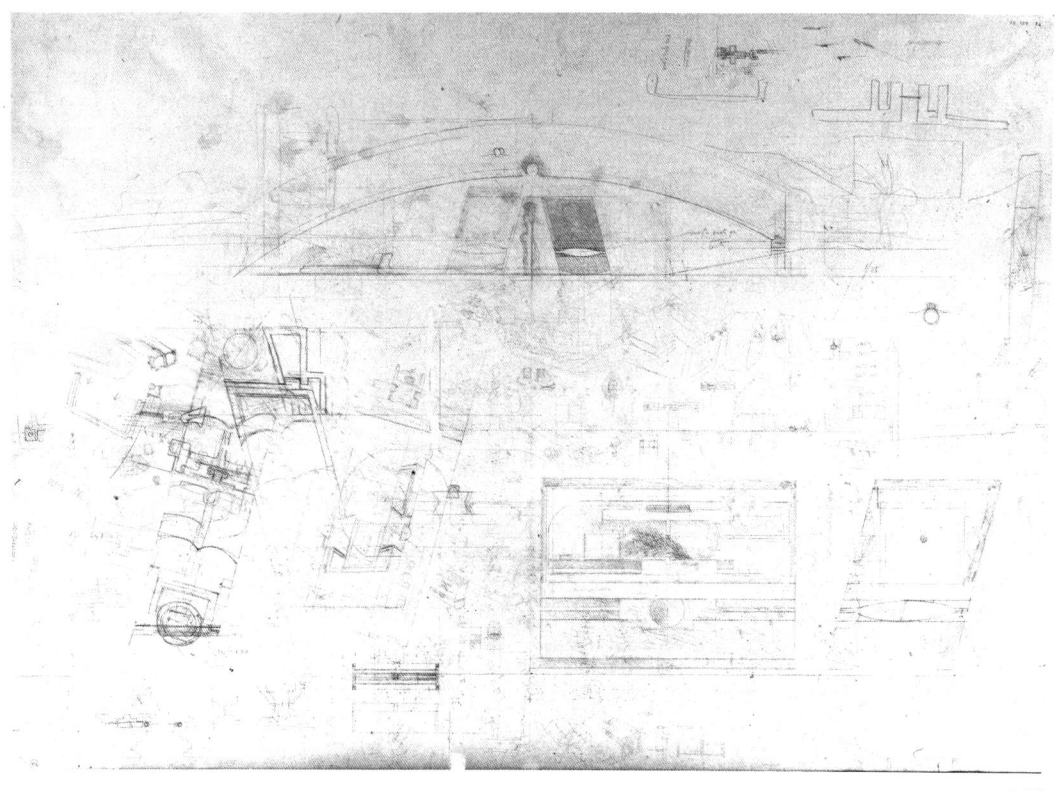

299

300

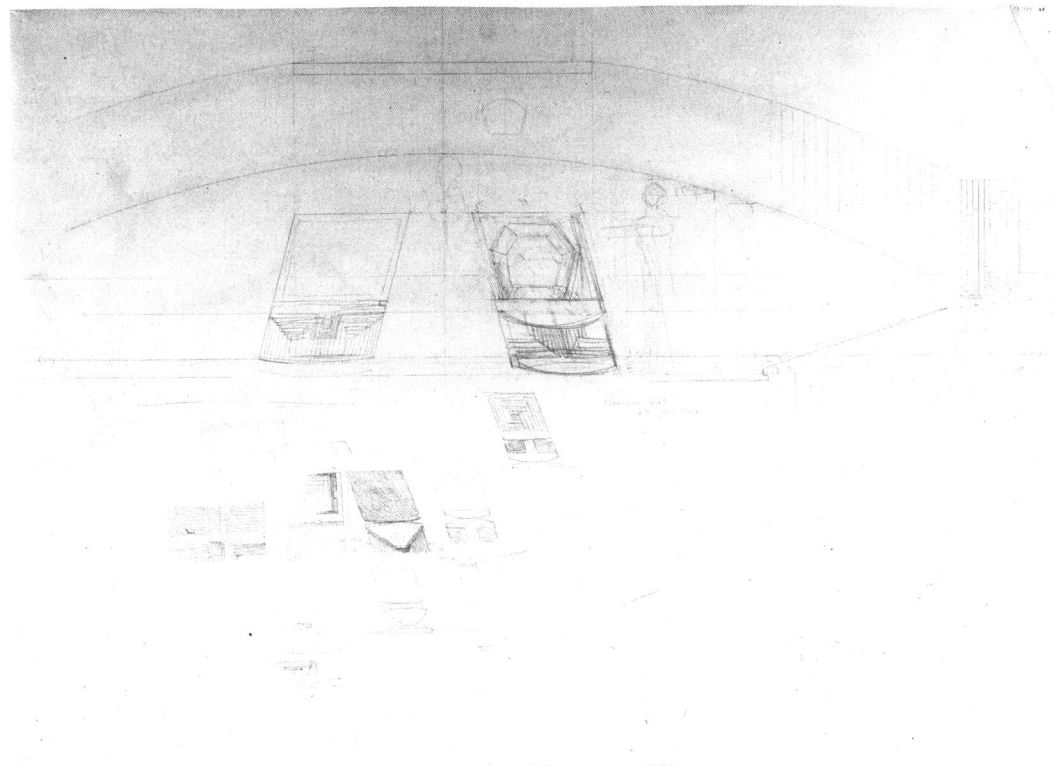

301

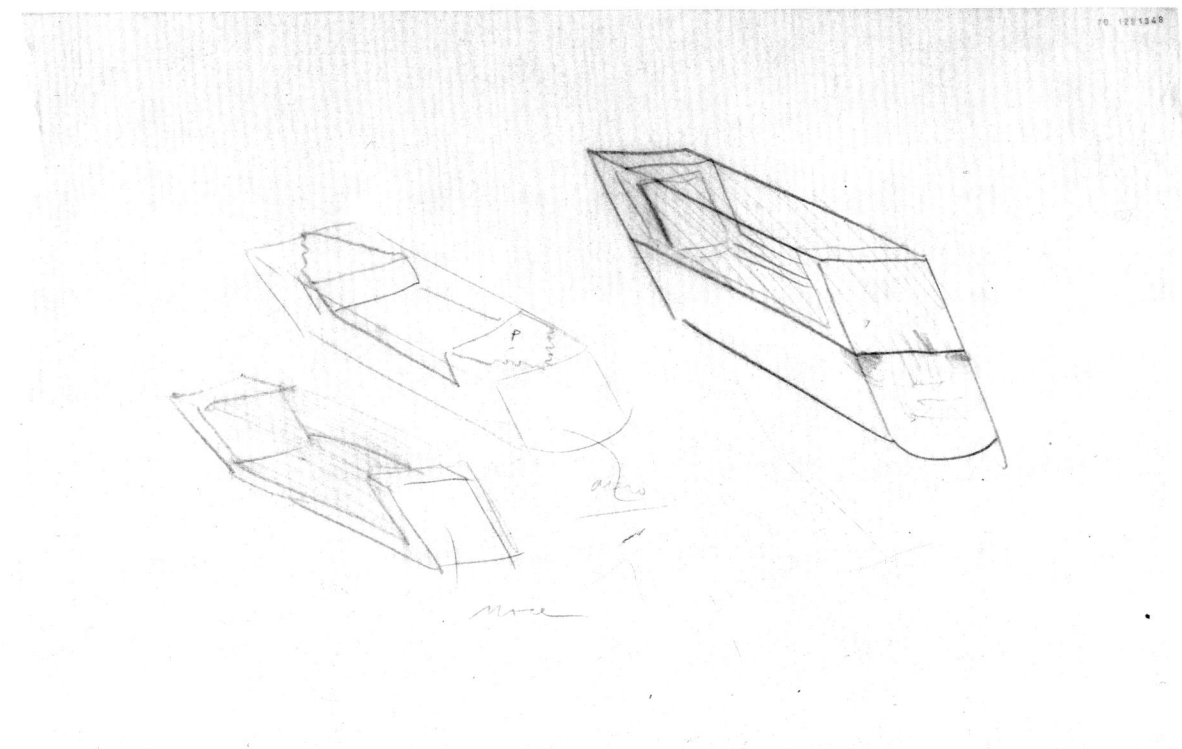

302

180

303

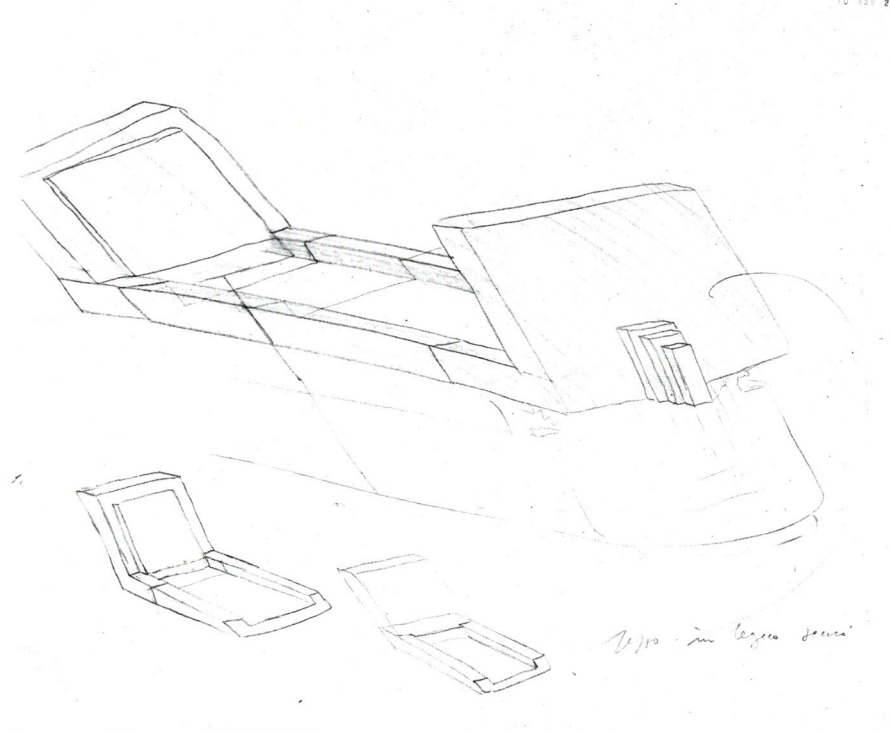

304

181

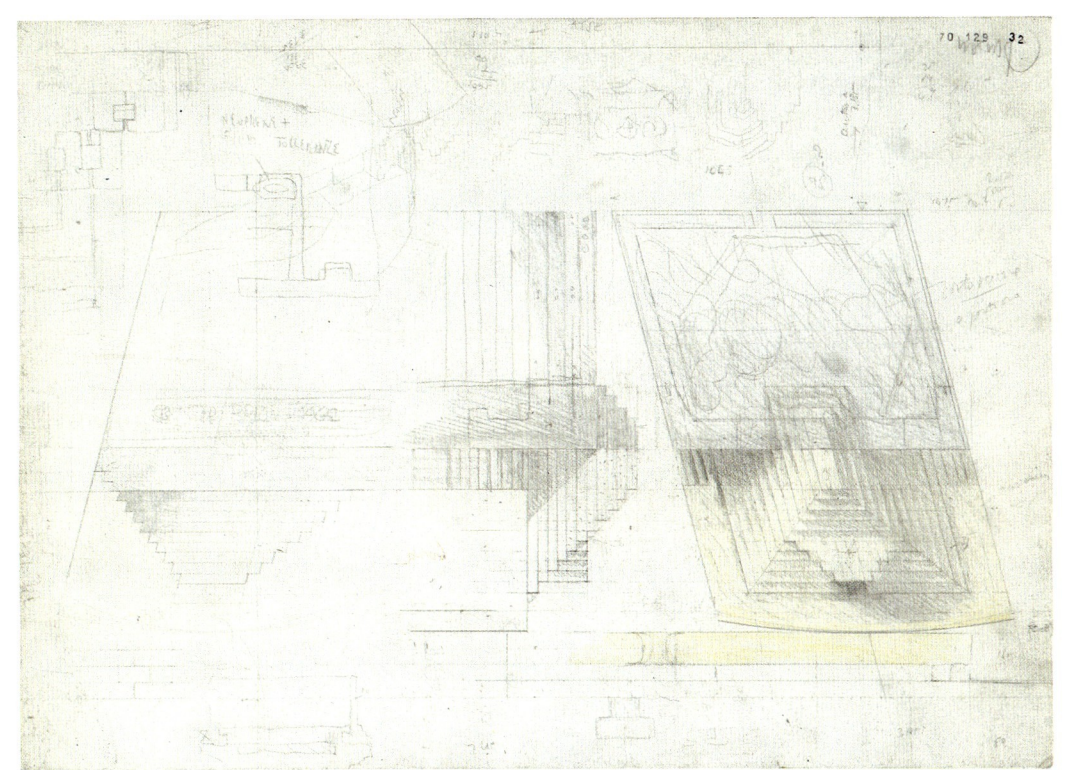

305

306

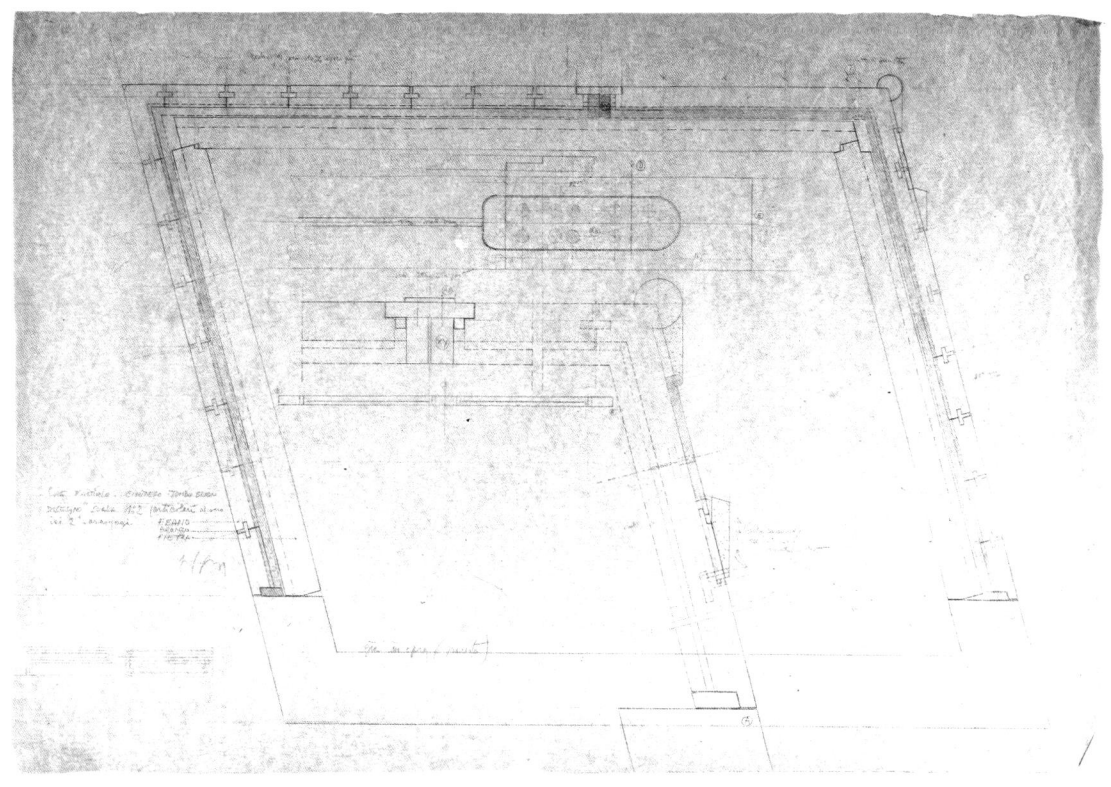

Inscription: ivory-inlaid ebony/Inschrift: Ebenholz mit Elfenbeinintarsie

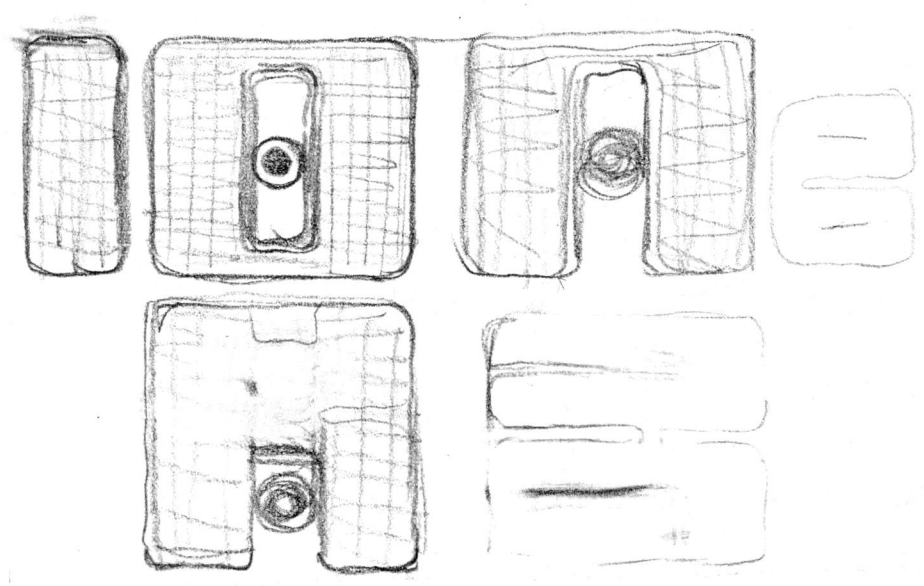

309

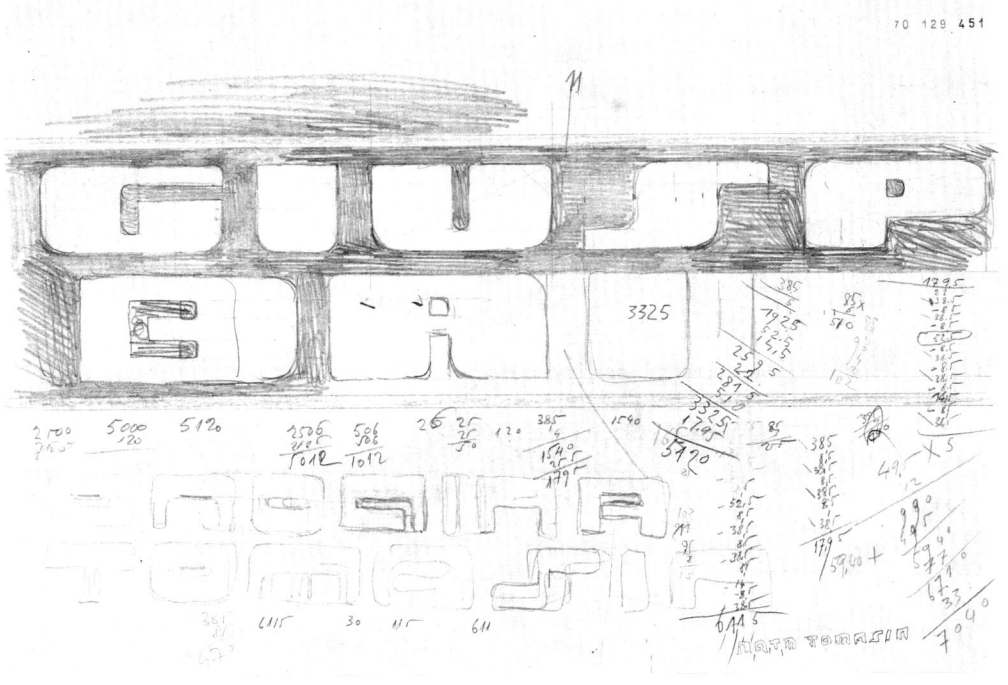

310

184

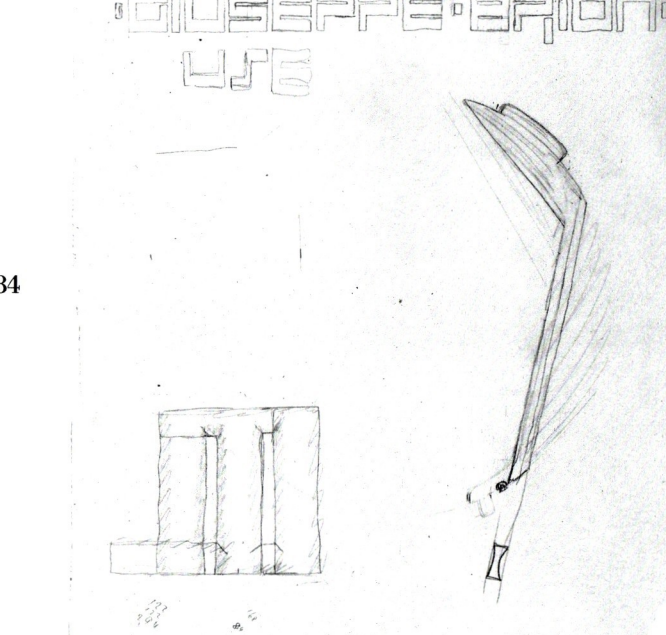

311

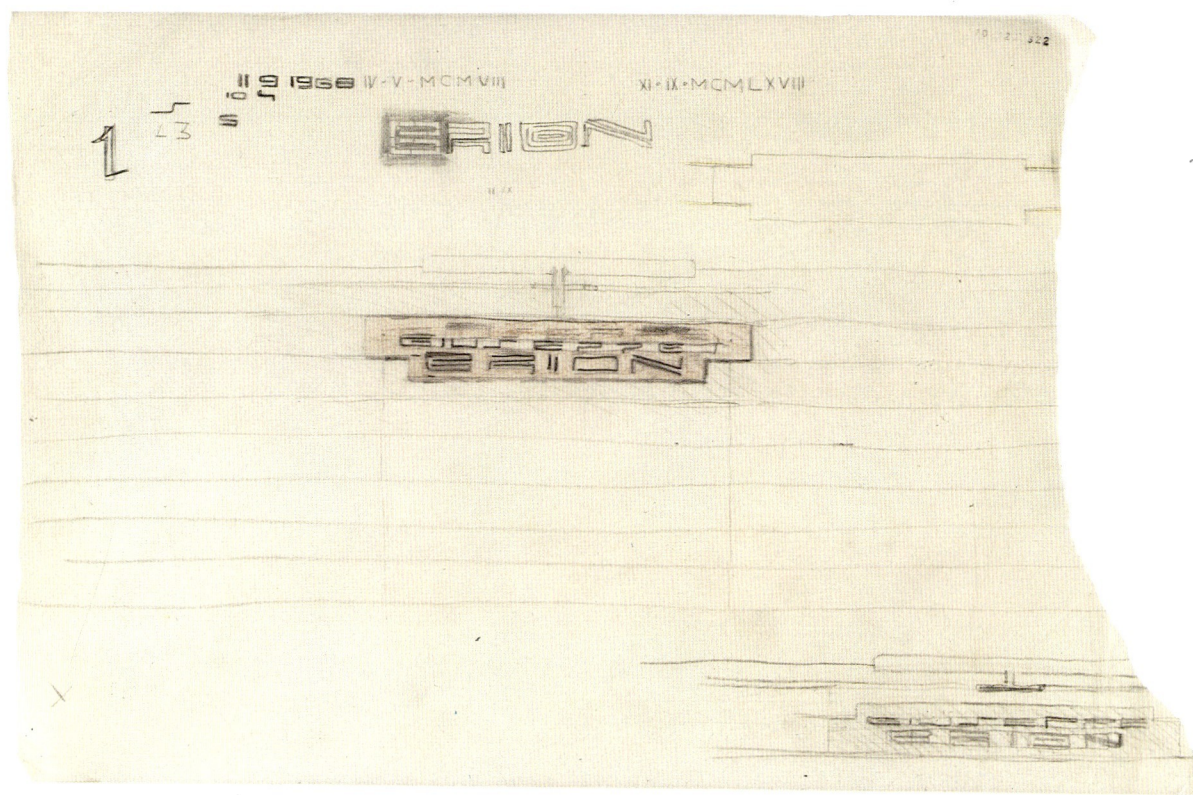

312

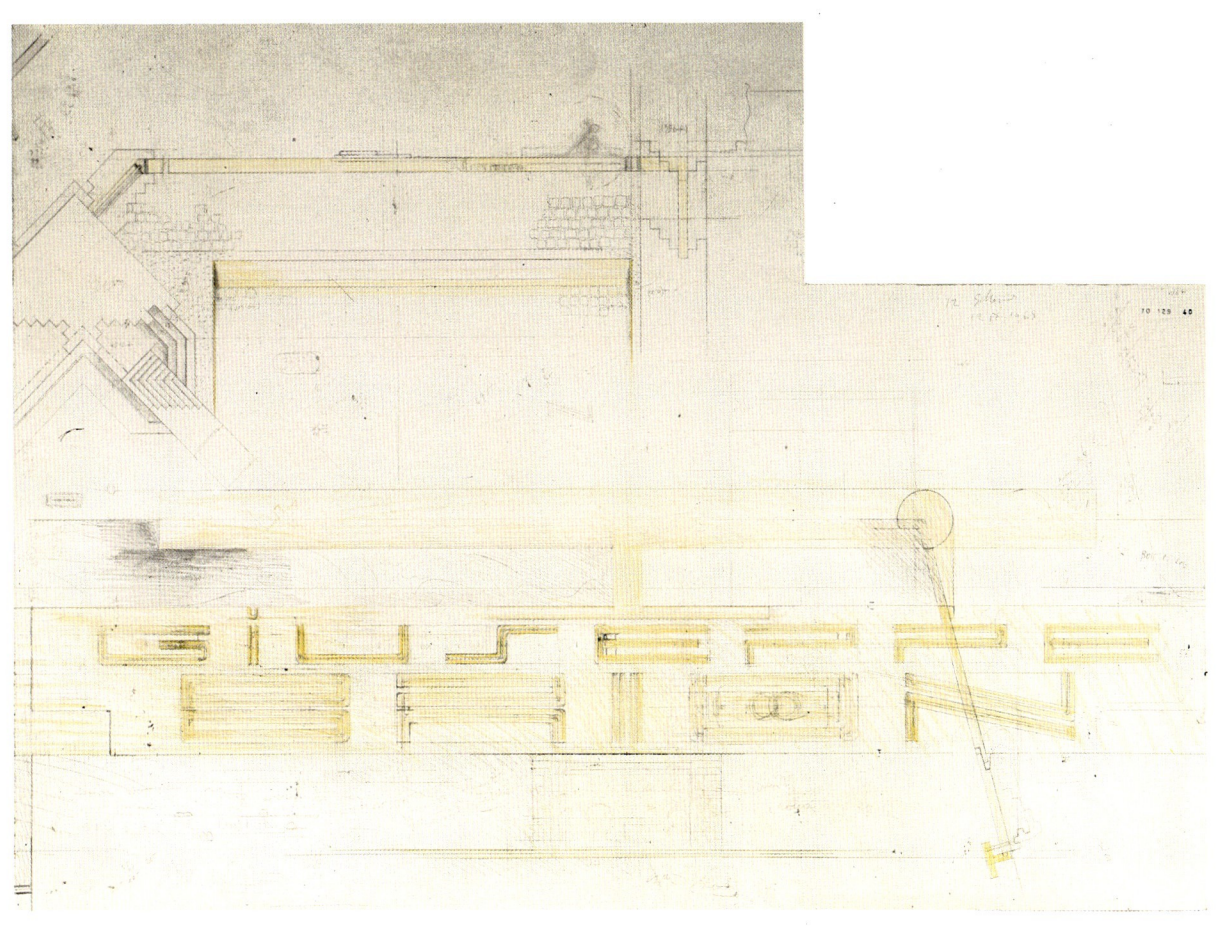

185

313

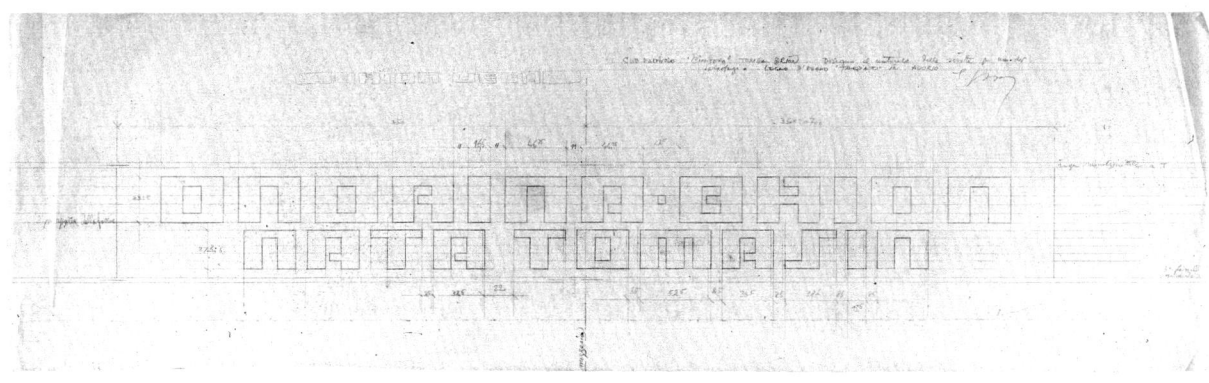

Floor: circular fascia/Fußboden: kreisrunde Einfassung

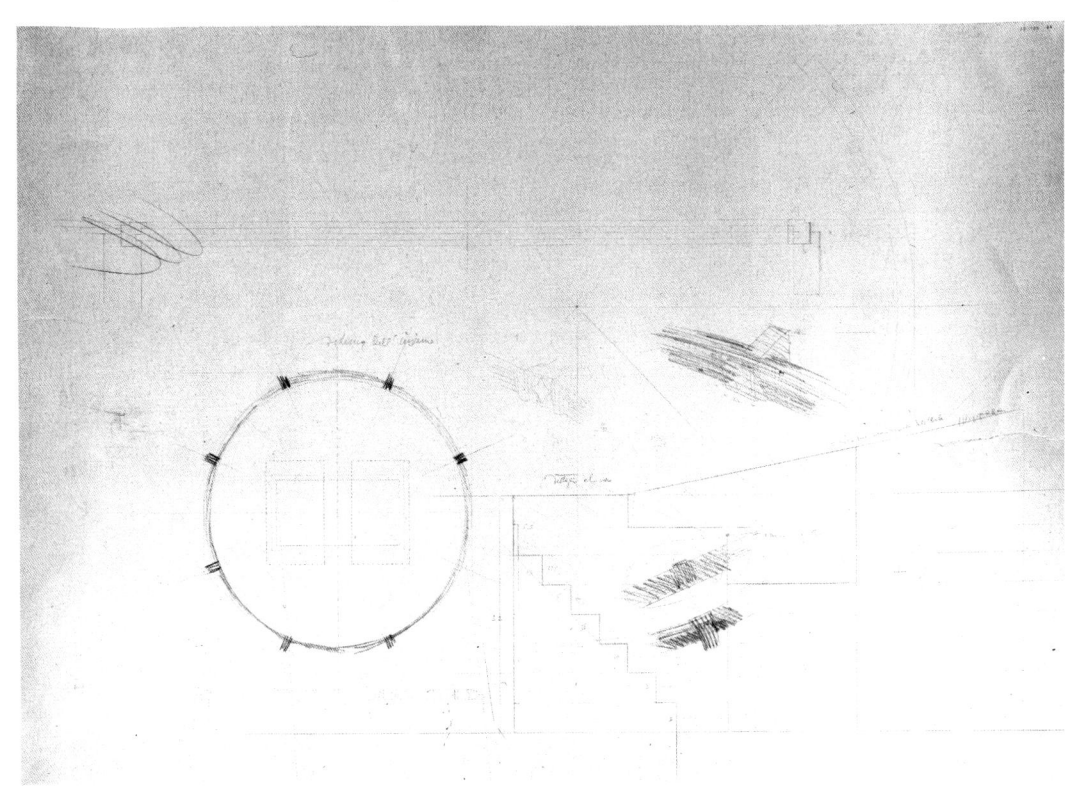

316

317

188

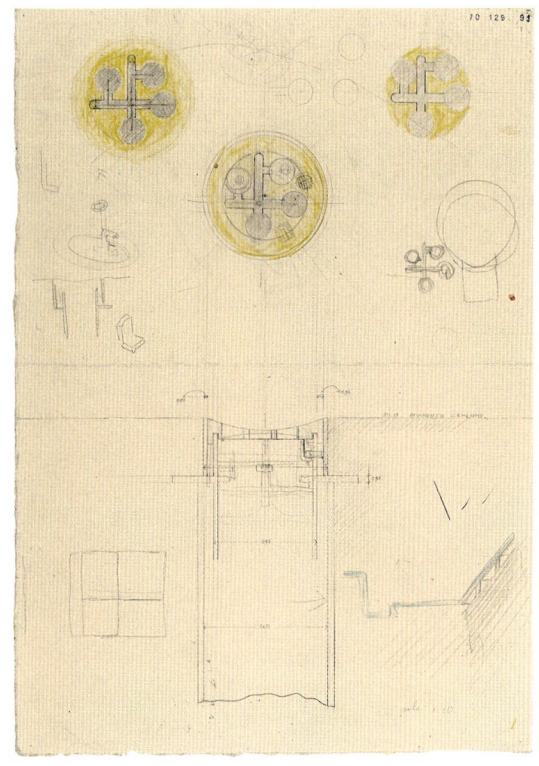

318

Sundial and waterway/Sonnenuhr und Wasserquelle

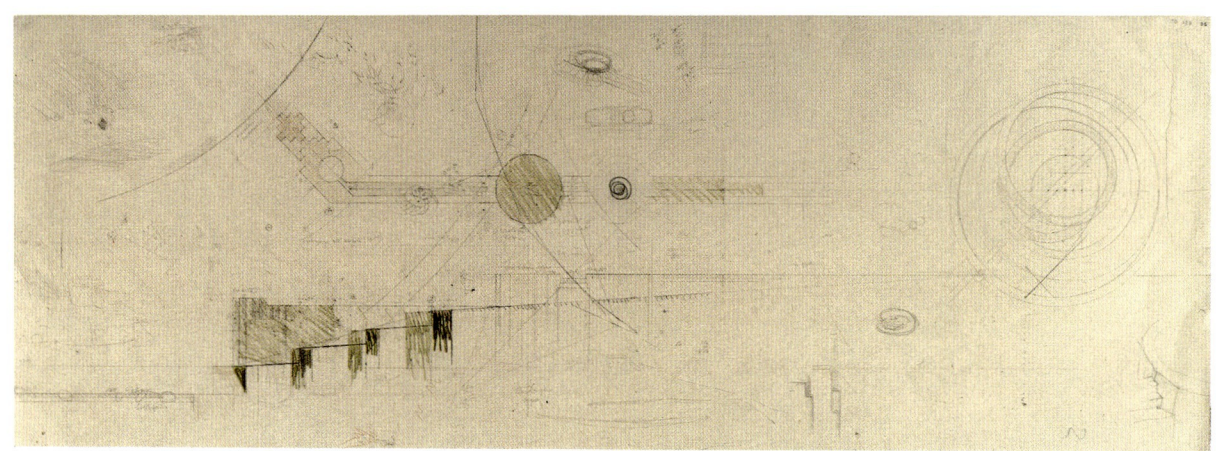

319

CHAPEL/DIE KAPELLE

Plans, Floorplans/Pläne, Grundrisse

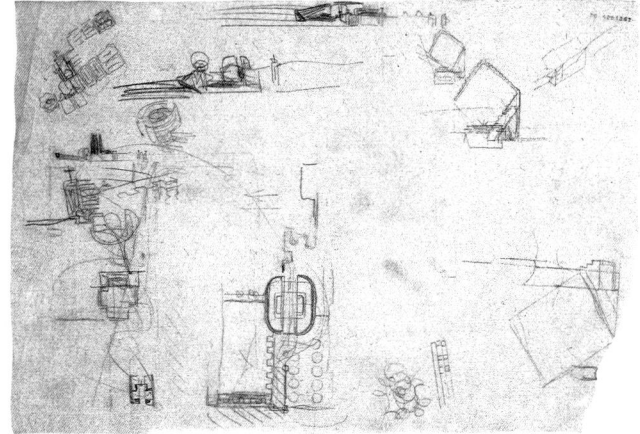

320

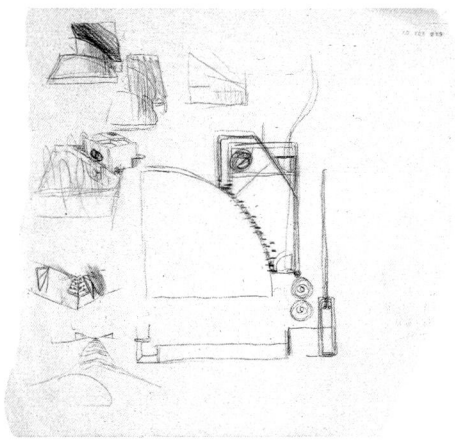

321

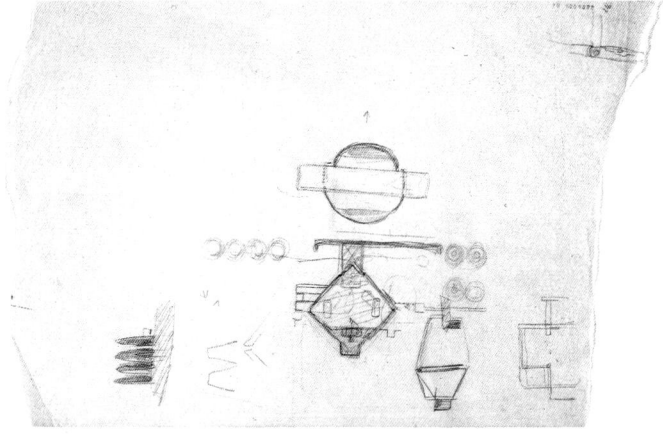

322

191

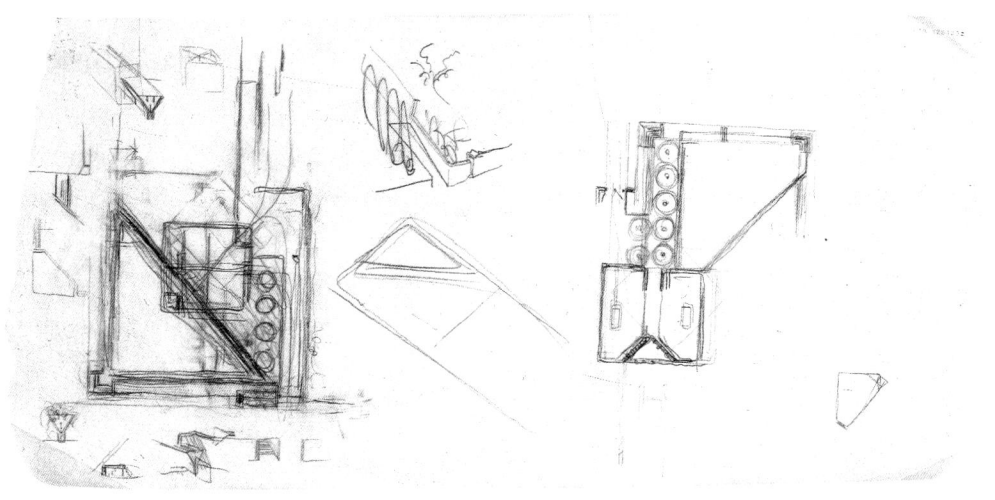

323

324

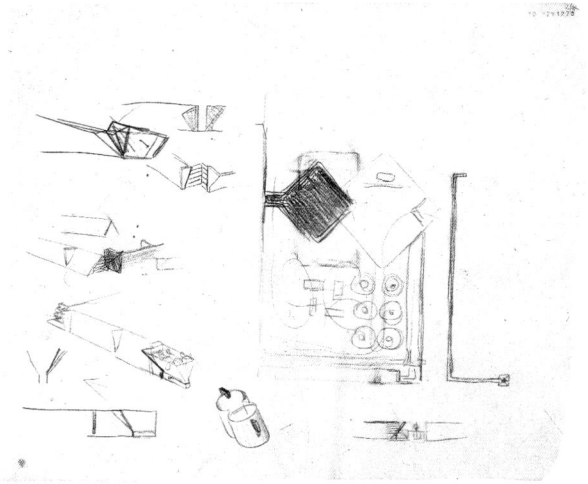

325

192

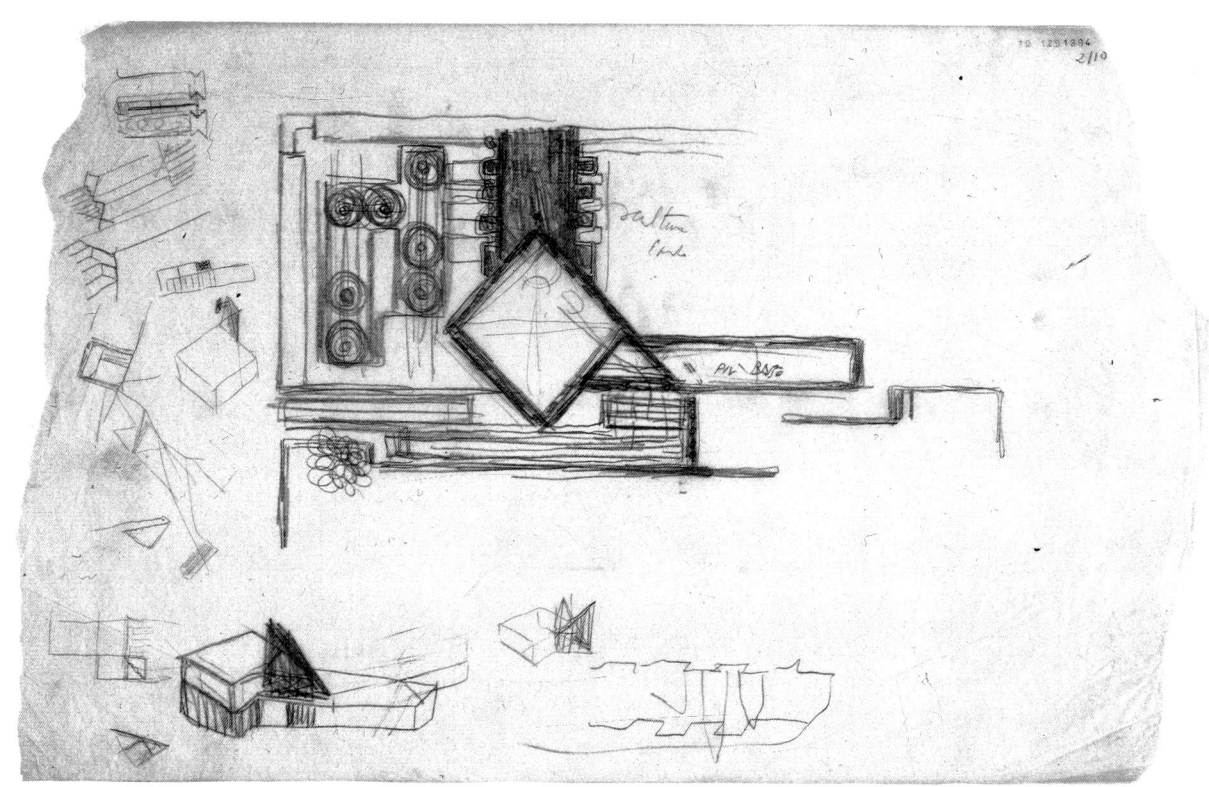

326

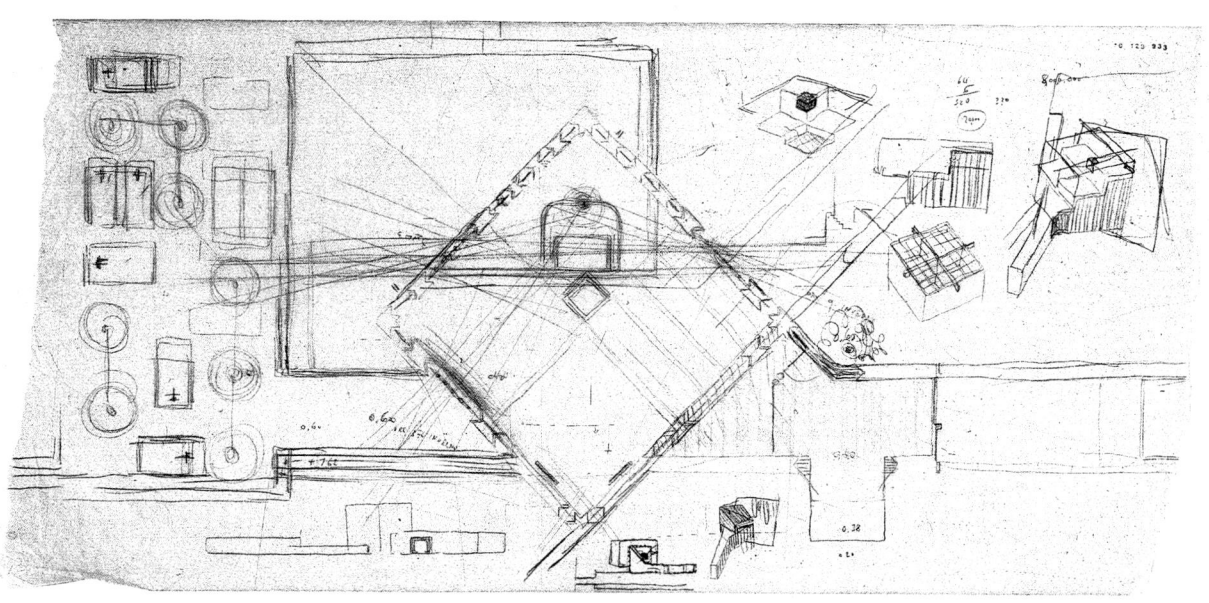

327

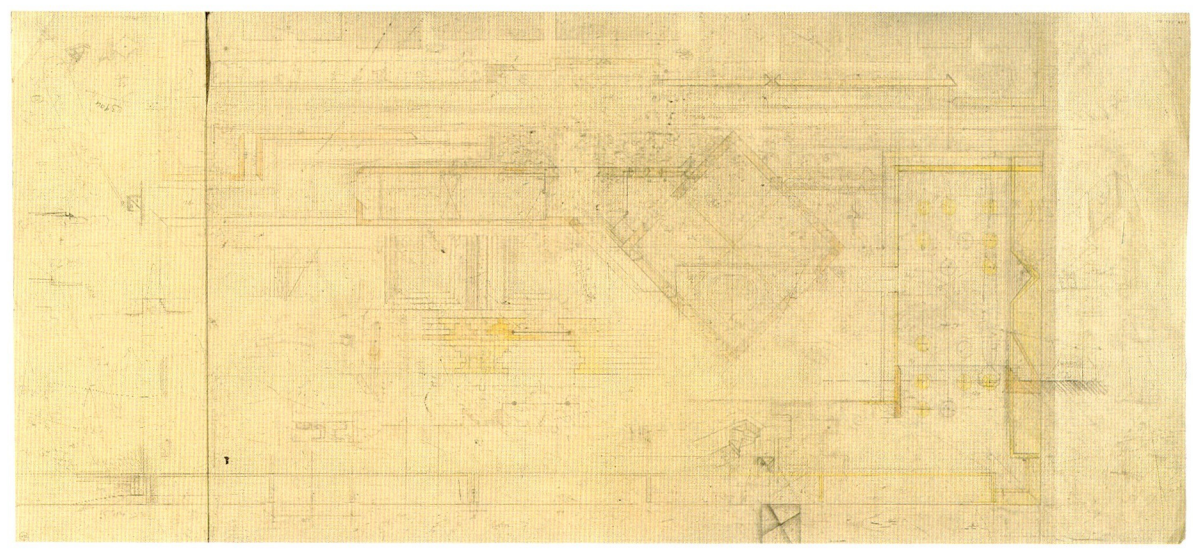

328

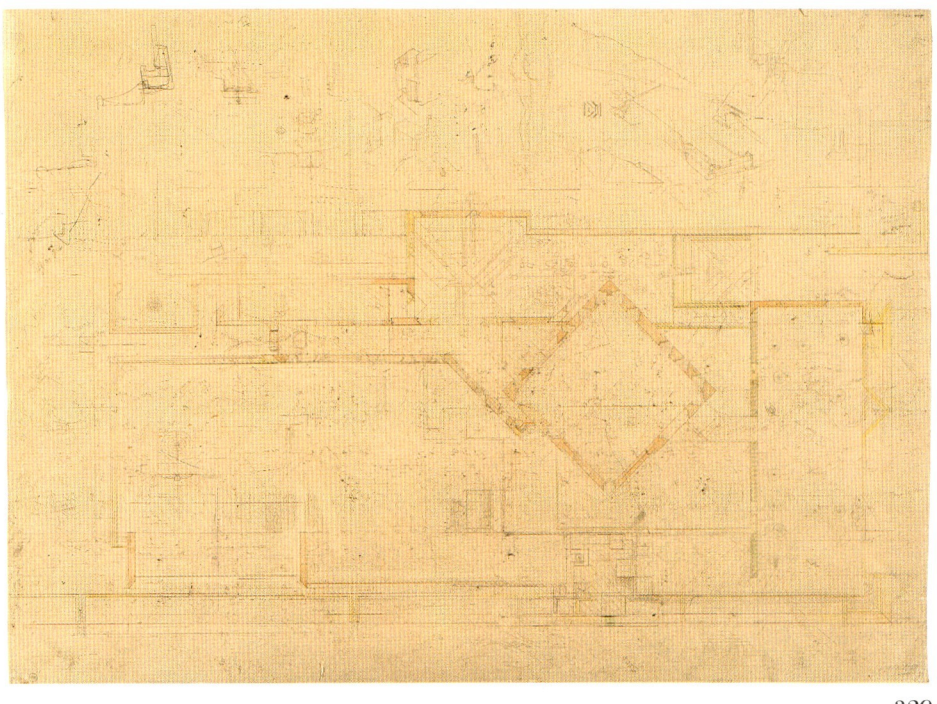

329

Views/Ansichten
Northeast/Nordseite

194

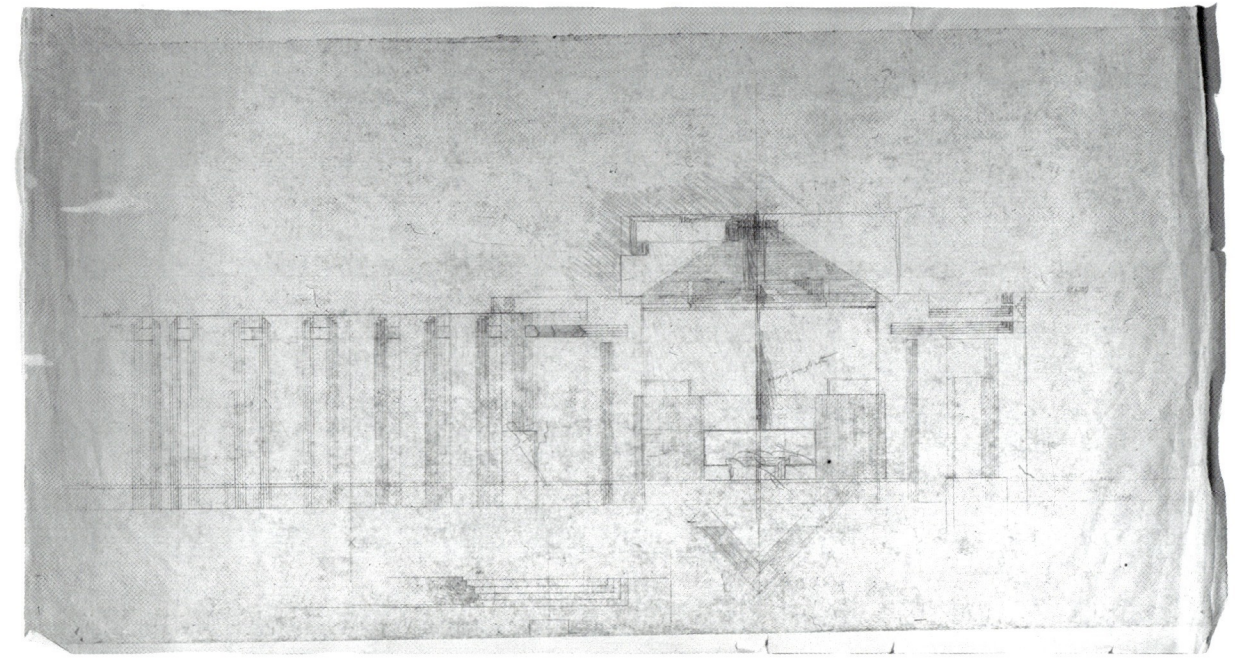

330

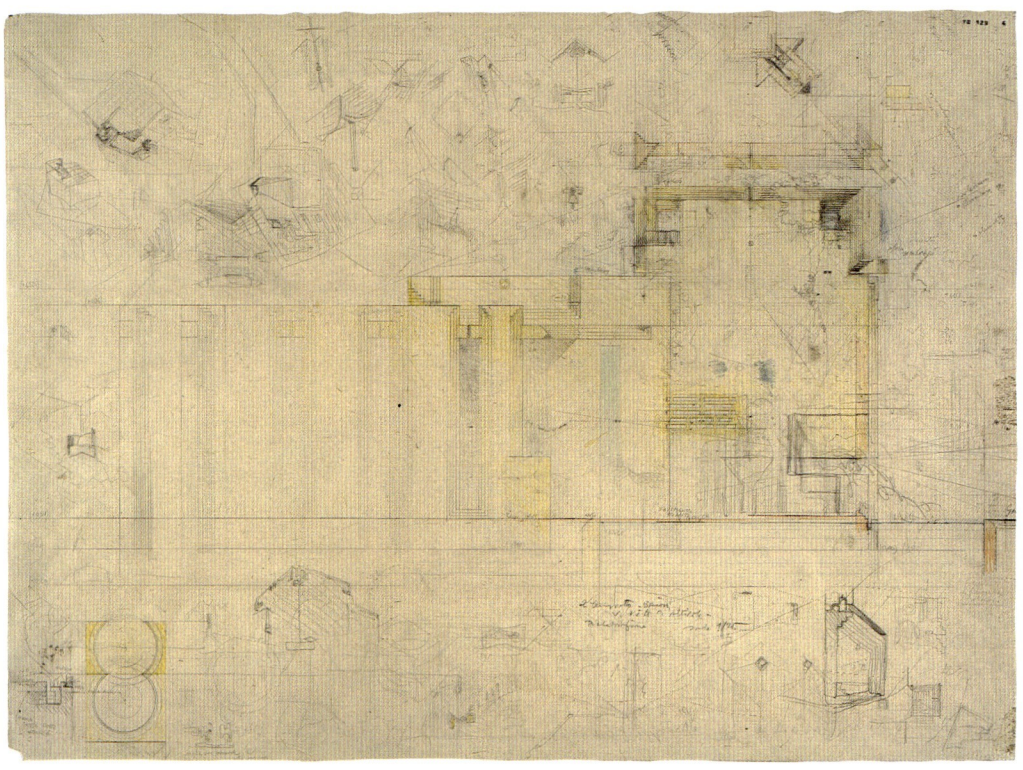

331

332

333

Northwest/Nordwestseite

334

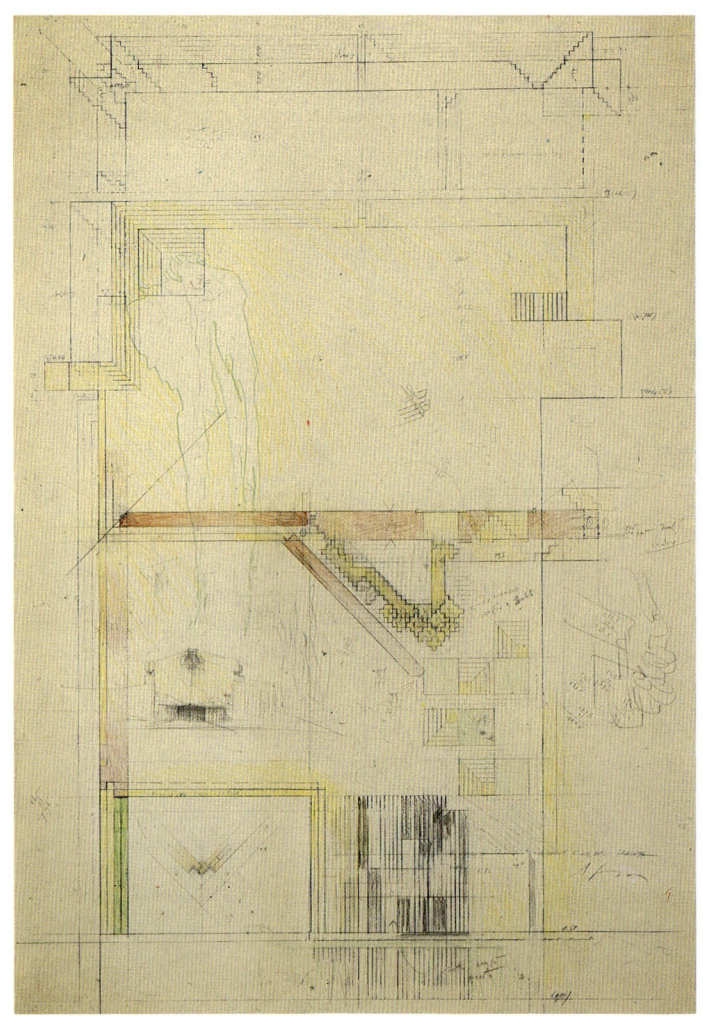

335

336

Sections/Schnitte

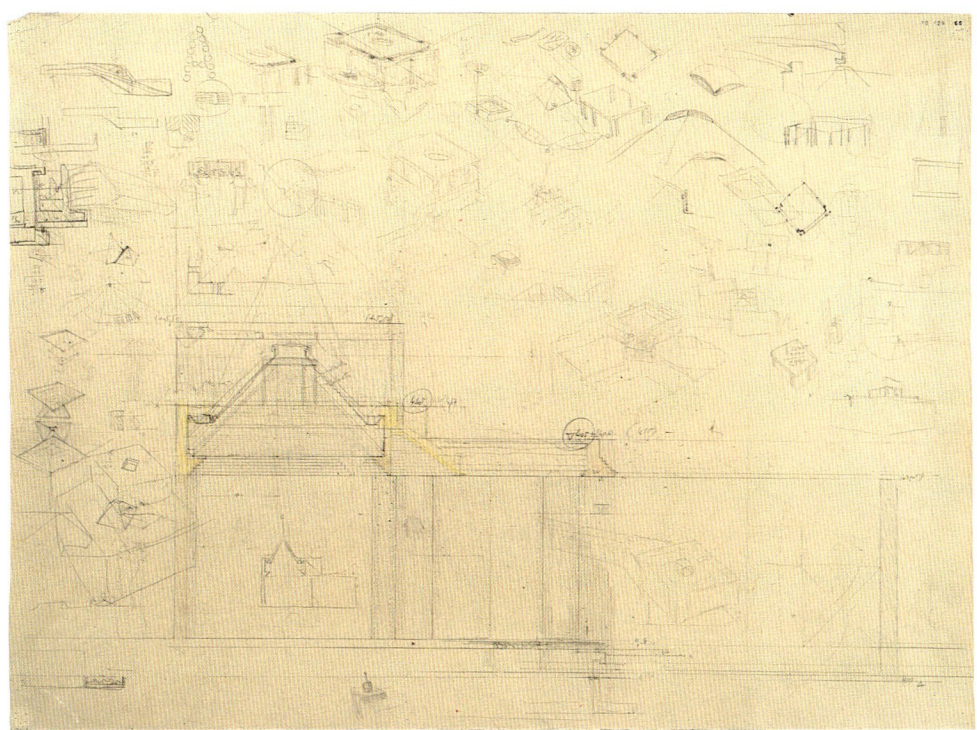

197

337

338

339

Cupola/Kuppel

340

341

342

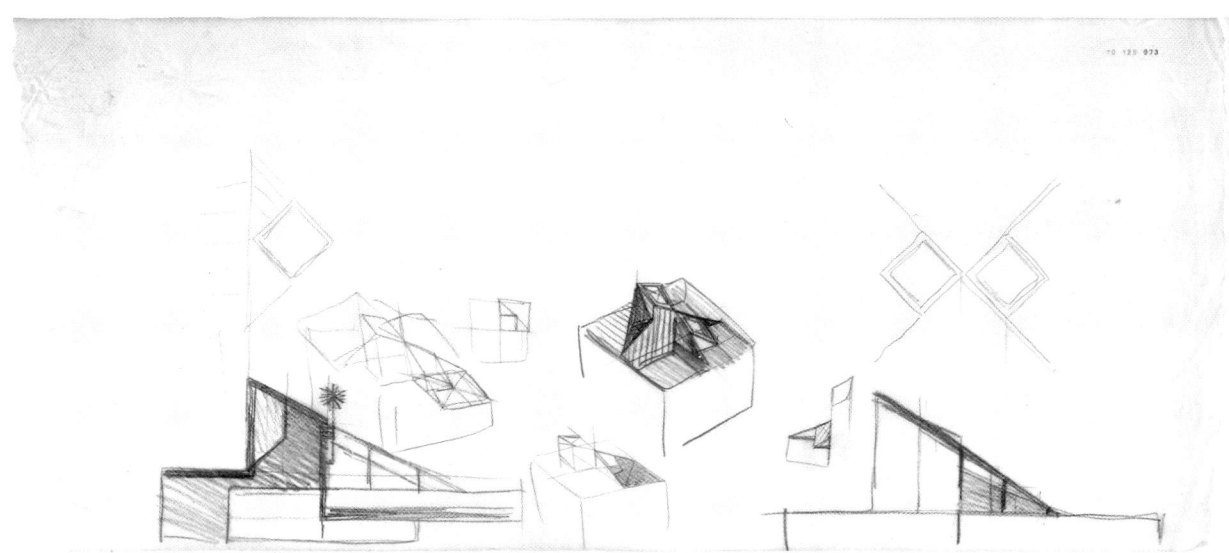

343

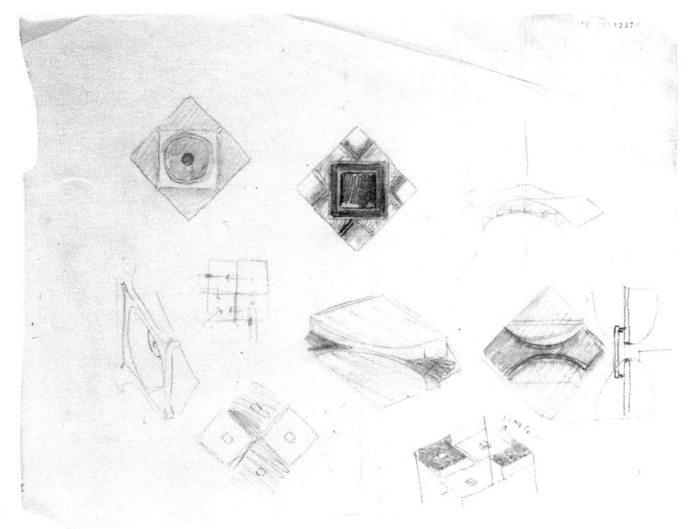

344

345

346

347

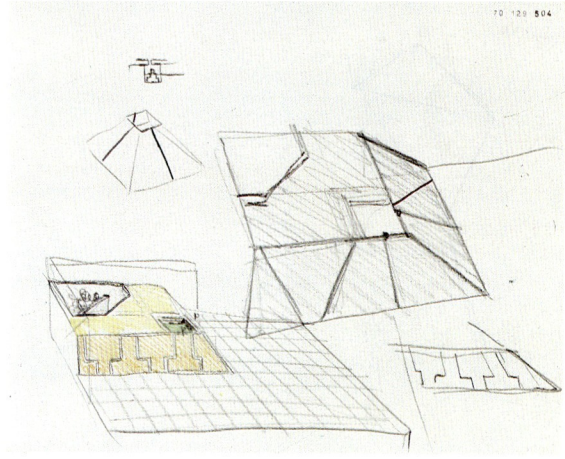

348

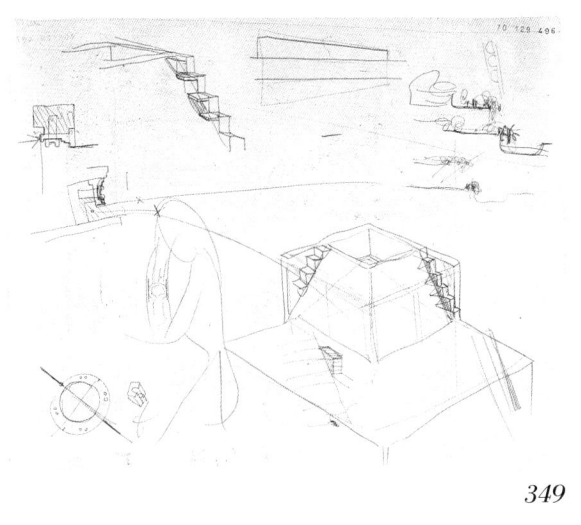

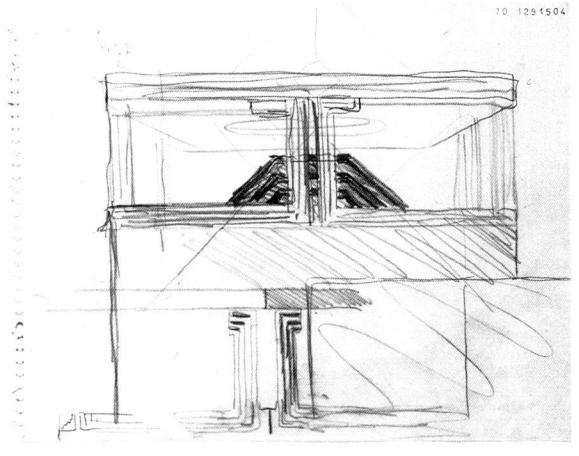

349

350

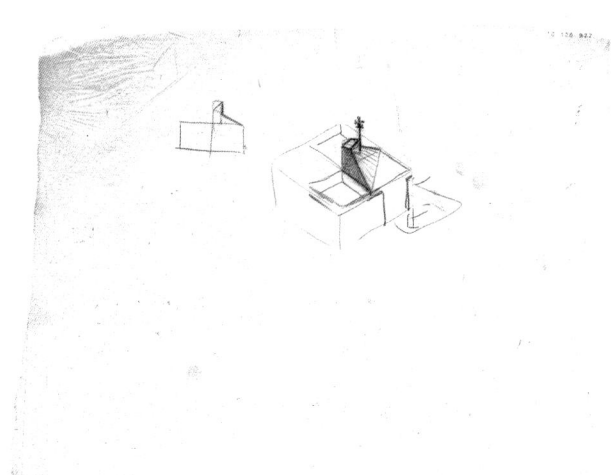

351

352

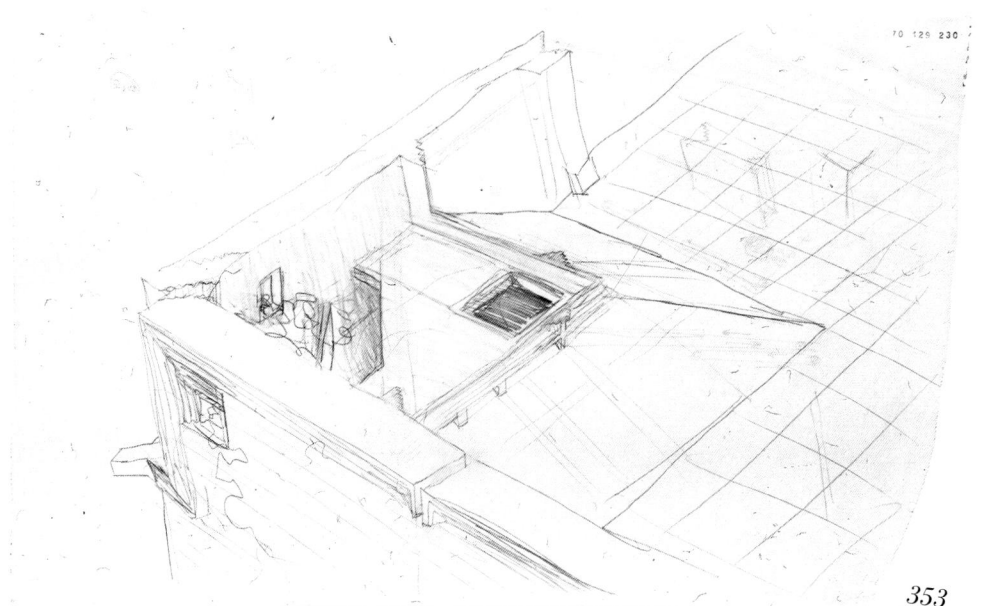

353

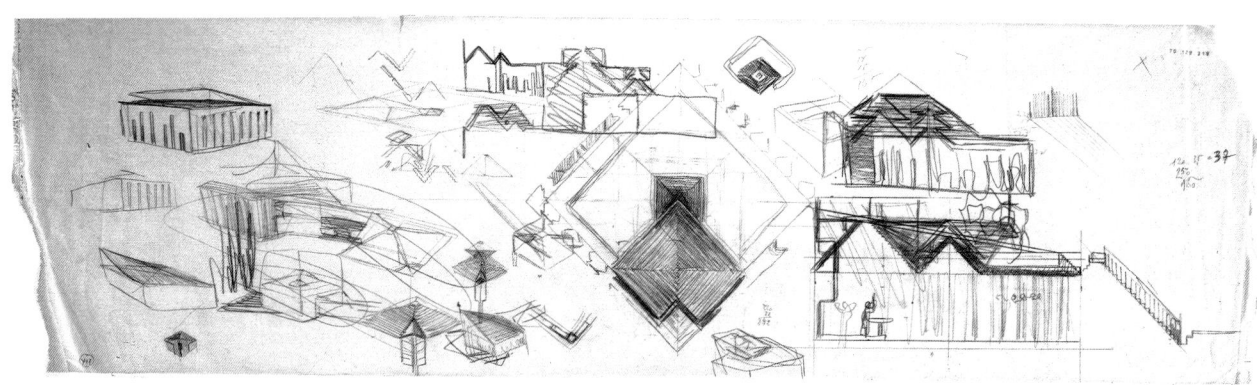

354

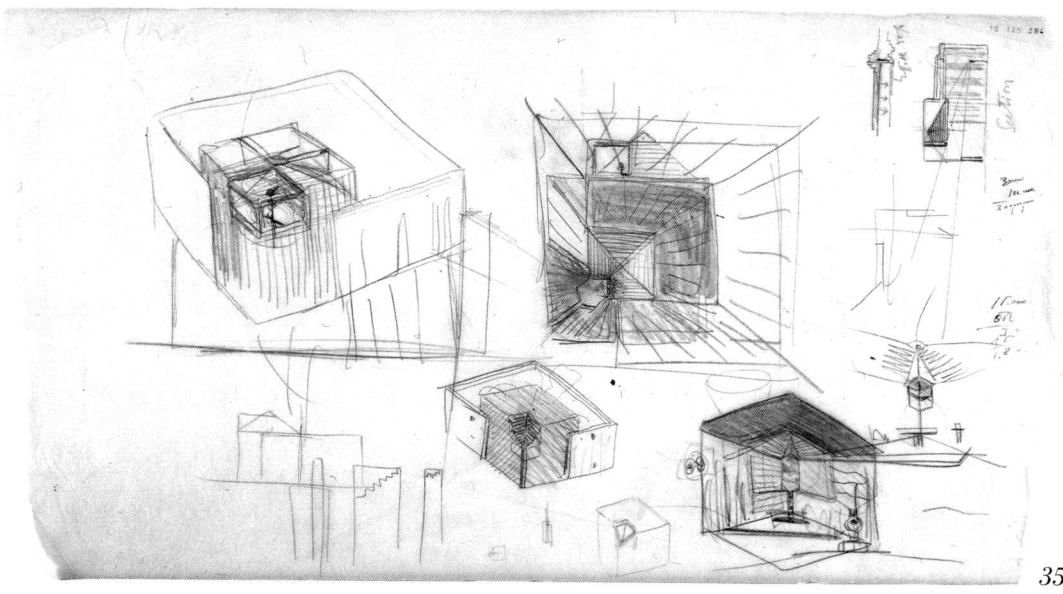

355

356

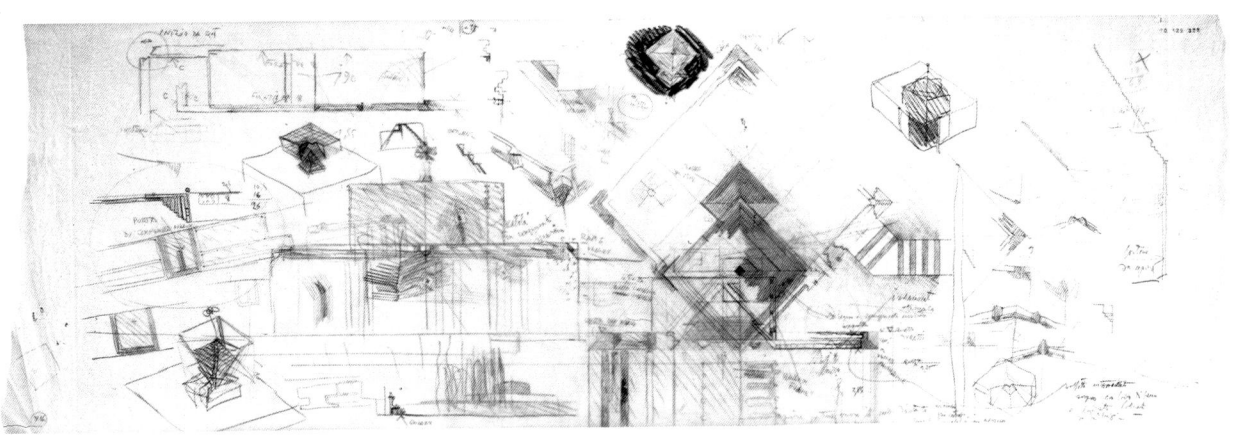

357

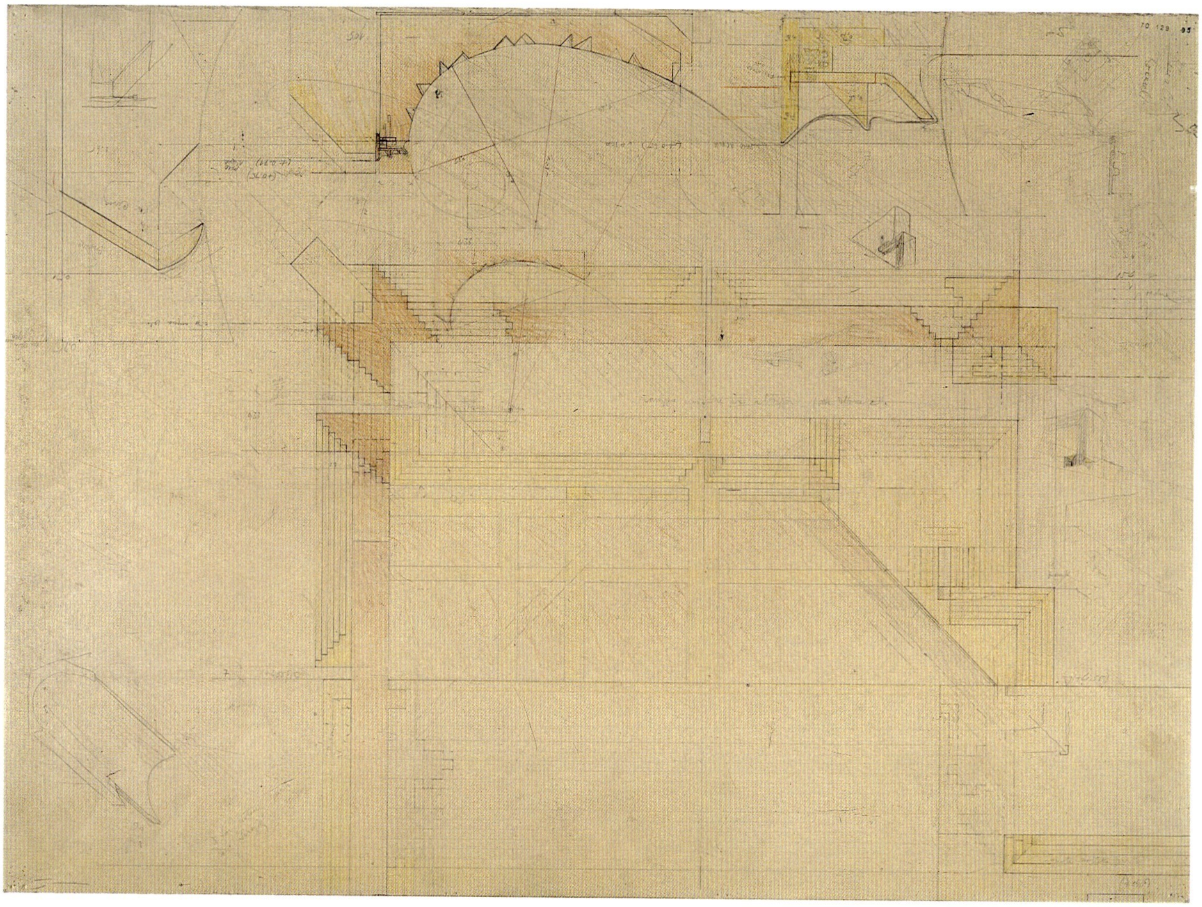

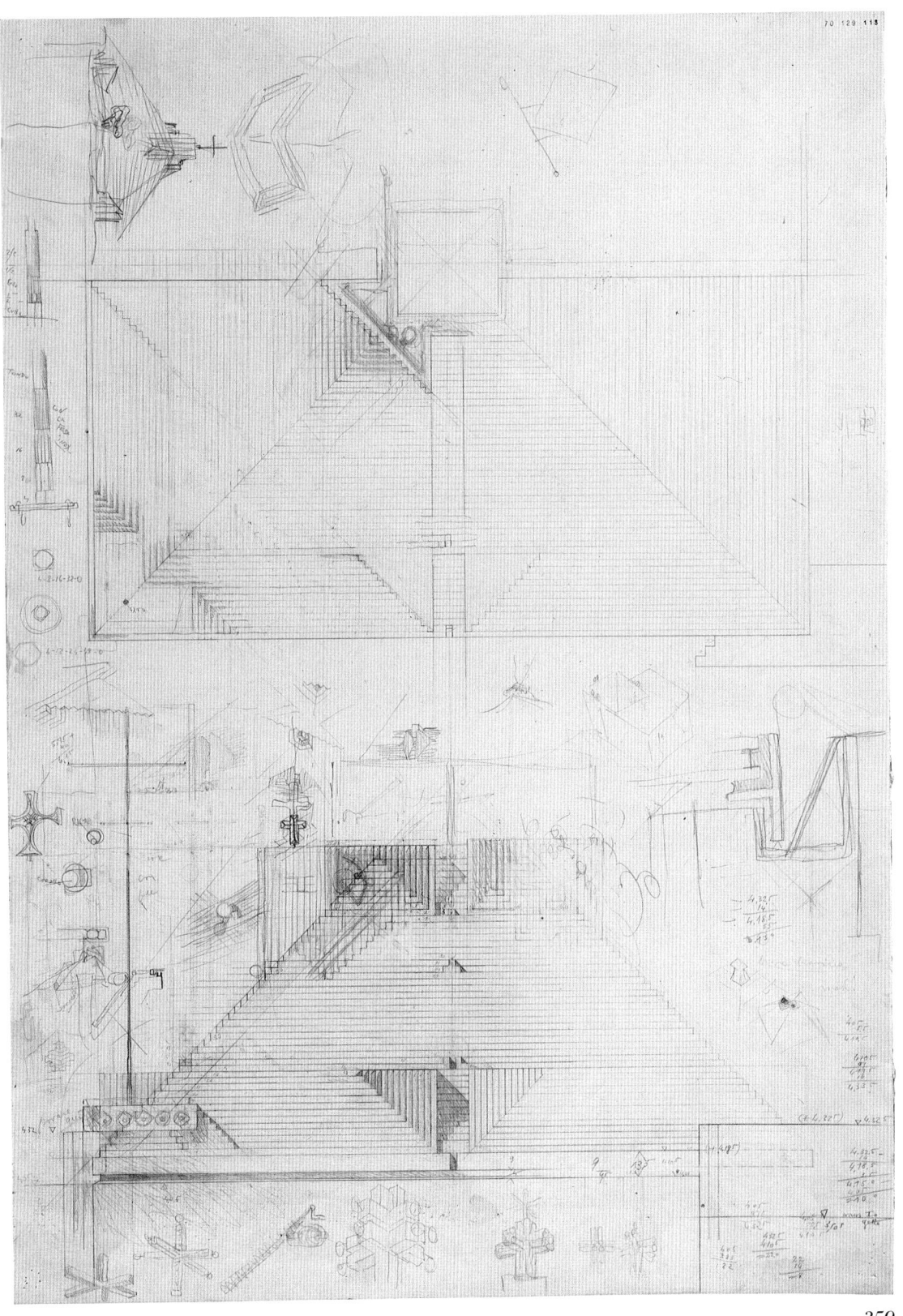

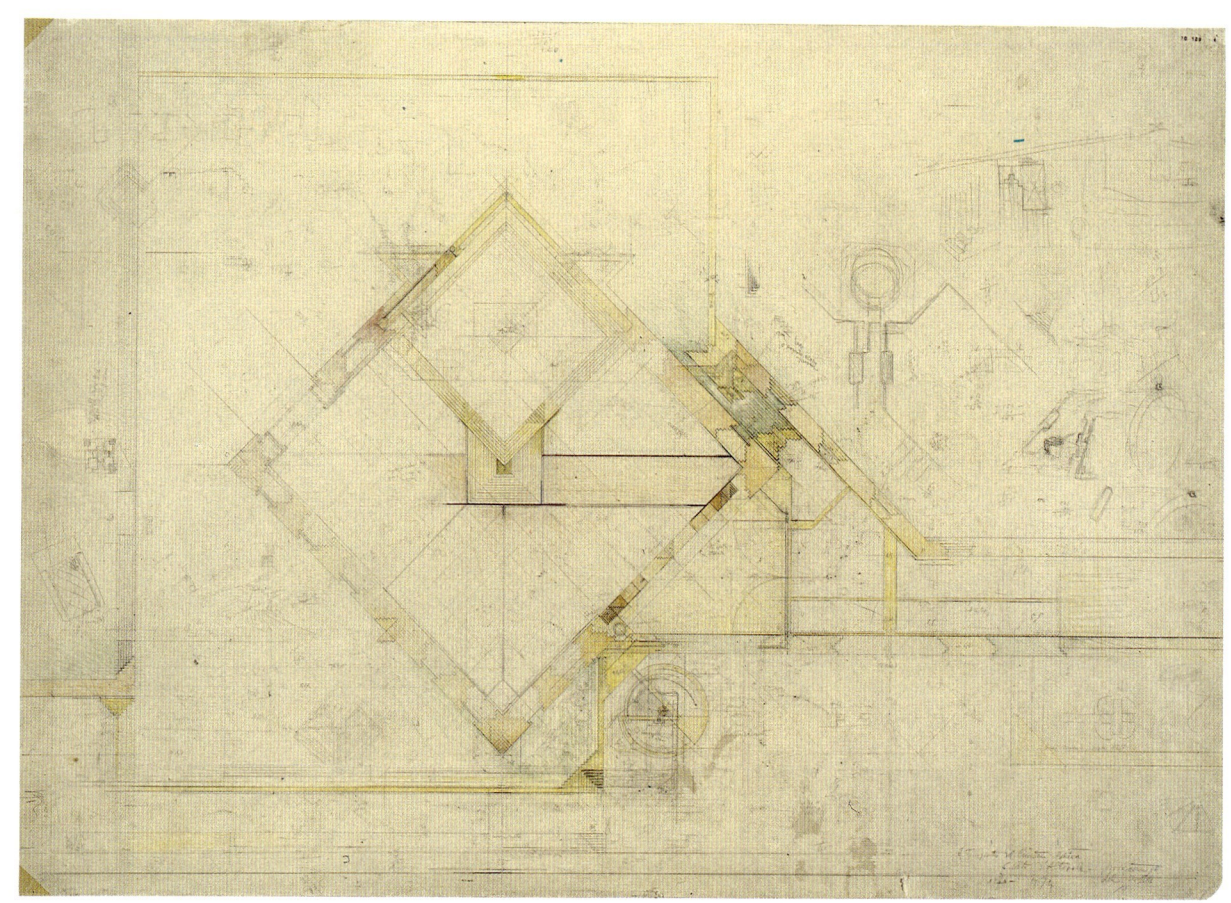

Ceiling lens (adjustable)/Oberlichtfenster (zu öffnen)

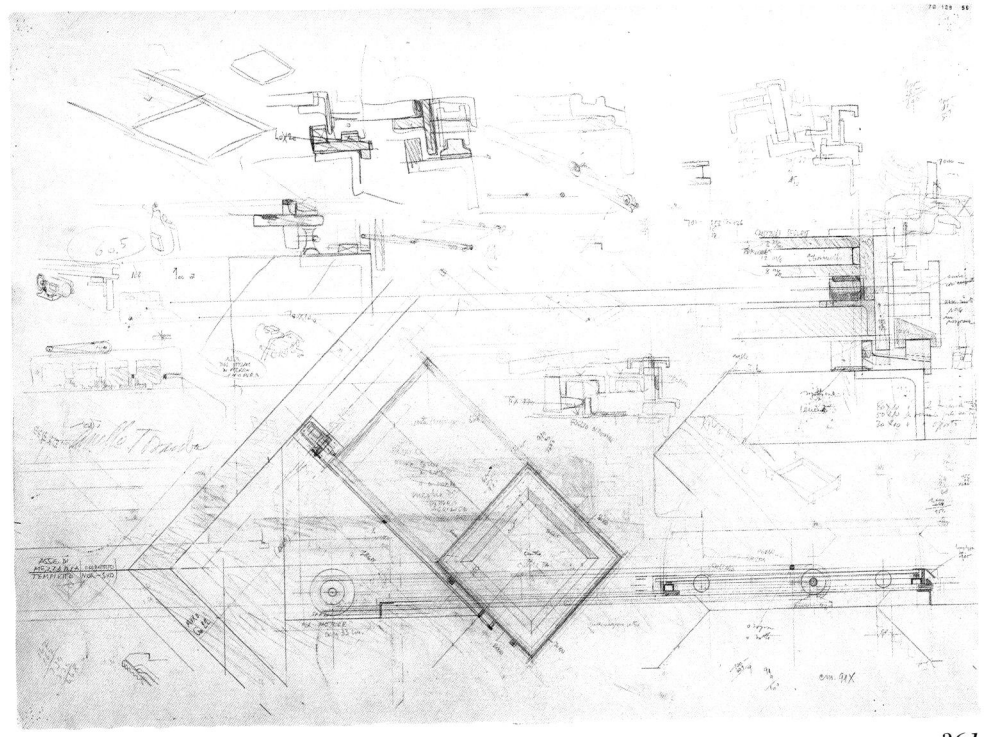

361

362

"Ufficium sepulcri"; angel of death/„Ufficium sepulcri": Todesengel

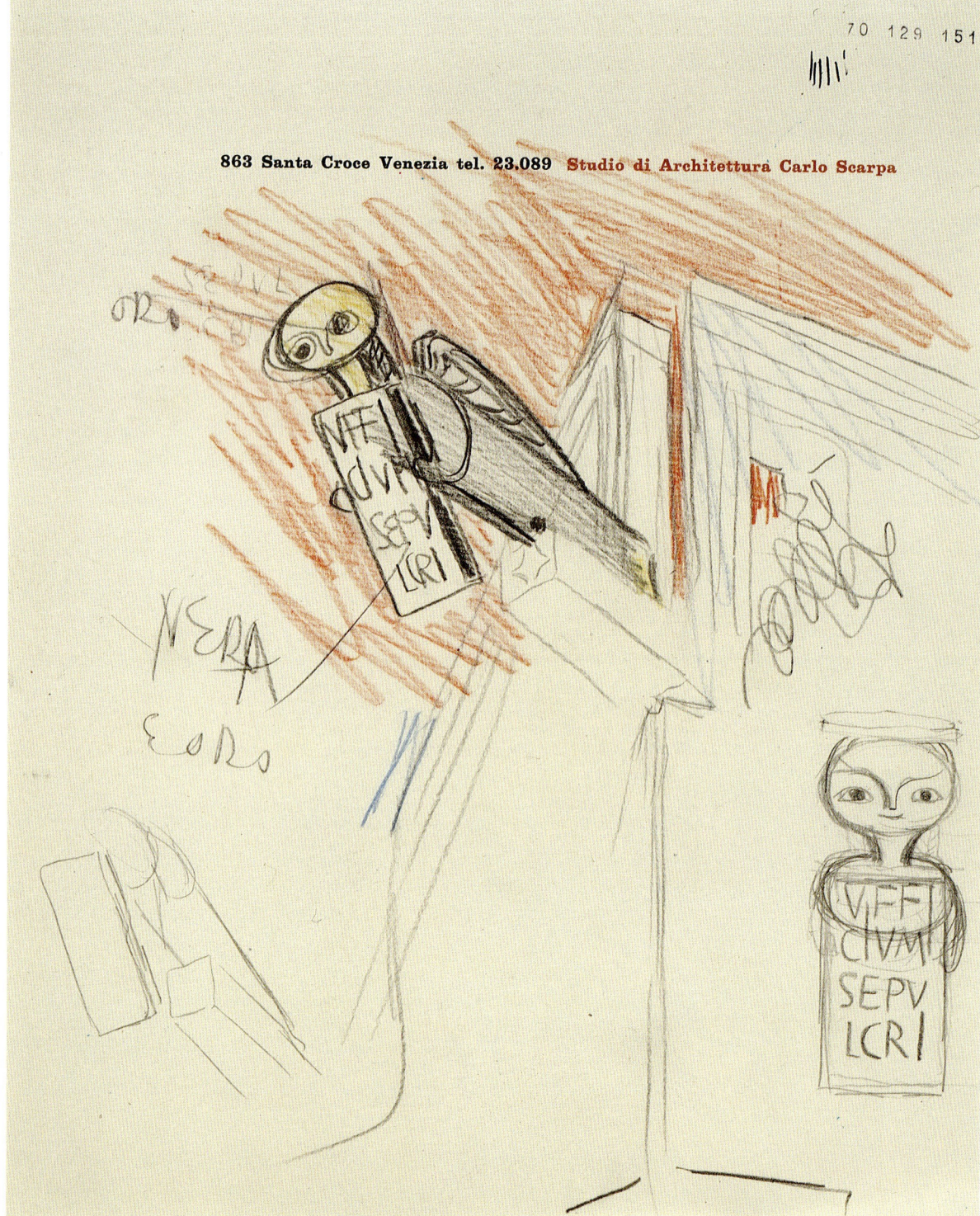

364

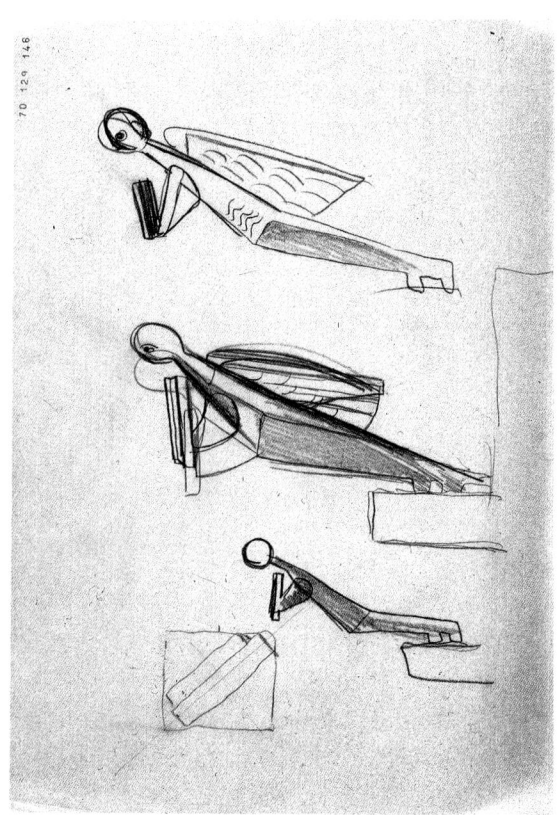

365

366

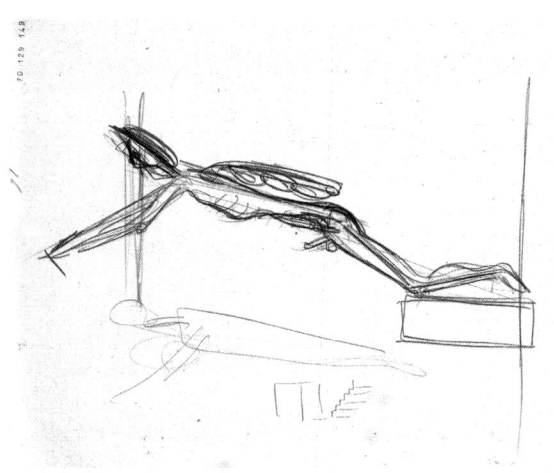

367

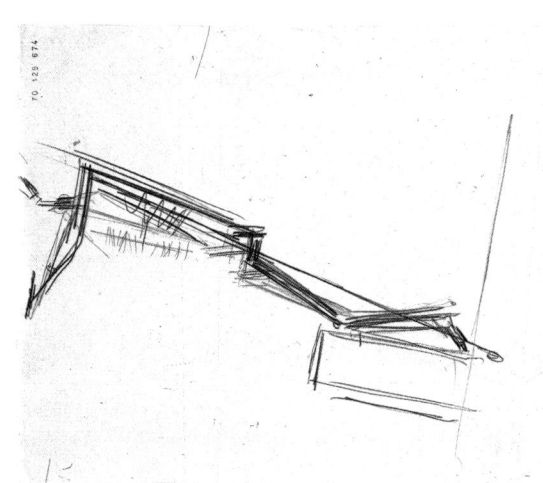

368

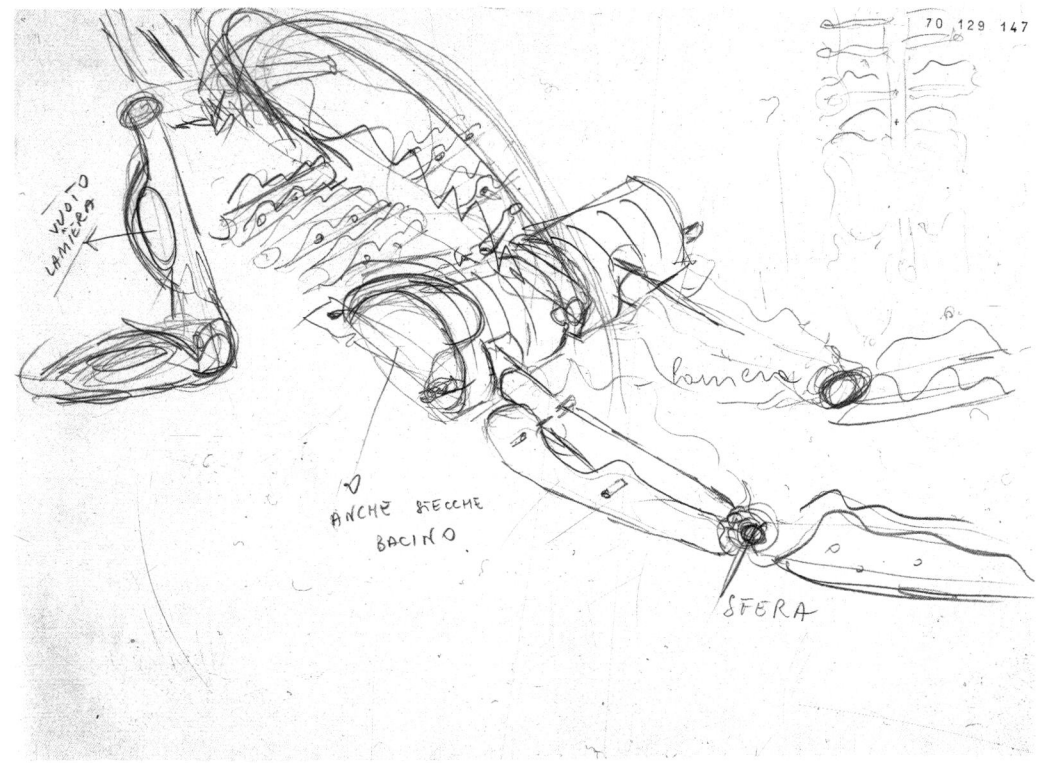

369

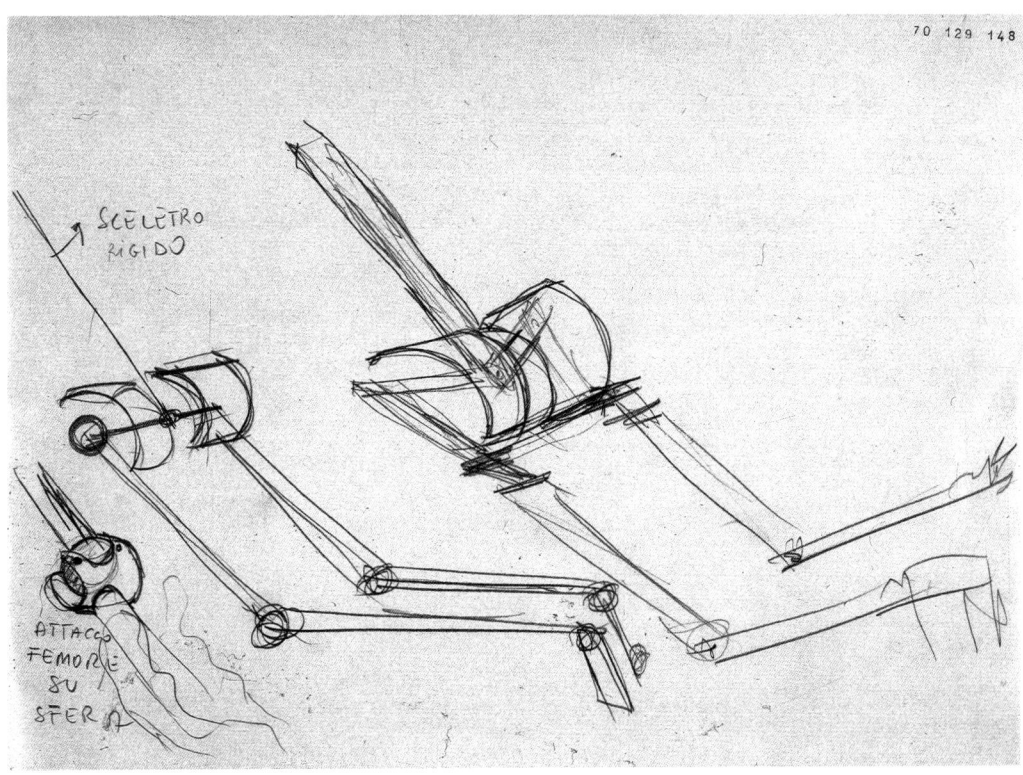

370

Floor/Fußboden

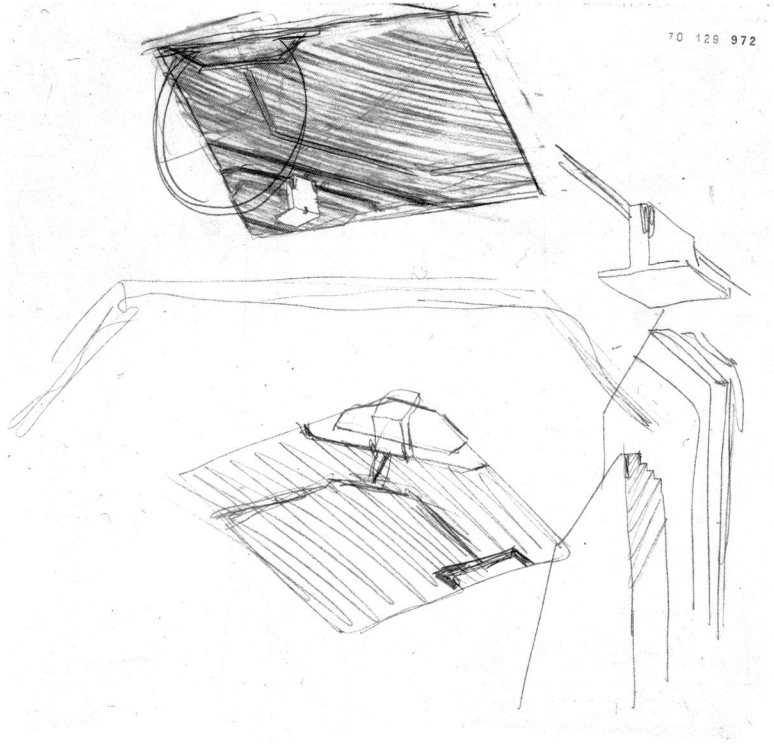

212

371

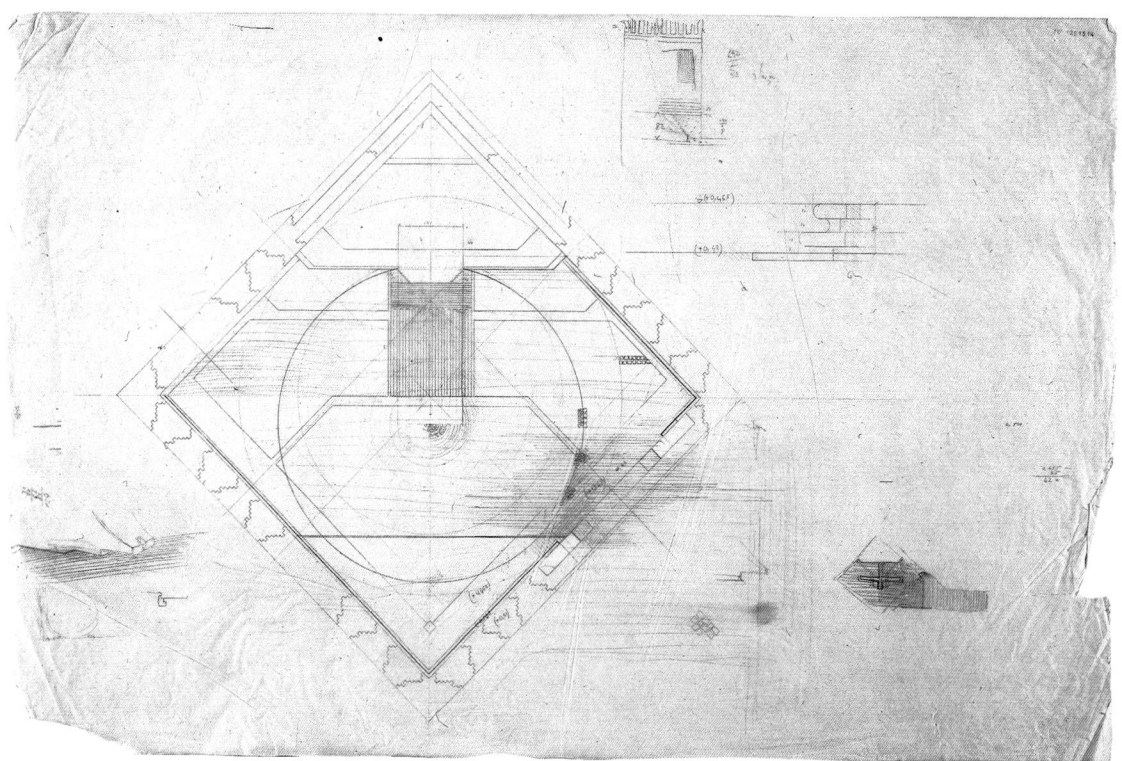

372

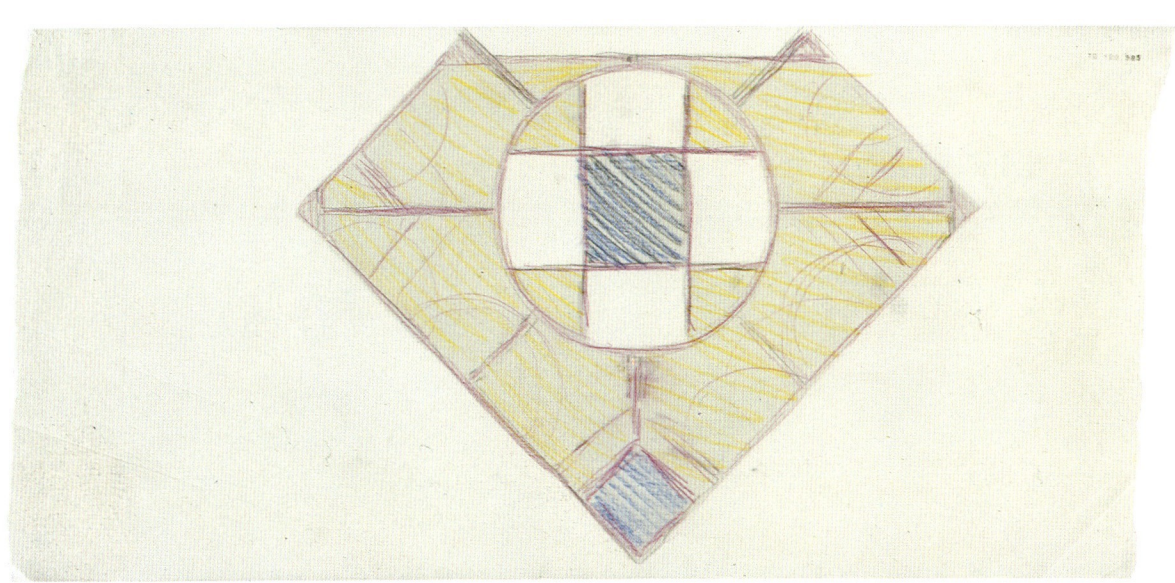

373

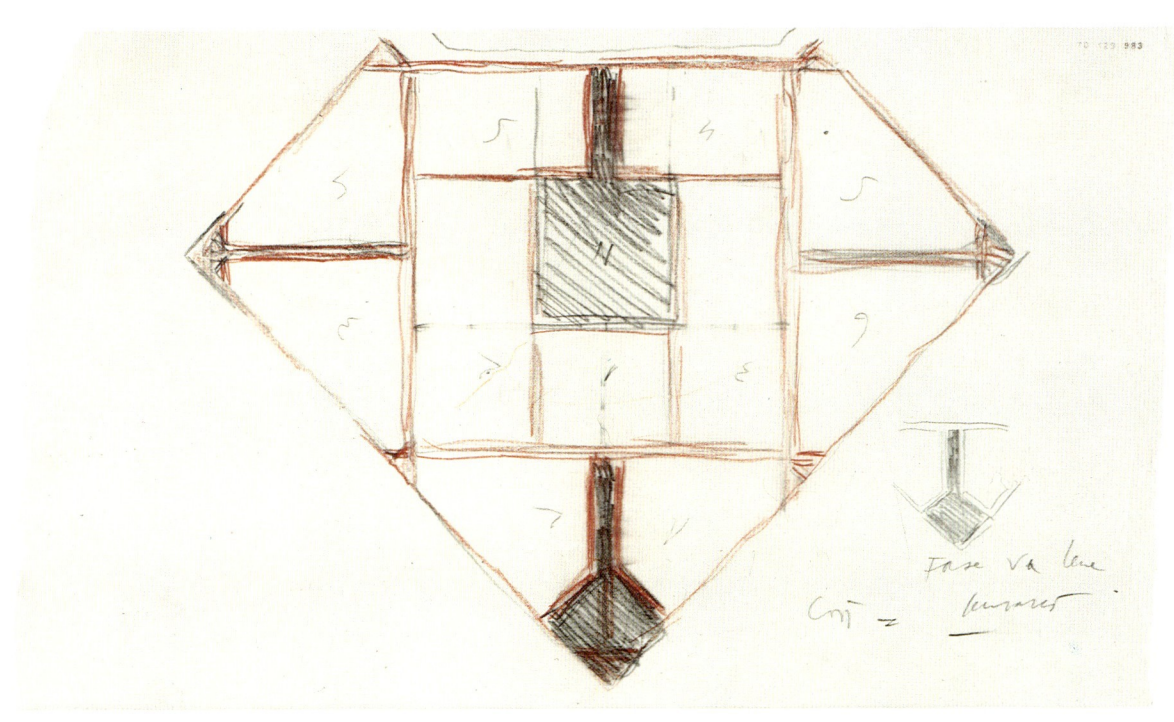

374

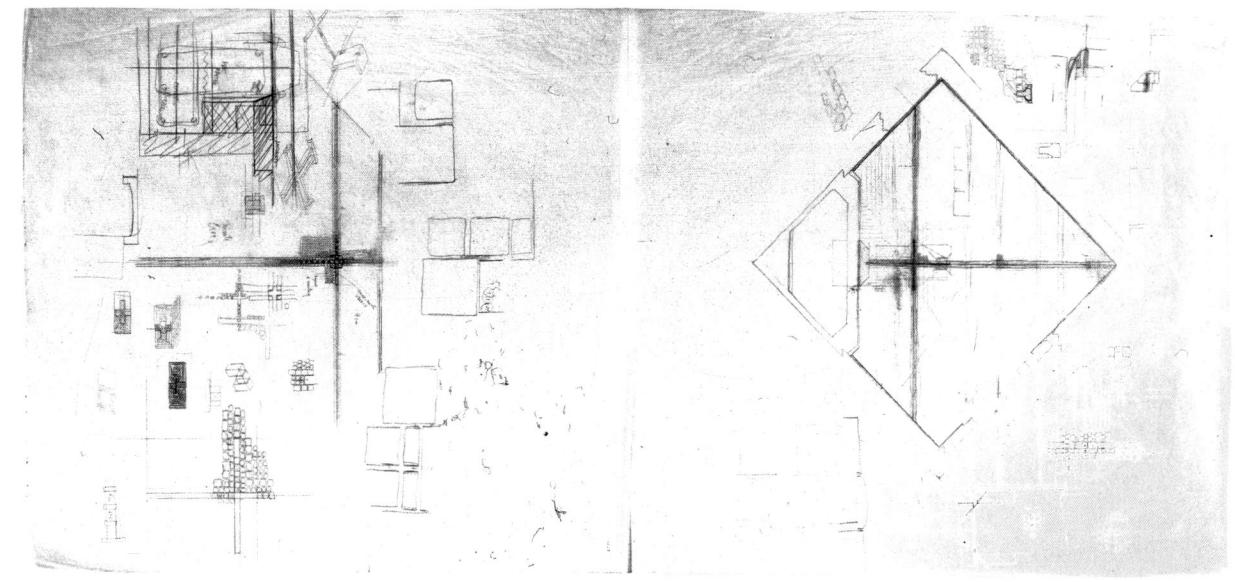

375

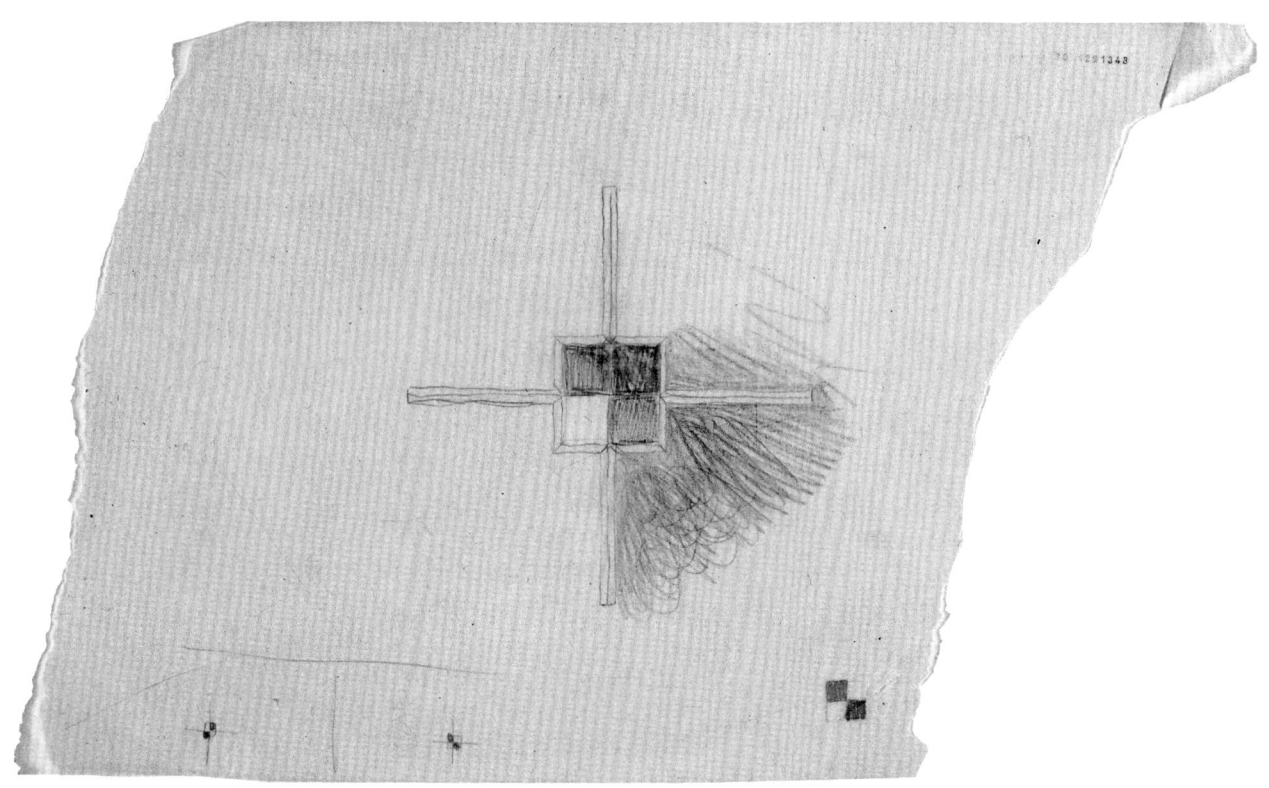

376

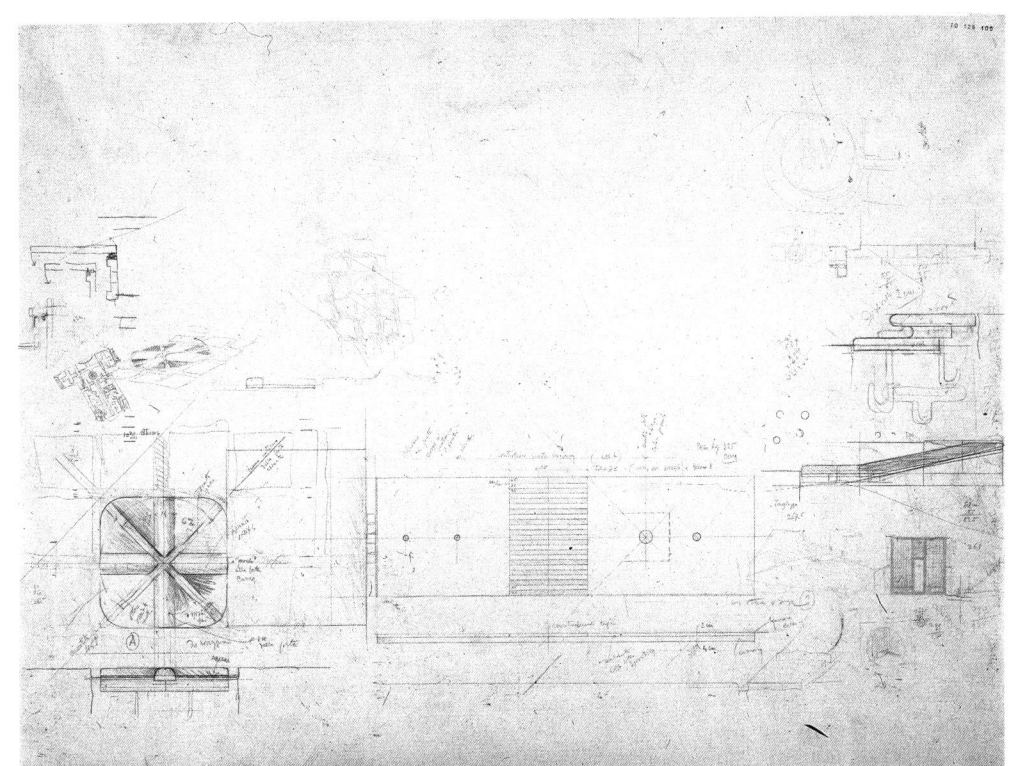

377

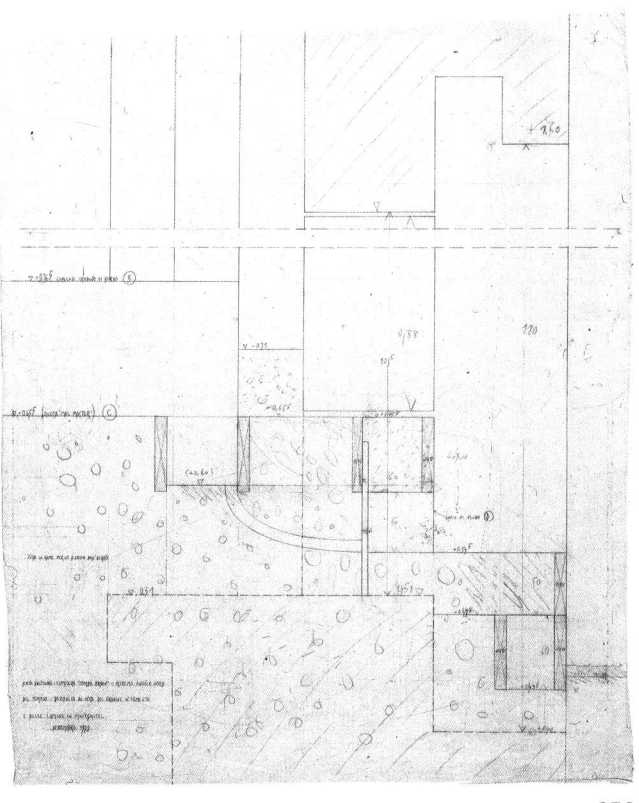

378

Mainportal/Hauptportal

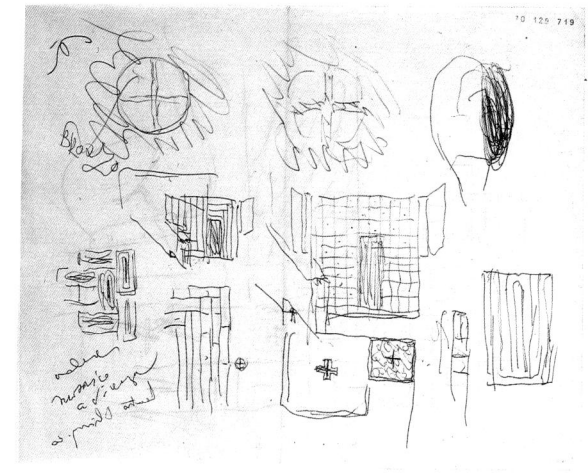

379

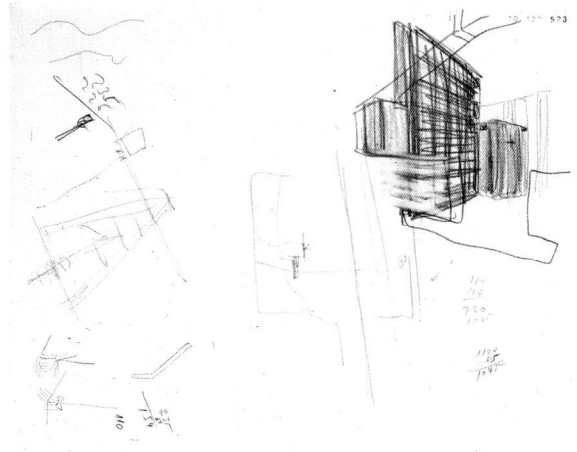

380

381

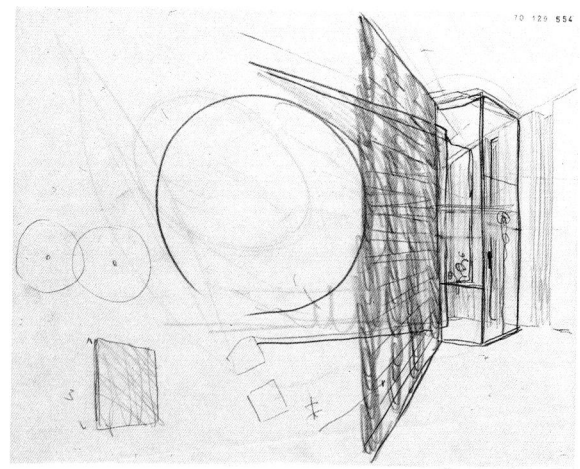

382

383

217

384

385

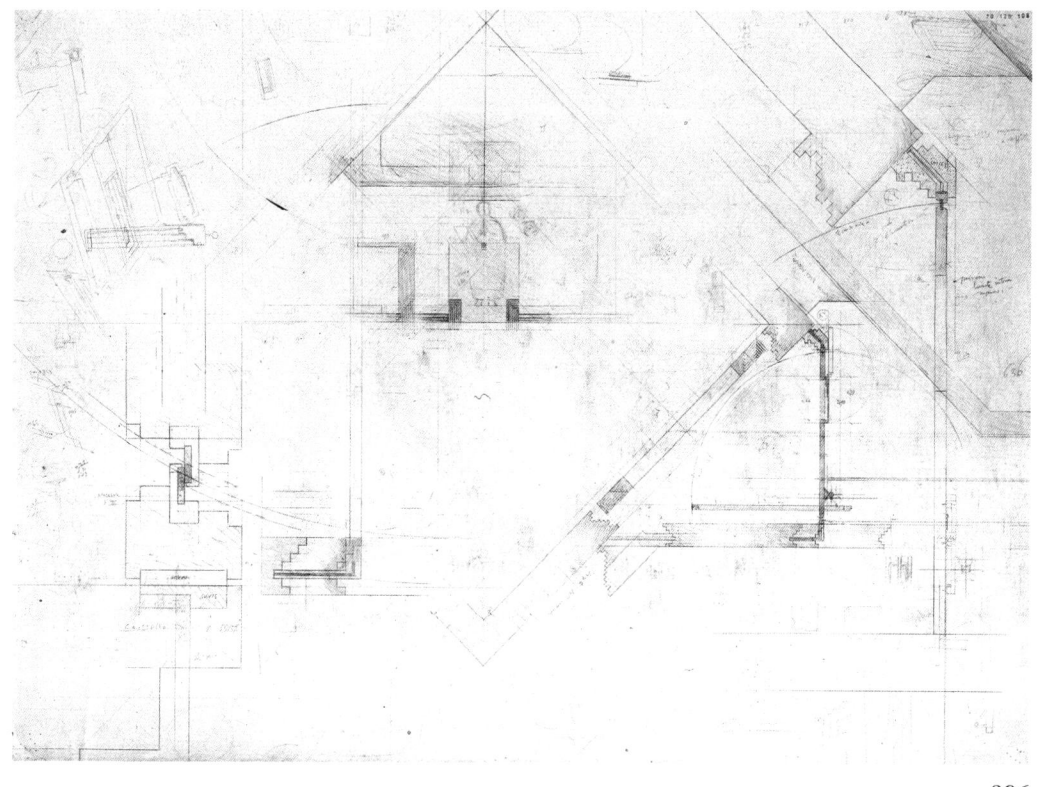

386

Metal hinge/Metallscharnier

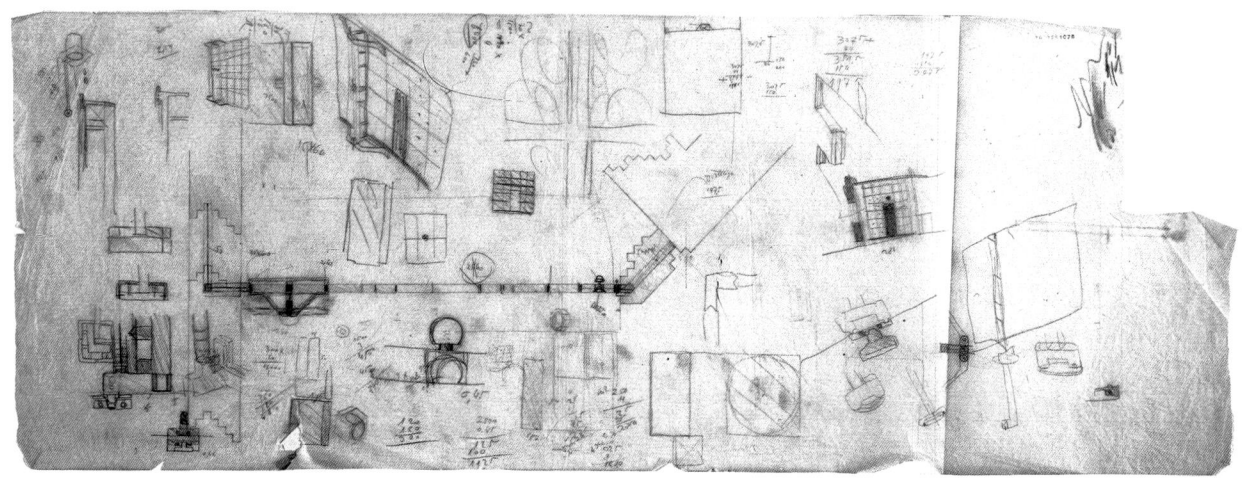

387

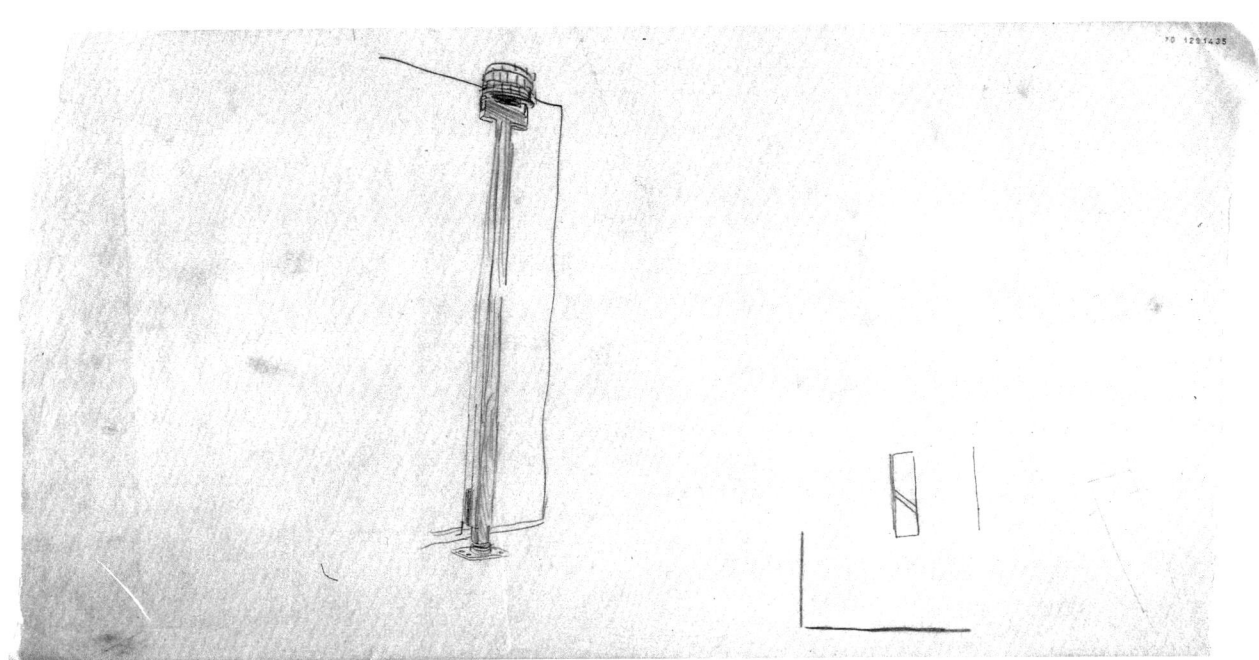

388

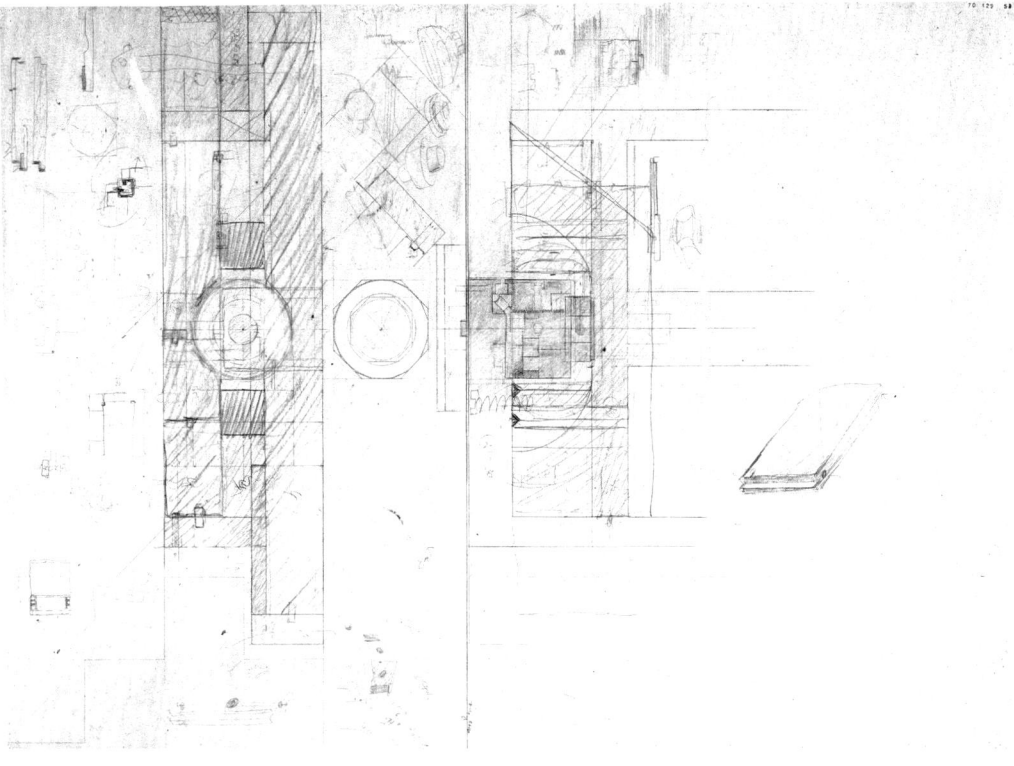

389

220

390

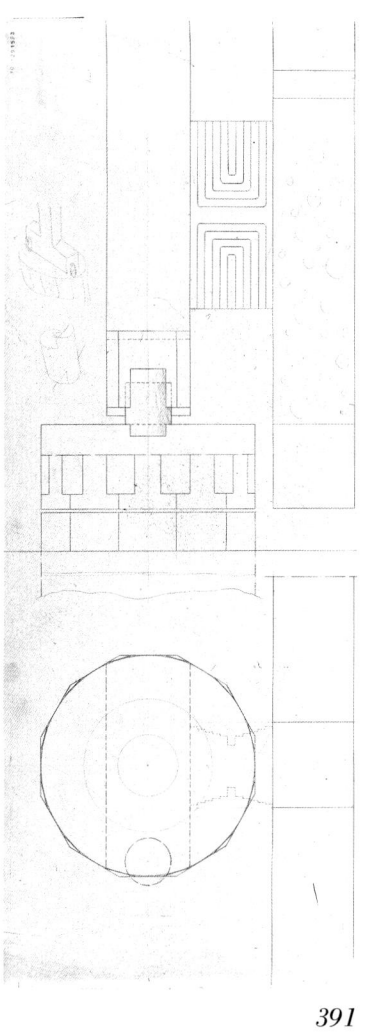

391

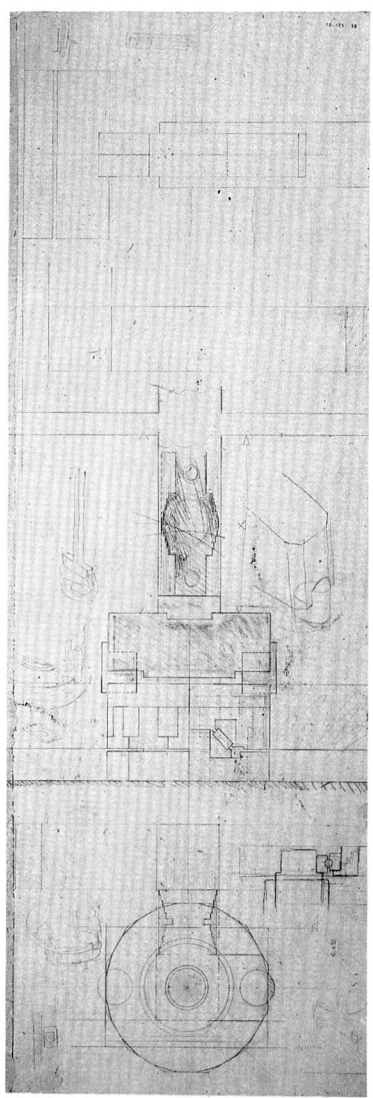

392

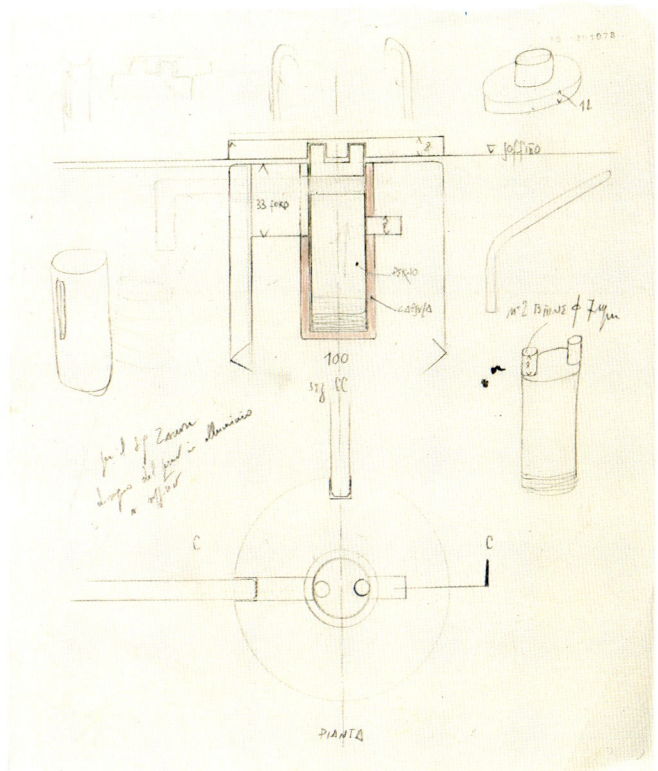

393

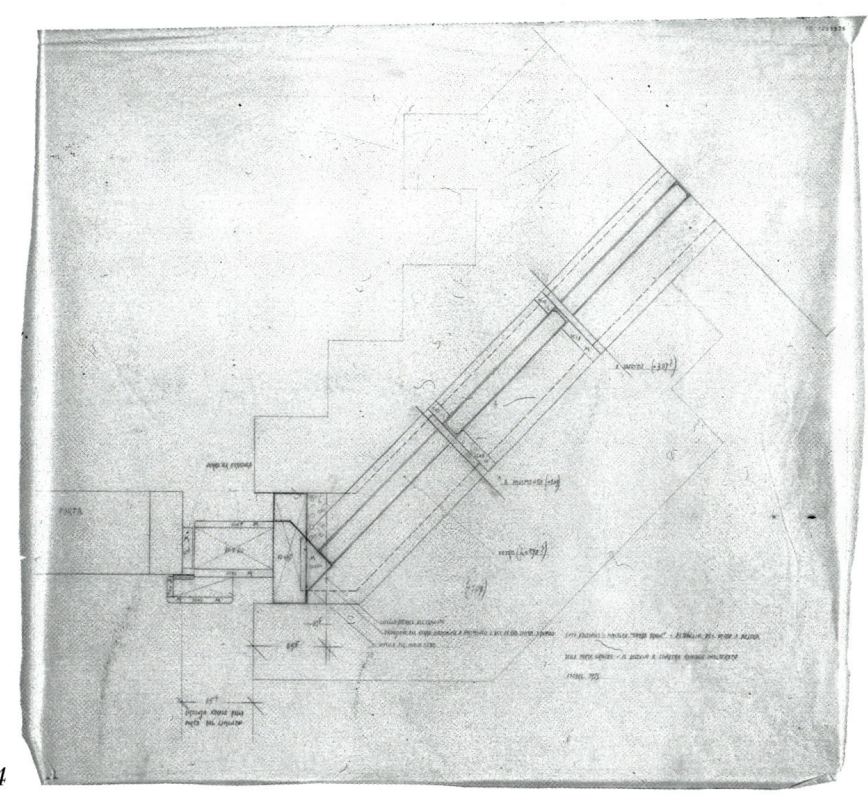

394

Small ebony door in the main portal (1973–1974)
Ebenholztürchen im Hauptportal (1973–1974)

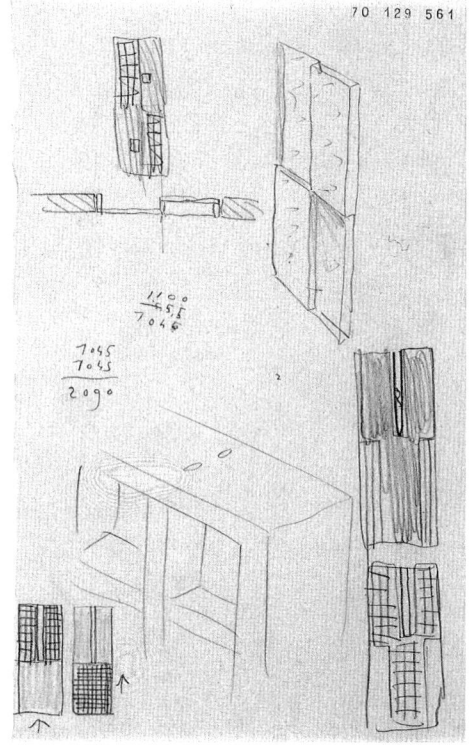

395

396

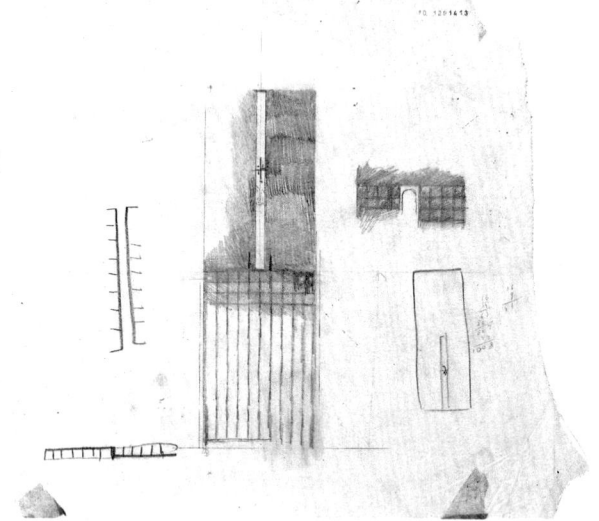

397

398

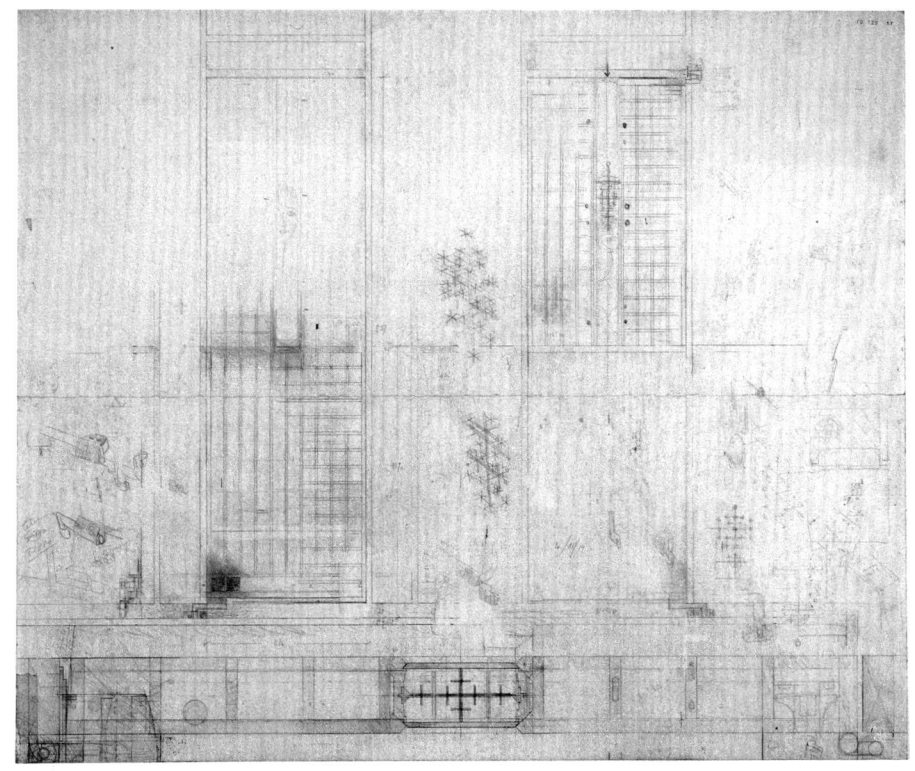

399

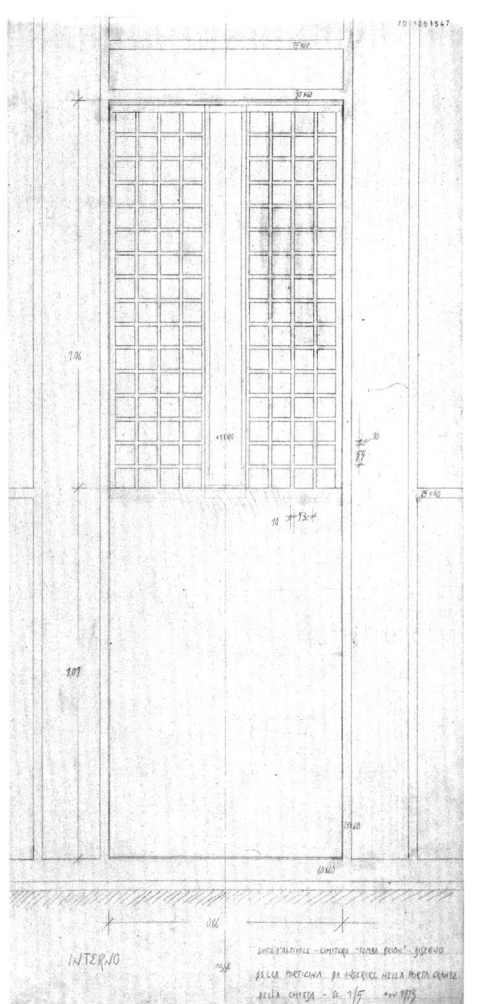

400

402

401

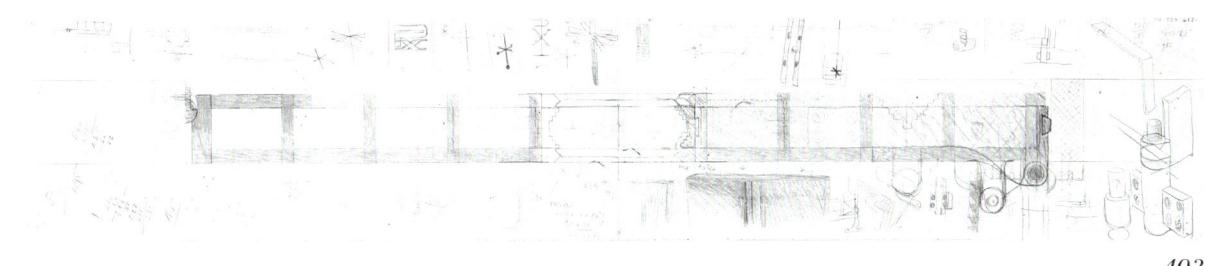

403

225

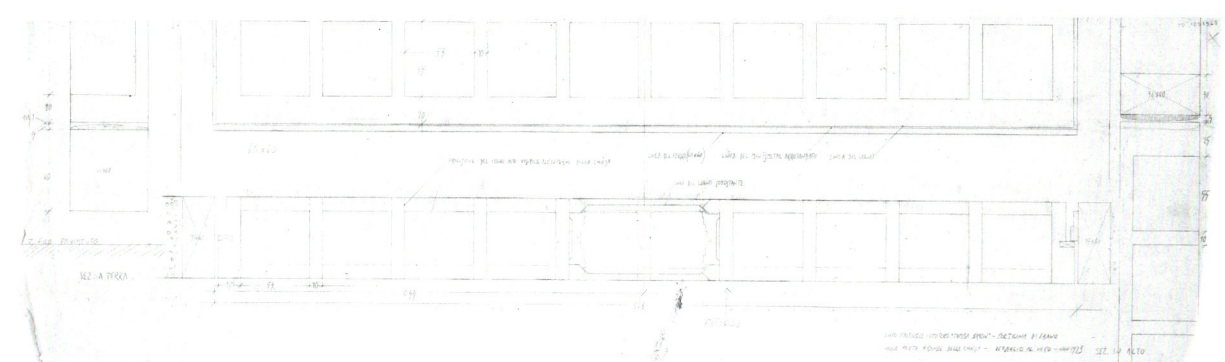

404

405

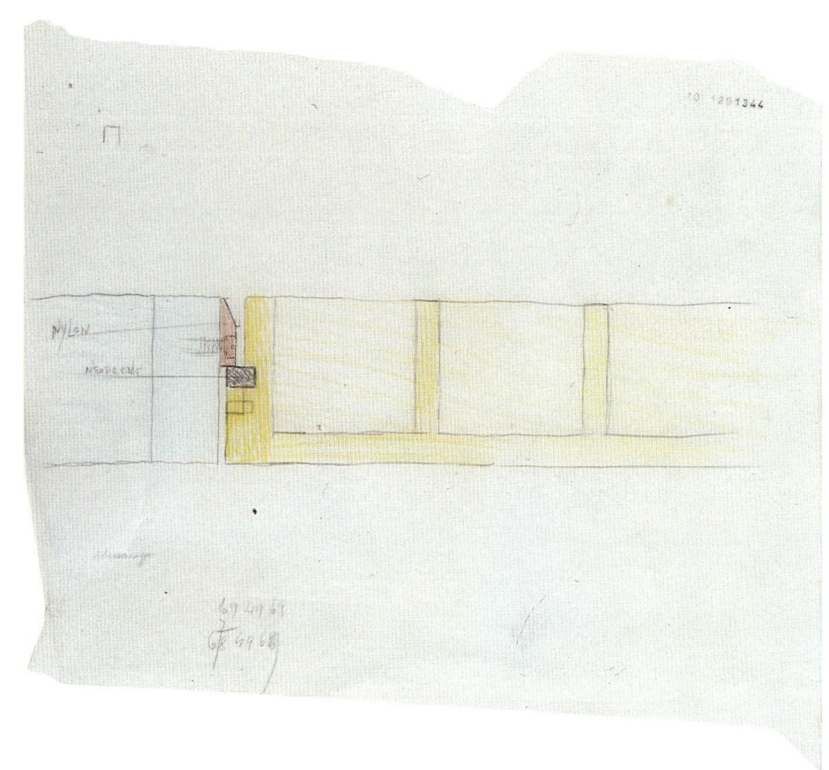

406

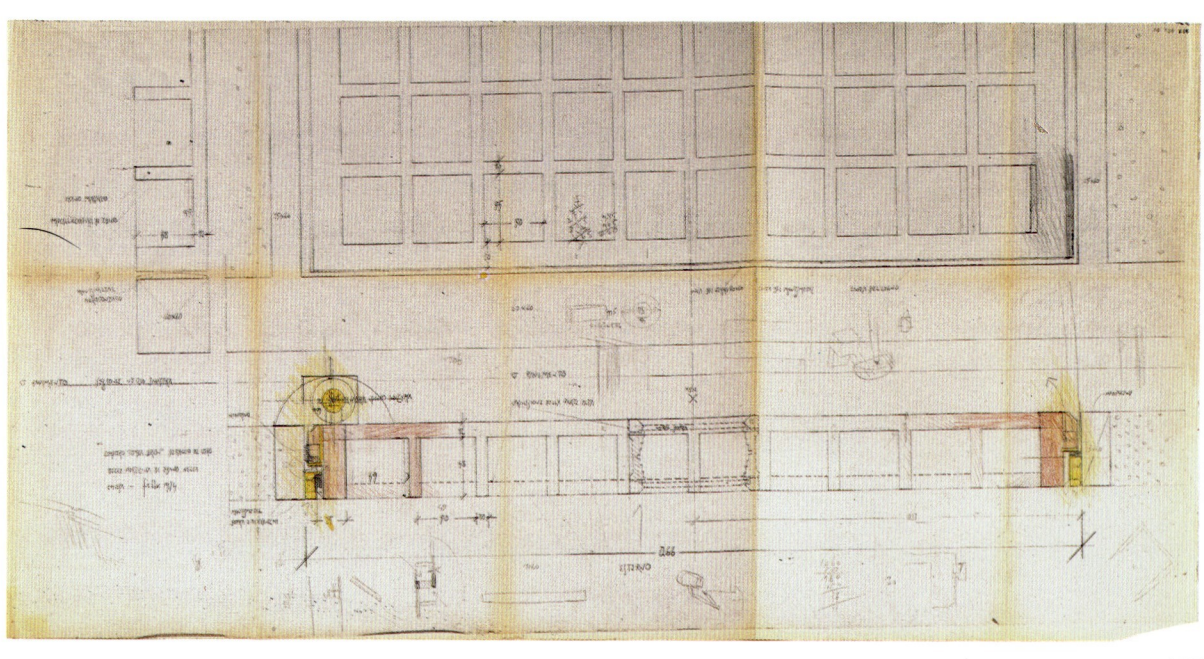

407

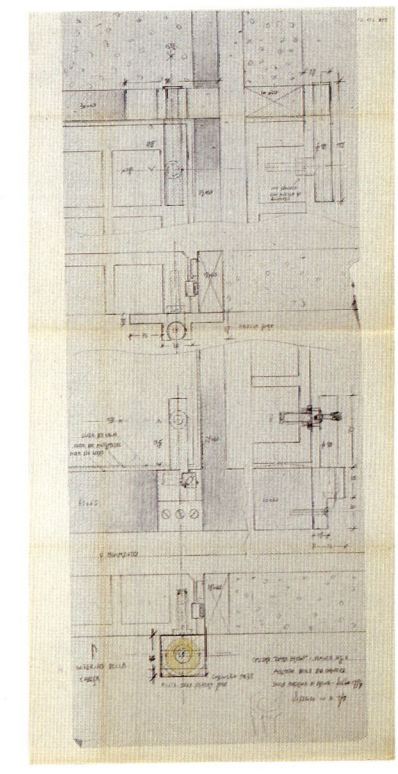

227

408

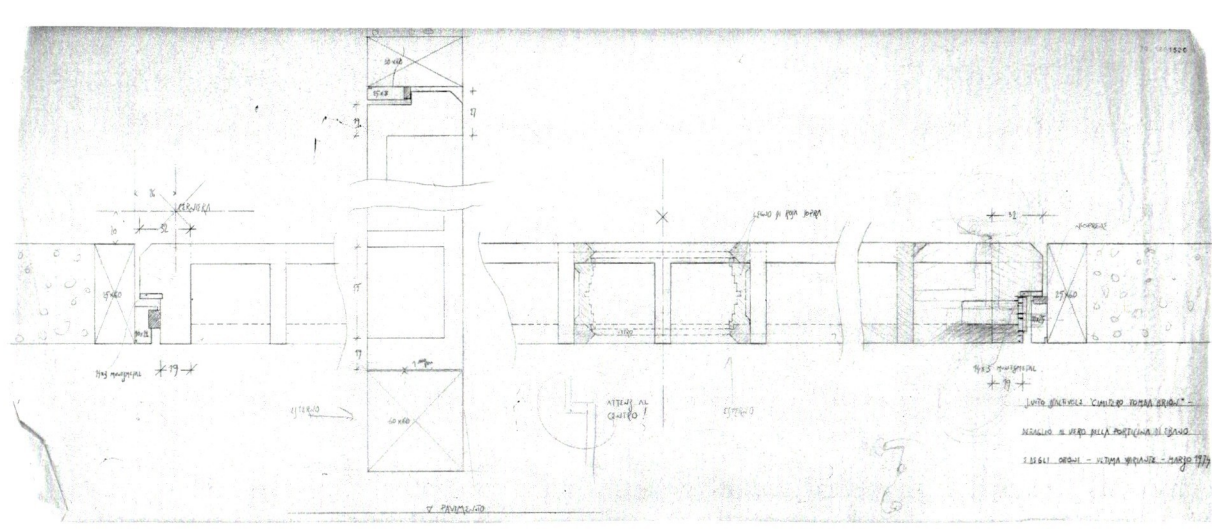

409

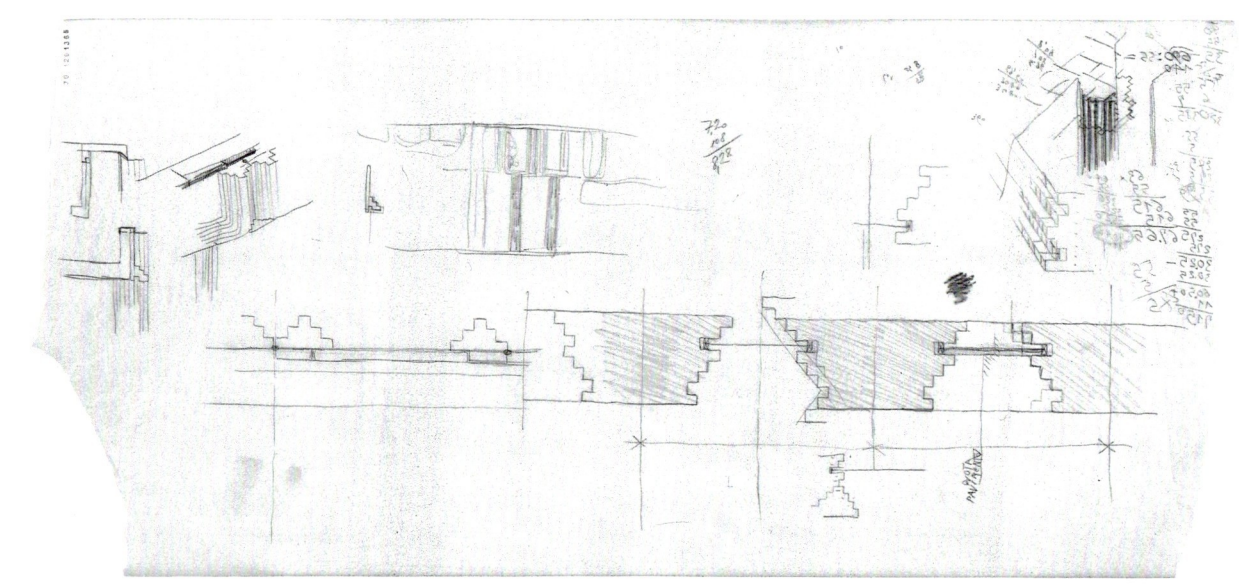

410

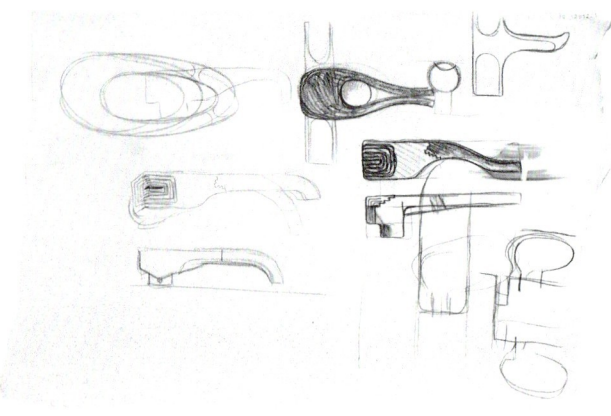

411

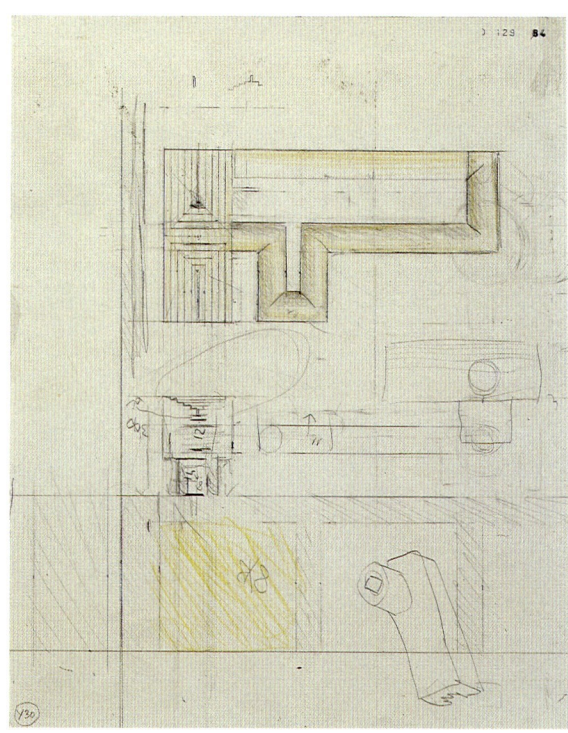

412

Font/Weihwasserbecken

229

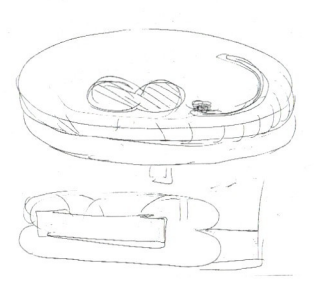

413

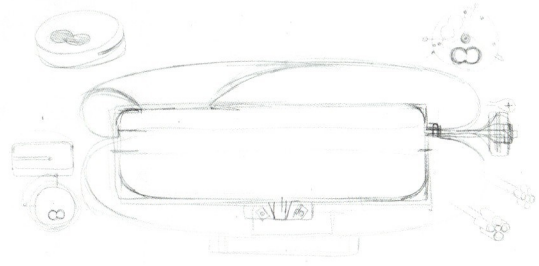

414

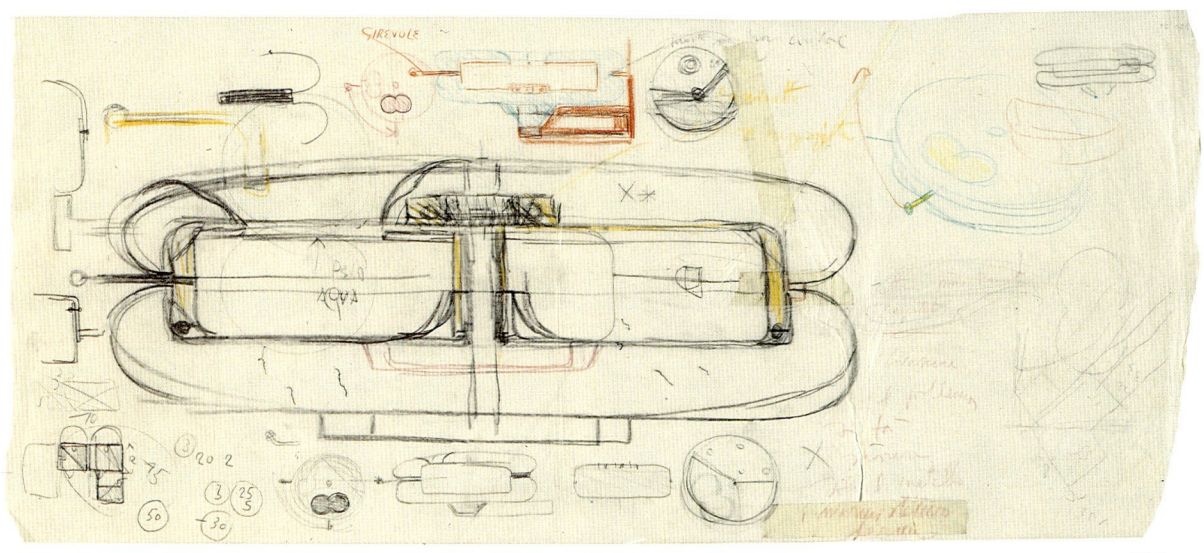

415

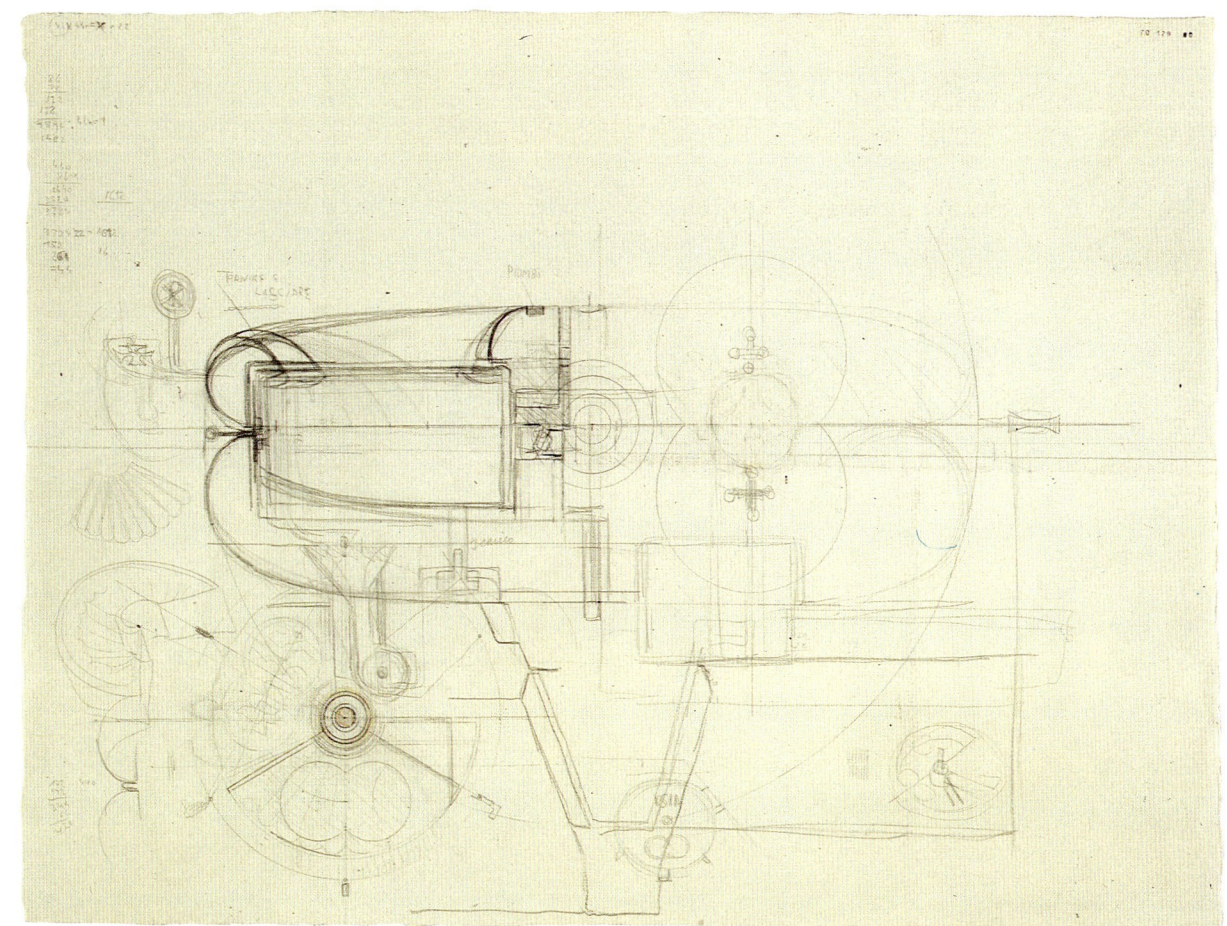

416

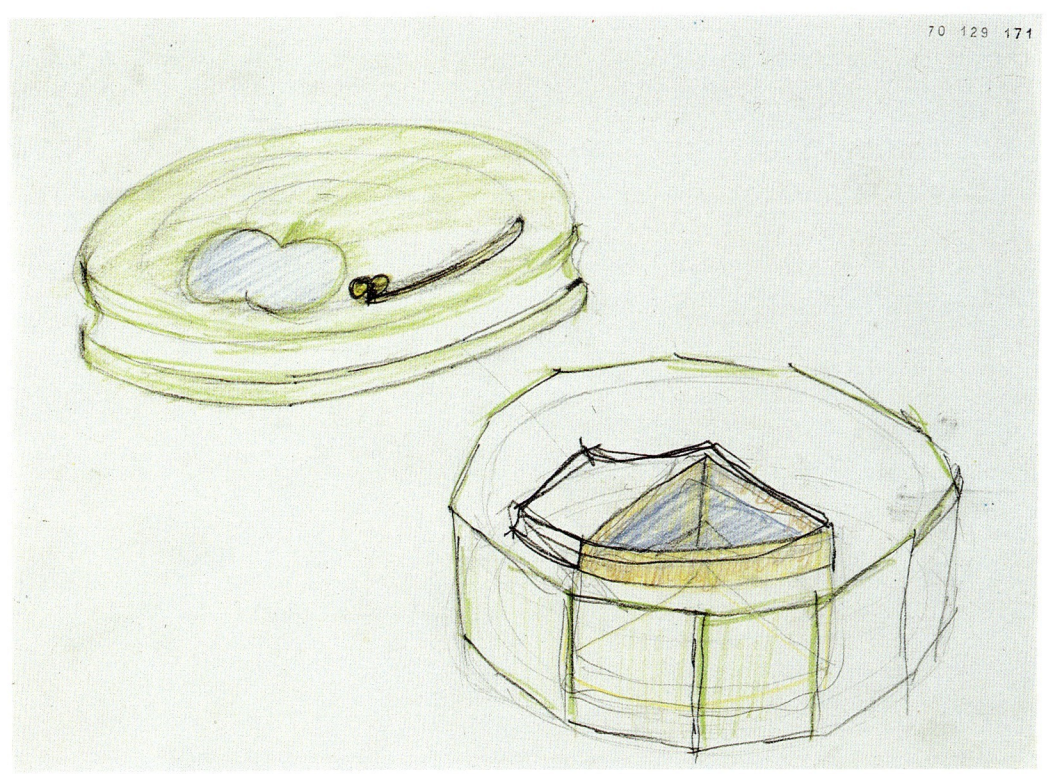

417

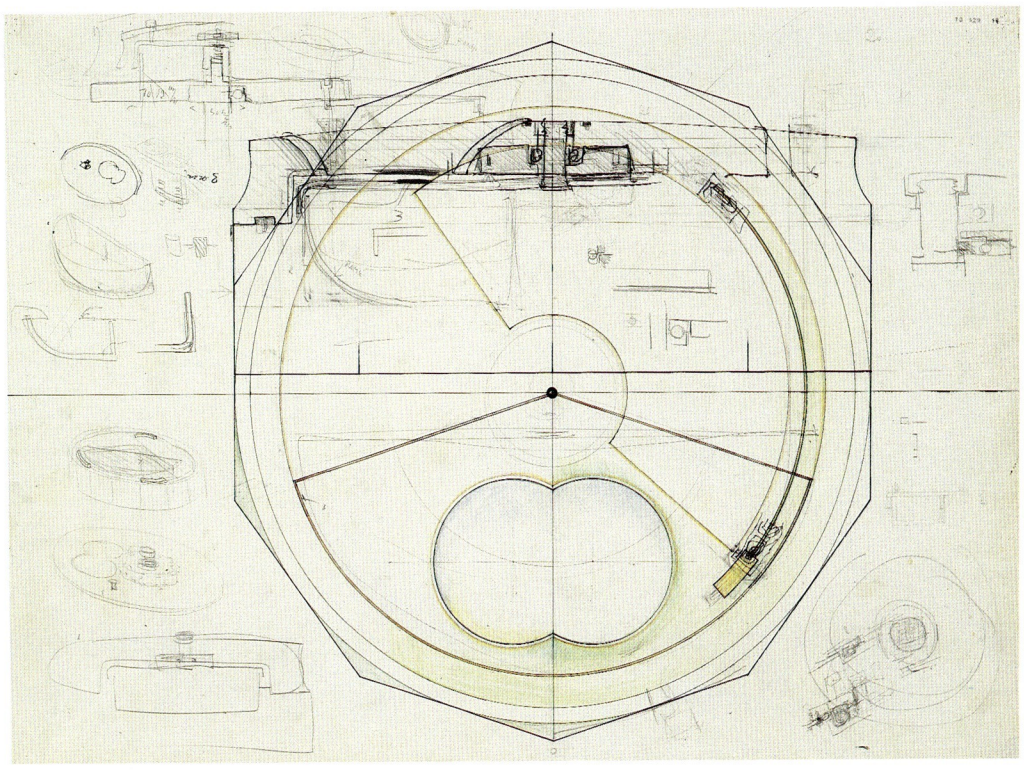

418

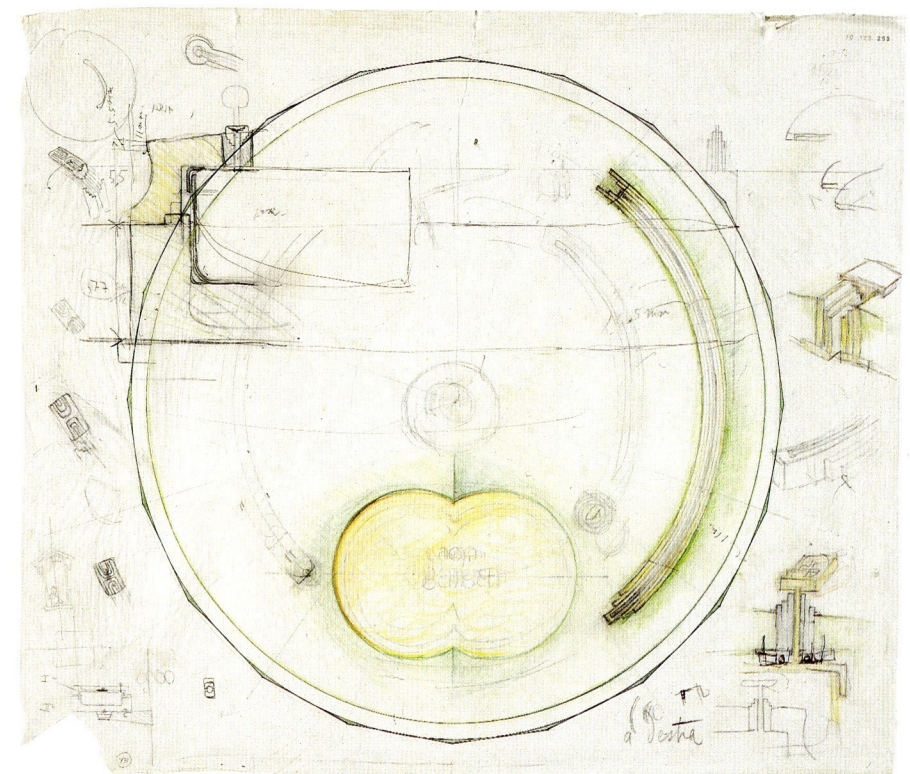

419

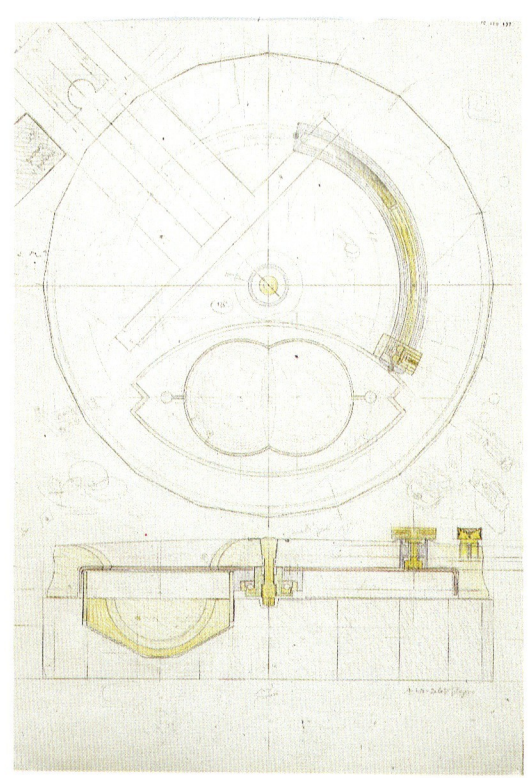

420

421

233

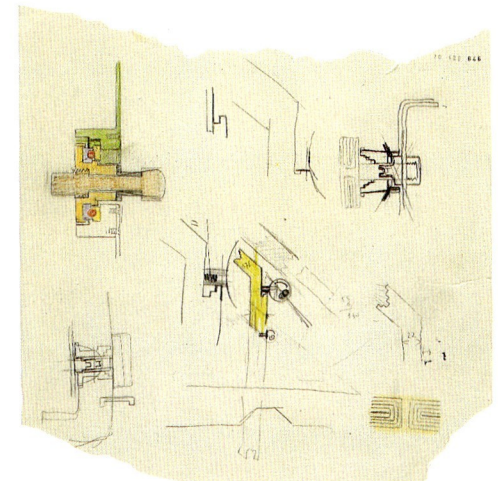

422

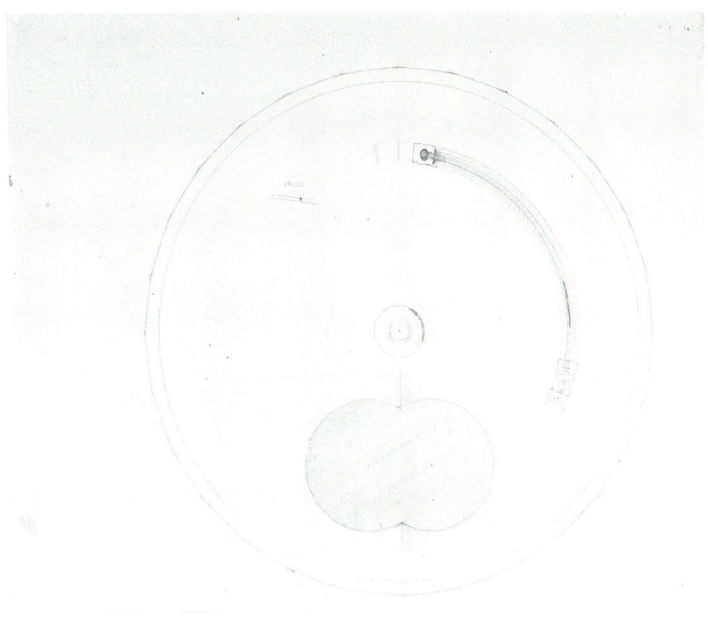

423

Circular portal/große Rundbogentür in der Kapelle

424

425

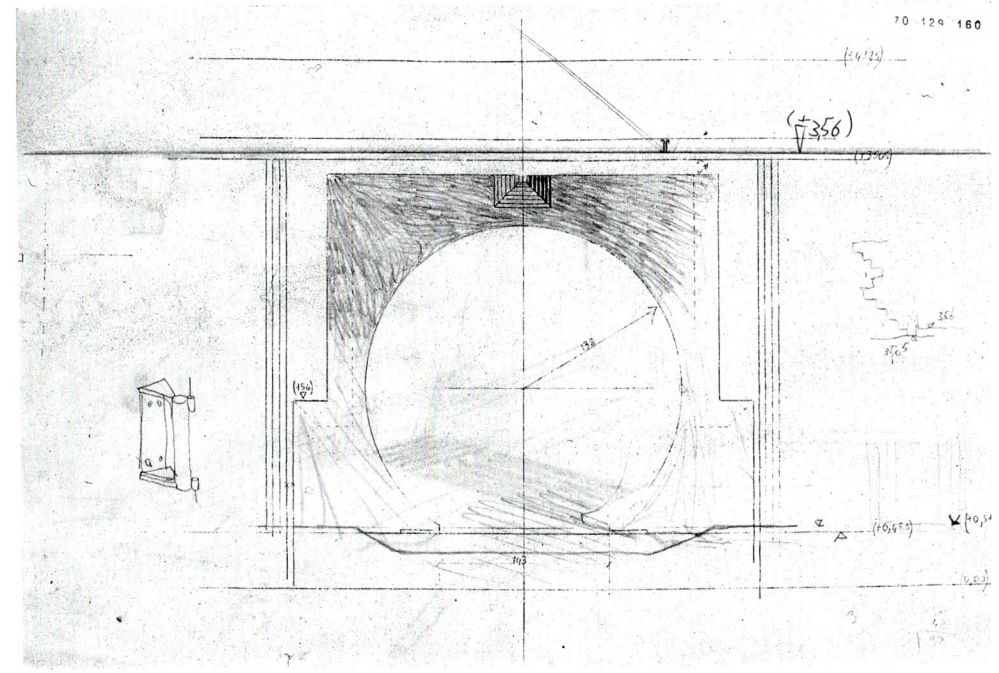

426

427

236

428

429

Windows/Fenster

High windows/Hochfenster

430

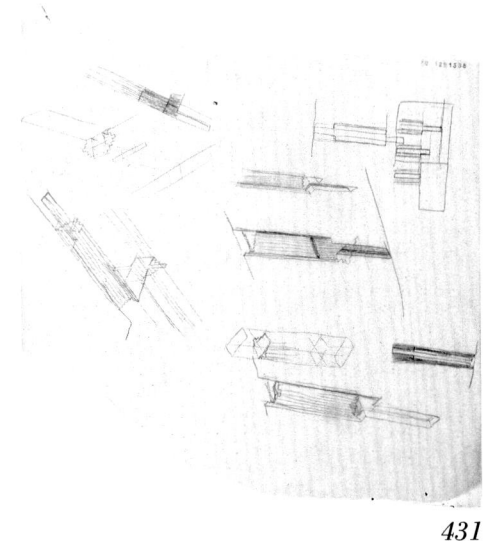

431

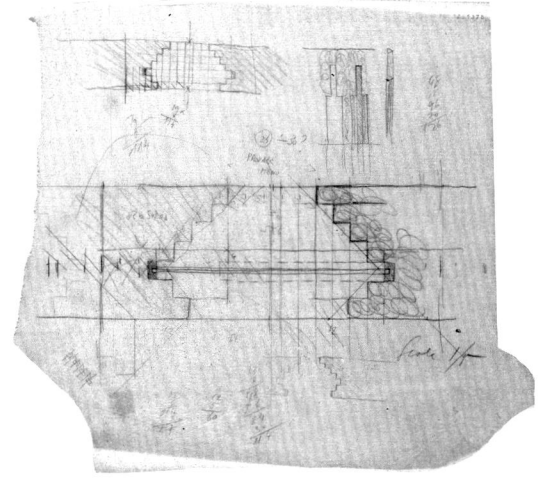

432

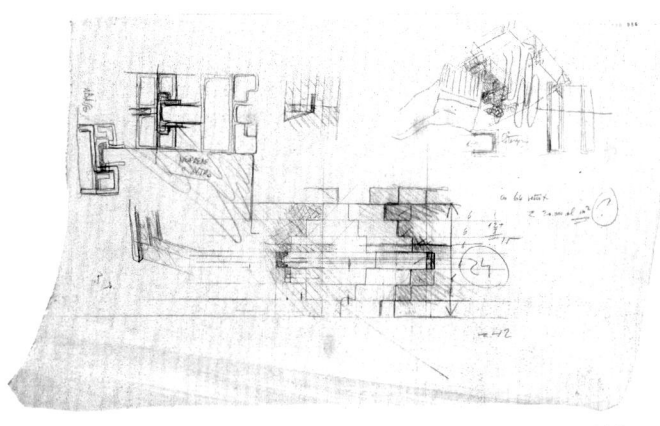

433

434

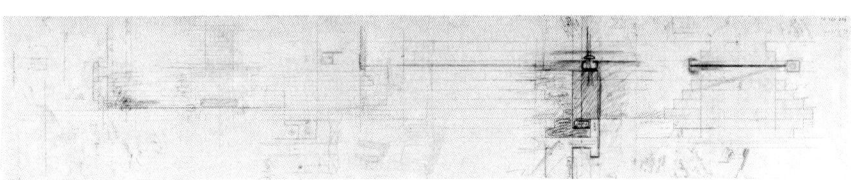

435

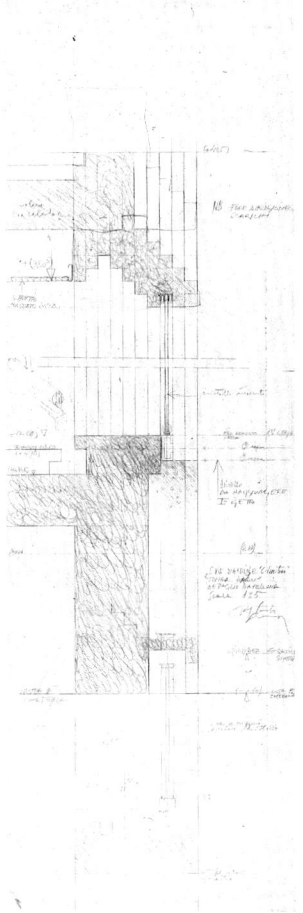

436

Square windows behind the altar/Quadratische Fenster hinter dem Altar

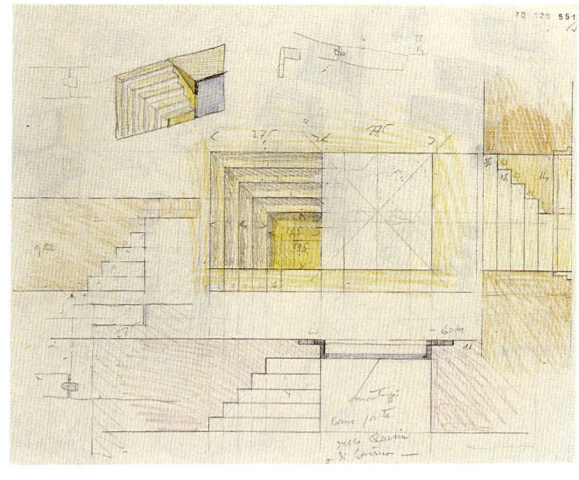

437

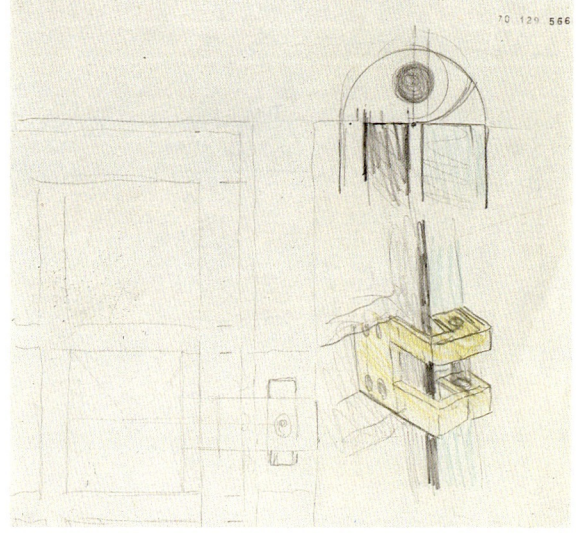

438

439

Altar/Der Altar

Location of the altar/Position des Altares

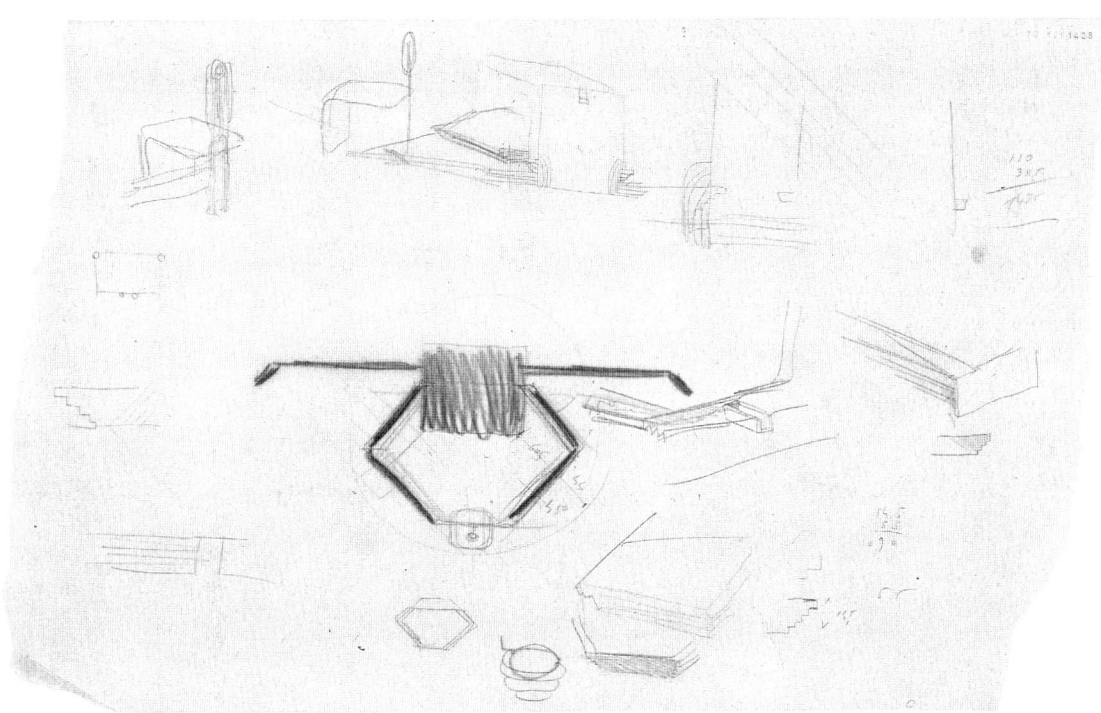

440

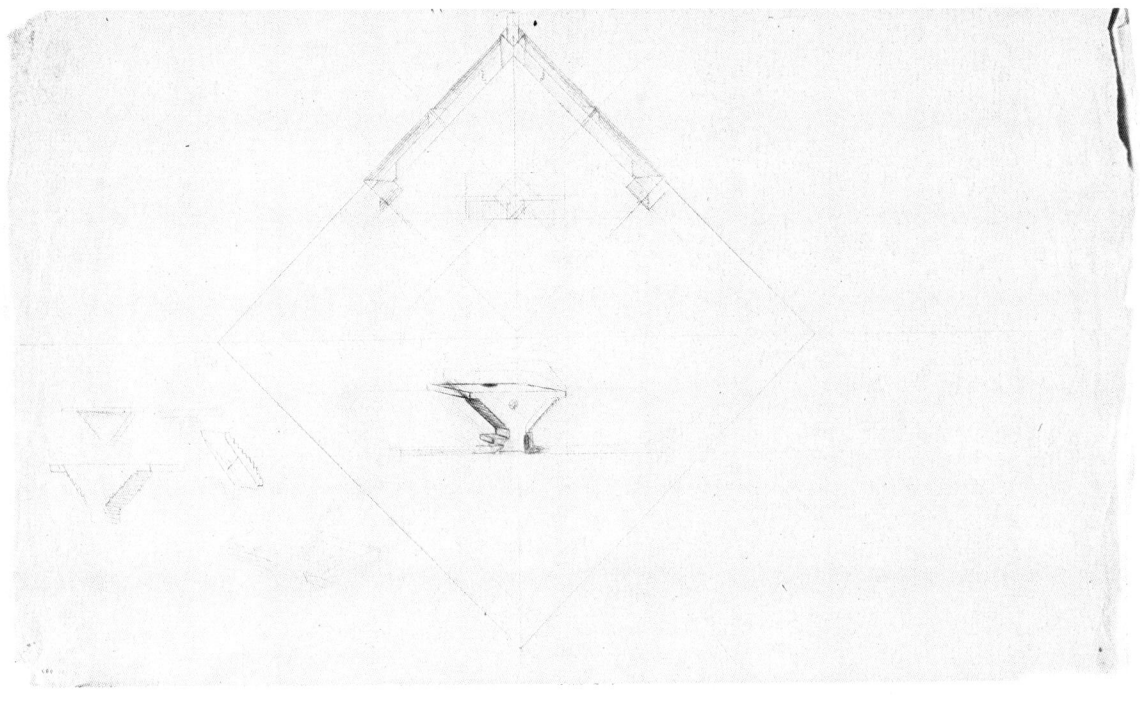

441

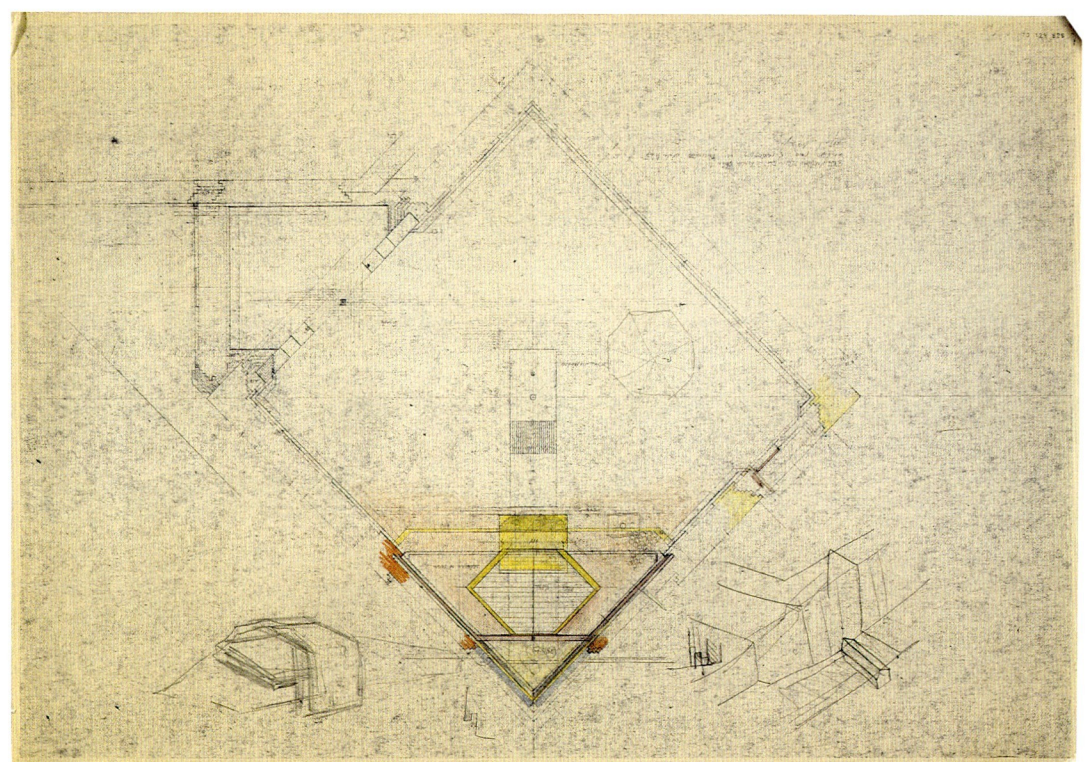

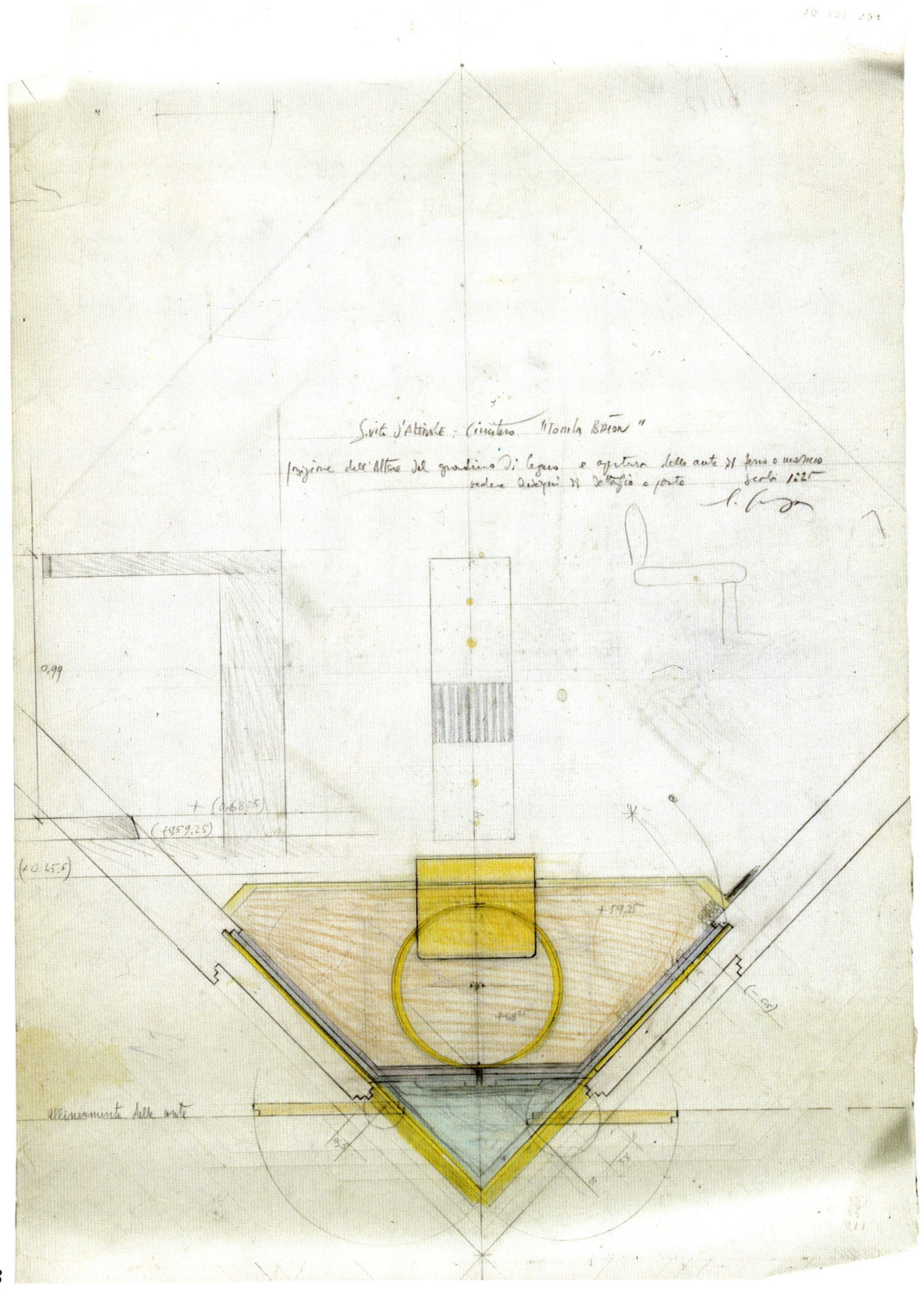

244

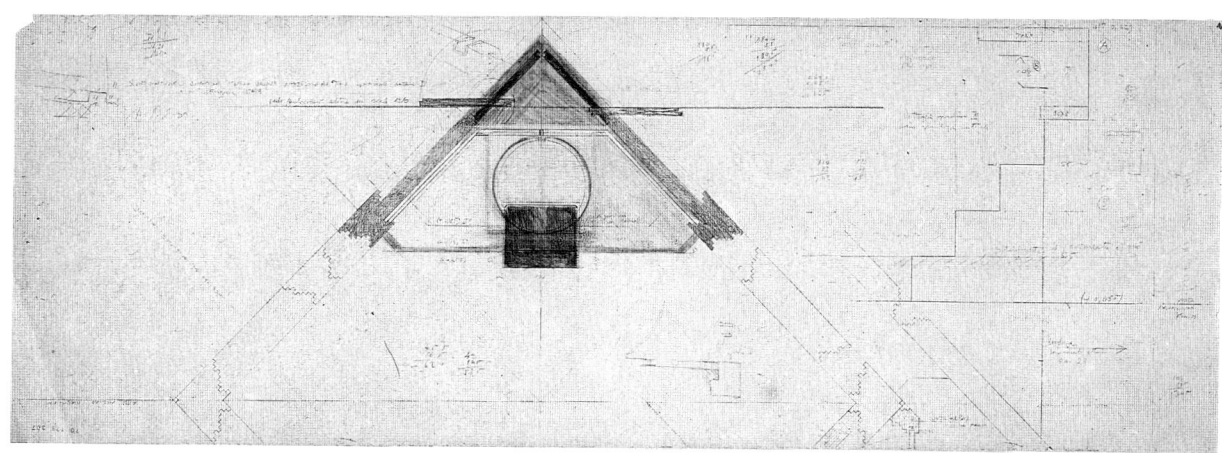

444

445

Arrangement of steps and altar/Anordnung von Stufen und Altar

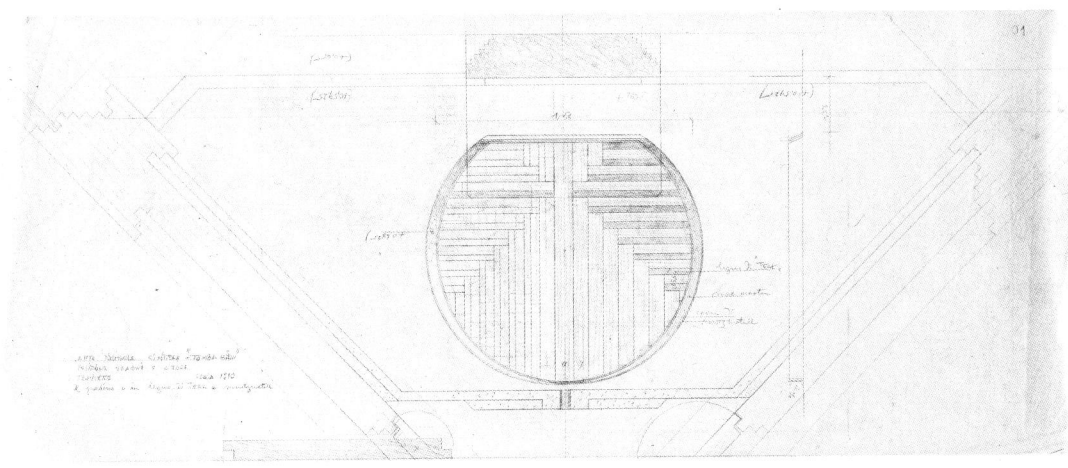

446

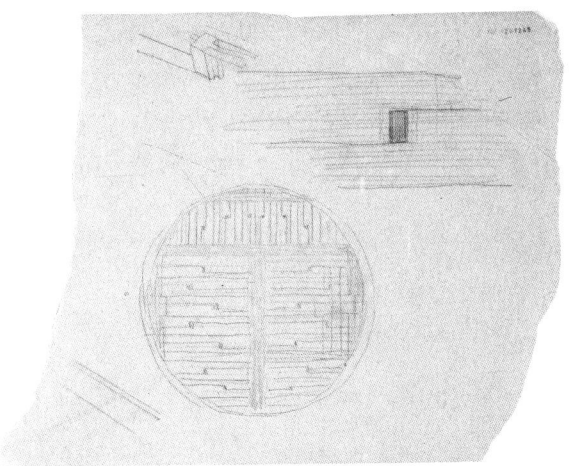

447

448

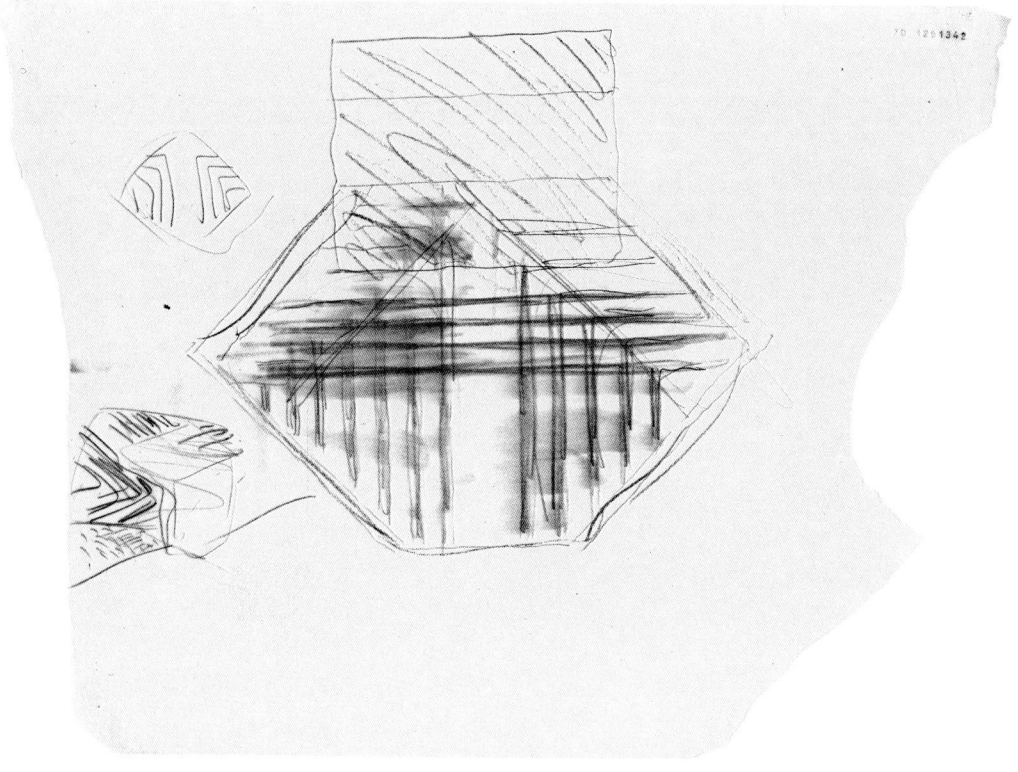

449

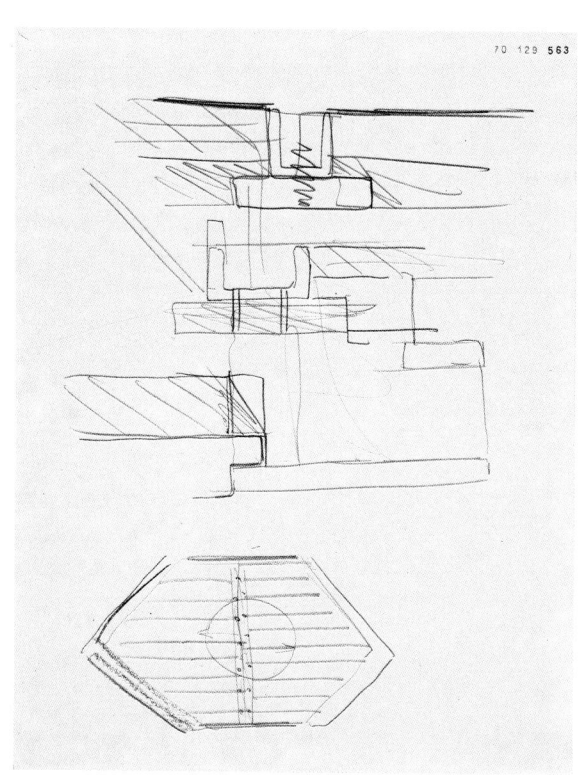

450

Dais under the altar/Sockel unter dem Altar

451

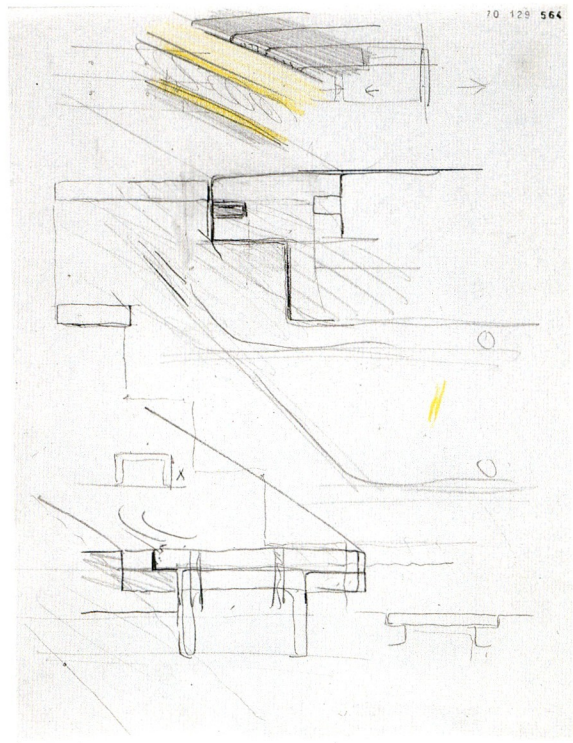

452

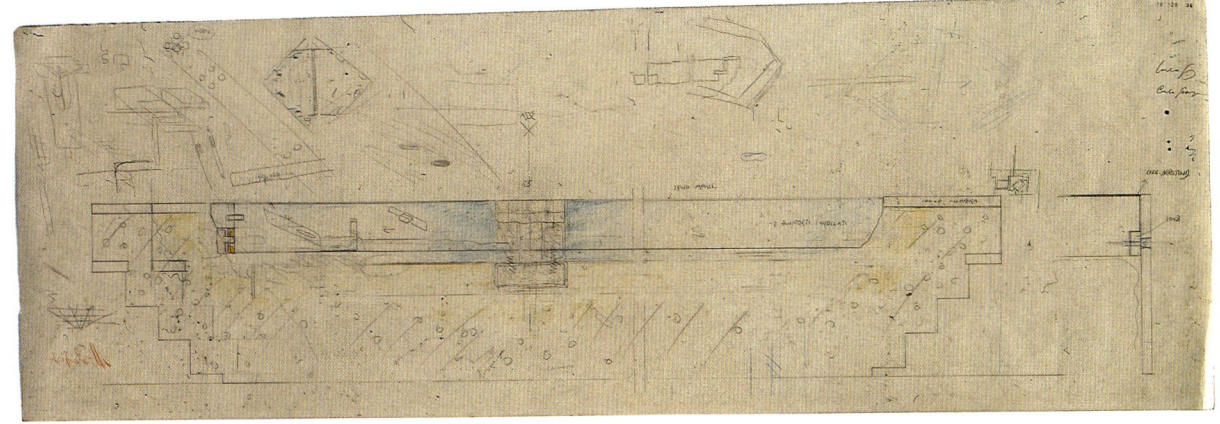

453

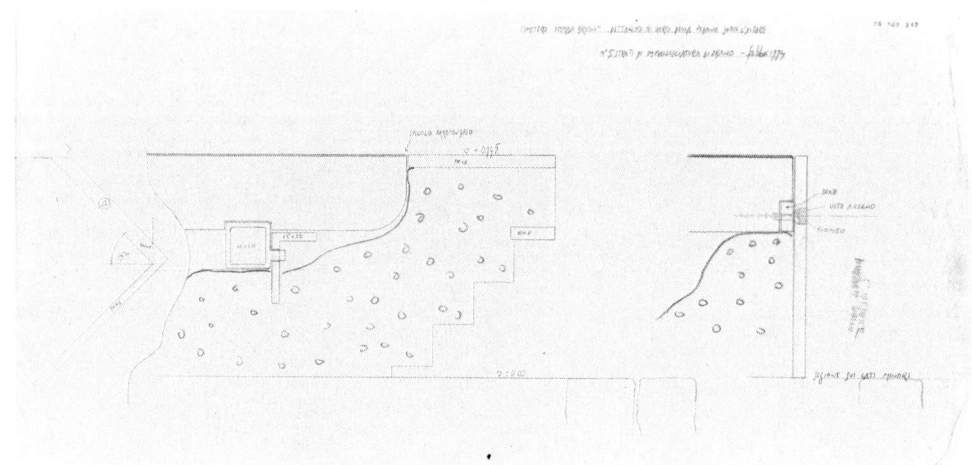

454

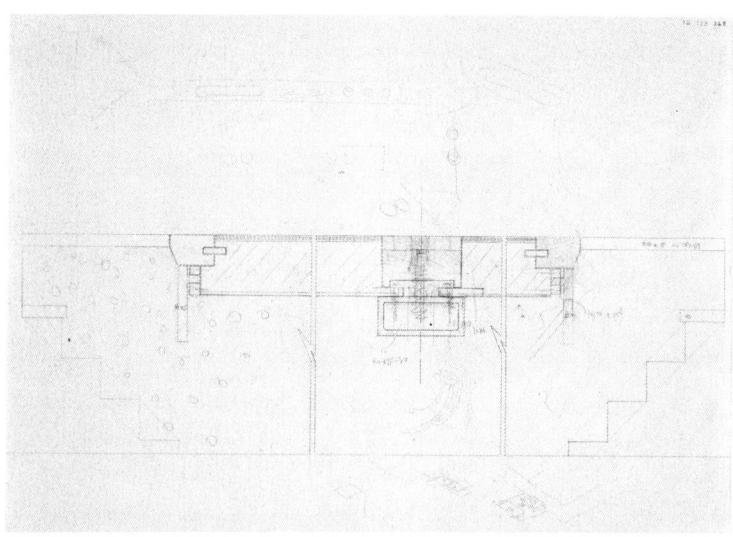

455

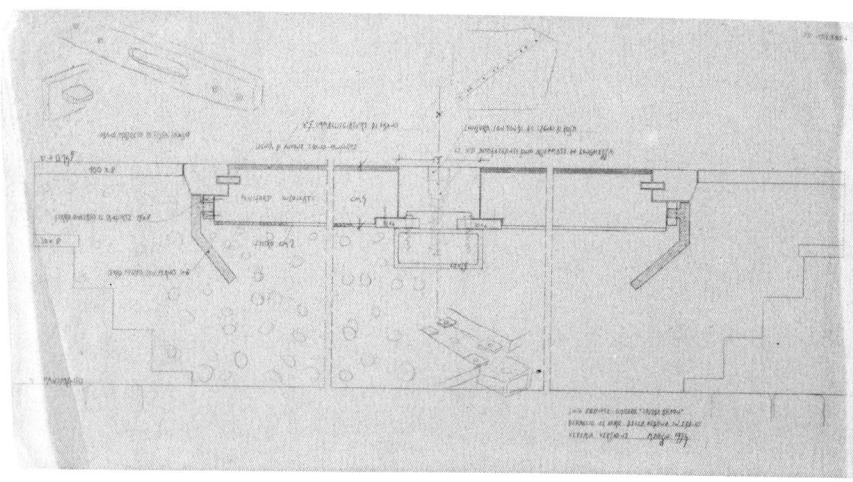

456

Altar / Der Altar (1971)

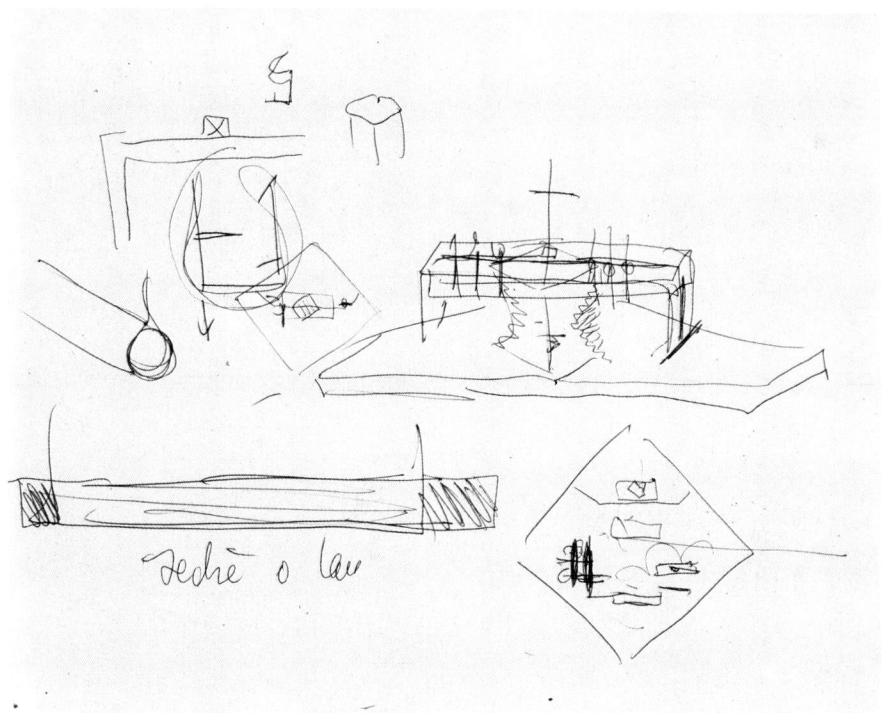

457

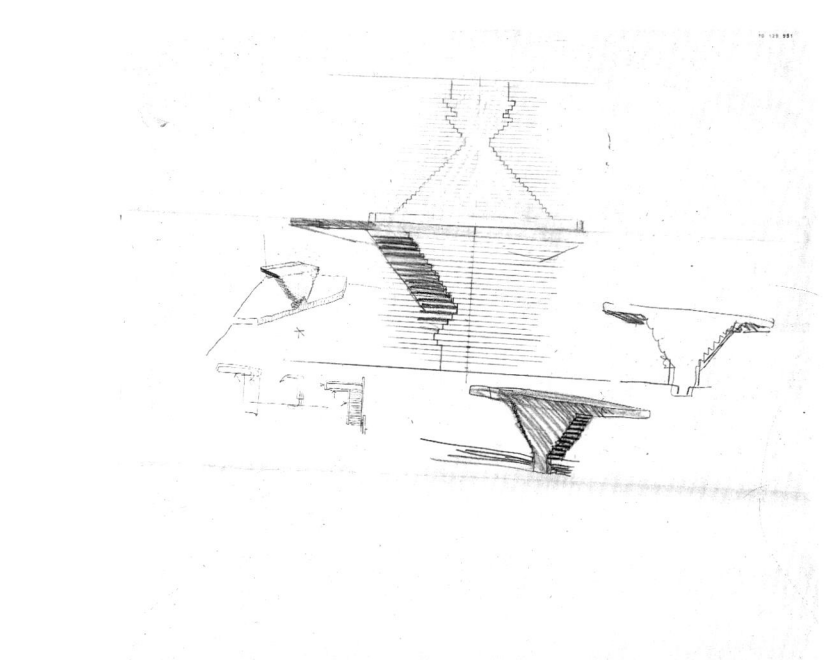

458

250

459

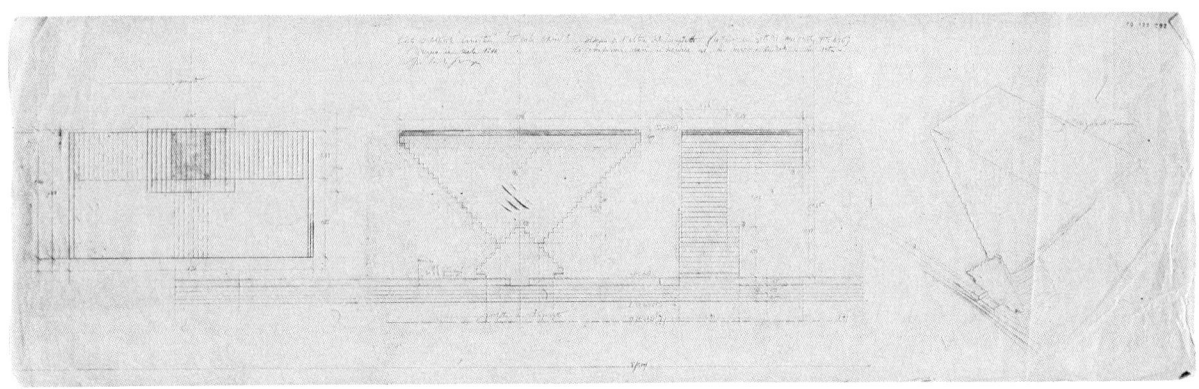

460

461

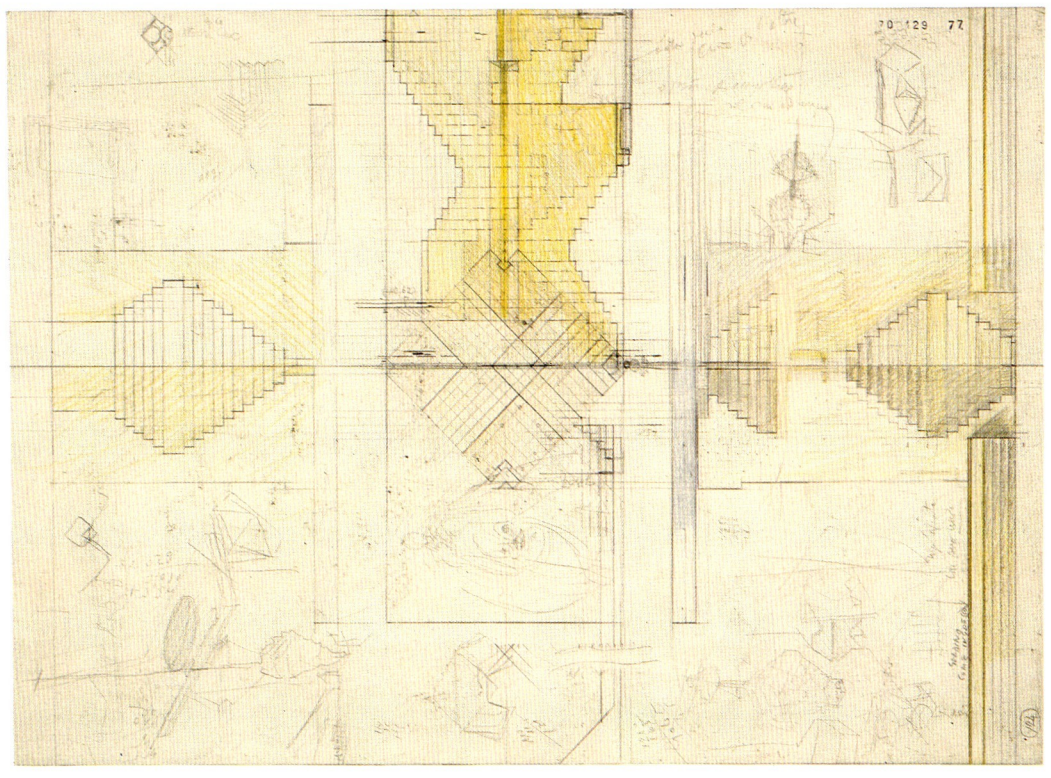

462

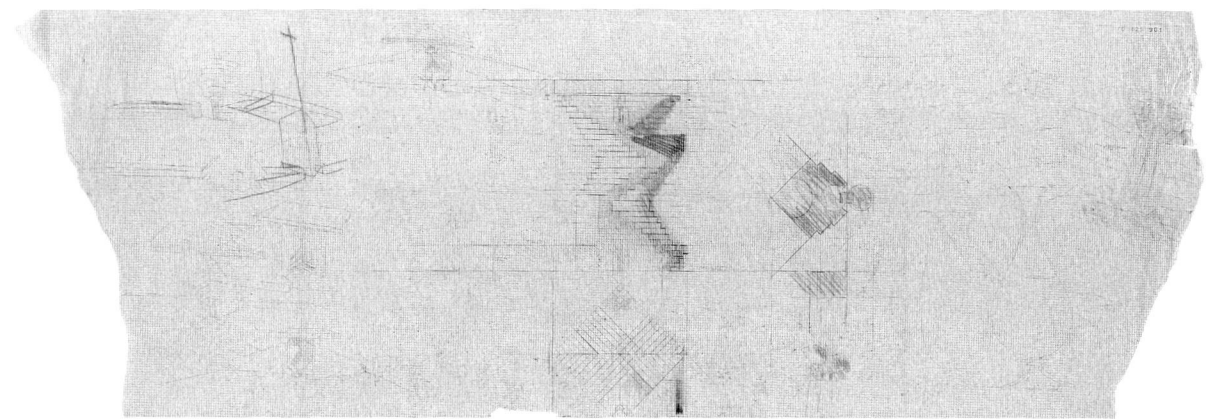

463

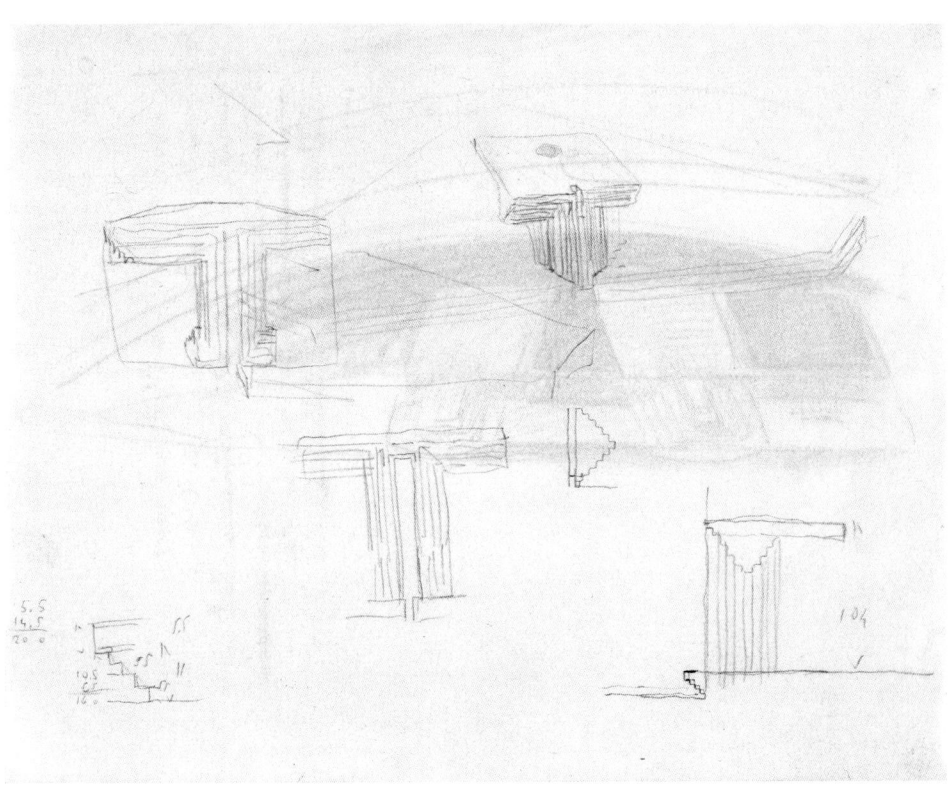

464

465

466

254

467

468

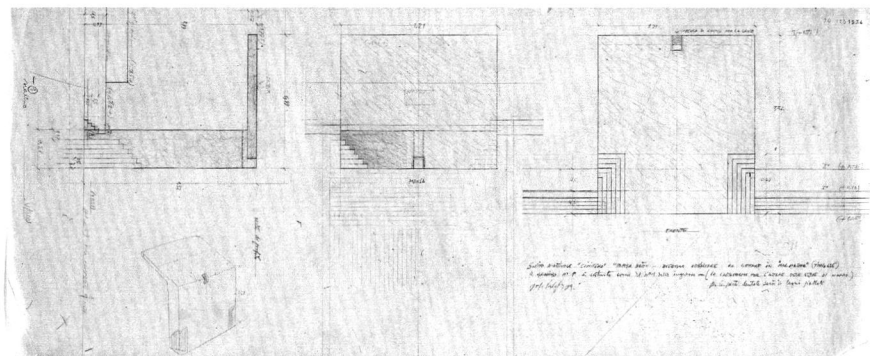

469

Sacrum

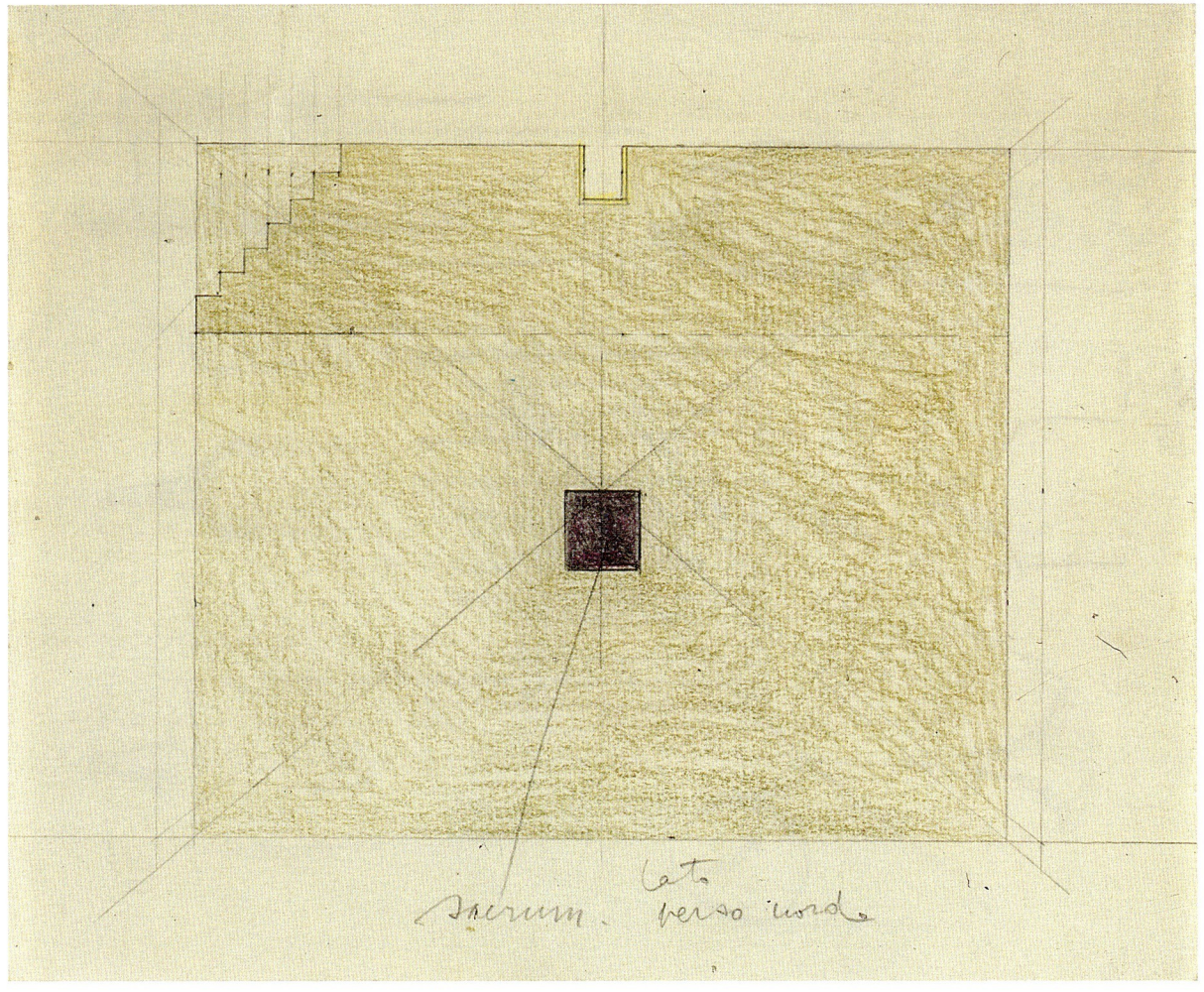

Sacrum. lato verso nord.

Chalice/Kelch

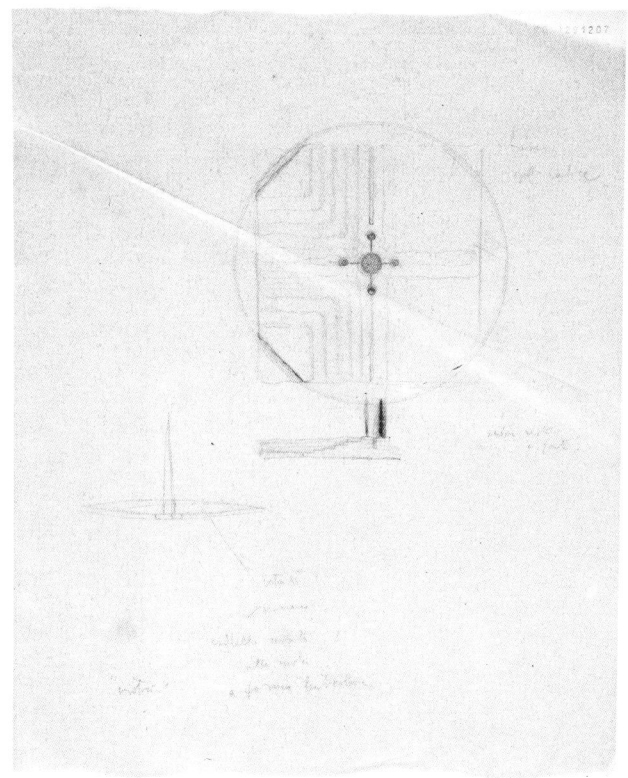

471

472

Crucifix/Kruzifix

257

473

258

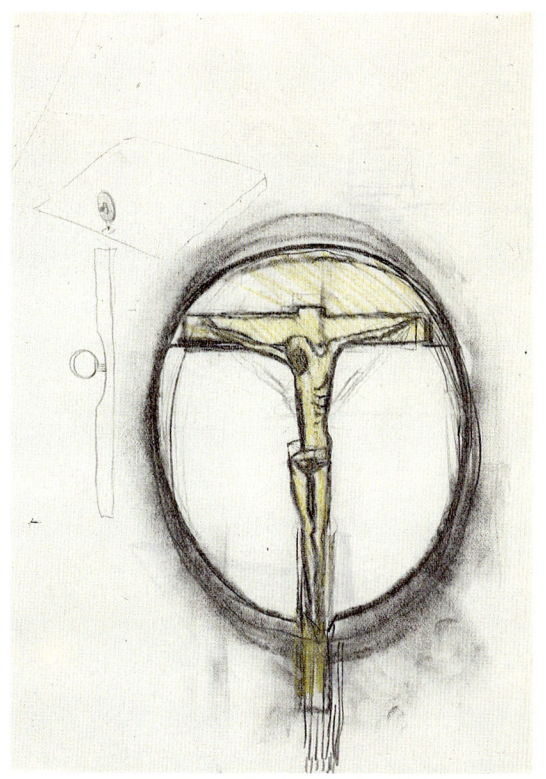

474

475

259

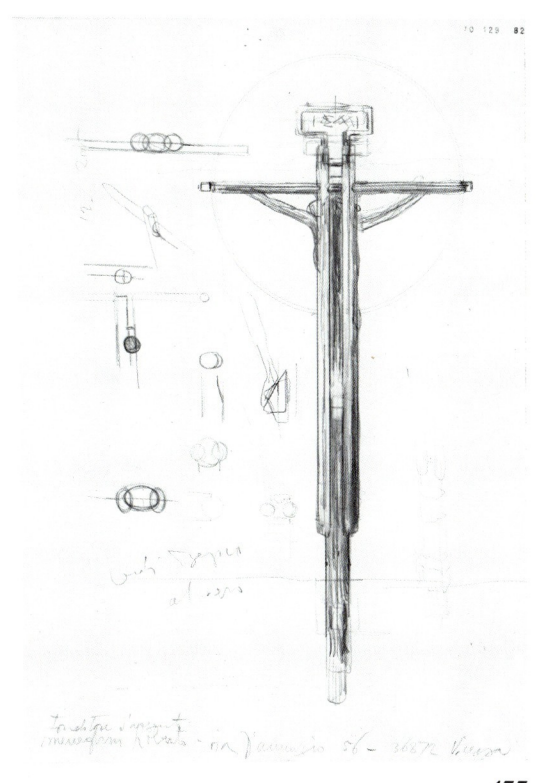

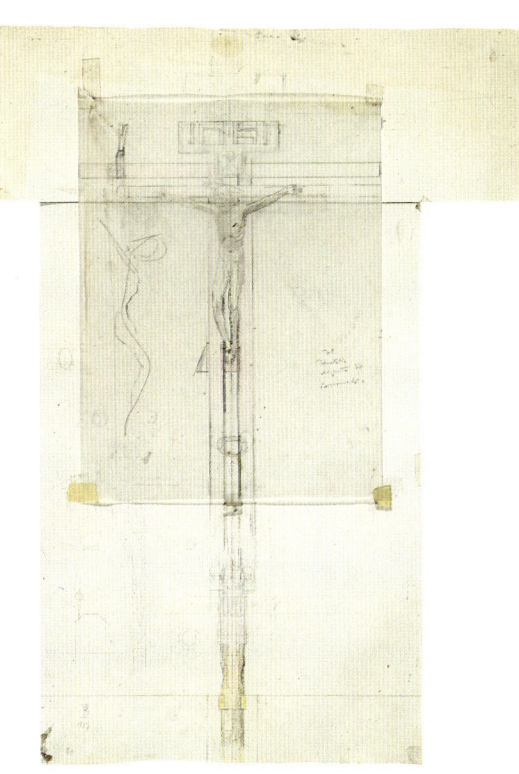

476

477

478

260

479

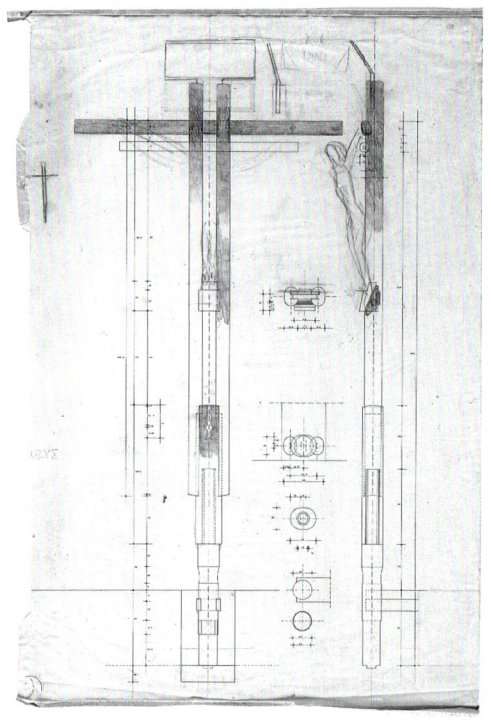

480

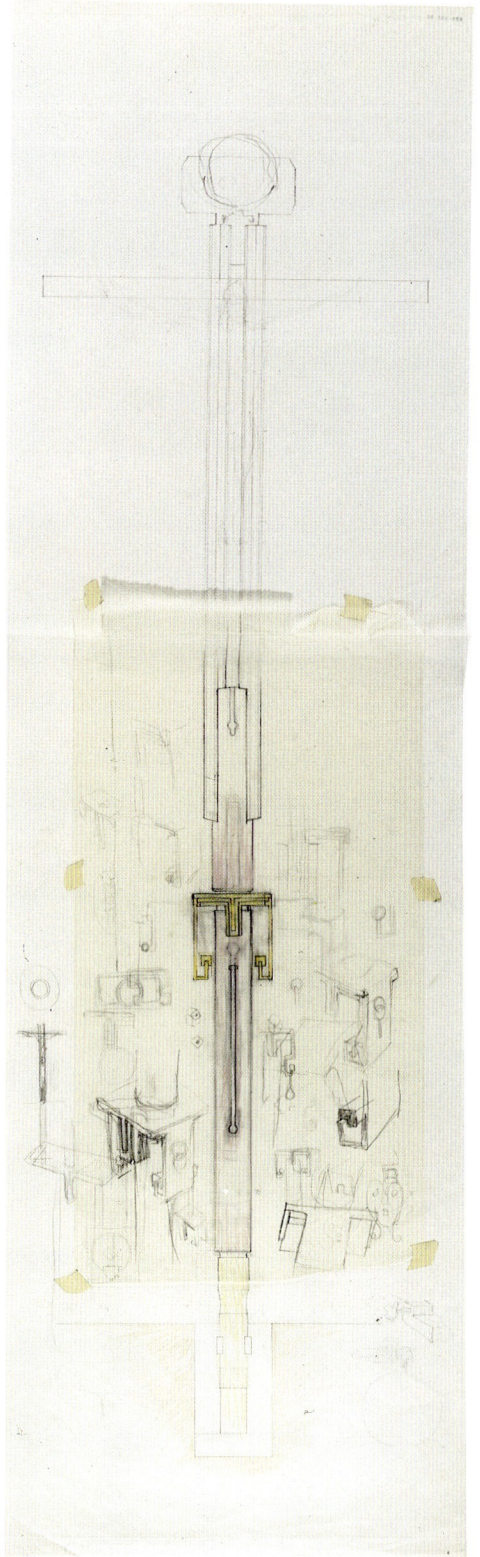

481

Suspended candelabra/Hängender Kandelaber

482

483

262

484

485

486

487

488

263

264

489

Candle holders/Kerzenhalterungen

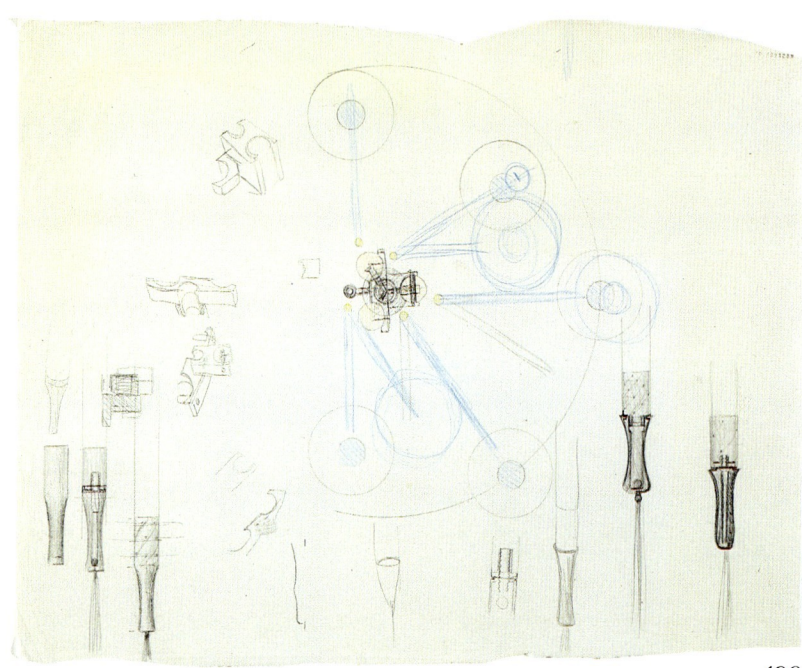

490

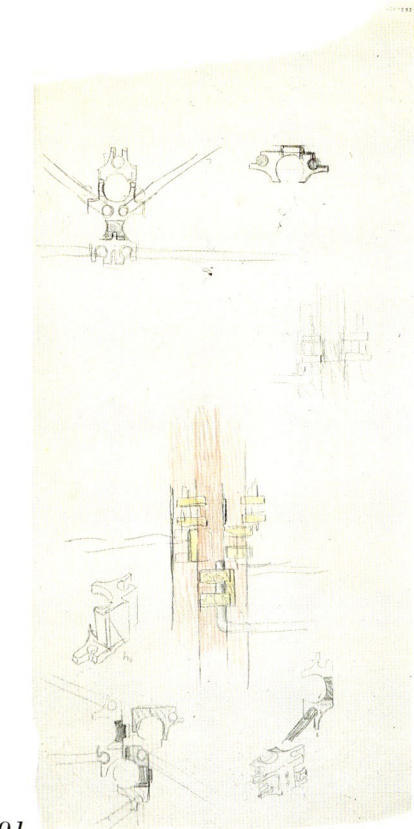

491

265

492

266

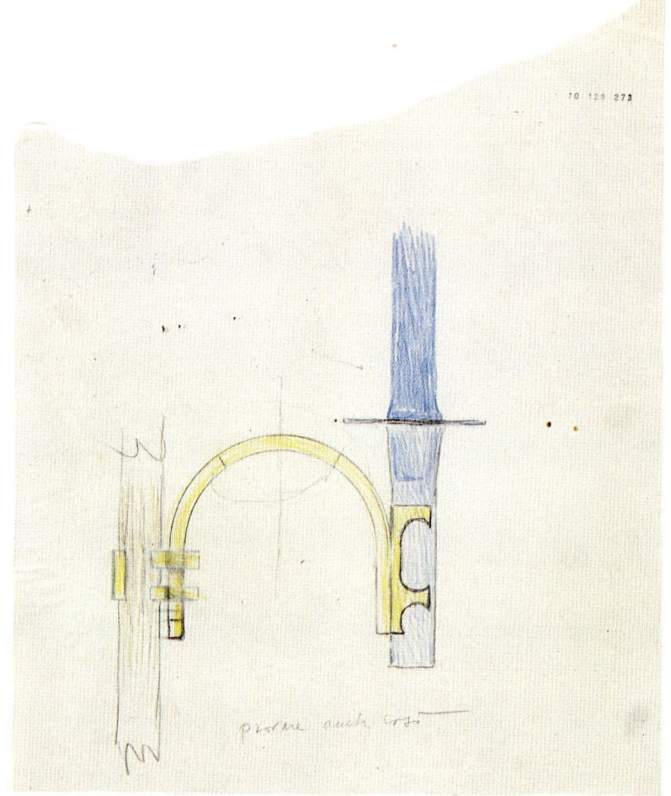

493

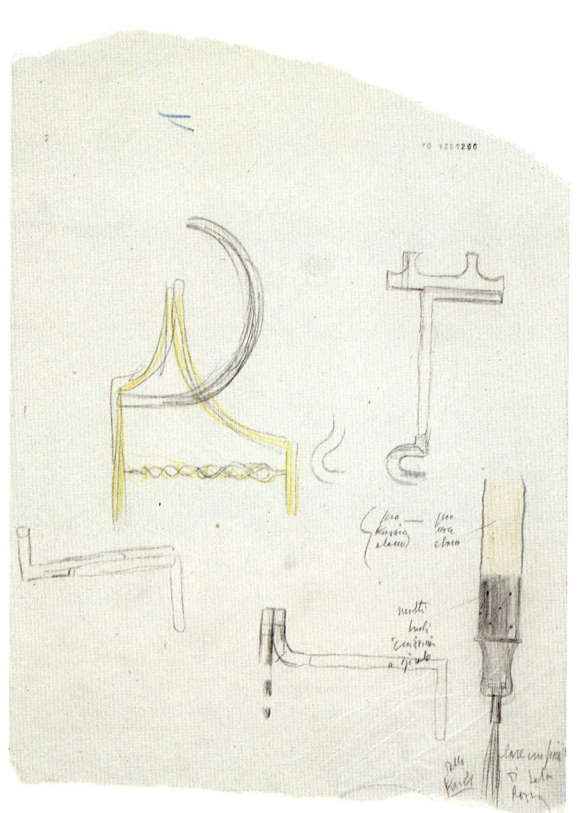

494

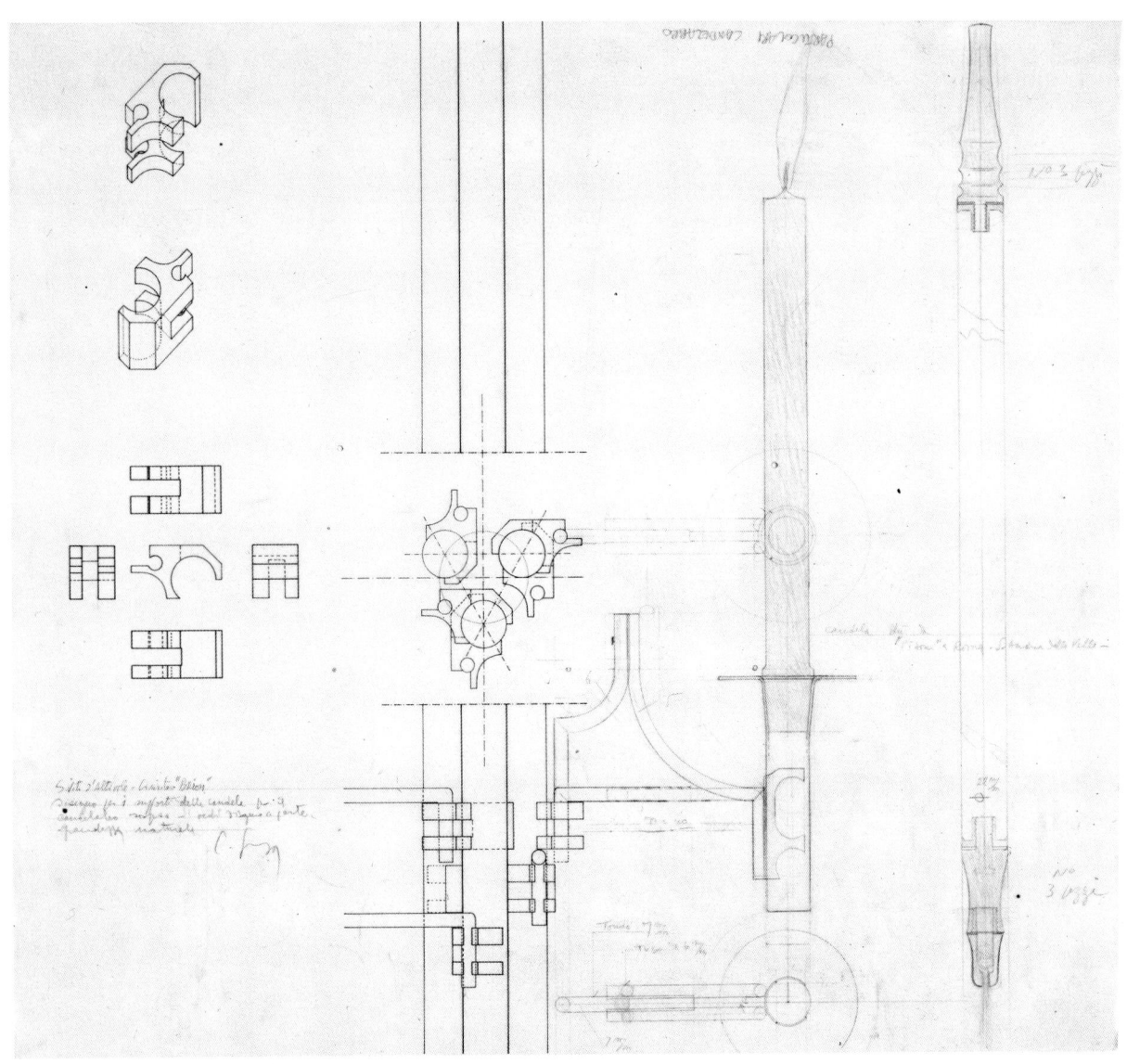

Ceiling pole mounts / Aufhängung der Stangen an der Decke

268

496

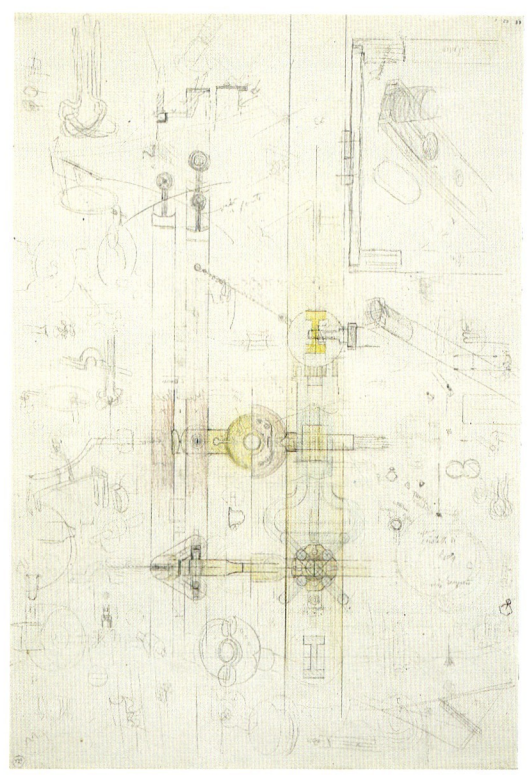

497

The three poles/Die drei Stangen

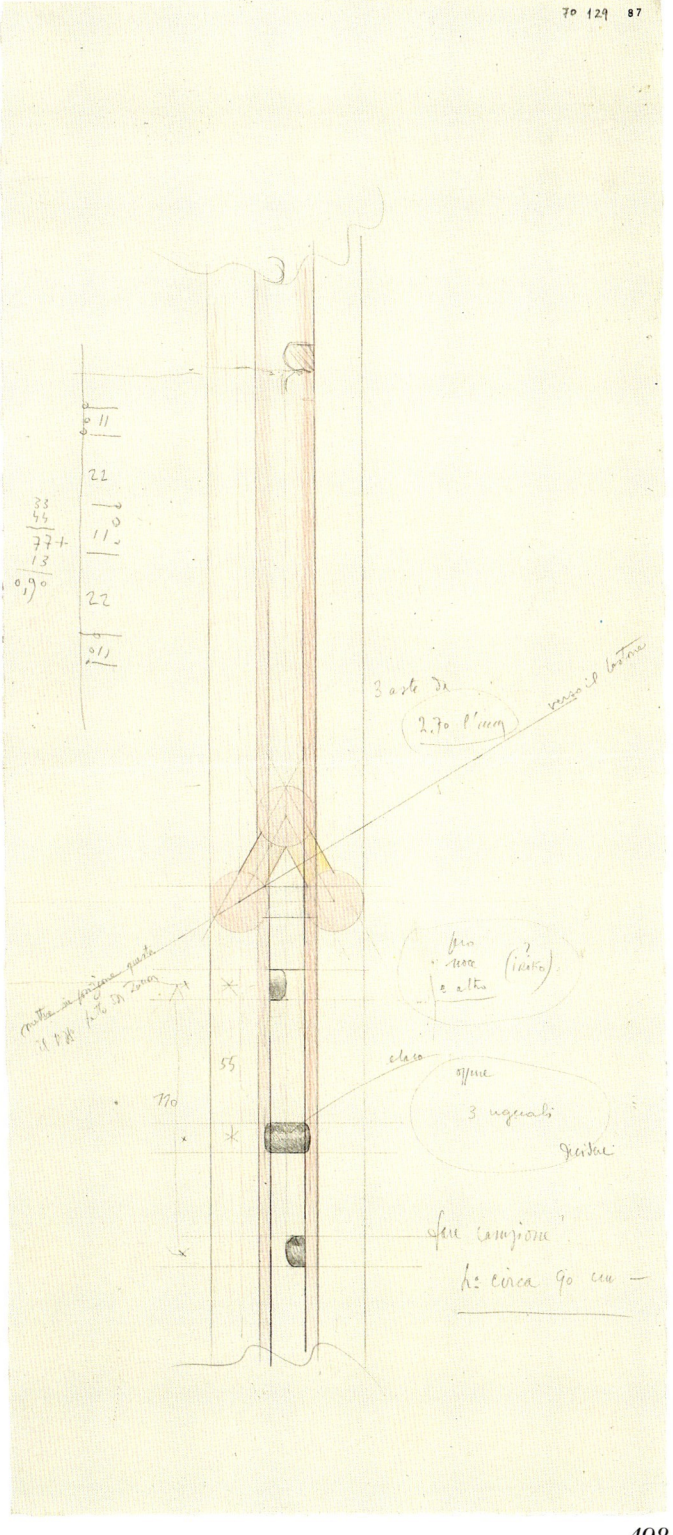

269

498

Marble antas behind the altar (1973–1974)/Kleine Marmortüren hinter dem Altar (1973–74)

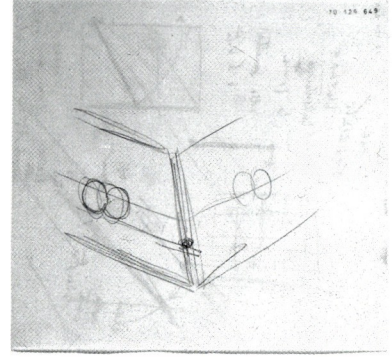

499

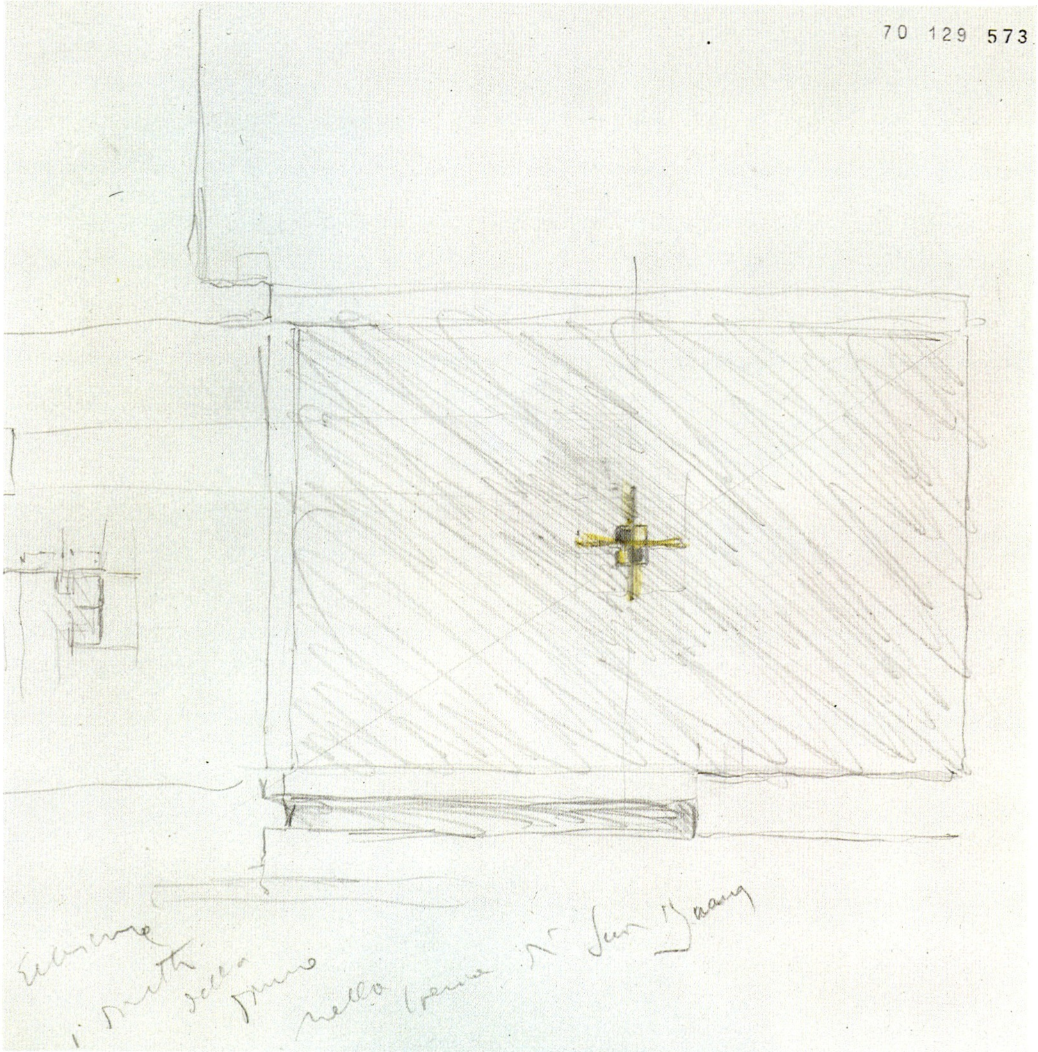

500

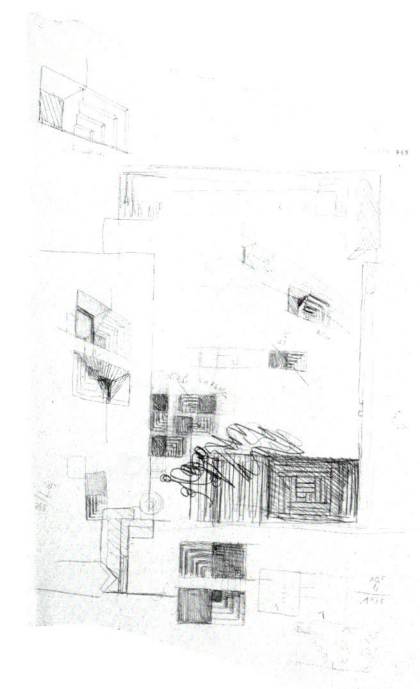

501

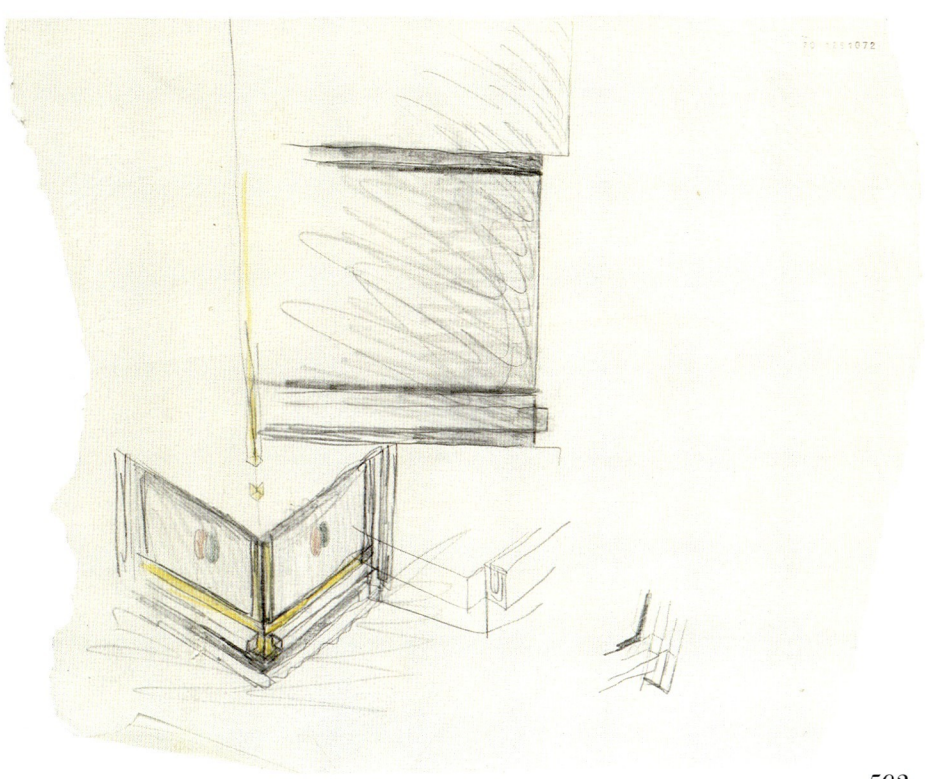

502

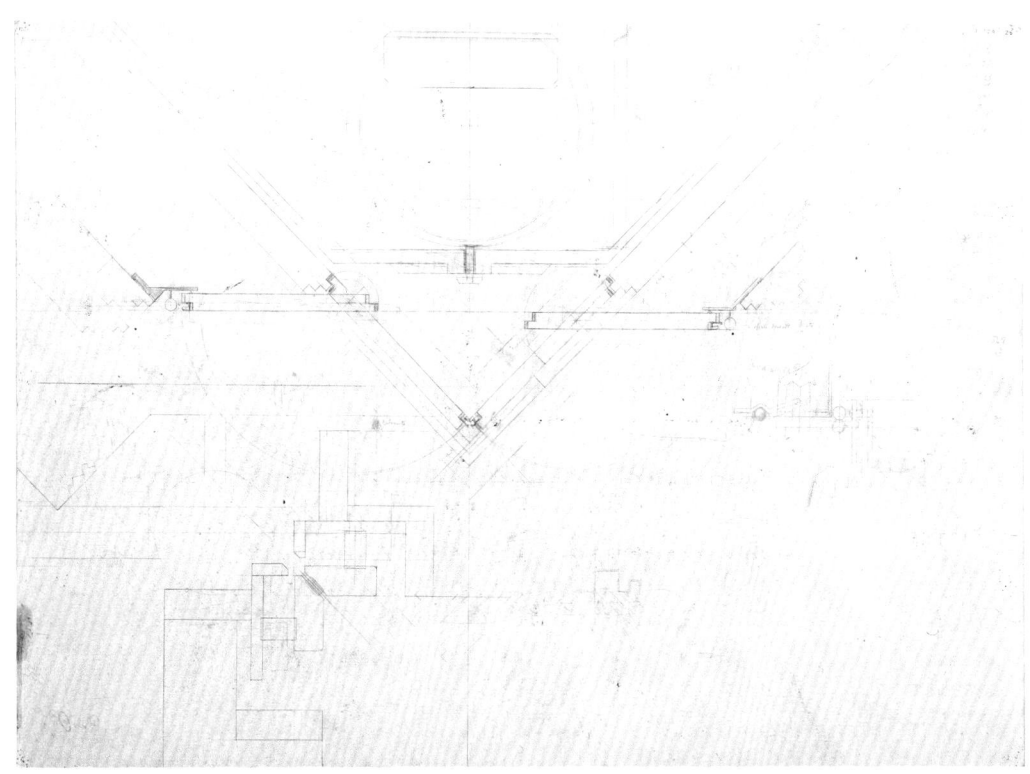

504

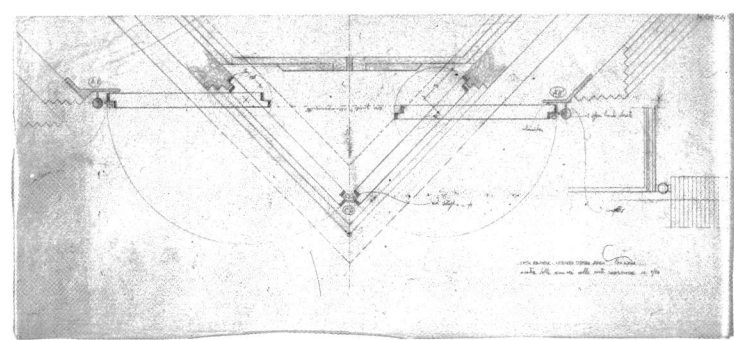

505

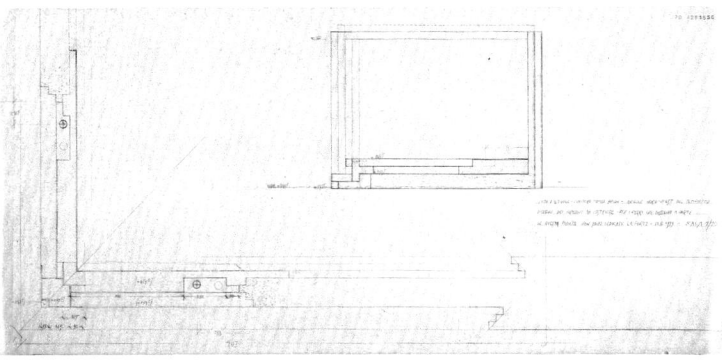

506

507

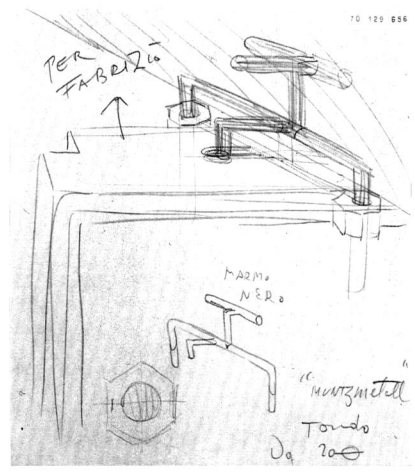

508

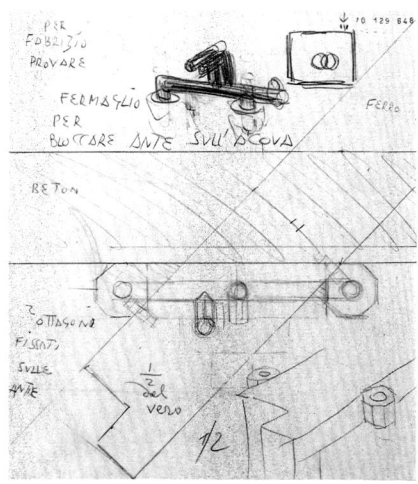

509

510

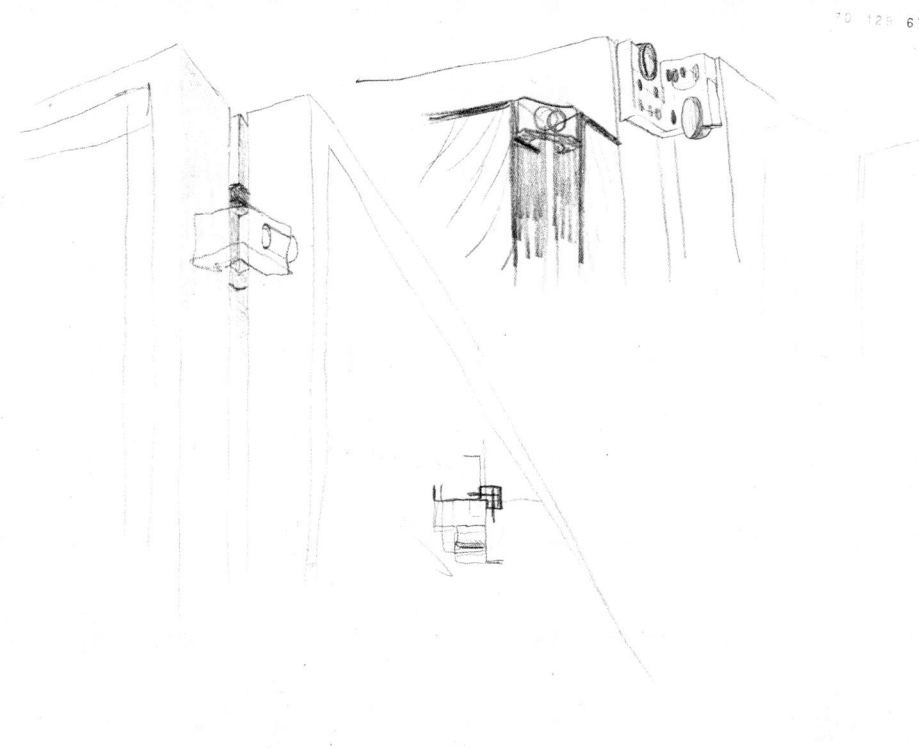

511

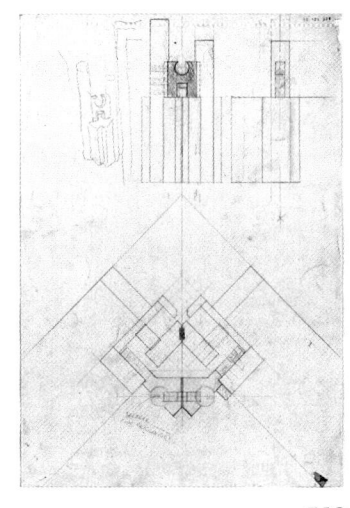

512

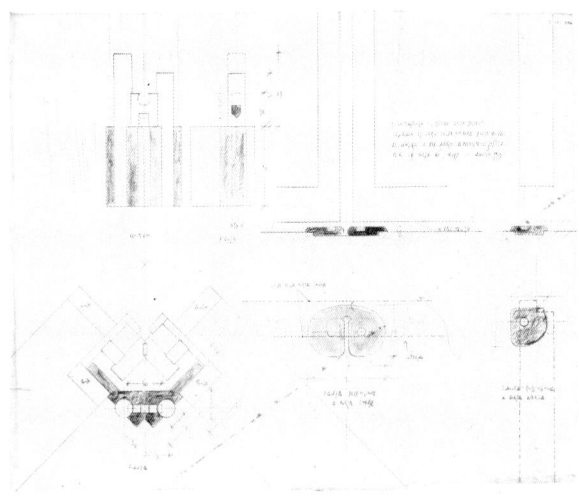

513

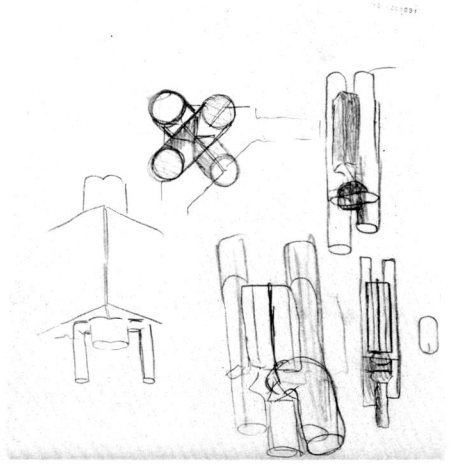

514

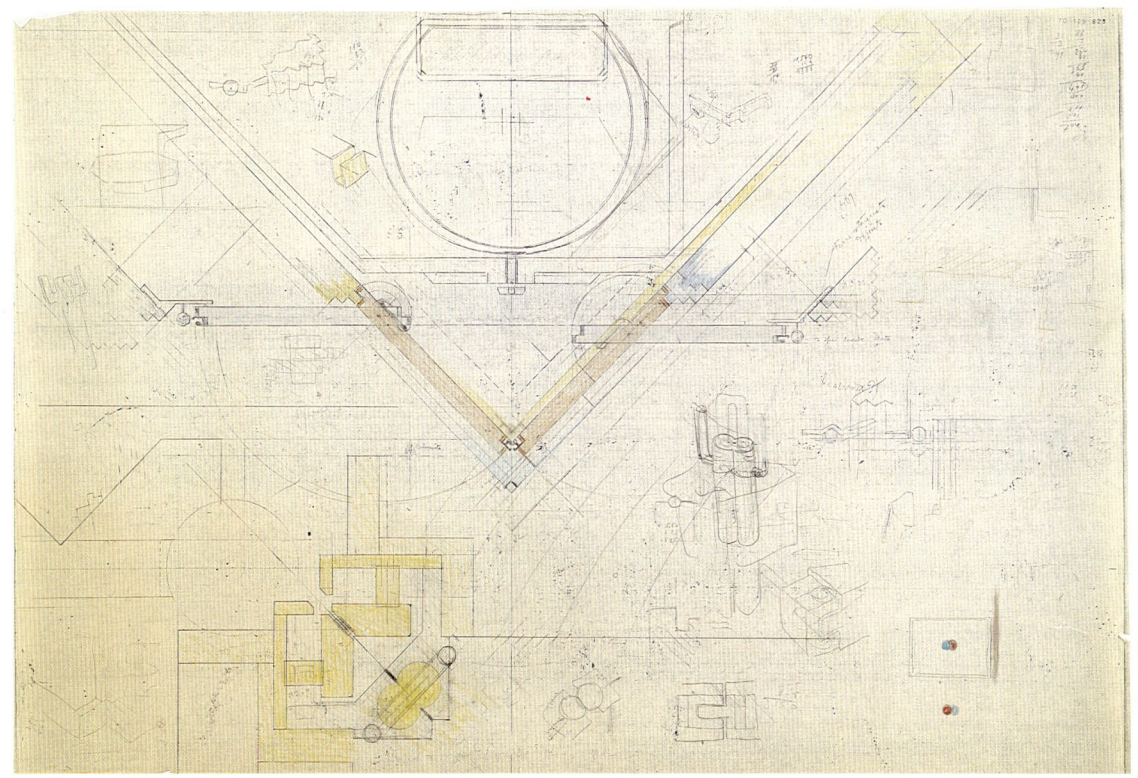

515

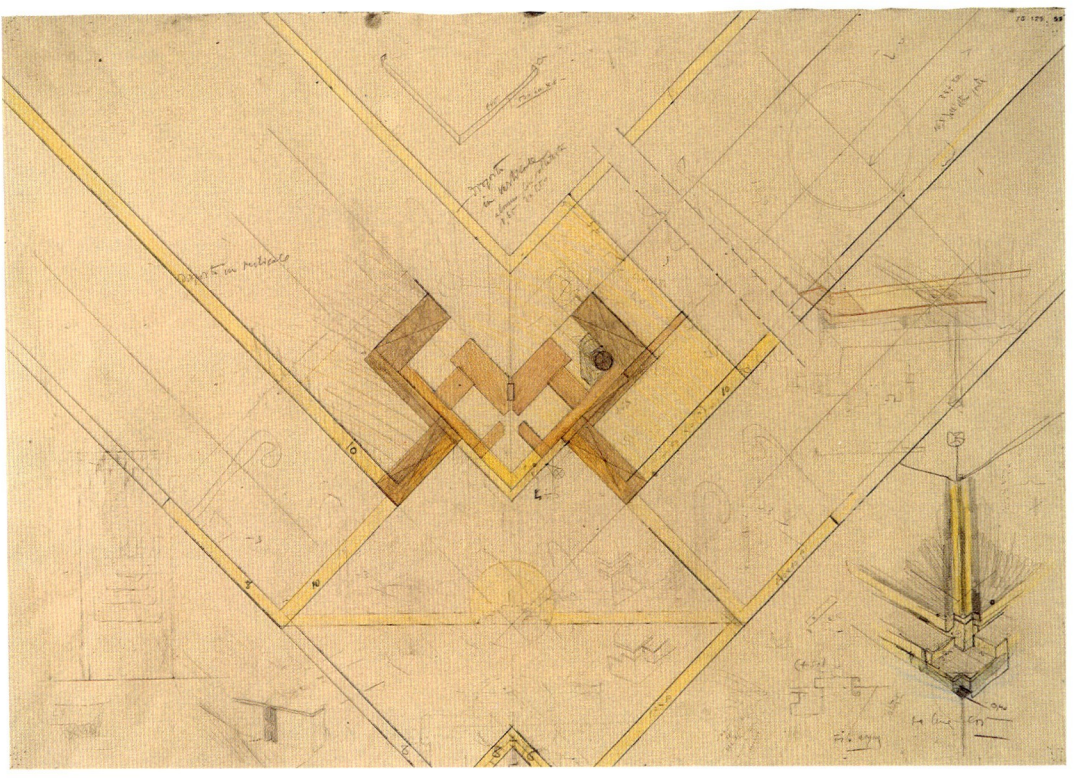

516

278

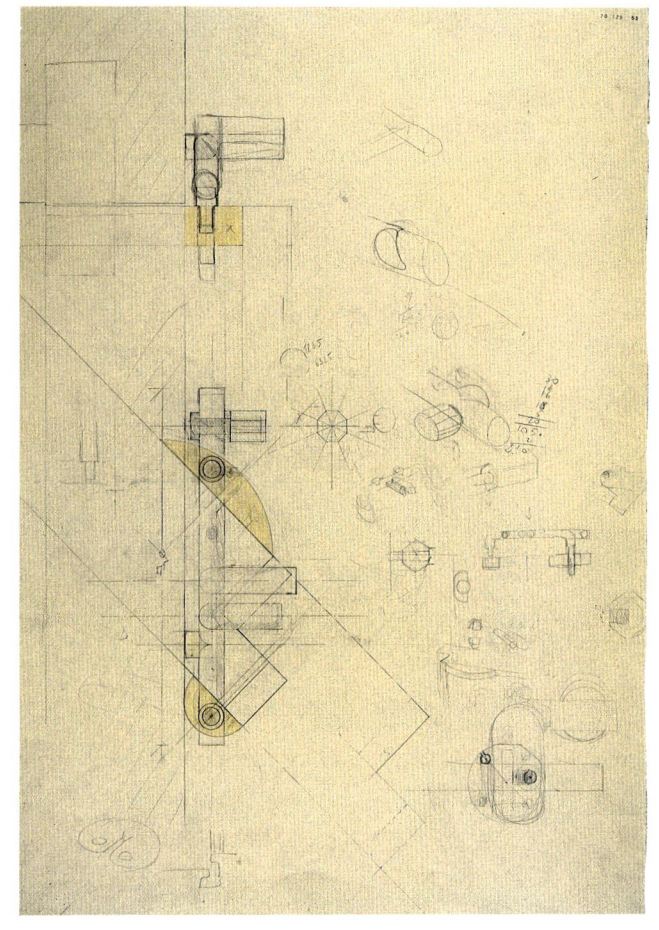

517

Gate to the cypress grove (1973–1975)/Tor zum Zypressenhain (1973–1975)

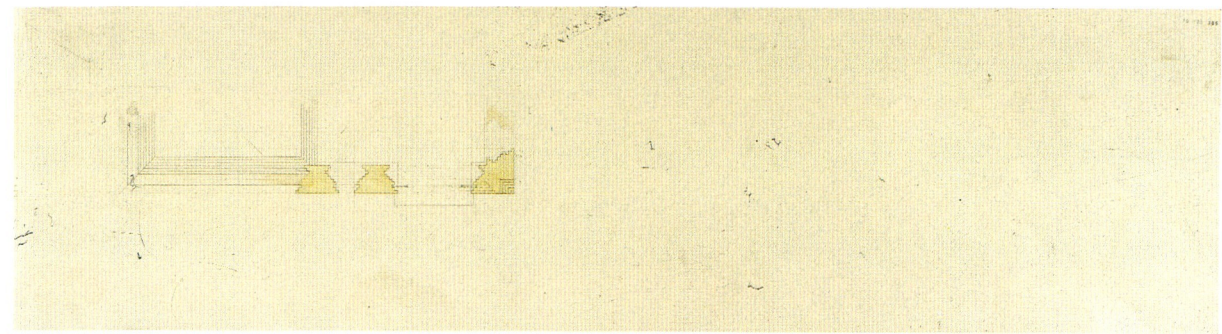

518

279

519

520

280

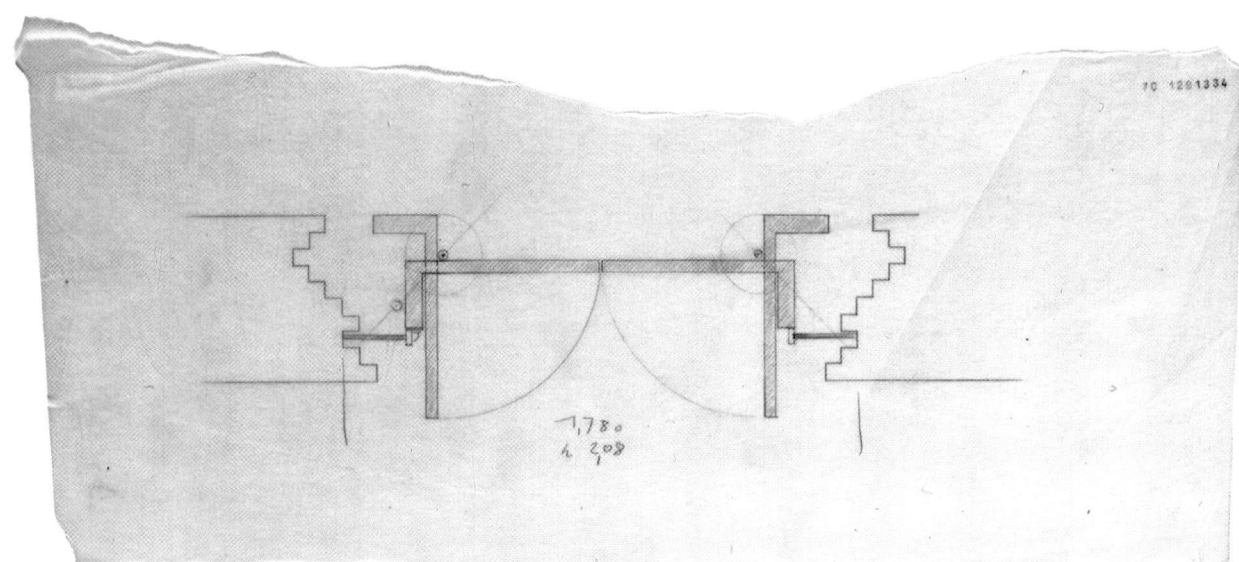

521

522

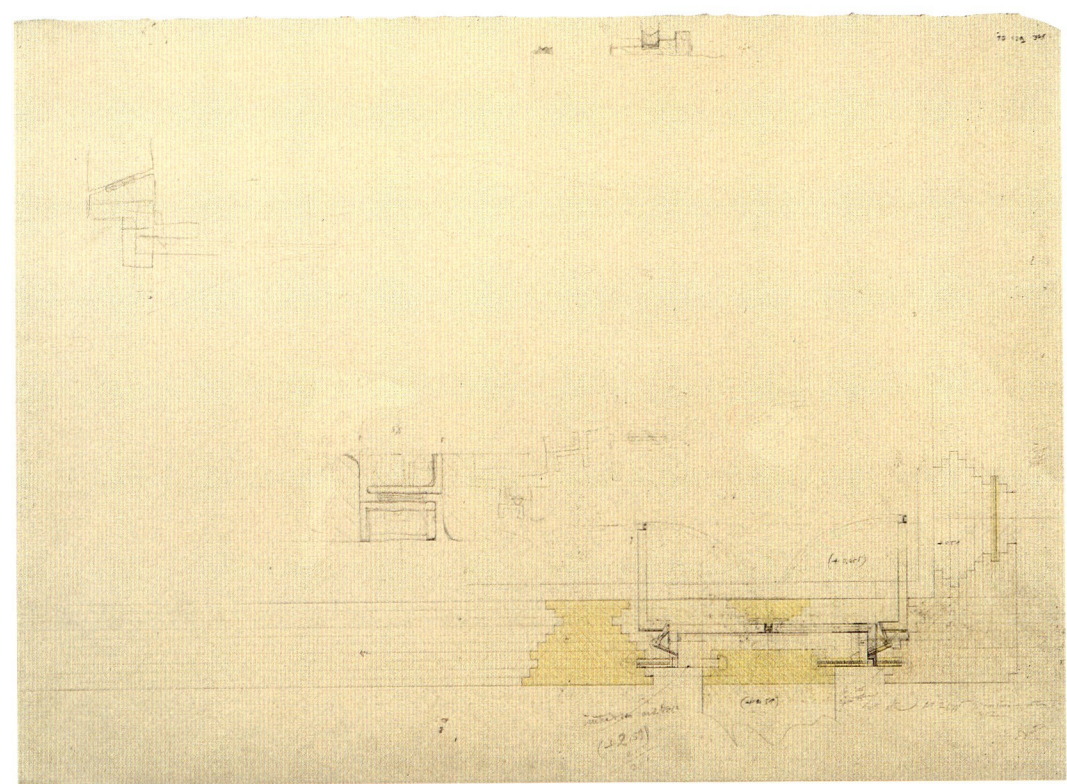

523

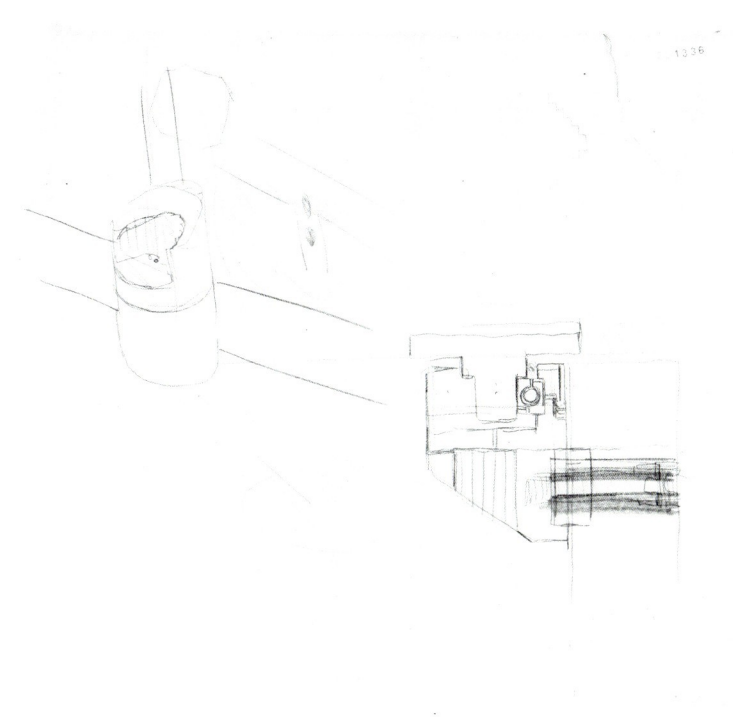

524

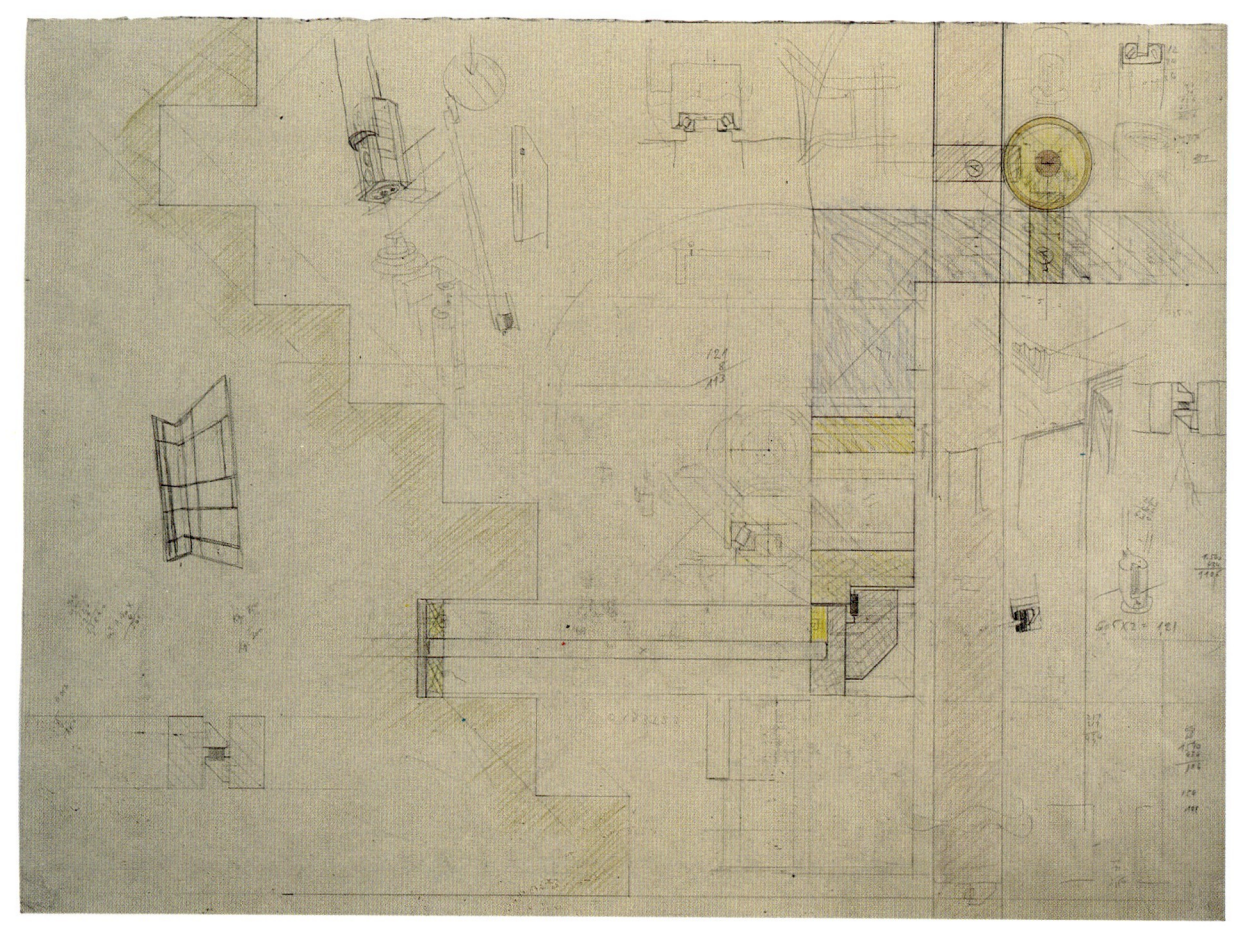

526

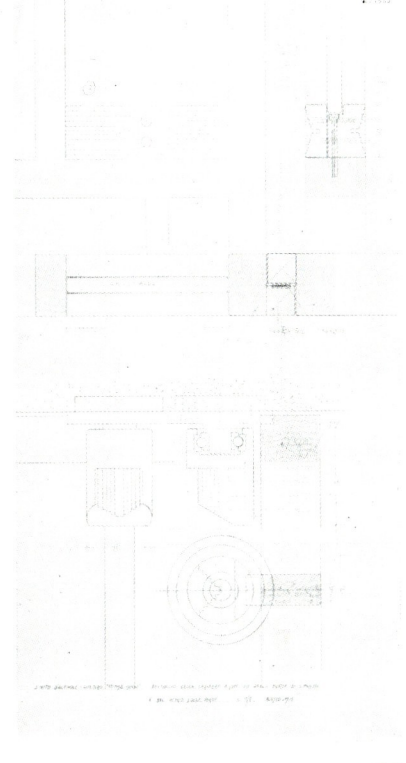

527

283

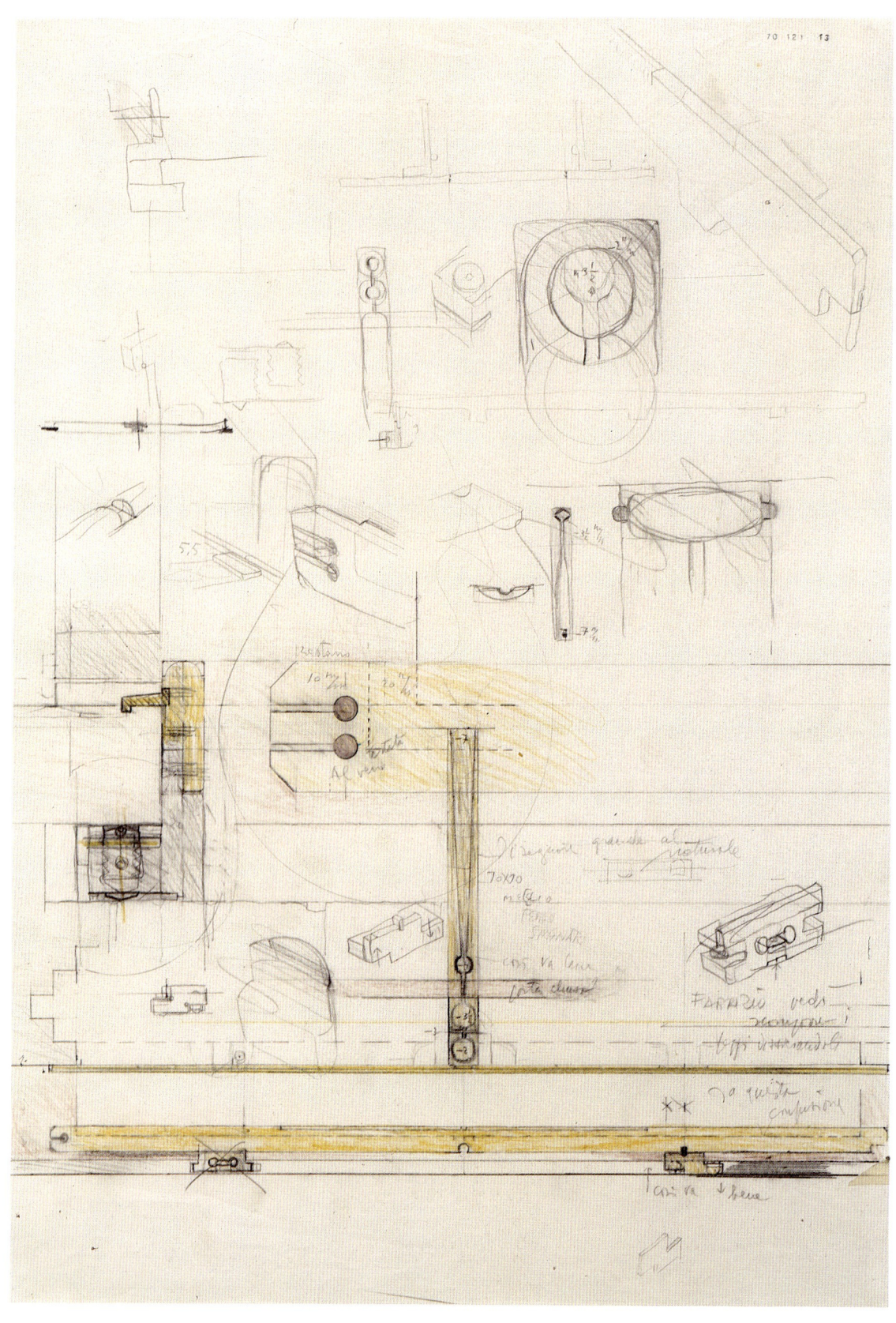

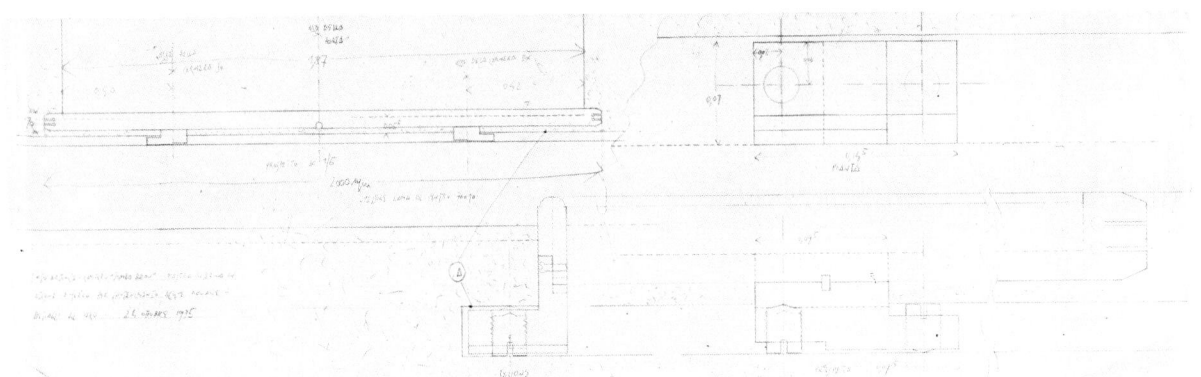

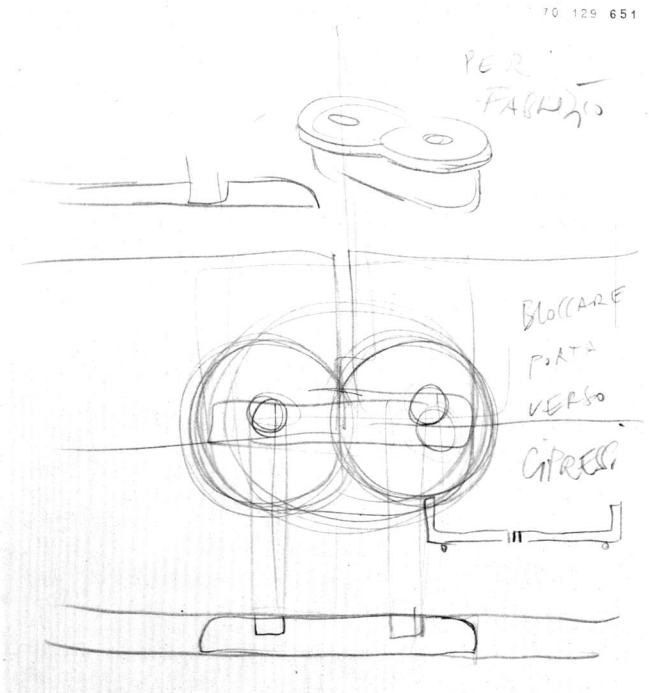

531

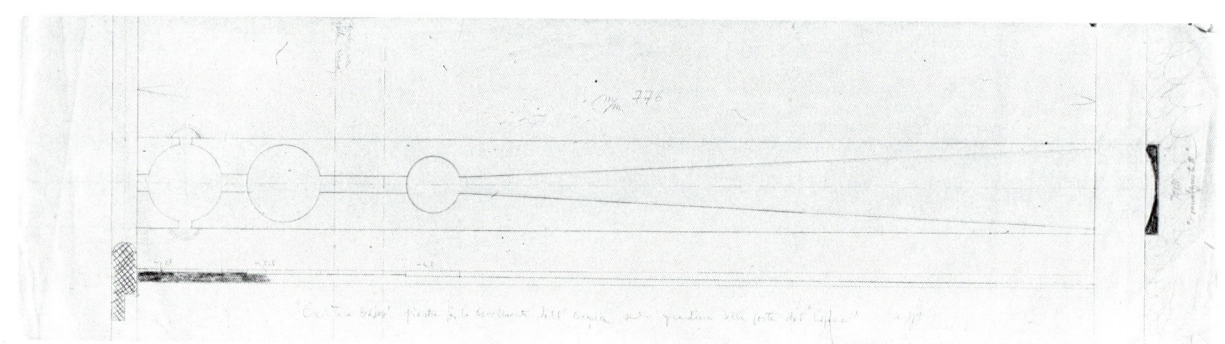

532

Entrance portal, open passage to the sacresty/Eingangsportal, offener Gang zur Sakristei

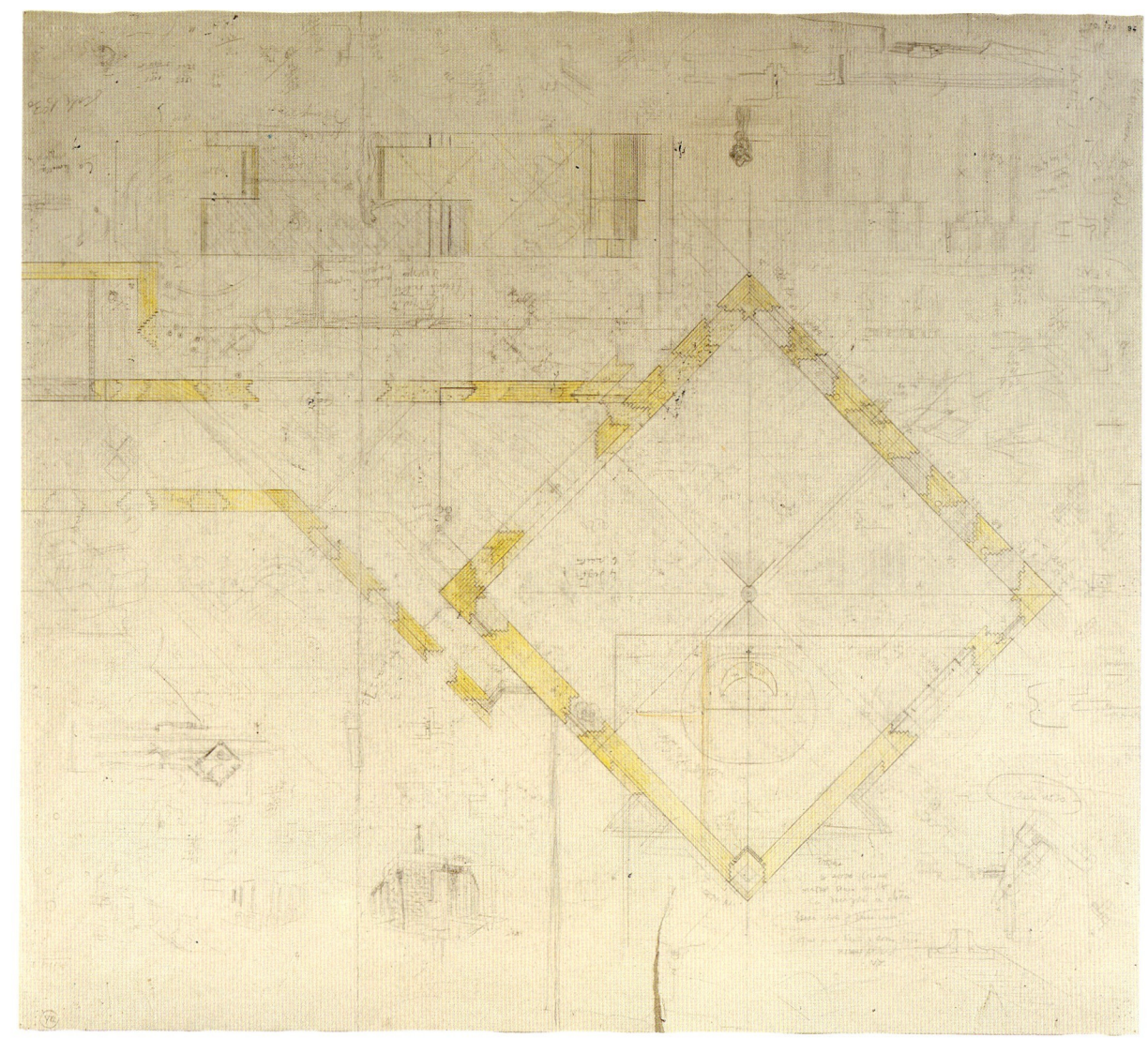

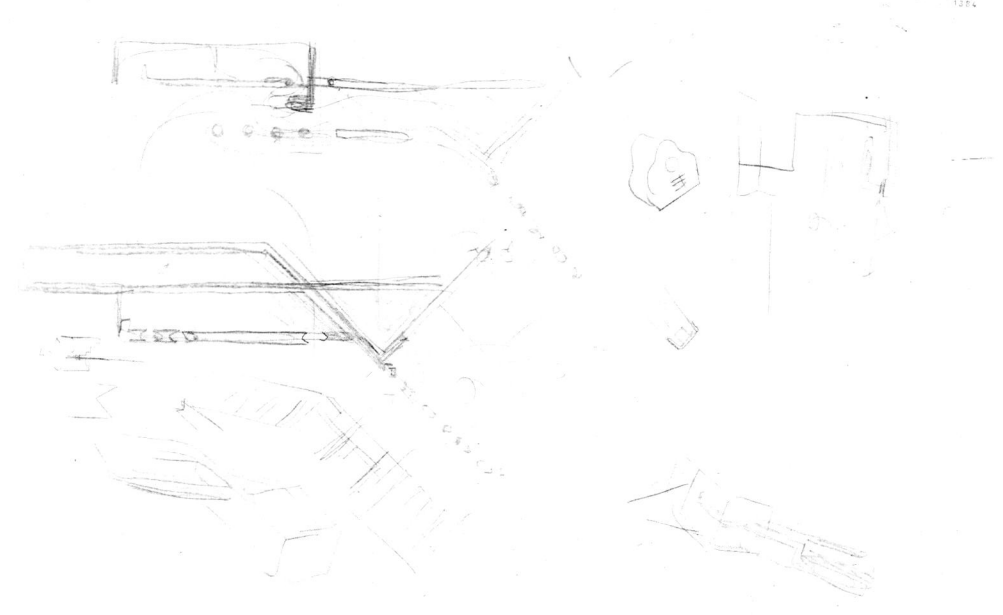

536

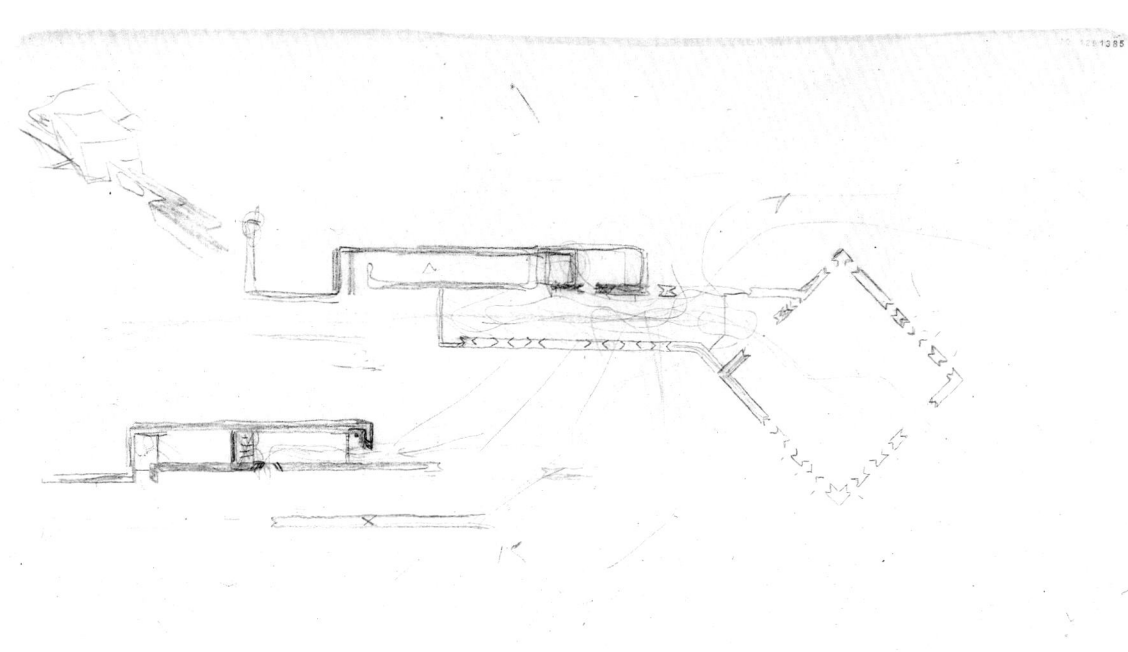

537

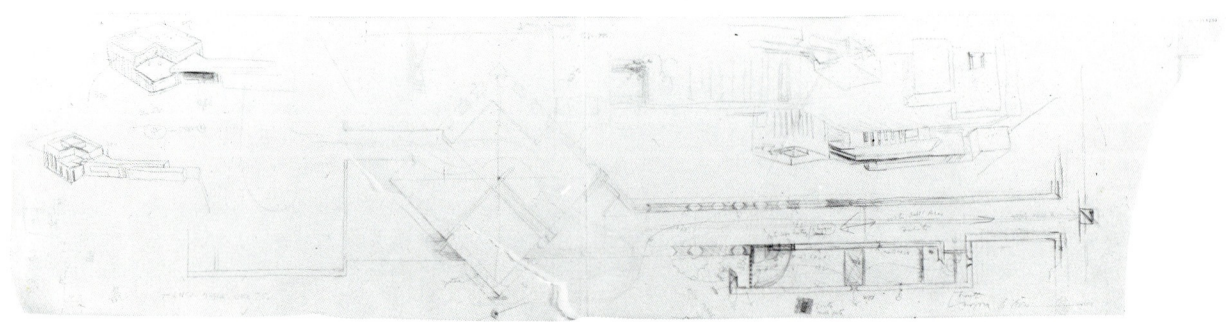

290

538

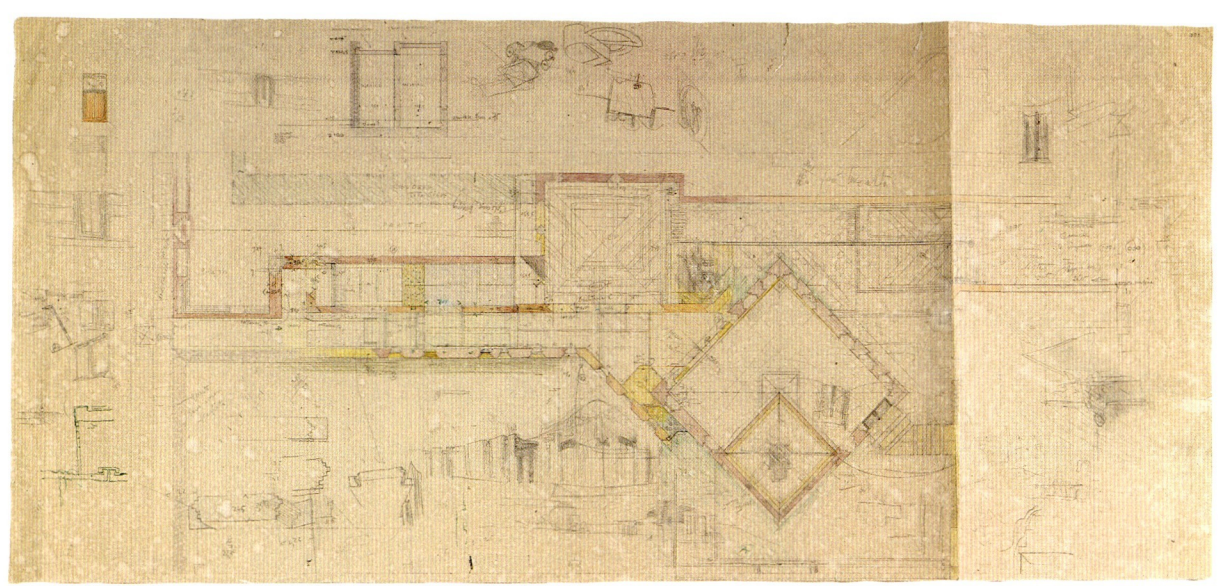

539

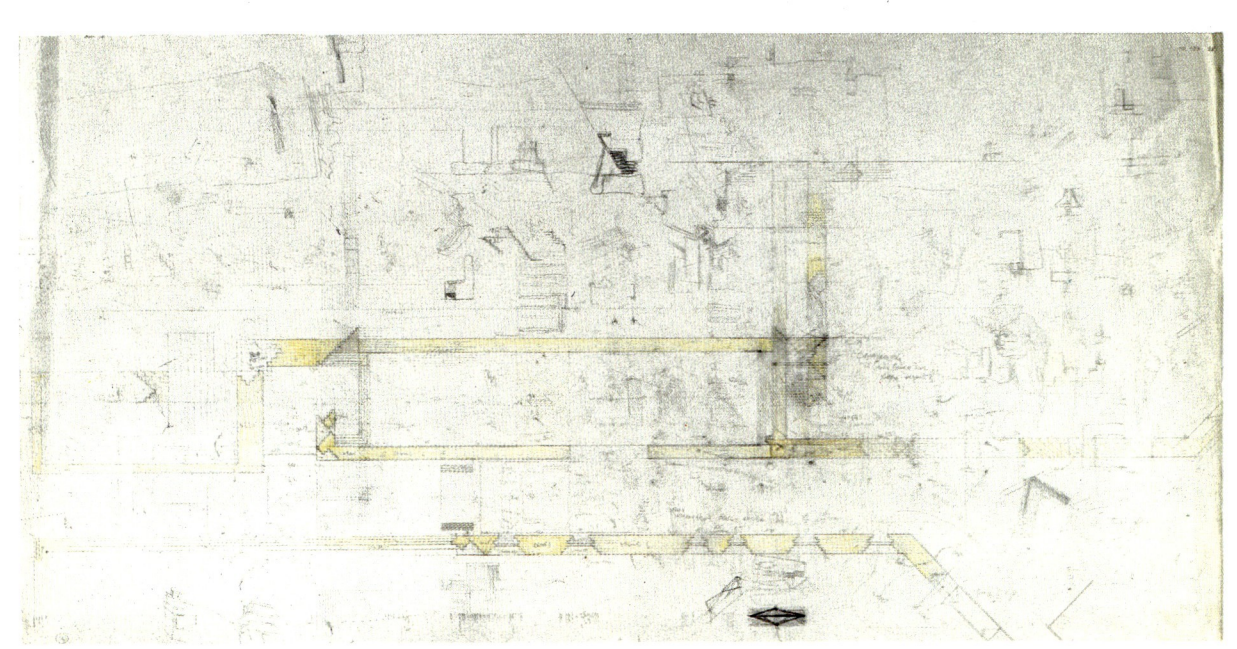

540

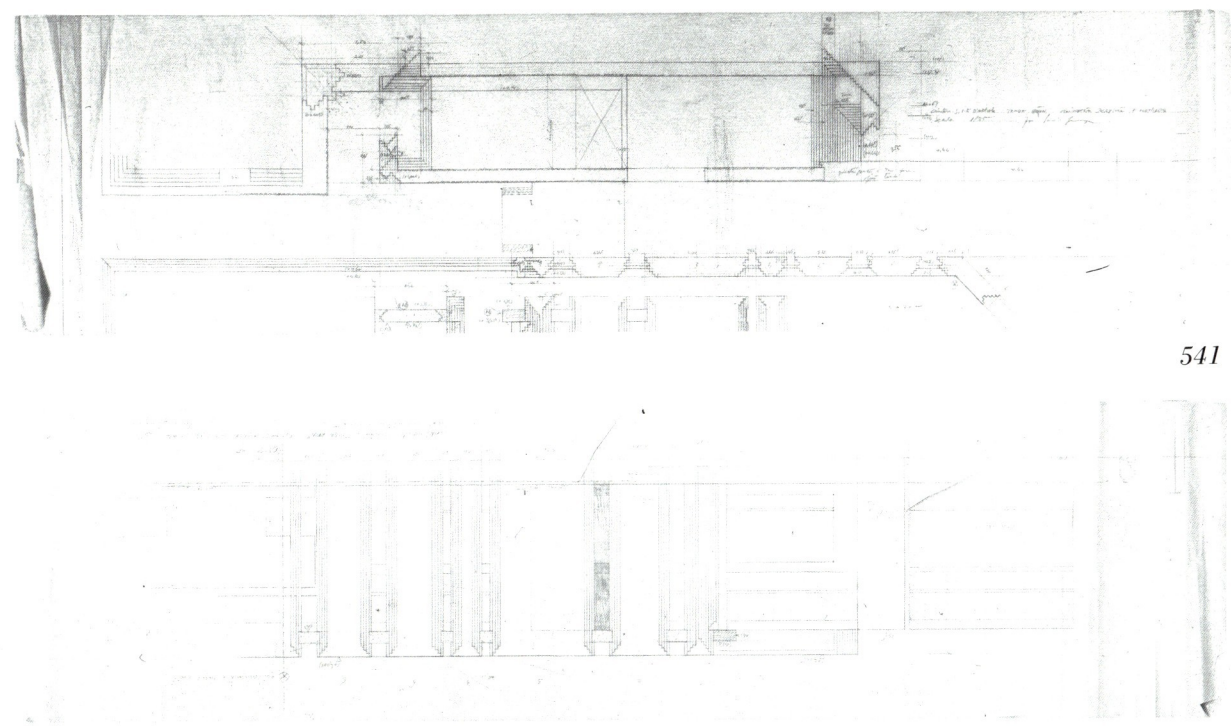

541

542

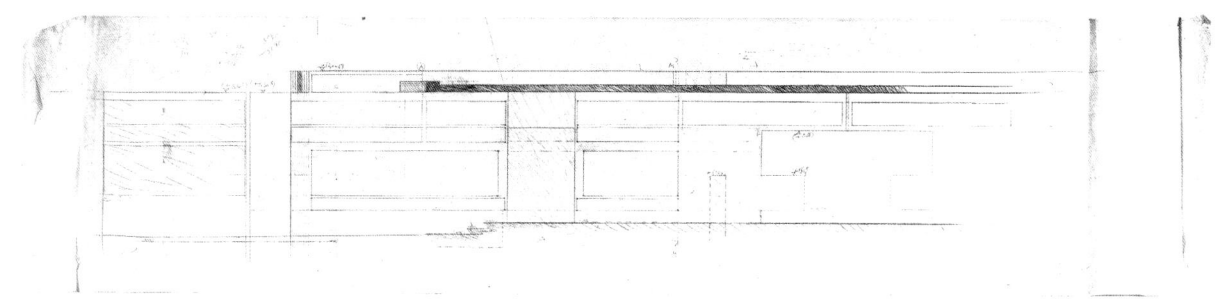

543

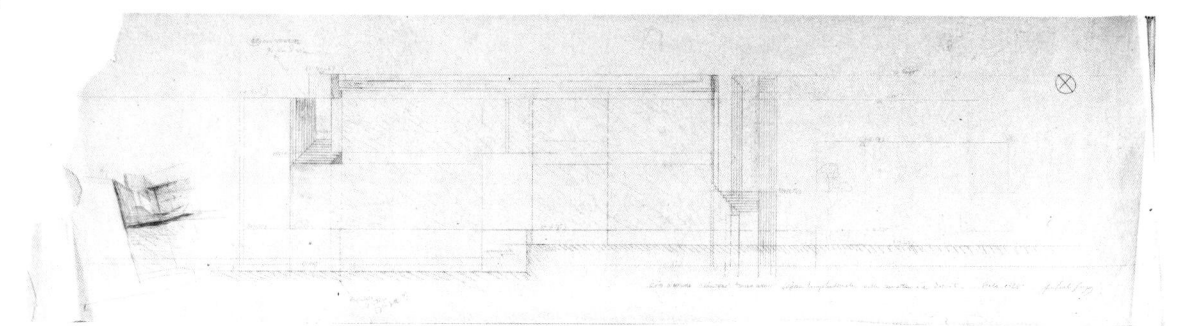

544

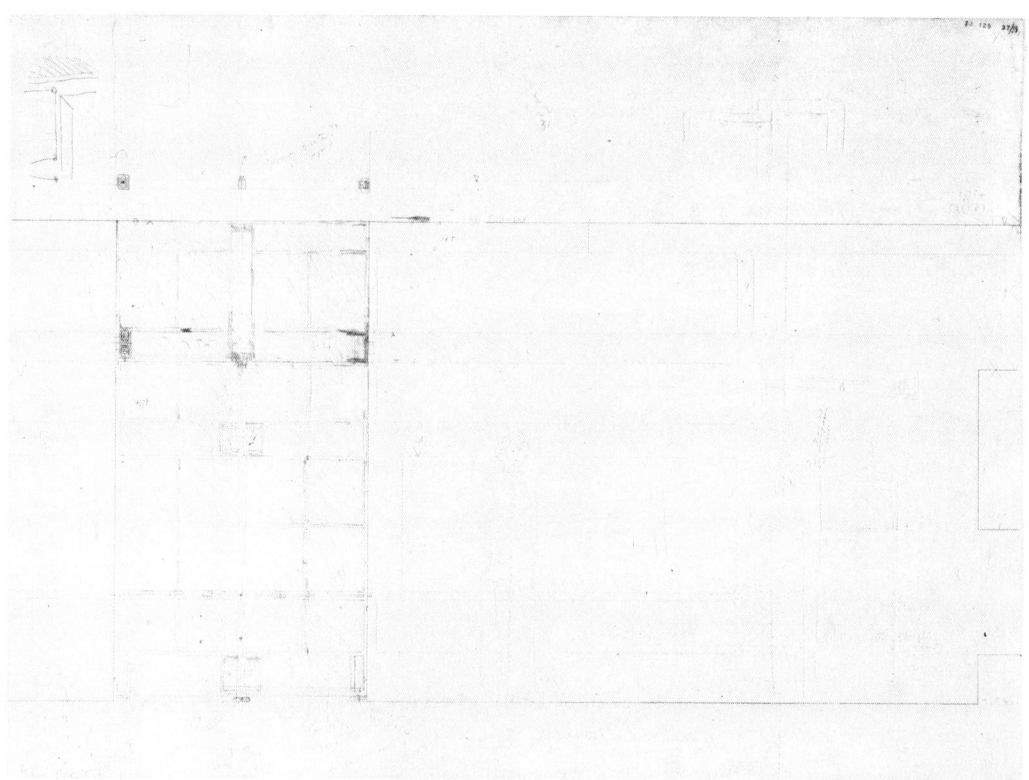

545

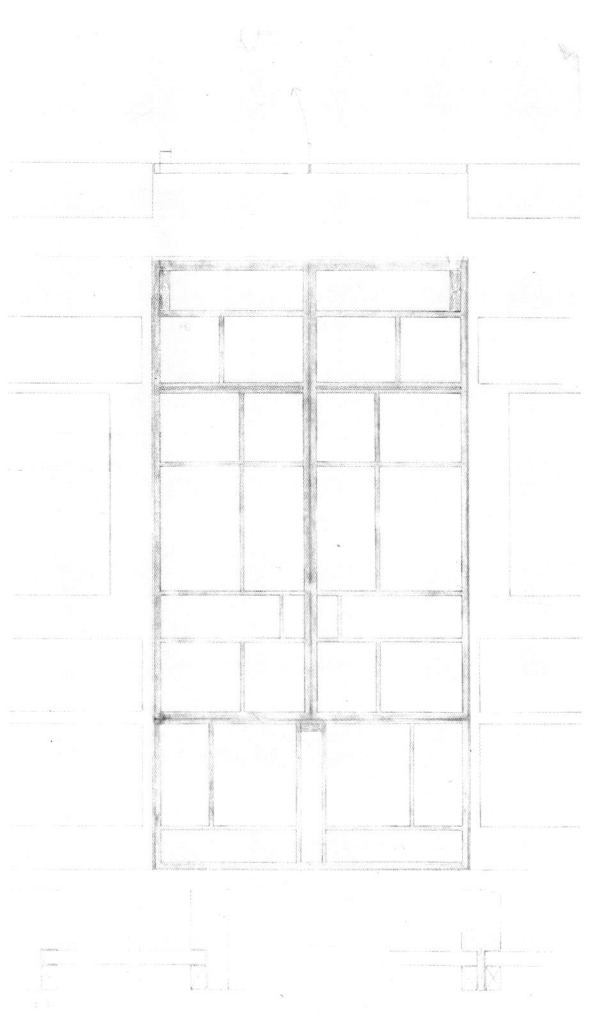

546

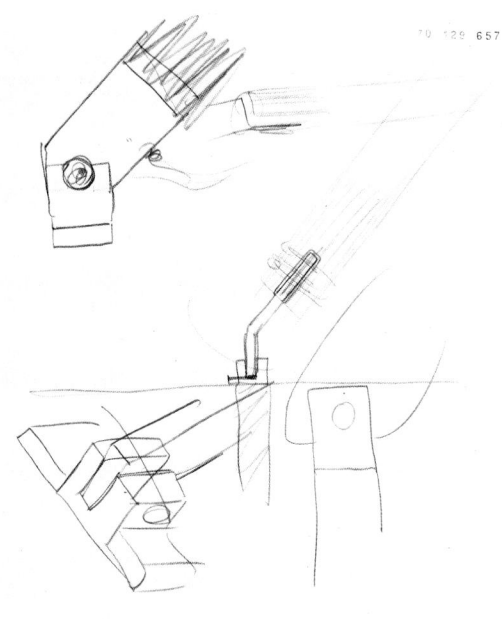

293

547

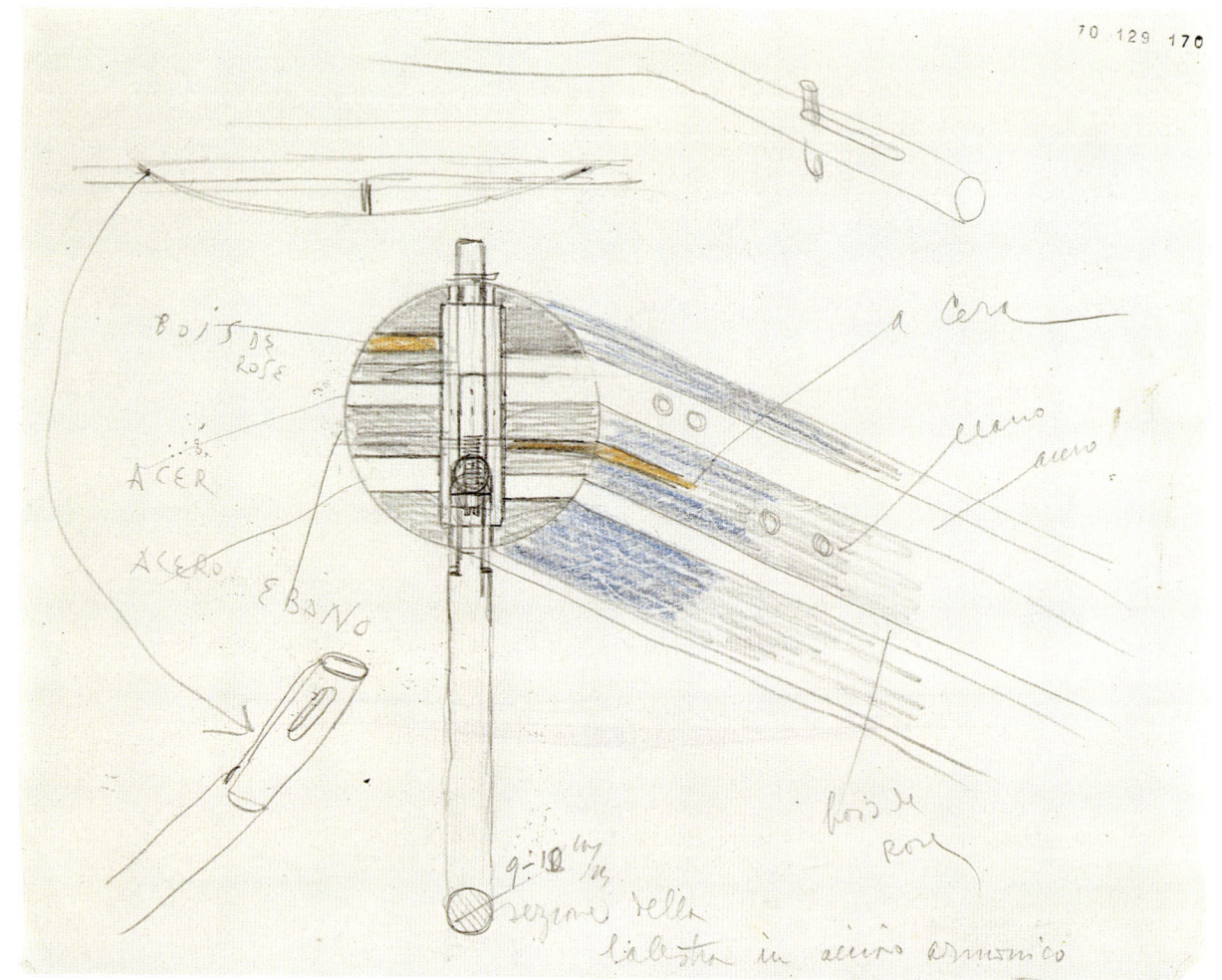

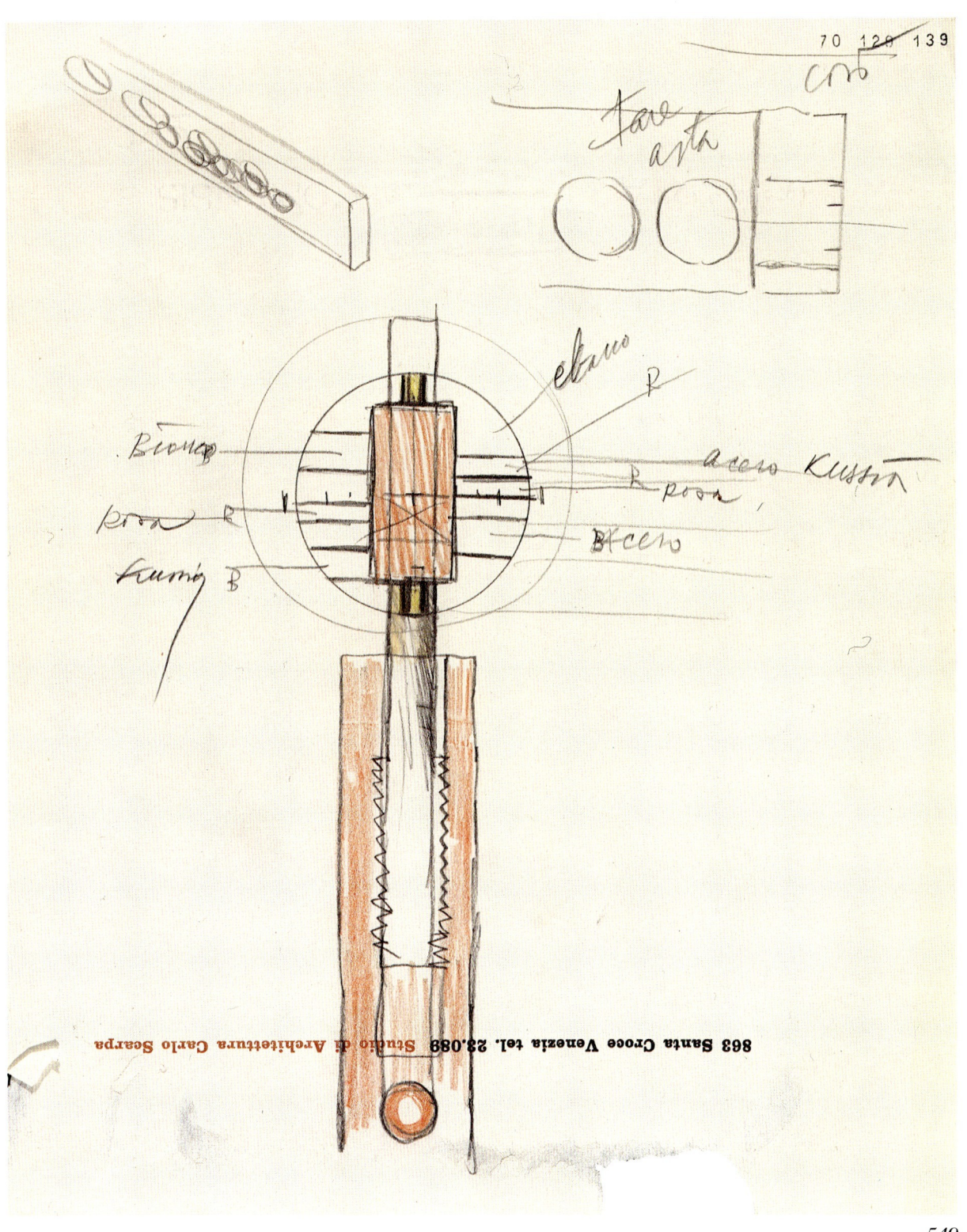

863 Santa Croce Venezia tel. 23089 Studio di Architettura Carlo Scarpa

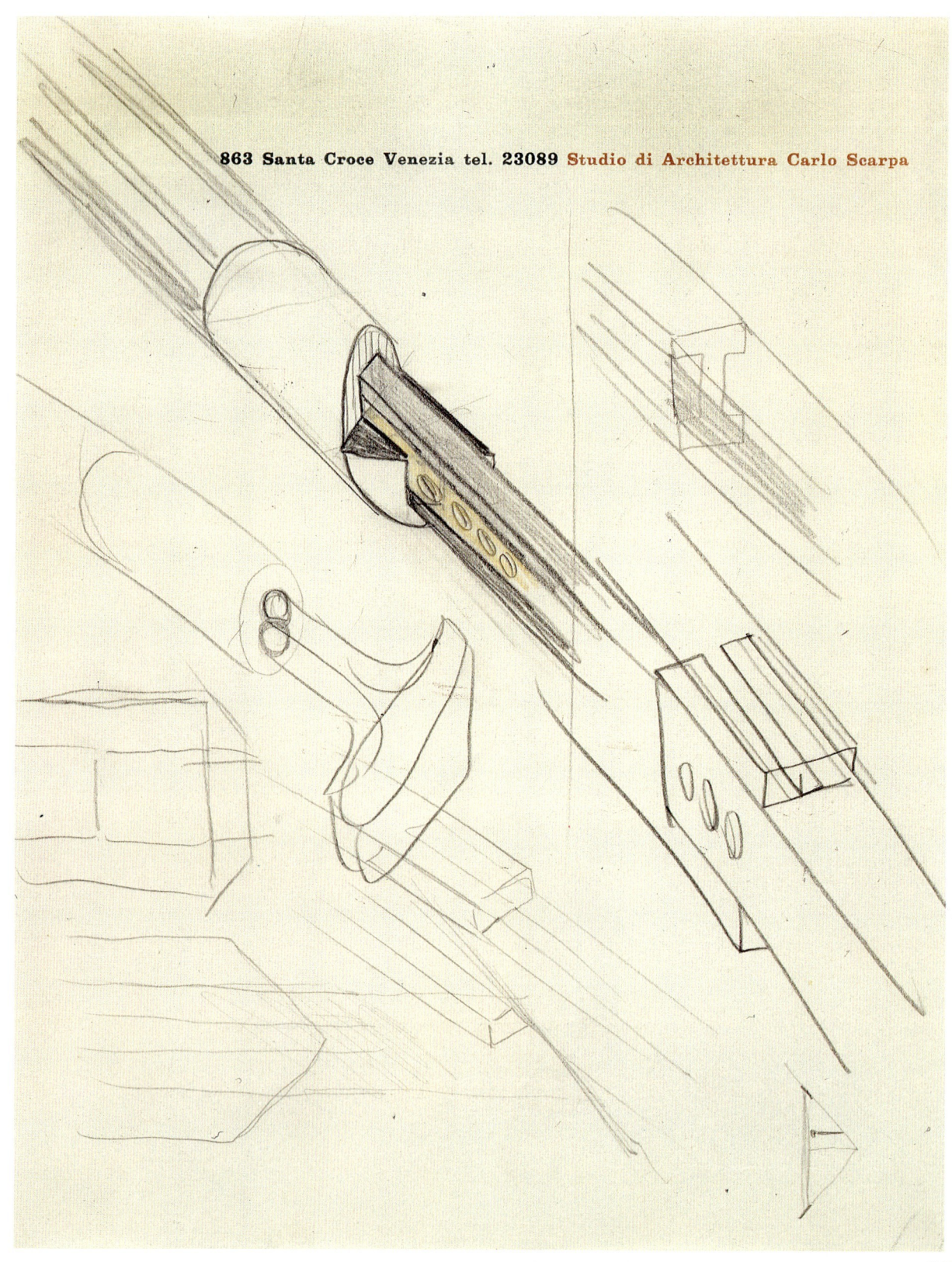

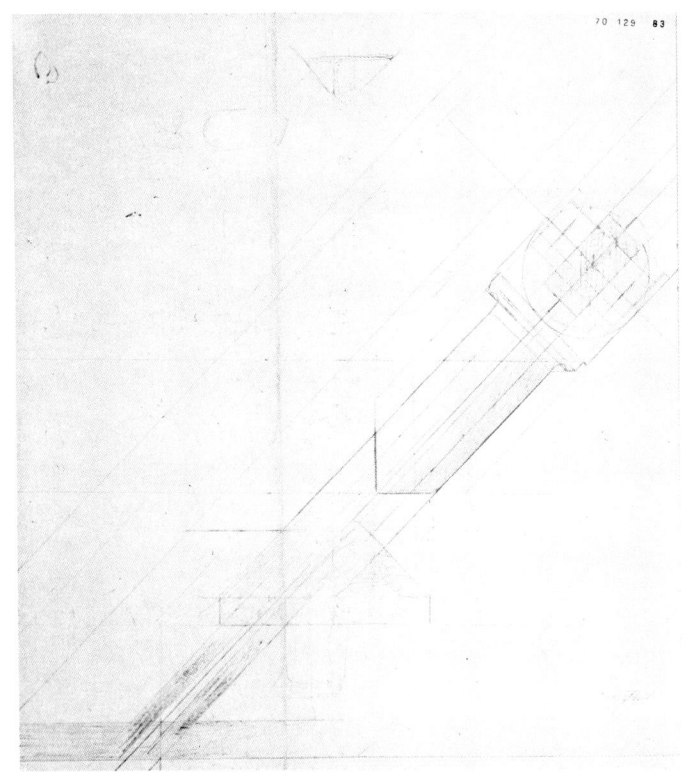

551

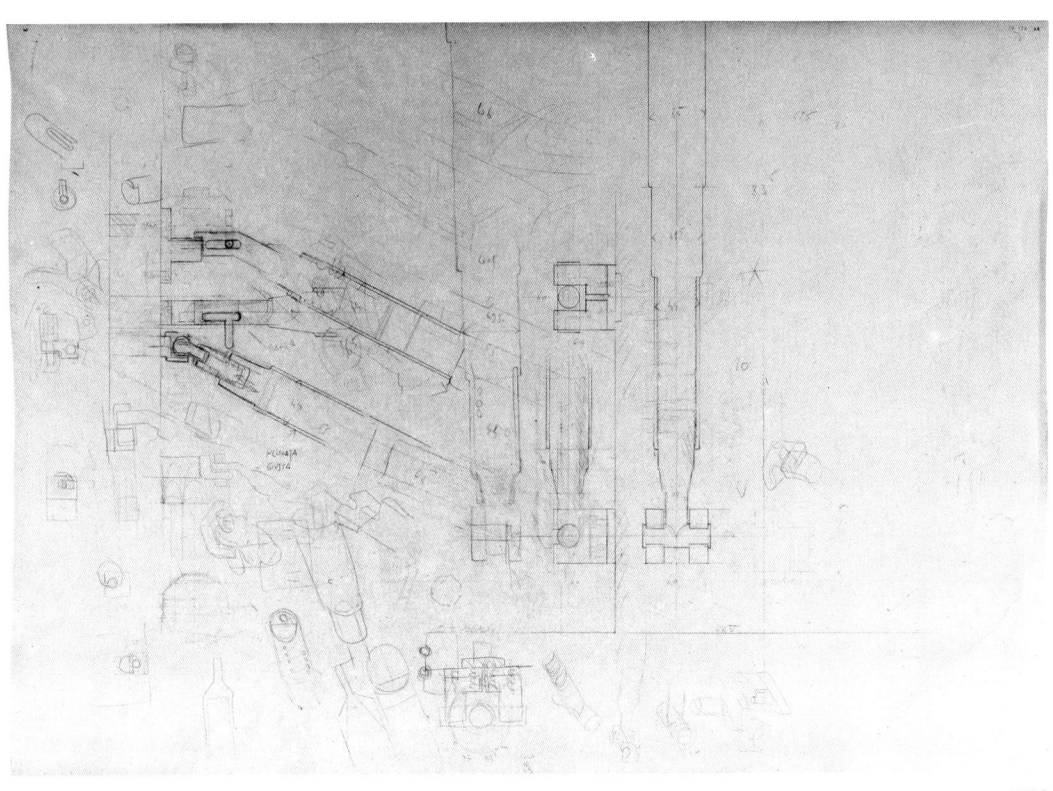

552

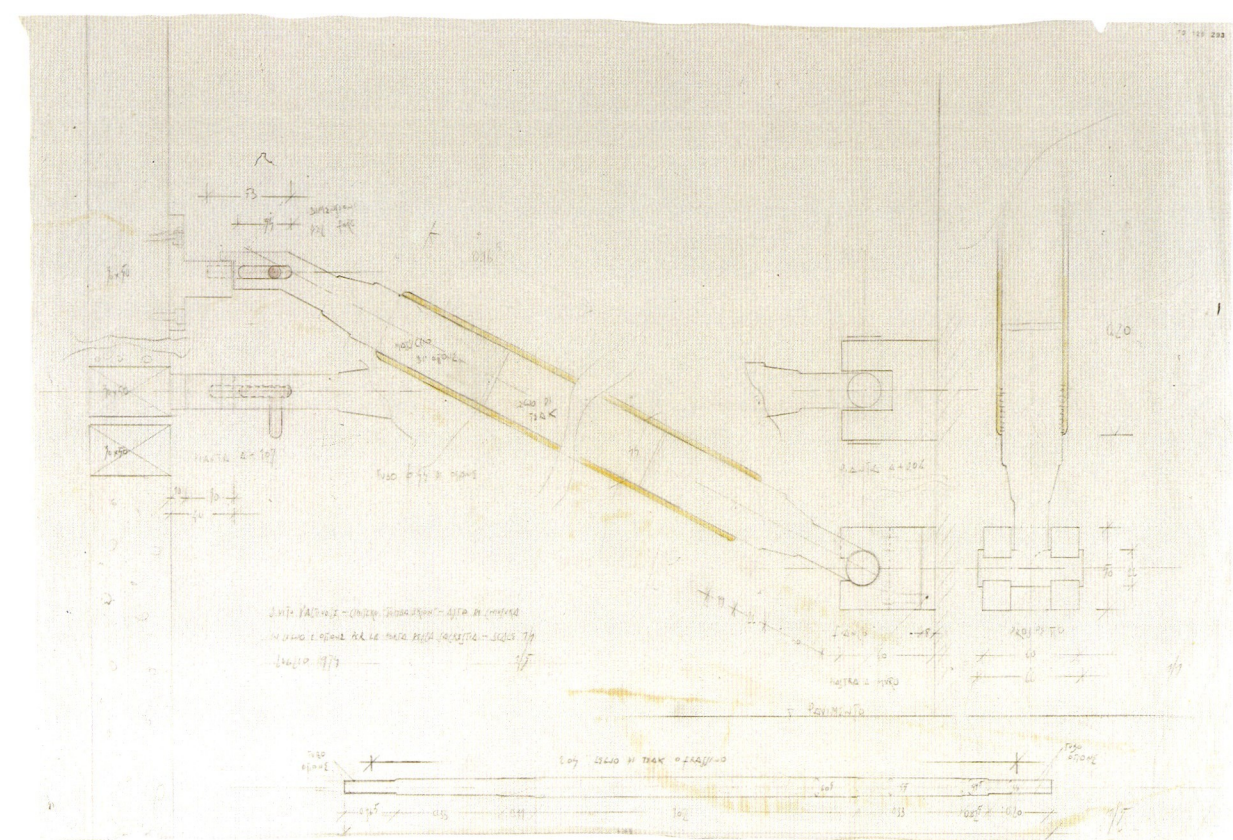

554

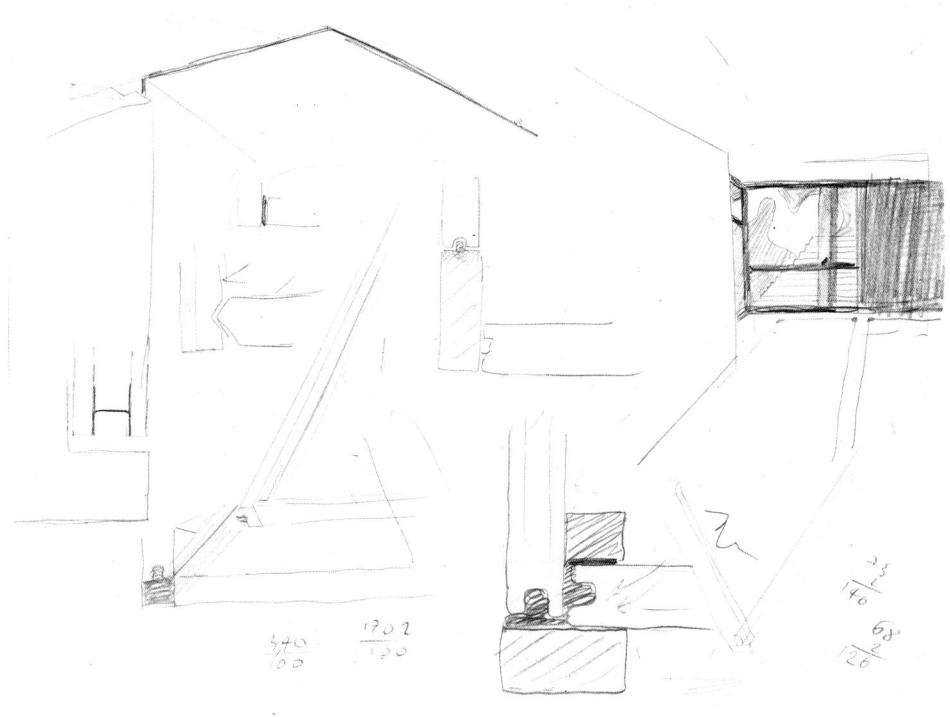

555

556

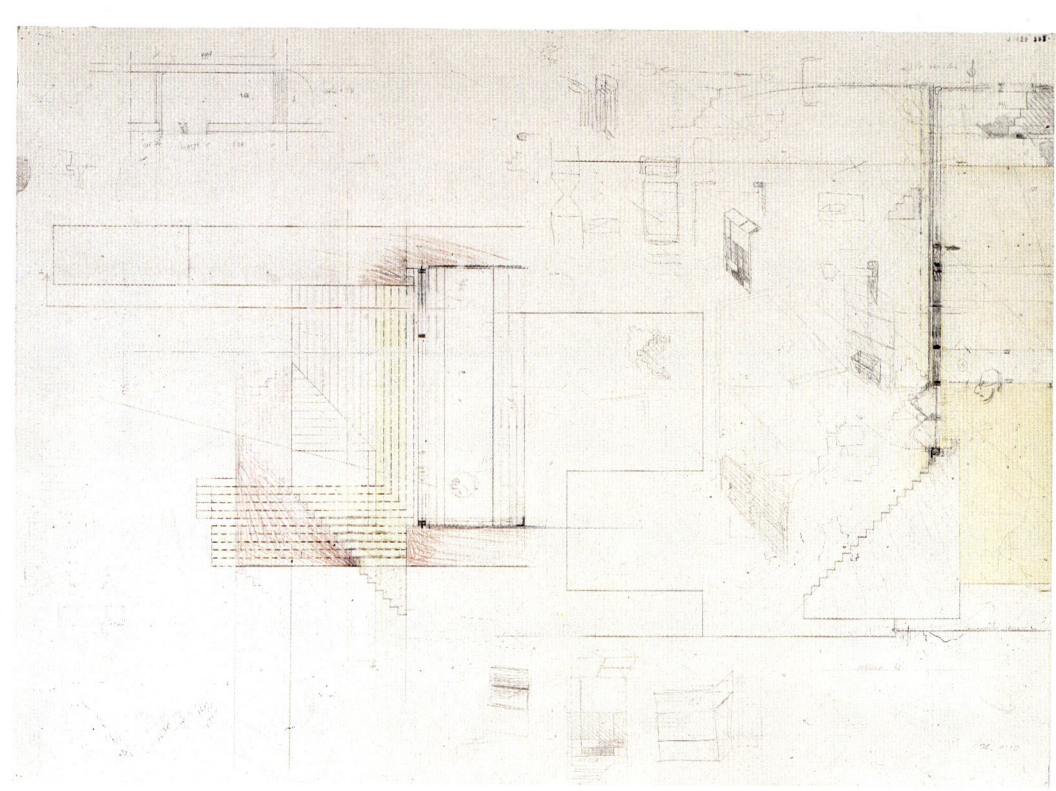

557

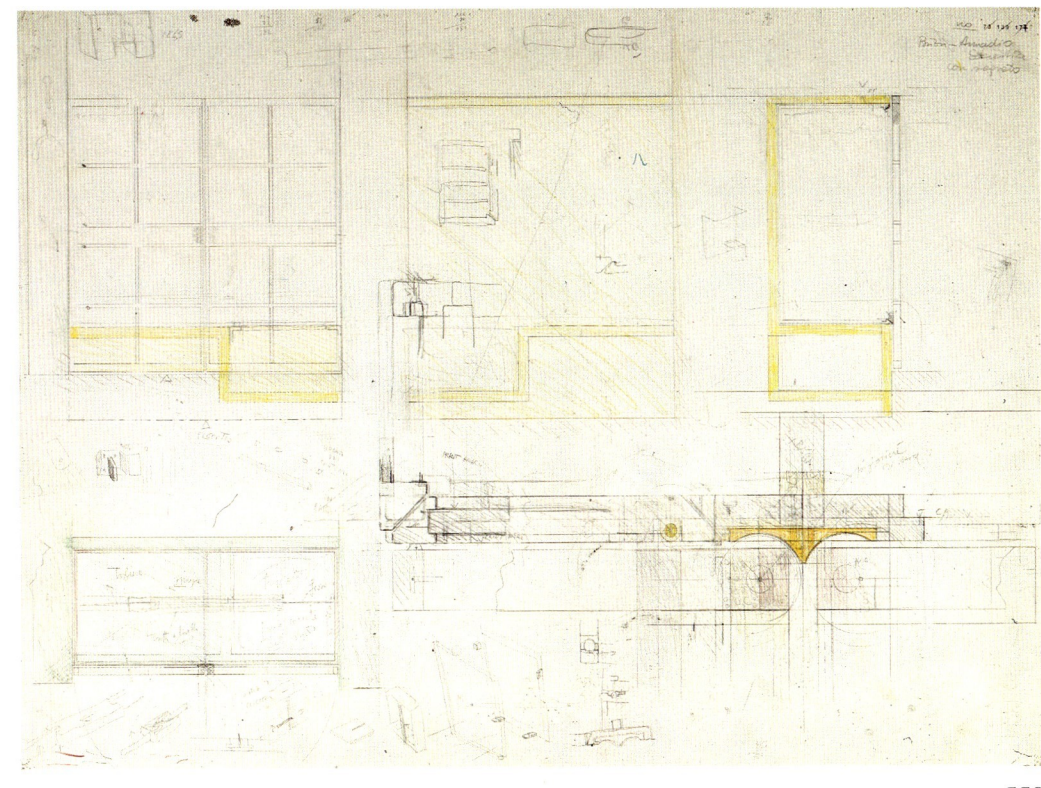

558

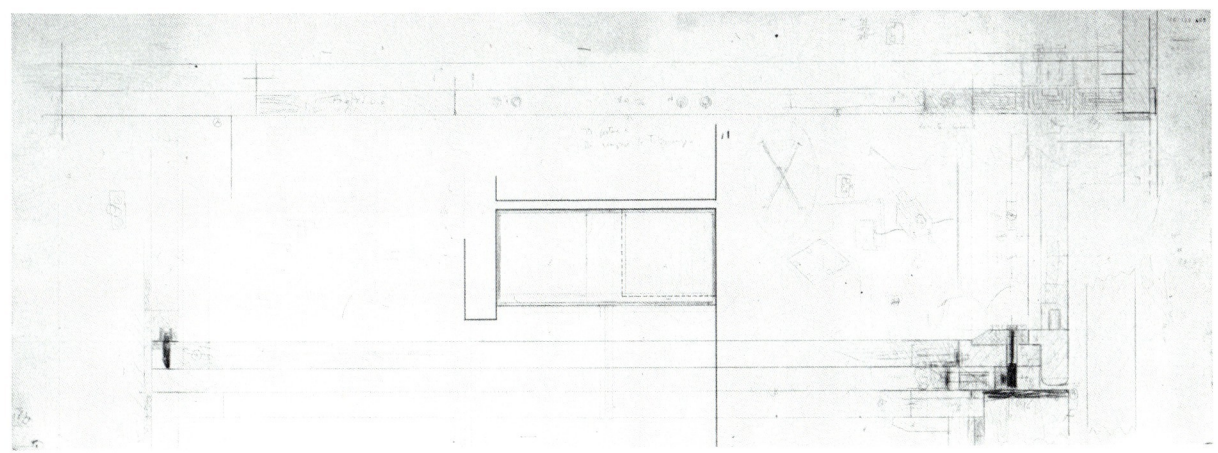

559

302

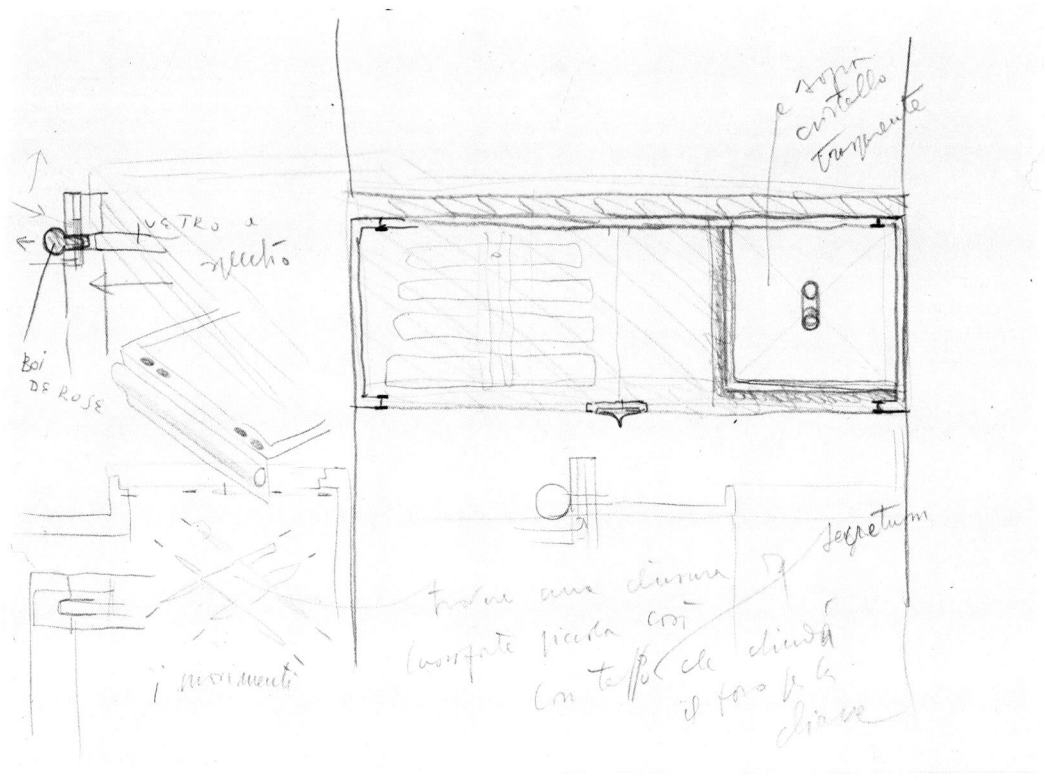

560

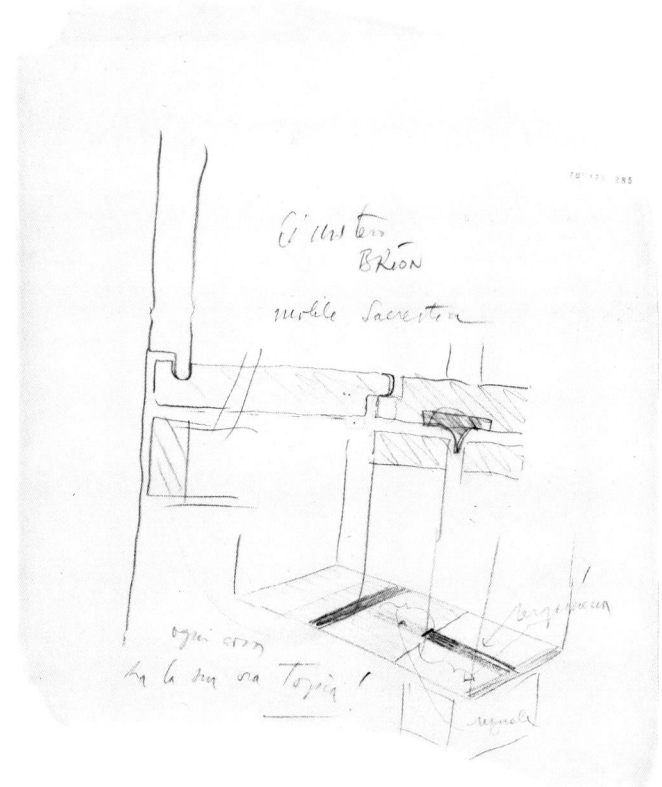

561

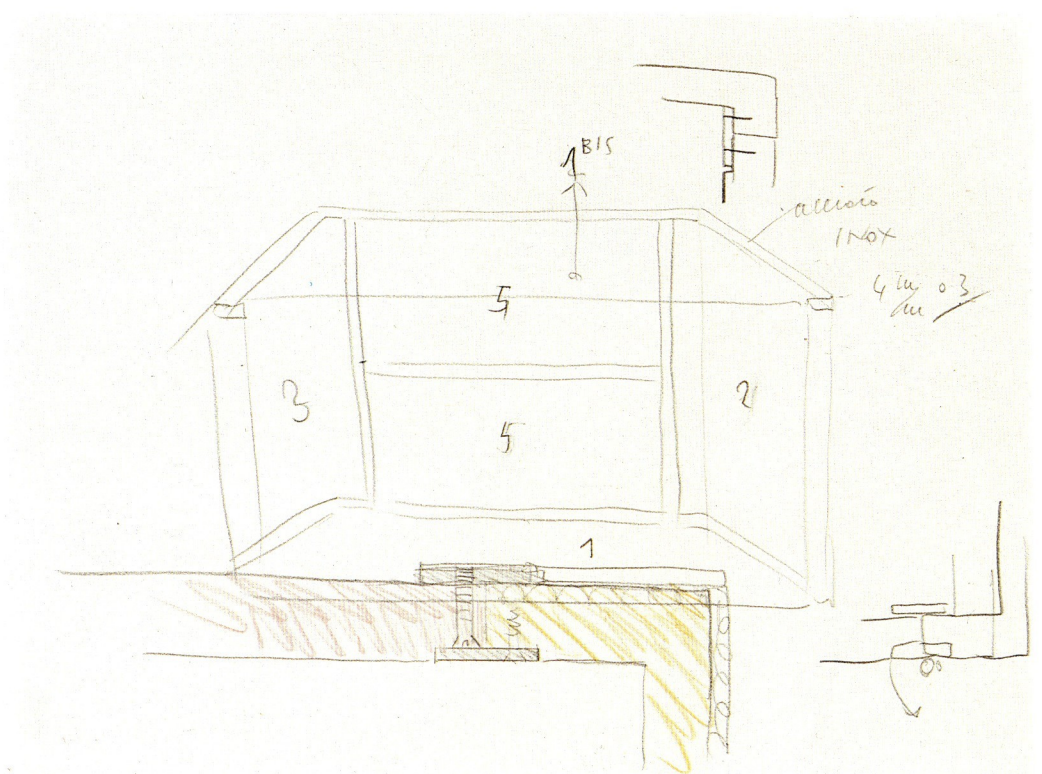

562

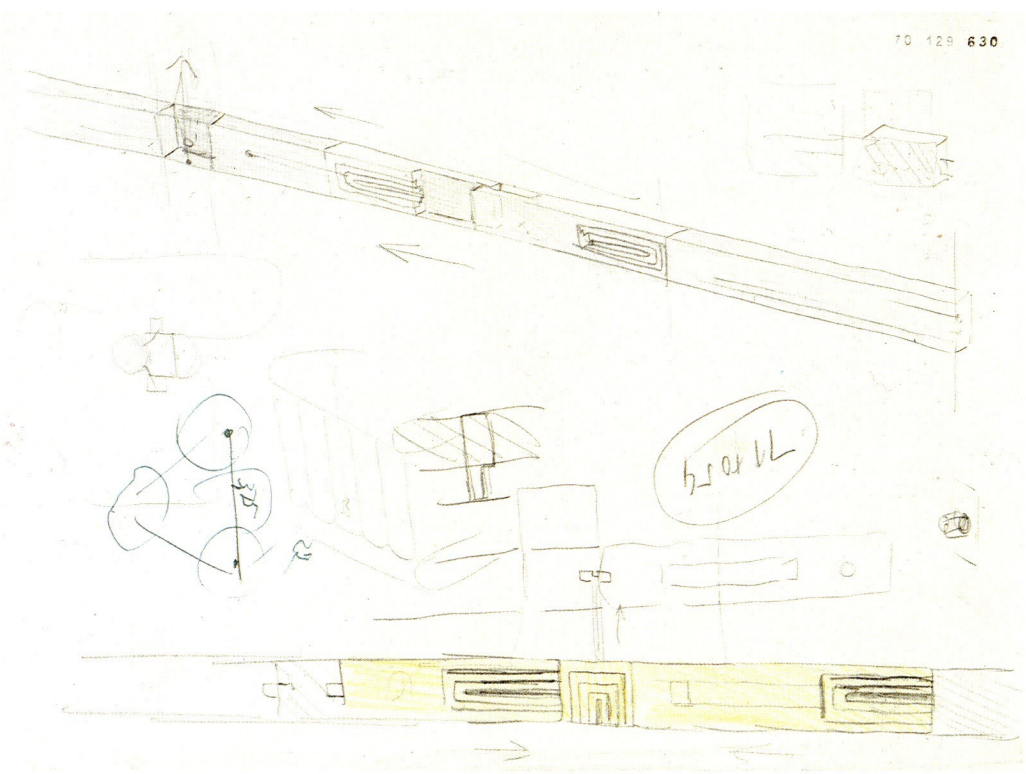

563

304

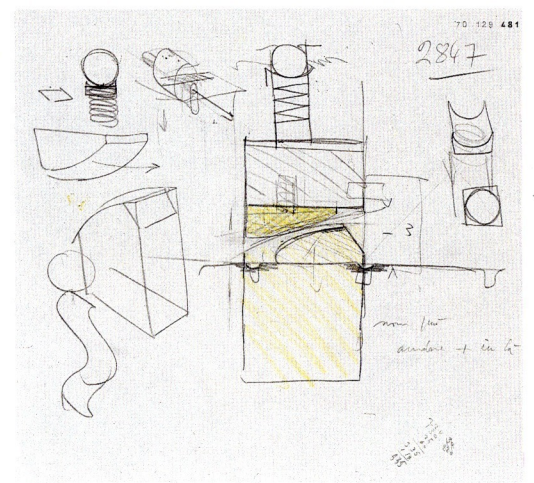

564

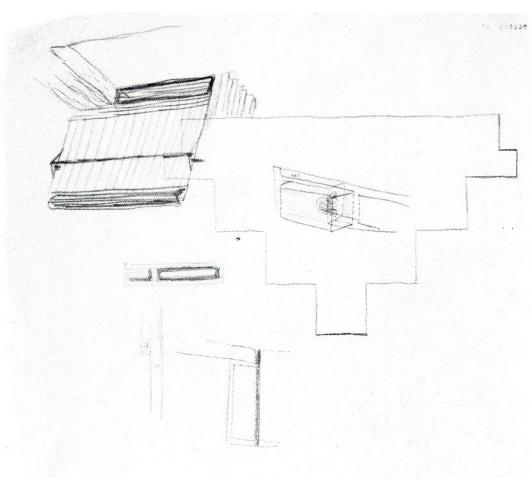

565

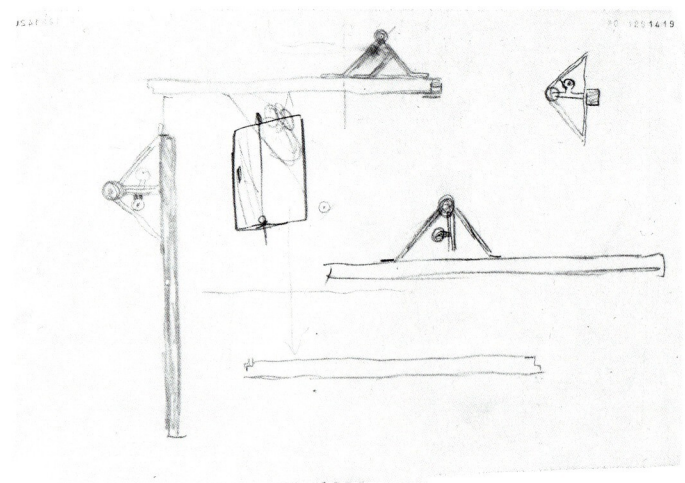

566

567

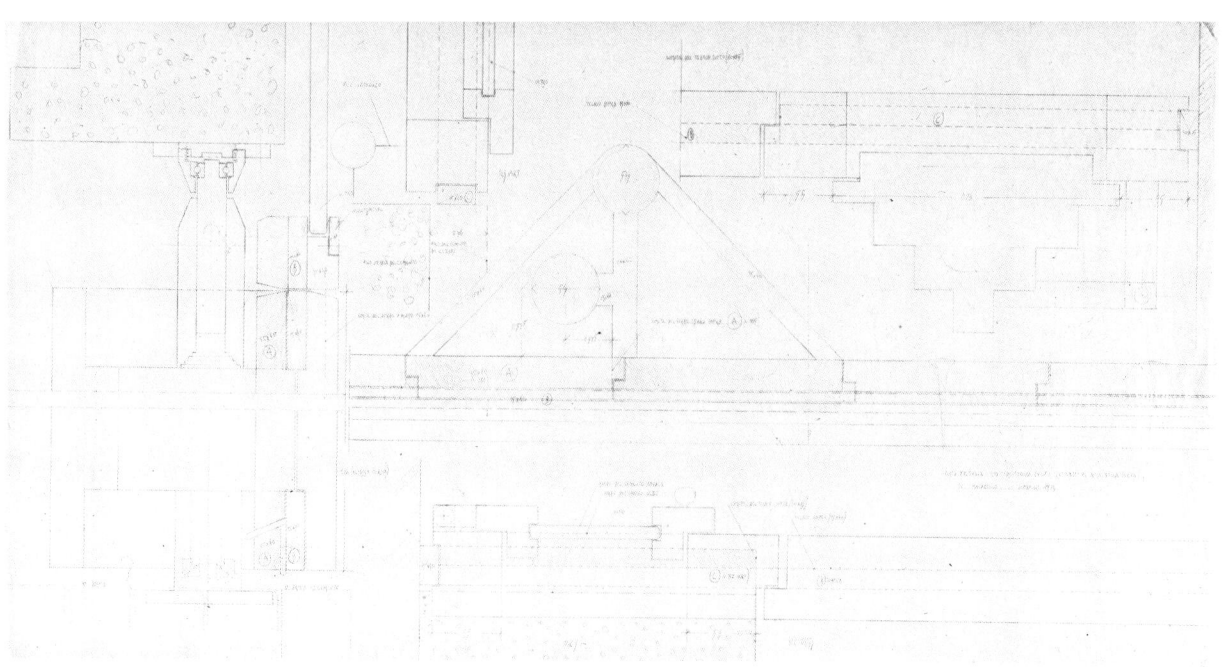

568

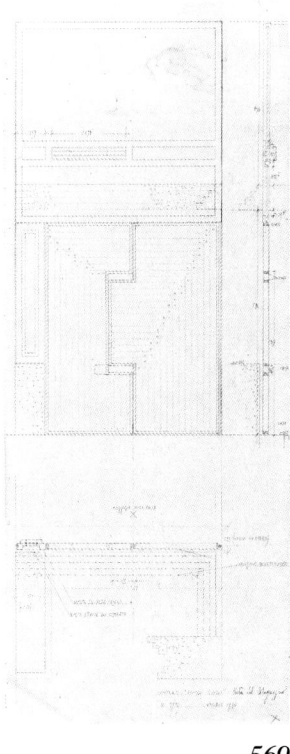

306

569

570

307

571

572

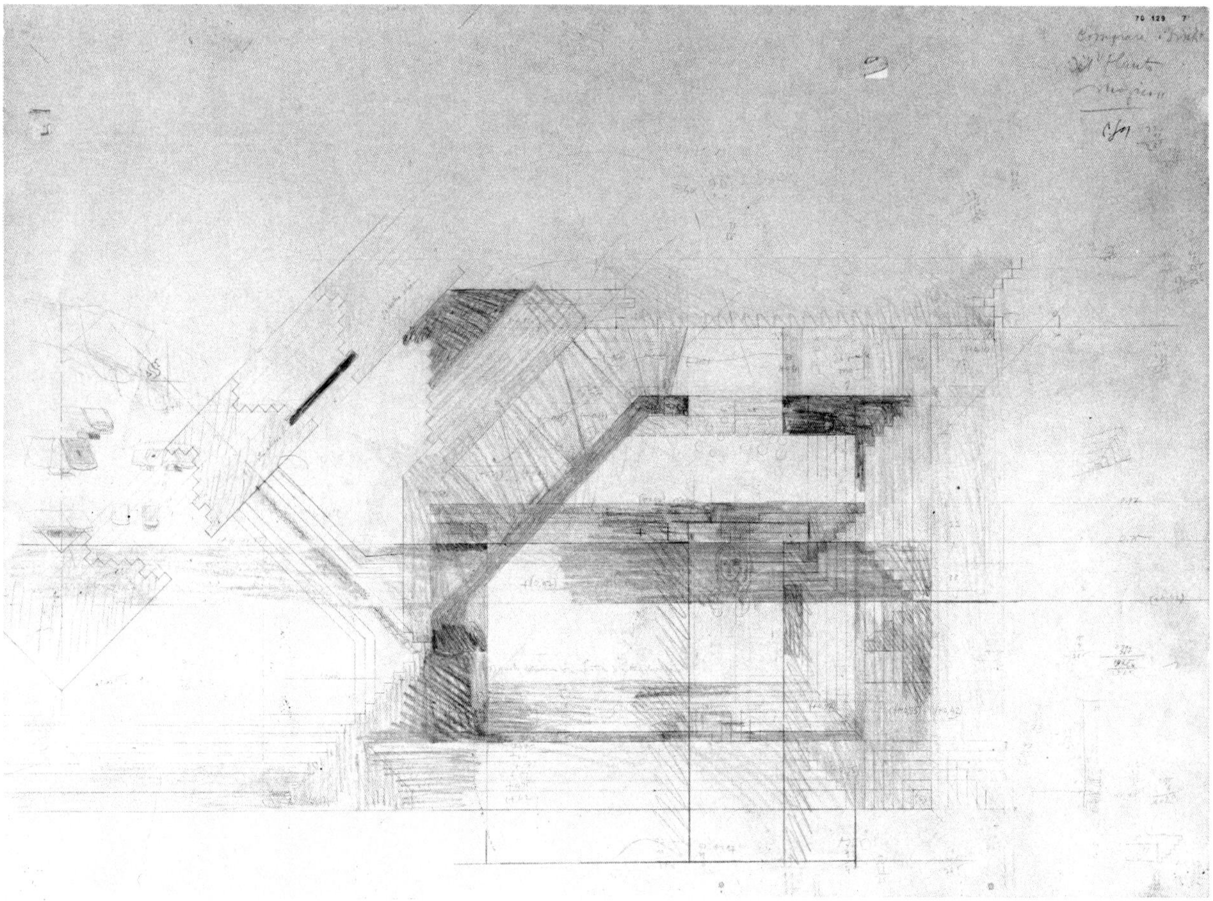

573

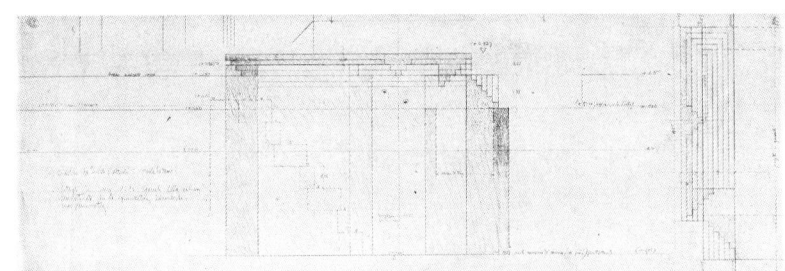

574

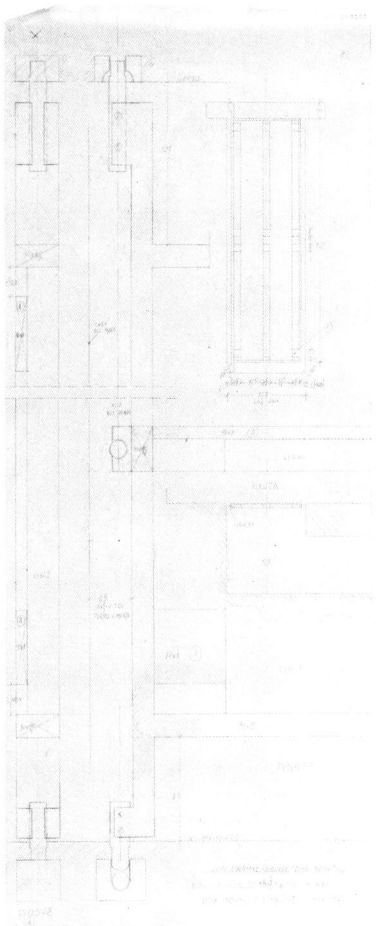

575

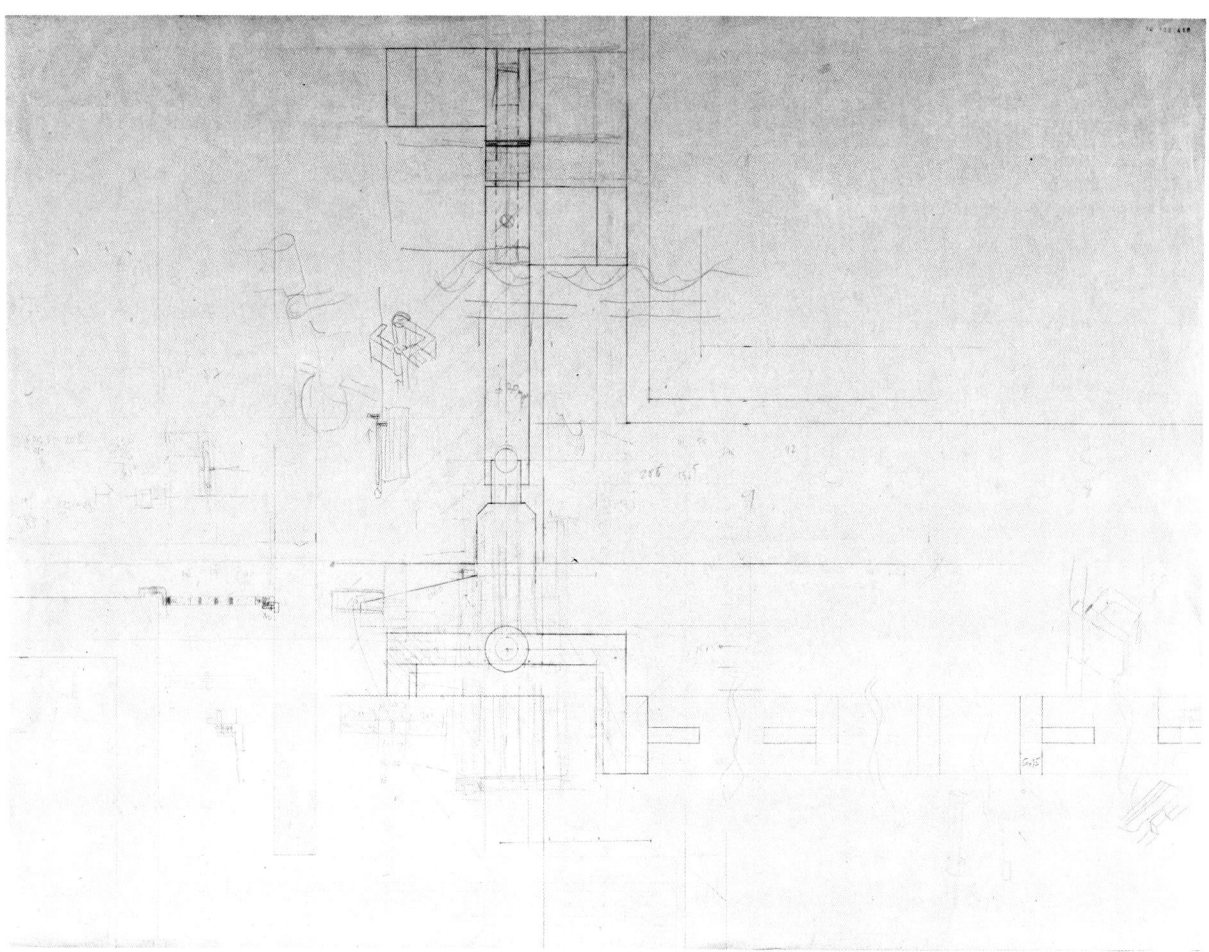

576

GARDEN LAYOUT
BEPFLANZUNGEN

312

579

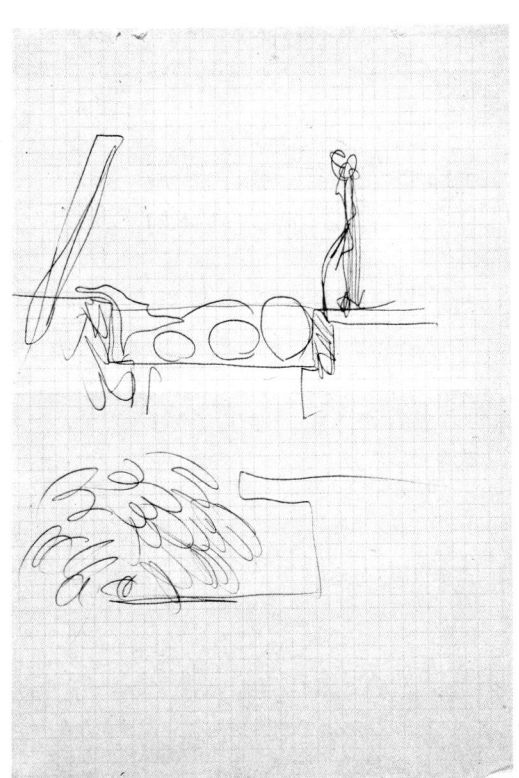

580

„DIE ANDERE STADT"
"THE OTHER CITY"

Manlio Brusatin

THE ARCHITECTURE OF LIFE

It is impossible to respond to Carlo Scarpa's biography without mentioning a few characteristic anecdotes that stand out like glowing stars.

A couple of times, when he wanted to get away from Venice, he spontaneously ordered the taxi-driver: "To Vienna!" And off he went. It was not unusual for him to spend a small fortune on such impulsive ideas. One time, annoyed with a client, he emptied the entire contents of his own wallet and allowed them to fall from the roof of a house under construction down onto the heads of passers-by. He was able to justify his reasons.

He was born in Venice in 1906. He was just two years old when he moved to Vicenza with his father, a high school teacher, and his mother, a tailor. It is for this reason that he sometimes claimed that he felt like a stranger to Venice, while the city of Palladios more than anything else had helped him form his idea of architecture. Stitch by stitch, like his mother's tailoring, his interest in design and drawing developed.

Scarpa regarded tailoring, with its precise cutting and "montage" of various parts, as the prime example of painstaking artistic work. Many of the Venetian artists and painters, such as Pisanello, had been trained in the simple family workshop. In this way they gained a certain artistic discipline and education which Plinius, as well as Alberti, for whom Scarpa had shown much admiration, thought absolutely essential: "No day without a line." Every day the architect's pencil, like a needle in its swiftness and perseverence, had to draw a line on paper, slowly building up an entire work: an architecture for life, deriving from a myriad of stitches, a myriad of lines.

This rare talent of his for drawing made Scarpa susceptible to daydreaming from the beginning on. After he finished technical school, his father took him to the entrance examination at the Accademia Reale delle Belli Arti–and, the first time, he failed (1919). This may seem unbelievable, yet it isn't when one considers how he left his drawings unfinished–and at the same time completed drawing assignments for his fellow students. This incident–which is documented–is characteristic of his overabundant generosity. This generosity never left him, and it was also the cause of his chronic lateness–yet, what did being punctual matter to him? To complete a work, and then leave it to itself–leave it free from its producer's will and vigilance and remove it from his authority–this is an attempt to preserve the work itself as a total artifact.

His architectural studies were pursued with painterly enthusiasm, by means of which, in addition to inner growth and technical refinement, his own style of drawing emerged. His drawings, always excessive and extravagant for architectural plans, filled the pages to the margins. This may be seen as a parallel to the rhythm and flow of life and creation.

From the beginning on his work was marked by his interrupted, but nonetheless finally completed, studies. One time he was asked to redo a project more clearly for a viaduct between Mestre and Venice–and was expelled on the grounds that–in his own words–his drawings were "unrestrained". And yet his drawings were even nicer than those of Otto Wagner and Tony Garnier. But after World War I the arts in Venice lay dormant, in a motionless mirror of emotion, polished and melancholy like glass and seaweed (see

Gabriele d'Annunzio, *Il Fuoco*, 1900, and Thomas Mann, *Death in Venice*, 1913, the two perfect tales of this "double" city). Scarpa's love of architecture grew with the appearance of a rather "failed" book, *Vers une architecture* by Le Corbusier (its first edition appeared in 1923, followed by a second in 1925) as well as Adolf Loos' book "Ins Leere gesprochen" *(Spoken into the Void)*. Even though he often claimed that the former was quite significant for him, he later addeds that it was Loos' book that had a lasting effect (he saw the Italian version of it in 1972; edited by Aldo Rossi, translated by his wife).

His architectural career was never a "determined" decision, but rather a "Scarpian" one in that, in addition to his work as an assistant to Guido Civilli (a true academic), he pursued with much more enthusiasm the works of Guido Costante Sullam, an excellent architect of Liberty, who was building on the Lido in Venice. Scarpa's request for entrance into the guild of architects was denied. His chronic misfortune (in reality due to a legal trifle), resulted in the fact that he had been practically and paradoxically barred (at least officially) from the very profession that made up his life.

Carlo Scarpa had not completed the studies that were necessary in order to be recognized as a professional with an official title; in other words, he was not allowed to sign his own works. Even his last great commission, the Brion Cemetery, was signed by his assistant. Indeed it bothered him his whole life that he had been sued in the '50s for illegal practice of a profession–in reality, however, because he had "disturbed architectural lectures": no other cause could be drummed up. But this stalemate with the law, which wrapped him up in one legal proceeding after another, marked him for life, woke him from sleep and dreaming: "Will the accused, Scarpa, please rise"–Carlo Scarpa often repeated it, jumped up, and played the role of the ironic Venetian who knows how bitter the laughter of the masks is.

In spite of all this, Carlo Scarpa was never really active as an architect during the twenty years from 1927–1947, the time of Fascism and the Second World War. He only developed a few, albeit outstanding "ideas", for example that of a new Ponte dell' Accademia in Venice (1932). It had an extremely sensible construction that took into account the tides, but only placed 10th (last) in a public contest.

Another more public, but nonetheless attractive commission was the interior design of the Aula Magna in the University of Ca'Foscari: He had the good fortune–or so he called it–to be able to tear it apart and build it up again with his own hands, taking meticulous pains to reuse the old wood in the magnificent new design (1954–55). This is where he erected, as supports, the "Tree-Columns", which are regarded as among the most important works in modern sculpture.

Carlo Scarpa kept aloof intentionally. Mostly he visited the workshops of the Murano glassblowers and those of his many artist friends: especially Arturo Martini, one of the greatest sculptors of our century, who presented Scarpa with a famous portrait drawing which could easily lead one to rave about his esprit and critical humor in the field of art.

In light of the instability of his early works as an architect, he worked as a design draftsman for glass with Cappellin and Venin. They were works of the highest order, which, due to their fragility, have been lost. We know little about glass production in Venice during the '20s and '40s. The world has been flooded with Venetian glass and yet is unaware of the high quality of the production from those years.

This particular production would deserve more considerate examination because it equals in quality the best products in the history of Venetian glass. Scarpa belongs to it. When Frank Lloyd Wright visited Venice and Murano in 1951, he–without knowing–stopped before Scarpa's glasses intending to order a large amount of them. These glasses were outstanding. They had remained from a very careful selection–out of a blown ball could thus emerge an excellent sculpture. This also meant the financial ruin of this work-shop in which Scarpa used to work. Yet the work-shop of the glass-blowers was a place of excellent handicraft and morals–it had its effect on Scarpa, and it shows in the rather secondary yet successful things that are made out of breath.

With the glassblowers, in an attentive and productive seclusion, ends a significant time in Scarpa's life. The second half begins with the rebirth of the *Facoltà di Architettura* under the direction of Giuseppe Samona in the year 1948, to which professors from all over Italy flocked, contributing to the school's later fame. Scarpa was already there and was, in fact, the one who initiated together with a group of students the fervent "Wright Period". After all of Bruno Zeris' propaganda in Italy, Wright received more appreciation than the "architettura organica", which was favored by the magazine "Metron", a weapon of the architects of the early '50s.

An important incident for both Scarpa and the city of Venice was when Frank Lloyd Wright designed a well known project for a house on the Grand Canal, the so-called Masieri Memorial. It was built in memory of Angelo Masieri, a student of Scarpa who had died in a car accident while on his way to see Frank Lloyd Wright in America. Scarpa himself suggested the setting forth of modern architectural emphasis in Venice–and to this end he engaged and got the drawings from Wright. They were promptly delivered after three weeks, and Scarpa guarded them jealously. He suggested a few small corrections necessary for the realization of the project: a dormitory to be erected on a prominent square in Venice, where the Grand Canal turns into the Rio Novo, between Palazzo Balbi-Valier and Ca' Foscari.

This project provoked one of the most severe controversies between innovative and conservative forces concerning the far-reaching problems of incorporating modern elements into the architectural fabric of Venice. In respect to the enormous uproar this case had caused with the public, local authorities and financiers were strictly against it. However, this stance also had the advantage that it could hold off trivial "modernization plans" proposed by a few architectural enterprises. Behind all this stood some powerful groups that voted decisively against Wright's project–although Wright, in turn, challenged theirs.

The "preservers" among the intellectuals were also against the project, for they assumed that after this borderline case architects would no longer put up with anyone less than Wright, and his style would be copied and reduced everywhere. The whole thing was not clearly directed against the *Facoltà di Architettura*, where no one would grow tired of international opinions being raised on the subject of modernism and classical antiquity in Venice–a question still being discussed today.

With regard to the Facolta, one can say that the school grew quite independently and in complete isolation from the city. This is still the case, with the exception of those professors and students who benefited from a study atmosphere until 1978–this was due to Carlo Scarpa's influence, this was also unusual and quite without comparison among the architectural schools in Europe.

This episode set the tone of Scarpa's relationship to Wright, and at the same time gave him the opportunity to show his colors. But today it is perhaps too easy to speak of Wright's direct influence on Scarpa, especially when one looks at the projects themselves. In fact, it was only in 1967 that Scarpa came across Wright's architecture, when he was entrusted with the erection of the Italian pavilion for the World Fair in Montreal. He laughed at the worship he received from the younger students; for instance, when he was invited to Talesia he had to undergo what he considered a rather silly ceremony: "They let me sleep in Wright's bed, the very thought of which would keep me from sleep. Still, I must say that I slept well on that mattress–it must have been made from the wool of an entire flock."

The true connection between the *Scuola di Archi-*

tettura and Venice goes back to Scarpa and his design of the Biennale. In fact, for a very long time Scarpa *was* the International Art Biennale. The story begins with the rather discreet design for Paul Klee's first exhibition in Italy in 1947 (for which Scarpa himself bore the costs); this was followed by the pavilion of books for the Biennale in 1950, the pavilion for Venezuela in 1954, one of his more famous yet today slightly neglected works, and last but not least those suggestions of his for the reinstallation of the Italian pavilion, one which really deserves more detailed analysis.

This period lasted from 1947 to 1968, until the XXIV Biennale, in the context of which Scarpa put up his own exhibition together with Louis Kahn (with whom he started a warm friendship in 1969). The exhibition consisted of selected examples of great architectural-sculptural mastery, as well as some examples of fully-developed solutions to various architectural problems. One may deplore the loss of Scarpa's major work, and at the same time discard any lingering doubts about "drawing teacher" in favor of professional architect. Despite numerous recommendations that he be promoted to the title "honoris causa", the degree was never officially bestowed upon him. This farce came to an end the moment Scarpa was appointed the head of the *Facoltà di Architettura*, regardless of the fact that he had no academic title.

The book pavilion, with which we concern ourselves here, is an excellent example of the architecture of the 20th century. During its installation at the Biennale of 1984 it caught fire, and the charred remains were only removed shortly before the official opening. I remember all this quite well. A burning work of architecture leaves the viewer only a few moments to perceive its design; as if in view of its transitoriness it reveals at last its idea. At times like this–when confronted with the small catastrophes of life, Scarpa would cite Matisse's three words: „calme, luxe et volupté".

Around 1950 Scarpa had not only passed the age of forty, but also had realized a kind of architecture that corresponds to the art of maturity.

With the *Palazzo Abatellis* in Palermo, the home of the *Gallerie d'arte di Sicilia* (1954), Scarpa became concerned with historical reference, particularly with a kind of modernism that derives a vital component from monuments and the past–today this movement is referred to as *"l'anima del restauro"*. The works which followed, such as the *Gipsoteca* in Possagno (Teviso) where you find the original plasters of Canova (1956–57), the restoration of the *Museo di Castelvecchio* in Verona (1958–64), and the *Pinacoteca Querini Stampalia* in Venice (1961), as well as the two shops "furnished in order to sell nothing" for Olivetti in Venice (1957–58) and Gavina in Bologna (1961), give a more vivid impression than method descriptions or annotations of these "minimi sistemi" which pulsate through Scarpa's architecture. These "systems" also correspond to a kind of "manierismo scarpiano", which sadly is missing from those works that were completed after his death (i. e. the *Casa Ottolenghi* in Bardolino, 1979; the entrance to the *Facoltà di Lettere di San Sebastiano* in Venice, 1979; the *Banca Mutua* in Verona, the so-called Palazzo Scarpa, 1980; the entrance to the *Facoltà di Architettura* in Venice, 1978)–they have tarnished the spiritual legacy Scarpa presented in his last great works.

The repertoire of "modi scarpiani" had already surfaced in both the Villa Veritti (Udini, 1955–61), and the Zenter house (Zurich, 1964–68). These examples testify to how difficult it was for Scarpa to realize a thing as simple as a house with a private client in mind: it was, above all, the product of an architect, a product which Scarpa, incidentally, intended to carry on with forever in regard to both detail and completion. The clients were taken aback by the architect's begrudging admission that, yes, one might live in the house *as well*. But to bring a house to completion was for Scarpa almost as difficult as to bring life to an end.

Like Gottfried Semper, Scarpa was convinced that

architecture was an art of interweaving: a simple yet magical handicraft which protests against the energy and inevitability of *chaos*. Architecture on the one hand combines things that by nature are distinct and separate, on the other hand, it distinguishes particularly intricate things from chance and custom. One need only look at how Scarpa deals with the point where ceiling and wall converge: horizontal and vertical lines, up and down... the opacity of a ceiling and the polish of a floor, or the angular connection of a wall with a ceiling. Scarpa reversed it and thus achieved an unexpected brightness as well as a reconciliation between up and down. This almost explains his famous "architectural stride" with *one's head in the air*: this was his way of looking, thus avoiding the rather "risky" light reflections of shining surfaces as opposed to dense and colorful materials.

Scarpa insisted that the true architect reveals himself by means of a tiny significant detail: that figure between wall and floor which the cleaning ladies call "battiscopa": the fateful point which can ruin the best exercise in architectural rhetoric. In places like this, Scarpa suggested the use of simple metal ridges removed from the wall, or "negative" marble frames whose connection to the wall reaches deeper than the surface of the floor. He loved these vital and yet "hovering" floors that could almost be called "archeological": when walking on them one almost expected something underneath it–something quite natural, such as water, or something artificial, like "a narrative" (consider the entrance of the Brion tomb). The hovering and elevated architectural works of Scarpa almost feel like bridges leading to hovering landscapes not unlike the architectural fantasies of Piranesi: narrow passages that multiply with different views.

In addition, the doors and openings of Scarpian gateways are rather narrow and solid, instead of being wide and dainty (as in rational and functional architecture). The gateways appear like narrow passages between giant walls. A simple door can thus amount to a significant passageway, the impression of its narrowness emphasized by the thickness of the walls which the passer-by brushes up against.

According to Scarpa, a vertical, linear, and absolute element could hardly support itself unless it had the dignity of a classical column: *the* encyclopedia of architectural elements. Besides the individual parts themselves, Scarpa preferred a doubling device–but which kind? Well, he doubled one element and then combined it "with itself". A gutter, doubled and bound, *became* architecture.

In a similar fashion he looked upon the hand as a type of "artificial limb" of human genius: single and in pairs. The hand, for example, can grip a handle, or–after changing directions and bending the wrist–grasp a stick. Or both hands may enclose something, connect with each other or other hands, entwining the fingers in joint-liability. The joint bindings of Scarpa are exemplary, like two parts joined together by the needle of a scale, or the hands of a clock. Scarpa had a special appreciation for the hand production af scales, which even at that time had started to die out. One day he called to my attention the high quality of a hand-scale, which indeed showed great resemblance to his iron and bronze works. He bought the scale from a blacksmith, although he had no place for it; and so he presented it back to the blacksmith as a gift, with the request that he not forget this art, the quality of which lay in the material as well as in the exactness of the instrument. I mention this only to show that his feeling for handicraft had nothing to do with *design*. The design-objects he made toward the end of his life demanded no technical refinements. What he was interested in was not the possibility of reproduction, but rather the perfection of execution. In addition to that he eagerly sought out those mythical images in which the form seems imprisoned in a labyrinth: as was the case in his works, especially his last works.

An idea of Scarpa's that simulated most this necessary conciliatory relationship was the intersection of two rings, circles or circle-like elements: often used as window openings. Two overlapping circles are clearly recognizable, yet at the same time they make room for a third to arise–which in turn combines and contrasts itself with the others.

The Brion tomb in San Vito d'Asolo, Scarpa's last work–begun in 1969 and completed in the year of his death, 1978–opens with these two interconnected circles which form a window that cannot be passed through–unless one cares to jump over the water that lies beyond it, as if coming into existence. This is the simplest and at the same time most complex mark of his last and most mature work. In this exhibition, "The Other City", one can see all the lines that made up the composition: a sheer infinite number of signs, some of them still visible on the stones, others having disappeared, yet all of them obeying some fantasy that gives us a vivid idea of how to approach architecture.

We have often, maybe too often, called this cemetery a *necropolis ludens* because of the peacefulness of its water and plants. The entire arrangement emerged within the walls of the old cemetery in the village from which the Brion family came. The actual tomb has the form of a bridge, toward which a clear stream (fed by an artificial lake within the sacred area) flows. A small island and a pergola face the arch of the bridge-tomb as well as the hills of Asolo in the distance behind the wall. On the side are the tombs of the family members and relatives of the Brions, in a sort of hut. All the paths in this garden lead to the core of the construction, the chapel. All this involves some multiform travelling–of the feet as well as the mind.

Scarpa decided to be buried here: although this might have seemed too simple a choice–the transition from author to owner. In order to avoid this, Scarpa decided to combine the part of the cemetery that was open *to all* with that which was reserved *for the few*. And he–he would settle somewhere between the two. During his lifetime he decided to be buried in a hidden and rather magical place: a place that became the cemetery of the cemetery, for it gathers the withering flowers of all the graves of this small world.

They finally agreed to give him the title "h.c.": the date set for this purpose happened to be the very day of his funeral. He would do anything to miss an appointment. But–what are missed appointments?

Manlio Brusatin

ARCHITEKTUR
DES LEBENS

Es ist unmöglich, an eine Biographie Carlo Scarpas ohne die Anekdoten zu denken, die wie helle Sterne sein Leben bestimmten.

Einige Male, auf dem Weg aus Venedig hinaus, befahl er dem Taxilenker aufs Geratewohl: „Nach Wien!".

Es lag in seinem Charakter, mit unvorhergesehenen Einfällen jeweils ein kleines Vermögen loszuwerden. So war es auch, als er einmal, verdrossen über den Auftraggeber, vom Dach eines Hauses, das gerade gebaut wurde, seine ganze Barschaft auf die Köpfe der Passanten hinunterflattern ließ, dabei seine Gründe dafür darlegte und alle mit seinem weise-unvernünftigen Tun überzeugte.

Er wurde im Juni 1906 in Venedig geboren und war gerade zwei Jahre alt, als er mit seinem Vater, einem Volksschullehrer, und seiner Mutter, einer Schneiderin, nach Vicenza übersiedelte. Daher beteuerte er auch einige Male, daß er sich Venedig gegenüber eher wie ein Fremder fühle, und sprach oft davon, daß mehr als alles andere die Stadt Palladios seinen Sinn für die Architektur gebildet hätte; so wie die Schneiderei zu Hause, in der Stich für Stich in geduldiger Arbeit das Werkstück entstand, seinen Sinn für Entwerfen und Zeichnen angeregt hatte. Scarpa pries die Schneiderei, mit ihrem präzisen Schnitt und der „Montage" der verschiedenen Teile, immer als die ursprüngliche *Natur* geduldigen und künstlerischen Tuns. Viele venezianische Künstler und Maler hätten sich, wie Pisanello, in der einfachen Werkstatt der Familie herangebildet und hätten dort jene künstlerische Disziplin und Bildung erworben, die schon Plinius forderte und die auch der von Scarpa so geschätzte Alberti vertreten hatte: „*Kein Tag ohne eine Linie*" („nulla dies sine linea"). Jeden Tag müßte der Bleistift des Architekten mit der Schnelligkeit und Ausdauer einer Nadelspitze eine Linie aufs Papier setzen, um ein gesamtes Werk zu ergeben: eine Architektur für das Leben, entstanden aus einer Myriade von Stichen, einer Myriade von Linien.

Diese seltene zeichnerische Veranlagung bestimmte Scarpa von Anfang an für eine Art wachen Träumens. Als sein Vater ihn nach der technischen Schule zur Aufnahmsprüfung an der Accademia Reale delle Belle Arti anmeldete, fiel er beim ersten Mal durch (1919). Das scheint unmöglich, ist aber verständlich, wenn man bedenkt, daß er, der besonders Begabte, die Zeichnungen für alle anderen machte – was belegt ist – und die eigene unfertig ließ. Diese Begebenheit ist auch kennzeichnend für seine übermäßige Großzügigkeit, die ihn sein Leben lang begleitete und ihn chronisch zu spät kommen ließ –, aber was hieß es für ihn, pünktlich zu sein? Ein Werk vollenden, und es dann sich selbst überlassen, es aus der Aufmerksamkeit eines Zeichners oder seines Willens zu lösen, es aus dessen Obhut entlassen, die das Werk als totales Manufakt behüten möchte.

Seine akademische Lehrzeit erfaßt die Architektur daher mit größter malerischer Begeisterung, die in innerer Reifung und technischer Vervollkommnung als „seine Zeichnung" gepflegt wird. *Seine Zeichnung,* die für einen architektonischen Entwurf immer überbordend und exzessiv war, so dicht und genau an den Rändern seiner vollgezeichneten Arbeitsbögen, entsprach dem Rhythmus und Fluß seines Lebens.

Von Anbeginn gleicht sein Werk einer zugleich *zerrissenen* und auch abgeschlossenen Lehre, als er gebeten wurde, das Projekt für ein Viadukt zwischen Mestre und Venedig weniger grob wiederzugeben und wegen – nach seinen Worten – „zeichnerischer Unbeherrschtheit" entlassen wurde. Und doch waren seine Zeichnungen bereits schöner als die von Otto Wagner und Tony Garnier. Aber Venedig lebte auch nach dem Ersten Weltkrieg noch im Kunst-Schlaf, in jenem regungslosen Spiegel der Gefühle, geschliffen und düster wie die Gläser und die Algen (siehe Gabriele d'Annunzio, *Il Fuoco*, 1900, und Thomas Mann, *Tod in Venedig*, 1913, die beiden *vollkommenen* Erzählungen dieser „doppelten Stadt"). Scarpas Liebe zur Architektur wächst mit der Literatur: mit einem „verpatzten" Buch, *Vers une architecture* von Le Corbusier (erschienen 1923; zweite Auflage 1925), von dem er oft sagte, daß es für ihn damals entscheidend war, viel später aber hinzufügte, daß das Buch von Adolf Loos *Ins Leere gesprochen* eigentlich *das* Buch schlechthin war, und das er 1972 auch in italienischer Übersetzung genießen konnte (Hrsg. Also Rossi, übersetzt von seiner Frau).

Der Weg zur Architektur war eine „nicht beschlossene" Entscheidung, und, wenn man will, eine „scarpianische", denn neben seiner Tätigkeit als Assistent bei Guido Civilli, einem echten Akademiker, am Instituto di Architettura (1926), verfolgte er mit wesentlich mehr Enthusiasmus die Arbeit von Guido Costante Sullam, einem ausgezeichneten Architekten des Liberty, der am Lido von Venedig baute. Scarpas Ansuchen um Aufnahme in die Gilde der Architekten wurde damals abgelehnt. Sein chronisches Unglück (in Wirklichkeit einer gesetzlichen Lappalie zuzuschreiben) schloß ihn in der Praxis für immer und paradoxerweise (zumindest offiziell) von jenem Beruf aus, der sein Leben ausmachte.

Carlo Scarpa hatte nicht jene Lehrzeit absolviert, die nötig war, um als Professionist mit Titel anerkannt zu werden, d. h. berechtigt, die eigenen Projekte zu unterzeichnen. Auch sein letzter großer Auftrag, der Cimitero Brion, ist von seinem Assistenten unterschrieben.

Tatsächlich bedrückte es ihn sein Leben lang, daß er in den fünfziger Jahren wegen widerrechtlicher Berufsausübung verklagt wurde, eigentlich aber deswegen, weil er „Architekturvorlesungen abgehalten hatte", etwas anders ließ sich nicht finden. Aber diese Pattstellung mit dem Gesetz, die ihn in eine ganze Reihe gerichtlicher Verfahren verwickelte, die zwar alle mit Freispruch endeten, zeichnete ihn für immer, trübte ihm Schlaf und Traum: „Der Angeklagte Scarpa erhebe sich" – Carlo Scarpa wiederholte es oft, sprang auf, und spielte den ironischen Venezianer, der weiß, wie bitter das Lachen der Masken ist.

Dabei war Carlo Scarpa während der zwanzig Jahre von 1927 bis 1947, der Zeit des Faschismus und des Zweiten Weltkriegs, als Architekt gar nicht wirklich aktiv. Er entwickelte nur einige, wenn auch hervorragende „Ideen", wie z. B. die für einen neuen Ponte dell'Accademia in Venedig (1932), mit einer äußerst sinnvollen Konstruktion, die die Gezeiten berücksichtigte, die aber im öffentlichen Wettbewerb nur den letzten (10.) Platz belegte.

Ein anderer, mehr öffentlicher, aber ein „dekorativer" Auftrag war die Ausstattung der Aula Magna der Universität in der Ca' Foscari: er hatte das Glück – so behauptete er – sie mit eigenen Händen zu zerstören und wiederherzustellen, wobei er peinlich darauf bedacht war, das Holz der alten Einrichtung in der prachtvollen neuen Ausstattung des Saales wiederzuverwenden (1954–55). Hier errichtete er als Stützen jene „Baum-Säulen", die zu den bedeutendsten Werken der modernen Plastik zählen.

Carlo Scarpa stand bewußt abseits. Er besuchte vor allem die Werkstätten der Glasbläser in Murano und die seiner vielen Künstlerfreunde – besonders Arturo Martini, einen der großen Bildhauer unseres Jahrhunderts, der ihm eine berühmte Portraitzeichnung schenkte, bei der man leicht ins Schwärmen über seinen Esprit und seinen kritischen Witz in Sachen Kunst geraten kann.

Bei der Instabilität seiner frühen Tätigkeit als Architekt arbeitet er als Entwurfszeichner für Gläser bei Cappellin und Venini. Es sind Werke von höchstem Rang, die aber wegen ihrer Zerbrechlichkeit verlorengegangen sind. Man weiß nur wenig über die venezianische Glasproduktion zwischen den zwanziger und vierziger Jahren. Die Welt ist mit venezianischen Gläsern überschwemmt worden, ist sich aber der hohen Qualität der Produktion aus jenen Jahren nicht bewußt. Sie würde eine genauere Erforschung verdienen, denn sie entspricht in der Qualität den besten Erzeugnissen in der Geschichte des venezianischen Glases. Scarpa gehört auch dazu. Als Frank Lloyd Wright 1951 Venedig und Murano besuchte, blieb er, ohne es zu wissen, vor Scarpas Gläsern stehen und wollte eine große Anzahl bestellen. Diese Gläser waren natürlich einzigartig, das Produkt einer äußerst strengen Selektion; aus einer geblasenen Kugel entstand z. B. eine einzigartige Plastik. Dies bedeutete allerdings den wirtschaftlichen Ruin der ersten Werkstatt, in der Scarpa arbeitete. Aber die Werkstatt der Glasbläser war ein Ort von hoher handwerklicher und menschlicher Moral, die Scarpas Haltung prägte und die auch in den so nebensächlichen und gelungenen Dingen, die mit dem Atem gemacht werden, präsent ist.

Mit den Glasbläsern, in einer wachen und produktiven Abgeschiedenheit, schließt ein grundlegendes Kapitel in Scarpas Lebensgeschichte. Das zweite beginnt mit der Wiedergeburt der *Facoltà di Architettura di Venezia* unter der Leitung von Giuseppe Samonà im Jahr 1948, als aus ganz Italien Professoren kommen und den späteren Ruhm dieser Schule begründeten. Scarpa war bereits da und initiierte jene fervente „Wright Periode" mit einer Gruppe von Schülern, die nach der Propaganda Bruno Zeris in ganz Italien Wright mehr schätzten als die *„architettura organica"*, die von der *Zeitschrift „Metron"*, dem Kampforgan der Architekten in den frühen fünfziger Jahren, propagiert wurde.

Ein wichtiges Ereignis für Scarpa und Venedig war es, als Frank Lloyd Wright ein berühmtes Projekt für ein Haus am Canal Grande entwickelte, das sog. Masieri Memorial. Es handelt sich dabei um ein Gebäude zum Gedenken an Angelo Masieri, einen Scarpaschüler, der auf dem Weg zu Wright in Amerika bei einem Autounfall ums Leben gekommen war. Scarpa selbst hatte den Vorschlag gemacht, in Venedig einen modernen architektonischen Akzent zu setzen und war daran interessiert, von Wright Entwürfe dafür zu bekommen. Sie wurden pünktlich nach drei Wochen geliefert, und Scarpa hütete eifersüchtig die Originale. Er schlug einige vorteilhafte kleine Änderungen vor, die für die Ausführung des Projekts erforderlich waren, das als Studentenheim an prominenter Stelle in Venedig stehen sollte: an der Biegung vom Canal Grande in den Rio Novo, zwischen Palazzo Balbi-Valier und Ca'Foscari.

Dieses Projekt entfesselte zwischen innovativen und konservativen Kräften eine der schärfsten Polemiken über das weit umfassendere Problem bezüglich moderner Einflechtungen in das architektonische Gewebe von Venedig. Autoritäten und Geldgeber waren entschieden dagegen, vor allem unter dem Eindruck des enormen Aufruhrs in der Öffentlichkeit, der damals zum ersten Mal rund um diese Geschichte entfacht wurde. Was zum Glück eine banale „Modernisierung" einiger architektonischer Unternehmungen bremste, die von jenen mächtigen Gruppen angestrebt wurden, die strikt gegen Wrights Projekt votierten, der wieder ihre Projekte offen angriff. Auch unter den Intellektuellen waren einige gegen das Projekt eingestellt, mit der Begründung, daß nach diesem Grenzfall sich kein Architekt mit weniger als Wright begnügen und egal wo seinen Stil kopieren und reduzieren würde. Das Ganze klang auch eindeutig als gegen die Facoltà di Architettura gerichtet, wo man nicht müde wurde, die internationalen Meinungen über Alt und Neu am Beispiel einer Stadt wie Venedig zu diskutieren, eine auch heute noch unlösbare Frage.

Was die Facoltà di Architettura betrifft, so kann

man sagen, daß sie in totaler Isolation und völliger Gleichgültigkeit der Stadt gegenüber gedieh: dieser Umstand dauert bis heute an, abgesehen von jenen Professoren und Studenten, die bis 1978 in einem von Carlo Scarpa geprägten Lernklima heranwuchsen, das einmalig und unter den Architekturschulen in Europa ohne Vergleich war.

Scarpas Beziehung zu Wright wurde von dieser Episode geprägt, die auch Gelegenheit bot, Farbe zu bekennen. Heute ist dies in den Projekten selbst, die allzu leicht einem direkten Einfluß des Amerikaners zugeschrieben werden, viel weniger spürbar. Erst 1967, anläßlich der Errichtung des italienischen Pavillons für die Weltausstellung in Montreal, sah Scarpa Architekturen von Wright in natura. Er konnte sich damals nicht genug über jenen Kult mokieren, den er unter den jüngeren Studenten bemerkt hatte, als er nach *Talisien* eingeladen war und dort einer von ihm selbst als lächerlich empfundenen Zeremonie unterzogen wurde: „Sie ließen mich in Wrights Bett schlafen, was jedem schon allein beim Gedanken daran den Schlaf raubte. Ich aber schlief herrlich, auf der Matratze, die aus der Wolle einer ganzen Herde gemacht war."

Die wahre Verbindung zwischen der Scuola di Architettura und Venedig wurde durch niemand anderen als Scarpa hergestellt, der die Biennale gestaltete. Tatsächlich *ist* Scarpa für lange Zeit die Internationale Kunstbiennale. Es beginnt mit der zurückhaltenden Gestaltung der ersten Ausstellung von Paul Klee in Italien (1947; Scarpa trägt selbst die Kosten), geht weiter mit dem Buchpavillon für die Biennale 1950, dem Pavillon für Venezuela (1954), einem seiner bekanntesten, heute aber leicht verwahrlosten Werke, bis zu jenen Vorschlägen für die Wiedererrichtung des italienischen Pavillons, der eine eigene, gesonderte Auseinandersetzung verdienen würde.

Diese Periode dauert von 1947 bis 1968, bis zur XXIV Biennale, in deren Rahmen er neben Louis Kahn (mit dem ihn 1969 eine herzliche Freundschaft verband) eine eigene Ausstellung einrichtete: ausgesuchte Beispiele großen handwerklichen Könnens im Architektonisch-Plastischen, Beispiele seiner ausgereiften Überlegungen zu einigen „Knoten" der Architektur.

Man wird hier den Verlust eines Hauptwerks von Scarpa beklagen müssen, *anhand* dessen sich auch die letzten Zweifel gegenüber dem „Zeichenlehrer" zugunsten des professionellen Architekten verflüchtigen. Der Titel konnte ihm trotz wiederholter Vorschläge für eine Graduierung „honoris causa" offiziell nicht verliehen werden aufgrund fortwährender Klagen wegen Pfuscherei: dieses fadenscheinige Argument fand paradoxerweise just in jenem Moment ein Ende, als Scarpa für zwei Jahre zum Leiter der Facoltà di Architettura gewählt wurde, ohne daß er selbst einen akademischen Titel hatte.

Der Pavillon des Buchs, um den es hier geht, ein ausgezeichnetes Beispiel der Architektur des 20. Jahrhunderts, geriet während des Aufbaus der Biennale 1984 in Brand und erst wenige Minuten vor der offiziellen Eröffnung wurden die hölzernen Trümmer weggekehrt. Ich erinnere mich lebhaft an all dies. Eine brennende Architektur läßt einige Momente lang ihren Entwurf erkennen, um angesichts ihrer Vergänglichkeit gleichsam ihre Idee zu erklären, quasi mit jenen drei Worten von Matisse, die Scarpa *vor* den kleinen Katastrophen des Lebens sagte: „calme, luxe et volupté".

Um 1950 hatte Scarpa nicht nur die vierzig überschritten, sondern auch eine Architektur verwirklicht, die moralisch und historisch einer Kunst der Reife entsprach.

Mit dem Palazzo Abatellis in Palermo, dem Sitz der Galleria d'arte di Sicilia (1954), beginnt sein Entwurf einer Geschichtsbezogenheit, mit einer Art Moderne, die von Denkmälern und Vergangenheit eine lebendige Komponente benützt und heute „l'anima del restauro" genannt wird. Die Gipsoteca in Possagno (Treviso), wo sich die Originalgipse von Canova befinden (1956–57), die Restaurierung des Museo di Castelvecchio in Verona (1958–64) und die

Pinacoteca Querini Stampalia in Venedig (1961–63); die beiden Geschäftslokale, „eingerichtet, um nichts zu verkaufen", für Olivetti in Venedig (1957–58) und Gavina in Bologna (1961) geben über Werkbeschreibungen und Kommentare hinaus einen lebhaften Eindruck von jenen „minimi sistemi" die in Scarpas Architektur pulsieren. Diese entsprechen auch einem „manierismo scarpiano", der leider mit den Werken, die nach seinem Tod ausgeführt wurden, zu Ende ging (i. e. die Casa Ottolenghi in Bardolino, 1979; der Eingang zur Facoltà di Lettere di San Sebastiano in Venedig, 1979; die Banca Mutua di Verona, der sog. Palazzo Scarpa, 1980; der Eingang zur Facoltà di Architettura in Venedig, 1978) – sie haben das geistige Vermächtnis, das in seinem letzten großen Hauptwerk enthalten ist, getrübt.

Dieses Repertoire von „modi scarpiani" hatte sich schon in den beiden großen Wohnbauten Villa Veritti (Udine, 1955–61) und Haus Zentner (Zürich, 1964–68) herausgebildet. Diese Beispiele belegen, wie schwierig es für Scarpa war, unter Einbeziehung der privaten Auftraggeber eine so einfache Sache wie ein Haus zu realisieren: von Anfang bis Ende das Produkt des Architekten, das Scarpa in jeder Weise ins Unendliche fortsetzen will, in Detail und Ausführung. Die Kunden sind verblüfft, wenn der Architekt meint, daß man in diesem Haus *auch* leben könne. Aber ein Haus zu Ende bauen, so meint Scarpa, ist schwierig, fast so wie ein Leben beenden.

Scarpa war, wie Gottfried Semper, davon überzeugt, daß die Architektur eine Kunst der Verflechtung sei: ein einfaches und doch magisches Handwerk, das aber gegen die Energie und Unabwendbarkeit des *Chaos* opponierte. Die Architektur vereint Dinge, die von Natur aus verschieden und getrennt sind, gleichzeitig aber unterscheidet sie die besonders komplizierten Dinge von Zufall und Gewohnheit. Man sehe nur, wie Scarpa das Aufeinandertreffen von Wand und Decke gestaltet: von Horizontale und Vertikale, von Oben und Unten... Die Undurchsichtigkeit einer Decke und der anzunehmende Hochglanz des Bodens, oder die eckige Verbindung einer Wand mit der Decke, sie wurden von Scarpa umgekehrt, wodurch eine unvorhergesehene Helligkeit und Annäherung zwischen oben und unten entstand. Das war auch indirekt ein Grund für sein besonderes „architektonisches Gehen" *mit dem Kopf in der Luft:* dies war seine Art zu schauen und die in Vergleich zu den dichten, farbigen Materialien „gewagten" Lichtreflexe der spiegelnden Oberflächen zu vermeiden.

Scarpa war davon überzeugt, daß der wahre Architekt sich in einem winzigen und wichtigen Detail zu erkennen gebe: jener Fuge zwischen Wand und Boden, die die Putzfrauen „battiscopa" (Besentod) nennen: der schicksalhafte Punkt, der auch die beste Übung architektonischer Rhetorik zu Fall bringen kann. Scarpa schlug hier einfache, etwas von der Wand abgerückte Metalleisten vor, oder „negative" Marmorrahmen, deren Verbindung mit der Wand tiefer lag als die Oberfläche des Bodens. Er liebte diese lebendigen und gleichsam „schwebenden" Böden, die man fast „archäologische" nennen könnte: beim Darübergehen erwartet man fast, daß sich etwas darunter befindet – etwas Natürliches wie Wasser, oder etwas Künstliches wie „eine Geschichte" (vgl. den Eingang zum Cimitero Brion). Die schwebenden und erhöhten Architekturen Scarpas sind wirklich, auch im Erleben, so etwas wie Brücken, die in schwebende Landschaften führen, ähnlich den Architekturphantasien Piranesis: enge Durchgänge, die sich in den Ansichten vervielfachen.

Darüber hinaus sind die Türen und Öffnungen dieser scarpianischen Passagen eher eng und massiv als weit und zierlich (wie in der rationalen und funktionalen Architektur). Die Durchgänge erscheinen wie enge Passagen zwischen riesigen Mauern, und so wird eine einfache Tür zu einem bedeutenden Durchgang, der durch die Mauerstärke den engen Eindruck noch betont, den Passierenden quasi streifend.

Nach Scarpas Meinung konnte ein vertikales, lineares und absolutes Element höchst selten allein bestehen, wenn es nicht in sich die Würde einer antiken Säule hätte, welches das Lexikon architektonischer Elemente schlechthin ist. Neben den einzelnen Teilen bevorzugte Scarpa eine Verdoppelung – welcher Art? Indem er jenes Element verdoppelte und „mit sich selbst" verband. Eine Dachrinne, verdoppelt und verbunden, *wird* Architektur.

In gleicher Weise betrachtete er auch die Natur der Hand, jener „Prothese" menschlichen Genies: einzeln und paarweise. So packt die Hand einen Griff, oder, indem sie die Richtung wechselt und das Handgelenk abwinkelt, eine Stange umfaßt, oder beide Hände erfassen etwas abwechselnd, verbinden sich miteinander oder mit anderen Händen, verflechten die Finger in entschiedener Bindung und Solidarität. Die Fugenverbindungen Scarpas sind hier beispielhaft, wie zwei Teile, die durch den Zeiger einer Waage oder Uhr verbunden werden. Die handwerksmäßige Herstellung von Waagen, die damals bereits im Aussterben war, genoß Scarpas ganz besondere Wertschätzung. Eines Tages machte er mich auf die hohe Qualität einer Handwaage aufmerksam, die tatsächlich große Ähnlichkeit mit seinen Werken aus Eisen und Bronze hatte. Er kaufte dem Schmied die Waage ab, wußte aber nicht, was er damit anfangen sollte; und so schenkte er sie ihm, mit der Bitte, diese Kunst nicht zu vergessen, deren Qualität im Material und in der Genauigkeit der Waage lag. Dies nur, um zu zeigen, daß sein Sinn für das Handwerkliche nichts mit *Design* zu tun hatte. Die Objekte, die gegen Ende seines Lebens entstanden, verfolgten Lösungen ohne technische Entwicklung. Was ihn interessierte, war nicht die Möglichkeit einer Wiederholung, sondern die ausgeführte Perfektion.

Daneben suchte er nach mythischen Bildern, die in einem Labyrinth eingefangen zu sein schienen: dies gilt für alle seine Werke, vor allem für sein letztes.

Jenes scarpianische Bild, das dieses ausgleichende Verhältnis von Notwendigkeiten am stärksten zur Geltung bringt, war die Überschneidung zweier Ringe, Kreise oder Kreiselemente – sehr oft als Fensteröffnung verwendet. Zwei sich überschneidende Kreise sind klar erkennbar, geben aber zugleich einer „dritten" Form Raum, die in ihrem Innern entsteht, sie vereint und sich selbst von ihnen abhebt.

Der *Cimitero Brion* in San Vito d'Asolo, Scarpas letztes Werk, 1969 begonnen und in seinem Todesjahr 1978 beendet, öffnet sich mit der Verbindung zweier Kreise, die ein Fenster bezeichnen, das nicht durchschritten, höchstens zum Vergnügen passiert werden kann, indem man über Wasser springt: als ob man ins Leben eintrete. Es ist dies das einfachste und zugleich komplexeste Zeichen seines letzten und reifsten Werkes. In dieser Ausstellung „Die andere Stadt" sind alle die für die Komposition notwendigen Linien zu sehen: eine fast unendliche Zahl an Zeichen, die sich auf den Steinen erhalten haben, oder verschwunden sind – auf alle Fälle einer Phantasie gehorchend, die uns noch eine lebendige Vorstellung der Architektur vermittelt.

Oft, vielleicht zu oft, haben wir diesen Friedhof wegen der Ruhe zwischen Wasser und Pflanzen als eine *necropolis ludens* bezeichnet. Die gesamte Anlage befindet sich innerhalb einer nach innen geneigten Mauer, angeschmiegt an den alten Friedhof des Dorfes, aus dem die Familie Brion stammt. Das eigentliche Grab hat die Form einer Brücke, zu der ein klares Bächlein fließt, das von einem kleinen künstlichen See innerhalb des heiligen Bezirks gespeist wird: eine kleine Insel und eine Laube blicken zum Bogen des Brücken-Grabes und auf die Hügel von Asolo hinter der Mauer. An der Seite finden sich in einer Art Hütte die Gräber der Familienmitglieder und Verwandten Brions, und schließlich führen alle Wege in diesem Garten zum Kern der Anlage, der Kapelle. Es handelt sich um eine vielgestaltige Reise, die sich unseren Schritten und nun auch unserem Geist erschließt.

Scarpa hatte beschlossen, sich hier begraben zu lassen. Aber das konnte zu einfach erscheinen – als ein Wechselspiel von Autor zu Besitzer. Dem auszuweichen, entschied sich Scarpa, den Friedhof, der *für alle* mit dem, der *für wenige* bestimmt war, zusammenzuschließen. Und er – er konnte sich *dazwischen* legen. An einem versteckten, magischen Ort, so sein Wille, wollte er begraben werden: ein Ort, der zum Friedhof des Friedhofs wurde, weil er die verwelkten Blumen aller Gräber dieser kleinen Welt versammelte.

Endlich hatten sie beschlossen, ihm den Titel „h. c." zu verleihen: das dafür festgesetzte Datum war der Tag nach seinem Begräbnis. Er hatte alles daran gesetzt, um eine Verabredung zu versäumen. Aber, welches sind die versäumten Verabredungen?

1976 – Carlo Scarpa in Vienna / Carlo Scarpa in Wien:
Zeev Aram, Carlo Scarpa, Walter Pichler, Aldo Businaro, Gerd Marquant

1976 – Carlo Scarpa in Vienna / Carlo Scarpa in Wien: Aldo Businaro, Carlo Scarpa, Katarina Noever, Walter Pichler

THE MERE DISTANCE, FREE FROM THE BURDEN OF PRESENT TIME...

DIE REINE FERNE, FREI VON DER LAST DER GEGENWART...

(Fernando Pessoa, Ode maritima)

In front of the cemetery / vor dem Friedhof

337

The Enclosing wall / Die Umfassungsmauer

Entrance to the Brion cemetery / Eingang zum Friedhof Brion

Chapel / Die Kapelle

Passageway to the municipal cemetery / Weg zum Ortsfriedhof

Passageway to the municipal cemetery; left: entrance to the open passage
Weg zum Ortsfriedhof; links: Eingang zum offenen Durchgang

Courtyard in front of the passageway to the municipal cemetery
Platz vor dem Durchgang zum Ortsfriedhof

Reinforced concrete door / Tor aus Eisenbeton

Reinforced concrete door (detail) / Tor aus Eisenbeton (Detail)

View through the open passage to the tomb
Blick durch den offenen Gang auf das Grabmal Brion

Open passage between the sacresty and the chapel / offener Gang zwischen Sakristei und Kapelle

View toward the chapel / Blick zur Kapelle

Main entrance to the chapel (right) / Haupteingang zur Kapelle (rechts)

Main entrance to the chapel / Haupteingang zur Kapelle

Chapel (view to the main entrance) / Kapelle (Blick zum Haupteingang)

Chapel (view from the main entrance to the Cypress grove) / Kapelle (Blick vom Haupteingang zum Zypressenhain)

Chapel, gate to the Cypress grove / Kapelle, Tor zum Zypressenhain

Cypress grove (view to the chapel) / Zypressenhain (Blick zur Kapelle)

Concrete sliding door (detail) / Schiebetür aus Beton (Detail)

Main entrance to the cemetery: concrete sliding door from inside
Eingang zum Friedhof Brion; Die Schiebetür aus Beton von Innen

Entrance (propyleion) from the municipal cemetery / Eingang (Propyläum) vom Ortsfriedhof

Entrance to the Brion cemetery (view from the municipal cemetery)
Eingang zum Friedhof Brion (Blick vom Ortsfriedhof)

Corridor (view towards the vertical sliding door) / Korridor (Blick zur versenkbaren Schiebetür)

Vertical sliding door / versenkbare Schiebetür

Entrance form the municipal cemetery / Eingang vom Ortsfriedhof

View from the corridor to the tomb / Blick vom Korridor auf das Grabmal Brion

The Tomb / Das Grabmal

The tomb Brion; left: the family tomb / Das Grabmal Brion; links: das Familiengrabmal

View from the tomb to the Pavilion / Blick vom Grabmal auf den Pavillon

373

The pavilion / Der Pavillon

The tomb of Carlo Scarpa / Das Grab von Carlo Scarpa

LIST OF ILLUSTRATIONS
(in brackets the inventory numbers of the Carlo-Scarpa-archive)

INITIAL PLANS/ FLOOR PLANS (1969–1970)

1. land registry deed: 68 m², Brion family burial vault area; scale 1 : 2000, colored heliographic print (888)
2. "first project": enlargement of the Brion area and survey of the existing burial vaults (east and north façades of the cemetery); scale 1 : 1, colored heliographic print (855)
3. drawings; tracing paper
4. 15—24 May 1969, land registry deed: "2200 m²", "Brion tomb" cemetery area; scale 1 : 2000, heliographic print

Black notebook

5. page 1: surveys (Brion burial vault, pilaster of the enclosing wall of the old cemetery and locule)
6. page 2: surveys (pilasters of the enclosing wall and entrance to the old cemetery)
7. page 4: drawings
8. page 8: drawings
9. page 11: view
10. page 13: drawings
11. page 15: drawings
12. page 18: details of the Brion tomb
13. page 19: 12 July 1969, plan and section of the Brion tomb

Drawings

14. heliographic print
15. scale 1 : 250, beige tagboard (71)
16. scale 1 : 250, tracing paper (254)
17. scale 1 : 250, tracing paper (253)
18. scale 1 : 250, tracing paper (248)
19. scale 1 : 250, tracing paper (1094)
20. scale 1 : 250, tracing paper (247)

6—9 March 1970, project approved by the Altivole town council

21. plan; scale 1 : 150, heavyweight tracing paper
22. east and west sections; scale 1 : 150, heavyweight tracing paper
23. east and west interior views; scale 1 : 150, heavyweight tracing paper
24. north and south interior views; scale 1 : 150, heavyweight tracing paper
25. north and east exterior views; scale 1 : 150, heavyweight tracing paper

ENCLOSING WALL

WEST: FAÇADE ADJACENT TO THE OLD CEMETERY

Fountain, spring, pool, waterside shed open to the General Public—Northwest Corner, Carlo Scarpa Tomb

26. view: drawing; tracing paper (1357)
27. plan and view; scale 1 : 10, white tagboard for printing photographs (421)
28. plans and section: drawings; tracing paper (1367)
29. plans and views: drawings; typing paper (718)
30. plan, section, view: drawings; scale 1 : 10, heavyweight tracing paper (282)

Propylaeum, Entrance, Passage, Access to Entrance Chapel, Passage Niches (1970—1974)

Façade facing the old cemetery

31. views, plan; scale 1 : 50, beige tagboard (61)
32. 15 November 1970, view, plan; scale 1 : 50, white satin tracing paper (1566)
33. plan; scale 1 : 25, colored heliographic print (837)
34. plan, view, section; scale 1 : 25; stairway details; scale 1 : 1, colored heliographic print (852)
35. view and section; scale 1 : 25, white satin tracing paper
36. view and section; scale 1 : 25, colored heliographic print of number 35 (299)
37. exterior view: drawing; scale 1 : 25, tracing paper (914)
38. interior view: drawing; scale 1 : 25, tracing paper (219)
39. interior view: drawing; scale 1 : 25, tracing paper (226)
40. interior view: drawing; scale 1 : 25, tracing paper (225)

Steps

41. view, section; scale 1 : 1, white tagboard (30)
42. view, section; scale 1 : 10 and 1 : 1, white satin tracing paper
43. drawings; tracing paper (1147)

East façade

44. drawings; typing paper
45. drawings; tracing paper (217)
46. drawings; tracing paper (243)
47. views, plan, section; scale 1 : 50, white satin tracing paper

Ceiling of the corridor

48. drawings; scale 1 : 25, yellow tracing paper (1155)
49. drawings; scale 1 : 25, yellow tracing paper (245)
50. plan and section; scale 1 : 25; section for the wooden strips; scale 1 : 1, white satin tracing paper

Coin-metal moulding of the entrance wing and in the center of the corridor

51. drawings; scale 1 : 20, 1 : 10 and 1 : 1, beige tagboard (404)
52. south façade, drawings; tracing paper (239)
53. south façade and center of the corridor, drawings; scale 1 : 10 and 1 : 1, beige tagboard (331)
54. center of corridor, drawings; beige tagboard (28)
55. north façade, drawings; beige tagboard of number 54 (27)

crystal glass and coin-metal doors along the corridor: vertical sliding door to prevent access to the large pool.

56. drawings; typing paper (442)
57. drawings; tracing paper (1324)
58. drawings; tracing paper (1408)

59   drawings; typing paper (434)
60   view, section, plan; scale
     1 : 10, white tagboard (75)
61   view, section, plan; scale 1 : 1,
     white tagboard (9)
62   October 1973, view, section,
     plan; scale 1 : 1; section; scale
     1 : 10, white satin tracing paper

iron counterweight, and bronze and stainless steel sliding door pulley system

63   view; scale 1 : 50,
     tracing paper on colored
     heliographic print (827)
64   view; scale 1 : 50,
     tracing paper (1441)
65   section; scale 1 : 10,
     colored heliographic print
     of number 62 (297)
66   drawings;
     tracing paper (1312)
67   drawings; typing paper (1499)
68   drawings; typing paper (759)
69   view and section of the
     pulleys; scale 1 : 1,
     white tagboard
70   section; scale 1 : 10; view and
     section of the counterweight;
     scale 1 : 1, beige tagboard (48)
71   March 1974, details; scale 1 : 1,
     white satin tracing paper
     (1153)

Bronze clasp on top of the east façade wall

72   drawing; scale 1 : 1, white
     satin tracing paper (1153)

SOUTH AND EAST

Flower Bed

73   drawings; tracing paper (246)
74   views, plan, sections; scale
     1 : 200, white satin tracing
     paper
75   plan, view; scale 1 : 200,
     colored heliographic
     print (867)

Large flower container above the pool

76   drawings;
     tracing paper (1165)

77   drawings; tracing paper (256)
78   drawings; tracing paper (252)
79   drawings;
     tracing paper (1121)
80   drawings;
     tracing paper (1130)
81   drawings; tracing paper (241)
82   details; scale 1 : 10,
     white satin tracing paper
83   section, view; scale 1 : 10,
     beige tagboard (70)

Sloping tiered wall

84   drawings;
     tracing paper (1164)
85   drawings; scale 1 : 10,
     tracing paper (251)
86   drawings; scale 1 : 10,
     tracing paper (906)
87   plan, view, section;
     scale 1 : 10,
     white satin tracing paper

NORTH: FAMILY TOMB

Corner Brackets

88   drawings; typing paper
89   view; scale 1 : 10; metal
     brackets; scale 1 : 1,
     white satin tracing paper
90   drawing: plan of the
     northwest corner; white satin
     tracing paper (1189)
91   drawings; yellow tracing
     paper (930)
92   drawing; tracing paper (250)

Family Tomb

exterior view

93   drawings; white satin
     tracing paper (233)

sections

94   drawings; typing paper (234)
95   drawings; white satin
     tracing paper (1020)
96   interior views; scale 1 : 25,
     beige tagboard (115)
97   interior views; scale 1 : 25,
     beige tagboard (22)
98   interior views;
     scale 1 : 25 (1548)
99   drawings: longitudinal view;
     scale 1 : 25, white satin
     tracing paper (235)

100 drawings: transversal view;
     white satin tracing paper (287)

slanted ceiling intrados—covering

101 drawings; white satin tracing
     paper (1019)
102 drawings;
     tracing paper (1146)
103 drawings;
     tracing paper (1047)
104 view; scale 1 : 25,
     beige tagboard (129)
105 drawings; white satin
     tracing paper (1026)
106 drawings; white satin
     tracing paper (1018)
107 chiaroscuro drawing;
     scale 1 : 25, white satin
     tracing paper (1519)
108 chiaroscuro drawing; scale
     1 : 25, colored heliographic
     print of number 107 (866)

Gutter

109 drawing; typing paper
110 drawings; typing paper
111 drawings; typing paper (117)
112 view; scale 1 : 10; detail; scale
     1 : 1, white satin tracing paper

Guttae and gold ball

113 drawings; typing paper (603)
114 drawings; typing paper (2470)
115 drawings; white satin
     tracing paper (1033)
116 drawings; tracing paper (189)
117 views; scale 1 : 10, white satin
     tracing paper (1282)
118 view; scale 1 : 1, white satin
     tracing paper (1029)

Gargoyle

119 drawings; typing paper (176)
120 drawings; typing paper (175)
121 plan, section; scale 1 : 1,
     beige tagboard (411)

Plan of the memorial stones

122 drawings; tracing paper (142)
123 drawings; tracing paper (185)

Memorial stones

124 drawings; white satin
     tracing paper (313)

125 drawings; typing paper
126 drawings;
white tagboard (181)
127 drawings; diary entry
"Friday, October 17"
128 drawings; typing paper (177)
129 section; scale 1 : 1, drawings;
white paper (11)
130 letters, drawings;
white graph paper (751)
131 letters, drawings;
tracing paper (1209)
132 letters, drawings;
tracing paper (1457)
133 entrance stairway, drawings;
tracing paper (198)

West: Entrance of the dead (Chapel Area)

134 drawings;
tracing paper (1187)
135 drawings; tracing paper (221)
136 drawing; white satin
tracing paper (1157)
137 view; scale 1 : 100, semihard
tracing paper (263)
138 plan and section; scale 1 : 100,
beige tagboard (93)
139 plan and view; scale 1 : 100,
beige tagboard (381)

Concrete sliding gate

140 drawings; white satin
tracing paper (971)
141 drawings; white satin
tracing paper (1190)
142 drawings; white satin
tracing paper (1192)
143 drawings; white satin
tracing paper (1200)
144 view; scale 1 : 10,
white tagboard (25)
145 view; scale 1 : 10; details;
scale 1 : 1, white satin
tracing paper

North: view towards the funeral chapels (old cemetery)

146 drawings; tracing paper (280)
147 drawings; typing paper
148 drawings; typing paper
149 view; scale 1 : 50;
details; scale 1 : 10,
beige tagboard (114)
150 views; scale 1 : 50; details;
scale 1 : 10, white satin
tracing paper (1549)

Reinforced concrete "anta" access to municipal cemetery (1974)

151 drawings; typing paper
152 drawings; typing paper (679)
153 drawings; typing paper (811)
154 views, plan; scale 1 : 10;
details; scale 1 : 1,
heliographic print (302)
155 drawing: plan; scale 1 : 10,
tracing paper (1272)

Solid brass mounts to hold doors open (1974)

156 drawings;
tracing paper (1080)
157 views, section; scale 1 : 10;
details; scale 1 : 1,
beige tagboard (69)
158 July 1974, views and section;
scale 1 : 10; details; scale 1 : 1,
tracing paper (295)

Enlargement of the "San Vito d'Altivole" cemetery proposals for the new enclosing wall (1971–172)

159 drawings on cadastral map;
scale 1 : 500, heliographic
print (818)
160 drawings; typing paper
161 7 October 1971, layout plan;
1 : 250, white satin
tracing paper
162 layout plan; scale 1 : 250,
yellow tracing paper (202)

West

163 7 October 1971, view; scale
1 : 100, white satin
tracing paper
164 entrance, plan, views,
sections; scale 1 : 25, white
satin tracing paper (1565)
165 entrance, drawings; tracing
paper (244)
166 views; scale 1 : 100 and 1 : 25;
details; scale 1 : 1,
beige tagboard (8)
167 10 February 1972, view, plan;
scale 1 : 100, colored
heliographic print (308)

PAVILION

Entrance plate: beam suspended over the large pool

168 plan, section; scale 1 : 50,
typing paper (1149)
169 section, view, plan; scale
1 : 10, beige paper (885)

Foundation—Central Plate

170 sectional plans and sections;
scale 1 : 25, white satin
tracing paper (1540)
171 detail; scale 1 : 10, white satin
tracing paper (288)
172 detail; scale 1 : 10, 1 : 25 and
1 : 1, white satin
tracing paper (1538)

Pavilion

173 plan; scale 1 : 50,
beige tagboard (44)
174 drawings; heliographic print
of number 168 (839)
175 drawings; typing paper
176 drawings; typing paper
177 drawings;
tracing paper (1086)
178 drawings;
tracing paper (1124)
179 drawings; tracing paper (242)
180 drawings; tracing paper (257)
181 drawings; tracing paper (238)
182 drawings; white satin
tracing paper (1537)
183 plan, sections; scale 1 : 50,
beige tagboard (109)

Sections

184 section; scale 1 : 10,
white tagboard (3)
185 drawings;
tracing paper (1139)
186 drawings; scale 1 : 50,
beige tagboard (47)
187 drawings; scale 1 : 25,
beige tagboard (2)
188 drawings; scale 1 : 25,
tracing paper (1125)
189 drawings; scale 1 : 25, colored
heliographic print (853)
190 drawings; scale 1 : 25, colored
heliographic print (842)

Wooden panels—the pavilion "Roof"

Exteriors

191 drawings; typing paper (547)
192 drawings; typing paper (143)
193 drawings; typing paper (1501)
194 drawings;
    tracing paper (1135)
195 drawings;
    tracing paper (1138)
196 drawings; white satin
    tracing paper (1158)
197 drawings; Bristol board (336)
198 drawings; tagboard (52)
199 longitudinal view; scale 1:10,
    heavyweight tracing paper

Interior

200 longitudinal view; scale 1:10,
    tracing paper (265)

Pilasters

201 drawings; typing paper (775)
202 drawings; typing paper (757)
203 drawings; tracing paper (193)
204 drawings;
    tracing paper (1407)
205 drawings; tracing paper (199)
206 drawings;
    tracing paper (1065)
207 drawings; tracing paper (201)
208 drawings; typing paper (587)
209 drawings; typing paper (142)
210 drawings; typing paper (172)
211 full-scale detail; scale 1:1,
    colored heliographic
    print (882)

Corners

212 drawings;
    tracing paper (1089)
213 drawings;
    tracing paper (1243)
214 vertical and horizontal
    sections; scale 1:1,
    semi-heavyweight
    tracing paper (184)
215 horizontal section; scale 1:1,
    white tagboard (97)

Entrance weing openings

216 view; scale 1:10,
    tracing paper (214)
217 drawings;
    tracing paper (1251)
218 drawings; tracing paper (216)
219 drawings; tracing paper (283)

Entrance stay bar

220 drawings; typing paper (791)
221 drawings; Bristol board (736)
222 drawings; white paper (12)
223 drawings;
    tracing paper (1232)

Structure

224 drawings;
    tracing paper (1389)
225 drawings;
    tracing paper (1414)
226 drawings;
    tracing paper (1434)
227 drawings;
    tracing paper (1134)
228 drawings; tracing paper (211)
229 plan; scale 1:10,
    white tagboard (81)
230 plan; scale 1:10,
    white satin tracing paper
231 plan: details; scale 1:10,
    tracing paper (264)

Lighting

232 drawings;
    tracing paper (1234)

Large pool

233 drawing; scale 1:50, yellow
    tracing paper (270)
234 details; scale 1:50, yellow
    tracing paper (276)
235 drawing; scale 1:50, colored
    heliographic print (304)
236 drawing; scale 1:100,
    heavyweight tracing paper on
    heliographic print (102)
237 drawing; scale 1:50, colored
    heliographic print (305)
238 drawing; scale 1:50, colored
    heliographic print (823)
239 drawing; scale 1:50, colored
    heliographic print (306)

Retaining wall near the pool

240 facade and views; scale 1:50;
    details; scale 1:10, white satin
    tracing paper (1539)
241 vertical section; scale 1:10
    and 1:1, white satin
    tracing paper (1533)

Bottom of pool

242 idea: plan;
    tracing paper (1076)
243 drawings; typing paper (804)
244 drawings; typing paper (471)
245 drawings; typing paper (803)
246 section; scale 1:50, yellow
    tracing paper (260)
247 drawings depicting flooding;
    typing paper

Views

248 draft of views; stationery
249 draft of views;
    stationery (128)
250 draft of views;
    stationery (127)

Bamboo Island

251 plan; scale 1:25,
    stationery (123)

Two rings

252 drawing; stationery (124)
253 drawing; stationery (129)
254 plan; scale 1:25,
    stationery (125)
255 section, drawings;
    stationery (130)
256 section, drawings;
    stationery (122)

Fountain or floating flower box

257 drawings; typing paper (133)
258 section; typing paper (121)
259 drawing; stationery (134)
260 plan, section; scale 1:25;
    details; scale 1:1,
    stationery (135)
261 plan; scale 1:10, colored
    heliographic print (873)
262 plan; scale 1:10, colored
    heliographic print (872)
263 plan; scale 1:10,
    tracing paper (629)

Edge of pool

264 sections; scale 1:10 and 1:1,
    colored heliographic
    print (823)

Hindrance near pool: cable barrier across lawn

265 view; typing paper (792)

266 drawings; typing paper (752)
267 drawings; scale 1 : 1,
white tagboard (424)

TOMB

268 drawings;
white Bristol board (164)
269 drawings;
white Bristol board (493)

6—9 March 1970, project approved by the Altivole town council

270 section and plan; scale 1 : 40,
heavyweight tracing paper
271 drawings; colored
heliographic print of
number 270 (864)

Arch over the sarcrophagi: Arcosolium

Extrados

272 drawings; typing paper (476)
273 drawings; typing paper (161)
274 drawings; typing paper (157)
275 drawings; typing paper (475)
276 section; scale 1 : 10,
beige tagboard (334)
277 plans; scale 1 : 25; section;
scale 1 : 10, white satin
tracing paper

Arch brace

278 drawings; typing paper (473)
279 drawings; typing paper (162)
280 drawings; typing paper (586)
281 drawings; tracing paper (209)
282 details viewed from below
looking up, and from above;
scale 1 : 10, tracing paper

Entredos mosaic

283 drawings; tracing paper (472)
284 plan; scale 1 : 25,
tracing paper (1353)
285 plan; scale 1 : 10,
beige tagboard (62)

Detail of the covering between the two spans above the sarcrophagi

286 drawings; white satin
tracing paper (1376)
287 sections; scale 1 : 10 and
1 : 25, white satin
tracing paper (1524)

Sarcrophagi

288 drawings;
tracing paper (1113)
289 drawings;
tracing paper (1106)
290 drawings;
tracing paper (1203)
291 drawings;
tracing paper (1112)
292 drawings;
tracing paper (1109)
293 drawings;
tracing paper (1100)
294 drawings;
tracing paper (1355)
295 drawings; white satin
tracing paper (1099)
296 drawings; tracing paper (212)
297 drawings; tracing paper (190)
298 views; scale 1 : 10,
tracing paper (1117)
299 views; scale 1 : 25 and 1 : 10,
beige tagboard (24)
300 drawings; tracing paper (236)
301 views; scale 1 : 25 and 1 : 10,
beige tagboard (65)
302 drawings;
tracing paper (1348)
303 drawings; tracing paper (213)
304 details; scale 1 : 2,
tracing paper (203)
305 views; scale 1 : 10,
white tagboard (32)
306 views; scale 1 : 10,
white Bristol board (74)
307 details; scale 1 : 2,
tracing paper
308 views; scale 1 : 5, colored
heliographic print

Inscription: ivory-inlaid ebony

309 drawings; piece of
stationery (468)
310 drawings; typing paper (451)
311 drawings;
tracing paper (1104)
312 drawings; tracing paper (322)
313 view; scale 1 : 1,
white tagboard (40)
314 view; scale 1 : 1, white satin
tracing paper

Floor: circular fascia

315 drawings; typing paper
316 full-scale detail; scale 1 : 1,
beige tagboard (66)

317 drainage, drawings;
tracing paper (1095)
318 drainage, plans and sections;
scale 1 : 10, beige
tagboard (91)

Sundial and waterway

319 plan and section; scale 1 : 10
and 1 : 1, beige tagboard (96)

CHAPEL

Plans/floorplans

320 drawings;
tracing paper (1362)
321 drawings; tracing paper (919)
322 drawings;
tracing paper (1372)
323 drawings;
tracing paper (1392)
324 drawings; tracing paper (911)
325 drawings; tracing paper
(1270)
326 drawings;
tracing paper (1394)
327 drawings; scale 1 : 50,
tracing paper (933)
328 drawings; scale 1 : 50,
beige tagboard (111)
329 drawings; scale 1 : 50,
beige tagboard (110)

Views

Northeast

330 drawings; scale 1 : 25, colored
heliographic print (849)
331 drawings; scale 1 : 25,
beige tagboard (4)
332 drawings; typing paper (159)

Northwest

333 drawings; scale 1 : 25, yellow
tracing paper (255)
334 drawings; scale 1 : 25, white
satin tracing paper (229)
335 drawings; scale 1 : 10, colored
heliographic print (863)
336 view and section; scale 1 : 25,
beige tagboard (104)

Sections

337 drawings; scale 1 : 25,
beige tagboard (60)

338 drawings; scale 1:25,
beige tagboard (51)
339 drawings; scale 1:25,
tracing paper (208)

Cupola

340 drawings; white
notebook paper (456)
341 drawings; white
notebook paper (1503)
342 drawings; tracing paper (975)
343 drawings; tracing paper (973)
344 drawings;
yellow tracing paper (1337)
345 drawings;
yellow tracing paper (204)
346 drawings; tracing paper (326)
347 drawings; tracing paper (905)
348 drawings; typing paper (504)
349 drawings; typing paper (496)
350 drawings; white
notebook paper (1506)
351 drawings; white satin
tracing paper (1399)
352 drawings; tracing paper (977)
353 drawings; white satin
tracing paper (230)
354 drawings; white satin
tracing paper (318)
355 drawings; tracing paper (284)
356 drawings; white satin
tracing paper (1304)
357 drawings; tracing paper (328)
358 plan and exterior view; scale
1:50, beige tagboard (95)
359 plan and exterior view; scale
1:50, beige tagboard (118)
360 ceiling plan; scale 1:50,
beige tagboard (1)

Adjustable ceiling lens

361 plan; scale 1:10; longitudinal
section; scale 1:1;
transverse section; scale 1:1,
beige tagboard (56)
362 plan; scale 1:10; longitudinal
section; scale 1:1;
transverse section; scale 1:1,
white satin tracing paper

„Ufficium sepulcri": Angel of Death

363 drawings; stationery (151)
364 drawings;
tracing paper (1332)
365 drawings; white satin
tracing paper (146)

366 drawings; typing paper (150)
367 drawings; typing paper (149)
368 drawings; typing paper (674)
369 drawings; typing paper (147)
370 drawings; typing paper (148)

Floor

371 drawings; white satin
tracing paper (972)
372 drawings; scale 1:25,
tracing paper (1514)
373 drawings; scale 1:25,
tracing paper (985)
374 drawings; scale 1:25,
tracing paper (983)
375 drawings; scale 1:25 and
1:1, tracing paper (1390)
376 inlays at the center of the
chapel; scale 1:1,
tracing paper (1343)
377 inlays at the center of chapel;
scale 1:1 and 1:100,
white tagboard (100)
378 edge step; scale 1:1,
white satin tracing paper

Mainportal

379 drawings; typing paper (719)
380 drawings; typing paper (523)
381 drawings; typing paper (524)
382 drawings; typing paper (554)
383 drawings; typing paper (163)
384 drawings; white satin
tracing paper (1320)
385 drawings;
tracing paper (1438)
386 plan; scale 1:50;
details; scale 1:10,
white tagboard (108)

Metal hinge

387 drawings;
tracing paper (1070)
388 drawings;
tracing paper (1435)
389 floor mount, section; scale
1:1, beige tagboard (58)
390 ground mount, plan, section,
view; scale 1:1,
white tagboard (35)
391 ground mount, plan, section,
view; scale 1:1,
tracing paper (1523)
392 ceiling mount, plan, section,
view; scale 1:1, white satin
tracing paper (1522)

393 aluminium ceiling support,
plan, section; scale 1:1,
tracing paper (1078)
394 October 1973, detail of the
pane to the right of the large
door; scale 1:1, white satin
tracing paper (1526)

Small ebony door in the main
portal (1973—1974)

395 drawings; white Bristol
board (561)
396 drawings; white satin
tracing paper (1051)
397 drawings;
tracing paper (1413)
398 drawings; tracing paper (192)
399 interior and exterior views;
scale 1:5; plane; scale 1:1,
white Bristol board (17)
400 November 1973, interior
view; scale 1:5, white satin
tracing paper (1547)
401 drawings; scale 1:5 and 1:1,
tracing paper (1416)
402 drawings; scale 1:5,
tracing paper (1350)
403 section; scale 1:1,
white tagboard (417)
404 November 1973, section; scale
1:1, white satin
tracing paper (1548)
405 section; scale 1:1, colored
heliographic print
of number 404 (832)
406 section, detail; scale 1:1,
tracing paper (1344)
407 February 1974, plan and
view; scale 1:1, colored
heliographic print (836)
408 February 1974, view of
hinges; colored
heliographic print (877)
409 March 1974, details; scale
1:1, tracing paper (1520)
410 March 1974, details of the
metal- and woodwork at the
center of the raised section;
scale 1:1, colored
heliographic print (833)
411 door handle, drawings;
tracing paper (1208)
412 door handle, view, section;
scale 1:1, white tagboard (84)

Font

413 drawings; typing paper
414 drawings; white satin tracing paper (1510)
415 vertical section; scale 1 : 1, tracing paper (1253)
416 vertical section; scale 1 : 1, white paper (80)
417 drawings; typing paper (171)
418 horizontal section; scale 1 : 1, white Bristol board (16)
419 horizontal section; scale 1 : 1, tracing paper (269)
420 horizontal and vertical section; scale 1 : 1, white tagboard (107)
421 pushing device, vertical section; scale 1 : 1, tracing paper (268)
422 pushing device, handle and opening, vertical section; scale 1 : 1 (646)
423 horizontal section; scale 1 : 1, white tagboard (14)

Circular portal

424 drawings; typing paper (710)
425 drawings; typing paper (498)
426 drawings; colored photocopy (160)
427 view and section; scale 1 : 10, beige tagboard (382)
428 plan and views; scale 1 : 20; detail; scale 1 : 10, beige tagboard (363)
429 floor mount; scale 1 : 1, beige tagboard (386)

Windows

High windows

430 drawings; typing paper (519)
431 drawings; tracing paper (1338)
432 horizontal section; scale 1 : 5, tracing paper (1378)
433 horizontal section; scale 1 : 5, tracing paper (956)
434 drawings; beige tagboard (393)
435 horizontal section; scale 1 : 10 and 1 : 5, white Bristol board (333)
436 vertical section; scale 1 : 5, white satin tracing paper

Square windows behind the altar

437 sections, view; scale 1 : 10, typing paper (551)
438 details; typing paper (566)
439 horizontal section; scale 1 : 1, beige tagboard (357)

Altar

Location of altar

440 drawings; tracing paper (1428)
441 drawings; white satin tracing paper (899)
442 drawings; scale 1 : 25, colored heliographic print (826)
443 drawings; scale 1 : 25, white satin tracing paper (291)
444 details; scale 1 : 25, 1 : 10 and 1 : 1, white satin tracing paper (1551)
445 drawings; scale 1 : 25 and 1 : 10, heliographic print of number 444 (307)

Arrangement of steps and altar

446 drawings; scale 1 : 10, white satin tracing paper
447 drawings; scale 1 : 10, tracing paper (1345)
448 drawings; scale 1 : 10, tracing paper (924)
449 drawings; scale 1 : 10, tracing paper (1342)
450 drawings; typing paper (563)

Dais under the altar (1974)

451 drawings; typing paper (562)
452 drawings; typing paper (564)
453 sections; scale 1 : 1, white tagboard (36)
454 February 1974, sections; scale 1 : 10 and 1 : 1, tracing paper (317)
455 sections; scale 1 : 1, white tagboard (349)
456 March 1974, sections; scale 1 : 1, tracing paper (1554)

Altar (1971)

479 view, section, plan; scale 1 : 1, white tagboard (112)
480 view, section, plan; scale 1 : 1, hard tracing paper
481 view; hard tracing paper (258)

Suspended candelabra

482 drawings; typing paper (763)
483 drawings; typing paper (787)
484 drawings; tracing paper (1430)
485 drawings; typing paper (136)
486 drawings; typing paper (1486)
487 drawings; scale 1 : 10, white tagboard (10)
488 view and section; scale 1 : 10, tracing paper on white tagboard (85)
489 drawings; scale 1 : 10, white tagboard (106)

Candle holders

490 plan; scale 1 : 1, tracing paper (1259)
491 drawings; tracing paper (1283)
492 view; scale 1 : 1, tracing paper (272)
493 drawings; scale 1 : 1, tracing paper (273)
494 drawings; scale 1 : 1, tracing paper (1260)
495 drawings; scale 1 : 1, hard tracing paper

Ceiling pole mounts

496 drawings; tracing paper (1379)
497 plan, section, view; scale 1 : 1, white tagboard (89)

The three poles

498 detail: plan, section, view; scale 1 : 1, white tagboard (87)

Marble antas behind the altar (1973—1974)

499 drawing; typing paper (649)
457 drawings; typing paper
458 view; scale 1 : 10, tracing paper (951)
459 4 November 1971, view; scale 1 : 10, white tagboard (34)
460 plan, view, section; scale 1 : 10, white satin tracing paper (292)
461 drawings; tracing paper (278)
462 plan, view, section; scale 1 : 10, white tagboard (77)
463 plan, view; scale 1 : 10 and 1 : 1, white satin tracing paper (901)

464 drawings; typing paper
465 drawings; typing paper (167)
466 drawings; typing paper (168)
467 drawings;
white drawing paper
468 drawings;
tracing paper (1424)
464 plan, section, view; scale
1 : 10, white satin
tracing paper (1534)

Sacrum

470 plan; scale 1 : 10, typing paper

Chalice

471 drawings;
yellow tracing paper (1287)
472 section; scale 1 : 1, tracing
paper on white paper

Crucifix

473 drawings; typing paper
474 drawings; typing paper
475 drawings; typing paper (145)
476 view; tracing paper (261)
477 drawings; white tagboard (82)
478 view, section; scale 1 : 1,
white tagboard
500 drawing; typing paper (573)
501 drawings; white satin
tracing paper (965)
502 drawings;
tracing paper (1072)
503 drawings;
beige tagboard (90/V)
504 plan; scale 1 : 10; details;
scale 1 : 1, white tagboard (26)
505 plan; scale 1 : 1, white satin
tracing paper (1564)
506 September 1973, view; scale
1 : 10, white satin tracing
paper (1550)
507 clip, drawing;
tracing paper (191)
508 clip, drawings;
typing paper (656)
509 clip, drawings;
typing paper (648)
510 clasp, drawings;
typing paper (771)
511 clasp, drawings;
typing paper (671)
512 clasp, plan and views;
scale 1 : 1 (338)
513 August 1974, clasp and
clamps; scale 1 : 1,
tracing paper (294)
514 clasp, drawings;
tracing paper (1091)
515 clasp, plans; scale 1 : 10, 1 : 1,
colored heliographic
print (825)
516 clamps, plan; scale 1 : 1,
beige tagboard (59)
517 clamps, plan; scale 1 : 1,
beige tagboard (53)

*Gate to the cypress grove
(1973—1975)*

518 plan; scale 1 : 25,
beige tagboard (386)
519 detail, access to the cypress
grove; typing paper (1502)
520 plan, view; scale 1 : 10; detail;
scale 1 : 1, white tagboard (73)
521 plan; scale 1 : 10,
tracing paper (1334)
522 August 1973, plan and view;
scale 1 : 10, white satin
tracing paper (1530)
523 plan; scale 1 : 10,
beige tagboard (375)
524 hinge, drawings;
tracing paper (1336)
525 hinge, drawings; scale 1 : 1,
beige tagboard (50)
526 floor hinge, plan and view;
scale 1 : 1, white tagboard (31)
527 August 1973, ceiling hinge,
plan, view; scale 1 : 1, white
satin tracing paper (1563)
528 step, drawings;
white paper (13)
529 25 October 1975, step, view;
scale 1 : 5; details; scale 1 : 1,
white satin tracing paper
530 clamp, drawings;
typing paper
531 panes, drawings;
tracing paper (1363)
532 detail; scale 1 : 1, white satin
tracing paper

*Entrance portal, open passage to the
sacristy*

533 view; scale 1 : 25, white satin
tracing paper
534 view; scale 1 : 25, white satin
tracing paper
535 plan, view; scale 1 : 25,
beige tagboard (94)
536 drawings;
tracing paper (1384)
537 drawings;
tracing paper (1385)
538 drawings;
tracing paper (1393)
539 plan; scale 1 : 25, colored
heliographic print (301)
540 plan; scale 1 : 25,
white Bristol board (29)
541 plan; scale 1 : 25, white satin
tracing paper
542 door to sacristy, north view;
scale 1 : 25, white satin
tracing paper
543 longitudinal section;
scale 1 : 25, white satin
tracing paper
544 longitudinal section;
scale 1 : 25, white satin
tracing paper
545 door, view; scale 1 : 10,
white paper (37)
546 door, plan, view;
scale 1 : 10 (1513)
547 door bolt, drawings;
typing paper (657)
548 bolt; typing paper (170)
549 bolt; stationery (139)
550 bolt; stationery
551 bolt, view; scale 1 : 1,
white tagboard for printing
photographs (83)
552 bolt, views; scale 1 : 1,
beige tagboard (46)
553 July 1973, bolt, views;
scale 1 : 1, heavyweight
tracing paper (293)
554 window, drawing;
typing paper
555 window, drawing;
typing paper
556 window, view; scale 1 : 10;
details; scale 1 : 1,
white tagboard (72)
557 window, sections; scale 1 : 10,
white tagboard (368)
558 cabinet with secret drawer,
drawings; scale 1 : 10 and
1 : 1, white tagboard (177)
559 cabinet, horizontal section;
scale 1 : 10 and 1 : 1,
white tagboard (405)
560 cabinet, drawings;
white paper
561 cabinet, detail;
white tracing paper (285)
562 cabinet, detail; typing paper
563 cabinet, detail;
typing paper (630)

564 cabinet, detail; typing paper (481)
565 store-room door, drawings; tracing paper (1330)
566 store-room door, drawings; tracing paper (1419)
567 store-room door, drawings; beige tagboard (399/V)
568 September 1973, store-room door, details; scale 1 : 1, white satin tracing paper
569 October 1973, store-room door, plan, view; scale 1 : 10, white satin tracing paper (1552)
570 water pumps, drawings; typing paper (526)
571 water pumps, drawings; white satin tracing paper (1170)
572 water pumps, drawings; white satin tracing paper (1167)
573 water pumps, plan; scale 1 : 10, beige tagboard (7)
574 water pumps, section; scale 1 : 10, white satin tracing paper
575 November 1973, water pumps, door to sacristy; scale 1 : 10 and 1 : 1, white satin tracing paper (1527)
576 water pumps, details; scale 1 : 1, white paper (410)

GARDEN LAYOUT

577 drawings; typing paper (707)
578 drawings; typing paper (144)
579 drawings; notebook paper
580 drawings; notebook paper

"DIE ANDERE STADT"

581 drawings; typing paper

VERZEICHNIS DER ABBILDUNGEN

(in Klammern die Invertarnummern des Carlo-Scarpa-Archivs)

ERSTE ENTWÜRFE UND GRUNDRISSE (1969–1970)

1. Kataster: 68 m² für Grabkapelle der Familie Brion; M 1:2000, kolorierte Blaupause (888)
2. „erstes Projekt": Vergrößerung des Gebietes für die Familie Brion und Aufriß bereits bestehender Grabkapellen (Ost- und Nordseite des Friedhofs); M 1:1, kolorierte Blaupause (855)
3. Skizzen; Aquafixpapier
4. 15.–24. Mai 1969, Kataster: 2200 m² für Friedhof „Grabstätte Brion"; M 1:2000, Blaupause

Das schwarze Notizbuch

5. Seite 1: Bauaufnahmen (Grabkapelle Brion, Pfeiler der Umfassungsmauer des Ortsfriedhofs und der Grabnische)
6. Seite 2: Bauaufnahmen (Pfeiler der Umfassungsmauer und des Eingangs zum Ortsfriedhof)
7. Seite 4: Skizzen
8. Seite 8: Skizzen
9. Seite 13: Skizzen
11. Seite 15: Skizzen
12. Seite 18: Details der Grabstätte Brion
13. Seite 19: 12. Juli 1969, Plan und Schnitte der Grabstätte Brion

Skizzen

14. auf Blaupause
15. M 1:250, beiger Karton (71)
16. M 1:250, Aquafixpapier (254)
17. M 1:250, Aquafixpapier (253)
18. M 1:250, Aquafixpapier (248)
19. M 1:250, Aquafixpapier (1094)
20. M 1:250, Aquafixpapier (247)

6.–9. März 1970, das von der Gemeinde Altivole angenommene Projekt

21. Grundriß; M 1:150, stärkeres Aquafixpapier
22. Schnitte gegen Ost und Nord; M 1:150, stärkeres Aquafixpapier
23. Innenansichten Ost und West; M 1:150, stärkeres Aquafixpapier
24. Innenansichten Nord und Süd; M 1:150, stärkeres Aquafixpapier
25. Außenansichten Nord und Ost; M 1:150, stärkeres Aquafixpapier

DIE UMFASSUNGSMAUER

WESTSEITE: FASSADE IN RICHTUNG ORTSFRIEDHOF

Brunnen, Quelle, Becken, allgemein zugängliche Wasserstelle, Nordwestecke mit Grab Carlo Scarpas

26. Ansicht, Skizze; Aquafixpapier (1357)
27. Grundriß und Ansicht; M 1:10, weißer Kunstdruckkarton (421)
28. Grundriß und Schnitt, Skizzen; Aquafixpapier (1367)
29. Grundrisse und Ansichten, Skizzen; Schreibmaschinpapier (718)
30. Grundriß, Schnitte, Ansicht, Skizzen; M 1:10, stärkeres Aquafix (282)

Eingang, Zugang zur Kapelle (1970–1974)

Fassade in Richtung Ortsfriedhof

31. Ansichten, Grundriß; M 1:50, beiger Karton (61)
32. 15. November 1970, Ansicht, Grundriß; M 1:50, satiniertes Pauspapier (1566)
33. Grundriß; M 1:25, kolorierte Blaupause (837)
34. Grundriß, Ansicht, Schnitt; M 1:25; Details der Treppen; M 1:1, kolorierte Blaupause (852)
35. Ansicht und Schnitt; M 1:25, satiniertes Pauspapier
36. Ansicht und Schnitt; M 1:25, kolorierte Blaupause von Kat.-Nr. 35 (299)
37. Außenansicht: Skizze; M 1:25, Aquafixpapier (914)
38. Innenansicht: Skizze; M 1:25, Aquafixpapier (219)
39. Innenansicht: Skizze; M 1:25, Aquafixpapier (226)
40. Innenansicht: Skizze; M 1:25, Aquafixpapier (225)

Stufen

41. Ansicht, Schnitt, M 1:10, weißer Karton (30)
42. Ansicht, Schnitt, M 1:10 und 1:1, satiniertes Pauspapier
43. Skizzen; Aquafixpapier (1147)

Ostseite

44. Skizzen; Schreibmaschinpapier
45. Skizzen; Aquafixpapier (217)
46. Skizzen; Aquafixpapier (243)
47. Ansichten, Grundriß, Schnitt; M 1:150, satiniertes Pauspapier

Decke des Korridors

48. Skizzen; M 1:25, amerikanisches Pauspapier (1125)
49. Skizzen; M 1:25, amerikanisches Pauspapier (245)
50. Grundriß und Schnitt; M 1:25; Schnitt für die Holzpanele; M 1:1, satiniertes Pauspapier

Rahmen aus „Muntzmetall" beim Eingang und in der Mitte des Korridors

51. Skizzen; M 1:20, 1:10 und 1:1, beiger Karton (404)
52. Südseite, Skizzen; Aquafixpapier (239)
53. Südseite und Korridormitte, Skizze; M 1:10 und 1:1, beiger Karton (331)
54. Korridormitte, Skizzen; beiger Karton (28)
55. Nordseite, Skizzen; beiger Karton, Rückseite von 54 (27)

Türe aus Kristallglas und „Muntzmetall" im Korridor: die vertikale Schiebetür versperrt den Zugang zum großen Wasserbecken

56. Skizzen; Schreibmaschinpapier (442)

57 Skizzen; Aquafixpapier (1324)
58 Skizzen; Aquafixpapier (1408)
59 Skizzen;
 Schreibmaschinpapier (434)
60 Ansicht, Schnitt, Grundriß;
 M 1:10, weißer Karton (75)
61 Ansicht, Schnitt, Grundriß;
 M 1:1, weißer dünner Karton (9)
62 Oktober 1973, Ansicht,
 Schnitt, Grundriß; M 1:1,
 Schnitt M 1:10, satiniertes
 Pauspapier

Gegengewicht aus Eisen und
Rollensystem in Bronze und
Inoxstahl für die Schiebetür

63 Ansicht; M 1:50,
 Aquafixpapier auf kolorierter
 Blaupause (827)
64 Ansicht; M 1:50,
 Aquafixpapier (1441)
65 Schnitt; M 1:10 kolorierte
 Blaupause von 62 (297)
66 Skizzen; Aquafixpapier (1312)
67 Skizzen;
 Schreibmaschinpapier (1499)
68 Skizzen;
 Schreibmaschinpapier (759)
69 Ansicht und Schnitt der
 Rollen; M 1:1,
 weißer dünner Karton
70 Schnitt; M 1:10; Ansicht und
 Schnitt des Gegengewichtes;
 M 1:1, beiger Karton (48)
71 März 1974, Details; M 1:1,
 satiniertes Pauspapier

Bronzeschließe im oberen Teil der
ostseitigen Mauer

72 Skizze; M 1:1, satiniertes
 Pauspapier

SÜD- UND OSTSEITE

Blumenbeet

73 Skizzen; Aquafixpapier (246)
74 Ansichte, Grundriß, Schnitte;
 M 1:200, satiniertes
 Pauspapier
75 Grundriß, Ansicht; M 1:200,
 kolorierte Blaupause (867)

Blumentrog über dem Wasserbecken

76 Skizzen; Aquafixpapier (1165)

77 Skizzen; Aquafixpapier (256)
78 Skizzen; Aquafixpapier (252)
79 Skizzen; Aquafixpapier (1121)
80 Skizzen; Aquafixpapier (1130)
81 Skizzen; Aquafixpapier (241)
82 Details; M 1:10, satiniertes
 Pauspapier
83 Schnitt, Ansicht; M 1:10,
 beiger Karton (70)

Schräge und abgestufte Mauer

84 Skizzen; Aquafixpapier (1164)
85 Skizzen; M 1:10,
 Aquafixpapier (251)
86 Skizzen; M 1:10,
 Aquafixpapier (906)
87 Grundriß, Ansicht, Schnitt;
 M 1:10, satiniertes
 Pauspapier

NORDSEITE:
FAMILIENGRABMAL

Ecklösungen

88 Skizzen;
 Schreibmaschinpapier
89 Ansicht; M 1:10;
 Metallträger; M 1:1,
 satiniertes Pauspapier
90 Skizze: Grundriß der
 Nordwestecke; satiniertes
 Pauspapier (1189)
91 Skizzen; amerikanisches
 Pauspapier (930)
92 Skizze; Aquafixpapier (250)

Familiengrabmal

Außenansicht

93 Skizzen; satiniertes
 Pauspapier (233)

Schnitte

94 Skizzen;
 Schreibmaschinpapier (234)
95 Skizzen; satiniertes
 Pauspapier (1020)
96 Innenansichten; M 1:25,
 beiger Karton (115)
97 Innenansichten; M 1:25,
 beiger Karton (22)
98 Innenansichten; M 1:25,
 satiniertes Pauspapier (1548)

99 Skizzen: Längsansicht;
 M 1:25, satiniertes
 Pauspapier (235)
100 Skizzen: Ansicht; satiniertes
 Pauspapier (287)

schräge Deckenleibung:
Überdachung

101 Skizzen; satiniertes
 Pauspapier (1019)
102 Skizzen; Aquafixpapier (1146)
103 Skizzen; Aquafixpapier (1047)
104 Ansicht; M 1:25,
 beiger Karton (129)
105 Skizzen; satiniertes
 Pauspapier (1026)
106 Skizzen; satiniertes
 Pauspapier (1018)
107 Zeichnung in chiaroscuro;
 M 1:25, satiniertes
 Pauspapier (1519)
108 Zeichnung in chiaroscuro;
 M 1:25; kolorierte Blaupause
 von Nr. 107 (866)

Dachrinne

109 Skizzen;
 Schreibmaschinpapier
110 Skizzen;
 Schreibmaschinpapier
111 Skizzen;
 Schreibmaschinpapier (117)
112 Ansicht; M 1:10; Detail;
 M 1:1, satiniertes Pauspapier

Tropfen und vergoldete Kugel

113 Skizzen;
 Schreibmaschinpapier (603)
114 Skizzen;
 Schreibmaschinpapier (2470)
115 Skizzen; satiniertes
 Pauspapier (1033)
116 Skizzen, Aquafixpapier (189)
117 Ansichten; M 1:10,
 satiniertes Pauspapier (1282)
118 Ansicht; M 1:1, satiniertes
 Pauspapier (1029)

Wasserspeier

119 Skizzen;
 Schreibmaschinpapier (176)
120 Skizzen;
 Schreibmaschinpapier (175)
121 Grundriß, Schnitt; M 1:1,
 beiger Karton (411)

Lageplan der Gedenksteine

122 Skizzen; Aquafixpapier (142)
123 Skizzen; Aquafixpapier (185)

Gedenksteine

124 Skizzen; satiniertes Pauspapier (313)
125 Skizzen; Schreibmaschinpapier
126 Skizzen; weißer Karton (181)
127 Skizzen; Kalenderblatt „Freitag, 17. Oktober"
128 Skizzen; Schreibmaschinpapier (177)
129 Schnitt; M 1 : 1; Skizzen; Aquafixpapier (11)
130 Buchstaben, Skizzen; kariertes Papier (751)
131 Buchstaben, Skizzen; Aquafixpapier (1209)
132 Buchstaben, Skizzen; Aquafixpapier (1457)
133 Zugangsstiegen, Skizzen; Aquafixpapier (198)

Westseite: Tor der Toten (bei der Kapelle)

134 Skizzen; Aquafixpapier (1187)
135 Skizzen; Aquafixpapier (221)
136 Skizze; satiniertes Pauspapier (1157)
137 Ansicht; M 1 : 100, stärkeres Aquafixpapier (263)
138 Grundriß und Schnitt; M 1 : 100, beiger Karton (93)
139 Grundriß und Ansicht; M 1 : 100, beiger Karton (381)

Schiebetür aus Beton

140 Skizzen; satiniertes Pauspapier (971)
141 Skizzen; satiniertes Pauspapier (1190)
142 Skizzen; satiniertes Pauspapier (1192)
143 Skizzen; satiniertes Pauspapier (1200)
144 Ansicht; M 1 : 10, weißer Karton (25)
145 Ansicht; M 1 : 10; Details; M 1 : 1, satiniertes Pauspapier

Nordseite: Richtung Grabkapellen (Ortsfriedhof)

146 Skizzen; Aquafixpapier (280)

147 Skizzen; Schreibmaschinpapier
148 Skizzen; Schreibmaschinpapier
149 Ansicht; M 1 : 50; Details; M 1 : 10, beiger Karton (114)
150 Ansicht; M 1 : 50; Details; M 1 : 10, satiniertes Pauspapier (1549)

Eisenbetontüre zum Durchgang zum Ortsfriedhof (1974)

151 Skizzen; Schreibmaschinpapier
152 Skizzen; Schreibmaschinpapier (679)
153 Skizzen; Schreibmaschinpapier (8119)
154 Ansichten, Grundriß; M 1 : 10; Details; M 1 : 1, Blaupause (302)
155 Skizze: Grundriß, M 1 : 10, Aquafixpapier (1272)

Vorrichtung aus massiven Messung zum Offenhalten der Tür

156 Skizzen; Aquafixpapier (1080)
157 Ansichten, Schnitte; M 1 : 10; Details; M 1 : 1, beiger Karton (69)
158 Juli 1974, Ansichten und Schnitte; M 1 : 10; Details; M 1 : 1, Aquafixpapier (295)

Erweiterung des Ortsfriedhofes von S. Vito d'Altivole
Vorschläge für die Umfassungsmauer (1971–1972)

159 Skizzen auf dem Katasterplan; M 1 : 500, Blaupause (818)
160 Skizzen; Schreibmaschinpapier
161 7. Oktober 1971, Bauaufnahme; M 1 : 250, satiniertes Pauspapier
162 Bauaufnahme; M 1 : 250, amerikanisches Pauspapier (202)

Westseite

163 7. Oktober 1971, Ansicht; M 1 : 100, satiniertes Pauspapier
164 Eingang: Grundriß, Ansichten, Schnitte; M 1 : 25, satiniertes Pauspapier (1565)

165 Eingang, Skizzen; Aquafixpapier (244)
166 Ansichten; M 1 : 100, 1 : 25; Details; M 1 : 1, beiger Karton (8)
167 10. Februar 1972, Ansicht, Grundriß; M 1 : 100, kolorierte Blaupause (308)

DER PAVILLON

Platte beim Eingang, Balken beim Wasserbecken

168 Grundriß, Schnitt; M 1 : 50, Aquafix (1149)
169 Schnitt, Ansicht, Grundriß; M 1 : 10, beiger Karton (885)

Fundament, zentrale Platte

170 Horizontalprojektionen und Schnitte; M 1 : 25, satiniertes Pauspapier (1540)
171 Detail; M 1 : 10, satiniertes Pauspapier (288)
172 Details; M 1 : 10, 1 : 25 und 1 : 1, satiniertes Pauspapier (1538)

Der Pavillon

173 Bauaufnahme; M 1 : 50, beiger Karton (44)
174 Skizzen; Blaupause von Nr. 168 (839)
175 Skizzen; Schreibmaschinpapier
176 Skizzen; Schreibmaschinpapier
177 Skizzen; Aquafixpapier (1086)
178 Skizzen; Aquafixpapier (1124)
179 Skizzen; Aquafixpapier (242)
180 Skizzen; Aquafixpapier (257)
181 Skizzen; Aquafixpapier (238)
182 Skizzen; satinietes Pauspapier (1537)
183 Grundriß, Schnitte; M 1 : 50, beiger Karton (109)

Schnitte

184 Schnitte; M 1 : 10, weißer Karton (3)
185 Skizzen; Aquafixpapier (1139)
186 Skizzen; M 1 : 50, beiger Karton (47)
187 Skizzen; M 1 : 25, beiger Karton (2)

188 Skizzen; M 1 : 25,
 Aquafixpapier (1125)
189 Skizzen; M 1 : 25, kolorierte
 Blaupause (853)
190 Skizzen; M 1 : 25, kolorierte
 Blaupause (842)

Holzpanele: „Dach" des Pavillons

Außen

191 Skizzen;
 Schreibmaschinpapier (547)
192 Skizzen;
 Schreibmaschinpapier (143)
193 Skizzen;
 Schreibmaschinpapier (1501)
194 Skizzen; Aquafix (1135)
195 Skizzen; Aquafix (1138)
196 Skizzen; satiniertes
 Pauspapier (1158)
197 Skizzen; Bristol-Karton (336)
198 Skizzen; leichter Karton (52)
199 Längsansicht; M 1 : 1,
 Aquafixpapier

Innen

200 Längsansicht; M 1 : 10,
 Aquafixpapier (265)

Eckpfeiler

201 Skizzen;
 Schreibmaschinpapier (775)
202 Skizzen;
 Schreibmaschinpapier (757)
203 Skizzen; Aquafixpapier (193)
204 Skizzen; Aquafixpapier (1407)
205 Skizzen; Aquafixpapier (199)
206 Skizzen; Aquafixpapier (1065)
207 Skizzen;
 satiniertes Pauspapier (201)
208 Skizzen;
 Schreibmaschinpapier (587)
209 Skizzen;
 Schreibmaschinpapier (142)
210 Skizzen;
 Schreibmaschinpapier (172)
211 Detail in Originalgröße;
 M 1 : 1, kolorierte
 Blaupause (882)

Ecken

212 Skizzen; Aquafixpapier (1089)
213 Skizzen; Aquafixpapier (1243)
214 horizontale und vertikale
 Schnitte; M 1 : 1, stärkeres
 Pauspapier (184)
215 Horizontalschnitt; M 1 : 1,
 weißer Karton (97)

Durchblick („occhio")

216 Ansicht; M 1 : 10;
 Aquafixpapier (214)
217 Skizzen; Aquafixpapier (1251)
218 Skizzen; Aquafixpapier (216)
219 Skizzen; Aquafixpapier (283)

Haltestange beim Eingang

220 Skizzen;
 Schreibmaschinpapier (791)
221 Skizzen; Bristol-Karton (736)
222 Skizzen;
 Schreibmaschinpapier (12)
223 Skizzen; Aquafixpapier (1232)

Struktur

224 Skizzen; Aquafixpapier (1389)
225 Skizzen; Aquafixpapier (1414)
226 Skizzen; Aquafixpapier (1434)
227 Skizzen; Aquafixpapier (1134)
228 Skizzen; Aquafixpapier (211)
229 Bauaufnahme; M 1 : 10,
 weißer Karton (81)
230 Bauaufnahme; M 1 : 10,
 satiniertes Pauspapier
231 Bauaufnahme: Details;
 M 1 : 10, Aquafixpapier (264)

Beleuchtung

232 Skizzen; Aquafixpapier (1234)

großes Wasserbecken

233 Skizze; M 1 : 50,
 amerikanisches Pauspapier
 (270)
234 Details; M 1 : 50 (276)
235 Skizze; M 1 : 50, kolorierte
 Blaupause (304)
236 Skizze; M 1 : 100, Pauspapier
 auf Blaupause (102)
237 Skizze; M 1 : 50, kolorierte
 Blaupause (305)
238 Skizze; M 1 : 50, kolorierte
 Blaupause (823)
239 Skizze; M 1 : 50, kolorierte
 Blaupause (306)

überhängende Stützmauer

240 Seite und Ansicht; M 1 : 50;
 Details; M 1 : 10, satiniertes
 Pauspapier (1539)
241 Querschnitt; M 1 : 10 und
 1 : 1, satiniertes Pauspapier
 (1533)

Beckenboden

242 Idee: Grundriß;
 Aquafixpapier (1076)
243 Skizzen;
 Schreibmaschinpapier (804)
244 Skizzen;
 Schreibmaschinpapier (471)
245 Skizzen;
 Schreibmaschinpapier (803)
246 Schnitt; M 1 : 50,
 amerikanisches Pauspapier
247 Skizzen für den Überlauf;
 Schreibmaschinpapier

Ansichten

248 Motivschema; Briefpapier
249 Motivschema;
 Briefpapier (128)
250 Motivschema;
 Briefpapier (127)

Bambusinsel

251 Grundriß; M 1 : 25,
 Briefpapier (123)

Zwei Ringe

252 Skizze; Briefpapier (124)
253 Skizze; Briefpapier (129)
254 Grundriß; M 1 : 25,
 Briefpapier (125)
255 Schnitt, Skizzen;
 Briefpapier (130)
256 Schnitt, Skizzen;
 Briefpapier (122)

Springbrunnen oder schwimmende
Blumenschale

257 Skizzen;
 Schreibmaschinpapier (133)
258 Schnitt; Schreibmaschinpapier
 (121)
259 Skizze; Briefpapier (134)
260 Grundriß, Schnitt; M 1 : 25;
 Details; M 1 : 1,
 Briefpapier (135)
261 Grundriß; M 1 : 10,
 kolorierte Blaupause (873)
262 Grundriß; M 1 : 10,
 kolorierte Blaupause (872)
263 Grundriß; M 1 : 10,
 Aquafixpapier (629)

Beckenrand

264 Schnitte; M 1 : 10 und 1 : 1, kolorierte Blaupause (823)

Absperrung vor dem Wasserbecken, Verspannung über der Wiese

265 Ansicht; Schreibmaschinpapier (792)
266 Skizzen; Schreibmaschinpapier (752)
267 Skizzen; M 1 : 1, weißer Karton (424)

DAS GRABMAL

268 Skizzen; Bristol-Karton (164)
269 Skizzen; Bristol-Karton (433)

6.–9. März 1970, das von der Gemeinde Altivole genehmigte Projekt

270 Schnitt und Grundriß; M 1 : 40, Pauspapier
271 Skizzen; kolorierte Blaupause von Nr. 270 (864)

Bogen über den Sarkophagen: „Arcosolio"

Bogenrücken

272 Skizzen; Schreibmaschinpapier (476)
273 Skizzen; Schreibmaschinpapier (161)
274 Skizzen; Schreibmaschinpapier (157)
275 Skizzen; Schreibmaschinpapier (475)
276 Schnitt; M 1 : 10, beiger Karton (334)
277 Grundriß; M 1 : 25; Schnitt; M 1 : 10, satiniertes Pauspapier

Verankerung des Bogens

278 Skizzen; Schreibmaschinpapier (473)
279 Skizzen; Schreibmaschinpapier (162)
280 Skizzen; Schreibmaschinpapier (586)
281 Skizzen; Aquafixpapier (209)
282 Details von oben und von unten gesehen; M 1 : 10, Aquafixpapier

Mosaik an der Bogenunterseite

283 Skizzen; Aquafixpapier (472)
284 Grundriß; M 1 : 25, Aquafixpapier (1353)
285 Grundriß; M 1 : 10, beiger Karton (62)

Details an der Bogenunterseite

286 Skizzen; satiniertes Pauspapier (1376)
287 Schnitte; M 1 : 10 und 1 : 25, satiniertes Pauspapier (1524)

Sarkophage

288 Skizzen; Aquafixpapier (1113)
289 Skizzen; Aquafixpapier (1106)
290 Skizzen; Aquafixpapier (1203)
291 Skizzen; Aquafixpapier (1112)
292 Skizzen; Aquafixpapier (1109)
293 Skizzen; Aquafixpapier (1100)
294 Skizzen; Aquafixpapier (1355)
295 Skizzen; satiniertes Pauspapier (1099)
296 Skizzen; Aquafixpapier (212)
297 Skizzen; Aquafixpapier (190)
298 Ansichten; M 1 : 10, Aquafixpapier (1117)
299 Ansichten; M 1 : 25 und 1 : 10, beiger Karton (24)
300 Skizzen; Aquafixpapier (236)
301 Ansichten; M 1 : 25 und 1 : 10, beiger Karton (65)
302 Skizzen; Aquafixpapier (1348)
303 Skizzen; Aquafixpapier (213)
304 Skizzen; Aquafixpapier (203)
305 Ansichten; M 1 : 10, weißer Karton (32)
306 Ansichten; M 1 : 10, Bristol-Karton (74)
307 Details; M 1 : 2, Aquafixpapier
308 Ansichten; M 1 : 5, kolorierte Blaupause

Inschrift: Ebenholz mit Elfenbeinintarsie

309 Skizzen; Briefpapier (468)
310 Skizzen; Schreibmaschinpapier (451)
311 Skizzen; Aquafixpapier (1104)
312 Skizzen; Aquafixpapier (322)
313 Ansicht; M 1 : 1, weißer Karton (40)
314 Ansicht; M 1 : 1, satiniertes Pauspapier

Fußboden: kreisrunde Einfassung

315 Skizzen; Schreibmaschinpapier
316 Detail in Originalgröße; M 1 : 1, beiger Karton (66)
317 Abfluß, Skizzen; Aquafixpapier (1095)
318 Abfluß, Grundriß und Schnitt; M 1 : 10, beiger Karton (91)

Sonnenuhr und Wasserquelle

319 Grundriß und Schnitt; M 1 : 10 und 1 : 1, beiger Karton (96)

DIE KAPELLE

Pläne, Grundrisse

320 Skizzen; Aquafixpapier (1362)
321 Skizzen; Aquafixpapier (919)
322 Skizzen; Aquafixpapier (1372)
323 Skizzen; Aquafixpapier (1392)
324 Skizzen; Aquafixpapier (911)
325 Skizzen; Aquafixpapier (1270)
326 Skizzen; Aquafixpapier (1394)
327 Skizzen; M 1 : 50, Aquafixpapier (933)
328 Skizzen; M 1 : 50, beiger Karton (111)
329 Skizzen; M 1 : 50, beiger Karton (110)

Ansichten

Nordostseite

330 Skizzen; M 1 : 25, kolorierte Blaupause (849)
331 Skizzen; M 1 : 25, beiger Karton (4)
332 Skizzen; Schreibmaschinpapier (159)

Nordwestseite

333 Skizzen; M 1 : 25, amerikanisches Pauspapier (255)
334 Skizzen; M 1 : 25, satiniertes Pauspapier (229)
335 Skizzen; M 1 : 10, kolorierte Blaupause (863)
336 Ansicht und Schnitt; M 1 : 25, beiger Karton (104)

Schnitte

337 Skizzen; M 1:25, beiger Karton (60)
338 Skizzen; M 1:25, beiger Karton (51)
339 Skizzen; M 1:25, Aquafixpapier (206)

Kuppel

340 Skizzen; Notizpapier (456)
341 Skizzen; Notizpapier (1503)
342 Skizzen; Aquafixpapier (975)
343 Skizzen; Aquafixpapier (973)
344 Skizzen; amerikanisches Pauspapier (1337)
345 Skizzen; amerikanisches Pauspapier (204)
346 Skizzen; Aquafixpapier (326)
347 Skizzen; Aquafixpapier (905)
348 Skizzen; Schreibmaschinpapier (504)
349 Skizzen; Schreibmaschinpapier (496)
350 Skizzen; Notizpapier (1504)
351 Skizzen; satiniertes Pauspapier (1399)
352 Skizzen; Aquafixpapier (977)
353 Skizzen; satiniertes Pauspapier (230)
354 Skizzen; satiniertes Pauspapier (318)
355 Skizzen; Aquafixpapier (284)
356 Skizzen; satiniertes Pauspapier (1304)
357 Skizzen; Aquafixpapier (328)
358 Grundriß und Außenansicht; M 1:50, beiger Karton (95)
359 Grundriß und Außenansicht; M 1:50, beiger Karton (118)
360 Deckenprojektion; M 1:50, beiger Karton (129)

Oberlichtfenster (zu öffnen)

361 Grundriß; M 1:10; Längsschnitt; M 1:5; Querschnitt, M 1:1, beiger Karton (56)
362 Grundriß; M 1:10; Längsschnitt; M 1:5; Querschnitt; M 1:1, satiniertes Pauspapier

„Ufficium sepulcri" Todesengel

363 Skizzen; Briefpapier (151)
364 Skizzen; Aquafixpapier (1332)
365 Skizzen; satiniertes Pauspapier (146)
366 Skizzen; Schreibmaschinpapier (150)
367 Skizzen; Schreibmaschinpapier (149)
368 Skizzen; Schreibmaschinpapier (674)
369 Skizzen; Schreibmaschinpapier (147)
370 Skizzen; Schreibmaschinpapier (148)

Fußboden

371 Skizzen; satiniertes Pauspapier (972)
372 Skizzen; M 1:25, Aquafixpapier (1514)
373 Skizzen; M 1:25, Aquafixpapier (985)
374 Skizzen; M 1:25, Aquafixpapier (983)
375 Skizzen; M 1:2 und 1:1, Aquafixpapier (1390)
376 Verlegemuster im Zentrum der Kirche; M 1:1, Aquafixpapier (1343)
377 Verlegemuster im Zentrum der Kirche; M 1:1 und 1:10, weißer Karton (100)
378 Stufenkante; M 1:1, satiniertes Pauspapier

Hauptportal

379 Skizzen; Schreibmaschinpapier (719)
380 Skizzen; Schreibmaschinpapier (523)
381 Skizzen; Schreibmaschinpapier (524)
382 Skizzen; Schreibmaschinpapier (554)
383 Skizzen; Schreibmaschinpapier (163)
384 Skizzen; satiniertes Pauspapier (1320)
385 Skizzen; Aquafixpapier (1438)
386 Grundriß; M 1:50; Details; 1:10, weißer Karton (108)

Metallscharnier

387 Skizzen; Aquafixpapier (1070)
388 Skizzen; Aquafixpapier (1435)
389 Skizzen; Befestigung am Boden; Schnitt; M 1:1, beiger Karton (58)
390 Befestigung am Boden, Grundriß, Schnitt, Ansicht; M 1:1, weißer Karton (35)
391 Befestigung am Boden, Grundriß, Ansicht; M 1:1, satiniertes Pauspapier (1525)
392 Befestigung an der Decke, Grundriß, Schnitt, Ansicht; M 1:1, satiniertes Pauspapier (1522)
393 Feststellvorrichtung aus Aluminium an der Decke, Grundriß, Schnitt; M 1:1, Aquafixpapier (1075)
394 Oktober 1973, Detail der Verglasung rechts neben der Tür; M 1:1, satiniertes Pauspapier (1526)

Ebenholztürchen im Hauptportal (1973–1974)

395 Skizzen; Bristol-Karton (561)
396 Skizzen; satiniertes Pauspapier (1051)
397 Skizzen; Aquafixpapier (1413)
398 Skizzen; Aquafixpapier (192)
399 Ansichten von innen und außen; M 1:5; Grundriß; M 1:1, Bristol-Karton (17)
400 November 1973, Ansicht von innen; M 1:5, satiniertes Pauspapier (1547)
401 Skizzen; M 1:5 und 1:1, Aquafixpapier (1416)
402 Skizzen; M 1:5, Aquafixpapier (1350)
403 Schnitt; M 1:1, weißer Karton (417)
404 November 1973, Schnitt; M 1:1, satiniertes Pauspapier (1948)
405 Schnitt; M 1:1, kolorierte Blaupause von Nr. 404 (832)
406 Schnitt, Detail; M 1:1, Aquafixpapier (1344)
407 Februar 1974, Grundriß und Ansicht; M 1:1, kolorierte Blaupause (836)
408 Februar 1974, Ansicht der Verschlüsse; kolorierte Blaupause (877)
409 März 1974, Detail; M 1:1, Aquafixpapier (1520)
410 März 1974, Details aus Holz und Metall in der Mitte des oberen Teils; M 1:1, kolorierte Blaupause (833)
411 Türgriff, Skizze; Aquafixpapier (1208)

412 Türgriff, Ansicht, Schnitt; M 1:1, weißer Karton (84)

Weihwasserbecken

413 Skizzen; Schreibmaschinpapier
414 Skizzen; satiniertes Pauspapier (1510)
415 vertikaler Schnitt; M 1:1, Aquafixpapier (1253)
416 vertikaler Schnitt; M 1:1, Schreibpapier (80)
417 Skizzen; Schreibmaschinpapier (171)
418 horizontaler Schnitt; M 1:1, Bristol-Karton (16)
419 horizontaler Schnitt; M 1:1, Aquafixpapier (269)
420 horizontaler und vertikaler Schnitt; M 1:1, weißer Karton (107)
421 Schiebeverschluß, vertikaler Schnitt; M 1:1, Aquafixpapier (268)
422 Schiebeverschluß und Griff zum Öffnen, vertikaler Schnitt; M 1:1 (646)
423 horizontaler Schnitt; M 1:1, weißer Karton (14)

Rundbogentür in der Kapelle

424 Skizzen; Schreibmaschinpapier (710)
425 Skizzen; Schreibmaschinpapier (498)
426 Skizzen; kolorierte Fotokopie (160)
427 Ansicht und Schnitt; M 1:10, weißer Karton (382)
428 Grundriß und Ansichten; M 1:20; Detail; M 1:10, beiger Karton (363)
429 Befestigung am Boden; M 1:1, beiger Karton (386)

Fenster

Hochfenster

430 Skizzen; Schreibmaschinpapier (519)
431 Skizzen; Aquafixpapier (1338)
432 horizontaler Schnitt; M 1:5, Aquafixpapier (1378)
433 horizontaler Schnitt; M 1:5, Aquafixpapier (956)
434 Skizzen; beiger Karton (393)
435 horizontaler Schnitt; M 1:10 und 1:5, Bristol-Karton (333)
436 vertikaler Schnitt; M 1:5, satiniertes Pauspapier

Quadratische Fenster hinter dem Altar

437 Schnitte, Ansicht; M 1:10, Schreibmaschinpapier (551)
438 Details; Schreibmaschinpapier (566)
439 horizontaler Schnitt; M 1:1, beiger Karton (357)

Altar

Position des Altares

440 Skizzen; Aquafixpapier (1428)
441 Skizzen; satiniertes Pauspapier (899)
442 Skizzen; M 1:25, kolorierte Blaupause (826)
443 Skizzen; M 1:25, satiniertes Pauspapier (291)
444 Details; M 1:25, 1:10 und 1:1, satiniertes Pauspapier (1551)
445 Skizzen; M 1:25 und 1:10, Blaupause von Nr. 444 (307)

Anordnung von Stufen und Altar

446 Skizzen; M 1:10, satiniertes Pauspapier
447 Skizzen; M 1:10, Aquafixpapier (1345)
448 Skizzen; M 1:10, Aquafixpapier (924)
449 Skizzen; M 1:10, Aquafixpapier (1342)
450 Skizzen; Schreibmaschinpapier (563)

Sockel unter dem Altar

451 Skizzen; Schreibmaschinpapier (562)
452 Skizzen; Schreibmaschinpapier (564)
453 Schnitte; M 1:1, weißer Karton (36)
454 Februar 1974, Schnitte; M 1:10 und 1:1, Aquafixpapier (317)
455 Schnitte; M 1:1, weißer Karton (349)
456 März 1974, Schnitte; M 1:1, Aquafixpapier (1554)

Altar

457 Skizzen; Schreibmaschinpapier
458 Ansicht; M 1:10, Aquafixpapier (951)
459 4. November 1971, Ansicht; M 1:10; weißer Karton (34)
460 Grundriß, Ansicht, Schnitt; M 1:1, satiniertes Pauspapier (292)
461 Skizzen; Aquafixpapier (278)
462 Grundriß, Ansicht, Schnitt; M 1:10, weißer Karton (67)
463 Grundriß, Ansicht; M 1:10 und 1:1, satiniertes Pauspapier (901)
464 Skizzen; Schreibmaschinpapier
465 Skizzen; Schreibmaschinpapier (167)
466 Skizzen; Schreibmaschinpapier (168)
467 Skizzen; weißes Zeichenpapier
468 Skizzen; Aquafixpapier (1424)
469 Grundriß, Schnitt, Ansicht; M 1:10, satiniertes Pauspapier (1534)

Sacrum

470 Grundriß; M 1:10, Schreibmaschinpapier

Kelch

471 Skizzen; amerikanisches Pauspapier (1207)
472 Skizze; M 1:1, Aquafix auf weißem Papier

Kruzifix

473 Skizzen; Schreibmaschinpapier
474 Skizzen; Schreibmaschinpapier
475 Skizzen; Schreibmaschinpapier (145)
476 Ansicht; Aquafixpapier (261)
477 Skizzen; weißer Karton (82)
478 Ansicht, Schnitt; M 1:1, weißer Karton
479 Ansicht, Schnitt; M 1:1, weißer Karton (112)
480 Ansicht, Schnitt; M 1:1, stärkeres Pauspapier
481 Ansicht; stärkeres Pauspapier (258)

Hängekandelaber

482 Skizzen;
     Schreibmaschinpapier (763)
483 Skizzen;
     Schreibmaschinpapier (787)
484 Skizzen; Aquafixpapier (1430)
485 Skizzen;
     Schreibmaschinpapier (136)
486 Skizzen;
     Schreibmaschinpapier (1485)
487 Skizzen; M 1 : 10,
     weißer Karton (10)
488 Ansicht und Schnitt; M 1 : 10,
     Aquafix auf weißem Karton (85)
489 Skizzen; M 1 : 10,
     weißer Karton (106)

Kerzenhalterungen

490 Grundriß, M 1 : 1,
     Aquafixpapier (1259)
491 Skizzen; Aquafixpapier (1283)
492 Ansicht; M 1 : 1,
     Aquafixpapier (272)
493 Skizzen; M 1 : 1,
     Aquafixpapier (273)
494 Skizzen; M 1 : 1,
     Aquafixpapier (1260)
495 Skizzen; M 1 : 1, stärkeres
     Pauspapier

Aufhängung der Stangen an der Decke

496 Skizzen; Aquafixpapier (1379)
497 Grundriß, Schnitt, Ansicht;
     M 1 : 1, weißer Karton (89)

Die drei Stangen

498 Details: Grundriß, Schnitt,
     Ansicht; M 1 : 1,
     weißer Karton (87)

kleine Marmortüren hinter dem Altar

499 Skizze;
     Schreibmaschinpapier (649)
500 Skizze;
     Schreibmaschinpapier (573)
501 Skizzen;
     satiniertes Pauspapier (965)
502 Skizzen; Aquafixpapier (1072)
503 Skizzen;
     beiger Karton (90, Rückseite)
504 Grundriß; M 1 : 10; Details;
     M 1 : 1, weißer Karton (26)
505 Grundriß; M 1 : 10; Details;
     M 1 : 1, satiniertes
     Pauspapier (1564)
506 September 1973, Ansicht;
     M 1 : 10, satiniertes
     Pauspapier (1550)
507 Verschluß, Skizze;
     Aquafixpapier (191)
508 Verschluß, Skizzen;
     Schreibmaschinpapier (656)
509 Verschluß, Skizzen;
     Schreibmaschinpapier (648)
510 Verschluß, Skizzen;
     Schreibmaschinpapier (771)
511 Verschluß, Skizzen;
     Schreibmaschinpapier (671)
512 Verschluß, Grundriß und
     Ansicht; M 1 : 1 (338)
513 August 1974, Verschluß;
     M 1 : 1, Aquafixpapier (294)
514 Verschluß, Skizzen;
     Aquafixpapier (1091)
515 Verschluß, Grundriß; M 1 : 10
     und 1 : 1, kolorierte Blaupause
     (825)
516 Haltevorrichtungen,
     Grundriß; M 1 : 1,
     beiger Karton (59)
517 Haltevorrichtungen,
     Grundriß; M 1 : 1,
     beiger Karton (53)

Tor zum Zypressenhain (1973–1975)

518 Grundriß; M 1 : 25,
     beiger Karton (386)
519 Detail, Zugang zu den
     Zypressen;
     Schreibmaschinpapier (1502)
520 Grundriß, Ansicht; M 1 : 10;
     Detail; M 1 : 1,
     weißer Karton (73)
521 Grundriß; M 1 : 10,
     Aquafix (1334)
522 August 1973, Grundriß und
     Ansicht; M 1 : 10, satiniertes
     Pauspapier (1530)
523 Grundriß; M 1 : 10,
     beiger Karton (375)
524 Angel, Skizzen;
     Aquafixpapier (1336)
525 Angel, Grundriß; M 1 : 1,
     beiger Karton (50)
526 Angel im Fußboden,
     Grundriß und Ansicht;
     M 1 : 1, weißer Karton (31)
527 August 1973, Angel an der
     Decke; Grundriß, Ansicht;
     M 1 : 1, satiniertes Pauspapier
     (1563)
528 Stufe, Skizze; Schreibpapier
     (13)
529 25. Oktober 1975, Stufe,
     Ansicht; M 1 : 5; Details;
     M 1 : 1, satiniertes Pauspapier
530 Haltevorrichtung, Skizzen;
     Schreibmaschinpapier (651)
531 Gläser, Skizzen;
     Aquafixpapier (1363)
532 Detail; M 1 : 1,
     satiniertes Pauspapier

Eingangsportal, offener Gang zur Sakristei

533 Ansicht; M 1 : 25,
     satiniertes Pauspapier
534 Ansicht; M 1 : 25,
     satiniertes Pauspapier
535 Grundriß, Ansicht; M 1 : 25,
     beiger Karton (94)
536 Skizzen; Aquafixpapier (1384)
537 Skizzen; Aquafixpapier (1385)
538 Skizzen; Aquafixpapier (1393)
539 Grundriß; M 1 : 25,
     kolorierte Blaupause (301)
540 Grundriß; M 1 : 25,
     Bristol-Karton (29)
541 Grundriß; M 1 : 25,
     satiniertes Pauspapier
542 offener Gang, Nordansicht;
     M 1 : 25, satiniertes
     Pauspapier
543 Längsschnitt; M 1 : 25,
     satiniertes Pauspapier
544 Längsschnitt; M 1 : 25,
     satiniertes Pauspapier
545 Portal, Ansicht; M 1 : 10,
     weißes Papier (37)
546 Portal, Grundriß, Ansicht;
     M 1 : 10 (1513)
547 Stange am Portal, Skizzen;
     Schreibmaschinpapier (657)
548 Stange, Skizzen;
     Schreibmaschinpapier (170)
549 Stange, Skizzen;
     Briefpapier (139)
550 Stange, Skizzen; Briefpapier
551 Stange, Ansicht; M 1 : 1,
     Kunstdruckkarton (83)
552 Stange, Ansichten; M 1 : 1,
     beiger Karton (46)
553 Juli 1974, Stange, Ansichten;
     M 1 : 1, stärkeres
     Pauspapier (293)
554 Fenster, Skizze;
     Schreibmaschinpapier
555 Fenster, Skizze;
     Schreibmaschinpapier

556 Fenster, Ansicht; M 1 : 10; Details; M 1 : 1, weißer Karton (72)
557 Fenster, Schnitte; M 1 : 10, weißer Karton (368)
558 Kasten mit Geheimfach, Skizzen; M 1 : 10 und 1 : 1, weißer Karton (177)
559 Kasten, horizontaler Schnitt; M 1 : 10 und 1 : 1, weißer Karton (405)
560 Kasten, Skizzen; weißes Papier
561 Kasten, Detail; Aquafixpapier (285)
562 Kasten, Detail; Schreibmaschinpapier
563 Kasten, Detail; Schreibmaschinpapier (630)
564 Kasten, Detail; Schreibmaschinpapier (481)
565 Magazintür, Skizzen; Aquafixpapier (1330)
566 Magazintür, Skizzen; Aquafixpapier (1419)
567 Magazintür, Skizzen; beiger Karton (399, Rückseite)
568 September 1973, Magazintür, Details; M 1 : 10, satiniertes Pauspapier
569 Oktober 1973, Magazintür, Grundriß Ansicht; M 1 : 10, satiniertes Pauspapier (1552)
570 Wasserpumpen, Skizzen; Schreibmaschinpapier (526)
571 Wasserpumpen, Skizzen; satiniertes Pauspapier (1170)
572 Wasserpumpen, Skizzen; satiniertes Pauspapier (1167)
573 Wasserpumpen, Grundriß; M 1 : 10, beiger Karton (7)
574 Wasserpumpen, Schnitt; M 1 : 10, satiniertes Pauspapier
575 November 1973, Wasserpumpen, Zugang; M 1 : 10 und 1 : 1, satiniertes Pauspapier (1527)
576 Wasserpumpen, Details; M 1 : 1, Aquafixpapier (410)

BEPFLANZUNGEN

577 Skizzen; Schreibmaschinpapier (707)
578 Skizzen; Schreibmaschinpapier (144)
579 Skizzen; kariertes Papier
580 Skizzen; kariertes Papier

„DIE ANDERE STADT"

581 Skizzen; Schreibmaschinpapier

CONTENTS
INHALTSVERZEICHNIS

Peter Noever
Reminiscenses 8
Erinnerungen 12
Tobia Scarpa
Venezia–Wien 10
Venezia–Wien 14
Luciano Benetton
Points of Reference 11
Bezugspunkte 15
Carlo Scarpa
Can architecture be poetry? 16
Kann Architektur Poesie sein? 22
Philippe Duboy
The other city 28
Die andere Stadt 32

Abbildungen/Illustrations
Initial plans and floor plans
Erste Entwürfe und Grundrisse (1969–1970) . 37
Enclosing wall/Die Umfassungsmauer 53
Pavilion/Der Pavillon 115
Tomb/Das Grabmal 161
Chapel/Die Kapelle 189
Garden Layout/Bepflanzung 311
„The other city"/„Die andere Stadt" 315

Manlio Brusatin
The Architecture of Life 319
Architektur des Lebens 325
Gerald Zugmann
the Mere Distance, free from the burden
of present time
die Reine Ferne, frei von der Last der
Gegenwart 335
List of illustrations 377
Verzeichnis der Abbildungen 387

Fotorepros: Georg Mayer, Atelier Prader, Thomas Rainagel
Cover/Umschlag
Luciano Svegliado
p. 21 Philippe Duboy
p. 7 Photogramma
p. 31, 35 Guido Pietropoli
Translations/Übersetzungen
Katharina Gsöllpointner, Regina Haslinger, Michael Huey,
David Marinelli, Johannes Wieninger, Oswald Zoeggeler